Forthcoming Books in the Dove on Fundraising Series:

Books Currently Available in the Dove on Fundraising Series:

Other Nonprofit Resources from Jossey-Bass

CONDUCTING A SUCCESSFUL FUNDRAISING PROGRAM

The Dove on Fundraising Series is a library of premier resource guides that combine practical instruction with real-world examples. In response to the ever-changing challenges nonprofits face, Kent E. Dove, The Indiana University Foundation, and Jossey-Bass have come together to develop and advance professional standards for fundraisers everywhere. Built on the successful fundraising model developed by veteran fundraiser and series editor Kent Dove, these publications provide a flexible campaign-based approach that recognizes fundraising as both a science and an art.

Clustered around the comprehensive *Conducting a Successful Fundraising Program,* each publication examines a key aspect of fundraising, and all authors bring years of experience and knowledge to their topics. Together, these guides present an integrated framework validated by research and practical results. **The Dove on Fundraising Series** seeks to provide nonprofit leaders, fundraisers, consultants, and students with not only time-tested principles, but also successful examples, strategies, and publications that readers can use to shape their own development programs.

CONDUCTING A SUCCESSFUL FUNDRAISING PROGRAM

A Comprehensive Guide and Resource

Kent E. Dove

JOSSEY-BASS
A Wiley Imprint
www.josseybass.com

Published by Jossey-Bass
A Wiley Imprint
989 Market Street, San Francisco, CA 94103-1741   www.josseybass.com

Jossey-Bass books and products are available through most bookstores. To contact Jossey-Bass directly call our Customer Care Department within the U.S. at (800) 956-7739, outside the U.S. at (317) 572-3986 or fax (317) 572-4002.

Jossey-Bass also publishes its books in a variety of electronic formats. Some content that appears in print may not be available in electronic books.

Credits are on page 963.

Library of Congress Cataloging-in-Publication Data

Dove, Kent E.
    Conducting a successful fundraising program: a comprehensive
guide and resource / Kent E. Dove.
        p.   cm.
Includes bibliographical references and index.
    ISBN 0-7879-5352-0 (acid-free)
    1. Fund raising. I. Title.
    HV41.2 .D68 2001
    658.15'224—dc21
            00-012939

HB Printing   10 9 8 7 6 5   FIRST EDITION

CONTENTS

PART TWO: THE FUNDRAISING RESOURCE GUIDE   365

PREFACE

Writing books is not my lot in life, or so I have always thought. I, like most who will read this, am a fundraising practitioner: I raise money for a living and love my work.

However, each of us owes a large debt to others who have encouraged us and instructed us in the skills and techniques of fundraising, especially in our beginning years. For those in my generation who started out thirty-plus years ago, formal education in this field was difficult to find. Most of us turned to mentors, if we were lucky enough to find them (and I was), fundraising seminars, short courses and conferences, and the limited available literature in the field.

I had wonderful mentors—Herman B Wells, Bill Armstrong, Curt Simic, Dick Edwards, Sam Cooper (to whom this book is dedicated), Will Miller, Bob Houser, and George Rupp. In that group I had the great benefit of learning from the best in all aspects of philanthropy and fundraising—fellow professionals, chief executive officers, and top volunteers.

They gave much to me, and each instilled in me a responsibility to give back, to share with others. That process began more than twenty years ago for me when I first began participating in conference programs as a speaker. From the start the capital campaign was my chosen area of concentration, and that led to many opportunities to make presentations, for capital campaigns were coming of age as a preferred method of fundraising then, a pattern that is perhaps even stronger today.

The progression of presentations led to a chapter titled "Changing Strategies for Meeting Campaign Goals," written for the second edition of the *Handbook on Institutional Advancement,* published by Jossey-Bass in 1986. That led to an invitation from that publisher to write *Conducting a Successful Capital Campaign,* a book that first appeared in 1988 and the second edition of which was released in 1999. That book has proved popular, and Jossey-Bass asked me to consider expanding my perspective in a new book—the one in your hands. Logically, this book should have preceded *Conducting a Successful Capital Campaign.* In that book, I drew on the fundamental principles that underlie any successful development program and enlarged them to capital campaign scale. However, the focus there remains tightly on issues and practices specific and particular to the capital campaign. In developing the present text, I have added much new material, expanded the selection of resources, and explored several additional dimensions of fundraising, but throughout both books runs a steady stream of bedrock material appropriate to any discussion of the principles of fundraising.

I still question whether I am the best person to have written these books, and I would not have attempted doing so had not some of the best minds and most able practitioners in the field agreed to contribute as well. But powerful memories remind me that we all have a responsibility to give back as we have been given, and it's now my turn to pass along the lessons I have learned to the next generation. Blessed by the mentors who guided me so well, I hope this text does them justice.

By the way, I still don't consider myself an author. I'm just a fundraiser who writes a little about what I know.

My central view of fundraising is deeply rooted in the campaign paradigm. It is equally appropriate for the annual effort to secure operating support or for the raising of huge sums of money for capital purposes. Much attention has been focused on the capital campaign model over the past half century, but less has been made of the organization of the annual campaign. Bigger dollar goals simply command more attention. But upon examination, all well-executed fundraising efforts are based on a campaign model; the parallels and similarities between the various campaign models are strong and compelling, and the differences are few. This book attempts to spotlight the similarities while noting differences too.

Fascinating—and very much to the point—is the experience of a small, private school in Indiana whose goal is to raise $500,000 annually. Year after year, using a single direct-mail appeal, a series of events, and personal calls on the top thirty to forty prospects realizes 75 percent of the school's annual goal. The rest of the activities combined raise the remaining 25 percent. The lesson here is that regardless of the size, nature, scale, or scope of your fundraising program, if it is to succeed, a few major donors will do a lot, and a lot of other donors will do the rest. Face-to-face solicitation (there is no substitute) is required to achieve top-level gifts, whether your top level is $250 or $250,000. The success of all fundraising programs will be determined by your organization's level of achievement in the ten essential areas outlined in Chapter One, and the degree of success will, above all else, almost always be determined by the "key three": a compelling written case statement, committed and educated key volunteers, and major donors who are ready and able to give.

The model of choice today is the campaign model, of which there is more than one. Experience and research reveal clearly and convincingly that the campaign model, broadly defined, permeates successful fundraising programs. Many core features of the complete, comprehensive fundraising program—annual giving, special gifts programs, gift clubs, planned and deferred giving, corporate and foundation relations, prospect research, donor relations and stewardship, use of technology in fundraising, and gift and account administration—are not in any fundamental way affected by the campaign model that an organization is using at a particular moment in time. Others—major gifts; public relations, publications, and communications; board involvement; volunteer participation; lead gift acquisition—are not changed fundamentally either except for the fact that when the stakes are higher, the spotlight shines brighter and the immediacy, relevance, urgency, and importance of fundraising are magnified.

Whether yours is an annual giving program seeking $500,000 in operational support in a relatively small midwestern town or a $2 billion, multiyear international capital campaign, the vast majority of the underlying principles, strategies, and processes discussed throughout this book will apply.

Audience

If you have read *Conducting a Successful Capital Campaign,* you may wonder whether this book is sufficiently different to warrant reading it. It is. Admittedly, the principles of fundraising do not change, and those immutable truths are contained in both books. But *Conducting a Successful Capital Campaign* is focused; it focuses tightly on capital campaigns. This book is broader; it provides a full-spectrum overview of the development process. It puts fundraising in a wider-ranging context. It offers a much expanded view.

Because of its comprehensiveness, this book will prove useful in appropriate ways to virtually everyone involved in the third sector—volunteers, board members, organizational administrators, fundraising professionals, all individual prospects and donors, and corporate and foundation grantmakers.

Overview of the Contents

The chapters in this book are organized around the fundamental issues and challenges that must be met if any fundraising program is to achieve success. Chapter One discusses the size of the third sector and its rapid growth, a brief history of philanthropy, and the ten prerequisites that predict success in fundraising. Chapter Two reviews the various fundraising program models, introduces a discussion of a continuous lifetime giving model, and concludes with a call for each nonprofit to consider all available options carefully as it frames its fundraising efforts.

Nothing is more important than stating the case for support. Chapter Three walks you through the process from developing a mission statement to developing an institutional profile to creating a strategic plan to stating the case for financial support of the current fundraising campaign, be it annual or capital.

Chapter Four defines the roles of leaders—governing board members, the chief executive officer, the chief development officer, and key volunteers.

Chapter Five establishes the procedures for mobilizing the large volunteer force vital to the success of both annual and capital campaigns. For the vast majority of nonprofits, development programs are volunteer-driven. This chapter tells how to make the most of volunteers' time.

Before an organization starts a campaign, it should select an appropriate strategy for soliciting gifts, and Chapter Six defines and presents the advantages and disadvantages of various asking strategies. Anyone planning a capital campaign should also establish, at the very start, a criterion for the gifts that will be reported as part of the campaign total over the course of the campaign. As an illustration, this chapter includes an accounting criterion for consideration.

The campaign structures for an annual campaign and a capital campaign are different. Chapter Seven offers a look at the many shapes and forms the annual campaign timeline and plan of action can take and details the more standard structures and timelines that guide successful capital campaigns.

Chapter Eight details one of the most fundamental components of any campaign: the standards-of-giving chart. It explains the formula for creating a gifts chart and, more important, the chart's efficacy in raising donors' sights, determining the adequacy of a prospect pool, relating required campaign gift levels to named gift opportunities, and keeping track of the campaign's progress.

Chapter Nine addresses the annual giving program, the foundation on which all fundraising programs are built. Direct mail, telemarketing, special events, and face-to-face solicitation for annual gifts are all covered in detail. Drawing on their backgrounds as the architects of one of the most successful annual giving programs in American higher education, Jeffrey A. Lindauer, director of annual giving and regional campus services at the Indiana University Foundation (IUF), and Carolyn P. Madvig, director of the IUF's office of special gifts and annual giving programs, have contributed much of the content of Chapter Nine.

Chapters Ten and Eleven describe the multistep process for obtaining the major gifts that are crucial to any campaign's success. Obtaining major gifts demands not just a strategy but also thorough research. In addition to the accurate evaluation, careful management, and systematic cultivation of prospects, it requires skilled soliciting techniques. IUF's Kathy K. Wilson, director of development services, and Vicky Martin, director of research, contributed heavily to the text on prospect research.

Chapter Twelve and Chapter Thirteen, written by Alan M. Spears, director of the office of major and planned gifts at IUF, is an extensive review of the complexities of planned and deferred gifts made understandable by his clear, straightforward explanations. Bequests, trusts, annuities, gifts of real property, life insurance, and more are covered. The text also discusses how to establish, administer, and market a planned gifts program.

Chapter Fourteen, written by Rodney P. Kirsch, vice president for development and alumni relations at Penn State University, and Martin W. Shell, chief operating officer and associate dean for external relations at the Stanford Law School, asks and answers several questions: Who makes lead gifts? What compels such acts of philanthropy? How do lead gifts come to pass? What, if anything, do lead gift donors have in common? And what environmental conditions influence such gifts?

Chapter Fifteen focuses on corporations and foundations. It explains how they determine where their support goes, how a nonprofit can successfully work with each, and how to put together a proposal, which is the method most often used to submit a formal solicitation to both foundations and corporations.

Several pieces of campaign literature in addition to those discussed in Chapter Three should be developed. These materials and their desired features are described in Chapter Sixteen.

Chapter Seventeen discusses two major board responsibilities, the validation of fundraising goals and the assessment of program performance. Various tools are discussed, particularly the market survey, an external test of the nonprofit's case for financial support and a validation of the feasibility of the fundraising goal, particularly for capital campaigns; and the program assessment, an internal review of the development program. An additional check, the Dove Preparedness Index, is presented.

The use of paid solicitors and consultants is discussed in Chapter Eighteen. Dos and don'ts for selecting them and the pros and cons of using them are covered.

In Chapter Nineteen, William V. West, a former senior management consultant with Andersen Consulting, former manager of information consulting at Ernst & Young, and past executive director of Alumni and Foundation Information Systems at Indiana University, helps define and determine technological needs and discusses how to select technology vendors, the best technologies to use in particular situations, and using the benefits of technology to the best advantage in fundraising.

The seldom noticed but extremely important processes associated with administering gifts and providing accountability once received are covered in Chapter Twenty—stewardship and donor relations, gift acknowledgment, gift and account administration, gift agreements, and investment policy are addressed.

Achieving financial success on schedule is the ultimate goal of all campaigns. Chapter Twenty-One discusses how to conclude the campaign successfully and take care of such post-campaign matters as writing final reports and assessing the campaign's productivity.

And that's just Part One. The even larger Part Two is devoted to useful resources, a sampling of literature from several organizations. The resources are included not only to illustrate the outcomes of processes described in Part One but also to serve as good examples so that readers may develop the support materials they need for any fundraising effort.

Today's typical educational, arts-related, religious, community, or healthcare organization is considering, conducting, or concluding a capital campaign, in addition to running an annual giving program, and yet many nonprofit organizations are inadequately prepared to plan, initiate, and manage such campaigns successfully. The resource section is intended to be a visual reference library for their use, provided in the knowledge that most organizations cannot afford to hire outside helpers and have many more essential tasks to complete than time permits.

December 2000   Kent E. Dove
Bloomington, Indiana

ACKNOWLEDGMENTS

In a review of *Conducting a Successful Capital Campaign*, the editor of *Contributions* wrote, "Dove, drawing on his own experience and that of other authorities . . ." The names of those authorities, too numerous to mention individually here, are liberally scattered throughout this book, too. To each and every one of you, I offer deep appreciation and sincere thanks. You have done this field a true service.

I have already lauded my mentors in the Preface. But there are of course a number of other people who merit special mention. Writing a book of this scope requires great effort and the accumulation and assimilation of a world of information. Although I am constantly communicating with people and reading in the field, it is the Indiana University Foundation (IUF) research team that holds the key to collecting and organizing information. Under the direction of Vicky Martin, the IUF team—particularly Marilyn Behrman, who is a frequent visitor to my office—takes great pride in assuring the accuracy and currency of the facts on which I must rely. Vicky tells me that they keep a file marked "Kent's books" and that the entire staff makes certain that all available pertinent pieces of information find their way into it. That kind of spirit is what makes Indiana University (IU) and the Indiana University Foundation the great places they are. We're a team, and everyone works hard, not only to do his or her own job but also to make it possible for others to do theirs. It doesn't matter who gets the credit; it matters only that we get things right and do things well.

The coauthors of Chapter Fourteen, Rod Kirsch and Martin Shell, are two very special individuals who in years to come will be among the small group of men and women providing top-level leadership in the field of fundraising. We couldn't be in better hands. Both possess great intelligence—and wisdom, too. Both have absolute integrity, a common touch, and great people skills. Both are tempered by the experiences of both success and struggle, hold to high standards and expect of themselves even more than they expect of others, and embrace a work ethic that fatigues even the young. I stand in awe of them.

For more than fifty years, IU and the IUF have produced leaders in the fundraising field and provided exemplary program models for all to emulate. I began my career here, and like the swallows to Capistrano or salmon to their spawning grounds, I have returned after serving more than one hundred nonprofit organizations in eight different time zones over a span of more than three decades. This place now harbors an extraordinary collection of talent, designing program models that will light the path to the future. The current staff, building on a tradition, is the best, the brightest, and the deepest we've ever had. What a joy it is to serve with them. I am truly fortunate to be here now.

Evidence of this program's quality is contained in every chapter of this book. It all begins with Curt Simic. During his tenure as IUF president, a strategic vision has been developed, programs capable of achieving the vision have been designed, and a staff to bring the program to life has been assembled. With the exception of Martin Shell, whom I met when he was at Hendrix College in Conway, Arkansas, every author contributing to this book is now or has been a vital part of this program. Carolyn Madvig and Jeff Lindauer manage a superior annual giving effort, and IU's telemarketing effort is currently one of the two best in American higher education—and Jeff is determined to surpass our good friends at the University of Michigan for the top spot. Alan Spears is a remarkable young man who has transformed IU's major gifts and planned giving programs. Rod Kirsch, an IU alumnus, was here as senior vice president for development before moving to Penn State. Bill West's knowledge of technology is leading-edge, and Jaci Thiede has brought with her to IU the next level of strategic direction and effective program modeling in her analytical development of the GIFTS project to implement A. T. Kearney's groundbreaking work at IU linking for-profit best practices in marketing compatibly with the culture, history, and traditions of philanthropy. Jaci is emerging as yet another bright star, along with Rod and Martin, who will lead the future of fundraising. And I must also acknowledge the many other talented, dedicated, and inspirational people who come to the IU campus each day to enhance the professionalism of its fundraising program.

Finally, I give thanks again to my friends at Jossey-Bass: former president and CEO Lynn Luckow; my editor, Dorothy Hearst; and my production editor, Xenia Lisanevich. The Jossey-Bass team is every bit as "world-class" as the IU team I work with daily.

This book is a reflection on my journey through fifty-six years of life, thirty-three of them spent as a professional fundraiser. I thank God for allowing me to continue to live such an interesting life and for putting me in a position to share my experiences for the benefit of others. It's been a remarkable trip—one that I consider a work in progress.

—K.E.D.

This book is dedicated to the memory of my mother.
Appropriately named Grace, Mom gave me unconditional love
and shared with me the ability to get to the heart of any matter
and a focused, determined, optimistic attitude toward life
that has carried me over some bumps in the road.
It is also dedicated to the memory of Sam Cooper.
Mr. Cooper taught me about the way the world works
and how to use that knowledge in fundraising.
Both taught me about people and the responsibility we all have
to respect and care for one another.
It is also dedicated to my wife, Sandy,
and our children, Jason and Kerrye, who have given
joy, purpose, and meaning to my walk along life's path.
All praise to God.

THE AUTHOR

KENT E. DOVE is the author of *Conducting a Successful Capital Campaign* (2nd ed., Jossey-Bass, 2000), widely heralded as the most important guide to planning and implementing a capital campaign ever published.

Dove's career began shortly after his 1968 graduation from Indiana University when he joined the Indiana University Foundation (IUF) staff as a publications writer for the university's 150th anniversary campaign. He also directed annual giving programs for several of the university's professional schools. Over the next decade he moved into positions of increasing responsibility—director of annual giving, assistant director of development, director of development—leading to his appointment as vice president of development at Drake University, coordinating the officers of development, alumni relations, public relations, and government relations. Only thirty-four at the time, he was the youngest chief advancement officer at a major university in America. Six years later he was counsel and resident director of the then-largest capital campaign for an American public university while also serving as a consultant to the largest campaign ever undertaken in Canada to that point in time.

Dove is considered the preeminent fundraising practitioner working in America today, and his career spans more than three decades. He currently serves as vice president for development at the IUF, to which he returned in 1993 to serve as executive director of capital campaigns, managing a six-year, $350 million endowment campaign for Indiana University, Bloomington, the largest campaign ever undertaken by the university. The campaign surpassed its goal in the summer of 1999, having raised $373 million more than a year ahead of schedule, and it is projected to conclude on December 31, 2000, more than $100 million over goal. Dove was named vice president for development in 1997, and in 1999 the Council for Advancement and Support of Education (CASE) recognized the IUF with its highest award of excellence for overall fundraising performance for the period 1993–1998.

Dove has held educational fundraising management positions at Rice University, the University of California–Berkeley, Drake University, the University of Alabama, Northwestern University, the University of Tennessee Center for the Health Sciences, and West Virginia University.

During three decades of involvement in capital campaigns, Dove has been associated with campaigns throughout the United States and Canada. As a practitioner, he has participated in the staffing and management of nine successful major campaigns and has provided consulting services to nearly fifty more. He has also served as a consultant to numerous other third-sector institutions.

From June 1989 to December 1993 he operated Kent E. Dove & Associates, a small firm offering personalized attention to a select client base. His areas of interest are assessment of institutional development programs, institutional planning, market surveys, management and supervision of capital campaigns, staff and board training, and management of nonprofit organizations.

Dove has served three terms on CASE's educational fund raising committee and one term on the board of directors of the Association of Fundraising Professionals (formerly National Society of Fund Raising Executives). In 1986 he received the CASE Steuben Glass Apple Award for Outstanding Teaching.

CONDUCTING A SUCCESSFUL FUNDRAISING PROGRAM

PLANNING AND IMPLEMENTING YOUR FUNDRAISING PROGRAM

TABLES, FIGURES, AND EXHIBITS IN PART ONE

INTRODUCTION

The term *development* is often considered a synonym, or even a euphemism, for *fundraising.* And certainly no development program can succeed without an effective fundraising operation to provide the necessary resources. But development in the broadest sense includes much more than fundraising per se. And the nonprofits that enjoy the greatest success in fundraising are those that understand the concept of development and know how to translate it into an effective fundraising operation. These nonprofits view development as an effort by the entire organization to realize its maximum potential and its highest destiny by performing three essential functions:

- Continuously analyzing the organization's mission, programs, and services
- Establishing strategic goals and objectives for the future
- Taking the necessary action to achieve those goals and objectives

This concept of development reaches far beyond the development office; it is a shared institutional responsibility. No development program can attain its full potential without a team concept and total institutional commitment. The most successful development programs are based on four things:

- A strategic planning process that identifies the kinds of resources and support that will be required to meet the organization's immediate and long-range goals

- A written plan of action for the development program, prepared by the professional staff and approved by the governing board
- A stewardship program that provides for the wise conservation, investment, and use of financial resources, both earned and contributed, and full accountability to the organization's donor-investors
- An expanding base of support that attracts new friends and new markets for the organization's programs and services

Development is a line function, equal in rank to the activities of the business office and other administrative units. The primary responsibility of the development office is to obtain the financial resources that will enable the organization to achieve its goals. It is headed by the chief development officer, who reports directly to the chief executive officer and enjoys the same professional stature as other direct reports. Even in a small organization, rarely can the chief executive officer personally carry out all the activities a strong development program entails; the chief executive officer must rely on competent development officers.

An effective development program includes the following components:

- Annual giving (to support current operations)
- Capital giving (including major gifts, special gifts, and the capacity to conduct periodic capital campaigns)
- Planned and deferred giving (such as bequests and life income plans)
- Prospect research (to identify and gather information on prospects)

Larger development offices may also have specialists in proposal writing, communications, marketing, and special events.

A comprehensive development program provides an organization with a number of significant advantages:

- A well-crafted strategic plan that extends several years into the future, helping the organization maintain an overall sense of direction.
- A clearly expressed vision that gives donors and prospects a sense of the organization's mission and programs and of what could be accomplished with additional resources.
- A market orientation that is based on matching the organization's goals with donors' interests. This means that the organization does not "plead" for gifts but rather presents donors with opportunities for investment. Donors act in willing concert as committed partners in helping the organization attain its full potential.

- Uninterrupted access by the organization and its donors to all methods of generating financial support, including annual, capital, and planned giving.
- Continuity in the fundraising program and all its components, as well as in the training and use of staff and volunteers.
- An expanding base of support, new friends, and new markets for the organization's programs and services.

   In essence, the purpose of an effective development program is to enable the organization to realize its full potential and its highest destiny—on behalf of all the people it serves and aspires to serve in the future. If the organization is to succeed, its development program must succeed—and the success of the development program is the success of the entire organization.

CHAPTER ONE

TRACING PHILANTHROPY'S ORIGINS AND DEFINING FUNDRAISING BASICS

Fundraising is big business, and it grows bigger by the day.

According to the American Association of Fund-Raising Counsel (AAFRC) Trust for Philanthropy (1997), in 1995 there were 626,226 organizations registered with the Internal Revenue Service (IRS) as charities, up from 422,103 in 1987. The following year the number was 654,186—up 4.5 percent in one year and a 55 percent increase over 1987 (AAFRC Trust for Philanthropy, 1998b). By 1997, the number was up again, this time to 692,524—a 5.6 percent increase over the year before and a 64.7 percent increase since 1987 (AAFRC Trust for Philanthropy, 1999).

Implications of Growth in the Nonprofit Sector

These impressive numbers are just the tip of the iceberg in measuring the size of the nonprofit sector in the United States. For example, these totals do not include many religious congregations—religious congregations are not required to register, although some do—nor do the local affiliates of such national organizations as Boys and Girls Clubs or the American Cancer Society register separately.

Even if religious congregations and local affiliates were counted, however, the picture of voluntary associations in the United States would still be incomplete.

Entities with gross revenues of less than $25,000 do not have to register, and there are more of them than one might imagine. Smith (1997) estimates that there are between thirty and one hundred organizations for every thousand citizens. This estimate implies that at least 90 percent of the voluntary associations in the United States are not reflected in IRS registration data, nor is giving to most of these organizations reflected in national statistics.

As the number of nonprofits grows, so do the number of organizations conducting larger-scale fundraising efforts. In August 1998, the Indiana University Center on Philanthropy released a new report, *The Philanthropy Giving Index (PGI)*, which states that some 33 percent of three hundred fundraising executives polled indicated that their organizations are engaged in capital campaigns and that another 21 percent planned to begin capital campaigns within the next six months. In the summer of 1999, the center reported that 32 percent of organizations were engaged in a campaign and 25 percent planned to start one.

What emerges from these statistics is the picture of a sector that has grown at the rate of nearly 50 percent over the past decade, with the real possibility that more than 50 percent of organizations in the third sector are conducting or planning greatly enhanced fundraising efforts. In this very large, rapidly growing field, the number of nonprofits will continue to increase and goals will go higher, even though they may level off for a period if present-value reporting methods are fully adopted (see Chapter Six). This growth points emphatically to the need for strategic institutional planning; for solidly drawn, carefully documented cases for support; and for volunteer campaign leaders of the first caliber.

A Brief History of the Philanthropic Tradition in the West

Robert L. Payton (1999, pp. 482–483) quickly traces the tradition of philanthropy:

> Several thousand years ago there emerged in the Middle East the first evidence of organized charity. In the oldest books of the Old Testament appear mandates from God to come to the aid of *the widow, the orphan, the stranger,* and *the poor.* Those categories identify the most vulnerable, those least able to sustain themselves in an agricultural society. "When you reap the harvest of your land, you shall not reap to the very edges of your field, or gather the gleanings of your harvest. You shall not strip your vineyard bare, or gather the fallen grapes of your vineyard; you shall leave them for the poor and the alien: I am the Lord your God" (Leviticus 19:5).

Another variant appeared in classical Greece and Rome:

Everybody knows that all of Rome's citizens, or a section of them, received every month, at a low price or free of charge, a certain quantity of corn, that these distributions were established in 123 [B.C.] by a law of the tribune Gaius Gracchus, and that they continued until the end of the Empire. They can be regarded as a "welfare-state" measure or else stigmatized as an encouragement to idleness, as by Cicero: "Gaius Gracchus brought forward a corn law. It was agreeable to the masses, for it provided food in abundance without work. Loyal citizens were against it, because they thought it was a call to the masses to desert industry for idleness, and saw that it was a drain upon the Treasury [Veyne, 1990, pp. 236–237].

The stories in the Old Testament are summarized and extended in a famous passage in the New Testament: "For I was hungry and you gave me food, I was thirsty and you gave me something to drink, I was a stranger and you welcomed me, I was naked and you gave me clothing, I was sick and you took care of me, I was in prison and you visited me" (Matthew 25:35–37).

By the time of Saint Thomas Aquinas 1,200 years later, that short list had been further expanded into two lists of "corporal alms" and "spiritual alms." Thomas's discussion lists seven of each. The corporal alms are: "feeding the hungry, giving drink to the thirsty, clothing the naked, giving hospitality to strangers, visiting the sick, ransoming prisoners, and burying the dead." The seven spiritual alms are: "instructing the ignorant, giving advice to those in doubt, consoling the sorrowful, reproving sinners, forgiving offenses, putting up with people who are burdensome and hard to get on with, and finally, praying for all" (Thomas Aquinas, 1975, p. 241).

Four centuries later, in 1601, the Statute of Charitable Uses was promulgated in England by Elizabeth I. It continues the Roman tradition of state assistance, and it includes reference to gifts and other support for "relief of aged, impotent, and poor people; some for maintenance of sick and maimed soldiers and mariners, schools of learning, free schools, and scholars in universities; some for repair of bridges, ports, havens, and causeways; some for education and preferment of orphans" (Chesterman, 1975, p. 25).

With the Reformation a new emphasis on individual charity appears, beyond what might be done by state or church, as in this sermon by John Wesley (1983, p. 463): "But let not any man imagine that he has done anything, barely by going thus far, by 'gaining and saving all he can,' if he were to stop there. . . . Add the third rule to the two preceding. Having, first, gained all you can, and secondly, saved all you can, then 'give all you can.'"

. . . I would here insert a reference to Madison on faction, to the First Amendment on freedom of assembly, and of course to Tocqueville on voluntary association. . . . Emblematic of one view is the famous statement by Sir William Beveridge in England in 1942 that heralded the coming of the modern welfare state: "He stated that in itself social security was 'a wholly inadequate aim'; it could not be part of a general programme. 'It is one part only of an attack upon five giant evils: upon the physical Want with which it is directly concerned, upon Disease which often causes that Want and brings many other troubles in its train, upon Ignorance which no democracy can afford among its citizens, upon Squalor . . . , and upon the Idleness which destroys wealth and corrupts men'" (Timmins, 1996, p. 24).

After three thousand years of debate one might expect consensus, but such is not the case:

> Isn't it time for the government to encourage work rather than rewarding dependency? The Great Society has had the unfortunate consequence of snaring millions of Americans into the welfare trap. Government programs designed to give a helping hand to the neediest of Americans have instead bred illegitimacy, crime, illiteracy, and more poverty. Our *Contract with America* will change this destructive social behavior by requiring welfare recipients to take responsibility for the decisions they make. Our *Contract* will achieve what some thirty years of massive welfare spending has not been able to accomplish: reduce illegitimacy, require work, and save taxpayers money [*Contract with America,* 1994, p. 69].

One theme running through it all is the fact of vulnerability and helplessness that generates a response of private and public assistance. There seems always to have been both, along with a debate about how responsibility should be apportioned: among self-help, mutual aid, government assistance, and philanthropy.

The Evolution of Fundraising

Philanthropy and charity are as old as humankind itself. Fundraising, however, is a modern phenomenon. If we trace the roots of giving in American society, as well as the development of the fundraising function, we find some benchmarks. In 1641, for example, Harvard College sponsored the first systematic effort to raise funds for higher education when it sent a trio of preachers to England on a begging mission to raise funds (Chewning, 1984). Once in England, the fundraisers found that they needed a brochure to support their appeal and relayed the need back to Harvard. In response came *New England's First Fruits,* written largely in Massachusetts but printed in London in 1643, the first of the public relations pamphlets and brochures that have ever since been a fundraising staple.

The first attempt to stage a community chest–type fund drive was undertaken in 1829 by Matthew Carey in Philadelphia. The net result of America's first federated fundraising effort was a total of $276.50 given by 137 subscribers. This effort contained, in embryo, the elements of modern fundraising: the paid solicitor, advance promotion, the classified prospect list, the federated drive.

Major gift fundraising became an established practice through both the rise of industrialization and the new willingness of major donors to give to third-sector institutions. During the late nineteenth and early twentieth centuries, such capitalists as Andrew Carnegie and John D. Rockefeller began underwriting libraries, museums, research projects, and even entire universities. Fundraising and public relations firms (for instance, the John Price Jones Corporation) were established to assist nonprofit organizations that did not have the staff or the expertise to conduct these efforts on their own.

Early in the twentieth century, one of the first successful major campaigns was directed by Charles Sumner Ward and his colleague Lyman L. Pierce, campaign directors for the YMCA. Over the course of three decades, Ward's fundraising techniques raised more than half a billion dollars for that organization. His efforts became the foundation on which today's modern campaigns are still built, earning him recognition as a master campaigner, and his strategies were copied by many other successful fundraisers.

Ten Prerequisites of Fundraising Success

To be successful, a fundraising program must be characterized by the following ten prerequisite elements:

1. Commitments of time and support from all key participants (the governing board, the chief executive officer, prospective major donors, key volunteer leaders, the professional fundraising staff, and the institutional family)
2. A clear organizational self-image and a strategic plan for organizational growth and improvement
3. Fundraising objectives based on important and legitimate institutional plans, goals, budgets, and needs
4. A written document that makes a compelling case for supporting the organization (larger, more complex organizations will need additional support materials)

5. Regular assessments of the institutional development program and, before a capital campaign, a market survey addressing internal and external preparedness
6. Enlistment and education of volunteer leaders
7. Ability and readiness of key donors to give substantial gifts early in the fundraising effort
8. Competent staff and, perhaps, external professional counsel
9. Adequate, even liberal funds for expenses
10. Consideration of other factors (as described in the following text), which, rather than determining whether the fundraising initiative should be undertaken, tend to determine the size of its goal and its timing in terms of both length and starting date

Other Influential Factors

As an organization plans its fundraising program, factors such as the ones discussed here will undoubtedly need to be considered from time to time. Although an institution that finds itself less than well prepared to meet these contingencies need not abandon its plans, it may have to slow its pace or postpone its efforts until it has acquired the necessary strength or until the situation has changed to the point where the program can proceed. Failure to consider these factors and contingencies can place a fundraising initiative at risk and may predestine its failure. Close adherence to a plan without varying the timeline is more necessary in the annual campaign than in the capital campaign, but it is nevertheless a good idea when running an annual campaign to be sensitive to these factors.

Age of the Organization

Older organizations tend to be better established than younger ones. They have longer track records of service and past success; they often have better-defined, older constituencies, and their support bases are often more developed. As a university president once asked, "Can you recall the last time a college more than a hundred years old had to shut down?"

Caliber of the Constituency

Research on patterns of charitable giving by Americans suggests that on the whole, heads of households contribute more than others. Contribution amounts are generally correlated with wage earners' income levels, occupations, employment status, educational levels, and ages (Gallup, 1982). Many of these conclusions are confirmed by another important piece of research commissioned by the Rockefeller Brothers Fund and conducted by Yankelovich, Skelley and White, Inc. (White, 1986). According to this survey, major influences on giving include income level, life expectancy, age, religious involvement, and marital status. Older, more prosperous individuals, especially the religious, give proportionately more. Organizations do better when their constituencies are older, wealthier, better educated, and more skilled. More recent research published by INDEPENDENT SECTOR (1996) confirms these earlier findings, which have all reached essentially the same conclusions. And a survey by the U.S. Trust (1998) reveals that the affluent give 8 percent of their after-tax income, compared to the general public, who gives 3 percent. The evidence can be seen in any community.

Wolpert (1993), studying giving patterns in American communities, documented the following facts:

- Americans are not uniformly generous but vary greatly from place to place in their level and targeting of donations.
- Generosity differences between communities have their greatest impact on services targeted to the lowest-income populations.
- Disparities in generosity levels were declining in the early 1990s, principally due to the harsher economic environment in the more generous places rather than greater generosity in the more parsimonious places.
- Generosity is greater where per capita income is increasing, where the political and cultural ideology is liberal rather than conservative, and in the smaller metropolitan areas, where distress levels are lower.
- Greater generosity is associated with greater targeting for educational, cultural, and health services rather than social assistance to the needy.
- The increased sorting of Americans into socially homogeneous communities has reproduced public and nonprofit service infrastructures in the suburbs often at the expense of support for center-city and rural institutions (the real growth of service provision is quite small).
- Gaps in basic services and quality of life are widening between the growing and declining states and metropolitan areas.
- The severely fragmented and atomized nonprofit sector contributes effectively to the variety and quality of life in American communities but lacks the resources and structure to address major service and regional disparities.

Williams (1995) in her research on the use of check-off and credit systems on state income tax returns to encourage philanthropy reaffirmed this pattern of variables that influence giving—local attitudes toward giving, the financial ability to give, and public policy supporting and encouraging giving.

Range of the Institution's Giving Program

The organization chart of a modern development program will take many sizes and shapes, but there is a standard model from which all development programs grow or into which all organizations aspire to grow if they are not yet fully developed and mature (see Figure 1.1).

The most productive fundraising programs characteristically include at least four key functional elements:

1. An annual giving program
2. A planned giving program
3. A major gifts program
4. A prospect research program

An organization that lacks any of these programs or that has failed to develop them fully tends to be less prepared for fundraising than an organization that

FIGURE 1.1. ORGANIZATION CHART
FOR A MODERN DEVELOPMENT PROGRAM.

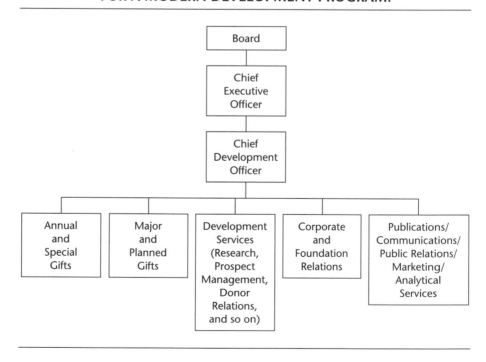

already has them in effective operation. As a result, the organization that lacks them may have to accept lower goals. Pickett (1984) demonstrated this point convincingly in his sampling of institutions of higher education.

Size and Geographical Distribution of the Constituency

The individual demographic factors mentioned earlier are certainly the most important determinants of the ability of a constituency to support a fundraising effort. It is also generally true, however, that organizations with larger constituencies tend to have a better base from which to work. (This will not always be the case, of course; an organization that provides services for indigent or low-income groups may well have a very large client list but few major gift prospects within this constituency who are able and willing to give at the levels required to support a campaign.)

The geographical distribution of the constituency is another factor to be considered in determining preparedness and the size of goal that is realistic. Less time and money and fewer staff are needed to organize and manage a fundraising program in a small geographical area, such as a city or one section of a city, than to conduct one over a wider area, which presents more complex organizational problems. National programs, especially those conducted by large educational institutions such as Harvard University, demonstrate this principle.

Previous Fundraising Success

Realism is necessary in determining fundraising goals. How long ago was the last effort conducted? What was the goal amount? Was the campaign successful? Past performance as well as current trends in giving must be analyzed to determine realistic goals. An institution annually raising $500,000 is unlikely to be prepared to mount a successful campaign for $30 million.

There is no ironclad prescription for using recent and current giving totals to project goals, but a random review of several successful recent capital campaigns suggests that organizations normally set goals that range from four to six times the current amount of total annual development income. A major consulting firm proposes that the cumulative total of gifts for the previous five years represents a good initial benchmark for determining a campaign goal; for example, an organization that has raised $20 million in five years will probably end up with a campaign goal of $35 to $45 million. If the comprehensive campaign model described in Chapter Two is used, however, one must be especially careful about employing such rules of thumb in determining a goal; it is too simplistic to use mathematical assumptions alone in making projections. It must also be remembered that part of the comprehensive goal is ongoing annual support, and the amount of this support should not be included in the capital component of the total goal. A further discussion of setting and adjusting the annual campaign goal appears in Chapter Eight.

Quality of the Program and Impact of Its Services

In determining fundraising preparedness and goals, two extremely important variables to be considered are the quality of the services being provided and the impact that these services have on the constituency or community being served. Institutions that provide higher-quality programs and a broader range of services tend to have greater access to a wider segment of the philanthropic market. High-quality organizations (such as the Mayo Clinic, Girls and Boys Town, the Girl Scouts of America, the stronger and more vibrant YMCAs and YWCAs around the country, and the dominant churches and synagogues in a community) are more competitive in the most competitive environments in their ability to reach known philanthropists, foundations, and corporations. These funding sources must always choose among numerous organizations requesting donations, and among the organizations meeting their giving criteria, they most often select those that demonstrate the highest qualifications.

The U.S. Trust survey (1998) reveals that 81 percent of affluent Americans (with incomes of $225,000 and above and a net worth in excess of $3 million) decide which nonprofits to support on the basis of the reputation and integrity of the organization; 79 percent give because they feel the organization meets an important need.

Location of the Organization

Organizations in urban areas tend to have a better climate in which to seek significant contributions than organizations in rural areas. Residents of larger cities and of geographical areas in which individual wealth and corporate and foundation headquarters are concentrated tend to be more experienced and sophisticated in fundraising and more generous in their support. Communities with United Way campaigns also tend to be more receptive to and supportive of other fundraising initiatives.

There are regional differences as well, both in the United States and in Canada. In the United States, organized fundraising by nonprofit organizations is generally more mature and sophisticated and involves more realistic expectations on the East Coast than in the Midwest or on the West Coast, and the same contrast holds between eastern Canada and western Canada, although there are specific exceptions in both countries.

There are other factors to be considered too. In the United States, there is a noteworthy concentration of foundation wealth on the island of Manhattan, and a significant portion of the support provided by these foundations tends to go to East Coast institutions. Texas has a number of large foundations, many of which restrict their giving to organizations in that state. In North Dakota, South Dakota, and Alabama, however, with fewer large foundations and corporate headquarters, there is comparatively much less charitable giving. The concentration of population or wealth and the institution's proximity to it are often important variables. Nevertheless, every community has a power structure, and any organization that is planning a fundraising initiative can maximize its potential by effectively involving its key community leaders.

Human Factors

Human emotion and motivation are factors that should never be underestimated. Three factors transcend all others in motivating people to give: urgency, importance, and relevance.

An earthquake hits Central America and destroys a hospital; a tornado rips through the Midwest and flattens a church—when there is an urgent need, people respond immediately. Never mind that the organization affected has no organized fundraising operation; donors will react to an urgent situation, and the decision to give is often spontaneous (Panas, 1984).

Importance is the second strong motivator. If something is important enough to people, they will see that it gets done. For example, if a community decides that a YMCA or YWCA building is important to it or that a program to shelter and feed the homeless and hungry should be at the top of its agenda, that importance alone can transcend other factors in getting the job done. Again, it is irrelevant that the organization falls short in critical ways; even if the prospective donor does not feel the urgency of the situation or does not deem it personally relevant, the prospective donor's support can be and will be generated if the need is perceived as important, particularly if it is perceived as important to peers and colleagues whose esteem the prospective donor values.

The third factor is relevance. People respond to stimuli that are personally relevant, often on a totally emotional basis. Individuals give emotionally, not cerebrally (Panas, 1984).

State of the Economy

Organizations that tend to feel the effects of a poor economy most immediately and often most dramatically are the community-based nonprofits that rely heavily on the nonprofessional white-collar middle class and the blue-collar working class for support to meet operating budgets. Middle-class donors' giving diminishes noticeably in times of high unemployment, strikes, and poor corporate performance, which in turn affect the amount of overtime available, the ability or willingness of companies to give raises or pay bonuses, and the overall psychology of workers who live from paycheck to paycheck.

Concrete evidence shows that over time, giving is relatively unaffected by the economy. But tell that to a nonprofit organization in Michigan when the automobile industry is suffering a downturn or to organizations currently involved in fundraising efforts related to British Columbia's forestry and mining industries. Overall, especially with larger donors, the state of the economy matters more psychologically than financially. Nevertheless, organizations generally tend to tread lightly in economic downturns and always hope to launch and conduct their fundraising initiatives in strong economic circumstances.

Competing and Conflicting Programs

The timing of other fundraising drives is another consideration. In the face of competing and conflicting capital fundraising efforts, an institution may decide to alter its own time frame, or it may choose to proceed more cautiously because the leaders it desires to attract are already committed to other efforts or because other efforts have already overextended its constituency's ability to give. In the annual fund, there is less chance to stall or postpone an effort, but it can be timed so as not to compete too directly with other, larger, more powerful efforts. In areas where the United Way effort is strong, many organizations keep a low profile while the United Way campaign is in high gear from mid-August to mid-November.

Trends in the Nonprofit Sector

Certain areas of the nonprofit sector seem to enjoy continuing and enduring support. Sometimes, however, there are attitudinal or mood changes directed toward a sector or within the nonprofit sector.

There are also new and emerging causes, and there are causes whose time is past. As an example of the first case, the HIV/AIDS epidemic has given rise to an entirely new cause in the past fifteen years. As an example of the second, when

Jonas Salk discovered the polio vaccine, the March of Dimes faced going out of business or reinventing itself; it chose to do the latter.

In addition, entire new sectors are emerging. In *Giving USA, 1986* (AAFRC Trust for Philanthropy, 1986), six sectors were identified: religion; education; health; human services; arts, culture, and humanities; and public/social benefit. *Giving USA, 1998* (AAFRC Trust for Philanthropy, 1998b) lists eight: the two new sectors are environment/wildlife and international affairs.

Unfavorable Publicity

Unfavorable publicity can crush a fundraising effort before it begins, and it can even have a dramatic effect on an initiative already in progress. The United Way of America felt such a backlash in the 1990s because of actions attributed to one high-profile individual. If the publicity is going to be short-lived, wait until the storm passes. If it is of a longer-term variety, plans may need to be altered, delayed, or abandoned in keeping with the nature of the negative publicity.

Local Issues

You may know of things happening in your own backyard that may affect your organization. Again, in keeping with the nature of the situation, actions and plans may have to be adjusted.

Challenge Gifts and Matching Grants

Never underestimate the power of a challenge gift. North Americans love the "buy one, get one free" concept, and the ability to leverage a gift is an irresistible temptation for many. Obviously, a 1:1 match—every dollar that the donor gives is matched by another dollar—is more appealing than a 1:2 challenge (a dollar is given for every $2 contributed by the donor), but even if the match is diluted by a factor of 2, it can still be very helpful. Challenges presenting less than a 1:2 incentive usually have significantly less appeal, and a richer challenge (2:1) greatly increases attractiveness, as the following examples illustrate.

• A magnificent $50 million challenge grant was among the forty largest gifts in U.S. history ever made to an institution of higher education by an individual ("Drake University," 1997). Opperman's was an especially rich match, with $10 million provided in a 2:1 ratio for gifts to Drake's Law School, of which he is a graduate; the remaining $40 million will serve as a challenge to all other alumni and friends on a 3:1 basis.

• In a two-year period, through the power of a matching gifts program, Indiana University more than tripled the number of endowed faculty positions that had been created in the university's first 175 years.

• The state of Florida sponsors the Major Gifts Trust Fund, which matches gifts of $100,000 and above for academic endowments at state colleges and universities on a progressive scale ranging from 1:2 at $100,000 up to 1:1 at $2 million and above. The state also sponsors the Facilities Enhancement Challenge Grant Program, which requires a specific legislative appropriation of the matching funds for a specific project. According to Paul A. Robell (personal communication, Sept. 1998), "Because of the great success of the program, the Major Gifts Trust Fund runs behind and donors' gifts are placed in a queue waiting for funding from the following legislative session. The University of Florida Foundation, Inc., has received well over $50 million from the Major Gifts Trust Fund and well over $30 million from the facilities program."

Matching gift programs can also be designed to assist nonprofits in their annual fundraising efforts:

• Margaret Skidmore (personal communication, May 2000), associate director of the Museum of Fine Arts, Houston, and its director of development, reports that one donor annually provides a substantial matching gift that is used up to the limits of the grant to increase current donors' giving and to encourage new gifts. The challenge is structured to assist the museum both to renew and expand its donor base and to increase annual support levels from current donors.
• A donor in support of a local effort on behalf of the American Diabetes Association recently provided a $1,000 challenge grant to coworkers, thereby increasing their company's support threefold from one year to the next.

Lightning can strike twice in the same place, too. Steve Bonchek, executive director of the Harmony School Education Center in Bloomington, Indiana (personal communication, Apr. 2000), reports a special, onetime "millennium grant" of $100,000 from a New York–based foundation "to strengthen Harmony School's core, its teachers and students." It was a 1:1 match, with all gifts made qualifying to meet the match. Shortly thereafter, the Lilly Endowment through the Community Foundation of Bloomington and Monroe County provided another challenge grant (see Exhibits 1.1 and 1.2). Harmony School successfully met both matches.

EXHIBIT 1.1. HARMONY SCHOOL LETTER TO PREVIOUS DONORS.

Harmony School Education Center
P.O. Box 1787
Bloomington, IN 47402
(812) 334-8349
Fax (812) 333-3435

April 14, 1999

Dear Friends:

Thank you for supporting us with your contribution several months ago. I now have both good news and "bad" news for you. The good news is that Harmony has been selected as a Community Partner by the Community Foundation of Bloomington and Monroe County. This means that Harmony will receive a $200,000 grant from The Lilly Endowment. The "bad" news is that we need your help again so soon after our last request because the Lilly grant is a CHALLENGE grant, and we must raise $100,000 by May 14th to receive it! Because it is an "all or nothing" challenge we again ask you to consider a contribution. So far we have raised $65,000 of the $100,000 we need.

In addition, The Lilly Endowment will add $25,000 to Harmony's $100,000 to set up a permanent endowment at the Community Foundation. The $200,000 from Lilly will be used on much needed repairs for our 1926 building (most likely first replacing our 1926 boiler). The $125,000 endowment will go toward supporting "the mission and purpose of Harmony School." Your tax-deductible donation will genuinely be a "gift that will keep on giving" because this endowment will forever contribute 5% per year to the school. I hope you can help.

I am including an article about another recent grant Harmony received which will allow us to reflect on our work at Harmony while we continue to help other schools.

Sincerely,

Steve Bonchek,
Director

Source: Harmony School Education Center. Printed with permission.

EXHIBIT 1.2. HARMONY SCHOOL LETTER TO NONDONORS.

Harmony School Education Center
P.O. Box 1787
Bloomington, IN 47402
(812) 334-8349
Fax (812) 333-3435

April 14, 1999

Dear Friends:

I was sorry that when I wrote to you last December, you were unable to make a contribution. However, now I am less disappointed because I need your help raising $100,000 by May 14th. You see, Harmony has been selected as a Community Partner by the Community Foundation of Bloomington and Monroe County. This means that Harmony will receive a $200,000 grant from The Lilly Endowment if we raise $100,000 by May 14th. Because it is an "all or nothing" CHALLENGE grant we again ask you to consider a contribution. So far we have raised $65,000 of the $100,000 we need.

In addition, The Lilly Endowment will add $25,000 to Harmony's $100,000 to set up a permanent endowment at the Community Foundation. The $200,000 from Lilly will be used on much-needed repairs for our 1926 building (most likely first replacing our 1926 boiler). The $125,000 endowment will go toward supporting "the mission and purpose of Harmony School." Your tax-deductible donation will genuinely be a "gift that will keep on giving" because this endowment will forever contribute 5% per year to the school. I hope you can help.

I am including an article about another recent grant Harmony received which will allow us to reflect on our work at Harmony while we continue to help other schools.

Sincerely,

Steve Bonchek,
Director

Source: Harmony School Education Center. Printed with permission.

Any institution that can develop a matching gifts program will enhance its fundraising potential and will help ensure the success of its campaign.

In situations like the last two, the intention is to both retain and increase the size of current gifts and to encourage both equally—that is, a 1:1 match across the board. However, if the nonprofit is particularly interested in, for example, growing its donor pool while still paying attention to its current donors, a 2:1 match for new gifts and a 1:1 match for increases on gifts is a successful way of promoting and emphasizing one aspect of the annual giving program without neglecting others.

CHAPTER TWO

CHOOSING A CAMPAIGN MODEL

The choice of a campaign model is a decision by the nonprofit as to how it will package and present its overall fundraising strategy to its constituents at a given point in time or over a long period of time. This chapter outlines the various models most commonly used, suggests a new model to be used in the future, and summarizes factors that influence the choice of a model.

Fundraising is a goal-driven process. The goal consists of organizational priorities expressed in terms of both institutional needs and the dollars necessary to fund those needs. These goals are arrived at through the case-stating process outlined in Chapter Three. The process also almost always includes a timeline or deadline. For the annual giving program, the timeline is generally one year. For larger-scale capital efforts, the timelines range from a few months to several years (see Chapter Seven).

Campaigns and the Forms They Take

A fundraising program is ordinarily referred to as a *campaign*. A campaign is organized (it has a structure); it is intentional (it follows a plan); it is systematic (volunteer enlistment and prospect cultivation and solicitation are from the top down); and it is strategic (movement and progress are plotted). Its approach to fundraising is delineated publicly as a set of priorities to be met and dollars to be raised in a specific period of time. Not all aspects of fundraising are campaign-bound, however. Planned giving, research, donor relations and stewardship, gift and account administration, and corporation and foundation relations are examples of fundraising activities that are ongoing and guided more by donors' timing and decisions than by institutional agendas and timelines.

But the paradigm that has emerged over the past century is the campaign model. Although the general principles of fundraising tend to be universally applicable to any type of organization, there are different campaign models. Four rather distinctive forms are found today:

1. The traditional annual campaign
2. The traditional capital campaign
3. The comprehensive campaign
4. The single-purpose campaign

Traditional Annual Campaign

Fifty years ago, the vast majority of third-sector institutions that engaged in fundraising ran annual campaigns seeking funds to provide for current programs and services and to pay for operating costs, in full or in part. This is the annual campaign in its purest form. Historically, when institutions decided a capital campaign was needed, the traditional campaign model was the one chosen, and the annual campaign was run as a separate, independent program. For reasons to be described shortly, this model is not used nearly as much today, although many organizations, usually smaller ones, still depend on the annual drive as their primary means of fundraising support. The United Way movement is the quintessential user of this model; community religious organizations and smaller nonprofits working in geographically focused areas depend largely on this model too. It features individual solicitation of the top prospects and is almost always supplemented by the use of direct-mail techniques to reach a larger number of prospects who cannot be contacted efficiently or effectively in person. Telemarketing is also used but is a less popular option. Electronic fundraising is the newest emerging feature now being used to supplement and enhance annual fund appeals, but its use may be less effective for small, local nonprofits.

Traditional Capital Campaign

The traditional capital campaign is a fundraising effort designed to secure gifts of capital assets to meet the capital needs of an organization, to build buildings, and in some instances to build the endowment—funds held in perpetuity with only a portion being spent each year. It is characterized by a highly motivated volunteer group working in a tightly organized and managed manner to meet a specific overall capital goal with one or more objectives during a specific period, usually three years or less. The volunteers make every reasonable effort to see all constituents and special friends on a face-to-face basis because the campaign is regarded as a once-in-a-lifetime program: traditional capital campaigns are typically spaced many years or even decades apart, and they usually occur only once during the major donor population's giving life. They are often superimposed on the ongoing development effort. In some instances, other fundraising efforts, especially annual campaigns, are suspended or downplayed during traditional capital campaigns. It is common to create a separate campaign office, budget, and staff for the sole purpose of supporting this type of effort.

The traditional capital campaign is still used in a variety of situations—the church is building an addition, the Y is constructing a swimming facility, the scout troop is founding a summer camp—but at least three important changes in campaigning have made the traditional model less fashionable today (and have led, increasingly, to the use of the comprehensive campaign and the single-purpose campaign):

First of all, a traditional capital campaign seeks gifts of capital assets to meet the capital needs of the institution. Today's capital campaigns are often designed to meet other needs, too; more gifts are being made to support all purposes, including capital.

Second, an institution conducting a traditional capital campaign runs the risk of restricting or damaging its other established, ongoing giving programs, and this is a risk that fewer and fewer institutions are willing or able to take.

Third, the traditional capital campaign attempts to reach all constituents and friends of the institution on a one-to-one, face-to-face basis. For many of North America's third-sector institutions, this is no longer possible either financially or logistically, given their number of constituents, the constituents' geographical distribution, and the high costs of fundraising.

Comprehensive Campaign

The comprehensive campaign is a major development program with specific goals and timetables. It almost always includes, under one umbrella, its current operations, onetime goals, and endowment objectives. It generally lasts for three to five years, although some campaigns are longer and some are conducted in phases. Gifts and pledges of all kinds, including annual as well as planned and deferred gifts, are often sought and counted in the campaign total. In many instances, the campaign is less dependent on volunteers, and there may be increased involvement of administrators and staff, not only as cultivators but also as solicitors, who concentrate on maximizing the gifts of major prospects through intense personal solicitation, often approaching both special and general prospects by telephone or direct mail. This type of campaign is related to the total development program and often encompasses other ongoing giving programs. The comprehensive campaign model is especially attractive to large, complex organizations that want to keep the total fundraising effort under one umbrella or want to work toward a more substantial goal above and beyond the "new money" goal set for dollars to be raised during the campaign, realizing that often the whole is greater than the sum of its parts, as Harvard demonstrated during its most recent successful campaign.

Single-Purpose Campaign

The single-purpose campaign raises money for an individual building, an endowment fund, or any other isolated objective. It is often targeted at one particular special-interest constituency, and it is generally not undertaken as part of the overall development effort; instead, it is supplemental to that effort.

Regardless of an institution's size or complexity, it is usually best to conduct a single, unified campaign. In large, administratively complex organizations, however, which use the single-purpose campaign almost exclusively, one unified campaign is not always possible or sometimes even desirable. Indeed, many institutions today are continually moving into and out of single-purpose campaigns—even, occasionally, into two or three or more at the same time.

It is becoming more and more common for this form of campaign activity to lead the institution to employ a full-time professional fundraiser, sometimes with a staff, whose responsibility is major and special gifts and who is given a job title to that effect.

Pros and Cons of the Capital Campaign

In 1980 a thought-provoking seminar for senior development professionals included a discussion of the capital campaign. The presenter, Joel P. Smith, left the audience with two questions: Is a capital campaign the right way to do fundraising? If not, how will fundraising get done?

In the essay that grew out of the ideas presented there, Smith (1981) developed the point that capital campaigns entail pros and cons. For twenty-five years, it has been an almost unchallenged axiom of fundraising that capital campaigns are a good idea. They are the centerpiece of fundraising programs in most institutions, and many institutions judge the success of fundraising programs by the magnitude and frequency of the campaigns they conduct. There is quite a persuasive case to be made for capital campaigns. Nevertheless, there is also room for more skeptical observations.

Pros

Capital campaigns provide valuable discipline in terms of planning, setting schedules, establishing goals, and providing an opportunity to manage by objectives—a rare opportunity in fundraising. Campaigns also inspire donors to make larger commitments than they otherwise would—commitments, to be sure, that may be spread over a considerable time but are nevertheless larger than they would be in the ordinary course of events.

A campaign produces results with long-term effects, and so the institution's ability to enjoy these results is not limited to the campaign period itself. Because standards have been raised during the campaign effort, it is reasonable to expect a higher level of giving afterward than was the case before.

A campaign also provides valuable, intensive experience for the development staff. Because so much is going on, and at such a level of intensity, there is an opportunity for dramatic professional growth that otherwise would not occur. There is so much to do that the staff, one way or another, learns how to do it and get it done, emerging as a group of experienced professionals. Moreover, campaigns provide not just discipline but also esprit de corps. They create a climate in which team members come together emotionally to accomplish some mutual objective. And because fundraising is a human, emotional activity, that spirit is a very valuable component in getting the job done.

These arguments amount to a really quite persuasive case. Therefore, it is not at all surprising that so many institutions have accepted these arguments and gone forward with campaigns. Indeed, some have gone forward with several campaigns over the past few decades. Nevertheless, there are some other, seldom aired, considerations.

Cons

When it comes down to the day of decision, a great many institutions are forced to conclude, reluctantly, that they simply do not have staff members with the requisite competence and experience to conduct a successful campaign. As a result, they turn to consultants or to short-term contract employees to conduct their campaigns. This is not to denigrate consultants or contract professionals—there are many honorable, able people who help numerous institutions in those roles—but turning to temporary help does have serious drawbacks. For one thing, the consultants and contract professionals will leave after the campaign. Therefore, the opportunity for professional growth, which is one of the most forceful arguments in favor of the campaign, is forfeited to some degree. Instead of building a professional staff that will be in place to conduct a refined fundraising program when the campaign is over, the institution has set up a situation in which some of the key players will leave, taking with them valuable knowledge and experience, no matter how conscientious they are about recording their knowledge in the institutional files. Furthermore, no matter how sophisticated consultants and contract professionals are, they may not be able to represent the institution with the same understanding, conviction, and depth of experience and local knowledge that the institution's professional staff can. And if there is a sine qua non of being a first-rate fundraiser, it is to have conviction and understanding about the place being represented.

Campaigns, almost by definition, place terrific emphasis on current results. The point of a campaign is to force as many gifts as possible over a prescribed period in order to achieve a goal that is often a stretch. Truly sophisticated fundraising is patient, and campaigns have no place for patience. Campaign deadlines, although they provide discipline, sometimes also encourage impetuousness. The emphasis on getting gifts now in order to reach the goal may cause an institution to accept, for example, a $50,000 gift now when a larger gift would have been available had the institution been more patient. There is a definite risk of haste and waste in campaigns.

It is difficult during a campaign to maintain the appropriate focus on an institutional agenda because there is so much attention directed to the bottom line, as well as such enthusiasm, eagerness, and determination to make the number on the bottom as large as it can be. But what is more important than amount is utility—not just bringing gifts to the institution but bringing in gifts that underwrite the institution's most important purposes. It is ironic that institutions lose this focus during campaigns, because campaigns are almost always preceded by months of discussion and planning about what it is important to raise money for. But the product of such discussion is often a comprehensive wish list rather than a rigorous evaluation of whether it is more important to have gifts for improving facilities or for expanding services. Assuming that the institution cannot have both, how is it to make the choice? Campaigns rarely force this kind of trade-off thinking; instead, they encourage the optimistic attitude that the longer the laundry list of desirable objectives, the more probable it is that the institution will achieve the vast dollar amount representing the total objective.

Campaigns make fundraising episodic. The institution pulls out the throttle for two, three, or four years; then it falls back, giving the volunteers and others some time off; then it regroups to think about another campaign; then it gears up for the next all-out assault. Most refined fundraising programs are not episodic, however. They are patient and sustained, they look to the long term, and they resist the temptation to be proud of their immediate accomplishments.

Then there is the matter of taking time off when a campaign is over. The conventional wisdom is that campaigns are so intensive and call for such effort, not only from the institutional team but also from volunteers, that everybody needs a rest. Furthermore, the argument runs, if the institution is successful in a really ambitious campaign, it will have picked all the pears there are on that particular tree and is going to have to take some time off to let new pears grow.

This is a really dangerous fallacy. It assumes that the body of prospects with whom the institution works is finite, that there are a certain number of interested people, loyal to the institution, from whom it is reasonable to expect gifts, and that the institution will go to them during the campaign and get an answer, yea or nay, so that when the campaign ends it is important to take time off, renew and regroup, and give these loyal supporters a rest.

But that is not what happens during a campaign. What happens is that a significant portion of the prospects give the institution an ambiguous answer. When the institution concludes its campaign and takes time off, *it forfeits the opportunity to follow through with those people.* Moreover, a campaign that covers three years lasts a long time, and the body of prospects is not some fixed constellation of individuals that remains static over that time. It changes by 20, 30, or 40 percent during the campaign. During that period, alliances emerge with people who become interested in and enthusiastic about the institution for the first time. To let down immediately after a campaign is to forfeit the opportunity to nurture alliances with these people, who have the potential to become important prospects over the next several years.

Campaign goals are also getting terribly large. The needs listed in a capital campaign today add up to a number likely to startle most people who care about the institution. Among those who are understanding and who are really close to the institution, an explanation of those needs will be received sympathetically. But with many, many people, the institution has the burden of making a case that is awfully difficult to make convincingly. How much credibility can there be in the claim that an unusually large goal is a realistic reflection of what an institution needs—that the institution has done the kind of soul-searching that warrants the assertion that these really are worthy objectives crucial to the quality of the institution? Is the institution coming across as grasping, as reaching for some dramatically large amount, hoping that somehow it might get it but willing to settle for less?

Clearly, whether to have a capital campaign is not the only issue. There is another very significant question: If a capital campaign will not be conducted, what are the alternatives? Surely no one can be satisfied with less than the most ambitious fundraising program appropriate to the institution's situation. The quality of all institutions is in jeopardy, and most have reached the point where their health can no longer be improved by the reduction of expenditures. The road to survival is not to sacrifice the quality of the organizations that constitute the third sector through radical cost cutting. The road to survival—for some, literal survival; for most, survival with a respectable level of quality—is somehow to bring in enough funds to underwrite the critically important objectives, the objectives that define quality for each institution and its mission.

A Proposed Solution: Continuous Lifetime Giving Program

The best answer to Smith's questions, and one that addresses many of his concerns, is the development program based on continuous lifetime giving. This approach requires many of the essential components of any successful campaign to be incorporated into the everyday life of the organization. The result of this approach is shown in Table 2.1 and Figure 2.1. It presupposes that an organization's administrative leaders have done careful, thoughtful analysis and planning and that the resulting objectives, in terms of both operations and capital, fit into the overall long-range strategic plan. It mandates that the board approve plans and, through the approval process, accept leadership responsibility. It requires that needs be real and compelling and that the case for them be articulate and stimulating. It directs that the case and the goal be tested and validated in the market before the campaign (annual or capital), insists that proper internal preparation take place, and appreciates that there must be a prospect pool able and willing to meet the fundraising goals that have been established.

FIGURE 2.1. CONTINUOUS LIFETIME GIVING: THE GIVING LIFE CYCLE.

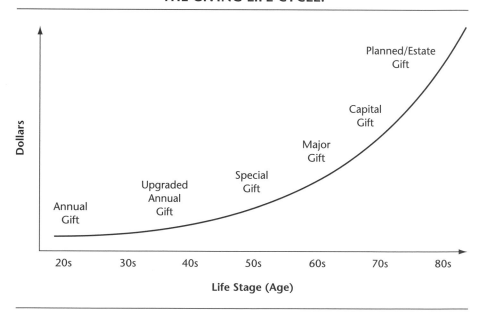

TABLE 2.1. CONTINUOUS LIFETIME GIVING PROGRAM—BROAD OUTLINE.

Type of Giving	Age of Prospects										
	20–25	25–30	30–35	35–40	40–45	45–50	50–55	55–60	60–65	65–70	70+
Annual gifts											
less than $1,000	X	X	X	X	X	X	X	X	X	X	X
$1,000–4,999			X	X	X	X	X	X	X	X	X
$5,000–24,999					X	X	X	X	X	X	X
$25,000+							X	X	X	X	X
Special gifts											
Programs, events (e.g., reunions)			X		X			X		X	
Major and planned gifts						X	X	X	X	X	X
Wills and bequests								X	X	X	X
Capital gifts							X	X	X	X	X

The A. T. Kearney Study

A. T. Kearney, Inc., based in Chicago and in operation since 1926, is one of the premier management consulting firms in the United States. In 1997 the firm performed an analysis of the giving trends, marketing practices, and strategic direction of the Indiana University Foundation (IUF).

The study was the first of its kind for Kearney. Although Kearney typically consults more with major corporations and commercial and service industry clients than with institutions of higher education that market "intangibles" in their giving programs, the firm's expertise in analyzing data and data trends was readily applied to over 200,000 donor records provided by IUF. In addition to analyzing these data, Kearney gained insight into the institution and its sector by interviewing Indiana University (IU) and IUF administrators, officers, and deans, as well as the presidents of five peer universities' fundraising foundations. Kearney gave IUF a rare opportunity to see how taking a for-profit approach to fundraising can bring it closer to achieving its objectives without compromising its nonprofit identity and integrity.

Overall, Kearney concluded, IUF did an excellent job of securing large gifts from top donors, but it did not spend adequate time and resources on younger, less mature donors who represented a sizable source of untapped funding. Kearney recommended that IUF work toward developing a "continuous lifetime giving" program—one that begins simply with participation when a student graduates from IU but evolves into a major or planned gifts effort over the life of the donor. Young donor acquisition and retention, coupled with continuous contact and cultivation, are essential phases in moving donors along in this giving cycle. Kearney recognized that each of IU's many schools and campuses had its own level of fundraising sophistication. To maximize giving to each school, IUF needed to implement a more strategic, tailored, targeted marketing effort than it currently had in place. Developing a continuous lifetime giving program required IUF to change the way it thought about marketing to its various donor segments.

This approach will be required in the future of organizations that want to move to the next level of support. It is true that giving in the United States increases nearly every year, and over the past fifty years, giving as measured by three-year rolling averages has risen continuously. It is also true that over more than a quarter century, the percentage of gross domestic product and the percentage of household income given to nonprofits have remained fairly constant (see Figures 2.2 and 2.3).

FIGURE 2.2. GIVING AS A PERCENTAGE OF GROSS DOMESTIC PRODUCT, 1968–1998.

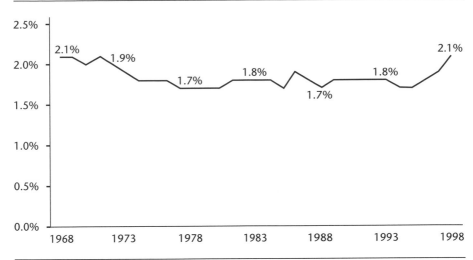

Source: American Association of Fund-Raising Counsel Trust for Philanthropy, 1999. Reprinted with permission.

FIGURE 2.3. GIVING BY INDIVIDUALS AS A PERCENTAGE OF PERSONAL INCOME, 1968–1998.

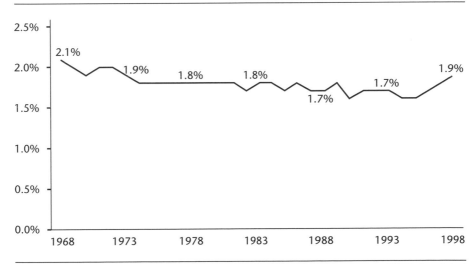

Source: American Association of Fund-Raising Counsel Trust for Philanthropy, 1999. Reprinted with permission.

- Between 1968 and 1998, according to the American Association of Fund-Raising Counsel Trust for Philanthropy (1999), giving has ranged from a high of 2.1 percent to a low of 1.7 percent of gross domestic product.
- In 1998, giving represented 2.1 percent of GDP, the same percentage as in 1968.
- To reach 3 percent of GDP, giving would have to have been more than $80 billion higher than it was in 1998.
- Over the same thirty-year span, personal giving has ranged from a high of 2.1 percent to a low of 1.6 percent of personal income.
- The 1998 estimate of personal giving of $134.84 billion represents 1.9 percent of personal income. If individuals had contributed 2.1 percent of personal income in 1998, personal giving would have reached $149.63 billion.
- There is some question about whether income is the appropriate measure by which to benchmark giving. Households that contribute large percentages of their income to nonprofits are often making such gifts out of assets or wealth, not from annual income. These households account for much of the nation's charitable giving.

The Kearney study opened eyes. IUF's development staff members, like those at most other institutions, were hired for their people skills and their fundraising expertise, not for their analytical and marketing skills. *Marketing* is a term that is broadly defined. To some it means sales or advertising; to others it means public relations or communications. IUF, like many other nonprofits, have people with all these skills. What was needed, Kearney stated, was analytically skilled people—marketers, statisticians, mathematicians, programmers—who could combine the expertise of their disciplines with the experience of the fundraisers to produce a new, more strategic, more focused, more productive, more cost-effective way of raising money.

Most organizations, in looking for the next major donor prospect, are manually combing through a haystack looking for needles. A better way is to do the looking with a magnet—a powerful one. The combination of technology and analytical marketing skills will create that magnet in the future for those nonprofits that use it.

But does this mean that nonprofits have to give up the old practices for the new ones or the new for the old? Nonprofits will not have to give up either if we can incorporate a sophisticated marketing department into our organizational structure. By identifying the most promising prospects, old and new alike, a marketing department will increase the efficiency and success of the development team: instead of having to search for the prospects, fundraisers will be able to devote maximum time and resources to developing and cultivating the relationships that are most likely to result in private support.

The mission of a marketing department is to facilitate and support any nonprofit's development division in its ongoing effort to maximize private support for its organization through the systematic, intentional implementation of a continuous lifetime giving program. This program will identify the varied financial resources and personal goals of an organization's constituency and will then match them with corresponding priorities of the organization.

The uniqueness of the nonprofit's "customer" is significant, according to a report (Thiede, 1998); for any nonprofit to be successful, it must convince its constituents to *give away* their resources, not for the sake of a tangible product that could benefit them directly, but rather for the satisfaction of knowing that their gifts have enhanced the lives of others. This approach makes fundraising a very emotional business—and different people are emotional about different things. Each organization will know, or needs to know, what its constituents are passionate about. The marketing department's job is to identify who is emotional about what and then to match appropriate prospects with the needs of the organization.

The overall objective of the marketing department, then, was to help development professionals secure private gifts. Within this framework, the specific objectives and responsibilities of the marketing department are defined by the five-part GIFTS program, outlined by Thiede (1998) and named for the first letter of each of its components:

1. *Gathering* information on current and prospective donors

    Keeping the database updated with pertinent demographic information

    Systematically recording all donor affiliations and activities

    Writing, conducting, and analyzing market survey projects for all institutional needs

2. *Identifying* donor segments for various giving programs

    Obtaining demographic information (age, income, property, names and number of children, and so forth)

    Establishing levels of loyalty (gift amounts and gift frequency)

    Making connections with donors (matching institutional needs with donors' affiliations, activities, and interests)

3. *Fostering* lifelong donor relationships through consistent, targeted communication

    Increasing emphasis on targeted direct-mail marketing programs

    Developing "brand loyalty" by increasing the quality and frequency of communications

    Developing donor- and project-specific marketing materials

    Personalizing communication materials whenever possible

Using the organization's Web site to maximize constituents' exposure to the organization

4. *Tracking* performance through systematic statistical analysis

Noting response rates to direct mail, customized correspondence, and personal solicitations

Calculating median gift amounts

Noting participation levels

Noting trends in giving (increases, decreases, or stagnation)

5. *Sharing* results and information

Disseminating "best practices" information throughout the organization, to help development professionals and programs achieve their own objectives

The Kearney report found that the groupings used to segment age (under 45, 45–65, and over 65) and income (under $75,000 and over $75,000) gave a good general illustration of how donors' life stages and income level can influence their levels of support (see Table 2.2). Nevertheless, there are segments within these segments, and each segment represents an opportunity to develop a more targeted and more effective marketing strategy. For instance, consider, on the one hand, a recent college graduate starting a first job and, on the other, a forty-year-old who has a successful business. If one makes $25,000 and the other $70,000, both donors might fall into the "under 45, single, under $75,000" segment, but their circumstances are obviously different, and each should be approached differently. This example shows the need to divide donors into smaller segments that keep relationships between age and lifestyle in mind (Thiede, 1998).

TABLE 2.2. SEGMENTING DONORS INTO NINE DEMOGRAPHIC GROUPS.

Group	Age	Income Level	Marital Status
1	under 45	under $75,000	N.A.
2	under 45	over $75,000	N.A.
3	45–65	under $75,000	single
4	45–65	under $75,000	married
5	45–65	over $75,000	single
6	45–65	over $75,000	married
7	over 65	under $75,000	single
8	over 65	under $75,000	married
9	over 65	over $75,000	N.A.

N.A., not applicable.

The Kearney report also recommended that donors' loyalty be examined to identify trends in giving for use in developing targeted marketing strategies for specific donor segments. In analyzing donors' loyalty, it is important to remember, once again, that fundraising is different from selling products like soap, bread, gasoline, or milk, which consumers are generally obliged to buy. Nonprofits' "customers" are people who give their money away, and so they are a unique kind of customer. Kearney (A. T. Kearney, Inc., 1997) defines three levels of loyalty:

- Loyal (donor has given four or five times in the past five years)
- Supportive (donor has given two or three times in the past five years)
- Erratic (donor has given once or not at all in the past five years)

However, basing loyalty analysis on the consistency and frequency of gifts given over a period of time is likely to paint an incomplete picture of loyalty (Thiede, 1998). To illustrate, Table 2.3 shows the gifts of two different donors over the same five-year period. Both donors have given five gifts over five years, and each donor has given a total of $750. If they were evaluated by the number of gifts made, both donors would be deemed loyal, and equivalent time and resources to retain their gifts would be spent. But the trends in their gift amounts reveal very different levels of loyalty, and these should be factored into the marketing strategy for each donor:

- Donor 1 has steadily increased his gift amount. Therefore, he should be acknowledged for consistent giving and asked either to maintain or slightly increase his gift.
- Donor 2 seems to have lost interest after year 2. Therefore, he requires cultivation to return to his previous level of giving.

Determining a donor's loyalty requires a more comprehensive look at the donor's giving history than can be gleaned from a single factor. Additional questions to be asked in determining a donor's loyalty include, but are not limited to, the following:

TABLE 2.3. COMPARISON OF
TWO DONORS' GIFTS OVER FIVE YEARS.

	Year 1	Year 2	Year 3	Year 4	Year 5	Total
Donor 1	$50	$100	$150	$200	$250	$750
Donor 2	$350	$250	$50	$50	$50	$750

- Has the donor's gift amount decreased, increased, or remained constant over the years?
- Has the donor been solicited every year?
- How was the donor solicited? By direct mail? Telephone? A personal visit? Some combination?
- Has the donor given each year, or did the donor make multiple gifts in one year?

Simultaneous evaluation of these kinds of questions will help develop more effective marketing strategies for different donor segments (Thiede, 1998).

Institutional leaders, realizing that there is a limit to the number of times extraordinary fundraising efforts can produce quick and effective solutions to today's problems, are accepting three premises: (1) that strategic organizational planning will become an accepted, even required, practice in all nonprofit organizations; (2) that strategic analysis such as Kearney prescribes will also become a requirement; and (3) that this type of planning and analytical thinking will eventually lead to better management practices and better managers for the institutions using it and for their development programs. Where strategic planning is used, development programs become multiyear efforts designed in supportive concert with institutional strategies. This approach results in perpetual campaigning to satisfy capital and other needs through a continuous lifetime giving fundraising effort, with major "subcampaigns" harmoniously integrated into the ongoing program. These subcampaigns are thus far less obvious as extraordinary fundraising efforts than is the case when the other models are used.

This is not to suggest that institutions using the strategic planning method will not, from time to time, continue to engage in intensive, time-specific "capital campaigns" with defined goals. They will. Apart from the sheer volume of dollars that can be raised when a heightened sense of urgency and importance is created, and apart from the psychological and motivational strategies that can maximize giving in the excitement of a campaign, sometimes an institution simply wants to bring to itself the special attention that a campaign provides. What is different in the future-oriented strategic planning environment is that those institutions that campaign will do so because they choose to do so, not because they have no other plausible alternative. Therefore, announced capital campaigns, as they have traditionally been known, will probably become less frequent; when undertaken, however, they will, curiously, have many of the traditional characteristics of the campaigns that Charles Sumner Ward first organized more than eighty years ago.

The selection of the campaign model to be used in a particular situation will be influenced by a number of factors:

- The commitment to and quality of strategic institutional planning
- The development program's current level of maturity and sophistication
- The development staff's experience and ability
- The availability of leadership for the campaign
- The impressiveness of the case to be made
- The potential of the major donor prospects
- The range and scope of the anticipated campaign effort

There is no one correct model for all institutions or all situations. In fact, the best way to serve a particular situation may be to incorporate features of more than one model.

CHAPTER THREE

BUILDING AND STATING THE CASE FOR SUPPORT

S eymour (1966) writes of the case statement, "This is the one definitive piece of the whole campaign. It tells all that needs to be told, answers all the important questions, reviews the arguments for support, explains the proposed plan for raising the money, and shows how gifts may be made, and who the people are who vouch for the project, and who will give it leadership and direction" (pp. 42–43).

What Seymour describes is the *case for financial support,* commonly called the *case* or *case statement,* the visible tip of the case-stating process iceberg. It is the finely produced document that constituents and the public usually see. What are not as often seen by many outside the close institutional family are the three additional building blocks that lead to its production: the mission statement, the institutional profile, and the strategic plan. This chapter examines each, building to the case for financial support for the current annual or capital campaign.

Mission Statement

A mission statement is a brief, clear, concise rationale for a nonprofit's existence—it establishes the organization's reasons for being (see Resource 1, "Mission Statements"). It has three elements:

- Core function—the organization's purpose
- Goals, both primary and secondary
- Philosophy or values statement

It should state who the organization's service users are and how the organization will satisfy their needs. If the organization is diversified, the rationale for diversification, which includes the breadth and scope of the portfolio, should also be included.

When established in 1936, the Indiana University Foundation's mission was as follows:

- To raise funds from the private sector for Indiana University (IU)
- To manage assets and invest endowment funds to maximize their value for IU
- To administer gift fund accounts in accordance with the donors' wishes for the benefit of IU

That mission has not changed, but how it is fulfilled (methods, techniques, programs) has, and dramatically, just as the institution has changed dramatically. In 1937 IU's main campus was in Bloomington, with three healthcare-related professional schools and a night law school branch in Indianapolis. Today IU has eight campuses spread throughout the state and an enrollment of 100,000 students. It is not a given that mission statements, once stated, do not change; they sometimes do. But if properly developed initially, the mission statement is the bedrock on which all that an organization does is predicated in the present and over time.

Outline of an Institutional Profile

The institutional profile is a centralization or documentation of all information describing the organization: needs, goals, objectives, strategies and tasks, staff, facilities, budget, institutional plans, financial history, personnel, staff competence to serve the mission, or the cause that the organization represents. It is literally a "database," a repository for data, according to the Association of Fundraising Professionals, which was formerly NSFRE (1985).

Thompson and others (1978) have drafted the following typical outline of an institutional profile for working purposes. The institutional staff can use this detailed profile as a checklist when pulling together material pertinent to the case for financial support.

Preface or Summary (This section should express the essence of the case in one or two pages and state overall goals to be achieved.)

I. *Institutional Mission*
   A. Role in society
   B. Philosophy of purpose
   C. Mission, goals, and program
   D. Salient factors in its history—heritage and distinctions that have endured
   E. Factors that appeal to
      1. Service users (a collective term used to describe those who receive services/benefits from a third-sector organization including students, patients, members, clients, recipients, etc.) and their families
      2. Institutional family
      3. Governing board members and volunteers
      4. Friends and community
      5. Past donors
      6. Potential leadership and financial resources
II. *Record of Accomplishment*
   A. Service growth—regular and special programs
   B. Service users—meeting their needs
   C. Institutional family
      1. Nature and quality
      2. Role in teaching, research, policy, preservation, collection, services
   D. Service users/constituents
      1. Further education/services
      2. Careers/specialty goals
      3. Civic leadership
   E. Community service
   F. Improvements in environment and physical facilities
   G. Financial growth
      1. Annual operations
      2. Capital—current and endowment
      3. Methods used to finance accomplishments
   H. Philanthropic support—distinctive gifts and bequests
   I. Where the institution stands today
III. *Directions for the Future*
   A. Distinctions that must continue to endure
   B. New directions
   C. Objectives, curriculum, programs, services

D. Service users

   1. Number to be served

   2. Nature of constituency

   3. Qualifications

E. Institutional and administrative projected requirements

F. Governance projected requirements

G. Financial policies

   1. For tuition, fees, charges

   2. For investment management

   3. For business management

   4. For private gifts and grants

   5. For public support

H. Physical facilities

   1. Campus/environment

   2. Buildings

   3. Equipment

IV. *Urgent and Continuing Development Objectives*

A. Priorities and costs

   1. Endowment for

      a. Service users

      b. Professional staff/faculty, physicians, curators

      c. Library/equipment restoration

      d. Laboratories/service units

      e. Operation of buildings

      f. Facility maintenance

   2. New buildings

   3. Redevelopment of present facilities

   4. Property acquisition

   5. Debt reduction

B. Master plan

V. *Plan of Action to Accomplish Future Objectives*

A. Goals

B. Programs

   1. Support current operations

   2. Support capital expansion

   3. Support special programs or projects

   4. Role of estate planning

C. Organization

D. Timing

      E. Resources
        1. Constituent sources
        2. Range of gifts needed—gift table
        3. Opportunities for memorials and tributes
        4. Methods of giving, including planned gifts and deferred giving
  VI. *The Institution's Sponsorship*
      A. Membership of the governing board
      B. Membership of the development groups
      C. Church/government sponsorship

This document is usually presented in a loose-leaf or three-ring binder, thus allowing for easy access and updating and keeping production costs low. It is most commonly an unadorned word-processed presentation in black ink on white paper. It is ordinarily distributed to primary institutional staff, board members, and a few key volunteers and donors only.

Strategic Plan

The first requirements for any fundraising program are a clear image of the institution and a plan for its growth and improvement so that it can fulfill its purpose. What is needed, in other words, is a strategic plan. Strategic planning is an approach that asks most institutions to be more intentional and more organized than they have been in the past.

Everywhere today, board members and local leaders are asking questions about the future of their third-sector institutions. They want to know the aims and goals. They are interested in assessing the development programs of the organizations that they are asked to support. Any development program presupposes, of course, that the institution knows what it is going to develop; no amount of public relations can substitute for an institution's having a reason for being. But an institution without a strategic plan is at the mercy of pressure groups. It is in danger of being manipulated by an influential individual's whim, a board member's pet project, or uninformed community opinion.

It is the business of all nonprofit institutions to do strategic planning, but many have neglected—or avoided—the self-analysis that would permit them to define aims and set goals. Without a strategy based on knowledge of the philanthropic marketplace, however, they will have only random ideas, without a guiding purpose. Lord (1996, pp. 32–35) puts it this way:

As the Roman philosopher Seneca said, "When a man does not know what harbor he is making for, no wind is the right one." Or, as Yogi Berra put it more recently, "You've got to be very careful if you don't know where you are going, because you might not get there." Many forces outside individual institutions are trying to legislate how they ought to be doing their jobs. So an institution has to have a plan for its future, particularly when it is preparing to embark on a fundraising campaign, if for no other reason [than] because people deserve to know how the institution intends to use the money—and what kind of benefits are expected. What makes planning even more valuable is the opportunity it presents for involvement. If an institution's leaders are on the ball, they will use the planning process to get people involved in mapping an organization's future—especially those people who have the power to bring about that future. Authentic involvement in a planning process promotes a sense of ownership among prospective donors and volunteers. People are simply motivated to work for and invest in the realization of plans they themselves have helped to develop.

The act of planning also focuses and clarifies thinking. This is another way in which the process itself is more important than the resulting document. Furthermore, with regard to fundraising, planning makes an institution look good. Most donors don't want to know all the details—but they do want to be assured that an organization knows its future and sees a path for getting there. They want to know that not-for-profit organizations are using the skills of the business world, and that they are treating the eleemosynary enterprise in an intentional, organized, and strategic manner. Any institution will make an excellent impression if it can tell those it is trying to attract, either as volunteers or as potential donors, that it has conducted surveys among the people it serves, designed a strategic plan, and produced a financial plan for the next three to five years or more.

This kind of planning is exactly what one philanthropist wanted when he asked a hospital trustee: "What's your mission? And I don't mean that formal stuff, either. What are you doing? What does your five-year plan look like? What services are you going to add? To abandon?" More and more prospects are asking these tough questions. Too many organizations still have no answers, or only the vaguest ones. The sharp organizations, those that are attracting big money, are ready with their plans. Corporations, foundations, and wealthy individuals, after all, are only asking that not-for-profits follow the same discipline that they—the prospects—have been practicing for years. Let's be clear, what's being talked about isn't the kind of "long-range planning" many organizations already do, but real strategic planning. The difference is important.

Bryson (1995) defines strategic planning as a disciplined effort to produce fundamental decisions and actions that shape and guide what an organization is, what it does, and why it does it. To deliver the best results, strategic planning requires broad yet effective gathering of information, development and exploration of strategic alternatives, and an emphasis on the future implications of present decisions. Strategic planning can help facilitate communication and participation, accommodate divergent interests and values, foster wise and reasonably analytical decision making, and promote successful implementation. In short, strategic planning at its best can prompt in organizations the kind of imagination— and commitment—that the psychotherapist and theologian Thomas Moore (cited in Bryson, 1995) thinks are necessary to deal with an individual's life conundrums. Bryson adds that strategic planning is clearly no panacea; it is simply a set of concepts, procedures, and tools designed to help leaders, managers, and planners think and act strategically. Strategic *planning* is not a substitute for strategic *thinking* and *acting*, Bryson says; only caring, committed people can think and act strategically. Used thoughtlessly, strategic planning can actually drive out precisely the kind of strategic thought and action it is supposed to promote. Nor is strategic planning a substitute for leadership: when it comes to using strategic planning to enhance organizational performance, there simply is no substitute for leadership. At least some key decision makers and process champions must be committed to the strategic planning process, or any attempts to use it are bound to fail (Bryson, 1995) (see Resource 2, "Strategic Plan," and Resource 3, "Strategic Plan Progress Report").

The Case for Financial Support (Case or Case Statement)

The institutional profile states the organization's reason for being in overarching terms; the case statement states the rationale for financial support at this moment in time, whether in connection with annual or ongoing fundraising or a capital campaign. When the comprehensive campaign model is used, the case statement must include both annual and capital aspects.

The lack of an effective case for financial support, or of someone able to formulate it properly, can waste precious time at the beginning of a campaign effort. Seasoned development professionals know that the preparation of a case statement is often the first challenge in any fundraising effort—and can be the most formidable. The case statement is one of the initial key management requirements for successful institutional development of a campaign.

Experience has shown that the most crucial elements affecting an institution's ability to attract financial support are a sophisticated and carefully developed case and the active involvement of key governing board members, other top volunteer leaders, and major potential donors. These elements—together with institutional planning, documented research and evaluation of the constituency, the enlistment of leaders, the organizing of volunteers, the existence of a qualified staff, and an adequate budget—represent a basic step in the direction of winning greater philanthropic support.

Pendel (1981) believes that the case statement must be a motivational document—that is, it must be persuasive, not merely an attempt at institutional glorification or an expression of the institution's need for survival. The case statement must accomplish the following things:

- It must justify and explain the institution, its program, and its needs so as to lead to advocacy and financial support.
- It must win the reader's endorsement of the vision that characterizes the leadership of the institution and reassure the reader of the wisdom and responsible nature of its management.
- It must make the organization distinctive (though not necessarily unique) in the reader's eyes.
- It must be positive, forward-looking, and confident, with all the facts and projections reasonable, clear, vital, and accurate.
- It must carefully set forth the fundraising plans in terms of policy, priorities, and enduring benefits. (The following questions must be anticipated from the reader: Why this institution? Why now? Why me? How?) The case statement must be clear and concise, even though it may be lengthy.
- It must be a substantial plan for the future, not a burdensome revisiting of the past, no matter how honored or glorious. In a real sense, it is a prospectus. It invites investment.

A case for financial support is a reasoned argument for an organization's receiving the support it can demonstrate it needs in order to continue as an essential community resource. Only after the institution has isolated, defined, and researched its target market (its donor market, its service market, and its client base) is it ready to develop its case. The case for financial support, then, poses the institution's mission, goals, plans, and programs in terms of the roles these play or can play in the life of the larger society. The case must be the institution in a nutshell. Its aim, above all, is to be persuasive—to motivate the reader to respond.

The institutional profile—the internal document—should contain a view of the organization and a brief history. This document is not an essay on the philosophy of the organization; rather, it is a statement about the perspective that the organization takes on the issues being addressed by the immediate campaign. It is most effective in the form of a loose-leaf binder of typewritten, photocopied pages—a draft document meant to be reviewed and revised, a working document that is updated periodically to remain always relevant. Distribution should be limited to board members and others who are interested enough in the organization to take the time to read it and who have the interest and ability to act on its recommendations and requests. Where good planning is being done, the case statement and the institution's strategic plan are companion pieces.

Organization of the Case Statement

The organization of a case statement can take many forms, and there seems to be no one formula for success (see Resource 4, "Case Statements"; Resource 5, "Case Statement with Companion Pieces"; and Resource 6, "Short-Form Case Statements"). Nevertheless, certain essential elements are always included, and a good case statement does the following things:

- It describes the organization's mission in terms of the human and social issues that are of central concern to the organization.
- It states the organization's objectives in specific, quantifiable terms.
- It describes a set of tasks or strategies for reaching the objectives within a given period of time.
- It reports on the facilities, staff assignments, and budget required to carry out the tasks and strategies, which will include control procedures for continuing evaluation.
- It identifies who will benefit from the services offered by the organization.
- It sets forth the reasons why someone should make a contribution to support the organization and thus the cause that it serves.
- It stresses the strengths of the organization. (Avoid the trap of publicizing weaknesses or needs; emphasize the positive by selling strengths, successes, and opportunities, demonstrating the potential of the institution, and showing how it can become even better, and therefore more valuable, if it is supported.)

In addition to these essential elements, the case statement should include the following kinds of information about the service area or environment in which the organization functions:

- An analysis of its market or service area, examining any significant changes that have occurred and the anticipated organizational impact of these changes (for example, a university's case statement may include a comparison of the institution's endowment with the endowments of similar universities; a healthcare facility's statement may compare that facility's patient-physician load per square foot with the same statistics at comparable facilities)

- Demographic and psychographic data in addition to socioeconomic indicators
- An outline of the institution's immediate, short-range, and long-range plans and a description of its expected future capabilities
- A list of its current and anticipated long-range needs, as well as annual, special, capital, and endowment requirements, all drawn from the institutional plan
- A list of the organization's personnel, including the brief biographies of key staff and members of the governing board
- An analysis of the organization's recent gift history
- The financial history of the organization, including recent financial statements and audits
- A general history of the organization

To be complete, a good case statement will also include messages of endorsement and commitment from top leaders, a detailed plan for using the resources sought (and a compelling rationale for their provision), a budget detailing the gift opportunities, and a list of the individuals who will lead the campaign and of those who have managerial responsibility for the institution.

In collecting, organizing, and presenting the written case—the printed document that grows out of the institutional profile and is shared publicly—it is best to have an experienced professional do the writing and to use highly qualified designers and printers. If such people are not immediately available, they should be sought out. There are professional firms that specialize in preparing case statements for public distribution and consumption, as well as highly talented individuals who work independently.

Preparation of the case statement provides an important opportunity for involving institutional insiders, prospective volunteer leaders and major donors, and the organization's power structure; in fact, the case cannot be properly developed without the benefit of their insights and perspectives. Research in the institutional files, personal interviews to gather pertinent data, and keen observation are all tools of the statement writer.

Uses of the Case Statement

Pendel (1981) identifies six ways in which the case statement is most profitably used:

- It is used by the institutional family as an internal document to resolve, sharpen, and focus planning and policies into a written statement that interprets the institution to others.

- An abbreviated form of the statement should be used in testing the market (that is, as a market survey).
- The statement serves to rally present leaders around the policy, planning, and fundraising story. It is the expression of the institutional policy and of the plans that have been agreed on by the governing board and that are being aggressively promoted by the professional development staff and by other, volunteer groups.
- The statement serves as a vital campaigning tool for the campaign leaders. It is easier to enlist new members for the governing board and top volunteers when there is a statement that argues the case for stability and security as well as for leadership and gift support. Communicating the case will also enhance the ability to recruit high-quality staff and administrators.
- The statement serves as a supporting tool in the solicitation of large annual, capital, and special gifts through tailored appeals to selected prospects who have considerable gift potential.
- It serves as a basic reference guide for proposed publications and communications of various kinds that will be distributed to the institution's various constituencies.

A thorough, honest case statement will transform apathy toward the institution into a sense of mission that prompts people to act. The case statement, properly prepared, can challenge the entire institution to provide greater service and engenders enthusiastic support for this direction.

Presenting the Case Statement

Although the traditional case statement is sufficient for most campaigns—a building drive to provide a shelter for the homeless, say, or a neonatal care unit for a hospital—many modern campaigns, especially for complex and large institutions, present the case through multiple publications. A series of documents can be more understandable, attractive, and effective in educating and persuading than a single piece. There is no standard way of dividing the case statement into components, but it is not unusual, particularly for a public institution (such as a tax-assisted college or university), to present the case statement in the following segments:

- A "historical piece" that indicates a long-established tradition of private support for the public good, if the institution has such a tradition of philanthropy (if it does not, a more general argument, based on a solid rationale, can still be made and is often required to persuade certain potential leaders and givers)

- A financial or economic impact statement that delineates the economic benefits derived from the institution by the community, highlights the role of private support in the budget, and encourages the investment of private dollars in the campaign
- A traditional program brochure that makes the arguments for the immediate campaign
- A companion piece that outlines gift opportunities and ways of giving

In complex organizations, such as large universities, museums, medical centers, and hospitals, it is not unusual to find several separate objectives within the overall campaign goal. In these situations, separate case statements are often prepared to support each of the major campaign objectives, and individual documents may also be prepared for each unit of the organization that has a major objective within the overall campaign goal (see Resource 5, "Case Statement with Companion Pieces").

The Case-Stating Process

Stating the case is a continuous process of communicating a message you want people to remember and even internalize. It is a repetitious, constant effort to make that message so clear, so understood, so believed that ultimately the leaders, volunteers, and prospects feed back to the institution its own message with conviction and enthusiasm.

According to Curtis R. Simic (personal communication, 1985), the case-stating process is "the process of making insiders out of outsiders." The case statement will continue to be the centerpiece in the presentation of capital campaigns; however, it is only part of the overall case-stating process. As Simic argues, volunteers' and prospective donors' acceptance of a campaign often depends on frequent and repeated reinforcement of the case statement's message. Therefore, the case-stating process usually involves a series of presentations—oral, written, and audiovisual— to introduce the campaign to all the organization's constituencies.

Leaders, on both the receiving and the giving side, must be fully informed about the campaign and its objectives. These vitally important constituents must also accept the premise of the campaign, understand its logic and its persuasiveness, and be moved to act on its behalf. What is most often required is a series of events, often repetitious, rather than a single presentation to any one group of key constituents. A single presentation cannot inform people of everything they need to know. A succession of events permits key individuals to ask all the questions they need to ask in order to be knowledgeable; to grasp the urgency, importance, and relevance of the campaign; and to commit to it fully.

The Short-Form Case Statement

Individuals who have the strongest ties to or involvement with an institution are at the center of the institution's orbit. They are the ones most likely to read and react to the case statement. Prospects more distant from the center have less intense interest, and so a short-form case statement, perhaps in the form of a program brochure accompanied by a question-and-answer pamphlet, is often more appropriate for use with these prospects (see Resource 6, "Short-Form Case Statements").

Compared to a full case statement, the short form has fewer pages and typographical features, is not as slickly produced, and is distributed to a larger number of people. The short form should of course be attractive, but not elaborate or lavish. It is often best to deliver this type of document by hand. If it is mailed, it should be accompanied by a personal note. The format should be flexible, particularly in a comprehensive campaign encompassing several objectives.

The short form—usually a brochure with four or six panels, consisting of briefly stated answers to the key questions *who, what, when, where, why,* and *why now*—focuses directly and concisely on the major objectives and issues of the campaign. As noted, it is designed for prospects who are currently not close to the organization or to the campaign and who will not give their attention, at least initially, to a lengthy, detailed argument for support. It is designed to be carried easily by a volunteer or a prospect and to be read in three minutes or less.

Many institutions mistakenly call their short form a case statement, but it is not; rather, it is often a shortcut taken because the institution has neither the will nor the ability to prepare a proper case statement. In truth, a short form does not and cannot replace the case statement. But it is an extremely useful supplement to it.

The short form is used in three distinct ways. The first is as an easy- and quick-to-read summary of a case statement developed to support a capital campaign for a large, complex organization, often presented in a question-and-answer format

The short form can also be used as the main printed promotional piece for smaller, single-purpose capital campaign. Remember that not all capital campaigns are big-goal, multiyear efforts. Two examples are presented in Resource 6. The Mission for Memphis campaign was done, start to finish, in five months; the IU East/Henry County Project was done in three months.

Finally, the case statement for an annual campaign is typically presented in the short-form format.

Conclusion

This progression of documentation prepares the nonprofit not only to understand itself but also to make itself understandable and appealing to the people it hopes to attract to its cause. Spare no effort and take no shortcuts in preparing these documents. There is simply no substitute for a nonprofit having a clear and compelling reason to exist, presented concisely and persuasively.

CHAPTER FOUR

DEFINING ROLES OF LEADERS AND TOP VOLUNTEERS IN FUNDRAISING

This chapter describes the roles of top institutional leaders—board members, the chief executive officer, the chief development officer, and key top volunteers—in fundraising. The primary focus in this chapter is on the leadership responsibilities and roles of each in the highest-level fundraising endeavors. Chapter Five goes into more detail about the broader role of volunteers in the fundraising program as the organization moves down the leadership ladder.

"A good fundraising program has two kinds of leadership—the layman who leads and the staff member who manages and serves. The better each is and the better they work together, the better the results will be. Leadership in itself, let it never be forgotten, is always the key factor in successful fundraising, whatever the cause, whatever the goal, and whatever the scope of the campaign" (Seymour, 1966, p. 179).

The chair of the governing board, the general chair of the campaign, and the chief executive officer of the institution have the principal roles in any campaign, especially in the early phases. They are responsible for setting the pace and establishing the right mood for fundraising. They also have to be confident that the planning stage is completed correctly and precisely and that all the tools necessary for a successful campaign are present. The success or failure of most fundraising efforts is ultimately attributable to these individuals.

In recent years the dramatic increase in fundraising competition has had a significant impact on the enlistment of top volunteers. Today there are more large, important campaigns and relatively fewer qualified, interested individuals to fill key leadership roles. Experienced volunteers now ask tough questions before they commit themselves to a project. Responsibility for enlisting and motivating these top volunteers falls to the chief executive officer, the professional staff, and key members of the board. It is they who must be prepared to win, convincingly, the commitment of top volunteer leaders.

Top Volunteer Leaders

The selection of leaders is of the utmost importance in a fundraising campaign. Top leaders should be excited and exciting, and leadership should come primarily from within. Any institution should be able to find the bulk of the leadership it will need during a campaign among its board members, its service users, its advisory groups, and its other "institutional family" constituents.

The power structure of a community may be a supplemental source of leadership. Community leaders fall into four main groups:

- Those who have inherited both wealth and its tradition of public service
- The newly rich and newly powerful (the Horatio Algers of the modern world)
- The top professional managers of key corporations
- Respected and admired men and women of the community

An absence of leadership at this level is an early warning sign that the institution is not yet adequately prepared to undertake a campaign.

For a campaign to be successful, its top leaders, whether they come from within the institution or from the community at large, must make a commitment of time, effort, and dollars. The top leadership group should consist of respected individuals who have the following characteristics:

- Immediate name recognition with the groups served by the institution
- A strong identification with the institution
- A history of association and active involvement with the institution
- A substantial record of major gifts to the institution
- The ability and willingness to be forceful, dynamic leaders
- Connections with colleagues and friends who are also leaders and who represent the institution's various constituencies

An organization chart and job descriptions should be prepared for the leadership group and should clearly describe specific responsibilities, as well as the amounts of time that will be required (this figure will include time spent in meetings). Recruitment should begin at the top and work down, so that these volunteers recruit the people who will be working for them (see Resource 8, "Volunteer's Job Description").

Construction of the Governing Board

Building a governing board is akin to piecing together a puzzle. It is a collection of individual pieces that when put together correctly forms a complete picture. And like puzzles, every governing board will look distinctive even if each has the same number of pieces.

The process of thoughtfully building a board for a small nonprofit is in many ways even more important than for the large, well-financed, fully staffed organization. Why? Because bigger organizations can employ staff and specialists, can afford vendors and consultants, and can pay for specialized services if they so choose. Their options are luxuries beyond the reach of many smaller nonprofits. Instead, these organizations must turn to pro bono sources and board members with professional expertise adequate to meet the organization's needs.

Many nonprofit boards require that certain members be appointed as representational members. Others will be added because of their complementary program or service expertise. Wouldn't it be a great idea to have an attorney who can help with planned giving? A marketer who can assist with marketing? A media person to aid with media relations? An accountant to help with financial matters? An investment professional if the nonprofit is supported by an endowment?

These board members must often be more actively involved in the day-to-day life of their nonprofits. Not all board members will be chosen because of their fundraising abilities, although all board members have a responsibility to be generous within their own means.

Look at your needs, and match your board members to them. Of course, you must be sure to pick board members who believe in your cause, who will be active in their advocacy, and who will give generously of themselves and their talents. Beware of the "professional" board member who agrees to serve to further his or her business or personal agenda rather than the organization's.

The Role of the Governing Board

The members of a governing board, according to Stuhr (1977, p. 46), have four main functions, which they must be capable of performing individually and collectively:

- To define the concept of the institution, set institutional goals, and approve plans for reaching them
- To approve top administrative officers and motivate them (rather than just rubber-stamp administrative recommendations), give affirmative support to administrators, and lend administrative support to board leaders
- To audit and assess the performance of the institution in all its parts, as well as the work of its top executives in the pursuit of established goals
- To take appropriate action on the board's assessments of what must be done to reach institutional goals and to build a more effective institution

To carry out these four functions effectively, a board is annually asked to endorse and support the annual campaign and is often asked, first, to make decisions that lead the institution into a capital campaign and, later, to act effectively within the campaign structure. In any campaign, individual board members' help is needed in a number of areas:

- Setting goals
- Encouraging the staff
- Formulating plans
- Identifying, cultivating, and soliciting major gift prospects
- Readily accepting major posts in the campaign (the community expects the institution's lay leaders to accept the key jobs)
- Taking on sufficient dollar goals for themselves to launch the campaign

Leadership from the governing board, according to Broce (1979), is the single most critical factor in the success of any campaign and even in whether an institution should conduct one. Without board members' visible and unanimous commitment, it will be difficult, if not impossible, to motivate others to participate. And it is the governing board members, independent of others, who must eventually commit themselves to seeing that a stated goal is reached because they themselves have unanimously determined that it will be reached.

Gerber (cited in Stuhr, 1977) reinforces Stuhr's points, stating that leadership from the top—in recruiting workers, cultivating prospects, soliciting support, and giving—is absolutely crucial to any successful campaign. Additional people will be needed as volunteer leaders, workers, and financial givers, but Gerber emphasizes that what governing board leaders give cannot be matched by any other group. More than anything else, the role of the governing board's members is to establish a policy framework within which the institution will operate and to set an example for others. Where the capital campaign is concerned, the board member sets an example for others by doing the following:

- Taking a place in the volunteer organization and becoming a worker
- Early in the campaign, making gifts that are generous and appropriate to his or her means
- Being informed and enthusiastic about the campaign and the institution
- Working to bring other volunteers into the program
- Communicating with others in the constituency about the institution and the campaign

The governing board as a whole must be significantly involved in any campaign from the start, according to Livingston (1984). For example, the board's executive committee, its finance committee, and its development committee must be informed about and supportive of the program. Because much of the money to be raised through the campaign will come through the efforts of board members, it is mandatory to get their approval to raise money, and it is imperative that they be sold not only on the project but also on the institution. The more enthusiastic they are about the institution's leaders and the institution itself, the more effective they will be in raising money.

As a part of its overall responsibility, the board should review the timing of the campaign. How does it relate to prior drives? What have similar institutions recently done, begun doing, or announced? Has anything happened recently to affect the institution and make this a particularly propitious or unpropitious time?

Another area of the board's responsibility, not generally considered part of fundraising but nevertheless very significant, is investment of the funds as they are received. The board's investment committee should determine in advance the amounts expected and should formulate an investment plan. If the funds will be needed relatively soon, some kind of short-term investment is probably called for; if the funds are earmarked for endowment, longer-term debt or equity may be considered. The most important thing is to put the donations to work.

The Role of the Chief Executive Officer

An institution's chief executive officer and its senior management determine the personality of the institution; they give it life and vitality. It is increasingly clear that chief executive officers are also central to the success of today's capital campaigns. Graves (cited in Stuhr, 1977, p. 72) says that the chief executive officer's role in fundraising can be described by four functions:

> The chief executive officer must personify the character and the goals of the institution being led. Every constituency of the institution expects this of the chief

executive officer. Successful results from development efforts depend on the chief executive officer's ability to exemplify the character and lifestyle, the hopes and aspirations of all those who comprise the institution at any given moment. Benefactors are becoming more discriminating in their selection of institutions to support. They want to know what the institution is trying to accomplish and how it expects to achieve its objectives. Therefore, any institution needs an easily recognizable image, one that is unusually appealing. It is the chief executive officer who must know the institution thoroughly.

Second, the chief executive officer must communicate these goals to the institution's constituent body. The chief executive officer must understand how the institution's constituents perceive its character and goals and must provide them with the synthesis, a structure within which [the volunteers and the chief executive officer can] carry out their representations. People respond most generously to institutions whose representatives exude clarity, solidarity, and confidence respecting their missions and the means for their pursuit.

Third, a chief executive officer must create a strong development staff. Chief executive officers need to find chief development officers with whom they can share their public relations and fundraising programs in an environment of complete confidence. These two should complement each other in administrative skills and working styles. Together, the chief executive officer and chief development officer must build and keep a strong staff, people who are creative in the production of institutional publications and . . . sensitive and talented in public relations activities, people who can find those who can be interested in supporting the institution and who can help the chief executive officer and the chief development officer cultivate this interest and consummate gifts.

Finally, the chief executive officer must be primarily responsible for fundraising. How the chief executive officer accomplishes this mission depends greatly upon individual personality and style of operation. No matter what other valuable contributions a chief executive officer makes to the quality of the individual institution being served, this person will have failed if the institution's financial needs are not provided for. This does not mean the chief executive officer cannot get a lot of help from others. In fact, the job cannot be done without it. If a chief executive officer has a good development staff, keeps the board informed and properly involved, . . . and has the cooperation of key staff members and just a little bit of luck, success in the everlasting quest for funds will be possible. But it falls to the chief executive officer to have money on the mind most of the time, not as an obsession, but in service of the institution's mission.

With the help of the board, the chief executive officer must see that the organization has plans that are specific enough to identify its needs. The plans must be institutionwide. The chief executive officer should participate in the planning process but not make the plans. The plans should include items that the development staff can clearly articulate and passionately believe in. These become the basis for any fundraising campaign. If the institution is worth supporting, the plans will have something exciting to sell.

Nobles, speaking to a development workshop in 1976, had this to say (cited in Stuhr, 1977, pp. 73–74):

There is no way that a chief executive officer of any organization can sidestep leadership in fundraising. In the areas of making solicitation calls, cultivating major gift prospects, and contacting foundations and corporations, the leadership of the chief executive officer is particularly important. But this individual's time must be conserved and well spent and [his or her] specific involvement tailored to play to personal strengths.

The chief executive officer must be prepared to manage the function as well as to lead it. This may well mean delegating responsibility and authority as well as exercising [them]. It is vital in the stimulation of volunteers to assist with these endeavors, but not necessary to directly become personally involved with everyone and every step of the process. The relationship of the chief executive officer to donors, but especially to major donors, should be personal and individual to the extent it can be. The chief executive officer is called on to represent the total institution to the best of [his or her] ability. A managed program involving strategic contact with, and continued interest in, those persons and organizations . . . best able to support an institution is the major basis for any large gift and represents the mode of operation for the chief executive officer not only during the capital campaign but also over a longer period of time. The staff and volunteers should assist the chief executive officer in this process, and the chief executive officer must not only let them assist but also delegate appropriate responsibility and authority to enable them to assist effectively.

The chief executive officer's enthusiasm, knowledge of [the institution's] direction, sensitivity to the climate of the institution and to the donor's particular interest in it, and strong articulation of [and belief in its mission] will provide the subject matter for any number of presentations during the campaign. Patience and perseverance in building through innumerable small steps . . . the interest of someone only peripherally interested in the institution [and] an alertness to every opportunity to speak for the institution—these are the characteristics that must be consciously built into the job of the chief executive officer during the campaign.

Indeed, the essential role of the chief executive officer in the development of private support is to be the energizing, vitalizing central force that will provide an institution with an enduring future. In this entire area of leadership, however, it cannot be forgotten that financial resources never take the place of ideas, convictions, and diligence in the making of a great institution.

In summary, the chief executive officer is to play the following roles:

- Lead the institutional planning process and advocate for the plan
- Open doors for fundraising to key constituents and prospects
- Build bridges of understanding and acceptance with all key constituencies
- Remove roadblocks that might impede or imperil a fundraising campaign's success, and overcome the objections of key prospective donors should they arise
- Be involved in the closing of gifts
- Express appreciation and gratitude to donors and workers for their involvement

Early Stages of Planning

The plan for a campaign is ordinarily developed by an institution's administration. Administrators are involved daily and are probably more aware of needs than outside board members are. This is not to say that there will never be occasions when the board suggests a campaign; the initial step, however, is usually taken by the chief executive officer of the institution in discussing a need with the chair of the governing board. This discussion will probably be followed by another with the board's executive committee. After preliminary approval has been granted, the staff is generally asked to prepare, for formal submission to the board's executive committee, a detailed report of the specific need and the costs and benefits involved. After the need has been reviewed and approved, perhaps with input from the board's finance and development committees, the concept is submitted to the full board for approval. If the board approves, the campaign is usually referred to the board's development committee, for planning and overall supervision of its implementation.

The development committee and the development staff are the likely organizers of any campaign. The board's role in this area is first of all to ensure that the campaign is properly planned. It should look at the organization and structure; the people involved; the individuals, corporations, and foundations to be solicited and how they will be solicited; how much they will be asked for; the timing of efforts; and the marketing aids to be used.

The Board's Role in Giving and Asking

Next, having approved the concept and the plan, the board members themselves should be asked to give. (First, however, they should be thoroughly cultivated and involved; see Chapter Five.) Their involvement in planning, both for the institution and for the campaign, is extremely important because involvement begets investment: the institution should evaluate both the potential and the probable giving ability of each board member and should also ask key board members to help rate fellow members. As a part of the involvement and cultivation process, board members should be shown the first draft of the case statement. Their reactions to it should be sought, as should their involvement in formulating the final draft. It is important that the institution not take board members for granted and that they be cultivated at the highest level.

Before board members are solicited, the possibility of a formula for board members' giving should be considered—a certain percentage of net worth or of annual income, for example. A policy should also be formulated for counting deferred and planned gifts from board members and others; this method may help board members enhance their participation in the campaign. The degree to which a board member's giving might be a leverage factor in setting the total goal should be considered as well: "If the board gives $1 million, we would have a chance of raising a total of $4 to $5 million." Most important, a key group of board members should be involved in resolving these matters and establishing the goal for the board's giving. Once this goal has been established and the board has been fully involved and properly cultivated, it is time to solicit gifts from board members.

Never forget that the single greatest mistake made in fundraising generally, and in capital campaigns specifically, is *not asking for the gift*. Early in the campaign, the institution must ask its board members to give and thus serve as an example to others (potential donors in the local community, major donor prospects, service users, and friends of the institution). But each solicitation should be carefully planned; no board member should ever give before having been asked to do so, because when board members' gifts (as well as gifts from others) are offered in advance, they are generally much smaller than if they had been properly solicited.

The solicitors should be carefully chosen, and each needs to have made a personal financial commitment first. Members of the board should be solicited by the chief executive officer or by other board members. Team solicitation, preferably with two callers on each prospect, is the most successful method. In making a solicitation, it is important to know the board member's areas of interest and relate them to the campaign: the biggest gifts will be generated when board members are asked to provide support in their areas of personal interest. It is also extremely important to note that capital gifts are not to be made in place of annual gifts. Careful consideration should be given to the method of asking (the separate ask, the double ask, or the triple ask; see Chapter Seven) before board members or others are approached.

In successful campaigns, contributions from board members and from the foundations and firms they control can range from 20 percent to more than 50 percent of the total goal. There are exceptions, of course, but there must always be a core or nucleus group ready to provide this kind of financial leadership, and it most often includes strong participation on the part of the governing board. In a capital campaign, 100 percent participation from the board is a powerful signal to other donors that the institution has vitality, vigor, and the confidence and enthusiasm of its governing board, who should know the institution better than anyone.

Once board members have given, their role becomes that of solicitors. Every board member should be responsible for some part of the campaign. It is not necessary that the campaign chair be a board member; ideally, however, all members of the board should be in leadership positions and should have groups of nonboard solicitors working for them and with them. This arrangement makes the board's involvement better known and demonstrates the board's backing of the program. It also provides the nonboard solicitors with people who are knowledgeable about the institution and who can answer their questions and accompany them on calls.

Board members should be used to identify potential solicitors, such as people with past, present, or future involvement with the institution. Board members, presumably, have useful contacts in the community, and so they should, as solicitors, use those contacts to bring in people who could be significant givers. They should ensure that enough of the right people are involved to get the job done in an organized manner and also that the people brought in have sufficient contacts to be useful solicitors or significant contributors themselves.

Several such people should also be on the institution's board. Board members should be asked to make important fundraising calls; their participation will add to the significance of these calls. They need not be involved with all the calls, however: being a board member is a part-time responsibility, and most board members probably have other obligations; they cannot afford to spend a great deal of time making calls, and so the calls that board members will make should be carefully selected. Board members are most helpful in calling on people they know or on people of similar standing in the community or the corporate world. If an institution's board includes the chief executive officer of a significant corporation, the institution should use that person to make calls on other corporate leaders.

Legon (1997) concludes that board members who are effective fundraisers share the following characteristics:

- A natural relationship with or commitment to the institution
- Willingness to contribute
- Willingness to use the appropriate method of asking and thus persuade others to give
- Enough interest in the institution to ask tough questions and ensure that staff members carry out their administrative responsibilities
- A sense of passion about the institution and its mission and a willingness to become advocates on its behalf
- Thorough knowledge of the institution, including its past and present, its traditions and values, and the likely direction of its future

In summary, then, these are the responsibilities of the board in a campaign:

- To review the need for the campaign
- To help structure the organization and timing of the campaign
- To suggest people as solicitors and potential donors
- To set giving levels for prospects
- To ensure proper research on prospects
- To review all printed material that will be used in presentations
- To make early lead gifts commensurate with its members' ability to give
- To be volunteer solicitors in the campaign
- To follow up with and cultivate other major donor prospects, as appropriate
- To ensure that there are proper investment plans for the funds

Foundation Boards and Development Councils

Today many public universities and large national organizations have headquarters at one location and affiliates or branches some distance away. A prevalent arrangement in such institutions is to have the fundraising program assisted by a foundation, a development council, or an advisory board that has focused responsibility for fundraising but does not have broader responsibility for governance and oversight. Under this arrangement, the institution's fundraising staff faces a special set of challenges in working with the volunteers provided by such foundations, councils, or advisory boards.

An advisory board or development council of this type is different from an institutional governing board. First, this type of group, because it has focused responsibility for raising money—indeed, that is its primary, if not only, purpose—should consist almost totally of influential, affluent individuals. (A governing board is necessarily attentive to issues of representation and must appoint members who reflect the diversity of the organization; this kind of group need not do so.) Second, because of its highly focused responsibility, this group's members are often not in a position to make institutional policy, set priorities, direct investments, or directly shape the future of the institution. Therefore, the challenge for the institution's development staff and top administrators is to involve this group in a meaningful way so that the members' inability to control the organization's direction does not defeat their enthusiasm, desire, and singular ability to help.

To further this purpose, it is imperative that the institution's governing board make itself accessible to this group. For example, one or two members of the governing board should serve in the group and ask its members for advice, listening carefully and thoughtfully to what they have to say. The group's members should be substantially and deeply involved in the processes of planning the campaign, setting priorities, and making the case for giving. If they are to seek—and give—substantial investments, they must be included and feel important.

The Role of the Campaign Chair

The campaign chair generally has the following duties:

- Serving as the campaign's chief executive officer
- Enlisting chairs for the principal functioning units of the campaign organization
- Cultivating and soliciting a limited number of appropriate prospects
- Assuming specific responsibility for personal and corporate commitments from members of the campaign steering committee and from all the principal operating chairs
- Serving as chair of the campaign steering committee and presiding over its meetings
- Making day-to-day decisions regarding the problems of the campaign, in consultation with the chief executive officer, the chief development officer, and others at the institution when important considerations arise
- Acting as campaign spokesperson for all news stories, campaign publications, special events, and other functions

The general campaign chair is the chief operating officer of the campaign. Therefore, the best that an organization has to offer may be barely good enough; no one is too big or too important to be asked to take this leadership post. The person who accepts it will be the key to the campaign and, more often than not, the measure of its success. The general campaign chair should have the following characteristics:

- Demonstrated capabilities
- Both influence and affluence—and the willingness to use them on behalf of the institution
- Dedication to seeing that the job is done on schedule
- Ability to command respect without demanding it
- A personality and character to which others will readily respond (people give to and work for people, not for causes)
- Intimate knowledge of the institution and the full scope of its program
- Persistence that compels others to follow suit
- Accessibility
- Willingness to follow the campaign plan and procedures and to accept direction
- Willingness to devote sufficient time to leadership
- Awareness that the early phases of planning and recruiting may require a considerable contribution of personal time
- Determination to overcome obstacles and invalid excuses
- Willingness and ability, at the start of the campaign, to make a personal pledge that is generous, thoughtful, and proportionate (in the event that the chair represents a corporation, a significant commitment from the company should set an example of leadership for other business and industry prospects)

The Role of the Chief Development Officer

In any campaign, the institution's chief development officer will be the catalytic force—educator, manager, researcher, communicator, facilitator, leader, guide, and stimulator. The principal purpose of the chief development officer in fundraising is to obtain understanding and support for the total program. This professional should hold a rank equal to that of other administrative officers and should report directly to the chief executive officer. The chief development officer must be an effective manager of staff and should provide support for the chief executive officer, the governing board, and key volunteers, ensuring that calls on prospects are actually made, not just planned and talked about. The role of the development staff is often in the background, not in the limelight. That belongs to the volunteers and the donors on the one hand and to the institution's chief executive officer on the other. More than anything else, the role of the chief development officer is to give structure and direction to any campaign effort.

How is this done? Every manager is different, and each has an individual style (moreover, no single management style is always best in all situations). Nevertheless, it can be said that most of today's professional development staff and volunteers believe that the following characteristics can be attributed to the manager of successful fundraising programs:

- Less orientation toward authority and more orientation toward the provision of good working conditions
- Helpfulness in solving problems and accomplishing goals
- Capacity to keep out of the way and, to the degree possible, to permit people to manage their own work
- Ability to provide a climate where staff members can gain confidence in each other, where goals are felt to be understandable and meaningful, and where everyone can participate successfully

The management function is important to the overall production of the entire staff and all volunteers. The chief development officer should have two primary goals: to be a contributor through actual involvement in the campaign and to provide leadership and guidance for both the staff and the volunteers. Actually, the manager's function today is considered to be more coordination of effort than actual fundraising. The roles are interdependent. Because most staff members and volunteers will agree that the chief development officer, who often also serves as the campaign manager, leads through demonstration, this individual should possess considerable knowledge of the profession, proven and recognized skills, and an ability to employ successful techniques in making a contribution to the campaign.

The chief development officer works in a group environment where all functions are interdependent and interrelated. Therefore, this individual must take advantage of the diverse talents of the group members, staff and volunteers alike. Rather than working through others in the traditional sense of assigning tasks to subordinates, he or she should have the ability to work with peers, associates, and even superiors to get the job done. This desired ability, of course, places a premium on strong, flexible personal qualities. The chief development officer, while building the overall approach on the best practices of traditional management, should augment this approach with new directions, techniques, and attitudes.

The chief development officer's role should be built on the recognition that a great deal of the organization's planning, organizing, directing, and controlling can and will be accomplished by others who are also managers, if only of their own time and effort. In other words, the chief development officer should provide the necessary climate to facilitate the best work of all subordinates, whether staff or volunteers.

A successful chief development officer generally serves the following functions:

- Recognizes the needs of staff and volunteers
- Delegates authority or responsibility (or both)
- Solicits and cultivates donor prospects
- Involves staff and volunteers, as appropriate, in decision making at every level
- Provides meaningful support, direction, and leadership
- Recognizes the challenge of changing times and human motivations
- Provides adequate feedback and recognition of achievement

More details of this role in a capital campaign are given in Chapter Eight.

CHAPTER FIVE

RECRUITING, EDUCATING, AND MOTIVATING VOLUNTEERS

The selection of volunteer leaders is perhaps the most crucial of all the decisions to be made in fundraising. There are three things every volunteer has to give—time, talent, and resources. However, each volunteer will have these to give in varying degrees and combinations. In other words, all volunteers are not equal.

Volunteers offer to perform services of their own free will, and there is no substitute for the influence that a volunteer leader can have on certain prospective donors. In many cases, the influence of the institution's staff is negligible compared to that of the right volunteer. Always remember, however, all volunteers can do some things, but only a few can do a lot. Since the success of any campaign usually depends on a handful of donors, it becomes critically important to the success of the campaign that the right volunteer leaders be enlisted "right" meaning that they have the ability to influence the people who will make or break the undertaking.

Every volunteer will do something, within reason, to help the institution, but most volunteers usually wait to be asked to do something specific. Attending meetings is not a gauge of a volunteer's power, and some volunteers are of great importance solely because of the contact they can make with a top-flight prospect. It is the responsibility of the staff to be certain that the best assignments go to volunteers who have demonstrated records of performance or the best credentials and that other volunteers are brought along, through training, to higher levels of performance. Always make assignments on a peer-to-peer basis (for example, corporate chief executive officer to corporate chief executive officer) or on a peer-down basis (for example, corporate chief executive officer to corporate vice president), and always be certain that the top volunteers are assigned to the top potential donors.

Almost every institution has access to top volunteer leaders, although some institutions do not believe they do. (If an institution truly lacks such access, it probably cannot mount a successful campaign.) The top volunteer leaders are characterized by certain recognizable traits:

- They are respected in the community.
- They are visible.
- They are able to influence others.
- They are success-oriented.
- They are involved in causes outside their work.
- They are able to attract other top leaders.
- They are self-assured and comfortable in most settings.

In looking for volunteers who are willing to work for the institution, first look to the organization's own family of constituents. If it is a college or a university, then its alumni, the parents of its alumni or current students, and its friends constitute the closest family members. For many community service organizations, those closest would include the individuals who use the services of the organization and their families. Other places to find volunteers include the corporate community, religious institutions, other volunteer organizations, and groups of local citizens.

The Importance of Volunteers

The trend, some will suggest, is away from using volunteers and toward having staff-driven campaigns. The suggestion is that volunteers today ask too many questions, express too many opinions, and sometimes forget their place. There is also an obvious and growing problem of supply and demand: good volunteers are in short supply and in great demand. However, do not be seduced by the short-term simplicity of believing, or of trying to convince others in your organization, that identifying, training, and staffing volunteers is more trouble than it is worth. Nothing could be further from the truth—as research consistently and abundantly shows (see, for example, the results of a Gallup Organization investigation in INDEPENDENT SECTOR, 1996). The American Association of Fund-Raising Counsel Trust for Philanthropy (1997) highlights the following findings:

• Among individuals who volunteer for nonprofit organizations, 90 percent also make financial contributions to charities, whereas among those who do not volunteer, 59 percent contribute. These percentages have been relatively stable over time. These results indicate that nonprofits able to increase volunteers' participation can boost giving levels—moderately during recessions and measurably when the economy improves.

• In 1993, the average gift among households with volunteers was 55 percent higher than among households with no volunteers. Among volunteers, the average contribution represented 2.6 percent of household income, whereas in households without volunteers the average was 1.1 percent of income.

Key volunteers are at least as valuable as key prospects. Good ones are fewer in number and will have multiple impacts that go beyond making gifts. Organizations that incorporate volunteers meaningfully into the fundraising structure will make the giving environment immeasurably more conducive to the acquisition of large gifts. Genuine involvement of volunteers includes their proper orientation, personalized professional staffing, shared planning and decision making, and allowing for honest differences of opinion. It means making a conscious decision about the selection of each volunteer for every role that the institution envisions. It requires the same thoughtful commitment to peer-to-peer personal recruitment as used in solicitation of major donors, and it recognizes that volunteers' time is often more valuable to them than money.

Volunteers' active participation in guiding the development of the case for financial support, creating strategies for others' involvement, and providing peer influence and leverage on solicitation calls all lead effectively to the attainment of large gifts. Use your volunteers or risk losing them—and if they go, realize that your donors, who are also volunteers, are also being lost.

The staff must always remember that most volunteers agree to serve on boards or committees in the hope that they can be of constructive help. Typically, volunteers look to the institution and ask it to show them how they can best serve. They assume that the institution will be wise enough to give them tasks that are within their experience and capabilities and that are important to the institution's goal. They expect to be used wisely and successfully.

Linda and Jack Gill reside in Houston, Texas, but have business interests that take them around the world. Both serve on local, regional, and national boards, and they have established the Gill Foundation. They tell me (personal communication, Apr. 2000), "Sure, we give as donors, but our time, contacts, and relationships are more valuable than our money. That's why we are dedicated volunteers, serving on boards of foundations, hospitals, and symphonies. 'Of those to whom a lot has been given, a lot is expected.' We feel privileged and obligated to support education needs in every way we can."

Recruiting Volunteers

Any organization wants the most capable, highest-profile, and most committed people out front. The people for such roles are usually found among the prominent members of the organization's constituency or community. They are immediately recognizable, not only for what they do for particular institutions but also for what they do in the professional, civic, or political arena. Ask busy people to do the job. The secret in using the time of busy people is to have them do what is crucial to the project, but no more; the next level of volunteers can do what is at the next level of importance.

Recruitment of volunteers is a shared task and is usually done most successfully from the top down. The campaign chair should be recruited by the top people in the organization. Before recruiting the chair for a capital campaign, the institution should have searched for the right person, figured out what it wants from that person, and as an enlistment aid, prepared the institution's case statement. Having done all these things, the institution should not send in a low-level manager to ask for the commitment. Send top guns—the chief executive officer and the board chair. And what, in turn, do the volunteers expect from the nonprofit seeking their services? John F. (Jack) Kimberling, a retired Los Angeles attorney who has served on local, regional, and national boards and also as co-chair of a national capital campaign and is the largest donor in the history of the Indiana University Bloomington School of Law, "I expect staff to be knowledgeable and up to date, using best practices as well as sharing them with me." He adds, "Staff should be dedicated to the principles and goals of their institution, to be hardworking, and to work for the good of the organization, not personal glory" (personal communication, Apr. 2000).

In recruiting the next level of volunteers—co-chairs and the campaign cabinet—the campaign chair reviews the pool of potential draftees with the staff and then participates in the recruitment visits. The campaign chair should do the actual asking but should be accompanied by the chief executive officer and the board chair. Some people feel that the chief executive officer and the board chair need not be involved, but that just isn't so. The last thing an organization wants to do is convey to its newly committed campaign chair that he or she must do the job all alone. The organization must come across as a well-built, well-staffed, smooth-rolling bandwagon. The development staff can assist the division chairs, the cabinet, in the recruiting that they do. This process continues all the way down through the organization until, ultimately, volunteers are recruiting other volunteers without staff assistance.

Recruitment is also a key part of the training and motivation process. No clear-thinking volunteer will accept a responsible assignment without asking a lot of pertinent questions. The institution must anticipate such questions and organize accordingly. Inform, but do not propagandize. Explain problems. The objective is to inform volunteers fully about the project and the campaign objectives and to give them confidence that they can do their assigned tasks successfully and enjoyably. In fact, enjoyment is one of the greatest motivators, and it is the staff's responsibility to make volunteering a satisfying experience. According to Kughn (1982), the best way to do this is to choose the right people for the right tasks and thereby ensure success.

Because the kinds of people sought for the top jobs are known in the community, it is not difficult to learn a great deal about them, and it behooves the organization to learn as much as it can. The more an institution knows about these top leaders, the better prepared it will be when the time comes to ask them for their help in achieving its goals. Hale (1980) provides a partial checklist for ensuring a successful first encounter in the recruitment of a key leader:

- Relying on the case statement, point out in some detail the importance of the campaign to the institution in general, those who will benefit from the services of the organization, and those who will come later. Stress the philosophical side of the case. People respond to ideas first, mechanics second.
- Meet personally with the prospective volunteer leader at a place and time most conducive to an unhurried discussion.
- Make it clear what the job is that is being offered.
- Assure the prospective volunteer that the institution will provide all of the backup needed to conduct a successful campaign.
- Assure the prospective volunteer that the top leadership of the institution on the board and among the institution's friends will be willing to help.
- Clarify the amount of time needed to do the job.
- Describe the goals and how they were set. Let the prospective volunteer see that they are obtainable.
- Answer all questions fully.
- After providing the institutional background, describe aspects of the program that the institution thinks will be most meaningful to the candidate.
- Decide before the meeting who among those calling on the person will actually ask the person to take a volunteer assignment in the campaign. Try to work out ahead of time how the prospective volunteer will be approached.

Communicating with Volunteers

The organization's staff serves behind the scenes in a supporting relationship to the top volunteer leaders. In working with these volunteers, the staff function should be carried out with a passion for anonymity. Staff members should coordinate and stimulate. They should furnish technical know-how, supply mechanical and clerical support, furnish resource information, and keep records. Finally, staff members help motivate and energize the volunteers, but at the center of the activity—in the spotlight—are the volunteers themselves.

Dunlop (1981) recommends that the staff be guided by the following principles:

• Before the first meeting with a volunteer leader, it is good for the staff to find out certain things (birth date and birthplace, religious affiliation, business background, family status, location of home, directorships, political affiliations, clubs, honors, awards). Some people might question the value of taking the time for such details, and some of the benefits are obscure; attention to these details is worthwhile, however, if only to avoid embarrassment. For example, warm reference to a spouse from whom the prospect is now divorced or to a former business associate who is now a competitor can ruin an otherwise positive encounter.

• At the initial meeting with the volunteer leader, first impressions are important. The staff member should try to appear presentable, considerate, reliable, well organized, and knowledgeable. Don't try to look too different. People feel more comfortable around people who seem similar to themselves. Individual manner, speech, and dress will affect how volunteers feel about staff.

• To show consideration, begin the first meeting by asking how much time the volunteer leader has to spend at this meeting. Do not take up any more time than that. Respecting the time limit shows that the staff recognizes the demands on the volunteer's time and values the time given.

• To appear well organized, make open use of an agenda. Give the volunteer leader the original, and work from a copy. Let the volunteer see that items are checked off as they are covered. Doing this reinforces a sense of accomplishment and refocuses attention on the agenda items still to be discussed.

• To build confidence in the staff's reliability, take notes openly. Doing so stresses the significance attached to the thoughts and ideas being discussed.

• To show that the staff is well organized and plans ahead, consult the volunteer leader about the stationery to be used in his or her work for the institution. Some volunteers may permit the use of their own business stationery, and others will not. Some volunteers have several other pieces of stationery from which to choose. The staff should understand the criteria for the use of each piece. Also ask whether the volunteer's secretary can provide samples of the volunteer's writing style, as a guide for drafting letters and other material. If the staff will be preparing printed materials to go out over the volunteer's signature, ask for three or four sample signatures in black ink, and have a pen with black ink and paper ready for the volunteer, of course, when this favor is asked. Ask whether the staff may consult the volunteer's secretary for the salutation to be used in writing to the key people with whom the volunteer will be dealing on behalf of the campaign. By giving attention to these details, staff members demonstrate to the volunteer the forethought that they have given to all aspects of the volunteer's work.

• An additional show of consideration comes in asking the volunteer leader about the best times for the staff to call.

• To give a sense of urgency to the work that the staff plans to do with the volunteer leader, set the time and place of the next meeting. Doing so suggests a general time frame for the accomplishment of tasks even if specific deadlines have not been set.

• In routine contact with the volunteer leader, be prompt. The emphasis on promptness should go beyond being on time for appointments. It is a matter of faithfully delivering whatever has been promised (a report, the draft of a letter, an opinion, a staff member for a meeting) on time. Courtesy also requires that staff members not keep the volunteer leader waiting on the phone. If an organizational secretary places calls for staff members, it is wise to have the staff member on the line before the volunteer picks up so as not to keep the volunteer waiting.

• Document the work accomplished at each meeting with the volunteer leader. Put each key decision, strategy, or plan in writing, and then invite the volunteer to make additions or corrections. This practice not only makes sure that there is mutual understanding of decisions but also provides a timely reminder and reference for the work being done.

• A volunteer leader's suggestion should never be rejected at the time when it is offered, no matter how unworthy it may seem. If no merit can be found in the volunteer's idea, simply say that it is something the staff would like to consider further or that the idea is new and there is a need to consult others about it. Then hope that at least some worthwhile element can be found in the idea. This delayed response not only allows the volunteer to save face but also gives everyone more time to consider the suggestion.

• Never delegate the proofreading of material that will bear a volunteer leader's signature. It is the staff's responsibility to make sure the copy is perfect. When it is perfect, submit it to the volunteer "for your consideration and approval," not "for your signature." No matter how many drafts have been gone through, always be graceful about giving the volunteer an opportunity to make additional changes. Remember that when anyone is asked to sign something, it becomes that person's work, and the person therefore has the final say in its preparation.

• Be candid with the volunteer leader. Sometimes staff members are tempted to offer optimistic encouragement rather than candor. It may be acceptable to project optimism in publicly announcing or discussing the campaign's progress but not in talking with a volunteer campaign leader.

- Staff behavior shows an attitude; keep it on the professional side. The objective of staff relationships with the volunteer leader is not to become a pal or bosom buddy. As Seymour (1966) noted, a party may be a party to the layman, but to the staff member, it's a business meeting.
- Don't pretend to have all the answers. A know-it-all attitude defeats the very relationship that the staff is trying to build with the volunteer campaign leader.

Educating Volunteers

The adage "easier said than done" certainly applies to educating volunteers. Orientation is necessary, and so are meetings. The campaign needs the power and stimulus that result when people come together to consider and attack a problem. To have a successful training session or meeting, however, the staff needs to take the following steps:

- Provide plenty of advance notice to the volunteers
- Draw up a well-planned agenda, with a copy for everyone, and mail it in advance
- Give the meeting a purpose
- Envision a result of the meeting (decisions made, actions taken)
- Make sure that the minutes of the meeting summarize what is to be done as a result of the meeting
- Put someone in charge of the meeting who will start on time, keep the meeting on track, and end on time

Volunteers expect professionalism from staff members. The staff must provide good training and the tools to complete the campaign successfully. As professionals, they must do their work in a businesslike manner and in a businesslike atmosphere, with well-prepared materials and a comprehensive training program. The ultimate objective of the institution is to have the volunteers catch fire with enthusiasm. A carefully planned volunteer training session can help do this, and carefully planned meetings can keep fanning the flame. Among the points to be covered at any orientation session are the following:

- A clear explanation of each person's role in the campaign (a chart will help)
- The points in the case statement that have caused the campaign to take on philosophical meaning
- Information and effective tools for each person to complete the assignment
- Complete answers to volunteers' questions

- Instructions for the volunteers (what they are to do, with whom, when, where, and why)
- Careful selection, rating, and assignment of prospects
- Guidelines on preparing for a successful call
- Clear instructions on what to do and what not to do on a call
- Instructions on what to do after a call
- Where to phone if there is a problem
- How to handle objections
- The importance of large gifts

A number of other elements may be included, as appropriate:

- A tour of the institution's facilities
- Presentation of architectural designs and floor plans, if a renovated or new building is a goal of the campaign
- Role-playing of a solicitation call on a prospective major donor
- Presentation of any audiovisual aids that have been prepared to make the case or assist the volunteers
- A timeline for making solicitations
- Appropriate remarks from the board chair, the chief executive officer, and the campaign chair
- Introduction of the staff members and the assignment that each one will have during the campaign

The quality of the orientation session depends on the person in charge, the individuals in attendance, expectations before the meeting, the planning that has gone into the meeting, where the meeting is held, how the room is arranged, the program, and the enthusiasm of the leaders.

During the volunteer training session, the explanation of the campaign plan, the campaign timetable, and the campaign objectives should be the shared responsibility of the institution's chief executive officer, the top campaign leader (usually the campaign chair), and the chief development officer. If the chief development officer is also serving as campaign director, it is especially important that the volunteers recognize this fact so that they will know this person as their contact within the organization. During the training session, the campaign director should be the one to explain the mechanics of the campaign and the materials in the worker's kit (see Resource 9, "Annual Campaign Volunteer's Kit," and Resource 10, "Capital Campaign Volunteer's Kit"). This is important not only because the professional knows the materials best but also because it demonstrates the competence of the director and builds confidence that the program is well conceived and carefully planned.

There are many kinds of volunteer training sessions, including workshops. For a nationwide campaign, the institution needs to recruit campaign leaders far in advance, usually six to ten months before the campaign begins, so that it can be certain of getting the workshop included in the busy schedules of its key volunteers. Once at the workshop, the volunteers will have ample opportunity to meet key institutional personnel and, ideally, some of the beneficiaries of the institution's services, as well as to hear firsthand about the institution and its objectives.

Bringing campaign leaders to the institution or to a local resort for a one- or two-day workshop requires a tremendous investment. Nevertheless, a meeting at a resort, or at any off-site location, means that there can be no distractions by phone calls or other intrusions. Volunteers who have come back to the area from far away may be returning for the first time in many years. That can be inspirational and should help prepare them further for their leadership work; they can also see who else is involved, and this alone can be rewarding. Even a local or limited-area campaign should also bring volunteer leaders on site, of course, but the logistics are not as difficult.

The volunteers should be prepared to answer the major questions that will be asked by prospective donors. The staff must prepare all the explanatory materials that will enable each volunteer to be a complete advocate of the program. These materials will be found in the volunteer worker's kit, a staff responsibility, which contains the following elements:

- The case statement
- Campaign objectives
- A description of the campaign plan
- Information about how to give noncash gifts
- Pledge cards
- Prospect rating instructions
- Information about the range of gifts needed
- Report forms and envelopes

The kit will also include other supporting materials. Chief among them is a volunteers' guide. This type of guide can be prepared in many different forms and formats, but it should always stress the following points to each volunteer:

- Know the case. Be able to present it concisely and with enthusiasm.
- Make your own gift. It gives you a psychological boost and helps you ask others.
- Be positive; never be apologetic. Assume that the prospect is going to give. Remember, you are asking not for yourself but for an institution worthy of support.
- Make personal calls only. Meet prospects face to face; do not use telephone calls or letters except to arrange or confirm meetings. (If volunteers will not do this for the organization, then it will be better not to use their services.)

- Keep your sights high, and emphasize that this is an important campaign. Ask the prospective donor to consider the amount suggested on the rating card.
- Go back to see the prospect again, as necessary. It is best not to leave the pledge card to be returned later. If the prospective donor wants to consider making a gift, say that you will return at a specified time. Decisions for major gifts take time; therefore, be prepared to make a number of visits if you need to.
- Obtain multiple-year (usually three- to five-year) pledges if it is a multiyear campaign. Most donors can give more if they can spread the payments over a period of years. Some donors, however, will not pledge for more than a year but will make a gift. If that is the situation, ask whether the institution can seek a renewal of the gift each year. Many donors are receptive to this approach.
- Get the job done—do not procrastinate. Take the best prospects first. Success will build your confidence. Report gifts promptly so that others will see your success and so that the institution will be able to announce progress toward its campaign goals.

At this point, it is also necessary to discuss what can be done about hesitant or reluctant solicitors and what staff members can do to help:

- Recommend that volunteers make their own gifts first. It is a fact that the volunteer's commitment is a source of psychological strength in asking another person to make a commitment.
- Suggest that volunteers team up to make calls on their prospects so that one volunteer can bolster another. The team approach should be used anyway for most major prospects; therefore, suggest it to novice or reluctant volunteers.
- For some volunteers, asking for the gift is the most difficult part of the personal call. Give them phrasing that helps take the sting out of the request. For example, the prospective donor cannot be offended if the volunteer asks, "Would you consider giving [the rating amount] over the next three years to help [name of organization] reach the goal?" The solicitor is asking for consideration of a request, not telling the donor what to do. This approach makes the appeal, but not in a hard-sell, aggressive way.

Staffing Volunteers

It is an axiom of any fundraising program that no institution can hire enough development staff to do the job of fundraising alone. Volunteers are of enormous value in research (the basic element of all fundraising), and they are indispensable in cultivating prospects and selling the program. Therefore, according to Kughn (1982), servicing volunteers is vital: it is not often that they provide their own steam, try to solve the problems that crop up, or motivate themselves.

The key to using volunteers effectively is to assign them tasks that they can and want to do in the campaign. Those tasks must also be important. Thus volunteers should have assignments consistent with their interests, as well as with their abilities. Before giving a volunteer an assignment, it is necessary to ask, "Is success possible for this volunteer?"

The organization has the right to expect certain things from volunteers. In addition to taking specific assignments, volunteers should take responsibility for the following areas of communication:

- Informing the staff if something occurs that has affected their ability or willingness to do the job
- Promptly reporting all progress concerning their prospects
- Never overstepping or exceeding the scope of their assignments without first clearing the changes with the staff
- Letting the staff know if conflicting interests arise that could put the institution at a disadvantage
- Checking with the staff before departing from agreed-on plans

Using Volunteers to Say "Thank You"

Peer-to-peer solicitation is an accepted and proven technique in fundraising. It is the best way to maximize giving. Therefore, peer-to-peer recognition should follow as naturally as night follows day. But often it does not. Today there is a growing tendency to overlook volunteers when recognizing and thanking donors.

Kimberly Ruff is a marketing professional, mother, and wife. She is a past president of Amethyst House, which operates two homes in Bloomington, Indiana, for housing recovering alcoholics and addicts and their dependent children. Amethyst House has an office staff of three along with twelve others who help full or part time in its houses. Its annual budget is $300,000. In fiscal 1999–2000 it raised $70,000 from a prospect pool of fifteen hundred names. Ruff explains, "A simple thank-you and the appreciation of the executive director and my fellow board members" are all the recognition she desires. Like the vast majority of volunteers, she serves Amethyst House "because I was asked. They needed someone with a marketing expertise, and I had an interest in the cause" (personal communication, May 2000).

Organizational leaders and campaign chairs, in their eagerness to express appreciation from the top—a perfectly legitimate and appropriate gesture—often fail to share these special moments. These moments of triumph should be treasured and savored with the individuals directly involved in delivering the gift, including the volunteers (or lower-level staff members) who closed it. Failing to share the glory is a mistake, too. The next time the opportunity presents itself, ask a volunteer to express thanks on your behalf to five donors instead of asking five prospects to give. Watch their reaction. And make a note of the results. Never forget that this type of involvement is yet another way of building on your personal relationship with the volunteer doing the thanking and the donor being thanked.

It has often been repeated that an institution receives important sums by having important people ask important prospects for the support of important projects. Give volunteers the time, attention, and service they require and deserve. Such attention will pay great dividends.

CHAPTER SIX

COORDINATING THE CAMPAIGN STRUCTURE AND SOLICITATION PROCESS

The first part of this chapter emphasizes the structure for a capital campaign, which is not essentially different from the structure for an annual campaign but is usually more fully developed and elaborate. (Campaign models for the annual campaign are covered more fully in Chapter Nine.) This chapter then moves on to examine the solicitation process, encompassing both annual and capital campaign models. It concludes with a discussion about accounting for gifts and pledges in institutional totals.

Staffing the Campaign

The responsibility of professionally staffing a campaign falls primarily to the chief development officer, the campaign director, and the development staff. The chief development officer should bear primary responsibility for preparing a comprehensive campaign plan, organizational chart, and campaign schedule before the campaign is launched (see Resource 11, "Annual Campaign Plan," and Resource 12, "Capital Campaign Plan"). These elements should include a leadership recruitment system and schedule and a public information plan and schedule covering media, printed materials, typescript materials, and audiovisual materials. The development staff should see that provisions are made for production of a prospect list as well as for an evaluation system for all campaign prospects; this system should include evaluation committees for larger gift prospects and formulas for giving for smaller gift prospects. There must also be a campaign budget and a system for controlling expenses, a system for recruiting volunteer workers, informational meetings for those recruited, and training workshops for volunteers and leaders.

It is important that the development staff establish a progress reporting and control system for prospects. It should include a system for assigning prospect pledge cards, a system for assigning workers and tracking their activity, a schedule for report meetings, mailings of progress reports, and a prospect reassignment system with a redistribution system for pledge cards. Systems for tabulating gifts and auditing the campaign should be well thought out and planned for in advance; they should include posting of the section listing and the master listing, as well as the auditing of all cash and pledges. Steps should also be set forth to address organizational issues, volunteer recruitment and training, public announcement of the campaign, subsequent report meetings, and the follow-up and cleanup necessary to the success of area campaigns. There should also be systems for acknowledging gifts, collecting pledges, and conducting the final follow-up.

It is important for the campaign director to work effectively with the volunteer organization and the top levels of institutional administration, but this officer must also make sure that the entire institutional community is aware of the campaign and feels that it has an active part to play. Key administrators should be consulted on or informed of all proposals and fundraising activities related to their specific areas. At the same time, key institutional personnel should be actively involved in the cultivation and solicitation process.

Campaign Organization

An organization chart for a typical capital campaign will generally resemble that shown in Figure 6.1. Organization charts can and do take many forms. Nevertheless, every campaign's organizational pattern should incorporate at least the structural features shown in the figure; this is the basic pattern from which other, more complex patterns are developed.

The exact structure of any campaign organization will have the following determinants:

- The method chosen for the campaign
- The ask method chosen
- The extent to which the organization intends to rely on a "rifle shot" approach versus a "shotgun" approach (the latter requires a more extensive volunteer structure)

FIGURE 6.1. CAPITAL CAMPAIGN ORGANIZATION CHART.

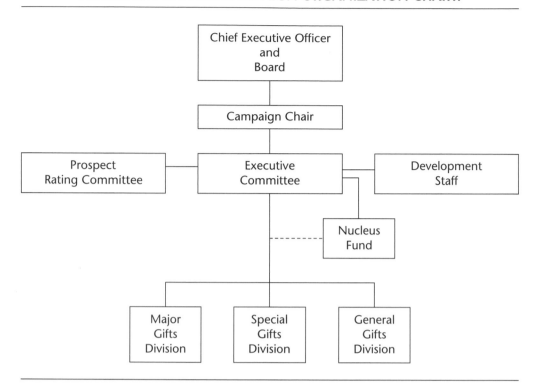

- The size and diversity of the institutional constituency
- Whether the campaign is a community campaign or a wide-area campaign
- The extent to which the campaign will rely on volunteers for solicitation
- The mix of face-to-face, telephone, and direct-mail solicitation that will be incorporated into the campaign structure

As discussed in detail in Chapter Five, a chair and members for each committee should be enlisted according to the following pattern: the board chair and the chief executive officer should enlist the general campaign chair in a personal visit; and the general campaign chair, the board chair, and the chief executive officer, working as a team or, as applicable, in pairs, should enlist members of the campaign's executive committee (these appeals, too, should be made in person). Enlistment should be as official and dignified as possible. Each volunteer should be given a job description, with definite assignments and specification of the results that will be expected within a definite period. Professionals find that sharing the results of the market survey or a preliminary version of the case statement is often very helpful in selling top prospective leaders on the campaign; doing so makes the prospective leaders feel that they are in on the ground floor—and they are.

Volunteer enlistment is a top-down process. Once the board chair and the chief executive officer have enlisted the campaign chair, and once the three of them have enlisted the key campaign leaders, all the members of the volunteer structure should in turn be expected and required to enlist the individuals who will work with them throughout the campaign. In every case, even at the level of special and general gifts, it is best for leaders to be enlisted through personal visits.

The success of any campaign depends on an overall volunteer organization designed to facilitate rather than restrict the effective solicitation of prospects. Organizational concepts must be realistic and practical. Overorganization can be cumbersome and stifling. The best organizational structure permits an efficient flow of communication and easy performance of functions by everyone involved. The size of a volunteer organization is dictated by the scope of the campaign, the size of the constituency, and geographical requirements. The effective rule of thumb regarding volunteer solicitors and prospects is that there should be one prospect per volunteer at the major gifts level, two or three prospects per volunteer at the special gifts level, and five prospects per volunteer at the general gifts level. Often the pattern followed is three to five major gift prospects per volunteer, four to seven special gift prospects per volunteer, and occasionally, ten or more prospects per volunteer for solicitation of general gifts. This pattern is less effective because busy people are being asked to do more; nevertheless, it is reality for many organizations.

Committee Responsibilities

Any campaign structure requires a number of committees, or at least one committee functioning in a number of ways. A typical campaign includes a policy committee, an executive committee, and committees on prospect evaluation, major gifts, special gifts, general gifts, and public relations (the role of public relations is discussed in Chapter Eighteen). Depending on the campaign model and structure chosen, there may also be a need for an institutional family campaign committee, a community campaign committee, a corporate campaign committee, and a foundation campaign committee.

The development committee of the governing board generally functions as the policy committee. It determines the general policies of the program and sets the goals. It approves the organizational pattern, staffing and budget requirements, and proposed timetable. It also sets guidelines under which memorial gifts or named gift opportunities may be established and determines guidelines for gift acknowledgment and donor recognition. The top development officer staffs this committee. Its recommendations are presented for approval to the full governing board.

The executive committee provides general direction and active management of the program. It coordinates the activities of volunteers and sets the operating schedule. The executive committee generally includes the chairs of the several campaign operating committees, advisory groups, and top administrators. The chief executive of the institution and the board chair should be ex officio members. This committee, too, is served administratively by the top development officer. This committee normally reports to the chief development officer or the chief executive officer (or both).

The prospect evaluation committee should be active early in the program, measuring both interest and financial capability. It evaluates what the prospects can give (not what they will give) in terms of both effort and contributions. Confidentiality and anonymity are absolutely essential to this committee. The research staff of the development office is assigned to this committee.

The major gifts committee has the critical task of evaluating, cultivating, and soliciting the institution's most important prospects. Because 80 percent or more of the campaign goal will probably come from a very small number of lead and major donors, it is important that the most affluent and influential group possible be enlisted to serve on this committee. The members of this committee must be the best volunteers who can call on the best prospects at the appropriate time to secure maximum investments. Committee members are often assigned only one or two prospects to work with at a time. This group constitutes one of the most important task forces in the campaign organization. It is the responsibility of this team, under the direction of its chair, to persuade its members to take appropriate assignments and to keep them in steady and productive pursuit of their prospects. Because this committee is so important, the selection of its chair should be carefully considered. Generally, the chair should be a resident of the community in which the campaign is taking a place (or in the case of a wide-area campaign, be able to commute readily to the organization's location), be capable of making a major gift, be active in the business or social community, have considerable influence, and not be afraid to ask for major gifts. In brief, the tasks of the major gifts chair are as follows:

- To put together a strong committee willing to seek gifts in the major gifts range
- To work closely with the campaign chair in all matters affecting the committee's responsibilities

- To make a generous personal gift within his or her financial means
- To ask for certain major gifts personally
- To hold regular meetings of the committee in which its members can screen and rate new prospects, take additional assignments, and report on progress
- To follow up periodically with members of the committee and make regular, timely reports to the committee on the progress of the campaign
- To see that members of the committee are fully informed about the campaign and that each member has made a personal commitment in accordance with his or her ability
- To work with the other committee chairs to identify and develop other individual leadership gifts throughout the campaign structure

The special gifts committee deals with substantial gifts just below the major gifts level. The duties of committee members are similar to those of members of the major gifts committee. The ratio of one worker to two to four prospects is commonly used. Liaison may be provided by development staff other than the top development officer.

General gift solicitation is generally the cleanup phase and in most modern campaigns is targeted to the general constituency of the institution. Personal solicitation is encouraged, but telephone solicitation and direct-mail solicitation are often used. For personal solicitation, one worker to five prospects is the generally accepted ratio. Telephone solicitation, second in effectiveness to direct-mail solicitation, is growing increasingly popular; mail techniques are the least effective of the three. Some campaigns have recently reported success with combination phone and mail programs.

The Solicitation Process

As repeatedly demonstrated over many years of fundraising, personal solicitation is both the most economical and the most effective form of campaign solicitation. Telephone solicitation is an extension of the personal visit but usually is not nearly as effective. Phone-and-mail solicitation, which should be used for prospects the institution cannot reach personally, is an increasingly popular method, although some observers believe that overuse is already causing it to lose some of its effectiveness. The principal purpose of a broad mail campaign is to attract new interest and cultivate donors who may give more later. If mail must be used for individual solicitation, pave the way by telephone whenever feasible.

But how, exactly, does an institution go about structuring its gift solicitation and determining the scope of solicitation for its particular campaigns, particularly when the comprehensive campaign model is used or when single-purpose campaigns are being conducted concurrently with the annual campaign? Evans (1978, 1979) outlines three distinct approaches to asking that gifts be considered: the "separate ask," the "double ask," and the "triple ask."

The Separate Ask

With the separate ask, donors are solicited at two separate times, once for an extended commitment to a capital gift and once each year for annual giving. There are three advantages to this approach:

- Two separate solicitations clarify the difference between capital giving and annual giving.
- Worker training may be made easier because those who volunteer to solicit capital funds need only inform the donor that the capital fund is distinct from annual giving and that donors will be asked at a different time to consider annual support.
- A special solicitation may lend annual giving more emphasis because it will not appear subordinate to the capital campaign.

A separate ask also presents problems:

- Donors may resent a second request that comes only a few months after they have made a major commitment to a capital campaign.
- More volunteers may be required if the annual fund solicitation is to involve more than direct mail.
- If solicitations come at separate times, some donors may merely shift their annual giving to the capital campaign, declining later on to support the annual fund and thus not increasing their total contributions.

Although this approach can be used with any of the types of campaigns described in Chapter One, it is not particularly well suited to the comprehensive campaign, because the institution that has chosen the comprehensive model has done so to create harmony and unity within its total program, and this approach creates division.

The Double Ask

Among institutions that have continuing capital programs and reasonably satis-fying experience in annual campaigns, the double ask—soliciting the donor for the capital gift and the annual gift at the same time—is a popular method of coor-dinating the annual and capital campaigns. People who are not ready to be solicited for capital gifts continue to be solicited for annual gifts; those who are ready are asked for both. The advantages of the double ask are as follows:

- If capital funds are solicited personally (and with major donors they must be), this system automatically provides for face-to-face solicitation of the annual gift as well.
- This system provides an efficient use of volunteers because the volunteer for capital solicitation will handle annual giving at the same time.
- It reduces "harassment" of the donor by providing for a single approach dur-ing the year.
- It keeps the concept of annual giving alive while also bringing attention to the capital campaign.

The double ask also presents some problems, however. Donors may not appreciate the distinction between the types of gifts and may simply say, "I'll make a gift to the institution, and you divide it up as you want." It may also make worker training more difficult—the more forms of solicitation a worker must present, the greater the potential for confusion.

The double ask can take two forms. The first is the *multiple-year capital, one-year annual* form. Here the donor is asked to make a pledge to the capital campaign, to be paid over a period of years, and at the same time is asked to make a contribution to the current annual fund, with a reminder that another solicitation for annual giving will occur each year while the capital pledge is being paid. The second is the *multiple-year capital, multiple-year annual* form. Here the donor is asked to make a pledge to contribute over the next three to five years, allocating a portion to capi-tal giving and a portion to annual giving. The disadvantage of this approach is that it limits the possibilities of presenting the case to the donor annually, if the donor has made a commitment to both the capital and the annual funds.

The Triple Ask

With the triple ask, not only are the capital and annual gifts solicited at the same time, but a planned gift commitment is also sought. The advantages and disad-vantages of the triple ask are similar to those of the double ask. This is a very sophisticated form of solicitation, requiring both an extremely well planned approach by staff and volunteers and a prospective donor who is extremely knowledgeable. It is to be used selectively and sparingly—only where the situation warrants it.

Scope of Solicitation

Having considered the ways in which the annual fund and the capital campaign can be combined, Evans (1978, 1979) suggests that an organization must consider the scope of each solicitation: Will the organization solicit everybody for everything, or will it limit solicitation of certain prospects to capital gifts and solicit others only for annual gifts? Once an organization has decided to continue annual giving in some form while conducting a capital campaign (and this is almost always the case), the traditional practice has been to solicit all constituents for both gifts. The advantages are obvious: everyone is given ample opportunity to participate in the several elements of the total development program; and the organization, by going to the entire constituency with the capital funds campaign, may have the opportunity to discover a few major donors not previously known to it. There are also problems with this approach, however. Maximum solicitation of constituents requires maximum commitment of staff and volunteers (as noted in Chapter One, it may be impossible for an institution with limited numbers of staff and able volunteers to approach its entire constituency), and soliciting everyone for everything is expensive—indeed, it may not be cost-effective.

Each time a solicitation moves to a larger number of prospects, the sights of the donors drop. When ten donors give a total of $10 million, the level at which people are contributing is perfectly clear. When five thousand givers contribute a total of $500,000, the level of giving is equally clear but less impressive, and the sights of major donors may be reduced. When it is known that everyone will be asked to provide the capital funds required, the burden is lifted from the handful with potential for major support, and they may wait for the masses to provide the funds needed. This puts the institution at peril because the masses, without lead and major gift support, will never provide all the funds needed.

A new concept is now emerging in capital fund solicitation: for capital gifts, solicit only prospective donors with capital potential; for annual giving, ask all others. To make use of this concept, an organization must identify the people capable of making significant multiple-year capital gifts and solicit them for that purpose; all other constituents will be solicited only for annual giving because the organization has made the judgment that they do not have capital potential at present. The advantages of this type of approach are twofold. First, it allows the organization to focus staff time and its best volunteers on the top major prospects. As an organization moves a campaign to larger and larger numbers, it dilutes staff time and volunteer attention; by focusing only on major donors for major gifts, the organization can more effectively use the "rifle shot" approach. Second, this approach makes the annual fund an integral part of the overall objectives; it requires a total development goal that includes annual giving, and its inclusion permits annual donors to feel that they are part of the program.

There are four problems with this type of approach:

- Major donors may resent the fact that only a small number are being asked for capital gifts.
- The masses may feel they have no role in "laying the bricks" if their gifts go only for current operations. (It is possible to overcome this feeling by emphasizing the total development program and especially by highlighting the relative merits of sustaining the ongoing program while the capital drive is in progress.)
- If only selected capital prospects will be approached for capital giving, the organization must continue a never-ending search for new major donors, and this will require a strong annual giving program as a means of identifying capital donors.
- Unless the masses clearly understand their vital importance in meeting the overall objectives, they may develop the habit of letting the big donors do it all. The large number of annual donors should not come to believe that an institution is dependent on only a handful of people.

Reporting and Valuing Gifts

Once the institution has decided whether to drop the annual fund or integrate it into the campaign effort, whether to exercise the separate, double, or triple ask, and whether to solicit select constituents for capital gifts or everyone for every purpose, the next important task is to coordinate this package with the planned or deferred giving program. Again, the institution has a few options. One is to exclude planned giving—any charitable life income trusts, annuities, or promised bequests—from the campaign results (if a donor died, however, such funds might come to the institution during the campaign). A second option is to count everything, even a future bequest from a four-year-old. A balance somewhere in between is suggested, and an approach is proposed at the end of this chapter.

In planning for a major development program, it is reasonable to include in the goal an expectation for income trusts, annuities, and other irrevocable commitments. This approach allows the institution to talk to potential donors about irrevocable gifts with retained life interest. A donor may be more apt to make a decision knowing that establishing a life income trust will count as participation in the campaign.

Bequests are a bit more difficult. On the one hand, it is certainly unwise (and perhaps even dishonest) to include in an institution's campaign results a potential bequest from a very young person. On the other hand, it may be unwise to completely exclude a future bequest from a donor who is advanced in years and is willing, for the satisfaction of participating in the total development program, to add a codicil to his or her will for a major gift.

Institutions should think about both what is fair and what will serve as a good incentive for fundraising and then set up clear guidelines in advance. For example, an institution may decide to include all estate notes from people over sixty-five and all promises of bequests from those seventy and older. In any event, the institution should make its decision before it sets its goal. It would certainly be unwise if a goal reflected only direct needs for the cash that will be required in the near future but the institution then counted toward that goal all promises of bequests, some of which might not materialize for many years. It is extremely important to exercise good judgment in a campaign where bricks and mortar are a major issue. It is imperative not only that an institution receive commitments to build the structure under consideration but also that a cash flow be established to pay for construction and reduce debt in a timely and equitable fashion. Using planned gifts to meet payment schedules for construction is extremely risky.

A final consideration is not only what to count but also, for the purposes of accounting and recording, how to value gifts, especially noncash gifts. In the educational sector, the guidelines provided in the *CASE Management Reporting Standards* (Council for Advancement and Support of Education, 1996b) are becoming an accepted approach to resolving this issue. These guidelines can be obtained from CASE, 1307 New York Avenue N.W., Suite 1000, Washington, DC 20005; http://www.case.org. The following organizations endorse the *CASE Campaign Standards: Management and Reporting Standards for Educational Fund-Raising Campaigns* (Council for Advancement and Support of Education, 1996a, p. 91):

American Association of Colleges of Nursing

American Association of Community Colleges

American Association of Fund-Raising Counsel

American Council on Education

American Prospect Research Association

Association of Community College Trustees

Association for Healthcare Philanthropy

Canadian Council for the Advancement of Education

College Board, Council of Graduate Schools

Council of Independent Colleges

Hispanic Association of Colleges and Universities

Lilly Endowment, Inc.

National Association of College and University Business Officers

National Association of Independent Colleges and Universities

National Association of Independent Schools

National Association of State Universities and Land-Grant Colleges

National Council for Resource Development

National University Continuing Education Association

Any organization can look to these guidelines as a model approach, realizing that different circumstances may suggest the need to modify the standards to make them applicable and useful.

The Association of Governing Boards of Universities and Colleges, while supporting the CASE standards, urges institutions to go even further, especially in reporting deferred gifts in capital campaign totals. A 1996 statement from that organization said, "The Board of Directors of the Association of Governing Boards [AGB] of Universities and Colleges commends CASE for developing the *CASE Campaign Standards*. AGB endorses the standards except for those provisions addressing testamentary bequests and deferred gifts. AGB urges institutions to count bequests only when actually realized. With regard to deferred gifts, AGB urges that campaign totals be based on present value only" (Council for Advancement and Support of Education, 1996a, p. 92). The point is well taken, but there will be understandable initial reluctance on the part of institutions to take this further step, for three primary reasons.

First, over the short haul, changing to these standards will create a series of practical "public relations" problems as it relates to donors. Donors accustomed to being given credit and public recognition for the face value of deferred gifts will now be "credited" for smaller gifts. As an illustration, consider the gift of a $100,000 life insurance policy from a fifty-year-old donor. Under current standards, the donor is recognized as a $100,000 donor; in terms of the policy's present value, however, the donor's credited gift will be appreciably less. Will this kind of adjustment dampen donors' enthusiasm? And to use another life insurance policy as an example, what is the public relations effect if two campaign co-chairs each want to give a $100,000 life insurance policy—two "equal" gifts—but one is fifty years old and the other is fifty-eight? In terms of the gifts' present value, the two co-chairs will be credited with "unequal" gift amounts. Again, will this have a harmful effect?

Second, North Americans are intensely competitive; we keep score. This is a far less compelling consideration than the first one, but it is nevertheless real. Therefore, which institutions, particularly among those that insist on comparing themselves to others in their sectors, will be the first to step forward and institute these new standards? What type of commitment to the new standards will it take for an institution to tell a potential donor, one who has multiple philanthropic interests, that his $100,000 life insurance policy will be credited at its present value when other institutions are still crediting it at face value?

Third, it is axiomatic that campaign goals are constantly going higher. When these new standards are implemented, however, it is clearly possible—in fact, it is likely—that campaign goals, at least for a while, will actually be lower than they are now. What impact, if any, will this development have on the energy and commitment of volunteers who are asked to lead these campaigns with seemingly smaller goals? Will it limit the vision of the donors who are asked to support these campaigns, causing them to lower their own sights? It should not matter, but will it? Campaign goals are not (or at least should not be) established to set records; rather, they should be established to meet legitimate institutional priorities that are consistent with the institution's mission and with its current and future needs.

The further transition that AGB encourages should occur, and governing boards should take the lead in supporting this movement. It is fiscally responsible and intellectually honest to do so. Movement in this direction will take time, however, and it needs to be phased in. One possible way to do that (and some organizations have already done so) is to begin reporting gifts in terms of both face value and present value. This practice can lead to a transition process, as seamless as possible, toward the point where it becomes acceptable for goal reporting to be based on present value alone.

With these observations and caveats in mind, an institution might consider the guidelines shown in Table 6.1 as a basis for consideration and discussion. It is important to establish such guidelines when they can be considered (and perhaps adopted) in a calm, rational way, without influence from the pressures that often exist when an institution is midstream in its fundraising effort and pressing to achieve success.

TABLE 6.1 FUNDRAISING ACCOUNTING GUIDELINES.

Type of Gift	Public Value	Internal Value	What Will Count	What Will Not Count
Cash	Full amount	Full amount		
Securities	Fair market value of securities on date of transfer	Fair market value of securities on date of transfer		
Real estate	Appraised value at time of gift	Appraised value at time of gift	Real estate received during the campaign	
Personal property	Appraised value at time of gift	Appraised value at time of gift	Personal property received during the campaign	
Pledges	Full amount	Full amount	Signed pledge card or letter from donor Pledges fulfilled within five-year period	Verbal pledges
Bequest expectancies	Face value	Discount based on donor's age	Copy of will or excerpt from will Donor society enrollment Signed gift agreement Letter of intent from donor Letter from donor's attorney or financial adviser	Contact report Contingencies Donor under sixty-five years old

TABLE 6.1 FUNDRAISING ACCOUNTING GUIDELINES, Cont'd.

Type of Gift	Public Value	Internal Value	What Will Count	What Will Not Count
Realized bequests	Full amount	Full amount	Monies actually received from an estate or trust distribution	Gifts that were counted in prior campaigns as bequest expectancies
Charitable gift annuities	Face value	Value of charitable remainder interest	Annuity agreement in place	
Charitable lead trusts	Face value of annual income received during the campaign and discounted value of annual income after the campaign	Amount of annual income	Copy of trust agreement	
Pooled income fund	Full value of contribution to the fund	Discount based on donor's age	Contributions to pooled income fund	
Charitable remainder trusts	Face amount	Value of charitable remainder interest	Trust agreement in place Copy of trust agreement (or excerpt) if an outside trust	
Retirement plan assets	Face amount	Discount based on donor's age	Signed gift agreement Letter of intent from donor	
Insurance	Face value	Discount based on donor's age	Organization as owner of the policy Fully paid-up policy	

Note: In general, the following will not count: gifts or pledges counted in previous campaigns, investment earnings on gifts, and governmental funds.

CHAPTER SEVEN

ESTABLISHING THE CAMPAIGN TIMELINE

This chapter addresses an area where there are fundamental differences in approach between the capital campaign and the annual campaign. The timeline of any annual campaign is by definition twelve months. Most organizations use the calendar year, it is easier to relate to, given the rhythms of our culture and individual giving habits and patterns, but some use the fiscal year. Either is acceptable. The great variable in annual campaigns is the fundraising methods used—face-to-face solicitation, direct mail, telemarketing, special events, and, increasingly, technology (see Chapter Nineteen). Within the framework of the twelve-month campaign, there are as many variations on the campaign content, methods used, and timing of various appeals as there are organizations doing annual campaigns. Other than the fact that most organizations focus their efforts heavily on the last three or four months of the calendar year, when as much as 70 percent of all gifts in any given year are made, annual campaigns have little else in common.

The capital campaign, by contrast, generally follows a very typical pattern but may be completed in a few months or take several years to accomplish, depending on the size and complexity of the organization and the campaign goal.

What follows is a look at several organizations and how each designs its annual campaign. Also presented are a typical organizational pattern for any capital campaign and one organization's approach to maintaining a distinctive annual fund program while also planning to conduct a capital campaign.

Approaches to the Annual Campaign

Organizations of different types and sizes take different approaches to the annual campaign. Let us look at six in Indiana, ranging from small to large.

Harmony School

Located in Bloomington, Indiana, the Harmony School Education Center offers educational programs from preschool through high school. Its current enrollment is 185 students; and it has more than a thousand alumni, former students, and friends on its prospect list. The school's budget is $1.1 million annually; it employs twenty-five people and has no fundraising professional on staff. Steve Bonchek, the school's executive director, is its chief fundraiser.

Its annual program consists of personal calls, one direct mailing a year, and four or five special events—two runs, a golf tournament, and rummage and plant sales. Bonchek reports that the school raises $500,000 annually (personal communication, Sept. 1999). Three gifts account for $175,000, and thirteen hundred other gifts total $275,000, including individual gifts generated through special events. Ten donors give $10,000 or more annually, six donors give between $5,000 and $10,000, twenty-four donors give $1,000 to $5,000, and twenty donors give $500 to $1,000.

Eiteljorg Museum

The Eiteljorg Museum of American Indians and Western Art, located in Indianapolis, Indiana, is a relatively young and rapidly growing museum under the able leadership of John Vanausdall, who serves as president and CEO. It maintains a broadly based fundraising program that is volunteer-driven. It uses personal solicitation, direct mail, memberships, telemarketing, gift clubs, and special events including an auction to generate revenues—a total of $2,676,155 in 1998–99. The museum's operating budget is $3,573,214, and it has a staff of fifty-six, with seven persons in development and a development budget of $299,953. Total annual giving including grants is $2,327,730. The annual fund receives approximately three thousand gifts totaling more than $850,000. Less than 10 percent of the donors to the annual fund give more than 85 percent of the total, according to Sharon Hunt, director of major gifts, and Lynn Lambuth, vice president and chief advancement officer (personal communication, July 1999).

Indianapolis Museum of Art

The Indianapolis Museum of Art has a most effective and efficient fundraising program under the direction of Linda Hardwick, who explains, "Annual giving in the museum has traditionally referred only to unrestricted gifts from corporations, foundations, and individuals. It has not included funds that are restricted to the annual program. This has been true of most museums. Now they break their giving areas into unrestricted, temporarily restricted (annual restricted programs), and permanently restricted—endowments, art purchase funds, and so on—really broadening their range of gifts and appeals and increasing membership" (personal communication, July 1999).

The museum's development budget is $900,000, including salaries for a staff of ten. There are 8,000 donors and a prospect pool of 56,600. For the year ended December 31, 1998; the museum reported $1,491,358 from annual gifts and memberships, $264,367 in restricted giving, $1,707,249 from activities even though the museum sponsors no special events, and $316,962 from grants. About one-third of the museum's annual giving ($600,000) come from 350 donors who support its major gift club. Total giving in 1998 was $28,412,347.

The Children's Museum of Indianapolis

Arguably one of the best children's museum in the world, the Children's Museum of Indianapolis is supported by one of the finest fundraising programs in America. The museum has a development staff of fourteen and a development budget of $830,970. It raises $4 to $5 million annually, depending on the capital needs to be funded. It does not do event fundraising, but one major event is held each year to benefit the museum: a haunted house put together by the Children's Museum Guild. In addition to this event and to the personal solicitation efforts, the museum's annual fund schedule was as shown in Exhibit 7.1.

EXHIBIT 7.1. CHILDREN'S MUSEUM OF INDIANAPOLIS, 1999 ANNUAL FUND SCHEDULE.

January	Tax letter to all 1998 donors
February	Tributes with reply envelope
March	First solicitation to current and three-year-lapsed donors
	Annual report with reply envelope
May	Tributes with reply envelope
June	Second solicitation to nonrespondents to the first nondonor members in selected ZIP codes
July-August	Telemarketing to one- to three-year-lapsed donors and nondonor members
August	Tributes with reply envelope
October	Third solicitation to current donors and three-year-lapsed donors
	Special project mailing
November	Telemarketing to nonresponding current donors
	Tributes with reply envelope
December	Fourth solicitation and second ask to donors who have made a gift to the 1999 campaign

Source: The Children's Museum of Indianapolis. Reprinted with permission.

On average the museum has about 3,500 donors. Says Jessica White, former director of development (personal communication, July 1999), "Because we prospect from the museum membership, our prospect pool is about thirty thousand. However, we actually have a moves strategy, a plan to take specific cultivation or solicitation actions, on about 250 individuals and 250 corporations. The foundation's prospect pool changes as our projects change." In breaking down its results, the museum finds that one corporation accounts for 10 percent of its corporate giving, four more corporations give the next 30 percent, and ten additional give 50 percent. All the rest give the final 10 percent. The giving by individuals follows a similar pattern—10 percent from one donor, 30 percent from three additional donors, and 60 percent from all of the rest.

Indianapolis Zoo

After relocating on the banks of the White River near downtown Indianapolis little more than a decade ago, the Indianapolis Zoo is one of America's most vibrant and fastest-growing zoos. In 1998 the Indianapolis Zoological Society also embraced a sister institution, White River Gardens, to become America's only accredited zoological park, botanical gardens, and aquarium. Meg Gammage-Tucker, former director of institutional advancement, reports that the institution currently raises $3.3 million on a development budget of $675,000 with a staff of nine (personal communication, Sept. 1999). This total comes from 5,000 donors with 50 percent of the total from the top 30 donors, 10 percent from the next 350 donors, and the remaining 40 percent from approximately 4,600 donors.

Because the society is growing so rapidly, it is developing a five-year, dual-track fundraising strategy to encompass both its annual program and its capital needs. A preliminary form of the plan is presented in Exhibit 7.2.

EXHIBIT 7.2. INDIANAPOLIS ZOO'S FIVE-YEAR FUNDRAISING STRATEGY.

Strategic Goals for Institutional Advancement, 1999–2003

Mission	Goal	Fundraising Goal
To provide recreational learning experiences for the citizens of Indiana through the exhibition and presentation of natural environments in a way to foster a sense of discovery, stewardship, and the need to preserve the Earth's plants and animals.	To provide adequate human and financial resources to support the organizational mission—this goal to be accomplished through a stabilization of resources strategy while continuing to position the Society for future growth.	To merge all fundraising efforts of the organization into a unified strategy. Focus will be on raising capital and endowment funds ($69 million) while continuing effective growth of operational support ($16 million and 10,000 new donors).

EXHIBIT 7.2. INDIANAPOLIS ZOO'S
FIVE-YEAR FUNDRAISING STRATEGY, Cont'd.

Unified Campaign Outline for Institutional Advancement, 1999–2003

Goal	Fundraising Goal	Fundraising Objectives
To provide adequate human and financial resources to support the organizational mission—this goal to be accomplished through a stabilization of resources strategy while continuing to position the Society for future growth.	To merge all fundraising efforts of the organization into a unified strategy. Focus will be on raising capital and endowment funds ($69 million) while continuing effective growth of operational support ($16 million and 10,000 new donors).	*Year 1(a):* Conduct campaign feasibility research. Launch 100,000-piece donor acquisition test mailing.
		Year 1(b): Secure lead gifts of $40 million for campaign. Mail 300,000 letters to recruit 2,000 new donors.
		Year 2: Secure $25 million in additional leadership or major gifts. Mail 500,000 letters to recruit 4,000 new donors.
		Year 3: Secure $15.25 million in major and mid-level gifts. Mail 1 million letters to recruit 6,000 new donors.
		Year 4: Launch public campaign for last $4.75 million. Mail 600,000 letters to recruit 4,000 new donors lost to attrition.
		Year 5: Reach campaign goal. Mail appropriate lapsed and acquisition pieces to revitalize and access new donors lost to attrition.

EXHIBIT 7.2. INDIANAPOLIS ZOO'S
FIVE-YEAR FUNDRAISING STRATEGY, Cont'd.

Unified Campaign Detail for Institutional Advancement, 1999–2003

Fundraising Goal[a]	Deadline
Subdivide projects and units available	Jan. 15, 1999
Completion of gift range charts	Jan. 15, 1999
Establish feasibility of plan and structure	Jan. 19, 1999
Identify staff impact and responsibility	Jan. 19, 1999
Identify leadership	Feb. 15, 1999
Committee development	Feb. 15, 1999
Completion of cash flow projections	Feb. 15, 1999
Development of theme and campaign materials	Mar. 15, 1999
Development of recognition opportunities	Mar. 31, 1999
Development of reporting procedures	Mar. 31, 1999
Development of event strategies and activities	Mar. 31, 1999
Committee and solicitation training	Apr. 15, 1999
Kickoff—board	Apr. 30, 1999
Kickoff—staff	May 30, 1999
Kickoff—leadership gifts	June 15, 1999
Solicitation of resources	Aug. 1999–Dec. 2002
Start of recognition	Aug. 1, 1999
Campaign celebration activities	Oct. (each year)
Annual review process	Dec. (each year)

Gift Range Chart, Unified Campaign for Institutional Advancement, 1999–2003

Range	Number of Gifts	Number of Prospects	Total per Range
$20,000,000	1	5:1 = 5	$20,000,000
$10,000,000	2	5:1 = 5	$20,000,000
$5,000,000	2	5:1 = 5	$10,000,000
$2,000,000	2	5:1 = 5	$5,000,000
$1,000,000	10	4:1 = 40	$10,000,000
$500,000	10	4:1 = 40	$5,000,000
$250,000	10	4:1 = 40	$2,500,000
$100,000	40	3:1 = 120	$4,000,000
$50,000	50	3:1 = 150	$2,500,000
$25,000	50	3:1 = 150	$1,250,000
$10,000	150	2:1 = 300	$1,500,000
$5,000	250	2:1 = 500	$1,250,000
$2,500	350	2:1 = 700	$875,000
$1,000	500	2:1 = 500	$500,000
Under $1,000	2,500	2:1 = 5,000	$575,000
Totals	3,927	7,560	$85,000,000

[a]Staff responsible and project status would ordinarily be indicated for each activity as the campaign progresses.

EXHIBIT 7.2. INDIANAPOLIS ZOO'S
FIVE-YEAR FUNDRAISING STRATEGY, Cont'd.

Institutional Advancement Goals and Objectives, 1999–2003

1. Develop, implement, and evaluate institutional image for the Society.

2. Plan and prepare materials for campaigns related to the next two phases of the Master Plan.

3. Develop Society case statements.

4. Establish policies and procedures manual.

5. Improve institutional advancement communications media and materials.

6. Establish, monitor, and evaluate board development activities.

7. Effectively develop and use Institutional Advancement Committee. Work with other Board committees as appropriate.

8. Implement staffing plan to ensure that all goals and objectives can be met.

9. Install and evaluate effectiveness of planned giving program.

10. Establish $22 million in pledged and realized endowment funds.

11. Establish policies and procedures to use and invest bequests and trust income to enhance endowment fund development.

12. Adjust donor relations program to support goals of unified campaign with special emphasis on development of new and effective stewardship of long-term relationships.

13. Continue to staff Nussbaum Committee effectively. Grow the Society by 20 percent in three years.

14. Grow Zoobilation event to 3,000 attendees and stabilize income to $500,000.

15. Establish annual New Year's Gardens event.

16. Increase donor base by 10,000.

17. Implement annual telefund program.

18. Stabilize travel program and ensure that financial goals are met.

19. Enhance interaction with membership department and effectively integrate activities to meet needs and goals of both departments.

20. Increase corporate and foundation donors by a minimum of 15 percent.

21. Establish improvements in corporate relations and integrate corporate members more effectively in Society activities.

22. Fully develop government and foundation grant initiatives.

23. Continue to support the Zoological Guild in its activities and help it focus on membership leadership enhancements.

24. Guide creation and development of White River Gardens support association and club.

Source: Indianapolis Zoological Society, Inc. Printed with permission.

The successful undertaking of such a comprehensive model in an organization this size depends primarily on four key factors:

- Employment of the ask strategies outlined in Chapter Six.
- Availability of enough able volunteers to do everything, and do it all well.
- Sufficient prospect pool.
- Adequate staff and budget.

United Way of Central Indiana

One of America's most successful United Way programs, in 1998 the United Way of Central Indiana raised $33,711,158 from a six-county area that has slightly over 1.2 million residents. Jim Smith, vice president for resource development, reports that his resource development budget is $2.96 million and that he has a staff of twenty-five with and additional five support staffers. Also, thirty to thirty-five loaned executives are available on a full-time short-term basis from mid-August until early November and are sponsored by their employees (personal communication, July 1999).

Of its 108,000-plus donors, Smith reports that one company and its employees accounted for 20 percent of the 1998 campaign total, one foundation for another 10 percent, and the top ten companies for 35 percent of the total.

Long recognized as the premier planner and organizer of annual campaigns, the United Way's annual timeline (see Exhibit 7.3) is the most comprehensive model for all. (See also Resource 8, "Volunteer's Job Description," and Resource 11, "Annual Campaign Plan.")

Typical Capital Campaign Timetable

Capital campaigns have been known to be organized and conducted in very short periods of time. For example, a campaign in Memphis took five months from start to finish, and another, in New Castle, Indiana, took only three. But it is more typical for a campaign to require between six and eighteen months of preparation and then two or three years, sometimes longer, for the active phase.

A capital campaign is an undertaking of great complexity (see Resource 12, "Capital Campaign Plan"). An organization's constituencies must be fully informed, prospective donors must be identified and classified in terms of their giving potential, and prospects must be carefully assigned for solicitation. Various committees must launch their solicitation activities at appropriate intervals. Finally, follow-up activities and meetings must be carried out in the closing weeks of each

EXHIBIT 7.3. ANNUAL CAMPAIGN TIMELINE, UNITED WAY OF CENTRAL INDIANA, 1998.

Committee	Area	Task	Completion Date	Report Progress Date
February, 1998				
Team A, B, and New Business Development	Meetings	Orientation	2-26-98	
Campaign Chair	Cabinet	Recruit volunteers	2-25-98	
Campaign Chair/ Co-Chair	Training	Attend Executive Roundtable	2-9-98	
Combined Federal Campaign	Advertising	Submit ad for PCFO	2-1-98	
Marketing	Simulcast	Gain commitment for 1998	2-26-98	
Marketing	Plan	Marketing plan approved	2-26-98	
New Business Development	Recruitment	All mag 7 big 40 volunteers recruited	2-26-98	
March, 1998				
All	Meeting	Annual Meeting	3-11-98	
All	Meeting	Campaign Cabinet	3-12-98	
Combined Federal Campaign		Select PCFO	3-15-98	
Combined Federal Campaign	Training	OPM Workshop	3-22-98	
Hamilton County	Meeting	Form Campaign Cabinet	3-30-98	
Loaned Associate	Recruiting	Recruit volunteers	3-15-98	
Loaned Associate	Communication	MBS sends letter	3-15-98	
Loaned Associate	Solicitation	Contact companies regarding participation in LA program	6-18-98	
Leadership	Recruiting	Recruit volunteer chairs	3-12-98	
Leadership	Prospecting	Identify prospects	3-30-98	
Marketing	Research	Accept focus group findings	3-17-98	

EXHIBIT 7.3. ANNUAL CAMPAIGN TIMELINE, UNITED WAY OF CENTRAL INDIANA, 1998, Cont'd.

Committee	Area	Task	Completion Date	Report Progress Date
March, 1998 (continued)				
Minority Key	Recruiting	Recruit Minority Key Club Cabinet	3-30-98	
New Business Development	Meeting	Report on volunteer selection and determine training dates	3-12-98	
New Business Development	Blitz	Call upon targeted park 100 companies	3-31-98	
Team A & B	Recruiting	Recruit Area Leaders	3-12-98	
Team A & B	Training	Train Area Leaders	3-30-98	
Team A & B	Recruiting	Area Leaders recruit Account Executives	4-15-98	
UWCI Agency Rep.	Recruiting	Recruit volunteers	3-15-98	
April, 1998				
All	Meeting	Campaign Cabinet	4-16-98	
Campaign Chair/ Co-Chair	Meeting	Community Leaders Conference	4-23-98	
Campaign Chair/ Co-Chair	Solicitation	CEO calls/Briefings	5-14-98 On-going	
Combined Federal Campaign	Applications	Mail applications to local agencies	4-29-98	
Counties	Recruiting	Recruit volunteers	5-14-98	
Hamilton County	Solicitation	CEO calls	5-14-98	
Hamilton County	Meeting	County Campaign Cabinet Meeting	TBD	
Leadership	Recruiting	Recruit Leadership Giving Council members	4-1-98	
Leadership	Meeting	Identify prospects and assigned calls		
Leadership	Solicitation	de Tocqueville and Platinum calls	6-28-98	
Loaned Associate	Solication	Calls to companies	On-going	

EXHIBIT 7.3. ANNUAL CAMPAIGN TIMELINE, UNITED WAY OF CENTRAL INDIANA, 1998, Cont'd.

Committee	Area	Task	Completion Date	Report Progress Date
April, 1998 (continued)				
Marketing	Materials	New campaign materials ready	4-16-98	
Minority Key Club	Meeting	MKC Cabinet Meeting		
Minority Key Club	Materials	MKC directories completed	4-16-98	
New Business Development	Event	Youth Day of Caring	4-18-98 4-21-98	
New Business Development	Training	Train volunteers	TBD	
Team A & B	Training	Train Account Executives	4-30-98	
Team A & B	Solicitation	CEO calls/Briefings	5-14-98	
UWCI Agency Rep.	Solicitation	Contact all UWCI member agencies	5-14-98	
May, 1998				
All	Meeting	Campaign Cabinet Preliminary goal set	5-14-98	
Campaign Chair/ Co-Chair	Solicitation	CEO calls/Briefings	On-going	
Combined Federal Campaign	Application	Local applications due	5-29-98	
Counties	Training	Volunteer Orientation	TBD	
Hamilton County	Solicitation	CEO calls	On-going	
Hamilton County	Meeting	County Campaign Meeting	TBD	
Leadership	Meeting	Identify prospects and assign accounts	TBD	
Leadership	Solicitation	de Tocqueville, Platinum and Gold	On-going	
Loaned Associate	Solicitation	Calls to companies	On-going	
Minority Key Club	Meeting	MKC Cabinet Meeting	TBD	
New Business Development	Meeting	Mag 7 Big 40	5-14-98 5-28-98	
New Business Development	Solicitation	Prospect calls CEO Briefing	On-going TBD	

EXHIBIT 7.3. ANNUAL CAMPAIGN TIMELINE, UNITED WAY OF CENTRAL INDIANA, 1998, Cont'd.

Committee	Area	Task	Completion Date	Report Progress Date
May, 1998 (continued)				
Team A & B	Solicitation	CEO Calls/Briefing	On-going	
UWCI Agency Rep.	Marketing	Send co-marketing materials	5-14-98	
June, 1998				
All	Meeting	Campaign Cabinet	6-18-98	
All	Event	Wine, Art, & Roses	6-28-98	
Campaign Chair/ Co-Chair	Solicitation	CEO calls	On-going	
Combined Federal Campaign	Applications	Notice of agency eligibility	6-10-98	
Counties	Training	Volunteeer Orientation	TBD	
Hamilton County	Campaign	Pacesetter	8-31-98	
Hamilton County	Solicitation	CEO calls complete	6-18-98	
Hamilton County	Prospecting	Identify new businesses	TBD	
Leadership	Meeting	Identify prospects and assign accounts	TBD	
Leadership	Solicitation	de Tocqueville, Platinum, Gold and Silver	On-going	
Minority Key Club	Meeting	MKC Cabinet	TBD	
New Business Development	Meeting	Mag 7 Big 40	6-11-98 6-25-98	
New Business Development	Solicitation	Prospect calls CEO Briefing	On-going TBD	
Team A & B	Campaign	Pacesetter Kick-off	8-31-98 TBD	
Team A & B	Solicitation	CEO calls complete	6-18-98	
Team A & B	Prospecting	Identify new businesses	6-18-98	
July, 1998				
All	Meeting	Campaign Cabinet	7-16-98	
Campaign Chair/ Co-Chair	Solicitation	CEO calls	On-going	

EXHIBIT 7.3. ANNUAL CAMPAIGN TIMELINE, UNITED WAY OF CENTRAL INDIANA, 1998, Cont'd.

Committee	Area	Task	Completion Date	Report Progress Date
July, 1998 (continued)				
Combined Federal Campaign	Materials	Design campaign materials	7-31-98	
Counties	Solicitation	CEO calls	7-31-98	
Hamilton County	Campaign	Pacesetter	On-going	
Hamilton County	Meeting	County Campaign Cabinet	TBD	
Hamilton County	Solicitation	Calls on prospects	On-going	
Leadership	Solicitation	de Tocqueville, Platinum, Gold and Silver	On-going	
Loaned Associate	Interviews	Sponsored LAs	8-7-98	
Loaned Associate	Training	LA Orientation	7-15-98	
Marketing	Materials	Produce Simulcast	TBD	
Minority Key Club	Meeting	MKC Cabinet	TBD	
New Business Development	Meeting	Mag 7 Big 40	7-9-98 7-23-98	
New Business Development	Solicitation	Prospect calls CEO Briefing	On-going TBD	
Team A & B	Campaign	Pacesetter	On-going	
Team A & B	Training	Employee Campaign Coordinator	7-28-98	
Team A & B	Solicitation	Company calls	On-going	
August, 1998				
All	Meeting	Campaign Cabinet	8-20-98	
All	Campaign	Colts Kick-off	8-22-98	
Campaign Chair/ Co-Chair	Solicitation	CEO calls	On-going	
Combined Federal Campaign	Materials	Materials delivered and sorted	8-31-98	
Counties	Campaign	Kick-off	TBD	
Counties	Campaign	CEO Briefings	TBD	

EXHIBIT 7.3. ANNUAL CAMPAIGN TIMELINE,
UNITED WAY OF CENTRAL INDIANA, 1998, Cont'd.

Committee	Area	Task	Completion Date	Report Progress Date
August, 1998 (continued)				
Hamilton County	Campaign	Pacesetter complete	8-31-98	
Hamilton County	Meeting	County Campaign Cabinet	TBD	
Hamilton County	Solicitation	Call on prospects	On-going	
Leadership	Solicitation	Call on prospects	On-going	
Loaned Associate	Meeting	Welcome Reception	TBD 8-18 – 8-20	
Loaned Associate	Training	6½ day training	8-24-98	
Marketing	Materials	Quality PSA placement	8-31-98	
Minority Key Club	Event	Social	TBD	
Minority Key Club	Campaign	Review Direct Mail letter	TBD	
New Business Development	Solicitation	Prospect calls CEO Briefing	On-going TBD	
New Business Development	Meeting	Mag 7 Big 40	8-13-98 8-27-98	
Team A & B	Campaign	Pacesetter complete	8-31-98	
Team A & B	Campaign	Fall Campaign Preparations/Calls	On-going	
September, 1998				
All	Meeting	Campaign Cabinet	9-17-98	
All	Campaign	Day of Caring and Kick-Off	9-12-98	
Combined Federal Campaign	Campaign	Train key workers	TBD	
Combined Federal Campaign	Campaign	Kick-off	TBD	
Counties	Campaign	Solicit work-place employees	On-going	
Hamilton County	Campaign	Solicit work-place employees	On-going	

EXHIBIT 7.3. ANNUAL CAMPAIGN TIMELINE,
UNITED WAY OF CENTRAL INDIANA, 1998, Cont'd.

Committee	Area	Task	Completion Date	Report Progress Date
September, 1998 (continued)				
Hamilton County	Meeting	County Campaign Cabinet	TBD	
Hamilton County	Campaign	Trouble Shooting	On-going	
Leadership	Solicitation	Call upon prospects	On-going	
Loaned Associate	Campaign	Accounts assigned	9-2-98	
Marketing	Campaign	Direct Mail sent to individuals and businesses	TBD	
Minority Key Club	Meeting	MKC Cabinet	TBD	
New Business Development	Solicitation	Prospect calls CEO Briefing	On-going TBD	
Team A & B	Campaign	Solicit work-place employees	On-going	
October, 1998				
All	Meeting	Campaign Cabinet	10-15-98	
All	Campaign	Trouble Shooting	On-going	
All	Prospects	Call upon new accounts	On-going	
Hamilton County	Meeting	County Campaign Cabinet	TBD	
Leadership	Solicitation	Call upon prospects	On-going	
Loaned Associate	Meeting	MBS presentation to LAs	TBD	
Marketing	Campaign	Second Direct Mail Letter to individuals and businesses	TBD	
Minority Key Club	Meeting	MKC Cabinet	TBD	
New Business Development	Recognition	Luncheon	TBD	
November, 1998				
All	Meeting	Campaign Cabinet	11-18-98	
All	Campaign	Trouble Shooting	On-going	

EXHIBIT 7.3. ANNUAL CAMPAIGN TIMELINE, UNITED WAY OF CENTRAL INDIANA, 1998, Cont'd.

Committee	Area	Task	Completion Date	Report Progress Date
November, 1998 (continued)				
All	Prospects	Call upon new accounts	On-going	
Hamilton County	Campaign	County Campaign Cabinet	TBD	
Leadership	Solicitation	Call upon prospects	On-going	
Loaned Associate	Event	Thank you Reception	TBD 11-10 – 11-12	
Marketing	Campaign	Third Direct Mail letter to individuals and businesses	TBD	
Minority Key Club	Meeting	MKC Cabinet	TBD	
New Business Development	Solicitation	Prospect calls Presidential Breakfast	On-going TBD	
December, 1998				
All	Meeting	Campaign Cabinet	12-17-98	
January, 1999				
All	Meeting	Post-campaign analysis	TBD	

Source: United Way of Central Indiana. Printed with permission.

of the separate phases. All these activities must be scheduled with careful regard for each volunteer's time.

It is sound campaign practice to seek the biggest gifts first; therefore, early moves have uncommon significance, and premature action can be dangerous. The following simplified outline of activities shows the timing of solicitation during a three-year "public phase" campaign. This calendar illustrates the principles of working from the top down. It also shows that the larger the gift, the longer the donor may need to consider it before making the decision to give.

1. First Phase: Before the Public Announcement (12–15 months)
   - Complete the institution's strategic plan
   - Organize development and campaign office
   - Retain counsel (as necessary)

- Draft plan and timetable
- Draft preliminary case statement
- Conduct market survey
- Enlist campaign chair
- Enlist other key campaign committee members
- Review campaign plan with committee
- Build prospect lists
- Identify, research, evaluate, and cultivate primary major prospective donors for early approach (lead gifts)
- Develop basic print-based and audiovisual materials
- Seek lead gifts
- Enlist and educate major gifts committee(s)
- Solicit members for campaign committee
- Begin enlisting and educating special gifts committee(s)
- Enlist general committee chair
- Publicly announce campaign (major event)
- *End first phase:* deadline for 50 percent of campaign dollar objective (no public announcement unless a minimum of 30 percent of goal has been met)

2. Second Phase: Major/Special Gifts (18–24 months)
   - Continue adding names to lists of major and special gift donors
   - As necessary, continue prospective donor contact
   - Continue major gifts solicitation
   - Solicit members for special gifts committee
   - Launch special gifts committee solicitations
   - Continue distribution of campaign information to news media
   - Enlist, organize, and train general campaign leaders
   - *End second phase:* deadline for 80 percent of campaign dollar objective

3. Third Phase: General Gifts, Cleanup (12–18 months)
   - Formally launch general gifts solicitation
   - Continue solicitation by major and special gifts committees
   - Continue distribution of campaign information to news media
   - Launch final campaign thrust, followed by final report meeting for top volunteers
   - Victory event
   - *End third phase:* deadline for 100 percent of campaign dollar objective

The capital campaign is, of course, a collection of individual campaigns, each with its own leaders and timing. The time schedule, once established, must be respected. In some instances, a general campaign will need to be supplemented by area or regional campaigns. The following calendar is typical for an area campaign (the time required will vary according to the area, the number of prospects to be solicited, and the size of the gifts to be solicited).

First Week

1. Chair and staff representative(s) meet to
   • Determine number of campaign workers needed to solicit prospects on the basis of completed prospect evaluation
   • Select names of prospective division leaders
   • Set up campaign calendar, including dates of all organizational meetings, the solicitation committee meeting, the announcement event, and the report and planning meetings
   • Determine and tentatively engage places for solicitation committee meeting and announcement event
   • Discuss arrangements for processing the necessary letters to be mailed over the chair's signature
2. Chair begins enlistment of division leaders

Second Week

1. Chair, division leaders, and staff representative(s) meet to review the campaign program and begin enlistment of other volunteer workers
2. Chair's invitation to the announcement event is mailed to those on the guest list
3. Division leaders begin enlistment of team members

Third Week

1. Letter announcing date of solicitation committee meeting is mailed to campaign workers as they are enlisted
2. Announcement of chair's appointment is released to appropriate news media
3. Area campaign goal is set

Fourth Week

1. Chair calls division leaders to check on progress in enlisting team members
2. Letters announcing date of solicitation committee meeting continue to be mailed

Fifth Week

1. Campaign solicitation committee meets; training and information session is held; workers are assigned prospects
2. Workers call assigned prospects to remind them of the announcement event

Sixth Week

1. Announcement event
2. One day later, brochure and chair's letters are mailed to all constituents in the area who are not scheduled for personal solicitation
3. Solicitation of campaigners begins on the day following the reception (chair solicits division leaders, division leaders solicit team members)
4. Solicitation of all prospects begins
5. After announcement event, weekly progress reports are mailed to all solicitors through a campaign newsletter prepared by area chair and staff representative

Seventh Week

First report meeting held

Eighth Week

Second report meeting held

Ninth Week

Third report meeting held

Tenth Week

Fourth report meeting held

Eleventh Week

1. Fifth report meeting held, as necessary
2. Final check made on outstanding pledge cards
3. Chair sends letter of appreciation to all campaign workers
4. Victory celebration held with workers at final report meeting as goal is achieved

CHAPTER EIGHT

CONSTRUCTING AND USING THE STANDARDS-OF-GIVING CHART

The standards-of-giving chart or gifts table is most commonly thought of in terms of its uses during a capital campaign. In fact, it is a necessary element of any fundraising effort, large or small, annual or capital. The first part of this chapter addresses its uses in detail, with an emphasis on its applications in capital campaigns. The chapter concludes with a discussion of the similar importance top-end gifts play in annual campaigns.

Important to volunteers and donors alike, the gifts table can and should serve several functions throughout the course of any campaign:

- It indicates the number and size of the various gifts that will be needed if the institution is to reach its goal.
- It serves as a reality test, especially with the board and the major donors from whom leadership gifts are expected.
- It is a vital part of the market survey used to determine the feasibility of a capital campaign goal.
- Once firmly established, the gifts table defines the goals that must be met in order for the campaign to succeed. (It is also to be hoped that the gifts table will raise the sights of prospective donors.)
- It establishes specific guidelines for volunteers to use in patterns of gift solicitation.

- It is an essential management tool, providing the purest and truest indicator of progress to date in any given campaign.
- It is a valuable evaluation tool after the campaign.

Constructing a Gifts Table

Certain mathematical assumptions are followed in arranging a gifts table. The 80/20 rule says that 80 percent of the money will come from 20 percent of the donors. This is a common rule of thumb, although many campaigns in recent years have seen 90 percent of the money come from 10 percent of the donors, and in a growing number of cases, 99 percent of the money is coming from 1 percent of the donors. In his book on fundraising principles, Seymour (1966, p. 32) states the rule of thirds. This rule, succinctly put, says that the top ten gifts in any campaign will represent 33 percent of the goal, the next hundred will represent another third of the goal, and all the rest of the gifts will represent the final third of the campaign goal. All these equations, when plotted on the gifts table, generally work out mathematically to about the same kind of representation. Tables 8.1 through 8.5 present typical gift charts for a $2 million campaign, a $4 million campaign, a $6 million campaign, a $25 million campaign, and a $60 million campaign, respectively.

TABLE 8.1. STANDARDS OF GIVING NECESSARY FOR SUCCESS IN A $2 MILLION CAMPAIGN.

Gift Type	Gift Range	Number of Gifts	Total
Major gifts	$400,000	1	$400,000
	250,000	1	250,000
	150,000	1	150,000
	100,000	2	200,000
	50,000	2	100,000
Special gifts	25,000	10	250,000
	10,000	15	150,000
	5,000	25	125,000
General gifts	less than 5,000	all others	375,000
			$2,000,000

TABLE 8.2. STANDARDS OF GIVING NECESSARY FOR SUCCESS IN A $4 MILLION CAMPAIGN.

Gift Type	Gift Range	Number of Gifts	Total
Major gifts	$500,000	1	$500,000
	300,000	1	300,000
	200,000	2	400,000
	150,000	3	500,000
	100,000	5	500,000
Special gifts	50,000	10	600,000
	25,000	14	400,000
	10,000	25	375,000
General gifts	less than 10,000	all others	425,000
			$4,000,000

TABLE 8.3. STANDARDS OF GIVING NECESSARY FOR SUCCESS IN A $6 MILLION CAMPAIGN.

Gift Type	Gift Range	Number of Gifts	Total
Major gifts	$750,000	1	$750,000
	500,000	1	500,000
	300,000	3	850,000
	200,000	4	800,000
	150,000	4	700,000
	100,000	6	600,000
Special gifts	50,000	10	600,000
	25,000	14	400,000
	10,000	25	375,000
General gifts	less than 10,000	all others	425,000
			$6,000,000

**TABLE 8.4. STANDARDS OF GIVING
NECESSARY FOR SUCCESS IN A $25 MILLION CAMPAIGN.**

Gift Type	Gift Range	Number of Gifts	Total
Major gifts	$2,500,000	1	$2,500,000
	1,000,000	4	4,000,000
	500,000	6	3,000,000
	250,000	10	2,500,000
	150,000	12	1,800,000
	100,000	30	3,000,000
Special gifts	50,000	50	2,500,000
	25,000	60	1,500,000
General gifts	10,000	135	1,350,000
	less than 5,000	all others	2,850,000
			$25,000,000

**TABLE 8.5. STANDARDS OF GIVING
NECESSARY FOR SUCCESS IN A $60 MILLION CAMPAIGN.**

Gift Type	Gift Range	Number of Gifts	Total
Major gifts	$6,000,000	1	$6,000,000
	5,000,000	1	5,000,000
	2,500,000	3	7,500,000
	1,000,000	6	6,000,000
	750,000	8	6,000,000
	500,000	10	5,000,000
	250,000	12	3,000,000
	100,000	20	2,000,000
Special gifts	50,000	50	2,500,000
	25,000	100	2,500,000
General gifts	less than 25,000	all others	14,500,000
			$60,000,000

A traditional gifts table is constructed as follows: The lead major gift—the single largest gift needed—is calculated to be 10 percent of the campaign goal. Thus in a $1 million campaign, the lead major gift needed to predict the campaign's success is $100,000. Then each successively smaller gift needed is half the amount of the previous one, and the number of donors needed is doubled, as illustrated by Table 8.6.

Of course, this simplistic approach does not always produce an appropriate gifts chart; one reason is that, in the majority of campaigns with goals of less than $25 million, there is a clear trend toward fewer and fewer major gifts accounting for more and more of the total goal. For example, reports from recent campaigns suggest that at times as few as four to six gifts, and often no more than ten to fifteen, account for 50 to 70 percent of the total goal in successful campaigns within this goal range, and gifts tables are now being designed to reflect this trend (see Tables 8.1, 8.2, and 8.3). The trend is evident in larger campaigns, too. Table 8.7 shows that 35 percent of the goal in a $51 million campaign was provided by just twelve gifts, and Table 8.8 shows 48 percent of a $25 million goal coming from only eleven gifts. Moreover, in very large campaigns (those with goals of more than $100 million), the projected amount of the lead major gift is sometimes set at less than 10 percent of the total goal (see Tables 8.9 and 8.10). In this situation, however, the percentage of the overall goal expected to be met by major gifts is not reduced; rather, the portion of the goal that is expected to come from other major gifts is increased, to compensate for the smaller lead major gift that is expected.

A standards-of-giving table is a sobering thing, and rightly so. It says, in effect, that without gifts on the order indicated, the entire effort has little, if any, chance

TABLE 8.6. ILLUSTRATION OF A MATHEMATICALLY DEVELOPED TRADITIONAL GIFTS TABLE—$1 MILLION GOAL.

Gift Type	Gift Range	Number of Gifts	Number of Prospects Needed	Total
Major gifts	$100,000	1	4	$100,000
	50,000	2	8	100,000
	25,000	4	16	100,000
Special gifts	12,500	8	24	100,000
	6,250	16	48	100,000
	3,125	32	96	100,000
	1,560	64	128	80,000
General gifts	less than 1,500	many	many	320,000
				$1,000,000

TABLE 8.7. MAJOR GIFTS CHART OF A CAMPAIGN WITH A GOAL OF $51 MILLION.

Gift Range	Number of Gifts Required	Number of Gifts Received	Amount Required	Amount Received	Percentage of Goal
$1,000,000	10	12	$14,000,000	$19,200,000	35
500,000	12	14	7,000,000	9,000,000	16
100,000	80	82	10,500,000	15,100,000	28
50,000	75	64	5,000,000	4,100,000	7
			$36,500,000	$47,400,000	86

TABLE 8.8. A CAMPAIGN THAT SUCCEEDED WITHOUT ITS LEAD MAJOR GIFT.

Gift Type	Gift Range	Donors Needed	Donors Committed	Total Gifts Requested	Total Gifts Received
Major gifts	$2,500,000	1	0	$2,500,000	$ 0
	1,000,000	4	7	4,000,000	9,536,107.51
	500,000	4	4	2,000,000	2,500,000.00
	250,000	6	6	1,500,000	1,513,000.00
	150,000	10	10	1,500,000	1,934,520.10
Special gifts	100,000	23	12	2,300,000	1,319,890.00
	50,000	42	15	2,100,000	897,783.80
	25,000	54	35	1,350,000	1,031,990.37
	10,000	135	58	1,350,000	709,192.52
		279	147	$18,600,000	$19,442,484.30

TABLE 8.9. STANDARDS OF GIVING NECESSARY FOR SUCCESS IN A $270 MILLION CAMPAIGN.

Gift Amount	Number of Gifts Needed	Total
$20,000,000	2	$40,000,000
15,000,000	2	30,000,000
10,000,000	3	30,000,000
5,000,000	6	30,000,000
2,500,000	10	25,000,000
1,000,000	20	20,000,000
750,000	30	22,500,000
500,000	40	20,000,000
250,000	75	18,750,000
100,000	100	10,000,000
less than 100,000	many	23,750,000
		$270,000,000

TABLE 8.10. STANDARDS OF GIVING NECESSARY FOR SUCCESS IN A $1 BILLION CAMPAIGN.

Gift Range	Number of Gifts	Total
$10,000,000+	7	$125,000,000
5,000,000+	20	175,000,000
2,500,000+	30	100,000,000
1,000,000+	125	150,000,000
100,000+	1,000	230,000,000
25,000+	2,000	100,000,000
All other gifts	200,000+	120,000,000
		$1,000,000,000

for success. In the mood of urgency created by this awareness, campaign leaders are better prepared to offer specific suggestions to prospective donors, and volunteers are better able to base each approach on the specific standards of giving needed to ensure the campaign's success. Inevitably, goal setting and gifts tables are interrelated, certainly to the extent that one of the important ingredients in setting a campaign goal has to be a realistic assessment of what the potential is for big gifts (Addison L. Winship II, personal communication, Mar. 1986).

The mathematical development of the gifts table should take account of known information about major gift possibilities. For instance, if a campaign goal of $25 million is contemplated, and if it is felt that a single gift of $10 million is a virtual certainty, then a gifts table should be established that includes a gift of $10 million, even if the circulation of the table is limited until the gift is actually received. This practice falls outside the guidelines provided by the mathematical principles and other standard assumptions that normally guide the construction of such a table, but in these circumstances it is reasonable. It demonstrates sound logic and common sense if it is properly used as a sight-raising technique or as a technique for securing that single potential donor who may ultimately make this magnificent gift. Be certain of the gift, however, before circulating the table publicly: if the gift fails to materialize, such a skewed gifts table will obviously create problems for the campaign from the beginning.

Known gift needs should also be taken into account. For example, one institution, in a recent campaign, included in its goal forty endowments to partially fund professorial positions. The gifts table (see Table 8.9) was designed with the knowledge of this need and reflected it. If a $10 million building has three floors, and if each floor can be named for a $2.5 million gift, then show three $2.5 million giving opportunities available in the gifts table. If there is a need for fifteen endowed scholarships at $100,000 per scholarship, then show at least fifteen $100,000 gift opportunities. It is a sign of poor planning, and a source of possible embarrassment, to have a list of named and memorial gift opportunities that is not in concert with the gifts table.

The Gifts Table as an Essential Management Tool

During the market survey, the gifts table is used to show survey respondents the size and number of the gifts that will be needed to ensure the campaign's success at the dollar level that the survey is testing. Indeed, one of the most vital pieces of information that any market survey provides is the respondents' assessments of the tested goal's feasibility in relation to the gifts table. Thus, used as part of the market survey, the gifts table is one of the strongest indicators of whether a goal has been set at a level that is too high, too low, or appropriate. Often, as one result of a market survey, the campaign goal must be decreased, and the gifts table for the campaign itself must be correspondingly adjusted.

After the gifts table has been designed, it is important for the institution to do solid prospecting. It is a generally accepted rule of thumb that an institution must have at least four legitimate gift prospects for each major gift required (see Table 8.6). As the institution moves down the gifts table, fewer prospects are required for each gift—three prospects for each special gift, and two for each general gift—because a prospect who is in the upper gift ranges, but who does not give a gift as large as anticipated, may give a smaller gift, thereby contributing to the goal set for a lower category on the gifts chart, even before the campaign phase corresponding to that category is undertaken.

Once the campaign commences, the gifts table becomes an essential management tool. It is not uncommon to hear a campaign director report, "We have 80 percent of the goal in hand and ten months to go in the campaign." On the surface, this may appear to be a favorable report. Nevertheless, if the lead major gift—the top gift on the chart—has yet to be received, and if there is little or no probability that it will be received, then the report is far less encouraging than it might be if in fact all the gifts at the high end of the range had been secured and the campaign needed only to conclude the general gifts phase. Volunteers and staff should use the gifts table as a "scorecard" during the campaign.

Table 8.7 illustrates how a gifts table can be used to indicate the number of gifts required in a range, as well as those received to date. It is a far more accurate indicator of progress in a campaign than any other representation. The actual campaign from which this example is taken exceeded its goal of $51 million by nearly $4 million, and 86 percent of the total funds were received from fewer than

3 percent of the donors. As the table indicates, the amount received in all the top major gifts ranges exceeded the requirements that had been projected at the beginning of the campaign. This gifts chart confirms a trend now obvious in many capital campaigns: a greater proportion of funds received is coming through major gifts at the high end of the range in successful campaigns.

In addition to the campaign illustrated in Table 8.7, at least two other very recent indicators confirm this trend. One indicator was reported by Addison L. Winship II (personal communication, Mar. 1986), who shared his experience of supervising a campaign at Dartmouth College. The review of the gifts table strongly suggested that a successful campaign would be expected to raise between 45 and 50 percent of its goal in gifts of $1 million or more. Winship surveyed six other large university campaigns with goals of more than $100 million. His evaluation of these campaigns showed that 74 percent of the total gifts to these six campaigns had come in amounts of $100,000 or more. The second indicator was noted by Anderson (1986), who reported the same findings from a survey of campaigns with goals ranging from $300,000 to $300 million. In the campaigns he surveyed, consistently 75 percent of the campaign goal was received in gifts of $10,000 or more. He also reported that the overall mean value of the top ten gifts in these campaigns came to around 45 percent of the campaign total. This pattern was fairly consistent for all campaigns covered in this analysis, and the Winship survey of larger campaigns showed only a slightly different pattern. The trend in all campaigns is clear and consistent: 95 to 99 percent of the goal will come from 1 to 2 percent of the donors because this campaign model counts all donors and gifts, including annual gifts. In these situations, there is a need for a new, more relevant way of instructing institutions about what is realistically needed to achieve goals. A review of more than fifty comprehensive campaigns conducted over the past quarter century suggests that a new standard should be established: in campaigns with goals under $100 million, 80 percent (or more) of the total goal will come through the top 50 (or fewer) gifts; in campaigns with goals between $100 million and $500 million, 80 percent (or more) of the total goal will come through the top 200 (or fewer) gifts; in campaigns with goals of between $500 million and $1 billion, 80 percent (or more) of the goal will come through the top 400 (or fewer) gifts; and in campaigns with goals of $1 billion and above, 80 percent (or more) of the total goal will come through the top 750 (or fewer) gifts. Therefore, if your organization does not have a pool of ready and able lead and major gifts prospects that can produce these numbers, then prospect identification, education, and cultivation remain to be done.

Can a campaign succeed without receiving the lead major gift that has been established on the gifts table? Yes, it can. Table 8.8 provides an example of an actual campaign that succeeded without receiving its projected lead major gift.

But a campaign probably cannot succeed unless the total of the major gifts received equals or exceeds the amount represented by the percentage of the total goal that is expected to come from major gifts. Tables 8.7 and 8.8 show the results of two actual campaigns that more than met their goals for major gifts. With success at the major gifts level, even if the lead major gift is not received, a campaign can succeed; without success at this level, a campaign is almost certainly doomed to failure.

An Unworkable Gifts Chart

One of the most common fallacies regarding gift ranges and distribution patterns is the notion that a campaign can succeed if everyone in the constituency gives the same amount. For the purpose of illustration, this theory suggests that a campaign with a prospect universe of one thousand possible donors can achieve a $1 million goal by having each prospect give $1,000. It never works. Why? This type of approach is not fair or equitable to donors. Wealth is not distributed democratically in this society. If all are asked to make gifts that are "generous within their own means," each donor will not be expected to give the same amount; much will be expected of a few, and many more will be expected to do as much as they can. Not only will everyone not give the same amount to any given campaign, but many will choose to give nothing at all. In addition, this approach limits the amount asked from those who could give more, and donors seldom give more than they are asked to give.

The Gifts Table as an Evaluation Tool

The gifts table can be a helpful evaluation tool after the campaign is completed. Table 8.8, from a recent campaign, illustrates the growing trend toward an emphasis on major gifts and the weakening of support in the traditional "special gifts" range. The same trend is in evidence in the campaign depicted in Table 8.7, and this phenomenon is being reported by other campaign directors across the country. The trend may be appearing because the middle class has less disposable discretionary income available today. Indeed, some research suggests that the middle class is shrinking and that if some in this group are moving up the economic ladder, more are falling back down (Rose, 1986).

For example, a study done for the American Association of Fund-Raising Counsel Trust for Philanthropy by the Gallup Organization (1987) compares individual giving in 1985 and 1986. It shows that 42 percent gave more in 1986 than in 1985. Fifty-seven percent of those who gave more said they had done so because they had more to give. Twenty-eight percent of those who gave less said they had done so because they had less to give.

Similarly, INDEPENDENT SECTOR (1996) found that the total percentage of households reporting charitable contributions was lower in 1995 (68.5 percent) than in 1987 (71.1 percent) but that the percentage of income from contributing households increased between 1987 and 1995, from 1.9 percent to 2.2 percent, and that average household giving had therefore increased because of higher levels of giving from a narrower base of supporters. Of the households surveyed for this study (a sample including households that gave nothing), the average household reported 1995 contributions equal to 1.7 percent of its annual household income—the same as in 1993. (Similarly, the American Association of Fund-Raising Counsel Trust for Philanthropy, 1997, estimates that the average percentage of household income contributed from all households in 1995 was 1.9 percent.) Further, according to INDEPENDENT SECTOR (1996), the average household gift, after adjustment for inflation, increased by 2 percent between 1993 and 1995, whereas giving from contributing households only (that is, from a sample excluding those households that gave nothing) increased almost 10 percent after adjustment for inflation.

Other studies, notably one by Schervish and Havens (1995), have found that the percentage of household income contributed increases with household wealth and that the question of whether a household contributes at all is strongly related to its wealth. Moreover, almost all households whose net worth is more than $50 million contribute, and contributions from those households represent, on the average, 18 percent of income (p. 101). INDEPENDENT SECTOR (1996) also indicated that income is a determinant of the decision to make contributions and that households with higher incomes give to charity more frequently than lower-income households do. Further evidence for this point is provided by the University of Michigan, which in 1997 raised $1,415,162,693, or 141.5 percent of its goal, in a campaign with a goal of $1 billion. Roy E. Muir writes:

> Our experience in the Campaign for Michigan demonstrated once again the absolute essential importance of a leadership gift program in a comprehensive campaign. We received 55% of the total from gifts of $1 million and above. In fact, we received 27% of the total from donors of $5 million and above. I believe that most of the true campaign "increment"—that which would not have been raised if we had not mounted the campaign—came from donors of $1 million and above.
>
> One major goal for Michigan's campaign was the $350 million sought for endowment. This was a significant change in the giving patterns and habits of

our donors—most of whom had not given to endowment in the past. Virtually all of the $377 million raised for endowment came from gifts of $1 million and above—certainly it came from gifts of $100,000 and above [personal communication, 1998].

Using the Standards-of-Giving Chart in Setting the Annual Fund Goal

The mathematical construction of a gifts chart for the annual fund closely parallels that of the capital campaign. Ten percent of the donors will need to give 60 percent of the goal; the next 20 percent of donors will need to give another 20 percent of the goal; and the remaining 70 percent of donors will give the remaining 20 percent of the goal.

If an organization has a prospect pool of 1,000 names, its rate of participation is 20 percent, and the goal is $100,000, the organization will receive 200 gifts. If the goal is $100,000, a total of 10 percent, or 20 donors, need to give $60,000. That averages to $3,000 a donor, but gifts in a range never all hit the average. The next 40 donors will give $20,000 in total; and the remaining 140 donors will give the remaining $20,000. These are the realistic expectations that guide the development of an annual giving goal. The similarities with the major gifts chart constructed for the capital campaign are apparent.

In setting the annual fund goal, look at the pattern (size and number) of gifts received last year. Look at the pattern (size and number) of gifts needed to achieve this year's goal. See if the size of the prospect pool has grown or shrunk. See how many of last year's donors can be upgraded. Consider the additional, if any, programmatic initiatives that can be undertaken to enhance the current effort and decide if the additional use of techniques (two mailings instead of one) might yield greater than average results. Other institutional fundraising programs, such as a capital campaign, and their relative priority and importance in the view of the governing board and management must be considered as well.

At times nonprofits will arrive at their annual fund goal by projecting income and expenses and, assuming the expenses are greater, set the fundraising goal at the difference between the two numbers. This is both foolish and dangerous. Pie-in-the-sky thinking will usually yield just desserts.

In a favorable economic and stable fundraising environment, growth of 6 to 10 percent a year can reasonably be projected. Higher projections must be validated against the factors already cited. Goals projecting slightly less modest growth, 3 to 5 percent, may be entirely reasonable too, given the age and maturity of the annual giving program when considered in combination with other factors.

Jim Smith describes the United Way of Central Indiana's goal-setting process as follows (personal communication, July 1999):

> We call it "potential-based," as opposed to "need-based." The process begins with a detailed analysis of the previous campaign, looking particularly at average gift and rate of participation in participating companies. (Workplace campaigns account for about 55 percent of the total campaign.) Based on growth in the previous campaign and areas where the potential for growth remains the greatest, a range of percentages—high, medium, low—is presented to the volunteer campaign leadership. During this time, personal calls are being made on the chief executive officer of the top fifty companies to enlist their continuing support and to get their input on how much their own company campaigns might—or might not—grow in the coming year. In June the campaign volunteer leaders, known as the Campaign Cabinet, determine their recommendation for the goal, with that recommendation being presented to the full board of directors for approval in August.

Jessica White (personal communication, July 1999) adds these comments about the Indianapolis Children's Museum during her tenure there:

> The development department constructs a goal based on the projects we will be doing for the next year and what we know of our prospects. We try to make this realistic yet challenging. This is then matched with what the museum marketing plan will be for the year. This applies mainly to securing sponsorships that need to be marketed. The budget is then submitted to our budget committee, which reviews it along with earned revenue budgets and expenses categories. As you might guess, there are always more expenses than revenue, and so adjustments are made. If programs are dropped, we make sure that development is in the loop so that the associated revenue is also cut. Sometimes we are asked to increase the goal. If that is done, it is a negotiated process between myself and the budget committee to ensure that the final number is realistic.

Tables 8.11 through 8.14 illustrate the size and number of gifts needed to achieve success in annual funds with goals of $100,000 and $1 million, respectively. Obviously, it matters significantly how proven the potential donor pool is (see Chapter Ten). "Prospects" and "expects" hold more promise as donors than "suspects"; it therefore takes more suspects than it does prospects and expects to meet a particular goal. In testing a goal against these standards, the questions are simple: Does the organization have donors capable and willing to give the amounts needed in the numbers needed at each level? Does it have a large enough prospect pool to support such a goal?

TABLE 8.11. STANDARDS OF GIVING FOR AN ANNUAL CAMPAIGN WITH A GOAL OF $100,000 AND A RELATIVELY UNPROVEN SUSPECT POOL.

Gift Range	Donors Needed	Prospects[a] (Ratio)	Total
10% of Donors = 60% of Goal			
$5,000	2	14 (7:1)	$10,000
2,500	6	42 (7:1)	15,000
1,000	18	108 (6:1)	18,000
500	34	170 (5:1)	17,000
20% of Donors = 20% of Goal			
250	48	192 (4:1)	12,000
100	80	240 (3:1)	8,000
70% of Donors = 20% of Goal			
Less than 100	412	1,236 (3:1)	20,000
			$100,000

[a]Total prospect pool: 2,002.

TABLE 8.12. STANDARDS OF GIVING FOR AN ANNUAL CAMPAIGN WITH A GOAL OF $1 MILLION AND A RELATIVELY UNPROVEN SUSPECT POOL.

Gift Range	Donors Needed	Prospects[a] (Ratio)	Total
10% of Donors = 60% of Goal			
$50,000	2	14 (7:1)	$100,000
25,000	6	42 (7:1)	150,000
10,000	18	108 (6:1)	180,000
5,000	34	170 (5:1)	170,000
20% of Donors = 20% of Goal			
2,500	48	192 (4:1)	120,000
1,000	80	240 (3:1)	80,000
70% of Donors = 20% of Goal			
Less than 1,000	412	1,236 (3:1)	20,000
			$1,000,000

[a]Total prospect pool: 2,002.

TABLE 8.13. STANDARDS OF GIVING FOR AN ANNUAL CAMPAIGN WITH A GOAL OF $100,000 AND A PROVEN PROSPECT POOL.

Gift Range	Donors Needed	Prospects[a] (Ratio)	Total
10% of Donors = 60% of Goal			
$5,000	2	8 (4:1)	$10,000
2,500	6	24 (4:1)	15,000
1,000	18	54 (3:1)	18,000
500	34	102 (3:1)	17,000
20% of Donors = 20% of Goal			
250	48	96 (2:1)	12,000
100	80	160 (2:1)	8,000
70% of Donors = 20% of Goal			
Less than $100	412	824 (2:1)	20,000
			$100,000

[a]Total prospect pool: 1,258.

TABLE 8.14. STANDARDS OF GIVING FOR AN ANNUAL CAMPAIGN WITH A GOAL OF $1 MILLION AND A PROVEN PROSPECT POOL.

Gift Range	Donors Needed	Prospects[a] (Ratio)	Total
10% of Donors = 60% of Goal			
$50,000	2	8 (4:1)	$100,000
25,000	6	24 (4:1)	150,000
10,000	18	54 (3:1)	180,000
5,000	34	203 (3:1)	170,000
20% of Donors = 20% of Goal			
2,500	48	96 (2:1)	120,000
1,000	80	160 (2:1)	80,000
70% of Donors = 20% of Goal			
Less than 1,000	412	824 (2:1)	200,000
			$1,000,000

[a]Total prospect pool: 1,258.

All of this information, taken collectively, suggests that major gifts at the high end of the gifts chart will be more and more important to the success of any campaign. This suggestion is a strong argument for concentrating efforts at the high end, and the implication is that institutions with a particular interest in entering into a capital campaign must have prospects able and willing to give at the major gifts level if the institution is to have any real hope of success, regardless of the size of the campaign goal.

CHAPTER NINE

LAYING THE FOUNDATION: BUILDING THE ANNUAL FUND

Kent E. Dove
Jeffrey A. Lindauer
Carolyn P. Madvig

An annual gift is any gift that can reasonably be expected from the same donor on an annual basis. Size does not matter, although most tend to be smaller gifts. What matters is whether they are to be repeating or not. The annual giving program, commonly known as the *annual fund,* is the fundraising program designed specifically to attract annual gifts. Most nonprofits consider the annual fund the mass marketing arm of the organization. It is the vehicle whereby the majority of supporters make contributions, with most asks coming through mail or phone appeals. Special events are also used by most nonprofits to raise annual gifts, and technology will play an increasingly important role in annual fund programs (see Chapter Nineteen). For larger annual gifts, face-to-face solicitation remains the preferred method.

Usually, an annual fund is the primary source for attracting new donors to the organization, and it also renews donors up to a certain level—typically, $1,000 or $5,000 per year. "Annual fund" is an apt name for the process, which occurs on a yearly basis and provides the support necessary to fund annual budgets and provide ongoing services. Goals of the annual fund are to bring in new donors while keeping current donors and encouraging them to increase the size of their gifts over time.

Why is it important to have an annual fund? After all, if an organization has a sufficient major donor base to pursue a major gifts strategy, it can get funding much more quickly by contacting just a few individuals and asking them to make significant gifts. To employ that approach alone is extremely shortsighted, however, and can cause significant problems in the long-run. Programs, even those that focus on larger gifts, need a steady stream of new prospects to ensure that the pipeline does not run dry. To be an annual fund success, an organization needs to be visionary, looking not only at what sources are available today but also at ways to identify and nurture its major donors of tomorrow.

The annual fund is the foundation of all fundraising efforts. If one thinks of fundraising as a pyramid, the annual fund is the base of that pyramid—bringing in smaller dollars but the largest number of donors. The annual fund's goal is to create the habit of philanthropy—to work hard in order to get the first gift (the hardest one to get) and then continue to provide compelling reasons for future gifts that will increase in size until a few donors identify themselves as serious major gift prospects. Every annual fund should work closely with major and planned giving programs—in essence, the annual fund is in the business of identifying the major donors of the future.

Although face-to-face approaches seeking larger gifts are the most effective fundraising option, they are also the most expensive, often requiring months or even years of cultivation prior to receipt of the first major gift. Compared with contact by mail (the least effective but also the least expensive option) or telephone (more effective but also more expensive than mail), it's easy to see why the annual fund needs to be the vehicle through which most small, annual donors are attracted and retained.

A good annual campaign has three major aspects:

1. *A personal touch.* As fundraising efforts continue to increase and nonprofits proliferate, people become increasingly discerning, and "Dear Friend" mass approaches won't work as they once did. As a result, it is important to incorporate as much personalization as possible into a program, from personalized salutations to having as much information about the individual available as possible when making phone calls.

2. *A focus on prospect and donor interests.* To draw prospects in, an organization needs to keep the prospects' interests in mind at all times. Staff members need to think not so much about what the organization needs as about what would make an investment in your organization appealing to prospects. Perhaps it is allowing a designation in honor of a specific individual; perhaps the ask should come from a peer rather than a national volunteer; perhaps the appeal should recognize a specific segment of an organization rather than the more conventional and typical appeal on behalf of the overall organization. All of these are effective ways to keep the prospects' interests uppermost in the process.

3. *A solid overall plan that includes feedback, good judgment, and extensive research.* Nothing about the campaign should be haphazard. And the plan should include a method for evaluating returns in order to determine whether the staff's initial

instincts were on target. Research helps ascertain potential market segments to target, thus improving overall results. It is important to follow up on efforts with statistical analysis in order to confirm that initial instincts about a particular segment are correct. Remember, you are not your audience.

Establishing an annual fund plan is the first step in undertaking an annual fund. First, figure out where the program stands today. Take stock, and be realistic. Then decide where the organization would like to be and how it can get there. When putting together an annual fund plan, the most common vehicle to use is a solicitation calendar (see Chapter Seven). It will show all efforts to be made, in what order, by what date they need to be completed, what follow-up evaluation will occur, and by what standard success will be measured. It is essential to have such a plan in place in order to accurately and adequately capture information that will be vital to future success.

Such a plan needs to be well thought out and based on a solid sense of what the organization feels will be most successful with its particular prospects. Depending on the audience, try a mailing first; if there is insufficient response within a designated length of time, follow up with a phone call—or try the reverse if that seems to be the more promising approach.

If it is the organization's first year to have an annual fund, or if it's simply time to have a baseline year, contact all prospects by mail or phone—this provides an opportunity to have a control group analysis that will determine segments to target going forward.

It is also important to keep some specific facts in mind when preparing a solicitation calendar. For instance, large universities need to coordinate efforts not only within the development office but also with the university's alumni association, with specific school efforts, and so on. Remember that to these particular prospects, all contact from the university is likely to be perceived as coming from the same source. Thus it behooves all parties to coordinate efforts—it will maximize results for all.

Even smaller organizations find it important to consider timing issues. Most solicitations, particularly mailings, go out toward the end of the calendar year. A mailing sent at this time runs the risk of being lost in a sea of donor options and holiday greetings. It may be wiser to send a mailing in September or October—arriving near the end of the year but probably among the first giving options prospects will see. Also, organizations that benefit from public proclamations, such as National Heart Month, do well by timing appeals to arrive at such times of heightened visibility. Some experts suggest that certain months of the year are best for fundraising, but in fact any time can be effective, depending on the audience. It is far more important to have a good, high-quality solicitation than to restrict efforts to one particular time on the calendar.

Volunteers as Partners in the Annual Fund Campaign

One way to draw individuals into your program, and also to encourage larger gifts, is to ask them to assist you as volunteers. Volunteer leaders can accomplish everything from providing additional publicity of your program through positive word-of-mouth to actually soliciting friends and associates on behalf of your program.

Annual funds use volunteers in all of these ways—in smaller programs, volunteers may man the phones during a telemarketing campaign; in larger programs, they may be the major gift contributors who, after having made their own gift, go along with a staff person to assist in soliciting a colleague, or even go alone. All of these jobs tie volunteers more closely to the program they are supporting while providing a wonderful resource to the organization they serve (see Chapter Five).

How to Determine Success

One way to measure success is to compare your results to industry standards, such as typical pledge or response rates for phone and mail efforts. Another effective measurement is to determine cost per dollar raised—how much money was spent on the effort, including staff costs, compared to the amount of money raised?

Particularly regarding nondonors, however, the long-term effects must also be measured. If a nondonor solicitation loses money in year one, remember that the new donors obtained will be easier to renew in year two, thus producing a long-term positive impact that would otherwise not have been possible.

From a practical standpoint, the information needed to calculate many of the important measurements related to annual funds includes the following:

- *Pledge or response rate.* This is the number of positive responses, divided by the number of prospects solicited, expressed as a percentage. What percentage of the people solicited agreed to make a pledge or gift?
- *Average pledge or gift.* This number is calculated by dividing the amount pledged or contributed by the number of positive responses. How much are donors giving on average?
- *Net income.* Add up all of the costs associated with a specific mailing or phone program. Then subtract that number from the total of the gifts received. A positive net amount is the hoped-for result.

When determining which individuals are the best prospects for a particular project, look for those who have connections with your organization or a similar one. Most universities, for instance, look first to their alumni. Often, however, friends of the university, perhaps residents of the community where the university is located, parents of current students, and faculty and staff should also be considered. In the case of service organizations, likely candidates include those who have benefited from the services offered, such as grateful patients from a hospital, patrons of an art museum, or visitors to a zoo. In general, the best prospects are found among people or organizations that have an already established interest in the particular program or cause.

Typically, annual funds break prospects into four categories, based on giving patterns:

- *Current donors*—people who gave in the current year
- *"Lybunts"*—people who gave "last year but not this" year
- *"Sybunts"*—donors who have given in "some year but not this" year
- *Nondonors*—people who have never made a gift to the organization

Depending on the mode of contact, varying rates of success will be achieved with these different groups.

"Lybunts" and *current donors* are the most responsive groups to solicit. These are individuals who indicate with their ongoing support that they understand your mission and are willing to make a contribution to support your endeavors. This is one area where it often makes most sense to send a mailing as a first attempt at renewal (see Exhibit 1.1 in Chapter One). Because the cost of a mailing is significantly less than that of a call and because these prospects may have fewer questions about the program (since they are already supporting it, and you will have done a good job of keeping them involved via newsletters, honor rolls, and other means), a mailing can be a very effective way for donors to make continued gifts (see Exhibit 9.1). A mailing to current or prior-year donors can have as much as a 50 percent response rate.

Reclaiming *"sybunts"* is a different matter. These are individuals who at one time supported your cause but have apparently decided to end that support. Either a mailing or a phone call can request a continuation of past support (see Exhibit 9.2). A typical mail response with this group would be approximately 10 to 12 percent, while a phone program might achieve 32 to 35 percent.

With either method, it is imperative to indicate that you are aware that these people have ceased their support—and indicate why you are interested in having them rejoin your rolls. A "we've missed you!" theme is employed frequently, primarily because it is effective in letting sybunts know that you want them back as donors. Another method is to be increasingly specific regarding uses for which gifts can be earmarked or designated. Yet another is to include a survey with your solicitation, requesting feedback as to ways in which you can serve your donors better and what type of appeals or information would be most helpful to them in the future.

EXHIBIT 9.1. DONOR RENEWAL PROGRAM.

Criteria

All telefund and mail donors who made a gift of below $1,000 to their unit between January 1, 1995, and June 30, 1996, who have not yet renewed for the 1997 fiscal year. Individuals who give as a result of any phase will be excluded from subsequent phases.

Calendar

Phase 1:	Unified Donor Renewal Mailing	September 15, 1996
Phase 2:	Donor Renewal Telefund #1	November 1996
Phase 3:	Donor Renewal Telefund #2	March 1997

Projections

Phase 1: Direct Mail

Prospects:	1,797
Gifts (@ 35% response):	629
Total $ (@ $50 annual gift):	$31,450
Expenses (@ $0.50 apiece):	$899
Net income:	$30,549

Phase 2: Telefund #1

Prospects:	1,168
Contacts (@ 70% reach rate):	818
Pledges (@ 72% pledge rate):	589
Total $ pledged (@ $55 annual gift):	$32,377
Total $ received (@ 80% ful.):	$25,902
Expenses (@ $5.97 per contact):	$4,883
Net income:	$21,019

Phase 3: Telefund #2

Prospects:	579
Contacts (@ 65% reach rate):	376
Pledges (@ 68% pledge rate):	256
Total $ pledged (@ $50 annual gift):	$12,800
Total $ received (@ 75% ful.):	$9,600
Expenses (@ $5.97 per contact):	$2,245
Net income:	$7,355

Total Donor Renewal

Total number of donors:	1,292
Total $ received:	$66,952
Expenses:	$8,027
Net income:	$58,923

Mail programs to *nondonors* can be an effective way to gain future donors (see Exhibit 1.2 in Chapter One), particularly if you have a compelling case or a specific event to capitalize on (your organization is celebrating its twenty-fifth year of service, for instance). Mailings to nondonors can typically expect a 1 to 2 percent response rate. All too often mail program organizers concentrate on the number of prospects contacted—"If I mail to one hundred prospects and each of them gives just $25, I'll have met my goal of $2,500!" They should realize that in actuality, only one or two of the one hundred prospects will come through with a gift—and hence the gross income from the mail effort will be $50. That is a far more realistic expectation.

EXHIBIT 9.2. LAPSED DONOR RETRIEVAL PROGRAM.

Criteria

All telefund and mail donors who made a gift of below $1,000 to their unit between July 1, 1991, and December 31, 1994, but have made no gift since then. Individuals who give as a result of any phase will be excluded from subsequent phases.

Calendar

| Phase 1: | Lapsed Donor Retrieval Telefund #1 | August–October 1996 |
| Phase 2: | Lapsed Donor Retrieval Telefund #2 | March 1997 |

Projections

Phase 1: Telefund #1

Prospects:	992
Contacts (@ 66% reach rate):	655
Pledges (@ 36% pledge rate):	236
Total $ pledged (@ $52 annual gift):	$12,272
Total $ received (@ 75% ful.):	$9,204
Expenses (@ $5.97 per contact):	$3,910
Net income:	$5,294

Phase 2: Telefund #2

Prospects:	756
Contacts (@62% reach rate):	469
Pledges (@ 32% pledge rate):	150
Total $ pledged (@ $48 annual gift):	$7,200
Total $ received (@ 70% ful.):	$5,040
Expenses (@ $5.97 per contact):	$2,800
Net income:	$2,242

Total Lapsed Donor Retrieval

Total number of donors:	282
Total $ received:	$14,244
Expenses:	$6,710
Net income:	$7,534

Telemarketing can be a more viable way of converting nondonors and is often better than mail, even though the initial cost is higher. The major reason for this is the dialogue that occurs between the prospect and the caller, which provides an opportunity to tell more about the project in question, as well as to answer any objections to giving that the prospect may have.

A program's response rate via phone is dependent primarily on the number of times prospects have been asked to give—typically, a negative response in one year doesn't preclude prospects from getting additional calls, as their situation may change, and they may be more favorably disposed toward giving later (see Exhibit 9.3). As a general rule, prospects who have not been approached may pledge support over the phone at a 16 to 18 percent rate, while more hard-core nondonors, those who have not supported for several years, may respond at a lower rate.

EXHIBIT 9.3. DONOR ACQUISITION PROGRAM.

Criteria

All graduates who have not given to the unit since July 1, 1991. Individuals who give as a result of any phase will be excluded from subsequent phases.

Calendar

Phase 1:	Unified Donor Acquisition Mailing	October 1, 1996
Phase 2:	Donor Acquisition Telefund	December 1996

Projections

Phase 1: Direct Mail

Prospects:	7,804
Gifts (@ 0.5% response rate):	39
Total $ (@ $50 annual gift):	$1,950
Expenses (@ $0.15 apiece):	$1,171
Net income:	$779

Phase 2: Telefund

Prospects:	7,765
Contacts (@ 50% reach rate):	3,883
Pledges (@ 18% pledge rate):	699
Total $ pledged (@ $50 annual gift):	$34,950
Total $ received (@ 65% ful.):	$22,718
Expenses (@ $5.97 per contact):	$23,182
Net income:	($464)

Total Donor Acquisition

Total number of donors:	493
Total $ received:	$24,664
Expenses:	$24,349
Net income:	$315

Direct Mail

It is important to have a good feel for the real cost of the programs being undertaken. A mailing's cost can vary widely, depending on whether it is sent first-class or bulk-rate, for example, or whether it is a simple letter or includes a sophisticated brochure as well. As a general rule, annual fund mailings may cost between 35 and 80 cents apiece, including printing, design, photographs, production, mail vendor costs, and postage.

Some years ago a fair amount of time was given to arguing the merits of certain types of paper, colors of paper, fonts, and other details, and whether they were more or less likely to bring a good response rate. Today it seems clear that the two most important aspects of any mailing are the text of the letter—how compelling a case it makes for the cause at hand—and getting it into the appropriate hands.

Nevertheless, following a few guidelines typically does lead to better letters. The Fund Raising School (1995) says:

- Grab attention: hook your reader in the first sentence. It is often your last chance.

  "At first, I didn't believe what the nurse told me. We found the baby in a shoe box. She weighed less than five pounds."
- State the problem. Tell a story.

  "Marie—that's what the nurses named her—was the first abandoned baby I treated at Memorial . . . but she wasn't the last. I want to tell you about . . ."
- Pose a solution. Explain how your organization's program or cause is attacking the problem.

  "With proper medical attention and love and care, babies like Marie still have a chance."
- Tell how the reader can help or participate—by making a gift.

  "This vital, lifesaving work at Memorial is only possible because of the gifts we receive from . . ."
- Tell the reader the benefits of becoming involved.

  "By making a gift, you will be paid back one hundred times over with feelings of joy and the knowledge . . ."

  "Your gift to Memorial will insure that . . ."
- Ask for a gift—today. Be specific about dollars.

  "Your gift of $25 or $40 or as large as you can possibly afford is urgently needed. Please respond today."
- Say thank you.
- Add a postscript. Postscripts should always urge action or have strong emotional appeal. Readers commonly look first at the opening sentence or two and then at the end of the letter.

The direct-mail package contains four essential items—outer envelope, letter, response device, and reply envelope. It may also include additional inserts (see Resource 13, "Direct-Mail Solicitation Letters: Sequential Annual Mailings," and Resource 14, "Direct-Mail Solicitation with Insert"). Be certain always to reflect an image in your pieces that is consistent with the overall character of your organization.

Depending on the sophistication of the piece, it may be decided that it can be produced in-house using current staff and computer equipment; if the number of pieces or staff availability should make such an endeavor prohibitive, however, there are a number of mailing vendors who can assist you by sending your mailing to the list of prospects you provide.

Typically, such vendors go through a bidding process that is triggered by your providing them with the specifications of your mailing. As is true with most bids, it is not necessarily wise to automatically pursue the lowest bid. Request a client list; get feedback from customers who are not on the list also, if at all possible; and do a reference check prior to awarding the bid to a particular mailing house.

There is a real advantage to using the same vendor from year to year as long as its bid remains competitive and the company works hard to provide a quality product. The reason for this is simple: as mailings become more and more sophisticated, having a ready partner who understands exactly what you want your final product to be is highly advantageous.

Another type of vendor who can prove valuable is the list broker. Not all nonprofits are fortunate to have ready-made mailing lists. And even if they do, they may want to add to their lists, particularly for acquisition purposes, or trade their lists with similar organizations or with list brokers, who maintain lists of individuals with similar interests.

Lists of prospective new donors are the single most important element in direct mail. There are four basic types of lists:

- Organizational donor, membership, and former donor lists
- Magazine and newsletter subscriber lists
- Mail-order buyer lists
- Compiled lists (lists arranged by ZIP code, professional directories, voting lists, lists of foreign car owners, and so on)

According to the Fund Raising School (1995), organizations should focus primarily on the first two types; with expert guidance, they might also want to test the third or the fourth. Lists of the following individuals contain the best prospects:

- People who share an interest in your mission or goals.
- People who match your current donors' profile. This may include such factors as age, sex, income level, geography, family composition, education level, political affiliation, and profession.
- People who already donate to nonprofit causes. Resist the temptation to convert masses of nongivers into philanthropists.
- People who are mail-responsive. Individuals who give gifts or buy merchandise through the mail are said to be mail-responsive. Because most compiled lists are not created through direct mail, the percentage of individuals who are mail-responsive is much lower than with other lists. Compiled lists usually do not work well for nonprofit fundraising.

Mailing lists are also available for onetime use on a rental or exchange basis. Depending on the quality of the list, you will pay a variable fee for a list rental. Many list owners or brokers require a minimum rental of five thousand names. Many list owners will also trade their lists for yours, again for one use only. Your only expense is typically a 20 percent broker's fee based on the rental rate.

Nonprofits that fail to trade their lists can be limiting their own future. Trading can play a critical role in developing a direct-mail program. Experience shows that you will not lose your donors due to trading. An organization may be very concerned about donor privacy and the security of the list when trading or renting names to another institution. A good list broker can explain the mechanics and ethics involved in list trading that have been developed to protect both the list owner and the list mailer. Donors may specify that their name not be traded.

List brokers manage lists for list owners. List brokers make a commission on both rentals and exchanges. The only efficient way to rent or trade for a number of lists is through a list broker. The right list broker can be your best friend and a valuable resource in developing a profitable direct-mail program.

List brokers help direct mailers in the following ways:

- Recommending lists to test
- Helping evaluate tests and selecting lists for rollouts
- Obtaining approval for list rentals or exchanges (this often involves submitting a sample of your letter to the list owner)
- Handling all rental and exchange arrangements

Only use a broker with experience and expertise in nonprofit fundraising lists. Some brokers specialize in certain types of nonprofit lists and organizations. Examples include specialists for religious, public interest, and politically conservative and liberal lists. To look for list brokers, consult fundraising magazines and journals, references from nonprofits similar to yours, and Association of Fundraising Professionals conferences and fundraising day exhibits.

Telemarketing

Telemarketing continues to be a vital part of any annual fund program. Even though some individuals are not comfortable giving over the phone, telemarketing is very successful, particularly with younger prospects. Like any other program, however, these phone calls have inherent costs that need to be figured when determining any particular project's success.

Telemarketing is more expensive because it requires not only what is often a long-distance phone call but also the equipment needed to make such calls—typically, a bank of phones large enough for a volunteer or paid staff and for a qualified supervisor to track their progress and provide advice and options for improvement. As a result, telemarketing efforts can cost anywhere from $4 to $10 per completed call.

Phone programs, however, can yield as much as a 70 percent pledge rate and also allow the donor continued interaction with a live individual, who will thank them for their continued support in a very personal way.

As a result, telemarketing is an important tool for any annual fund effort. Proper planning, training, and execution are all necessities for a successful phone program. With today's proliferation of telemarketers, nonprofits may see slight reductions in the efficiency of telemarketing, but it remains an effective way of acquiring new donors as well as of renewing past donors.

Telemarketing offers an opportunity to gain support, interact with donors, receive feedback, and educate prospective donors. It also allows you to update your records and build friendships with individuals who support your cause.

Telemarketing must of course be coordinated with the direct-mail, personal solicitation, and other methods you use. Careful attention must be paid so as not to overlap other solicitations, which could have a negative effect on the overall success of the annual fund.

Proper planning is essential for any phone program, as many decisions must be made in advance of calling. Beyond coordinating with other solicitations, it is important to decide whether to conduct the campaign using volunteers or paid callers or to hire an outside vendor, to prepare scripts and information packets, and to plan for follow-up mailings for fulfillment of pledges.

Planning also includes a determination if this particular annual fund project is appropriate for telemarketing. Programs that cannot be easily explained over the telephone, for example, might lend themselves more to personal solicitation or direct mail.

Many organizations choose to conduct in-house "phonathons" using either hired or volunteer callers, while others choose to hire outside vendors to conduct calling campaigns for them. Both methods can be rewarding to an annual fund program, so this is an important choice that will affect the entire campaign.

Although in-house phonathons offer more direct control over day-to-day operations, they can be very time-consuming. Constant recruitment of callers, training, and on-site supervision can easily devour large blocks of time for one or more members of the staff. In-house phone programs should therefore be conducted only by organizations willing to invest the time and effort needed to ensure a quality experience for all.

Hiring an outside vendor is often an appropriate decision. For organizations that are unable to dedicate human resources to a phone program, there are many excellent telemarketing vendors from which to choose. There are also less reputable vendors, so choosing a vendor is important and should be done with care. Consult with peer groups that outsource their telemarketing programs. Ask about pricing, success, reliability, and quality control measures. Choose a vendor you are comfortable with, as the telemarketer may well be the only human link prospects have to your organization.

If you choose an outside vendor to conduct your calling campaign, it will hire callers, train them, and generally walk you through the process. If you choose to conduct your own campaign, expect both a challenging and rewarding experience.

Volunteers are another possible resource to tap for a phone program. Individuals who have shown an interest in the organization are often best suited to speak with prospects and share personal stories about the reason they support the cause, making them valuable representatives for the annual fund. These same volunteers can also be difficult to recruit and hard to train and may not always feel comfortable asking for money!

Hiring callers allows more control over the script, it may lead to fewer problems with recruitment and retention, and callers can be told exactly what to say and how to say it. After all, it is easier to supervise a caller you are paying to do the job than a donor who has volunteered for the phone program.

Whether you hire callers or use volunteers, incentives such as food, T-shirts, bonus items, and other trinkets can help improve morale, retain callers, and improve productivity.

The ideal telemarketing representative for any organization is enthusiastic, articulate, and knowledgeable about the mission and goals of the annual fund. Keep in mind that each of your prospects is being bombarded by telemarketing calls each and every day. Callers that represent your organization need to be different and must be good enough to make your call stand out among the others (see Exhibit 9.4).

Volunteer applicants that are not suited for calling might be reallocated for stuffing envelopes, answering questions, or providing other support to the calling program. The same may be true of hired callers that aren't working out on the phones—the ones you wouldn't want to fire but prefer not to use as telemarketers often make excellent clerical helpers.

At least one part of the hiring process should be an interview by phone. Having a caller read a mock script over the phone provides valuable insight into his or her future as a telemarketer.

Training Callers

Proper training of callers is essential to a phone program's success. Callers should be provided with materials and information that will help them make top-quality phone calls. This information should include all of the following:

- Facts and information about the organization and the annual fund
- Scripts or outlines of a proper call (see Resource 15, "Telemarketing Scripts")
- Ways to deal with objections they might hear (see Exhibit 9.5)
- Samples of mailings sent by the organization recently

EXHIBIT 9.4. HOW TO MAKE A GOOD
FIRST IMPRESSION OVER THE TELEPHONE.

Whether you are a teacher, a salesman, a doctor, a lawyer, or a telefund caller, first impressions count! Often the first five to ten seconds of a conversation will determine if a prospect will listen or hang up on you. Here are some ideas and strategies to help you make a good first impression.

- *Be enthusiastic.* If you've ever received a phone call from a credit card company, a magazine company, or any other firm, you may have noticed a lack of enthusiasm. Put a smile on your face and in your voice and it will make all the difference in the world! A prospect can hear your attitude, and if you sound happy and excited about your job, your cause, and the call you are making, chances are the prospect will feel the same. Remember that enthusiasm is contagious!

- *Use inflection.* The prospect will start yawning if you don't have any inflection in your voice. Imagine having a book read to you in a monotone. Pretty boring, isn't it?

- *Sound credible.* Everything you do in the phone call affects your credibility, from beginning to end. To maintain credibility, you should speak clearly, avoid hesitancy ("uh" or "um"), and speak proper English (avoid using slang).

- *Introduce yourself.* You're not only introducing the program, you're introducing yourself! Give the prospect your entire name and state who you are, giving enough information to establish yourself as an individual who has a good reason to be making this phone call.

- *Be respectful.* You are calling somebody you don't know. Don't address the prospect by first name unless specifically invited to do so. When calling, ask for "Mr. John Smith" at first, and then refer to the prospect as "Mr. Smith." Also, using the person's name throughout the call will let the person know that you know you're relating to an individual, not just another phone number on your list.

- *Make the case.* When stating the reason for the call, be clear and concise. Don't try to fool people into thinking you're not asking for money—they *know* you're asking for money; they want you to explain *why* you're asking for a contribution at this time. Refer to your screen and other materials for the specific goals for your program.

- *Call back if necessary.* If your prospect is unavailable and you reach a spouse or other family member, maintain your respect and your enthusiasm. Thank the person and say you'll call again. You don't want prospects to be told that "another nasty telemarketer" phoned; you want them to look forward to your call!

EXHIBIT 9.5. DEALING WITH OBJECTIONS.

People say no for a reason. That reason could be that they don't have the money, they have kids in school, they're retired, or many other reasons. We know they'll say no. We also know that people who say no several times can eventually be persuaded to say yes. We just need to be prepared for the no and able to deal with the objection.

The most important thing you can do to deal with an objection is *listen*. If you don't listen to the prospect, you'll never know what the objection is. "Not interested" isn't really an objection—it's the first thing people say, but it's not the real reason they're saying they won't support this program. We need to find out why they aren't interested. How do we do that? *Ask!*

Of course, when you ask why they aren't interested, you must be polite. A good way to ask when they say they aren't interested and don't give a reason is to say (with a big smile in your voice), "Oh, I'm surprised to hear that! Many of the people I've called for this program have been interested. Do you mind if I ask why?"

Prospects will ordinarily give you an objection that you can deal with.

There is an easy formula for dealing with an objection: *reflect, deflect, ask again.*

> *Reflect:* Talk about the objection. If the prospect is retired, ask about retirement. If the prospect has kids in school, ask where they are going and what they are studying. If the person is unemployed, ask what type of work he or she used to do or is looking for.

> *Deflect:* Let the person know that he or she isn't alone. "We talk to lots of unemployed people who want to support our program!" "Kids in school? Let me tell you about our Parents Fund. It's one of our most popular programs." You get the idea.

> *Ask:* Remember that you're required to continue asking until you've completed the gift ladder. Ask with a smile, believe all prospects can give, and they will!

Common Objections and Sample Responses

> *Objection:* I'm sorry, I only give through the mail.

> *Reflect:* I've talked to others who've said that—you're not alone. There are really two reasons we call everyone: It's so much more personal and we can get some important feedback about the school. Making phone calls is also the most cost-effective way to reach everyone we need to contact.

> *Deflect and Ask:* What I like to let people know is that if we can write them down for a pledge, even an amount smaller than they know they'll give, we'll send them a pledge card with their name on it and all the necessary information so they'll know we're legitimate and so your gift will be designated as you wish. Then, if they send more, it's icing on the cake. Most people have felt comfortable with this. Let me mention something I think you could do. . . .

> *Objection:* I can't afford to give, I've got kids in college. Thanks for calling!

> *Reflect:* You've got kids in school! That's great. Where are they going? What are they studying?" *(discuss with the prospect)*

EXHIBIT 9.5. DEALING WITH OBJECTIONS, Cont'd.

Deflect and Ask: You know, Mr. _____, I've talked to a lot of people in your situation, and they didn't want to make a large commitment, but most of them wanted to be a part of this effort because participation is the most important part of our program. Many of them felt more comfortable when I mentioned a gift of $_____; it would be great if I could put you down for that!

Objection: I can't commit now. I need to talk this over with my spouse.

Reflect: That's great that you want to help! I talk to a lot of people who say just the same thing, and I can understand that. Unfortunately, we have so many people to call that we really don't have the resources to call everyone twice. It sounds like you want to help, so let me make a suggestion. . . .

Deflect and Ask: What most people have wanted to do is make a small pledge they *know* they can handle in the next month or so. Then, when they get their pledge card, they can talk to their spouse and decide if they want to make a larger gift. That way we know we have everyone's participation this year, and if you decide to do more, it's just icing on the cake! Let me suggest a much more popular gift, it's just $_____.

Objection: I just can't give this year, but I promise to give next year.

Reflect: I've talked to a lot of people who've said that, and I know this is kind of sudden, with us just calling out of the blue.

Deflect and Ask: As you probably know, our annual fundraising relies on the support of many individuals to pool their gifts and make a big difference. It sounds like you want to help, and many people in your situation have wanted to make a small gift this year to show their support and then consider something more significant in the future. Some have felt more comfortable when I mention a gift of $_____. It would be great if you could help with that this year!

Objection: I can't give; I'm unemployed.

Reflect: Oh, I'm sorry to hear that. What type of work are you looking for? How are things going with your search?" *(discuss the job search)*

Deflect and Ask: Ms. _____, I've spoken with a few people in your situation, and I'd like to wish the best of luck in your job search. Your degree from this university is going to be a great asset in your job search, and I'm sure a new position is just around the corner! Others who have been between jobs haven't felt comfortable making a large gift either, but they still wanted to be a part of this year's effort with a minimal gift. A few people in your situation have felt comfortable with $_____; is that something you would feel comfortable with?

Callers should introduce themselves and state the case for support. The case for support must be clear and concise, as prospects may not be willing to listen for five or ten minutes.

When asking for money, it is often more successful if the caller asks for specific dollar amounts (see Exhibit 9.6). These amounts may be linked to specific giving groups or clubs or may be arbitrary round numbers. Either way, a prospect is much more likely to give when asked for a specific amount than when simply asked, "Would you like to support this effort?"

In any call, the most common answer is no. Callers must know how to overcome objections they will hear often. Lack of money, no interest in the organization, and refusal to make pledges over the phone are common, though each organization will also have objections specific to its program. In each case, callers should be trained to deal with these objections tactfully while continuing to ask for the prospect's support.

Most important, callers must be trained to remain polite under any and all circumstances. They will be insulted and will encounter extremely rude people when calling. Regardless, they must maintain their composure and be polite and respectful representatives of your organization.

Telemarketers should have access to phones, pens, pencils, and other equipment needed for the calling program. If the nonprofit does not have facilities appropriate for a phone program, local banks, real estate offices, visitors' bureau, or other organizations may be willing to allow their offices to be used for a calling program for a short period of time.

Each caller should be provided with a substantial number of prospects at the beginning of the calling session. Names, addresses, phone numbers, affiliations, and past giving should be indicated on a form that has ample space to make notes. Callers will want to write down pledges and refusals, as well as calls that reach answering machines, uncompleted calls, and other outcomes. If conducting a calling program that covers several time zones, care should be taken to ensure that prospects are not called too early in the morning or too late in the evening.

Accurate record keeping is essential. Pledge cards should be sent as soon as possible to facilitate fulfillment, and copies should be retained. In the event that pledges are not paid on a timely basis, a system for follow-up reminders should be in place. In many cases, this includes reminder notices when pledges are one month, two months, and three months past due. Some organizations also conduct phone programs to call individuals who have not yet paid their pledges. These efforts will help increase fulfillment and overall net income for the annual fund.

One technique that works well when calling to upgrade donors is presenting them with the opportunity to belong to some sort of giving society that lends prestige to that level of gift. For instance, introducing named categories for gifts of

EXHIBIT 9.6. MAKING THE ASK.

Just asking for a pledge is important, but the *way* you ask makes the difference between a pledge and a refusal. You must put enthusiasm into your asks and believe that everyone can make a pledge.

Think back to your childhood. When the ice-cream truck would drive by, which of the following requests do you think would be more successful?

"Um, could I have some change for an ice-cream?"

or

"Ooh, the ice-cream man! I would really, really like an ice-cream. It'd be so yummy! Please could I have some change for an ice-cream?"

The first request is kind of blah. There isn't any real urgency about the ice-cream or your need for some change to buy one. In the second ask, however, there's no doubt that you're excited about the ice-cream and the idea that a donation would get you something yummy.

The same is true when asking a prospect to make a pledge. If you don't sound like you believe in the program or your prospects' ability to pledge, you won't get the gift. If you are excited about the program and believe that prospects will make a pledge, they will.

Following are some ideas you can use when asking for a pledge:

- "The first gift I want to mention is a prestigious gift of $1,000, which can be set up as four installments of $250 to make it a little easier. It would be terrific if you'd be the next to make such a prestigious pledge!"

- "Let me share something many more people have been able to do—it's a gift of $500, which can be broken into four installments of $125. I'd love to put you down for that!"

- "A much more popular pledge for this program has been a gift of $50 this month and $50 next month for a total of $100. That's probably something you'd be more comfortable with."

- "It sounds like you want to help with this effort, so let me share something with you. For every ten people we speak with that give $50, we'll have $500 for this important effort. It would be terrific if we could put you down for $50!"

- "I don't want to leave you out of our efforts, because participation is the most important aspect of our program. We know that if every single person we call can provide just $35, we'll meet all of our goals. I'd love to get your participation with a gift of $35!"

$500, $1,000, and $2,500 may provide an incentive for a donor who is currently making a gift of $250 to give at a higher level in the future.

Although it is very important to promote the value of giving for philanthropy's sake, it can be effective to equate the size of a gift with specific donor benefits. For instance, donors of $500 may be eligible for inclusion in an invitation-only event, or donors at the $1,000 level can be listed on the organization's honor roll in a prominent place.

When coming up with names for your giving levels, one good option is to tie it to the organization in some way. For instance, the Parents Fund at Indiana University uses the following giving levels:

$500	Graduate Circle
$1,000	Faculty Circle
$2,500	Provost's Circle
$5,000	Chancellor's Circle

It can also be quite effective to recognize lifetime gifts or consecutive years of giving with a special society. This is particularly effective in renewing and retaining current donors (see Resource 16, "Membership Club, Donor Club, and Giving Society Brochures").

With proper planning and preparation, telemarketing can have a very positive impact on an annual fund's bottom line. As with any annual fund program, peer input is extremely valuable when planning a telemarketing program. Consult with others, borrow ideas and scripts, and enjoy the benefits of this important annual fund component.

Face-to-Face Contacts

It is true that there are occasions when a personal ask, face to face, is the most productive, especially if such contact is valuable for other reasons (such as public relations) and is cost-effective. Increasingly, annual fund programs are expanding to take on face-to-face efforts with specific groups of prospects that seem to warrant such individual attention.

If, for instance, a new donor is identified via a telemarketing program who agrees to make a contribution of $1,000 with little persuasion, there may be merit in arranging a follow-up thank-you from a staff member or a volunteer. The logic here is that any prospect who is willing to make such a gift with little reflection is likely a good prospect for larger contributions.

Such a thank-you is the first step in an ongoing relationship that can bear fruit in future years, when the ask could come in person rather than by mail or phone. Likely prospects for this kind of special attention include current donors in the $1,000–$10,000 range and young potential donors who stand to inherit wealth or earn substantial sums through their own efforts.

The next step is to make an appointment with the prospect, on his or her own turf—the fundraiser should always be willing to go to the donor. When making your appointment, be straightforward about the reason for your visit. Explain that you want to get feedback about your program as well as talk about the possibility of continuing support. It is always best to be honest from the outset; a donor or prospect must never end up feeling hoodwinked or sandbagged.

Ask how much time the donor can give you, and don't let your meeting run longer unless the donor wants to keep talking. You need to let the donor lead the way in conversation while still keeping control of the solicitation. You must absolutely not forget to ask for specific support. Most important, follow up after the visit with a thank-you, at the same time answering any trailing questions and letting the donor know that you have completed any tasks asked of you.

Special Events

Organizing special events has long been a popular fundraising strategy. Funds may be raised in advance as well as during an event, but the event itself is the focus of the fundraising activity. However, special events are often labor-intensive and, when all factors are considered, may not be particularly efficient if fundraising is the organization's primary purpose. This is not to say that some events are not highly successful fundraisers. Some are. Indeed, for some organizations, an annual signature event defines the organization in the public's eye and raises significant dollars.

But often the major purposes of special events go beyond the raising of money. Publicity is frequently a main benefit. An event can call attention to an organization at a critical point in its life. Publicity from the media is most desirable, but publicity from the people who attend can assist as well. Events can also attract new friends and potential donors to an organization. Organizations like educational institutions and healthcare providers have built-in mechanisms for generating new prospects—incoming students and new patients. But most organizations have no inherent access to a potential donor pool. A special event can provide a distinctive setting that attracts potential prospects and donors and encourages interest and involvement. Information garnered from this initial contact can be used subsequently to generate more interest and involvement. For many nonprofits, this may be the single largest benefit derived from special events, especially with appropriate follow-up.

Events are also a valuable way to reward donors, involve volunteers, and recognize leaders. Such events can be used to build morale, say thank you, and encourage further involvement and giving.

The Fund Raising School (1995) lists the following criteria for choosing a special event:

- Who is the audience?
- What do you want from this audience?
- Could you reach the audience through a less labor-intensive strategy?
- What will attract the audience?
- What will this audience be willing to pay for admission to the event?

It further raises the following questions to consider before beginning the actual planning:

- Is the event you have chosen appropriate? For example, a beer bash may attract a new audience, get publicity, and make money, but it is inappropriate for an alcohol recovery program. Dances are neutral in many places but offensive in some communities.
- Does the event promote your organization's image? You need to find an audience sympathetic to your cause as well as desirous of attending the event.
- Can you afford to plan this event? You must have sufficient cash available to pay all the up-front costs before you can make any money from the event.

The Fund Raising School also advises the establishment of an events committee, a primary leadership committee of five to seven people whose main job is to plan events and organize other people to perform the necessary tasks. If the committee is too large, meetings become events in themselves. The committee should also draw up a list of tasks, with deadlines attached. These tasks should indicate "what," "when," and "who" and should also include all tasks that will cost money. This list in turn becomes the expense budget.

The types of events you might host are virtually limitless, bounded only by your organization's imagination (within the confines of appropriateness). Some of the most commonly used events are the following:

- Lunches, dinners, galas
- Dances
- Sales (book sales, bake sales, rummage sales)

- Auctions
- "Thons" (runathons, walkathons, rockathons, telethons)
- Fashion shows
- Outings (golf, tennis)

"The key to any great special event is in the details," says nationally known events planner Anne Coulter (personal communication, Aug. 1999), "so walking through an event fills in a lot of the detail questions; so does visiting a similar event to see what you like or don't like." Here is a special-events checklist based on Coulter's recommendations:

1. *Purpose:* What is the purpose of the event? To raise funds, friends, awareness?

2. *Audience:* Determining your audience will help you with all of the other decisions.

3. *Date and time:* Might it conflict with another major event or activity your audience may be interested in attending?

4. *Site*

    Electricity: Will the event involve an audiovisual presentation? Will there be music? Will you be using electric lights, candles, or sunlight?

    Bathrooms: Are there restrooms, or will you need port-o-lets?

    Accessibility: Is the site handicapped-accessible?

    Weather: If your event is outdoors, what will you do if it is extremely hot or cold or windy? What if it rains?

    Sights, sounds, and smells: If any of these is offensive, your guests will not enjoy the event.

5. *Food and drink*

    What kind of food are you serving? Be sure you will have more than enough.

    Will there be an open bar or cash bar or a specialty drink?

    Will you be able to accommodate people on special diets?

6. *Entertainment or program*

    What will it cost?

    Is this form of entertainment a good choice for this event and this audience?

7. *Responsibilities*

    Itemize every task, and assign someone to it.

    Be sure you have a backup for each responsibility.

8. *Schedule*

> Walk through your event mentally, minute by minute or hour by hour, and put every step down on paper.
>
> Distribute your written notes or prospectus to *all* key individuals associated with the event.
>
> Have a production meeting so that everyone involved can go through the details.

9. *Invitations and tickets*

> Always send out more invitations than you think you need—remember, you will not obtain a 100 percent response.
>
> How will RSVPs be handled—over the phone, by mail, by e-mail?
>
> Are you going to mail tickets or hold them at the door?
>
> What will you do about orders that come in late?
>
> Who will staff your "will call" area?
>
> What will you do about such things as lost tickets, late reservations, and selling tickets at the door?

10. *Ambiance*

> What kind of decorations do you need?
>
> Does your site have any limitations in terms of decorations?

11. *Permits*

> Do you need any permits to use your site, to serve alcohol, to run a raffle or offer a door prize, to have the activity you are planning?
>
> Do you have a security and medical assistance plan in place?
>
> Does your insurance company know about your plans?

12. *Publicity*

> How do you plan to let people know about this event? Advertising or advertising trades for tickets? Newsletters? Invitations? Press releases? In other creative ways? (Remember, there are always a lot of events and activities competing for people's time.)
>
> Will board members or community leaders lend their name or support to attract guests to the event?
>
> Are you using volunteers from the community to maximize your time?

13. *Signage:* Make sure the guests can find your event.

14. *Services and supplies*

What services and supplies do you need for this event? Think about floral, catering, audiovisual support, tablecloths, chairs, highchairs, golf carts, photographer, transportation (buses, vans, carriage, animal?), special guests services, music, rental items (podium, china, crystal, and so on).

Try to arrange for as many services and supplies as possible to be donated. There will always be last-minute expenses that you could not have anticipated and will have to pay for, so you must try to make your budget go as far as possible.

15. *Morning after:* Review every aspect of the event after it is over.

What were you most pleased with? What could you have done better? What do you never want to do again?

Get comments from your committees. They will have noticed details you did not.

Remember that a great event takes at least a year to plan well. You should constantly be looking ahead. If you start late, you will end up paying for a lot of things you might have gotten donated, or you will not have a good event and your guests will remember this for a long time to come.

Don't forget to say thanks and issue gift receipts.

Special Events: Planning for Success (Harris, 1998) contains checklists that address budget, equipment, audiovisual needs, catering, bar, floral and decoration needs, program, and the involvement of VIPs. Any organization can use these as a basis for developing its own checklists. (See also Resource 17, "Special-Events Planning Checklists.")

Making Giving as Easy as Possible

No matter how people give to the annual fund, it remains very important to ensure that doing so is easy. For example, make the reply card easy to read and fill out, with blanks large enough to hold the information you are requesting.

Provide a preaddressed envelope in which the donor may send the gift. Some organizations feel that the envelopes should be postage-paid, but research has indicated that providing the envelope alone may be all that is necessary to encourage a response.

Give the donor a variety of options for contributing, including installment plans, credit card gifts, and automatic bank withdrawals. Now that credit card companies have developed advantage cards, more and more donors are using their cards to make charitable contributions.

Also of particular interest of late is the idea of electronic fundraising, particularly through a Web site. As consumers become more convinced that security precautions protect their credit card numbers on-line, more and more donors will be at ease with the idea of making gifts over the Internet. All organizations should pay close attention to developments in this area in response to donor wishes—there is no doubt that this trend will gain momentum as time goes on (see Chapter Nineteen).

Remain sensitive to the needs, requests, and desires of your donors, and adapt your program accordingly. Such special efforts will go a long way toward encouraging initial contributions and ensuring continued allegiance over time.

Making Donors Feel Appreciated

It is of the utmost important to thank every donor, accurately and promptly, for every contribution, as well as to ensure that donations are recorded in such a way that donors are able to take any tax advantages that accrue to them for their gifts (see Chapter Twenty).

Recognition of contributions is part of the stewardship function, which is integral to all aspects of fundraising. Stewardship and good planning are vital to the idea of a continuous lifetime giving program—a concept that more and more annual funds are adopting. This change in thinking involves ensuring that you are looking at the long term as well as the short term when planning an annual fund. What are you doing to move your current annual donors up the ladder? What strategies can you employ that will prove most advantageous to your program? By keeping these questions uppermost in your mind, the maximum possible benefit can be attained, both now and in the future.

CHAPTER TEN

IDENTIFYING, RESEARCHING, AND RATING INDIVIDUALS AS MAJOR GIFT PROSPECTS

It is impossible to overemphasize the importance of major gifts to the success of any fundraising program. But major gifts do not just happen; someone makes them happen as a result of a well-thought-out plan. To obtain major gifts, an organization must involve itself in the process of identifying, cultivating, and soliciting major donors. This chapter, together with Chapter Eleven, discusses the steps involved in successfully generating major gifts from individuals, who give between 85 and 90 percent of all gifts. (Giving by corporations and foundations is discussed in Chapter Fifteen.)

Defining Major Gifts

Major gifts are defined as the top 10 to 20 percent of gifts received by an organization that account for 70 to 80 percent or more of its gift income. In larger organizations, it is not unusual to see a major gift defined as $100,000 or more. For smaller and newer organizations, major gifts may be defined as $2,500 to $5,000 or more. For institutions between the two extremes, the majority of all nonprofits, the definition of a major gift will range from $5,000 to $10,000 or more, based on individual circumstances. A *lead gift* is a gift that serves to establish a trend for giving by others believed to be capable of making gifts at the same level. It is possible to secure lead gifts in the major, special, and general divisions of the gift table.

However, most commonly, lead gifts are associated with the top gift or gifts in a given campaign. To satisfy this definition, a lead gift should represent 10 percent or more of the campaign goal, be it annual or capital. A *nucleus gift* is a gift received at the earliest stages of the campaign—usually a major or lead gift, most often given by an institutional "insider"(a board member or previous major donor). Nucleus gifts collectively provide core funding and give momentum to the campaign. An *ultimate gift* is the largest single gift a donor ever makes. (Some organizations define it as the largest single gift a donor ever makes *to that organization*.) True ultimate gifts are almost always estate gifts.

All of these types of gifts are considered major gifts.

Characteristics of Major Donors

Gibson (1999) identifies the following characteristics of lead gift donors (see Chapter Fourteen): most are self-made, have a history of giving, have personal ties to the institutions they support, are generally sixty-five years of age or older, and are passionate about the causes they fund.

Major donors have strong values and deep beliefs, according to Campbell (1985). They believe in people and have great respect for knowledge. They often seek to provide opportunities they did not themselves have, to help the less fortunate, to improve the quality of life, to solve problems in society, and to preserve and perpetuate values of humankind, especially those that they hold dearest. Major gift donors are usually quite religious, have a deep belief in the free enterprise system, and are generally conservative. They already know someone in or something about the institution they will be asked to support. Someone has already made an impression on them. They have come to believe in someone or something the institution represents—the chief executive officer, a member of the board, a volunteer, a professional staff member, or some part of what the institution stands for. They have values that are comparable with the institution's, and they are probably regular donors to the institution or to one that is similar.

They view giving as an investment, and through their investments they desire to solve a problem or resolve an issue and find ways to express themselves (self-actualization). They also expect to see and understand the "return" on their investments. They will not openly seek but will accept (and in fact expect) recognition. They may want to honor or memorialize someone else rather than themselves, although many will indeed honor themselves. They have the resources to make a major gift. In some instances, these resources may not be liquid at the moment. Their spouses and families are usually involved in the gift decision. Major donors tend to stay with programs and activities that have been of interest to them over a long period. Those who will give major gifts to an institution in the future have generally given to it in the past.

Seeking to quantify the traits that motivate wealthy people to make charitable contributions, Price and File (1994) studied more than eight hundred individuals and developed seven basic profiles (see Exhibit 10.1). The general perspective on philanthropy embodied in each profile suggests a specific and unique approach to fundraising for different kinds of nonprofit organizations.

EXHIBIT 10.1. THE SEVEN FACES OF PHILANTHROPY.

The Communitarians: Doing Good Makes Sense

Communitarians, the largest segment (26.3%), give because it makes good sense to do so. Communitarians are typically local business owners who find that service on boards and committees of local nonprofits can be good for business, because of the relationships that often develop in such settings. The other reason Communitarians believe active philanthropy makes good sense is that they help their own communities prosper by supporting local charities.

The Devout: Doing Good Is God's Will

The Devout are motivated to support nonprofits for religious reasons: they say they believe it is God's will for them to help others. Almost always members of a local church, which is part of a regional or national religious group, the Devout channel nearly all (94.6%) their giving to religious institutions. The Devout make up the second largest group (20.9%) of major donors.

The Investor: Doing Good Is Good Business

Investors are affluent individual donors who give with one eye on the nonprofit cause and one eye on personal tax and estate consequences. Investors calibrate their giving to take advantage of tax and estate benefits and therefore want to work with nonprofits that understand these concerns. To achieve their tax, estate, and philanthropic interests, Investors donate to a wide range of nonprofits and are the segment most likely to support umbrella nonprofits such as community foundations (22.5%). About 15.3 percent of major donors are Investors.

The Socialite: Doing Good Is Fun

Socialites find social function benefiting nonprofits an especially appealing way to help make a better world and have a good time doing it. Socialites are members of local social networks with which they interact to select nonprofits for support and to leverage in fundraising activities. They seek opportunities to create fundraisers and social events benefiting nonprofits and are less interested in participating in the day-to-day operations of the nonprofit or activities directed at constituents. Socialites, who tend to support the arts and education as well as religious nonprofits, make up 10.8 percent of major donors.

EXHIBIT 10.1. THE SEVEN FACES OF PHILANTHROPY, Cont'd.

The Altruist: Doing Good Feels Right

Altruists embody the popular perception of the selfless donor—the donor who gives out of generosity and empathy to urgent causes and who modestly "wishes to remain anonymous." Altruists give because they believe it is a moral imperative and because it helps them grow as human beings or evolve spiritually. Altruists make giving decisions without the input of advisers and are not usually interested in active roles in the nonprofits they support. A far greater proportion of Altruists than any other group focus their philanthropy on social causes. Nine percent of major donors are Altruists.

The Repayer: Doing Good in Return

Repayers tend to have been constituents first and donors second. A typical Repayer has personally benefited from some institution, often a school or medical center, and now supports that institution from a feeling of loyalty or obligation. Repayers concentrate their philanthropy on medical charities and educational institutions. Repayers are 10.2 percent of major donors.

The Dynast: Doing Good Is a Family Tradition

Unlike other segments, Dynasts typically inherit their wealth. The philanthropic motivation of Dynasts stems from their socialization. Giving is something their family has always stood for, and they believe it is expected of them to support nonprofits. However, younger Dynasts will seek out different philanthropies than their parents. Although Dynasts have been significant figures in philanthropy for some time, they now comprise 8.3 percent of major donors.

Source: Price and File, 1994, pp. 14–16.

Women's Expanding Role

The role that women play in all phases of philanthropy is growing and will continue to grow. Women have long controlled the majority of wealth; they outlive men on average. Only in the past twenty-five years, however, have they emerged in large numbers as an active, independent force in philanthropy. Today's nonprofit boards are heavily populated, and in some situations dominated, by women. Corporate boardrooms are seeing more and more women too. Women in growing numbers are rising to the topmost rungs of the corporate ladder, and they are populating the executive and staff ranks of nonprofit organizations and development programs as well.

And women are now giving big. For example, Miller and Nayyar (1998) report on a Princeton University study (Capek, 1997) showing that the number of women whose net worth exceeds $600,000 increased 28 percent between 1992 and 1995 and on research by INDEPENDENT SECTOR (1996) showing that average charitable contributions by women increased 26 percent between 1993 and 1995. The correlation here is not that because women now have more money they are giving big but rather that giving big requires the ability to do it. Interest in the case and involvement with the organization remain the predominant reasons people make large gifts.

According to the Women's Philanthropy Institute (1999):

- 43 percent of Americans with assets greater than $500,000 are women.
- Women own 36 percent of U.S. businesses. Women are starting new businesses at three times the rate of men.
- Companies owned by women employ 35 percent more people than the Fortune 500 firms employ worldwide.
- 29 percent of working wives make more than their husbands.
- 74 percent of men and 71 percent of women invest in stock funds, and both sexes allocate 46 percent of their portfolios to equities.
- 78 percent of women business owners volunteer. Of all business owners, 56 percent volunteer.
- 88 percent of charitable dollars in the United States come from individual donors.
- 71 percent of women and 65 percent of men gave to charity in 1995.
- Both men and women donate an average of 2 percent of their annual income to charity. In 1995, women's average annual gift was 93 percent as much as men's.
- $10 trillion will be passing to the baby boomers in the next thirty years, and women outlive men by an average of seven years.
- In the first half of the twenty-first century, $41 trillion will be transferred from one generation to the next, and women will most probably outlive men by even more than seven years.

According to Gwinn Scott ("Exploring Women and Philanthropy," 1998), for more than a century women philanthropists have been bringing dramatic change about in America, whether they were creating colleges, as Sophia Smith did in 1871 with a gift of $393,000, or working to save the planet, as Harriet Bullitt and Patsy Bullitt Collins did when they announced in 1994 that they would give most of their $375 million fortune to fund environmental causes. In fact, women respond to a wide variety of needs and give to all kinds of institutions and organizations, and yet only recently have they begun to realize their full potential as philanthropists—and only recently have many nonprofits taken action to identify and cultivate women as key sources of financial support. Scott finds that women tend to prefer outright gifts over multiyear commitments, are driven more by causes than by competition between and among themselves, base their choices on where they can have the most impact, are moved to respond to cases that stir their hearts and evoke passion, are more likely to give anonymously or to name things for others, and give most readily to organizations that include them and target programs toward them.

Shaw and Taylor (1995) identify the "six *C*'s" that motivate women: desire to *change, create, connect, commit, collaborate,* and *celebrate.*

Research shows that men give out of loyalty to the institution, support the traditions of the institution to which they give, are more likely to give before volunteering, and are generally comfortable talking about money. Women, by contrast, want their gift to make a difference. They are more likely to volunteer before giving, usually prefer personal over public recognition, prefer to work as part of a team toward a goal, and are generally uncomfortable talking about money.

Donor education programs can help make women more comfortable with their potential or actual role as philanthropists while increasing their sense of connection with the institution.

Giving by People of Color

The next frontier for mainstream philanthropy to address is giving by ethnic minorities. Little information is available in this area today, but increasing attention is being paid to it. *Giving USA Update* (Issue 2, 1999) focuses on the subject.

It is too early in the research cycle to make generalizations about people of color as a whole, but differences in income, length of time in the United States, extent of religious observances, and education are some of the factors that may contribute to differences within ethnic groups.

In a study of ethnic philanthropy in the San Francisco Bay Area, Smith, Shue, Vest, and Villarreal (1994) note that sometimes "subtle gift-giving rituals can signal appropriate degrees of honor and shame, reaffirm cultural precepts, and allow positive channels for 'face-saving' behavior. In such cultural contexts, giving a gift or being asked to give (particularly by a stranger) can easily create suspicion on the part of the potential donor or inadvertently create a situation in which the gift-giver perceives that he or she has been placed in a subservient position" (p. 7).

Berry (1999) notes that Native American cultures place a high value on sharing, exchange, reciprocity, and community involvement. Traditional giveaway rituals can be key to building relationships and organizing social structures. Philanthropy, however, is often associated with receiving gifts from outside the community, reinforcing long-standing hierarchies of dependence on U.S. governmental programs.

For many Latin American immigrants, in their home countries the government and the church—rather than nonprofit organizations—assume primary responsibility for dealing with social issues.

Researchers working in African American, Asian American, Latino, and Native American communities all report that addressing critical needs is the number one priority of donors. When crises occur in the family, extended family, or neighborhood, resources may be fully allocated there and not reach the mainstream nonprofit sector. The U.S. Census Bureau (1999) describes almost 25 percent of African American households as "other families with children." They do not conform to the mainstream pattern of a married couple and its children. This suggests that many African Americans are using their resources to care for children in their extended family or community at large—a generous act, but not formal philanthropy.

Most minority communities have long traditions of charitable behavior and are strong supporters of the nonprofit sector in the United States ("Charitable Giving by People of Color," 1999). Nevertheless, anecdotal and survey evidence suggest that many people of color are somewhat less involved in the formal nonprofit sector than their white counterparts. If people of color as a whole are to be included more fully in institutional philanthropy, the nonprofit sector must connect its fundraising practices to the giving patterns and cultures of a wide range of communities.

Nonprofits must demonstrate a commitment to including ethnic communities in the philanthropic process. This can include hiring and training more minority fundraisers and teaching people already working in development to be sensitive to the concerns of different groups. The third sector must also educate communities of color. This includes introducing people to the language and institutions of mainstream charitable giving, as well as clarifying the financial benefits that donors can incur by making gifts to nonprofits.

Finally, organizations must make an effort to cultivate and seek contributions from different communities. In some cases, this will entail transforming development programs to meet the interests and financial profiles of these donors. For example, community foundations that have been successful in recruiting donors of color often make it possible for people to make relatively small contributions to pooled funds, rather than requiring a substantial minimum contribution. On a more basic level, cultivation and solicitation efforts can include translating fundraising materials into other languages, recruiting volunteers or spokespeople from different communities, and adding a personal touch to the solicitation process, something that is effective in all communities.

Identifying Prospects

There are three levels of potential donors: expects, prospects, and suspects.

An *expect* is a donor who has given a lead or major gift to the organization in the past and can be expected to do so again if properly stewarded, cultivated, and solicited.

A *prospect* is a donor who has given to the organization before but not at the level now being requested. For example, someone who has been giving at the $1,000 level annually is a legitimate prospect for consideration for a $5,000 or larger gift to a multiyear campaign while continuing ongoing support at the current level.

A *suspect* is a potential donor who is not a prospect. To be a legitimate prospect, one must have not only money available for giving but also something more—interest or involvement in the organization and, generally when the focus is on lead or major gifts, a prior history of giving at a significant level. Pursuing suspects in the hope of turning them into prospects is a generally futile chase that all too many organizations engage in, wasting time, energy, and resources that are better directed to individuals who do care and will give, when properly motivated and asked.

Where there is potential but not yet probability, it is mandatory for the institution to move these prospects through what G. T. Smith (personal communication, June 1986) describes as "the cultivation cycle." The cultivation of potentially large donors is a systematic and continuing effort to develop a power structure, either actual or potential, for an institution. It involves four steps: *identify, inform, involve, invest.* In nearly every instance, the final three steps constitute a continuing cycle of learning additional information about potential donors, heightening their interest through the dissemination of information (via personal contact and mailings), encouraging a meaningful involvement (such as volunteer service or active participation), and ultimately receiving significant financial investment. Involvement is the highest level of cultivation in that it requires that the prospect be brought into active contact with the organization through service on a committee, membership on the board, or some other equally important way.

Effective Research

Martha Murphy, director of Prospect Research at Valparaiso University, offers a good definition of prospect research: "Prospect research is an important step in the process of increasing the philanthropic resources of an institution. We seek to identify the shared values between an organization and its prospective donors through the collection, organization, and presentation of significant information for development purposes" (Murphy, 2000).

The basic principles of prospect research are as follows (Fund Raising School, 1995):

1. *It is ongoing and cumulative.* One piece of data leads to another in a never-ending succession.
2. *It is selective.* Researchers must narrow their focus on whom they research and what information they gather.
3. *It is confidential.* All information obtained by research must be held in the strictest confidence.
4. *It is accurate.* All information should be verified or attributable to a source.
5. *It is personal.* The best information on a prospect will always come directly from the prospect or someone who knows the prospect.
6. *It is tied to funding needs.* Researchers need to know the priorities set by the administrators of their institution and work within those guidelines.

The key factors in conducting basic research are linkage, ability, and interest, known as the *LAI principle.* Linkage is the first essential. A prospect can be linked in any number of ways—for example, through personal connections, professional associations, or geographical location. Ability to give is a second requisite; though often obvious, it is not always easy to verify. And interest is also indispensable. You must determine a prospect's roles and responsibilities in life and his or her priorities among these to determine where your organization fits (see Figure 10.1). Although most researchers like to start by determining the prospect's ability to give, linkage and interest are far more important. Without linkage or interest, ability doesn't matter.

As you uncover facts by gathering information about the ownership, control, influence, and wealth of individuals, corporations, and foundations, the larger task becomes how to reduce great quantities of information to readable, understandable, concise reports pertinent to your current goal.

To meet these objectives, the professional staff must correlate, control, and interpret data in order to carry out the following five tasks:

1. To develop a strategy for action
2. To determine appropriate projects to which the prospect can be assigned
3. To identify the prospect with the right groups
4. To assign the right people to cultivate the prospect
5. To establish a schedule for implementation of the cultivation and solicitation program

FIGURE 10.1. WHEEL OF ROLES AND RESPONSIBILITIES.

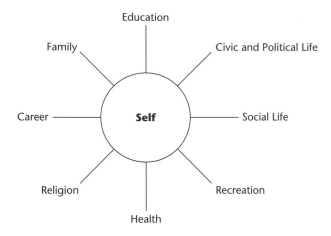

Source: The Fund Raising School, 1995. Reprinted with permission of The Fund Raising School, The Center on Philanthropy, Indiana University.

The best prospects for major gifts to any organization are people who are committed to the organization and have been donors in the past. Many will already have accepted leadership positions in the organization. Prospect research involves both basic and sophisticated processes. Whittaker (1983) outlines the basic information that must be gathered:

- Name, nickname
- Home address (or addresses)
- Business name, job title, address, and phone number
- Telephone, fax, and cell phone numbers, e-mail address
- Date and place of birth
- Education (secondary and higher, along with academic major)
- Job history
- Marital status
- Spouse's name
- Spouse's education and business
- Number, names, and ages of children
- Family connections to the organization
- Family connections to other organizations
- Honors and achievements
- Clubs and organizations
- Political affiliation
- Religious affiliation

- Personal interests
- Estimated net worth
- Net salary
- Stock holdings
- Directorships
- Family foundations
- Favorite charities
- Gift record
- Names of secretaries
- Name of attorney
- Name of banker
- Names of close friends

The best research is done in the field, not in the office. A twenty-minute face-to-face conversation with a prospect or donor will often yield more information and give more insights than hours of in-house or on-line research. People will tell amazing things about themselves if you show genuine interest and listen to them. There is no substitute for being with prospects. And with the prospect is the only place to be if you want the competitive edge that comes from having a strategic piece of information or a perceptive bit of insight no one else has. That's truly valuable research information: it's the kind that produces gifts.

Therefore, it is vital to keep a record of the prospect's contacts with the organization. A contact report needs to be clear and concise, with a meaningful summary—something that quickly reveals if this is relevant to a specific fundraising activity. Details of a contact report may include the following:

- Date of contact
- Place and purpose of last contact
- Result of the contact
- Next steps to be taken
- Staff assigned
- Volunteers assigned

Among the sources of this information are institutional records (including the records kept in the development office, in the chief executive's office, and in the alumni or public relations office), institutional publications, and institutional staff members. Other especially good sources of information are board members, service users, and friends who can provide information from their own personal knowledge. The following printed and published materials are excellent sources of information:

- Chambers of commerce
- *Chronicle of Higher Education*
- *Chronicle of Philanthropy*

- Clipping services
- Corporate annual reports
- Corporate filings
- Foundation annual reports, directories, and grant indexes
- *The Foundation Directory*
- Local, regional, and national newspapers
- Magazines such as *Forbes, Fortune,* and *Business Week*
- Various volumes of *Who's Who*
- *Philanthropic Digest*
- Standard & Poor's, Dun & Bradstreet, and Taft corporate directories
- State directories of corporations and executives

According to Kathy K. Wilson, director of development services at the Indiana University Foundation (personal communication, Jan. 1998), the Internet, online services, and the CD-ROM medium have reduced the number of printed and published materials that research offices purchase and review. Part of a research budget should include the proper hardware and software and the maintenance of these in order to conduct the necessary research. High-speed Internet access is essential. Because of the expense of on-line and CD-ROM products, it is advisable for smaller operations to work with local librarians in formulating search strategies for on-line services and, perhaps, to share the expense of CD-ROM products. It is imperative that one develop a solid search strategy *before* incurring costs on-line. One useful tool is Lexis/Nexis Academic Universe, which is typically available through an institution of higher education. This database offers the following:

- General news topics (major newspapers, regional sources, major trade journals)
- Company news (major newspapers, regional sources, major trade journals)
- Company financial information (Hoover's Online, Companies Online, U.S. private company reports, company intelligence, Standard & Poor's corporate descriptions)
- Biographical information

A CD-ROM product that is used extensively is *Biography and Genealogy Master Index;* the microfiche version is called *Biobase.* A good on-line source for individual, corporate, or foundation research is Dialog. This, too, can be accessed via the World Wide Web (http://www.dialog.com) and allows a researcher to browse more than 6 billion pages of text and 3 million images, all of which can be searched in seconds. A few favorite resources include the Marquis *Who's Who* series, the *Wall Street Journal,* ABI/Inform, Business Dateline, Foundation Directories, *Biography Master Index,* Dun & Bradstreet, and products published by Gale Group.

One of the best ways to stay informed and ask questions is through PRSPCT-L (http://www.egroups.com/group/PRSPCT-L), an electronic discussion group that allows people who conduct research a way to share information via e-mail. Another resource for individual and corporate research is the on-line *Internet Prospector.* This combination Web site and monthly newsletter has a "People" section for searching individuals, with articles and links to other sites. One of *Internet Prospector*'s best-known features, especially for beginners, is David Lamb's Prospect Research Page (http://www.PRESBYTERIANCHURCHUSA.com/lamb), which includes an annotated list of links to companies, people, foundations, commercial information providers, search engines, and more. Additionally, more and more research offices are developing their own Internet home pages with links to helpful sites.

One needs to be aware of the explosion of information that has become available on the Internet in recent years. There are many sites that offer free or fee-based information so that a shop with even the smallest of budgets can do effective research over the Internet. Vicky Martin, director of research, has prepared a list of Web sites that have been helpful to the Indiana University Foundation research office (see Exhibit 10.2).

EXHIBIT 10.2. USEFUL BOOKMARKS FOR DOING ON-LINE PROSPECT RESEARCH.

Address, Phone, and ZIP Code Sites

AmeriCom Area Decoder: *http://decoder.americom.com*

AnyWho: Find Telephone Number, E-Mail, Home Page URL, Fax, Toll-Free Number, and Address: *http://www.anywho.com*

Directory Assistance: *http://www.555-1212.com*

ZIP Code Lookup and Address Information: *http://www.usps.gov/ncsc*

News Sites

American Journalism Review News Link: *http://www.ajr.org*

@The Premier Network for Business, Technology, and Knowledge Management: Forums, Articles, Magazines, Events, Resources, Analyses, and News: *http://www.brint.com*

Business Wire 1999: *http://www.businesswire.com*

CFO Magazine and Treasury and Risk Management Home Page: *http://www.cfonet.com*

Dow Jones Reuters Business Interactive LLC: *http:///www.bestofboth.com/index.html*

Folio: The Magazine for Magazine Management: *http://www.foliomag.com*

Gebbie Press: PR Media Directory: Newspapers, Radio, TV, Magazines: Press Releases, Faxes, E-Mail, Publicity, Freelance, Journalism, Marketing: *http://www.gebbieinc.com/index1.htm*

EXHIBIT 10.2. USEFUL BOOKMARKS
FOR DOING ON-LINE PROSPECT RESEARCH, Cont'd.

Minority Business Entrepreneur Magazine Home Page: *http://www.mbemag.com*
NewsDirectory: Newspapers and Media: *http://newsdirectory.com*
News Headlines from Interlope News: *http://www.interlope.com*
NewsHub—Headline News Every Fifteen Minutes: *http://newshub.com*
PointCast Download Page: *http://www.pointcast.com*
WallStreetReporter.com: *http://www.wallstreetreporter.com*

Corporate Information Sites

CEO Express: *http://www.ceoexpress.com*
CommerceInc: Homepage *http://www.commerceinc.com/index.shtml*
Company Sleuth Home Page: *http://www.companysleuth.com*
Corporate Information: *http://www.corporateinformation.com*
CorpTech Database of Fifty Thousand U.S. Technology Companies: *http://www.corptech.com*
Dun & Bradstreet: *http://www.dnb.com/dnb/dnbhome.htm*
Financials.com—Annual Reports, Stock Quotes, and More: *http://www.financials.com*
FirmFind: Main Menu: *http://udese.state.ut.us/cgi/foxweb.exe/firmfind*
Global Corporate Information Services: *http://www.gcis.com*
Hoover's Online: *http://www.hoovers.com*
Industry.net: *http://www.industry.net*
InvestorGuide—The Leading Guide to Investing on the Web: *http://investorguide.com*
Online Investor: *http://192.41.31.102/onlineinvestor.index.html*
Search SEC EDGAR Archives: *http://www.sec.gov/cgi-bin/srch-edgar*
10K Wizard Quick Search Menu: *http://www.tenkwizard.com*
Thomas Register of American Manufacturers—Industrial Manufacturing Supplies, Equipment, Plastics, Valves, Fasteners, Motors, Compressors, Engineering, CAD/CAM, Sheet Metal Fabricating: *http:///www.thomasregister.com*
WSRN.com—Your One Stop for Financial Research: *http://www.wsrn.com*

Stock and Insider Information Sites

Quicken.com—Insider Trading: *http://quicken.com/investments/insider*
Stock Quotes: *http://www.streetnet.com/quote.html*
Stock Splits: *http://stocksplits.net*
Thomson Financial Wealth Identification: *http://www.wealthid.com*
Yahoo! Finance: *http://quote.yahoo.com/?u*

Foundation Information Sites

The Foundation Center: *http://fdncenter.org*
Welcome to GuideStar, the Donor's Guide to Nonprofits and Charities: *http://www.guidestar.org*
Quality 990: Improve IRS Form 990 Reporting: 990 in 2000: *http://www.qual990.org*

EXHIBIT 10.2. USEFUL BOOKMARKS
FOR DOING ON-LINE PROSPECT RESEARCH, Cont'd.

Biographical Information Sites

American Medical Association Doctor Finder: *http://www.ama-assn.org*

Ancestry.com—Online Genealogy: *http://www.ancestry.com*

Indiana Biography Index Overview: *http://199.8.200.90:591/ibioverview.htm*

International Directory of Finance and Economics Professionals:
http://linux.agsm.ucla.edu/dir

Martindale-Hubbell Lawyer Locator: *http://www.martindale.com*

Outstanding Americans: *http://www.oyaawards.com*

Welcome to LawOffice.com—Over One Million Lawyers and Information About the
Law: *http://www.lawoffice.com*

General Information Sites

The Careful Donor: *http://donors.philanthropy.com*

Chambers of Commerce and Other Related Associations on the Internet:
http://www.indychamber.com/chambers.htm

Council for Advancement and Support of Education Home Page: *http://www.case.org*

Guide to Understanding Financials: *http://www.ibm.com/FinancialGuide*

Indiana University Libraries Online Resources: *http://www.indiana.edu/~libfind*

KPMG Knowledge Management: *http://kpmg.interact.nl/publication/survey.html*

Lexis-Nexis Academic Universe: *http://web.lexis-nexis.com/universe*

Librarians' Index to the Internet: *http://sunsite.berkeley.edu/InternetIndex*

Primary Source Media: City Directories Online:
http://www.citydirectories.psmedia.com/index.html

Prospect Research Online: *http://www.rpbooks.com*

Travelocity—Online Airfares, Hotel and Car Reservations: *http://www.travelocity.com*

TravelWeb: Hotel and Flight Reservations: *http://www.travelweb.com*

University of Virginia Prospect Research:
http://www.people.virginia.edu/~dev-pros/index.html

Yahoo! Real Estate—Home Values: *http://realestate.yahoo.com/realestate/homevalues*

Search Engines

Alta Vista: *http://altavista.digital.com*
Dogpile: *http://www.dogpile.com*
Google: *http://www.google.com*

Source: Vicky's Bookmarks in *Special Events, Planning for Success,* by April Harris. Indiana University Foundation, 1998, pp. 104–107; 119–135. Reprinted with the permission of Vicky Martin.

Another tool for identifying prospects is the demographic screening service. Although screening is not new, such services have become more sophisticated with the use of computer-based methods. According to Barth (1998), screening companies often use a combination of tools to provide data. One such tool is geodemographic screening, or matching your constituents against the characteristics of their neighborhoods and against models of consumer behavior in order to rate their probable interests, lifestyles, and philanthropic giving trends. Among the companies that provide geodemographic screening are Grenzebach Glier; Marts & Lundy; and Econometrics. Another tool is asset screening, which compares publicly reported stock holdings and property ownership to the names in your database. Companies that provide this sort of data include Thomson Financial Wealth Indentification (formerly CDA/Investnet); Prospect Information Network (PIN); and Major Gifts Identification/Consulting (MaGIC), owned by Alexander Haas Martin and Partners. Lifestyle clustering assigns households to socioeconomic categories. Companies that fall into this category include Experian and Claritas. Regardless of the type of demographic service used, the data they provide should enhance, not replace, your own. Because these kinds of screening often increase the workloads of research staff by asking them to validate or negate the ratings for particular prospects, it is a good idea, before contracting with a screening vendor, to ask some questions: What would be the purpose of our using this service? What do we want to achieve? How will the results be processed? How much data can we process internally?

Once research is completed, the development team—fundraisers, researchers, and others—should review the results to determine whether all the needed information is there and whether the prospect belongs in the prospect pool. Prospects who do not belong should be deleted from the list early in the review process, and their names should be given to the annual giving staff. The next step is an in-house financial rating of the prospects. (A similar system used to obtain peer prospect ratings is described in Chapter Eleven. The rating systems complement each other.) The in-house rating includes prospects' *potential* to give (what they would give if the institution were their number one philanthropic cause and they wanted to make the biggest gifts of their lives) and a *probable* gift size (the gifts that they could pledge over the next eighteen months, without much solicitation, and that would be payable over the next three to five years). For an individual, figure the potential gift as 3 to 5 percent of total assets (excluding personal real estate and life insurance). To determine the probable gift, look at the prospect's giving history (including the largest previous gift), other obligations, financial health, types of investments and rates of return, family obligations (parents, children), attitude toward giving, ties (if any) to the institution, and conspicuous consumption (the visible signs of wealth—private schools, estates, vacation homes, and so forth).

Some factors to determine realistic expectations for research staff include

- Size of development program
- Number of researchers
- Other research staff members (support staff, hourly employees, and others)
- Additional research staff responsibilities

Once the potential and probable gift sizes have been determined, it is time to evolve a strategy. Look at the nature of the prospect's asset base. Is it liquid? Is it in securities? Define how the institution wants the prospect to give. Are there tax considerations? What are the prospect's possible interests in the institution, and how are those interests tied in to its priorities? Who is the best person to make the first contact, and who is the best to make the solicitation? Determine the next move: whether to get more information, visit the prospect, invite the prospect to attend some function, and so on.

Many times when specific projects need funding, certain key words can be searched using various CD-ROM and book resources. These key words (see Resource 18, "Nonprofit Key Word Search") rarely change and are matched with corporations and foundations that would appear to have an interest in the project in which you are seeking funding.

One of the best places to start as a beginner in research is to join the Association of Professional Researchers for Advancement (APRA). APRA has a mentoring program that pairs researchers new to the field with those who have a great deal of experience and knowledge. An increasing amount of information can now be found via the Internet, and APRA members can share the most helpful sites, as well as helpful tips for more effective on-line searching. Also, the Fund Raising School of the Indiana University Center on Philanthropy offers many classes and opportunities for learning more about the field of development in general.

Challenges in Research

Researchers face a number of challenges in their work. There is a constant need for more and better in-depth financial information on a prospect, which is a time-consuming and difficult task. Determining the personal interests of a prospect is difficult without the assistance of and information from the development staff, who knows the prospect or has information provided by the prospect personally. Another challenge is the ability to stay abreast of all the technological advances. Because research is ongoing and cumulative, it is important for researchers to be kept informed on the cultivation and solicitation progress of a prospect.

Researchers would like development staffers to provide answers to the following questions:

- Is the information current and up to date?
- Are there additional financial worth indicators or assessments?
- How does the prospect use his or her wealth?
- Who might be able to establish a relationship with this prospect?
- What is this person's giving capacity, based on the known liquidity of assets and other information?
- What causes does the prospect care most about?
- Are there particular projects of interest to this prospect?

Development staff need to be aware that researchers cannot produce profiles at the drop of a hat. Be sure to include researchers as part of the comprehensive development team—do not assume that they would prefer to stay in the stacks with books and computers. As with all members of the team, thanks should be expressed frequently and sincerely. If a staff member is visiting a prospect or donor, it is beneficial for researchers to be notified well in advance in order to prepare properly. Finally, communicate, communicate, communicate.

Researchers should not assume that the development staff understands and appreciates the steps involved in the research process. The importance of the work may need to be marketed to the entire development team. Researchers should view the development staff not as users but as customers and strive to be customer-driven in their daily work. What development staff meetings researchers attend might tell how they are perceived in the overall fundraising picture and indicate how hard they might need to "market" their services.

Finally, every research shop should develop an in-house code of ethics. Integrity, sensitivity, and confidentiality should be the driving force behind every development staff member's work (see Exhibit 10.3).

Rating Prospects

Once effective research has been done and prospects have been identified, the next step is to evaluate the prospects. Prospect rating is often done by staff members, but it must also be done by volunteers to validate the staff effort. The purpose of external prospect rating is to determine an individual's *potential to give* (see Table 11.1 in Chapter Eleven) The evaluator should not be concerned with what the individual *may* give or even with whether the person *will* give; further research subsequent to the evaluation, as well as future cultivation and solicitation activities, will address those questions.

EXHIBIT 10.3. APRA STATEMENT OF ETHICS.

Association of Professional Researchers for Advancement (APRA) members shall support and further the individual's fundamental right to privacy and protect the confidential information of their institutions. APRA members are committed to the ethical collection and use of information. Members shall follow all applicable federal, state, and local laws, as well as institutional policies, governing the collection, use, maintenance, and dissemination of information in the pursuit of the missions of their institutions. APRA members shall respect all people and organizations.

Code of Ethics

Prospect researchers must balance the needs of their institutions to collect, analyze, record, maintain, use, and disseminate information with an individual's right to privacy. This balance is not always easy to maintain. The following ethical principles apply, and practice is built on these principles:

I. Fundamental Principles
  A. Confidentiality
     Confidential information about constituents (donors and non-donors), as well as confidential information of the institutions in oral form or on electronic, magnetic, or print media are protected so that the relationship of trust between the constituent and the institution is upheld.
  B. Accuracy
     Prospect researchers shall record all data accurately. Such information shall include attribution. Analysis and products of data analysis should be without personal prejudices or biases.
  C. Relevance
     Prospect researchers shall seek and record only information that is relevant and appropriate to the fund-raising effort of the institutions that employ them.
  D. Accountability
     Prospect researchers shall accept responsibility for their actions and shall be accountable to the profession of development, to their respective institutions, and to the constituents who place their trust in prospect researchers and their institutions.
  E. Honesty
     Prospect researchers shall be truthful with regard to their identity and purpose and the identity of their institution during the course of their work.
II. Suggested Practice
  A. Collection
     1. The collection of information shall be done lawfully, respecting applicable laws and institutional policies.
     2. Information sought and recorded includes all data that can be verified and attributed, as well as constituent information that is self-reported (via correspondence, surveys, questionnaires, etc.).
     3. When requesting information in person or by telephone, it is recommended in most cases that neither individual nor institutional identity shall be concealed. Written requests for public information shall be made on institutional stationery clearly identifying the inquirer.
     4. Whenever possible, payments for public records shall be made through the institution.

EXHIBIT 10.3. APRA STATEMENT OF ETHICS, Cont'd.

5. Prospect researchers shall apply the same standards for electronic information that they currently use in evaluating and verifying print media. The researcher shall ascertain whether or not the information comes from a reliable source and that the information collected meets the standards set forth in the APRA Statement of Ethics.

B. Recording and Maintenance

1. Researchers shall state information in an objective and factual manner; note attribution and date of collection; and clearly identify analysis.
2. Constituent information on paper, electronic, magnetic or other media shall be stored securely to prevent access by unauthorized persons.
3. Special protection shall be afforded all giving records pertaining to anonymous donors.
4. Electronic or pager documents pertaining to constituents shall be irreversibly disposed of when no longer needed (by following institutional standards for document disposal).

C. Use and Distribution

1. Researchers shall adhere to all applicable laws, as well as to institutional policies, regarding the use and distribution of confidential constituent information.
2. Constituent information is the property of the institution for which it was collected and shall not be given to persons other than those who are involved with the cultivation or solicitation effort or those who need that information in the performance of their duties for that institution.
3. Constituent information for one institution shall not be taken to another institution.
4. Research documents containing constituent information that is to be used outside research offices shall be clearly marked "confidential."
5. Vendors, consultants, and other external entities shall understand and agree to comply with the institution's confidentiality policies before gaining access to institutional data.
6. Only publicly available information shall be shared with colleagues at other institutions as a professional courtesy.

III. Recommendations

1. Prospect researchers shall urge their institutions to develop written policies based upon applicable laws and these policies should define what information shall be gathered, recorded and maintained, and to whom and under what conditions the information can be released.
2. Prospect researchers shall urge the development of written policies at their institutions defining who may authorize access to prospect files and under what conditions. These policies should follow the guidelines outlined in the CASE Donor Bill of Rights, the NSFRE Code of Ethical Principles, and the Association for Healthcare Philanthropy Statement of Professional Standards and Conduct.
3. Prospect researchers shall strongly urge their development colleagues to abide by this Code of Ethics and Fundamental Principles.

Source: Association of Professional Researchers for Advancement (APRA), Sept. 30, 1998, http://www.aprahome.org/apra_statement_of_ethics.htm. Printed with permission from APRA.

During any rating session conducted by or with volunteer evaluators, the sole criterion should be what a donor *can* do, given his or her personal circumstances. Staff members should not participate in this evaluation other than to explain the purpose of the session, keep the session moving, and clarify and answer questions about form and procedure. Four rating-session procedures are commonly used:

1. In *group discussion*, evaluators engage in roundtable discussion until they agree on a rating. A group leader should conduct this session. A professional staff member should be present to record observations but should not make any comments that could influence the ratings. This is the best method of evaluation, but its success depends on the group leader's ability to initiate discussion and on the group's willingness to participate openly and forthrightly, as well as on the evaluators' ability to make informed ratings.

2. In *group/individual ratings*, each member of the group is given a rating book and works individually, without discussion, to rate the prospects and offer appropriate written comments. A professional staff member collects the evaluations at the end of the rating session and tabulates the information after the meeting. The major disadvantage here is lack of exchange of ideas or information within the group. The advantage is that the confidentiality of this method may lead the evaluators to provide higher evaluations as well as more pointed and more useful comments. The success of this kind of session often depends on getting someone who is well known and well connected to serve as host or hostess.

3. In the *individual/one-to-one* approach, a professional staff member meets individually with volunteer evaluators and verbally goes through the prospect list, recording pertinent comments on the evaluation form. The advantage of this process is that the evaluator can be completely assured of confidentiality: no one else will hear the comments or know the evaluator's personal feelings about the prospect. The disadvantage is that the validity of the evaluation is limited to the extent of the evaluator's knowledge: there are no second or third opinions. Moreover, the evaluator may not know a number of the prospects well enough to rate them, and so it will be necessary to hold additional rating sessions with other evaluators.

4. In the *individual/solitary* approach, evaluators are given a list of prospects and rating instructions and are left on their own. The evaluation book is either picked up or mailed back by a mutually agreed date. This procedure should be used only in special circumstances. Its advantage is that it gives the evaluator time to reflect on and consider the ratings and comments; properly used, this procedure generally leads to thoughtful, thorough evaluations. Its disadvantage is that individuals often put off doing the evaluations and thereby stall the process.

No matter which procedure is used, the evaluations should be done by knowledgeable individuals. Secondhand and hearsay information is of little or no value; speculation is just that. The best evaluators tend to be bankers, lawyers, investment counselors, financial planners, insurance executives, the socially prominent, and individuals actively involved in organized philanthropy in communities with organized efforts. Evaluation of individual prospects should continue until an adequate database is established. For each prospect, many institutions acquire at least three valuations, preferably all within a fairly narrow range (say, $10,000, $12,000, and $15,000), before assuming that the prospect's rating has been validated. This entire process must be conducted in a way that safeguards confidentiality. Many times raters find that evaluating certain individuals may present a potential or real conflict of interest. In any such case, the rater must ask to be excused from that particular rating.

Estimating an Individual's Giving Potential

When giving potential is being considered, any information known to the organization about an individual's financial circumstances should play a part. Factors to be considered in assessing potential include accumulated or inherited wealth, stocks and bonds, real and personal property, full or part ownership in business enterprises, access to family or other corporations, foundations or trusts, and annual income level.

There are no absolute rules to suggest how much an individual may be capable of giving on the basis of accumulated assets and income, but a useful framework for making decisions is shown in Table 10.1. These guidelines are suggestions and should be used only as a starting point to help focus institutional thinking about an individual's potential to make charitable gifts. Remember, the institution is rating *potential* to give, not inclination to do so; measurements of inclination tend to be less precise and more subjective. Factors to be considered include the prospect's level of interest as well as number of years of giving to the organization, involvement with the organization, and cumulative previous giving.

These evaluation sessions have a dual goal:

- To uncover fresh information about important prospects (first priority) and about all other prospects (second priority)
- To promote the cultivation and involvement of the volunteer evaluators who participate in the process

Other benefits may also accrue. For example, these sessions are often a valuable tool for staff training. They are a way of identifying suitable solicitors, they can raise the sights of volunteers who eventually will become donors, and they provide an opportunity to educate participants about the campaign.

TABLE 10.1. GIFT-GIVING POTENTIAL.

Income Level	Assets Accumulated	Gift Rating
$2,500,000 or more	$250,000,000 or more	$60,000,000 or higher
2,500,000 or more	150,000,000–250,000,000	40,000,000–60,000,000
2,500,000 or more	100,000,000–150,000,000	25,000,000–40,000,000
2,500,000 or more	50,000,000–100,000,000	10,000,000–25,000,000
2,500,000 or more	25,000,000–50,000,000	5,000,000–10,000,000
2,500,000 or less	20,000,000–25,000,000	2,500,000–5,000,000
2,000,000 or less	10,000,000–20,000,000	1,000,000–2,500,000
1,000,000 or less	7,500,000–10,000,000	500,000–1,000,000
500,000–1,000,000	5,000,000–7,500,000	250,000–500,000
100,000–500,000	2,500,000–5,000,000	100,000–250,000
100,000–250,000	1,000,000–2,500,000	50,000–100,000
less than 100,000	less than 1,000,000	10,000–25,000

Keeping Evaluation Sessions Manageable

It is extremely important to keep evaluation sessions manageable from the standpoint of the volunteers. It can be counterproductive if too many prospects are expected to be evaluated in one sitting. No evaluation session should be scheduled to last more than ninety minutes. How many prospects can be rated in this time? The answer depends on the rating method being used, the level of the prospects being evaluated, and the ability of the evaluators. Some evaluators, working alone, can rate as many as 500 prospects in one session, whereas a group discussion may cover only 100 to 150 prospects. If evaluators are asked to rate too many prospects, or if the session is too long, the level of concentration will drop off toward the end. Therefore, it is generally recommended that all prospect lists be kept as short as possible.

Storing the Information

Information from the rating sessions should be retained by the organization and stored in a secure place. This confidential file should include the following information:

- The name of each prospect who has been rated
- The individual who rated the prospect
- The level at which the prospect was rated
- Whether the rater can help in the cultivation and solicitation process (with more information or in other ways)
- Other comments made by the rater

The ratings are then entered into the prospects' records and into the system.

Because the rating sessions are confidential, raters' names and comments are not revealed except on a need-to-know basis with the specific development officers who are working most closely with the prospects. The research department can then take the top-rated prospects and either start conducting additional research or forward their names to their assigned development officers for validation of the ratings. Discussions and ratings that involve real or potential conflicts of interest, that strain personal discreteness or discernment, or that raise individual ethical concerns should be assiduously avoided at every point in this process. No one should be asked to do anything that creates an uneasy feeling.

CHAPTER ELEVEN

CULTIVATING AND SOLICITING MAJOR GIFT PROSPECTS

Once prospects have been identified, researched, and evaluated, the organization must begin to cultivate the most promising among them. Cultivation is a continuous process. It often takes several steps and anywhere from a few months to several years. Campaign directors indicate that it generally takes twenty-four to thirty months to successfully cultivate and negotiate major gifts.

Guidance System for Soliciting Major Donors

Bringing in major gifts is a matter of hard work, imagination, and good taste. Major gifts occasionally come from unexpected sources, but usually many cultivation contacts by staff or volunteers are necessary to bring prospects to the point of making major gifts. Therefore, the pursuit of the extraordinary gift should be a well-planned, properly funded, adequately staffed part of any fundraising effort.

Prospect management is a systematic approach to identifying and tracking major gift prospects. Prospect management systems, whether they use large and complex databases, straightforward word processing, or manual systems, both rely on and encourage careful planning and follow-through. By recording vital information on major gift candidates and donors, an institution may know at any given time who its best prospects are and where it stands in relation to them.

According to Baxter (1987):

The concept of prospect management is a relatively recent trend in development, made possible by the widespread use of technology in fundraising. Data-processing technology, which has revolutionized gift processing, acknowledgment, and record keeping, will now play an important role in shaping development activities on the front end—long before solicitation occurs.

Prospect management enables an institution to focus attention on the individuals and organizations that hold the most promise for major gifts. These top-tier prospects are generally a small percentage of an institution's database, but they account for the greatest proportion of gifts. Whether the threshold for a major gift at an institution is $500 or $50,000, the prospects with the potential to give that or a greater amount are candidates for prospect management.

All institutions with sound fundraising programs—no matter what their level of automation—practice some sort of prospect management with their major contributors and prospects. However, computer applications in prospect management allow an institution to record and track a greater level of detail on major prospects than is possible in any manual system, and they are safer than relying on the information that staff and volunteers carry around in their heads.

A well-designed and -maintained prospect management system can improve major gift fundraising and help an organization improve the effectiveness of its development program. It can provide detail on a single prospect, select all prospects with a common trait, or give an overall view of a campaign's progress. The objectives of most tracking systems are as follows:

- To manage effectively cultivation and solicitation processes that are highly individualized
- To identify and quantify measures of progress in the cultivation and solicitation process
- To maintain momentum over long periods of time
- To provide information that will educate, motivate, and reward volunteers and staff involved in the major gifts effort
- To focus attention on top prospects
- To facilitate regular reporting to volunteers and staff
- To develop a written history of prospect cultivation that will provide an institutional memory of communications with major supporters.

There are a number of tracking systems available today, ranging from manual types to those using word processing or spreadsheets through very sophisticated systems using state-of-the-art computer hardware and software. The criteria for selecting a tracking system include size of major prospect pool, size of development staff, complexity of fundraising program, existing computer capability, and budget. Systems developed for prospect management need not be complex, but they should accommodate all of the data needed for identifying, assigning, and tracking major prospects.

When planning for a prospect management system, an institution should consider its information needs, the size of its file, and its hardware and software. If the system is already in place in the office—both computer (hardware) and programs (software)—this will have an effect on the data and number of records that can be tracked. Ideally, the first two considerations—needs and size—should determine the kind of equipment selected. A number of systems are on the market that have been developed expressly for prospect management. Gifted Memory is an example of a stand-alone system. Most development software vendors also have prospect management modules. If one of these meets an institution's specifications for data, file size, and system cost, it will save developing a system from scratch.

It may also be possible to use an existing system for prospect management and tracking. If an institution's system is flexible, a means of flagging major prospects and the addition of a few fields may be all that is needed. However, it is not always feasible for institutions with very large master databases to add the prospect management feature because it focuses on such a small percentage of the file. Since it is a system tailored to an institution, the most important consideration is to provide the information that is essential to its development program. This will vary from institution to institution and may mean simply an alphabetical list of major prospects and a few details about them, something that can be managed easily on a word-processing system. If, however, it is important to be able to select prospects by geographical region, staff or volunteer assignment, rating, gift target, or a combination of elements, a more complex system will be required.

In setting up a system, an institution should plan for the kinds of routine reports needed as well as for the data it will need to call up at any given moment. Plan for growth, and if possible, select a system that is flexible enough to allow for modifications and newly identified information needs. Include all important data fields, but do not clutter the system with unnecessary data. Remember, the more fields in the system, the more maintenance required. An elaborate system that has outdated information or empty data fields is almost worse than no system at all.

To ensure that the prospect management system is a useful tool, Baxter (1987) emphasizes that information must constantly be relayed to the person or department responsible for data entry and system maintenance. This means documenting all contact between the institution and prospects and forwarding the information to the system, submitting any additions or deletions, and keeping the system manager apprised of changes in a prospect's status. Regular reports from the system can identify any information gaps or highlight errors.

Data Elements

Baxter (1987) suggests the following list of possible data elements as a guide in setting up a prospect management system. These are suggestions rather than hard-and-fast requirements because each institution has unique characteristics that influence system design.

Data Element	*Comments*
Identification	If possible, should be consistent with master file ID number.
Name	Prefix (title), last, first, middle, suffix.
Address, phone	Can allow for home, business, second home, and so on, but must keep in sync with master file.
Title	Business or professional position.
Salutation	Needed where prospect management system has word-processing capabilities.
Geographic region	Useful for institutions with constituents spread out over a large area, where location determines staff assignment, and for planning cultivation and solicitation trips and visits.
Source	Indicates type of prospect (alumnus, trustee, parent, corporation, foundation, and so on).
Wealth code	For those institutions whose lists have been screened by an outside vendor.
Class and degree	For educational institutions.
Gift rating	Prospect's capacity to give: usually a range of figures.
Interest rating	Prospect's involvement with the institution (readiness for solicitation).
Status	Where prospect is in solicitation cycle (cultivation, solicitation, stewardship, and so on).
Giving areas	Project, campaign, or type of gift the prospect is targeted for or given clearance for (can be more than one).

Staff	Staff member assigned to manage the prospect.
Volunteer	Nonstaff volunteer assigned to the prospect.
Moves	Contact between institution and prospect, generally a date and brief description of the contact. Systems can be designed to accommodate numerous entries, to record last contact and next move, or to have comment fields that summarize past activity and future plans.
Solicitation	Request date, amount, purpose, solicitor (if other than volunteer); response date, amount, purpose.
Connections	Other ties to institution: spouse, family, classmates, business associates, and so on.
Identifiers	Institutional codes that identify special populations (sometimes called list or select codes).
Tickler	Date for staff or volunteer to conduct follow-up.
Comments	Free-form text to flag special circumstances or provide additional information.

Whatever the choice of data elements and whatever the system's configuration, fields should be set up to allow for swift and easy information searches.

Five Subsystems

The prospect management system is an integral part of a comprehensive approach to pursuing the extraordinary gift. It should be designed to ensure that an institution's best prospects are identified, cultivated, and solicited according to a master plan and that all activities are monitored. Used conscientiously, it can measurably help those who have responsibility for the success of major campaigns. Five subsystems are usually found in a prospect management system for major donors: a rating system, a priority system, an approach system, an accountability system, and a report system.

Rating System

Step one in a program to obtain extraordinary gifts is identifying priority prospects. This system places a great deal of importance on the research function. Research and rating go hand in hand, and a solid records and research system is the foundation of any fundraising program. If not already in place, a research capability that will yield prospect ratings must be developed. The end result of a rating process should be not one but two rating codes: the prospect's giving capacity and the prospect's interest in the organization. A prospect's giving capacity is a collective "best judgment," after a review of all the pertinent rating and file information, of how much the prospect could contribute to the organization over three or five years if so inclined. The interest rating is a collective judgment of the prospect's interest in and concern for the organization. This rating is based on personal information, the prospect's giving record, and file information on hand. Table 11.1 shows the numerical rating codes that might be used in a typical system.

Priority System

By adding the two numerical ratings (capacity and interest), an institution can determine each prospect's priority rating. The higher the rating, the higher the prospect's priority. The higher the prospect's priority, the more cultivation "moves"—structured contacts designed to bring a prospect closer to making a major gift—an institution will want to make on the prospect in a given period, usually a calendar year.

As a guide to determining how much cultivation a prospect gets, it is recommended that the institution use a "cultivation quota"—the sum of the two numerical ratings, multiplied by 2. This figure represents the minimum number of

TABLE 11.1. PROSPECT RATING CODES.

Giving Capacity Code	Estimated Giving Capacity	Interest Code	Description
1	$2,500–5,000	1	Not involved, no record of interest
2	5,000–10,000		
3	10,000–25,000	2	Minimal interest, occasional donor, attends meetings infrequently, and so on
4	25,000–50,000	3	Moderately active or formerly very active
5	50,000–100,000	4	Very active, major donor, club member, committee person
6	100,000–250,000	5	Member of governing board, other boards, or executive groups
7	250,000–500,000		
8	500,000–1,000,000		
9	1,000,000 or more		

cultivation moves an institution should hope to make on a prospect each year. For example, if one prospect is rated 3 + 1 (capacity rating of 3, interest rating of 1) and another is rated 1 + 3 (capacity rating of 1, interest rating of 3), both would have cultivation quotas of 8. At the moment, the first is a rather unlikely prospect for a $10,000 gift; the other one is a fairly likely prospect for a $2,500 gift. Their cultivation quotas tell the organization to plan for eight cultivation moves on each of these prospects in a year. But the institution may have to decide which prospect will get its attention first: with the first prospect, a longer cultivation period may result in a larger gift; with the second, a smaller gift can be more readily realized.

Cultivation quotas are flexible guidelines. Staff and volunteers should have the authority to make more or fewer than the recommended number of contacts, as circumstances may dictate. Another important point is that ratings—and therefore cultivation quotas—can change during the year. To return to the previous example, in the opinion of the institution the person rated 3 + 1 has a gift-giving potential of $10,000 to $25,000 but has not demonstrated much past interest in the organization. Nevertheless, a staff member or volunteer who calls on the prospect discovers that the prospect has become much more interested. This discovery changes the prospect's interest rating to 3, and this change in turn increases the cultivation quota to 12. Therefore, four additional contact points will be called for over a year.

It must be clearly understood that ordinarily, the campaign's top leaders should be assigned to cultivate and solicit those with both the greatest capacity to give and the greatest interest. It is equally important that the entire campaign stay focused throughout on the best donor prospects. Little time should be given to prospects rated 1 + 1, but what about prospects rated 9 + 1 or 8 + 2? Should time be spent on them? Yes—but it must be a measured amount of time, and the effort should be disciplined. It usually takes a series of steps to move a prospect from the point of having little or no interest to the point of serving on the institution's governing board. This kind of cultivation is not accomplished in one leap. So even though great ability to give exists, the proclivity to give needs to be developed, and that often takes more time than is available in a limited-term, movement-intensive campaign. Leave some time for the long shots, and give some effort to their cultivation, but reserve the bulk of the effort for prospects with major gift potential who are already more involved.

Accountability System

Each major gift prospect should be assigned to a member of the staff whose duty it is to see that a personalized campaign is waged to get the best gift possible. To carry out this responsibility, a strategy needs to be developed for each prospect. A good strategy plan (see Exhibit 11.1) will contain a long-term goal to be achieved with the prospect, including specific steps to be taken leading to major gift solicitation, and an expected solicitation date. Each staff member becomes an account executive and acts as a catalyst, providing the initiative and the strategy. The institution should attempt to assign most prospects to one or more volunteers for cultivation and solicitation, and it should strive to give its volunteers the feeling that they are responsible for their prospects. Every two to four weeks, staff should report on gift prospect assignments. The reports should list all prospects (individuals, foundations, and corporations) for whom the staff person is responsible, the volunteer or volunteers assisting with each prospect, the number of cultivation or solicitation contacts that the campaign's master plan indicates should be made with each prospect during the year, and the number of contacts made to date. By reviewing these reports, staff members will readily see which prospects need attention and can plan accordingly.

EXHIBIT 11.1. INDIVIDUAL STRATEGY PLAN FORM.

Submitted by:_____   Date submitted: _____

Prospect name: _____   Capacity to give: _____

ID number: _____   Primary manager: _____

Title: _____   Co-managers: _____

Business: _____   _____

Address: _____   Strategy type: *(check one)*
          _____   ___ Cultivation
          _____   ___ Solicitation
                                                              ___ Stewardship

Telephone: _____   Volunteer: _____

                                             Prospect for: *(unit/project)*

INDIVIDUAL PLAN

Expected solicitation date: _____

Summary of analysis and objectives:
(12- to 24-month summary of actions planned and considered)

Approach System

Prospect contacts may consist of phone calls, letters, and personal visits by staff, by the chief executive officer, or by volunteers; the prospect's attending institutional functions and participating in leadership retreats; prospect involvement in key issues and programs; mailings to the prospect; firsthand briefings and information on important events; and recognition events. In most systems, contacts are weighted according to significance, importance, and impact. A typical weighted system looks like this:

Cultivation Contact	*Contact Points*
Letter from a staff member	1
Phone call from a staff member	2
Letter from a volunteer	2
Invitation to a major event	3
Phone call from a volunteer	3
Phone call from the chief executive officer	3
Visit by a staff member	4
Letter from the chief executive officer	4
Attendance at an institutional activity (off-site)	4
Visit by a volunteer	5
Attendance at an institutional event (on-site)	5
Firsthand information about important events	6
Meeting with the chief executive officer	7
Personal recognition	7
Leadership retreat	7

Report System

Follow-through is absolutely essential in making contacts with major donor prospects. There is no substitute for persistence and patience. A useful management technique is to require staff members to identify their top ten prospects. During regular staff meetings, each staff member assigned to these prospects should report on what is being done to move them closer to making major gifts, on who has the initiative, and on what is the next step. Then at the next staff meeting, each staff member should report any progress or difficulty in carrying out cultivation plans and should discuss the next sequence of steps to be taken. A call report should also be filed after every phone call or visit. A good call report includes the following elements (see Exhibit 11.2):

- *General:* A clear, concise, meaningful summary—something that tells the reader at a glance if the call is relevant to a specific fundraising activity.
- *Details:* Date of contact, name of the development officer who made the contact, identifying information on the prospect (whatever makes the prospect identifiable within the users' information keeping system), and distribution—who needs this information?

EXHIBIT 11.2. PROSPECT CALL REPORT FORM.

This is a confidential *record.*

Prospect name: _____   Contact date: _____

ID number:_____   Degrees (years obtained): _____

Title: _____   Cross-reference:_____

Contacted at: ____ Home ____ Business   Volunteer names and IDs:

Address: _____   _____

_____   _____

_____   Reported by: _____

Phone number: _____   Type of contact: *(check one)*

___Visit ___ Phone ___

___Other: *(specify)*

Purpose of contact: *(check one)* ___ Cultivation ___ Solicitation ___ Evaluation ___ Stewardship ___ Feasibility study ___ Volunteer recruitment ___ Volunteer follow-up ___ Committee meeting

SUMMARY OF CONTACT_____

DETAILS OF CONTACT _____

_____

Reminders and dates:

Next action:

Managing the Process

With its five subsystems, the guidance system for soliciting major donors is a control mechanism that ensures big gift prospects are rated, given priorities, assigned to staff members and volunteers, cultivated and solicited according to a master plan, and reported on. The system should be designed to help get results, not to stimulate scoring points for that sole purpose. It should encourage well-thought-out, appropriate strategic moves that the institution feels will bring its prospects closer to making major gifts. No one knows for sure how many contacts it will take to bring a prospect to the point of making a gift; the institution has to use something, such as cultivation quotas, as a guide. It is appropriate to rely on this guidance system as a tool for bringing human factors into play because human factors are, after all, the most important elements in getting the prospect ready to give.

Prospect tracking and management help an organization monitor its involvement with major prospects. Once someone is identified as a prospect, it is imperative that the institution involve that person in its life. Involvement precedes and often begets investment, and investment is the end game in the capital campaign.

In small to medium-sized organizations, it is possible, and where it is possible it is preferable, for the staff to meet, often with volunteers present, to review the status of prospects and their ongoing management. In larger, more complex organizations, it is a necessity to cover this process with an umbrella prospect management program or system.

Soliciting Major Gifts

Securing major gifts is both the natural and the hoped-for result of the cultivation process. Cultivation begins when the prospective donor first hears about a particular institution. It reaches its highest point when the donor asks, "How much will it cost?" Because tangible results are not usually obtained in a few weeks or months, cultivation demands a sensitive balance of patience and persistence.

Philanthropy is the act of expressing love for others, so major gifts are much more than money contributed to meet an institution's needs. They represent a personal investment, based on a deeply felt commitment. Solicitation is the delicate presentation of an opportunity to invest material assets in a way that brings mostly intangible rewards and a very real sense of fulfillment. Solicitation is not begging; it is a high form of seeking investments.

One advantage of the capital campaign is that it necessitates asking for major gifts within a definite time frame. An institution can occasionally jump immediately from identifying a project to asking for an investment, but this approach is not often successful. Nevertheless, more gifts have probably been lost through waiting for the perfect time than through asking too soon. *It is better to act, even imperfectly, than to wait forever for the perfect time.* Some factors to consider in timing are length of cultivation, date of the prospect's last major gift, the person's age and health, and the urgency of the project for which funds are sought.

Preparing to Make the Major Gift Call

Each negotiation is a campaign in itself, according to Campbell (1985). Do the necessary homework. Know the prospect—his or her needs, wants, hopes, and ambitions. Get all the help available. Find out who the prospect's family members, friends, and advisers are and which people at the institution the prospect knows and respects. Meet with those people and learn all they can tell you about the prospect. Identify at least two possible projects that correspond to the prospect's interests. Document the need for each project and the benefits that will accrue if it is funded. Prepare a presentation—flipchart, proposal, or letter—to take to the meeting with a prospect, and perhaps leave it with the prospect. Bring prospects to the institution regularly. Candidly discuss opportunities, issues, and problems. Ask for their counsel and advice. Follow up, report back, and show appreciation whenever it is possible to do so.

Select solicitors who have made major gifts themselves. Teams of solicitors, most commonly two or three people, usually work best on major gift calls. Develop a strategy for the major gift prospects, and review this strategy with these solicitors. If necessary, give them a script, and rehearse it with them until they have internalized it.

Use the phone, or see the prospect in person, and ask for time to talk about the institution's capital campaign. Confirm this appointment in writing. It may be useful to send the prospect some easy-to-read information about the institution's plans along with the confirmation letter. Select a meeting site where the prospect will be comfortable. Avoid noisy, congested sites. Reconfirm the meeting by phone beforehand.

Large gifts from individuals do sometimes result from personal conversations alone, without the aid of formal written presentations, but usually only when a donor is very closely identified and involved with the institution. Even then, a follow-up presentation in writing often helps firm up the appeal. A written statement may be anything from a letter to a highly individualized—and usually quite extensive—published document. Ordinarily, however, a typewritten proposal with a cover letter is adequate. The length of the proposal may vary from one page to as many as ten, with extensive supporting appendixes. (It is rarely necessary to exceed ten pages.) The written proposal should cover at least these four items:

- Statement of the opportunity or need
- Proposed action for meeting the need or fulfilling the opportunity
- Financial data, including information about costs, other funds available, and the amount being requested
- Summary statement of the benefits that the donor will derive from the gift

See Chapter Fifteen for further information.

Asking for large gifts should never be a hit-or-miss proposition, nor should such solicitations be made in casual conversation. It is a serious mission that requires preparation and planning before visits, an understanding of the techniques to be employed during visits, and the willingness to follow up after visits.

Making the Visit

During a visit, allow an initial period for conversation on topics of mutual interest, and then introduce the reason for the visit. Present the background that has led to the occasion of this presentation. Do not let the conversation become a monologue; allow ample opportunity for the prospective donor to participate. Ask questions. Listen carefully to everything that is said. Finally, ask for the prospect's participation, and be clear about how much the institution is hoping to receive.

Be aware of body language—dress, actions, eye contact. First impressions are important. Consider objections and criticisms as opportunities for discussion and indications of interest. Deal with them as such, but never argue with a prospect.

Take ample time in a solicitation. Arouse interest to the point where the prospect asks, "How much do you want?" Remember, people give to help people. Sell the institution's programs and concepts, not the costs. Logic, emotion, and enthusiasm are the best motivators. Tax advantages seldom play a part in major gift decisions. They are most often a secondary benefit.

Ask for the gift! Keep the sights up, and be specific about the amount. If you can, cite some other lead gifts in the major gifts range. It is not uncommon to ask for two to four times what it is thought a prospect will give, and there is no known case of a volunteer or a staff member suffering bodily harm for asking for too much. A large request, if it is within the giving ability of the prospective donor, is usually flattering.

Should the donor refuse, listen carefully to the reasons. Find out what must be done before a gift can be secured. Then leave the meeting without closing, and plan a strategy for the next visit. Gifts that are made in haste or that are made by an unconvinced donor tend to be minimal. Clearly establish the next move, including a date for a possible follow-up meeting. It is better not to leave the pledge card with the prospect, although some solicitors do this and some prospects insist on it: if the pledge card is left with the prospect, the solicitor loses a primary reason to follow up, and it is possible that the prospect will either fail to use it or make a minimal gift.

In discussing a major gift with a prospect, emphasize that the gift can be made not only as an outright gift but also in the form of securities and other property and that a gift can return a lifetime income if the donor so desires. In most capital campaigns, unless they are solely for construction purposes, bequests are generally welcomed too.

During many solicitations, the prospect will raise objections. Some objections are subliminal. For instance, some elderly donors who are alone or lonely will object to closing, not because they have an objection to the case or reservations about investing, but because they fear that after a gift decision is announced, the institution will stop giving them the attention they have received in cultivation and solicitation. Most objections are more straightforward, however: "This is a bad time for us financially. All our assets are currently illiquid" or "I do not agree with your chief executive officer's priorities."

Whatever the objection, hear it out completely. In discussing the objection with the prospect, restate it, and make sure it is understood in context. Explore ways that the objection could be overcome. Never let the objection lead to an argument, however, and do not make the objection bigger than it is. Respond to it with facts, and never make excuses. If the objection is weak, deal with it as quickly as possible and move on. It is perfectly legitimate to compromise on objections if in fact they will not be a hindrance to reaching the major goal.

Determine whether the prospect will donate if the objection can be overcome. If so, do what reasonably can be done to remove it. Always remember that objections are really questions and that the prospect's investment in the project will help overcome the objections. Keeping this fact in mind will help you convert objections into reasons for giving. If an objection cannot be overcome, move along to another prospect; do not waste time on prospects who for whatever reason are absolutely not going to give.

After the visit, write a short note of thanks for the prospect's time and interest. As appropriate, draft a further note of thanks from the chief executive officer and perhaps from the board chair. Prepare a complete summary report on the visit, giving particular attention to new information on the potential donor's special interests, background, and idiosyncrasies. Be sure to include at least the following information:

- Name of company, foundation, or individual visited, date visited, and place of meeting
- If a foundation or corporation, names and positions of people visited

- Who went on the visit
- Purpose of the visit
- Points highlighted or conveyed during the visit, and whether this was done successfully
- As much detail as possible about what happened at the meeting (what comments were made by whom, responses to those comments)
- Whether any materials were distributed during the meeting and, if so, what they were, whether there are copies in the development office's research files, and whether there is any pre- or postmeeting correspondence that others should have copies of
- What concerns (if any) were voiced by the prospect, and what positive comments were made
- Whether a request for funding or assistance was made and, if so, specific details
- Whether additional action or follow-up is needed and, if so, what types, by when, and by whom
- Whether other people should be alerted to the fact that this visit was made and, if so, who they are
- As appropriate, thoughts and recommendations on the best strategies or approaches for cultivating and soliciting the prospect

Errors to Avoid in Solicitation

The Public Management Institute (Conrad, 1978) has identified the fourteen most common major errors that are made in soliciting a major gift:

- Not asking for the gift
- Not asking for a large enough gift
- Not listening—talking too much
- Not asking questions
- Talking about the organization and its approach rather than about the benefits to its clients
- Not being flexible and not having alternatives to offer the prospect
- Not knowing enough about the prospect before the solicitation
- Forgetting to summarize before moving on
- Not having prearranged signals between solicitation team members
- Asking for the gift too soon
- Speaking rather than remaining silent after asking for the gift
- Settling on the first offer that a prospect suggests, even if it is lower than expected
- Not cultivating the donor before soliciting
- Not sending out trained solicitors

Study this list. These mistakes are all avoidable with the right preparation, approach, and presentation to the prospect.

Being asked to contribute has a powerful and positive effect on giving. In 1993, fully 84.1 percent of the households surveyed by INDEPENDENT SECTOR (1994) were asked to contribute, and 76.9 percent of those that were asked did so; by contrast, only 38.1 percent of the remaining households—those that were not asked—contributed anything, and this pattern has been observed consistently in the periodic surveys that INDEPENDENT SECTOR has conducted since 1987. Moreover, in 1993 respondents reported on how specific kinds of asking might affect their giving frequency. Being asked to give by someone the respondent knows well or being asked by clergy are the most significant factors that lead to higher giving levels; other methods of solicitation are not as effective, although some nevertheless do elicit giving. This finding strongly suggests the need to determine the type of contacts to be made, by whom, and how frequently.

Obtaining major gifts is a process—a cycle—open to everyone. Most of all, everyone must give this activity top priority in day-to-day and week-to-week efforts. Nothing must be allowed to divert attention from the greatest source of support for an institution: major donors.

Most of this discussion about major gifts has centered on individual donor prospects, and about 85 percent of the money given to all nonprofits does come from individuals rather than from foundations or corporations. But the process of identifying, cultivating, and soliciting major gift prospects can and should be used effectively for corporations and foundations too (see Chapter Fifteen). When all is said and done, the "six *rights*" of prospect research also apply to donor cultivation: securing major gifts involves finding the *right* person to ask the *right* prospect for the *right* gift in the *right* form for the *right* reason at the *right* time.

CHAPTER TWELVE

DEVELOPING AND MARKETING A PLANNED GIVING PROGRAM

Alan M. Spears

Chapters Twelve and Thirteen deal with the subject of planned giving. Increasingly, individual donors of significant means are using planned gifts to realize their dream and benefit the nonprofits they care about most. This chapter discusses the implementation and marketing of a planned giving program. The next reviews the various ways planned gifts can be made.

Even without a formalized planned giving program—and most small and medium-sized nonprofits do not have one—any nonprofit can encourage donors to make certain types of planned gifts. For example, it is very simple for an organization to suggest that donors consider including it in their will through a bequest. Nonprofits can also discuss with certain prospects the concept of a charitable remainder trust or a charitable lead trust, with the understanding that the person would need to be referred to counsel and the nonprofit would not be able to manage the trust. However, gifts to pooled income funds are not possible unless the organization has established such a fund, and charitable gift annuities may not be an option unless the organization is certified to offer them (see Chapter Thirteen).

For the nonprofit that wants to move beyond receiving an occasional planned gift to actively seeking a wide variety of planned gifts, consideration should be given to formally establishing a planned giving program. Before doing so, the nonprofit should be sure that its program meets the following prerequisites:

- The nonprofit has a positive community image and a well-established position in the community.
- There is a significant group of prospects and donors of relative affluence over age sixty.
- The nonprofit has sufficient current resources to meet its operational needs and can afford to defer the receipt of planned gifts to some point in the future.
- The board of the nonprofit is willing to support a planned giving program and to commit money and resources to fund it.

When establishing the planned giving program, the board should set policies and guidelines for the program. These policies and guidelines might include the following:

- Types of planned gifts to be sought
- Criteria for acceptance of gifts
- Procedures for evaluating the feasibility of certain assets as gifts
- Who will be authorized to accept gifts and to commit the nonprofit to planned giving arrangements

The board may want to set up an acceptance committee to review all planned gifts for which the organization would incur potential liability. In addition, if the board decides to offer gift annuities, the organization must apply for certification to do so.

Planned Giving Council

A nonprofit without its own planned giving capacity can organize a planned giving council, a group of volunteers who will agree to assist in identifying prospects and providing their specific expertise to the organization pro bono in support of its planned giving efforts. Bankers, attorneys, estate planners, investment brokers, and accountants are excellent choices. They should be leaders in the community and visible and respected in their field. They should also be individuals who are at a point in life where they are more interested in serving than in expanding their own client base. The nonprofit needs to understand and appreciate that these individuals will at times be prevented from assisting owing to real or potential conflicts of interest.

Managing a Planned Giving Program

Once a planned giving program has been established, it must be managed. One of the first steps is to develop a record-keeping system to track planned gifts. An inventory and filing system should be put in place to track bequests, annuities, charitable remainder trusts, insurance policies, gifts in kind, estates in probate, and anticipated estate distributions.

Planned gifts will not be received by the nonprofit for years to come. Therefore, it is important to have a system in place that tracks planned gifts so that regardless of staff turnover and other inevitable changes, the nonprofit will always know what gifts it can expect ultimately to receive.

Related to the record-keeping system, the nonprofit should also consider establishing a method for recognizing planned giving donors. Many organizations create a special recognition level for their planned giving donors to provide stewardship. Stewardship of planned giving donors is particularly important because of the long time span between the initial gift and its use by the nonprofit. It is also critical because your planned giving donors are your best prospects for additional planned gifts. Regular visits to the planned giving donors are essential. Donors who have a life income arrangement with the nonprofit should be given special attention to ensure that their payments are correct and on time and that tax information related to their life income gift is accurate and provided in a timely manner.

Marketing a Planned Giving Program

Experience has shown that donors are motivated to make planned gifts primarily as a result of psychological factors such as loyalty to the nonprofit, religious conviction, gratitude for services, desire to be recognized, and the desire to leave a legacy. Donors will certainly consider the financial benefits of making a planned gift, such as taxes and cash flow, in determining the type, size, and timing of their gift. However, financial benefits alone will rarely motivate a donor to make a gift. In many cases the donor will have practical considerations in making a planned gift, such as simplification of his or her life, relinquishing asset management, or maintaining control. These concerns may also carry more weight with donors than saving taxes and increasing income. When marketing planned gifts, the focus should not solely be on the numbers, for emotions drive donors to make their gifts.

An effective marketing program will show donors the advantages planned gifts present in helping them realize their philanthropic objectives. The most effective marketing will both appeal to the psychological motivations and offer financial solutions for the donors.

Planned giving marketing can be divided between the internal market and the external market. The internal market consists of the development staff, board members, volunteers, and current and retired staff. The external market will consist of current donors, new prospects, and professional advisers.

Internal Marketing

The first step in marketing planned gifts is to educate the internal constituency. Training sessions should be conducted for development staff members, regardless of their area of specialization. All members of the development staff should have a basic understanding of the methods of planned giving, the ability to suggest a gift plan, and the skill to recognize the clues and cues on when and how to involve those with planned giving expertise.

A presentation should also be conducted to the board on the benefits of planned giving. The board should be informed about the nonprofit's planned giving program and prepared for its oversight role. Board members should also be encouraged to refer individuals within their network of friends and associates in the community for whom a planned gift would be appropriate. The presentation to the board would also, ideally, result in board members' relating planned gift ideas to their own situations and prompt them to initiate discussions on their own planned gifts.

Volunteers should also be provided with basic planned giving training. Many nonprofits rely heavily on volunteers to assist in their fundraising efforts. Knowledge of planned gifts will equip the volunteers with the ability to suggest alternative giving methods to prospects they are soliciting and will stimulate further discussion of a potential gift.

External Marketing

The key to a successful external marketing program is to educate prospects and their advisers about planned giving vehicles and how these can be used to help meet the donor's needs while strategically assisting the organization at the same time. The external marketing should be focused on the prospects, current donors, and professional advisers to donors.

Current and Prospective Donors

To reach current and prospective donors, planned giving materials should appear continually over a sustained time period. Planned gifts rarely close immediately, and it is usually a culmination of consistent, repetitive marketing follow-up that will result in a donor's making a planned gift.

An essential part of the marketing effort is a "guide to charitable gift planning" brochure. This brochure will provide donors and prospects with an outline on the many different ways they can make a gift, using a variety of assets. The brochure should go into some detail about each available planned giving option, illustrate the various levels of giving, and discuss the tax benefits of planned giving. The brochure should also focus on the mission of the nonprofit and why it is worthy of donor support. This guide to giving should provide information to donors and prospects in such a way that it will invite inquiries and encourage them to contact the organization for additional information. The brochure can be mailed to donors who request information about ways to give to the organization and can be taken along by development officers and volunteers when they make personal visits.

It is recommended that the guide to giving include a response form that enables prospective donors who receive it to reply quickly and easily to the planned giving office. The response piece can be a perforated card or a card inserted into the binding of the booklet. The card should include a place for the prospect to list their name, address, telephone number, and date of birth. The response card should also provide a space for the donor to indicate the type of asset that might be used to make the gift and the value of the asset, as well as the cost basis. This will allow the planned giving office to prepare an illustration of the tax and financial benefits the donor will receive by making the planned gift. The nonprofit should furnish a business reply envelope in which the response card can be returned to preserve prospect confidentiality.

Newsletter. A newsletter is an excellent way to have regular communication with prospects and donors. The newsletter should discuss various charitable gift opportunities in the context of general estate planning and should be mailed on a regular basis, perhaps three or four times a year. Each issue can focus on a specific planned giving vehicle, such as charitable remainder trusts, charitable gift annuities, or gifts of real estate. Testimonials from donors are particularly effective in motivating prospects to consider a gift. The newsletter should be targeted to prospects and donors age sixty and up, as they are the primary market for planned gifts.

There are many vendors who specialize in assisting nonprofits with publication of a planned giving newsletter, including Stelter, Inc.; Endowment Development Services (EDS); and Pentera, Inc. If your nonprofit does not have the budget for a separate planned giving newsletter, then planned giving articles and testimonials should appear in the general development newsletter of your nonprofit.

Target Mailings. With targeted mailings, the nonprofits' constituency is segmented into groups with a common interest, and the mailing is tailored to that particular audience. An example of a targeted mailing is one sent to the prospects above the age of seventy who may be candidates for charitable gift annuities.

Advertisements. If the nonprofit does not have a natural constituency, it may be necessary to advertise in public media such as local newspapers. These ads can be used to expand the reach of the nonprofit to include individuals who may not have a natural affiliation with the organization and its mission. Respondents to ads in mass media are likely to be more interested in financial benefits than in philanthropy.

Seminars for Prospects and Donors. A seminar can be an effective and efficient way to educate prospects and donors about the benefits of planned giving. For a seminar to be successful, it should be targeted to a particular audience, personal invitations should be sent, and great care should be taken to ensure that the topic presented will appeal to the audience and the speaker will have credibility. The presentation must be done in lay language so as not to confuse or overwhelm the audience. A presentation that goes over the audience's head can sometimes produce negative results—the last thing you want to have happen.

Annual Fund Materials. Every nonprofit has some form of annual fund solicitation mailing and materials. Information can be included on the annual fund materials, which could incorporate a check-off box for the recipients to indicate if they have included the nonprofit in their will or if they would like to receive additional information on planned giving options. Similar information can be included on pledge cards.

Marketing to Professional Advisers

Professional advisers are an important part of the process of securing planned gifts. Professional advisers include attorneys, trust officers, financial planners, accountants, stock brokers, and insurance agents. Professional advisers have knowledge of their clients' net worth, tax situations, and real estate holdings. Professional advisers are able to counsel their clients regarding the need to make a charitable gift and are in a position to recommend your nonprofit as a recipient of their client's philanthropy. A successful marketing program will include a component directed at professional advisers. It is important to build relationships with professional advisers, as they will help facilitate gifts and are an excellent source of referrals.

As a start, the nonprofit should compile a list of professional advisers in your community who have demonstrated knowledge of estate, tax, or financial planning. These will be the key advisers on whom to focus the marketing efforts of the planned giving program. These advisers can be added to the mailing list to receive planned giving publications from the nonprofit.

Just as in working with prospects, personal visits to professional advisers can serve as a means of strengthening relationships. While many professional advisers are knowledgeable in their own particular fields, planned giving is an area of specialization with which they may not be familiar. Personal visits can be a way to educate them on the intricacies of planned giving.

You may also want to consider publishing a newsletter with technical information regarding estate, financial, and charitable planning. Again, there are vendors who can assist with this project, including those mentioned earlier in this chapter. This is another way to keep your nonprofit's name in their mind while providing a valuable service.

You may want to consider establishing a committee made up of the professional advisers in your community. This will give you an opportunity to have regular contact with local key professionals, and the committee can serve as a source of technical support for your planned giving program. The initial meeting can provide an opportunity to offer a review of the various planned giving vehicles and your mission, as well as to explain how charitable gift planning can be an important part of their clients' overall estate and financial planning. The advisory committee can also assist with the formulation and presentation of seminars on estate and charitable gift planning. Seminars can be developed that target other professionals and provide them with continuing education credit. Members of the advisory committee can present seminars directed toward prospects and donors in the community to educate them about planned giving. Members of the advisory committee who conduct the seminars benefit from increased visibility in the community among their peers and resulting new business referrals from the prospects and donors in attendance.

Professional advisers can be crucial to the success of the planned giving program. It is important that you build relationships with them, for they help facilitate gifts and are a valuable source of referrals.

Cultivating the Prospect and Closing the Planned Gift

Once the planned giving program has been established, planned giving techniques are clearly understood, and a comprehensive marketing effort has been undertaken; it is time to begin the cultivation of prospects with the hope of turning them into planned giving donors. To identify a planned giving prospect, you should look for the following characteristics:

• Planned giving prospects tend to be older than other development prospects. They are at a point in their lives where they have accumulated wealth and are now in a position to give a portion of it away. They are no longer in the wealth acquisition stage; they no longer need to save for a home or for children. Often their children are adults who are established in their own careers. Individuals who do not have children, surviving close relatives, or extended families are particularly promising prospects.

• Planned giving prospects tend to be wealthier individuals who are attracted by the financial and tax benefits offered by planned giving. Planned giving is also a tool for them by which they can make their most significant gift to the nonprofit.

• The surviving spouse of a couple that was connected to your nonprofit would be an excellent planned giving prospect. One compelling option is for the surviving spouse to make a planned gift to honor the memory of the deceased spouse.

• The best planned giving prospects will be those who are linked to the organization as donors, board members, or volunteers. They understand the mission of the organization and its needs and may have supported it for many years with their time, talent, and money. They will now be at a point in their lives where they are able to make a larger gift employing planned giving techniques.

Cultivation

The best way to cultivate a planned giving donor is through a face-to-face meeting. Mailings and brochures can help introduce a prospect to planned giving, but it is still the one-on-one contact that will close the gift.

Prior to the face-to-face meeting with the prospect, it is important to obtain background information to determine the person's connection to you, current financial situation, family responsibilities, and charitable objectives.

You should also examine the prospect's giving record with your nonprofit: at what level and frequency the person has made gifts in the past and how those gifts have been used by the nonprofit. A lack of a previous giving history is not, however, a disqualifying factor: organizations have been known to receive sizable gifts and bequests from virtual strangers.

At the meeting, listen to the prospect. Let the person discuss what areas or programs he or she wishes to support. Be prepared to discuss what the nonprofit needs to fulfill its mission, in case the prospect needs further direction. Specific information should be obtained at the meeting about possible assets that may be used to make the planned gift. The asset that may be used will help determine the best way to structure the gift and what planned giving vehicle may be best suited to the donor's financial needs and philanthropic goals. Important information related to the asset would be its market value, its cost basis, and how it is owned.

During the meeting, your focus should be on being a good listener. Listen to what your prospect is telling you about himself or herself, interest in your organization, and philanthropic goals. Discuss a charitable plan that will address the prospect's situation. Do not go to the meeting with the idea that you will "sell" the prospect on an annuity, bequest, or any other particular planned gift. Rather, listen to the donor's ideas and suggest how a planned gift will realize his or her personal, financial, and philanthropic objectives.

Information you gather at the initial meeting will permit you to prepare a financial illustration and proposal for the prospect to review. You can use readily available planned giving software to prepare the financial illustration, which should explain the financial benefits to the donor and the benefits to the institution. The proposal should also include a description of the project or program that will be funded by the planned gift and the amount the prospect will be asked to give. The options for funding the gift should be presented in the proposal and may include a comparison of planned giving alternatives or the combination of a planned gift with an outright gift. The proposal should be presented in a manner that is easily digested by the prospect. Wherever possible, graphics should be used to illustrate the financial and tax benefits. The proposal should be customized for the donor's particular situation and presented in an attractive manner.

There are several ways in which the proposal and accompanying financial illustration could be presented to the prospect:

- Meet with the prospect, and then at his or her direction, discuss the plan with the prospect's advisers.
- Meet with the prospect, who will then discuss the plan privately with his or her professional adviser.
- Meet with the prospect and the professional advisers at the same time.
- Forego the face-to-face meeting and send the proposal to the prospect by mail.

Care should be taken with the proposal so that it does not overwhelm the prospect with technical information. Follow up after the proposal is presented, and agree on the next steps, which may involve providing bequest language, sample gift annuity contracts, or trust agreements.

Closing the Planned Gift

Closing a planned gift is different from closing any other type of gift. Because of the many complexities involved in planned giving, the donor may take some time before making a decision regarding a gift. The development officer must respect this and be very patient while at the same time continuing with periodic follow-up to advance the decision-making process. This may involve additional meetings with the donor and his or her advisers and further revisions to financial proposals.

When the donor has decided to make a gift, the next step will be preparation of the documents necessary to transfer the asset to your organization. These documents will vary, depending on whether the donor is using securities, real estate, life insurance, personal property, or cash. Once the asset has been transferred, documents can be prepared if the gift will involve a life income vehicle. The documents will need to be prepared by outside counsel, or the donor's own attorney, if you do not have an in-house legal staff. If you do have an in-house legal staff, any documents prepared in-house must be reviewed by the donor's own counsel.

Gift Agreements

Many planned gifts will be used to establish programs or fund initiatives that will last into perpetuity. Most planned gifts will not provide funds for use by the nonprofit until after the donors have passed away. Every nonprofit should make it a priority to follow the donor's intended use for the gift. It is recommended that a gift agreement be prepared in consultation with the donor and his or her advisers, setting out the intended use of the donor's gift by the nonprofit (see Resource 19, "Gift Agreement Templates"). The donor should be advised that he or she may revise the gift agreement at any time during the donor's lifetime. Here are some guidelines for things that should be included in every gift agreement:

- Title the fund in the donor's name—for example, "Joseph R. Smith Endowment at XYZ Charity." Most donors enjoy seeing their name attached to the endowment. In some rare cases, you will have donors who choose to remain anonymous.
- Identify the parties creating the gift agreement—the donor or donors and the nonprofit.

- State how the endowment will be established: gift annuity, bequest, current gift, or some combination. Include language that allows additional gifts to be made to the fund by the donor or others.
- Include biographical information on the donor. Details of links with the organization and other achievements are helpful because they serve to memorialize the donor after the donor's death.
- Clearly state the donor's intended purpose for the use of the gift. For example, will the income be used to fund a scholarship, support a particular program, or used at the discretion of the nonprofit?
- Discuss financial administration of the fund. State whether or not principal can be invaded to make an award, or will only income be used. If there is a year in which an award is not made, will the income generated be accumulated for future awards or be reinvested to the principal?
- State any restrictions placed on the endowment. Restrictions may be geographical requirements, financial need, or a particular area of study. Donors should resist making their agreement so restrictive that the nonprofit is unable to make an award because few or no candidates meet the donor's criteria.
- Describe the selection process, if there is to be one. This may involve a selection committee composed of representatives of the nonprofit, board members, or persons selected by the donor. A selection committee representative should be referred to by title but not by name, in case circumstances change. The donor may serve as a member of the selection committee but is prohibited from acting alone in the selection of the recipient of the award.
- Include language that allows the nonprofit to find an alternative use for the fund if at some point it is unable to fulfill the original terms of the gift agreement. The donor should be informed that as time passes, the nonprofit may have to adapt its programs and mission to the changing needs of society. This is a crucial feature to include; it can avoid long legal proceedings.

Drafting the gift agreement in consultation with the donor will ensure that the donor's wishes are properly carried out by the nonprofit, and the resulting document will provide guidance to future staff members on the use of the gift.

Gift planning offers all nonprofits the opportunity to permit their donors to provide ongoing support as well as leave a legacy. Many of the planned giving vehicles will create an endowment that will support a nonprofit's mission into perpetuity. Life income vehicles can benefit your donors and ultimately your nonprofit. Bequests permit donors to make a larger gift at death than they could ever have made during their lifetime. Planned giving at some level should be an essential part of every nonprofit's development program.

CHAPTER THIRTEEN

STRUCTURING PLANNED GIFTS

Alan M. Spears

Increasingly, donors are making gifts to nonprofits in the form of planned gifts. There are many reasons why planned giving is attractive. A planned gift can be larger than a donor might have thought possible in any other form. For many donors, a planned gift is the best way, and perhaps the only way, to make a substantial gift. Planned giving techniques also permit a donor to be creative in making a gift. Because of the wide variety of assets that can be used to fund a planned gift, many more options are available.

Nonprofits will need to place greater emphasis on planned giving techniques in the years to come. Most of the country's wealth is held by individuals age sixty and older. As this population ages, the largest intergenerational transfer of wealth in the history of the United States will occur: an estimated $10 trillion is expected to pass from the Depression–World War II–Korean War generation to its baby boomer children. Over a longer timeline, Havens and Schervish (1999) project that more than $40 trillion will be transferred in the first half of the twenty-first century. Planned gifts offer an attractive way to secure current income, pass wealth on to children, and provide for charity while also receiving income and estate tax benefits (see Resource 20: "Rules Regarding Income Tax Charitable Deductions").

Planned giving, broadly speaking, consists of three primary types of gifts:

- *Outright gifts,* which allow the nonprofit to use the asset immediately. These gifts are often in the form of securities, tangible personal property, and some types of real estate.
- *Life income gifts,* whereby a donor in exchange for a present-day gift receives a stream of income for life, and upon the donor's death, the remainder value is transferred to the nonprofit.
- *Deferred Gifts,* which consist of gifts bestowed through wills and trusts that pass into the possession of the nonprofit upon the donor's death.

Outright Gifts

A variety of planned giving techniques are available to help you secure major gifts from donors. Which techniques are most appropriate for your organization and your donors will depend on your organization's resources and staff and your donors' financial and philanthropic goals.

Gifts of Tangible Personal Property

Tangible personal property is anything that can be held physically. Many different items of tangible personal property can be used to make a gift. Following are some examples:

Furniture	Artwork	Antiques
Jewelry	Clothing	Equipment
Automobiles	Aircraft	Livestock
Books	Collections (stamps, coins)	

Transferring ownership of or title to tangible personal property from the donor to the nonprofit requires that the property be physically transferred to the nonprofit by the donor and that the nonprofit sign a formal acceptance for the property. Usually a deed of gift is drafted to accomplish the transfer. The deed of gift is a document that identifies the property to be transferred and includes a statement of donative intent signed by the donor (see Exhibit 13.1). Certain types of tangible personal property have formal requirements for transferring title. For example, automobiles must be transferred at the appropriate state agency.

Tax Deductions. One of the benefits of making a gift of tangible personal property is the charitable income tax deduction the donor receives. The amount of the deduction for gifts of tangible personal property depends on the use of the property

EXHIBIT 13.1. DEED OF GIFT.

_____ , 200__

_____ , DONOR, of _____ , hereby confirms that he is the legal owner of and does hereby irrevocably and unconditionally give, grant, and convey an absolute, unconditional, and undivided interest in the items described on the attached list, identified as Exhibit A, to the XYZ Charity for the benefit of _____ , hereinafter referred to as DONEE. Title to the items and all associated rights are hereby vested in DONEE, without reservation and free and clear of all encumbrances. DONOR understands and agrees that the items may be displayed, loaned, retained, disposed of, or otherwise employed at the sole discretion of DONEE.

EXECUTED by DONOR at _____ on _____ , 200__.

Donor _____

ACCEPTED: ATTESTED:
XYZ Charity

By: _____   By: _____
_____ , President   _____ , Corporate Secretary

by the nonprofit. If the property has a use related to the exempt purposes of the organization, the donor may claim a charitable income tax deduction equal to the fair market value of the property, limited to 30 percent of the donor's adjusted gross income, provided that the property has been held by the donor for at least a year and a day to qualify as a long-term capital asset. For the property to have a use related to the exempt purpose of the nonprofit, it must be reasonably anticipated that the receiving organization will use the property in a way related to its mission (for example, artwork given to an art museum for display in its gallery).

If, however, the use of the gift is _not related_ to the organization's mission, the deduction is limited to the donor's cost basis in the property. For an unrelated use, the donor may claim a deduction of up to 50 percent of adjusted gross income. A donor who wants to make a gift of tangible personal property for which there is no related use may prefer to sell the property and make a gift of the proceeds from the sale. The donor is responsible for any capital gains tax due on the appreciation of the property. An example of a gift that would not meet the related-use test would be the donation of an item to be sold at auction. In this instance, the charitable income tax deduction is limited to the donor's cost basis in the gift.

The Internal Revenue Service (IRS) requires that a donor obtain a qualified appraisal when the amount of a noncash gift reported as a charitable income tax deduction exceeds $5,000, unless the donated property consists of publicly traded securities, stock that is not traded publicly worth $10,000 or less, or property donated by a legally constituted C corporation. The qualified appraiser is defined as an individual who is in the business of making such appraisals. The donor is required to attach a completed appraisal summary to his or her tax return.

If the donor claims a deduction for a gift of art in excess of $20,000, the donor must attach to his or her income tax return a copy of the completed signed appraisal (not an appraisal summary) along with an 8-by-20-inch color photograph or a 4-by-5-inch color transparency of the item.

Substantiation of Gifts When a noncash gift is made to a nonprofit, the IRS requires that the gift be substantiated. Both the donor and the nonprofit must follow certain procedures for reporting noncash gifts.

IRS Form 8283 (see Exhibit 13.2) must be filed by donors who make noncash charitable contributions. The need to file this form depends on the status of the taxpayer and the size and type of gift:

- *Gifts valued at $500 or less.* If a gift from an individual donor is valued at $500 or less, the donor need not complete Form 8283. However, if the donor has made a series of gifts in a given year each of which is $500 or less but the total exceeds $500, the donor is required to complete Form 8283, Part A.
- *Gifts valued between $501 and $5,000.* Gifts in this range must be reported on Part A of IRS Form 8283. An appraisal is not necessary; however, the nonprofit should retain a copy of the completed Form 8283 for its records.
- *Gifts valued over $5,000.* If the amount claimed as a charitable income tax deduction is in excess of $5,000, the IRS requires the donor to complete Part B of Form 8283. The qualified appraiser and an authorized representative of the charity must sign the form.
- *Gifts of non–publicly traded stock.* The stock is defined as nonpublic if it is not listed on an exchange or regularly traded. If the donor makes a gift of non–publicly traded stock, Part B of Form 8283 must be completed. This is true regardless of the value of the stock. If the value of the stock exceeds $10,000, a qualified appraisal is required.

EXHIBIT 13.2. IRS FORM 8283.

Form **8283**	**Noncash Charitable Contributions**	OMB No. 1545-0908
(Rev. October 1998)	▶ **Attach to your tax return if you claimed a total deduction of over $500 for all contributed property.**	
Department of the Treasury Internal Revenue Service	▶ **See separate instructions.**	Attachment Sequence No. **55**
Name(s) shown on your income tax return		Identifying number

Note: *Figure the amount of your contribution deduction before completing this form. See your tax return instructions.*

Section A—List in this section **only** items (or groups of similar items) for which you claimed a deduction of $5,000 or less. Also, list certain publicly traded securities even if the deduction is over $5,000 (see instructions).

Part I   **Information on Donated Property**—If you need more space, attach a statement.

1	(a) Name and address of the donee organization	(b) Description of donated property
A		
B		
C		
D		
E		

Note: *If the amount you claimed as a deduction for an item is $500 or less, you do not have to complete columns (d), (e), and (f).*

	(c) Date of the contribution	(d) Date acquired by donor (mo., yr.)	(e) How acquired by donor	(f) Donor's cost or adjusted basis	(g) Fair market value	(h) Method used to determine the fair market value
A						
B						
C						
D						
E						

Part II   **Other Information**—Complete line 2 if you gave less than an entire interest in property listed in Part I. Complete line 3 if conditions were attached to a contribution listed in Part I.

2   If, during the year, you contributed less than the entire interest in the property, complete lines a–e.

a   Enter the letter from Part I that identifies the property ▶ _____. If Part II applies to more than one property, attach a separate statement.

b   Total amount claimed as a deduction for the property listed in Part I: **(1)** For this tax year   ▶ _____ .
    (2) For any prior tax years ▶ _____ .

c   Name and address of each organization to which any such contribution was made in a prior year (complete only if different from the donee organization above):
    Name of charitable organization (donee)

    Address (number, street, and room or suite no.)

    City or town, state, and ZIP code

d   For tangible property, enter the place where the property is located or kept ▶ _____

e   Name of any person, other than the donee organization, having actual possession of the property ▶ _____

3   If conditions were attached to any contribution listed in Part I, answer questions a – c and attach the required statement (see instructions).

		Yes	No
a	Is there a restriction, either temporary or permanent, on the donee's right to use or dispose of the donated property?		
b	Did you give to anyone (other than the donee organization or another organization participating with the donee organization in cooperative fundraising) the right to the income from the donated property or to the possession of the property, including the right to vote donated securities, to acquire the property by purchase or otherwise, or to designate the person having such income, possession, or right to acquire?		
c	Is there a restriction limiting the donated property for a particular use?		

For Paperwork Reduction Act Notice, see page 4 of separate instructions.   Cat. No. 62299J   Form **8283** (Rev. 10-98)

EXHIBIT 13.2. IRS FORM 8283, Cont'd.

Form 8283 (Rev. 10-98) Page **2**

Name(s) shown on your income tax return	Identifying number

Section B—Appraisal Summary—List in this section only items (or groups of similar items) for which you claimed a deduction of more than $5,000 per item or group. **Exception.** Report contributions of certain publicly traded securities only in Section A.

If you donated art, you may have to attach the complete appraisal. See the **Note** in Part I below.

Part I   Information on Donated Property—To be completed by the taxpayer and/or appraiser.

4   Check type of property:

☐ Art* (contribution of $20,000 or more)   ☐ Real Estate   ☐ Gems/Jewelry   ☐ Stamp Collections
☐ Art* (contribution of less than $20,000)   ☐ Coin Collections   ☐ Books   ☐ Other

*Art includes paintings, sculptures, watercolors, prints, drawings, ceramics, antique furniture, decorative arts, textiles, carpets, silver, rare manuscripts, historical memorabilia, and other similar objects.

Note: *If your total art contribution deduction was $20,000 or more, you must attach a complete copy of the signed appraisal. See instructions.*

5	(a) Description of donated property (if you need more space, attach a separate statement)	(b) If tangible property was donated, give a brief summary of the overall physical condition at the time of the gift	(c) Appraised fair market value
A			
B			
C			
D			

	(d) Date acquired by donor (mo., yr.)	(e) How acquired by donor	(f) Donor's cost or adjusted basis	(g) For bargain sales, enter amount received	See instructions	
					(h) Amount claimed as a deduction	(i) Average trading price of securities
A						
B						
C						
D						

Part II   Taxpayer (Donor) Statement—List each item included in Part I above that the appraisal identifies as having a value of $500 or less. See instructions.

I declare that the following item(s) included in Part I above has to the best of my knowledge and belief an appraised value of not more than $500 (per item). Enter identifying letter from Part I and describe the specific item. See instructions. ▶ _____

Signature of taxpayer (donor) ▶   Date ▶

Part III   Declaration of Appraiser

I declare that I am not the donor, the donee, a party to the transaction in which the donor acquired the property, employed by, or related to any of the foregoing persons, or married to any person who is related to any of the foregoing persons. And, if regularly used by the donor, donee, or party to the transaction, I performed the majority of my appraisals during my tax year for other persons.

Also, I declare that I hold myself out to the public as an appraiser or perform appraisals on a regular basis; and that because of my qualifications as described in the appraisal, I am qualified to make appraisals of the type of property being valued. I certify that the appraisal fees were not based on a percentage of the appraised property value. Furthermore, I understand that a false or fraudulent overstatement of the property value as described in the qualified appraisal or this appraisal summary may subject me to the penalty under section 6701(a) (aiding and abetting the understatement of tax liability). I affirm that I have not been barred from presenting evidence or testimony by the Director of Practice.

Sign Here

Signature ▶	Title ▶	Date of appraisal ▶

Business address (including room or suite no.)	Identifying number

City or town, state, and ZIP code

Part IV   Donee Acknowledgment—To be completed by the charitable organization.

This charitable organization acknowledges that it is a qualified organization under section 170(c) and that it received the donated property as described in Section B, Part I, above on ▶ _____ (Date)

Furthermore, this organization affirms that in the event it sells, exchanges, or otherwise disposes of the property described in Section B, Part I (or any portion thereof) within 2 years after the date of receipt, it will file **Form 8282**, Donee Information Return, with the IRS and give the donor a copy of that form. This acknowledgment does not represent agreement with the claimed fair market value.

Does the organization intend to use the property for an unrelated use? . . . . ▶ ☐ Yes   ☐ No

Name of charitable organization (donee)	Employer identification number	
Address (number, street, and room or suite no.)	City or town, state, and ZIP code	
Authorized signature	Title	Date

✿

If the nonprofit sells, exchanges, or disposes of donated property having a value of $5,000 or more, other than cash or marketable securities, within two years of the date of the gift, the organization must complete and file IRS Form 8282 (see Exhibit 13.3) and send a copy to the donor. The IRS uses Form 8282 to monitor potential fraud. The donor's appraisal must be a realistic estimate of the true value of the item donated to avoid the appearance of fraud. Fraud may be suspected if the nonprofit sells the property for substantially less than the appraised value.

Gifts of Securities

Securities are among the most popular assets used to make gifts. Securities include publicly traded stocks, mutual funds, treasury notes, and closely held stock. Publicly traded stocks and mutual funds are increasingly being used to make gifts because the value of donors' stock portfolios and mutual funds have increased tremendously over time. Securities are used to make outright gifts as well as to fund life income vehicles.

Stock Transfer. The method for transferring securities to a nonprofit depends on how the securities are held by the donor. When the securities are held by the donor's stockbroker, the donor or the broker should call to inform the nonprofit that a gift of securities is about to be made. The nonprofit will need to provide the broker with its tax identification number and delivery instructions. Alternatively, the nonprofit may establish an account with the donor's broker in the nonprofit's name and transfer the stock from the donor's account to the new nonprofit account. Stock can then be sold directly from this account, with the proceeds delivered in the form of a check to the nonprofit (minus the broker's commission). The donor's broker should always be instructed not to sell the securities until they are in the nonprofit's account, or else the donor will be liable for capital gains tax on any appreciation.

Electronic transfer through the Depository Trust Company (DTC) is another way to make gifts of stock. This electronic transfer system permits securities to move from one account to another without any physical exchange of stock certificates. The nonprofit must notify its account manager to be on the alert for a transfer of securities via DTC so that the transfer may be properly credited to the nonprofit's account.

Often the donor will have physical possession of stock certificates used to make the gift. To accomplish this transfer, the donor should sign a stock power for each certificate to be transferred to the nonprofit. Stock powers can be obtained

EXHIBIT 13.3. IRS FORM 8282.

Form **8282**	**Donee Information Return**	OMB No. 1545-0908
(Rev. September 1998) Department of the Treasury Internal Revenue Service	(Sale, Exchange, or Other Disposition of Donated Property) ▶ See instructions on back.	**Give a Copy to Donor**

Please Print or Type	Name of charitable organization (donee)	Employer identification number
	Address (number, street, and room or suite no.)	
	City or town, state, and ZIP code	

Part I   Information on ORIGINAL DONOR and DONEE Receiving the Property

1a Name(s) of the original donor of the property	1b Identifying number

Note: *Complete lines 2a–2d only if you gave this property to another charitable organization (successor donee).*

2a Name of charitable organization	2b Employer identification number
2c Address (number, street, and room or suite no.)	
2d City or town, state, and ZIP code	

Note: *If you are the original donee, skip Part II and go to Part III now.*

Part II   Information on PREVIOUS DONEES—**Complete this part only if you were not the first donee to receive the property.** If you were the second donee, leave lines 4a–4d blank. If you were a third or later donee, complete lines 3a–4d. On lines 4a–4d, give information on the preceding donee (the one who gave you the property).

3a Name of original donee	3b Employer identification number
3c Address (number, street, and room or suite no.)	
3d City or town, state, and ZIP code	
4a Name of preceding donee	4b Employer identification number
4c Address (number, street, and room or suite no.)	
4d City or town, state, and ZIP code	

Part III   Information on DONATED PROPERTY—If you are the original donee, leave column (c) blank.

(a) Description of donated property sold, exchanged, or otherwise disposed of (if you need more space, attach a separate statement)	(b) Date you received the item(s)	(c) Date the first donee received the item(s)	(d) Date item(s) sold, exchanged, or otherwise disposed of	(e) Amount received upon disposition

For Paperwork Reduction Act Notice, see back of form.   Cat. No. 62307Y   Form **8282** (Rev. 9-98)

from a broker or a bank; some nonprofits may even keep a supply on hand. The stock power allows the nonprofit to sell the securities and retain the proceeds.

If the donor is mailing the stock certificates, the stock powers should be sent to the nonprofit separately. If the certificates and the stock powers were sent together and then lost or stolen, anyone could sell the securities. When the nonprofit has received both the stock powers and the stock certificates, it may proceed with the sale.

It is also possible for the donor to endorse the back of a stock certificate, which results in its becoming immediately negotiable, much like a personal check. This method should be used only if the donor is hand-delivering the certificates; it's best not to endorse the certificates until the moment of in-person delivery.

Valuation of Gifts of Securities The value of a gift of securities to a nonprofit is the average between the high and the low trading price of the security on the date of the gift. If a gift is made on a Saturday, Sunday, or holiday, the average of the mean values on the preceding and succeeding business days must be used.

The date of the gift depends on the method of delivery. If the donor sends the gift through the mail, the postmark on the envelope is the date of the gift. If the donor personally delivers the securities to the nonprofit, the date of delivery is the date of the gift. If the securities are transferred by a broker from the donor's account to a nonprofit's, the date the securities are actually delivered to the account of the nonprofit is the date of the gift.

Retirement Plan Assets

Qualified retirement plan assets present an often overlooked way to give. This example illustrates why.

Jack and Evelyn Shoemaker, ages sixty-one and sixty-three, have assets totaling $2.5 million. Of this amount, $1.8 million is in the Shoemaker's Individual Retirement Accounts (IRAs). The Shoemakers have been talking with a representative from their favorite nonprofit to determine the best way to make a significant gift. In addition to their other goals, Mrs. Shoemaker wants to leave an IRA worth $100,000 to her niece. What she did not realize prior to her discussions is that by doing this, the total amount that her niece would actually receive after taxes would be approximately $30,000. The other $70,000 would go to pay taxes. This results because the retirement assets are tax-deferred, so they are subject to income tax when withdrawn as well as any estate tax. In Mrs. Shoemaker's situation, these two levels of taxation result in the following situation:

$100,000	IRA balance
− _50,000_	Estate taxes (at an assumed rate of 50 percent)
50,000	Net of estate taxes
− _20,000_	Income taxes (at an assumed rate of 40 percent)
$30,000	Total to the niece net of all taxes

Because of this double taxation of retirement assets, the Shoemakers decide to use the retirement assets in their IRAs to fund their charitable contributions and use other assets as bequests to their family. By bequeathing the $100,000 IRA to their favorite nonprofit, the entire amount goes to the nonprofit, with no taxes due. No federal estate tax will be due because the estate tax charitable deduction is unlimited, and no income tax need be paid because the nonprofit is tax-exempt (see Exhibit 13.4). Please note that benefitting charity through a qualified retirement plan may affect the plan owner's lifetime mandatory distribution amount.

Real Estate Gifts

Real estate represents the largest single asset many donors own. It can be used to fund either an outright gift or a life income gift. It is important for the nonprofit to have a policy and procedures in place for the acceptance of gifts of real estate. Caution must be exercised in deciding whether or not to accept such gifts so that the nonprofit may avoid pitfalls associated with receiving unmarketable or environmentally hazardous gifts of real estate.

Essential Steps for Gifts of Real Estate. Real estate has tremendous potential as a gift. Donors can make a gift of their personal residence, vacation home, farmland, commercial property, or undeveloped lots. Real estate gifts can be donated outright or used to fund charitable remainder trusts and gift annuities. However, real estate also has the potential to create problems and liabilities for the nonprofit. Due diligence steps are required prior to acceptance of a gift of real estate.

Title to Real Estate. For the nonprofit to accept a gift of real estate, it is important to identify how the donor holds title to the property before accepting the potential gift. There are several ways in which a donor might hold title that could affect the ability to convey the property.

Appraisal of Property. A gift of real estate must be appraised by an independent, qualified appraiser to determine the property's value for gift purposes. The donor is responsible for arranging and paying for the appraisal. IRS rules provide that the

EXHIBIT 13.4. LEAD TRUST PROJECTIONS.

Benefits and Tax Consequences

ASSUMPTIONS:
Testamentary trusts established in 2000 for 20 years.
Lead trust makes annual end-of-period payments to nonprofit.
Original principal of $4,000,000.
Beneficiary's income is $100,000.
Value of donor's estate is $10,000,000. Prior taxable gifts are $0.
Income is 4%; capital appreciation is 4%.

	6% Charitable Lead Unitrust	No Trust
Donor's estate	$10,000,000	$10,000,000
Federal estate tax (paid 2000)	3,827,594	4,920,250
Gross principal	4,000,000	4,000,000
Average annuity to nonprofit	190,338	0
Estate tax deduction	1,986,647	0
Estate tax savings	1,092,656	0
Net federal estate tax on gross principal (paid 2000)	1,107,344	2,200,000
Net principal placed in plan	2,892,656	1,800,000
Remaining estate to family	3,279,750	3,279,750
Total management fees	659,839	0
Total income tax paid	0	960,366
Principal after 20 years	3,501,738	6,550,919
Unrealized capital gain	1,903,590	2,855,643
Potential capital gains tax	380,718	571,129
Benefit to family from plan after capital gains tax	3,121,020	5,979,791
Total distributed to nonprofit	3,806,761	0

IRS discount rate is 6.4%.

The information in this chart is general. Please see your tax adviser to verify all figures.

appraisal should be done no more than sixty days prior to the date of the gift but may be completed at any time up to the date of the donor's filing of a federal income tax return for the year in which the charitable deduction for the gift is claimed. The cost of the appraisal is a miscellaneous itemized deduction that the donor may claim on the tax return, to the extent that the donor's total miscellaneous deductions exceed 2 percent of adjusted gross income.

Restrictions and Easements. Real estate may be subject to restrictions or easements that affect its value or marketability. The deed needs to be closely reviewed to determine if there are any references to the existence of restrictions or easements, and a visual inspection of the property is necessary as well. It should be noted that a gift of real estate for which the donor retains an easement is considered a gift of a partial interest, and the donor receives no charitable deduction for such a gift.

Environmental Hazards. Real estate must be closely inspected to ensure that there are no environmental hazards that could result in potential liability for the nonprofit. It is highly recommended that a specialized firm conduct an environmental inspection, particularly if the gift involves commercial property or farmland.

Marketability. In most instances, the nonprofit will want to sell the real estate as soon as possible after the gift has been received. Marketability of the property is an important consideration before accepting a gift of real estate. A local real estate broker with knowledge of the local market can be helpful in determining the marketability of the property.

Life Estates. Another option is for the donor to donate the real estate but retain a life estate in the property. A retained life estate gives the owner the right to occupy the property for the remainder of his or her life. This applies only to a personal residence or a farm. The residence or farm need not be the donor's primary residence. As the life tenant of the property, the donor is obligated to pay real estate taxes, upkeep and maintenance, and insurance on the property.

The donor will retain the benefit of living in and using the property while also obtaining a current charitable income tax deduction. The property will also be free of federal estate tax so long as the life estate is created for the donor (or the donor's spouse) and the remainder is left to a nonprofit.

Should the donor wish to vacate a property that is subject to a retained life estate, the donor may relinquish the remainder of the life estate, giving the nonprofit the right to occupy or liquidate the property. The relinquishment of the life estate generates a new charitable income tax deduction for the donor based on the value of the donor's life estate at the time it is relinquished. In addition, the nonprofit could purchase the donor's remaining life estate for cash or an annuity.

If the nonprofit and the donor agree to sell the property, the proceeds of the sale can be distributed proportionally. The proportionate share of the nonprofit is based on the charitable remainder value in relation to the total value of the property. The donor's proportionate share is equal to the difference between the charitable remainder value and the total value of the property.

The donor will receive a charitable income tax deduction for the value of the remainder interest in a personal residence or farm that is donated to a nonprofit. He or she receives this deduction even though the gift is of a partial interest in the property. The deduction is based on the appraised value of the property minus the anticipated depreciation of the property over its estimated useful life.

Bargain Sales. A bargain sale results when a donor sells property to a nonprofit for less than its fair market value. In a bargain sale, the nonprofit receives the benefit of the excess of the property's market value over its cost. The donor relinquishes the property and receives the sale price of the property in return. The donor may deduct the difference between the fair market value and the sale price. For example, if a donor sells to the nonprofit property with a value and cost basis of $10,000 and the nonprofit purchases it for $6,000, the donor may deduct $4,000, the difference between the sale price and the purchase price.

However, if a donor has a bargain sale of appreciated property, it can produce a taxable gain that the donor must report. A donor's cost basis is divided proportionally between the sale portion of the property and the gift portion. To determine the amount of gain to report, the donor subtracts the basis attributable to the sold part of the property from the price the nonprofit pays for the property. The taxable gain is the excess of the price the donor receives over the basis of the part sold. This means that if the sale price of the property is 40 percent of the property's value, 40 percent of the entire property's basis is used to determine the gain.

For example, a donor sells property worth $10,000, with a $5,000 basis, to a nonprofit for a price of $3,000. The nonprofit has received a $7,000 benefit, and that amount is deductible by the donor. However, because the donor has received $3,000, some tax must be paid on the gain. The $3,000 sale price is 30 percent of the property's value, so 30 percent of the $5,000 basis must be used to compute the gain as follows:

Fair market value: $10,000

Purchase price = $3,000 = 0.30 basis proportion factor

Cost basis of $5,000 × 0.30 basis proportion factor = $1,500 basis for computation of the gain

$3,000 – $1,500 basis for computation of gain = $1,500 taxable gain

Bargain sales may be attractive to a donor who does not want to give up all of a property's value. It is a disadvantage to the nonprofit because it must pay for part of the gift, rather than receiving it outright. Before entering into a bargain sale agreement, a nonprofit should obtain an appraisal to determine the true value of the property being offered for sale.

Life Insurance

Most planned giving programs offer the opportunity for donors to give life insurance policies. Life insurance permits a donor to leverage a gift, in that for a relatively small sum of premium payments, the donor can produce a large death benefit for the nonprofit. However, as with bequests, it may be many years before the nonprofit receives the gift. Both fully or partially paid-up policies may be given to nonprofits.

When a donor makes an outright gift of life insurance, the nonprofit should be named as the owner and the beneficiary of the policy. The donor completely relinquishes ownership of the policy, waiving the right to assign or borrow against the policy or to change the beneficiary.

If the donor makes an outright gift of a paid-up policy, he or she will receive a charitable income tax deduction for the paid-up policy's replacement value—the cost to purchase an identical policy. If the replacement value exceeds the donor's cost basis in the policy, the deduction is limited to the cost basis. The donor's deduction is limited to 50 percent of adjusted gross income in the year of the gift. Any unused portion of the deduction may be carried forward for the next five tax years.

On many occasions, the donor names the nonprofit as owner and beneficiary on a new or partially paid-up life insurance policy. In this case, the nonprofit and the donor should agree at the outset how the remaining premiums will be paid. If the donor makes the payments directly to the charity and the nonprofit in turn forwards those to the insurance company, the donor will receive a charitable income tax deduction for the payments to the nonprofit. The deduction is limited to 50 percent of the donor's adjusted gross income. If the donor makes insurance premium payments directly to the insurance company, the charitable income tax deduction will be limited to 30 percent of adjusted gross income. The reason for the difference is that the payment to the nonprofit is considered a gift to the nonprofit, whereas a payment to the insurance company is considered "for the benefit of" the nonprofit.

If the partially paid-up policy has an accumulated cash surrender value, the donor may receive a charitable income tax deduction for the gift. The deduction is based on the "interpolated terminal reserve." This is defined as the amount that reflects the daily current value of the policy at the time of the gift and will usually be slightly more than the cash surrender of the value. The donor's charitable income tax deduction is limited to 50 percent of adjusted gross income.

If a donor claims a charitable income tax deduction of $5,000 or more for a gift of life insurance, it must be reported on Form 8283, as life insurance is considered a noncash gift. In addition, the donor must provide a qualified appraisal of the gift.

There are some cautions to bear in mind when accepting gifts of life insurance:

• Do not endorse any one company's products or services.
• Never provide a list of your donor names to an insurance agent. Your donors' confidentiality must be protected.
• If you are going to accept the role of owning and administering life insurance gifts, you must be sure that you have adequate staff to perform the necessary duties related to administering the policies.
• The nonprofit should develop a policy regarding how life insurance policies that are in danger of lapsing will be handled.

Flexible Endowment Gifts

Flexible endowment gifts are a relatively new form of planned giving. An endowment is money invested for future growth, with only a portion of the return being used today. A flexible endowment gift is one in which the donor agrees to provide the nonprofit with an annual gift equivalent to the expendable income that an endowment would generate if it were established. These annual gifts are available for immediate expenditure by the nonprofit. It is expected that at the same time the donor is making his or her annual gifts for current use, he or she will also make additional gifts to build the principal of the endowment, or there will be in place an estate gift that will fully fund the endowment at death.

A flexible endowment is an excellent planned giving alternative for donors who may not be in a position to fully fund an endowment at present. Many donors have illiquid assets such as closely held stock, real estate, or partnerships, which may provide them with an income sufficient to provide the annual gifts needed to establish a flexible endowment but not the liquidity needed to fully fund an endowment. Flexible endowments also appeal to elderly donors who already have a significant planned gift in their estate but would like to see their gifts benefit the nonprofit during their lifetimes.

If a donor wishes to create a $100,000 endowment using the flexible endowment approach and your nonprofit pays out 5 percent on an endowment annually, the donor agrees to give $5,000 each year until such time as he or she makes a gift totaling $100,000 separate from the annual payments. The nonprofit can spend the annual gift as it is received, and the donor retains the assets that may eventually make up the endowment principal for as long as needed.

Donors can make a gift to the endowment principal in the form of a lump sum or in installments. The installments are in addition to the annual gifts. As the installment gifts are made to build the endowment principal, they will generate endowment income, which will have the benefit of allowing the donors to lower their annual obligation. The timing of when the donor should pay the entire principal amount can vary, depending on the donor's circumstances. If the nonprofit and the donor are in agreement, the donor can defer funding the principal until after death through a testamentary planned gift.

When establishing a flexible endowment, the nonprofit should account for the effect that inflation will have on the purchasing power of the donor's annual and principal gifts. It is recommended that discussions with the donor focus on how the donor's annual and principal commitment in terms of current dollars will be adjusted annually for inflation. They might agree that the gifts will be adjusted annually to reflect some agreed-on measure such as the Consumer Price Index. Or they might agree that the funding level of the endowment will adjust to reflect the minimum funding level set by the nonprofit's board for that particular type of endowment gift.

The nonprofit should specify to the donor when it will consider the endowment fully funded. This could be when the market value of the principal in the endowment equals the value of the donor's original commitment, adjusted for inflation.

Principal endowment gifts may be revocable or irrevocable, depending on the purpose for which the gift was made. If the nonprofit assumes a financial obligation on the basis of the flexible endowment gift (such as construction of a new building), then the flexible endowment agreement should be made irrevocable and its payment guaranteed by the donor's estate through a will contract. The will contract will permit the nonprofit to enforce the donor's commitment against the donor's estate.

The donor will receive an income tax charitable deduction for gifts to the flexible endowment. The deduction is based on the total amount given to the nonprofit as an irrevocable gift each year, subject to applicable tax laws.

Flexible endowments provide donors with an opportunity to see the benefits of their gifts to the nonprofit at work during their lifetime. It also allows the nonprofit to recognize the donors for their generosity. Flexible endowments are a planned giving technique that offers many benefits to your nonprofit. It should be examined closely to determine its appropriateness for donors and your organization.

Life Income Gifts

Life income gifts are key to building a sound foundation for a planned giving program. They provide an opportunity for the donor to benefit the nonprofit while receiving an income and significant tax benefits. There are three primary types of life income vehicles: charitable gift annuities, charitable remainder trusts, and pooled income funds.

Charitable Gift Annuities

The charitable gift annuity allows the donor to make a gift to a nonprofit and receive an income for the rest of the donor's life and, if desired, that of one other beneficiary. Upon the death of the last beneficiary of the annuity, the nonprofit receives the remainder. The donor receives a charitable income tax deduction for the creation of the gift annuity.

The gift annuity is a contract between the donor and the nonprofit. In exchange for the gift, the nonprofit is legally obligated to pay the donor a fixed annuity for the remainder of the donor's lifetime. The annuity is backed by the assets of the nonprofit. An example of a gift annuity contract is presented in Exhibit 13.5.

Gift annuity rates are age-dependent. The older the donor, the higher the annuity rate. Also, the rate is dependent on whether or not there are one or two annuitants and their respective ages.

The American Council on Gift Annuities is a national organization that recommends annuity rates for nonprofits to offer to annuitants. These recommended rates are the same for both sexes and ages. Many types of planned giving software are available, which can be used to calculate a donor's annuity rate and charitable income tax deduction. Two popular software packages are PC Calc and Crescendo.

A deferred gift annuity is a variant of the charitable gift annuity. Simply put, the donor makes a gift to the nonprofit and the nonprofit agrees to pay the donor

EXHIBIT 13.5. CHARITABLE GIFT ANNUITY AGREEMENT.

THIS GIFT ANNUITY AGREEMENT, made and entered into this _____ day of
_____ , 200__ , by and between _____ (hereinafter called
"Donor"), residing at _____ , _____ , _____ , and
XYZ Charity (hereinafter called "Charity"), a not-for-profit corporation located in
_____ (city), _____ (state).

1. GIFT. Donor has this day contributed and voluntarily given to Charity
the sum of _____ Dollars ($_____), receipt of which is hereby
acknowledged, to ultimately benefit _____.

2. ANNUITY. Charity, in consideration of the transfer and delivery of such gift,
shall pay to Donor during the full term of Donor's natural life the sum of _____
Dollars ($_____) annually in quarterly payments on the last day of March,
June, September, and December in each year. The obligation to pay the annuity
shall terminate with, and no amount shall be payable for, the period subsequent
to the last date for payment immediately preceding or coincident with the death
of Donor, at which date it is expressly agreed that Charity shall be discharged and
forever released from any further responsibility or obligation whatsoever that it
may have assumed under this agreement. This annuity is nonassignable by Donor.

3. REPRESENTATIONS OF CORPORATION. Charity hereby represents and certi-
fies that it is a not-for-profit corporation, publicly supported and tax-exempt, that
has been established to solicit, receive, and administer gifts and bequests for the
benefit of XYZ Charity, located and established at _____ (city), _____
(state).

4. CONTRIBUTIONS. Both Donor and Charity acknowledge that the difference
between the fair market value of the gift and the present fair market value of the
annuity to be paid to Donor constitutes a contribution from Donor to Charity.

5. IRREVOCABILITY. This Gift Annuity Agreement is irrevocable.

6. NOTICE. A charitable gift annuity provided by Charity is not issued by an
insurance company, nor is it regulated by the state division of insurance or state
insurance commissioner. It is not protected by any state guaranty fund or protective
association.

IN WITNESS WHEREOF, the parties hereto have set their hand and seals on the
day and year first above written.

DONOR

_____

XYZ Charity

By: _____

_____ , President

ATTEST: _____

_____ , Secretary

(and no more than one other annuitant) a stream of income for life at an agreed-on date in the future. At the death of the last annuitant, the nonprofit receives the remainder of the annuity. Because of the deferral period from the date of the gift until the time the payments begin, the annuity rate for a deferred gift annuity will be substantially higher than for an immediate-pay annuity. The donor receives a current charitable income tax deduction at the time the annuity is created, even though payments are deferred until some point in the future. Deferred gift annuities are particularly popular with professionals who are seeking to supplement their retirement income.

Tax Consequences of Charitable Gift Annuities

Creation of a charitable gift annuity will have consequences for the donors that will affect their income, gift, capital gains, and estate taxes, as well as their charitable income tax deduction. Let us examine each affect one by one.

- *Charitable income tax deduction.* The value of the charitable income tax deduction is determined by subtracting the value of the annuitant's life income interest from the value of the gift, with the result being the remainder interest to the nonprofit, which is equal to the donor's charitable income tax deduction. Part of the calculation includes applying the IRS discount rate to the annuity payments the annuitants will receive over their life expectancy. The discount rate is defined as 120 percent of the Federal Midterm Rate, which changes monthly. The Federal Midterm Rate is the average market yield on all options of the U.S. market that have a maturity over three years and less than nine years. The donor can select the discount rate for the month in which the gift is made or the rate of either of the two preceding months. The higher the discount rate, the higher the charitable income tax deduction. If the donor uses cash to fund an annuity, the deduction is limited to 50 percent of adjusted gross income in the year of the gift. If an appreciated asset is used, the deduction will be limited to 30 percent of adjusted gross income in the year of the gift. In each case, any unused portion of the deduction may be carried forward for the next five tax years.
- *Gift taxes.* If the donor establishes a charitable gift annuity for the benefit of anyone other than the donor or the donor's spouse, the donor has made a taxable gift and may be required to pay a gift tax on the value of the charitable gift annuity. The taxable gift is based on the total value of the charitable gift annuity's projected income at the time the gift is made. If the payments to the third party begin in the year the annuity is created, the donor may use his or her $10,000 annual gift tax exclusion to eliminate or reduce the gift tax due on the creation of the gift annuity.

- *Capital gains and income taxes.* A donor who uses appreciated property to fund a charitable gift annuity will have to pay capital gains taxes on the portion of the property that is used to purchase the charitable gift annuity. If the donor is the sole beneficiary or the first beneficiary, the gain can be spread out by reporting it over the donor's life expectancy. If the donor is not one of the annuitants, all of the reportable gain will be taxed to the donor in the year of the gift. Also, the beneficiary's income is all taxed as ordinary income. Regarding income taxes on gift annuity payments, a portion of these payments will be considered a tax-free return of principle, a portion will be considered ordinary income, and to the extent appreciated property is used, the remainder is taxed as a capital gain. When the donor attains his or her life expectancy, as it was calculated at the time the annuity was created, the entire amount of the annuity payment is taxed as ordinary income.
- *Estate taxes.* If the donor is the only annuitant and the annuity ceases at the donor's death, the value of the annuity will not be taxed in the donor's estate. If the surviving spouse of the donor is the remaining annuitant, the spouse's interest will qualify for the estate tax marital deduction. If someone other than the donor's spouse is the remaining annuitant at the donor's death, the value of the annuity will be taxed in the donor's estate.

Let's look at an example (see Exhibit 13.6). Lila Carter is eighty-seven years old and wants to make a donation to her favorite nonprofit but also would like to receive an income stream for the rest of her life. After hearing about a charitable gift annuity, she decided that it would meet all of her goals. She decides to set up a $50,000 charitable gift annuity contract with her favorite nonprofit by transferring long-term appreciated stock. At her age, the nonprofit agreed to issue a gift annuity to Mrs. Carter for 9 percent of the amount transferred for as long as she lives no matter what the earnings from the amount used to fund the annuity. Since the entire asset base of the nonprofit backs the annuity contract, this contract will provide her with guaranteed annual payments of $4,500. Of this amount, for the first six years of the annuity, $1,817.10 will be tax-free, $1,211.40 will be taxed at her long-term capital gains rate, and $1,471.50 will be taxed at her ordinary income tax rate. After six years, the entire amount of the annual annuity payment will be ordinary income. This preferential tax treatment for the first six years combined with the $31,835.00 charitable income tax deduction to which she is entitled are benefits that Mrs. Carter receives in addition to her satisfaction of knowing that she has made a significant contribution to the charitable cause in which she believes.

Funding Annuities. Annuities may be funded with a variety of assets. These include cash, stocks, and real estate.

EXHIBIT 13.6. CALCULATIONS FOR
A 9 PERCENT CHARITABLE GIFT ANNUITY.

April 20, 2000

Deduction Calculations
Summary of Benefits

9% Charitable Gift Annuity

ASSUMPTIONS:

Age of annuitant	87
Principal donated	$50,000.00
Cost basis	$30,000.00
Annuity rate	9%
Payment schedule	quarterly at end

BENEFITS:

Charitable deduction	$31,835.00
Annuity	$4,500.00
Tax-free portion	$1,817.10
Capital gain	$1,211.40
Ordinary income	$1,471.50

Total reportable capital gain of $7,266.00 must be reported over 6.0 years, the expected lifetime of the donor, age 87.

After 6.0 years, the entire annuity becomes ordinary income.

IRS discount rate is 8%.

The information in this chart is general. Please see your tax adviser to verify all figures.

EXHIBIT 13.6. CALCULATIONS FOR
A 9 PERCENT CHARITABLE GIFT ANNUITY, Cont'd.

April 20, 2000

Deduction Calculations
Taxation of Gift Annuity Payments

9% Charitable Gift Annuity

ASSUMPTIONS:

Age of annuitant	87
Date of gift	4/20/2000
Principal donated	$50,000.00
Cost basis	$30,000.00
Annuity rate	9%
Payment schedule	quarterly at end

CALCULATIONS:

Charitable deduction	$31,835.00
Number of full payments in first year	2
Days in payment period (4/1/2000 to 6/30/2000)	91
Days in credit period (4/20/2000 to 6/30/2000)	72
Annuity	$4,500.00
Quarterly payment	$1,125.00
First partial payment	$890.11

BREAKDOWN OF ANNUITY:

	Capital Gain	Tax-Free Portion	Ordinary Income	Total Annuity
2000	$845.32	$1,267.97	$1,026.82	$3,140.11
2001–2005	1,211.40	1,817.10	1,471.50	4,500.00
2006	363.68	545.53	3,590.79	4,500.00
2007 onward	0.00	0.00	4,500.00	4,500.00

Total reportable capital gain of $7,266.00 must be reported over 6.0 years, the expected lifetime of the donor, age 87.

After 6.0 years, the entire annuity becomes ordinary income.

IRS discount rate is 8%.

The information in this chart is general. Please see your tax adviser to verify all figures.

The nonprofit must exercise caution if real estate is used to fund a charitable gift annuity. The annuity rate should be negotiated with the donor with the realization that the property may sell for less than the appraised value or that costs associated with selling the property may reduce the sale proceeds below the appraised value of the contributing property. The nonprofit should also decide how soon payments to the donor will begin, as there may be a delay between the time the property is accepted and the time it is sold and converted to cash to fund the annuity. It may be advisable to use a deferred charitable gift annuity when real estate will be the funding asset. The deferred annuity provides the nonprofit with time to sell the real estate before payments to the annuitants begin.

Regulation of Gift Annuities. Charities that offer gift annuities must comply with a wide range of state regulatory requirements. Because of the lack of uniformity among the states regarding regulatory requirements and registration procedures, you should check the requirements before issuing a gift annuity in a given state. Most states that regulate gift annuities require the following:

- A permit issued by the state department of insurance
- A segregated reserve fund dedicated to sustaining the life income payments to the donors
- Publication in the nonprofit's annual report of details on the balances held in the reserve fund
- Specific disclosure language in the gift annuity contract

Some states may also require the nonprofit to provide financial statements, by-laws, articles of incorporation, and proof of tax-exempt status (see Exhibit 13.7).

The American Council on Gift Annuities recommends that a nonprofit comply with the laws of any state in which it issues gift annuities and that it meet all registration requirements and obtain state approval before beginning to issue gift annuities in that state.

Charitable Remainder Trusts

Charitable remainder trusts have become increasingly popular as planned giving vehicles. They can generate substantial financial and tax benefits for the donor and significant revenues for the nonprofit. Charitable remainder trusts may be established during the donor's lifetime or at his or her death. Charitable remainder trusts may pay their income to the beneficiaries for life or a term of years not to exceed twenty. To qualify as a charitable remainder trust, the donor must make

EXHIBIT 13.7. REGULATION OF GIFT ANNUITIES BY STATE.

This chart summarizes the regulatory status of charitable gift annuities by the various states and the District of Columbia as of November 1999. This information is constantly changing, and there may be regulatory initiatives under way that could change a state's current status.

States That Specifically Exempt Gift Annuities from Regulation
(some require notification or have other conditions that must be met)

Alabama	Louisiana	North Carolina
Arizona	Maine	Ohio
Colorado	Massachusetts	Oklahoma
Connecticut	Michigan	Pennsylvania
Florida	Minnesota	South Carolina
Idaho	Missouri	South Dakota
Illinois	Nebraska	Texas
Indiana	Nevada	Utah
Kansas	New Hampshire	Virginia
Kentucky	New Mexico	

States That Regulate Gift Annuities

Arkansas	North Dakota	Washington
California	New Jersey	Wisconsin
Hawaii	New York	
Maryland	Oregon	

States in Which the Law Does Not Specifically Address Gift Annuities

Alaska	Iowa	Tennessee
Delaware	Mississippi	Vermont
District of Columbia	Montana	West Virginia
Georgia	Rhode Island	Wyoming

an irrevocable gift to the trust with the remainder interest going to a qualified nonprofit organization. There are two forms of charitable remainder trusts, the charitable remainder annuity trust and the charitable remainder unitrust. With both, the payout rate is negotiated between the donor and the nonprofit at the time the trust is created. That rate will generally be a factor of the age and the number of beneficiaries on the trust. By law, the rate may not be less than 5 percent or more than 50 percent.

The IRS has created forms to serve as templates for drafting charitable remainder trusts (see Resource 21, "Templates for Drafting Trusts").

The donor must name a trustee for the charitable remainder trust. The trustee may be a bank or trust company, an investment firm, or the nonprofit itself. Serving as trustee allows the nonprofit to maintain a close relationship with the donor and the beneficiaries of the trust and to control the investment allocation of the trust's portfolio of assets.

The charitable remainderman of the trust must be a nonprofit that is qualified under the Internal Revenue Code section 501(c)(3). A donor may name more than one charitable remainder beneficiary, and the donor may reserve the right to change the charitable beneficiaries without affecting the charitable nature of the trust.

Tax Consequences of Charitable Remainder Trusts

Charitable remainder trusts are creations of the Internal Revenue Code and have income, gift, and estate tax consequences for donors who set them up. These tax considerations are often a key factor in discussions with donors who are contemplating setting up such trusts.

• *Income taxes.* Income distributed from the charitable remainder trust to the beneficiary is taxed to the beneficiary, as the trust itself is a tax-free entity (so long as there is no unrelated business income for the trust). For income tax purposes, distributions from the charitable remainder trust are taxed in the following order: (1) ordinary income, (2) capital gain income, (3) tax-free income, (4) return of trust principal. There is no tax-free income or return of the initial principal until all ordinary and capital gain income earned by the trust has been distributed to the beneficiary.

• *Capital gains taxes.* If the trust is funded with an appreciated asset such as securities or real estate, the donor will avoid any capital gains taxes on the gain at the time the trust is created. However, to the extent the trust does not earn sufficient ordinary income to meet the distribution due the beneficiaries under the stated payout rate of the trust, capital gains will be distributed from the trust. So in effect the donor may only be postponing capital gains rather than eliminating them by creating the charitable remainder trust. It should be noted, however, that a donor's tax rate on ordinary income is usually higher than the 20 percent long-term rate on capital gains, meaning that if part of the payment is taxed as capital gains, it reduces the overall tax on the income the beneficiary receives.

• *Gift taxes.* If the donor or the donor's spouse is the beneficiary of the charitable remainder trust, there will be no gift tax consequences at the time of the trust creation. If the spouse is a beneficiary of the trust, the donor has made a gift to the spouse, thereby qualifying for the unlimited gift tax marital deduction and hence incurring no gift taxes. If the donor has named anyone other than a spouse as a current beneficiary of the trust, it is a taxable gift for which the donor may use his or her $10,000 annual gift tax exclusion to reduce or eliminate the gift tax. If the value of the gift exceeds the $10,000 annual exclusion, the donor can apply his or her unified estate and gift tax credit to eliminate or reduce any potential gift tax due. To avoid a current taxable gift, the owner may reserve the right by will to revoke the income interest of the nonspousal beneficiary.

• *Estate taxes.* If the donor creates a charitable remainder trust naming himself or herself as the beneficiary, the entire value of the trust assets as of the date of the donor's death will be included in the donor's estate. The gift will qualify for a 100 percent charitable estate tax deduction. If the donor and the donor's spouse are the beneficiaries, it will also be included in the donor's taxable estate but will qualify for the 100 percent marital deduction, exempting it from any estate taxes. If the trust is created paying income first to the donor and then to anyone other than a spouse, there will be estate tax consequences. There is a charitable deduction for the charitable remainder value of the trust on the date of death, and estate tax may be due on the life income interest of the nonspousal beneficiary. Typically, there will be estate taxes due on the life income interest of the nonspousal beneficiary who survives the donor.

• *Taxpayer Relief Act of 1997.* The Taxpayer Relief Act of 1997 established certain requirements a trust must meet to qualify as a charitable remainder unitrust or annuity trust. First, the act set a maximum annual payout rate of 50 percent of the fair market value of the trust assets. This requirement discourages extraordinarily high payout rates. The act also requires that the value of the charitable remainder interest be at least 10 percent of the net fair market value of the property transferred to the trust at the time of its creation. This requirement discourages the addition of younger or multiple beneficiaries, as well as too high a payout rate. In addition to these requirements, a charitable remainder annuity trust must pass a 5 five percent exhaustion test. This test provides that if there is a greater than 5 percent chance that the assets of the annuity trust will be depleted so that the nonprofit will receive nothing at the death of the donor, the donor will not be entitled to a charitable income tax deduction upon the creation of the trust.

Types of Charitable Remainder Trusts

There are two basic types of charitable remainder trusts: the charitable remainder annuity trust and the charitable remainder unitrust. Which will be more appropriate depends on the donor's particular circumstances and financial and philanthropic objectives.

Charitable Remainder Annuity Trust. A charitable remainder annuity trust pays the income beneficiaries a fixed, guaranteed payment for life or a term of years. The payment must be not less than 5 percent of the initial funding amount of the trust. As with gift annuities, the payout rate is age-sensitive. Unlike a gift annuity, there may be more than two beneficiaries on a charitable remainder annuity trust. To the extent income is not sufficient to meet the stated payout rate, the trustee may invade principal to meet the payment obligation due the beneficiaries. The annuity trust appeals to donors who seek the security of a fixed payment. Fewer annuity trusts are now being created because gift annuities provide the donors with similar benefits. Annuity trusts are still appropriate where a nonprofit may not offer a gift annuity program or if it is receiving a gift from a donor in a state for which the nonprofit is not authorized to offer gift annuities. It should be noted that once an annuity trust is established, no additional contributions can be made to it. Of course, a donor may establish more than one charitable remainder annuity trust with a nonprofit.

Charitable Remainder Unitrust. The charitable remainder unitrust has three variations: a straight unitrust, the net income unitrust, and the flip trust. Each has a different objective and affects the beneficiaries' payouts differently.

Straight Unitrust. The straight unitrust pays to the income beneficiary a fixed percentage of the fair market value of the trust's assets, as valued annually. The trustee determines the distribution due the beneficiaries by multiplying the percentage payout rate by the fair market value of the trust's assets as valued on the annual valuation date. If the assets of the trust appreciate in value, the income beneficiary will receive a larger distribution. Conversely, if the assets of the trust have decreased in value, the beneficiary will receive a smaller distribution. To the extent income is insufficient to meet the required distribution, the trustee must invade principal to make payment to the beneficiary.

It works like this: George and Anna Baltz, ages seventy-six and seventy-two, are giving $500,000 to their favorite nonprofit through a charitable remainder unitrust. The charitable remainder unitrust will pay the donors 6 percent of the fair market value of the trust's assets as revalued annually. The donors thus receive an annual income of $30,000 in the first year and a 6 percent payout each succeeding year based on the annual valuation of the trust. The fact that in positive markets the trust's annual value payments increase along with its principal makes this type of trust a popular way to provide a hedge against inflation. The donors can also make additional contributions to the trust at any time. The Baltzes will also receive a charitable income tax deduction of $212,945.00 based on an IRS discount rate of 8 percent. Since the Baltzes used appreciated property to fund their trust, they will be able to deduct up to 30 percent of their adjusted gross income on their tax return in the year that they set up the trust. If they are unable to use the entire amount of their charitable deduction, they may carry over any remaining amount for an additional five years.

Net Income Unitrust. A net income unitrust pays the beneficiaries the stated percentage or the net income earned by the trust, whichever is *less.* The trustee is not permitted to invade principal to make the distribution to the income beneficiaries. Therefore, if the trust earns no net income, no distribution is due the beneficiaries. Often a net income trust will be drafted with a makeup provision. A makeup provision provides that the income beneficiaries are entitled to a makeup of any income not distributed during the term of the trust. Thus if the income beneficiary receives distributions that are less than the stated percentage, the makeup provision allows the beneficiary to make up income in the future when the trust has net income in excess of the stated payout percentage. Net income trusts are often used by nonprofits when gifts of real estate are used to fund the trust. The net income trust allows the trustee to have time to sell the real estate before any payments are due the income beneficiary. Growth stocks are often used to fund net income trusts as well. The trustee can invest the growth stocks, which generally appreciate in value over time. At some point in the future, the trustee can convert the growth stocks to a mix of income-producing stocks and bonds. The income beneficiaries then receive net income produced or the stated payout percentage, whichever is less. This arrangement is often popular with donors who seek to use the net income unitrust as a way of supplementing their retirement income.

Flip Unitrust. IRS regulations now permit a planned gift vehicle known as the flip unitrust, which provides for a "flip" of the trust's payment method. Prior to a specified event, the trust distributes the lesser of the trust's net income or the fixed percentage amount. After the event occurs, the trust becomes a standard unitrust and the payments to the income recipients are then simply a straight percentage of the trust's net fair market value. Although the income stream would continue to fluctuate after the flip occurs, depending on the market performance of the trust, the payments would no longer depend on the *income earned* by the trust's assets.

Because the flip unitrust provides greater flexibility in determining the trust's income stream, such trusts are typically recommended in two circumstances: when assets are illiquid or when deferred income is desired.

- *Illiquid assets.* When funding a charitable remainder trust with illiquid assets, such as real estate or closely held stock, the flip unitrust may be particularly appropriate. Prior to the sale of the non-income-producing asset, the net-income restriction protects the trustee from the untenable position of making distributions to the income recipients from illiquid trust assets. When the trustee subsequently sells the property and diversifies the trust's portfolio, the trust will in the next calendar year provide an income stream based solely on the trust's fixed percentage payout.

• *Deferred income.* Donors who have little need for current income but expect that they will need such an income stream in the future may also choose a flip unitrust. By selecting a future date or event as the trust's flip date (a date not in any person's discretion), the donor receives a smaller income stream (subject to the net-income restriction) until the event occurs. Beginning with the year following the flip date, the trust provides an income stream based solely on the trust's fixed percentage payout.

Examples of permissible flip events are the income recipients' attaining a specified age, the arrival of a specified date, or the birth, death, marriage, or divorce of an individual.

Any makeup provisions used in a net-income unitrust to recover shortfalls and distributions must be forfeited once the trust flips. After the trust has flipped, it must remain a straight percentage unitrust.

It is anticipated that the flip trust will replace the net-income trust as the preferred vehicle for receiving gifts of real estate and other illiquid assets.

Charitable Lead Trust

The charitable lead trust is in many ways the opposite of the charitable remainder trust. With a lead trust, the trust will pay income to benefit the nonprofit, and after a term of years or a lifetime, the remainder is returned either to the grantor (with a grantor lead trust) or someone other than the grantor, usually the grantor's heirs (a nongrantor lead trust). A charitable lead trust is not required to meet the 5 percent minimum payout of a charitable remainder trust. The lead trust payout rate can be determined on the basis of current conditions in the economy, the nature of the funding asset, the term of the trust, and the tax benefits desired. The lead trust is most beneficial if the donor does not require current income from a particular asset but wishes to retain the asset for the benefit of his or her family. The unique nature of a lead trust allows a donor to transfer substantial amounts of wealth from one generation to the next at greatly reduced rates of estate and gift taxation and in many cases, tax-free.

In one situation, it worked this way (look back at Exhibit 13.4): Dorothy Bradford had been contemplating making a substantial gift to her favorite nonprofit, but she also wanted to pass on the bulk of her assets to her niece. In discussing her goals with the nonprofit, Ms. Bradford decided to make a gift of $4 million through her will to a charitable lead trust paying 6 percent for a period of twenty years. Based on an IRS discount rate of 6.4 percent, the donor receives an estate tax deduction of $1,986,647, which represents the present value of the income stream going to the nonprofit. The donor pays federal estate taxes of $1,107,344, which may be partially offset by the unified credit. The net principal placed in the trust is $2,892,656, which provides an estimated income to the nonprofit of $3,806,761 over the twenty-year trust term. As the amount in the trust varies over the term of the trust, the annual unitrust amounts payable to the nonprofit also vary.

At the end of the twenty-year trust term, Ms. Bradford's niece will receive the balance of the assets in the trust free of any additional taxes, which, based on a 4 percent rate of income and a 4 percent appreciation in capital, would be $3,121,020. If Ms. Bradford had transferred the asset directly to her niece without using the trust, the niece would have had to pay $2.2 million in estate taxes, leaving $1.8 million and no benefit to the nonprofit.

There are two primary types of charitable lead trusts, the grantor lead trust and the nongrantor lead trust. With the grantor lead trust, at the end of the trust term, the assets remaining in the trust are returned to the grantor. The grantor lead trust provides the grantor with a charitable income tax deduction; however, the grantor will be taxed on the income paid to the nonprofit each year. Because the tax benefits are minimal, grantor lead trusts are seldom used.

The nongrantor lead trust provides that at the end of the trust term, the remainder is transferred to someone other than the grantor; in most cases this will be the grantor's heirs. The grantor will not receive a charitable income tax deduction but will receive estate and gift tax benefits. If the grantor establishes a nongrantor charitable lead trust during his or her lifetime, the donor will obtain a gift tax charitable deduction for the present value of the income stream to the nonprofit. If the grantor establishes the trust upon his or her death, as a testamentary lead trust, the donor's estate will receive an estate tax charitable deduction for the value of the income stream passing to the nonprofit.

Lead trusts may make their distributions in the form of an annuity interest or a unitrust interest. With the annuity trust, the nonprofit receives a fixed payment each year, based on the initial funding amount of the trust. With the unitrust, the nonprofit receives a variable payment calculated by multiplying the payout rate by the annual market value of the trust. Like a charitable remainder unitrust, additional contributions are permissible to a charitable lead unitrust.

Lead trusts are a complex planned giving technique with many income, estate, and gift tax consequences. Whether or not a lead trust is the appropriate technique for a particular donor will involve much analysis and discussion among the donor, the nonprofit, and the donor's legal and tax advisers.

Pooled-Income Funds

Pooled-income funds are another life income vehicle for planned giving prospects and donors. A pooled-income fund is similar to a mutual fund in that a donor's gift is combined with gifts from other donors to create a pool of funds for investment purposes.

The payout rate from the pooled-income fund is market-sensitive and may increase or decrease, depending on the performance of the fund. A donor who makes a gift to a pooled-income fund will receive income for life. The donor may claim a charitable income deduction at the time of the gift; from the death of the donor, the nonprofit receives the remainder interest. The pooled-income fund permits donors to make smaller gifts than is possible with other life income vehicles.

Donors may use greatly appreciated securities to make their gift to a pooled-income fund. That allow them to avoid capital gains taxes on their gift and to convert stock that may be paying a low dividend into a higher-yielding investment.

In recent years, more and more organizations have been using charitable gift annuities and charitable remainder trusts as life income vehicles to offer their donors. However, the pooled-income fund still has a place in a planned giving program. If the nonprofit does not offer gift annuities, the pooled-income fund is a viable alternative. Also, because the size of the gift to a pooled-income fund is much smaller than that required to establish a charitable remainder trust, it can be useful to donors who seek a stream of income but may be unable to make a gift large enough to establish a charitable remainder trust.

Deferred Gifts

A gift is considered deferred when the nonprofit cannot make use of it immediately. Often a deferred gift does not become available until the death of the donor, which means that the deferral period may last many years before the gift can be put to its intended use.

Deferred gifts are central to a successful, mature planned giving program.

Bequests

Gifts made by bequest are the cornerstone of a nonprofit's planned giving program. The majority of all planned gifts are made this way. The bequest program is the simplest part of a planned giving program to start and administer. In fact, many nonprofits will receive bequests even when they do not have a formal planned giving program.

Bequests are gifts from donors' estates and will include gifts by will or through trusts. The irrevocable living trust has become a popular estate planning tool, and so the number of gifts left through them has increased and will continue to do so. Many donors prefer to make gifts through their estate because that arrangement permits them to maintain the use and control of their assets during their lifetime. In many cases, an estate gift is a donor's only realistic option.

To encourage bequests, the nonprofit should make sample bequest language available to its donors—for example, "I give, devise, bequeath (some portion/percentage/residue) of my estate to XYZ Charity, a not-for-profit corporation with principal offices located in Anywhere, USA, to be used for the purposes as set out in a gift agreement on file with said charity." An attorney can then incorporate the language into the will or trust agreement.

Bequests will likely come in the following forms:

- *Specific bequest.* A specific bequest is a distribution of a certain amount of cash, securities, or a particular piece of personal property—for example, a stated amount of money, a specific number of shares of stock, or a particular piece of artwork.
- *Percentage.* The charity will receive a stated percentage of the donor's estate—for example, "25 percent of my gross estate to XYZ Charity." A percentage of the gross estate will result in a larger gift to the charity than a percentage of the net estate, which is the value after the estate has been reduced by administrative expenses and taxes.
- *Residue of the estate.* The residue of the estate consists of the remainder of the donor's estate that has not been given to specific named beneficiaries. In many cases, the nonprofit will receive a percentage of the residue of the donor's estate.

Bequests are ideal for older donors and prospects. Donors who have consistently supported the nonprofit with annual gifts have demonstrated their commitment to your mission and are excellent prospects for bequests.

CHAPTER FOURTEEN

BUILDING LASTING RELATIONSHIPS AND DEVELOPING LEAD GIFTS

Rodney P. Kirsch
Martin W. Shell

In 1998 a total of $174.52 billion was contributed to American charities. The great majority of this amount, 85 cents of each dollar, came from living individuals or through bequests. The American Association of Fund-Raising Counsel (AAFRC) Trust for Philanthropy (1999) lists nearly four hundred gifts of $1 million or more from individuals to every part of the nonprofit sector—religion, education, healthcare, human services, the arts, the environment, and more. Most of these gifts came as lead gifts to capital campaigns. This chapter focuses on the conditions needed to bring about lead investments from individuals and on ways of positioning and using the positive dynamics created by such magnificent investments. And these major acts of philanthropy are indeed investments. They result from deep and meaningful relationships that span the course of time, and they are as much "given" as "solicited." In this respect, they represent the convergence of factors that go well beyond the mechanics of soliciting large gifts during campaigns (see Chapter Ten). But there are also some cautions and considerations to be raised about how fundraisers work to achieve lead gifts in the context of a campaign, considerations that take account of the many personal complexities in donors' lives.

The AAFRC Trust for Philanthropy (1999) reports that there are now nearly seven hundred thousand 501(c)(3) organizations registered as charities with the Internal Revenue Service. The great majority of these will not see their donors listed in the *Forbes* annual roster of largest gifts. This is not terribly important.

What matters is that your organization can certainly achieve success with lead gifts, a success to be measured less by your past achievements in this area than by the extraordinary potential that you have to bring about change in the community you serve.

Defining a Leadership Gift

Before considering the optimal conditions for inspiring leadership gifts, let us define such gifts. There are four traditional definitions.

An Inspirational Gift

Lead gifts and the donors who make them possess transformational qualities. In other words, the impact of these gifts is to move an entire organization or a significant part of the organization forward in a single leap. They create synergy for further philanthropy and define to the entire constituency the importance and value one donor holds for the organization. As one donor said about a lead gift, "It puts you on the map. Others will now more carefully consider the important contributions your organization makes."

Indeed, as the name implies, these gifts set a standard of leadership, perhaps beyond any anticipated level. In many cases, a lead gift can be truly historic, launching a new chapter in the life of the recipient organization.

In this way, leadership gifts are philosophical and inspirational. They are the kinds of investments to keep in mind as you consider this topic. Adopting this definition will raise your expectations and your donors' aspirations. Dare to dream big dreams!

Portion of the Donor's Wealth

The public does not ordinarily know what portion of a donor's wealth a gift represents. Often insiders don't know either. Most professional development officers and volunteers would consider a gift that represents 20 percent or more of an individual's net worth substantive, regardless of the amount, be it $50,000 or $50 million. Key volunteers, donors, and staff members must have a feel for the sacrificial nature of such gifts and should use this knowledge wisely to encourage other donors, discreetly and strategically.

Relationship to Other Large Gifts

Another traditional way to define lead gifts is to determine where they fit in relation to other major gifts over the course of a campaign. Being among the top 2 or 3 percent in gift size would certainly qualify for recognition. But be aware that this definition is *comparative;* it is not necessarily related to the true potential of the donor and so may fall short of what might have been obtained under the other two definitions.

Threshold Amount

Perhaps the most conventional way of defining a lead gift is by stipulating its amount. This will of course vary from organization to organization, but today's standard definition is 10 percent (or more) of the campaign goal. The danger with such an exact and arbitrary definition is that it can limit the potential of donors and lowers their sights. Donors capable of contributing much more will be content to meet the threshold level.

Shared Purpose and Passion

A lead gift typically grows out of a close association between a donor and an organization, an association based on a shared and deeply held vision, belief, or value. At first blush, this suggests that attention be paid to creating persuasive case statements and program brochures. But these standard campaign vehicles are preliminary and superficial instruments for inspiring lead gifts. Each non-profit organization should consider the constituencies it serves, the mission it holds dear, and the values it expresses when engaging individuals in the lead gift process. The organization's ability to articulate these important dimensions of its existence is essential to fostering an environment for lead gift possibilities.

Experienced development professionals know, both from surveys and from personal experience, that major philanthropy at its very core is primarily an emotion-based enterprise. This is particularly true where lead gifts are concerned. Many individuals, often without much forethought, write modest checks every day for good causes. But lead gifts—the kind that transform an organization—are usually tied to deeply held beliefs in the purpose of a nonprofit and are given with passion. The donor does expect accountability after the gift is made, and surely the tax implications are thoroughly examined during the decision-making stage. Nevertheless, the impulse to consult a financial adviser or concern over the measurable outcomes of a lead gift will stem from the donor's strong convictions about the purpose and the work of the organization. This kind of passion cannot be evoked by brochures or annual reports, which, from the donor's perspective, tend over time to make organizations seem more similar than different. Passion for an organization's purpose comes from involvement in the life of the organization.

Therefore, the heart of the matter is the development of meaningful, personal relationships with prospects and donors.

The most successful organizations find myriad ways of bringing individual donors inside, where they can help shape policy, test their values and interests against the organization's, fully understand the organization's mission, appreciate the organization's impact, and ultimately discover the right channels for expressing their passion for the organization's work through philanthropy. Involvement of this type does indeed beget significant investment, and organizations have the ability to choose just how and to whom they wish to extend this special level of involvement. It should be done with the understanding that practical considerations (time constraints, governing structures, budgetary limitations, program activities) allow for only a precious few individuals to see the organization in this special way. Therefore, those few should be carefully chosen. They will discover lead donors for your organization, make lead gifts themselves, or both.

Mature, Ongoing Relationships

Lead gifts from total strangers are wonderful but exceedingly rare. How many times have you personally been named beneficiary of a will drawn up by someone unknown to you? Lead gifts come almost invariably from individuals who have known an organization for a long time.

Endeavor daily to develop ever-deepening relationships with key stakeholders. The process of genuine engagement with volunteers must be extended to a broader circle of interested parties. It is a process of mutual selection, one whereby the donor selects the organization and the organization selects the donor for a long-term and even lifetime relationship. Nevertheless, one of the most critical errors made in securing lead gifts is failing to look beyond the immediate campaign to the lifetime value of a donor's relationship with the organization. The concept of a lifelong relationship, like the attitude of valuing lifetime friendships with donors, is central to creating an environment for lead gifts. Thinking, in a long-term context, about relationships with volunteers, donors, and other stakeholders brings several fundamental ideas into focus.

First, quality is more important than quantity. Creating a positive climate for lead giving, in and beyond the context of the campaign, is hardly a mass-production, assembly-line process; indeed, the richest 0.5 percent of the population owned 27 to 28 percent of the wealth in America in 1995 (United Auto Workers, 1997). Organizations are best advised to focus their time on and build mature relationships with individuals who can ultimately make the kinds of high-impact gifts that this chapter describes. This need not be a cold, calculating activity; rather, the organization's role is to serve as a catalyst in these relationships, and facilitating them is a process that is both consuming and rewarding—time-intensive but worthy of the organization's investment. It is more essential than ever to focus attention on building high-quality relationships with fewer individuals instead of seeking many relationships that never go beyond the superficial level. (If you do not believe this, reread Chapter Six.)

Second, multiple relationships inside the organization add value. The best volunteers and the most generous donors are those who extend their involvement in multiple ways. Over time, they may serve on different committees, contribute to different organizational programs, and form numerous relationships, whether with the chief executive officer or with clients served by the organization. For example, several years ago one institution discovered that a prospective donor had directed, over time, gifts of modest size to nearly twenty separate purposes within the organization. Needless to say, this donor had established multiple interests and many personal relationships at different levels, and these relationships contributed to a broad understanding of the organization's mission, as well as to the impact that the organization had on its constituency. When the time came for a multi-million-dollar lead investment in a single program, it was clear that this donor's many relationships had played a role in his continuing interest in the organization, as well as in his willingness to make a transformational gift—which he did, at the level of more than $20 million. In any organization, large or small, the focus should be on managing and, as appropriate, even creating multiple relationships inside the organization. Too often, however, the organization's first instinct is to direct prospects to the priority program rather than allowing them to explore their own interests. Organizations should encourage rather than restrict multiple contacts and connections.

Third, past donors are most likely to be future investors. Treat them well. There is nothing more fundamental than remembering past and current donors. The typical nonprofit organization, however, if it were to candidly examine where it places its priorities, would probably discover that it is much busier looking for the next big prospect than stewarding the last major donor. One college president, for example, complained that his staff relied too heavily on the "*Casablanca* method" of fundraising—"rounding up the usual suspects," as he put it—instead of broadening the base of donors. Every organization must of course find new friends in order to stay vibrant and keep moving forward, but an environment conducive to lead gifts evolves from careful stewardship of relationships with past and current donors. The challenge in the nonprofit sector is to focus as much energy on stewardship as on solicitation, thus creating an appropriately balanced environment for continuous lead giving.

The Act of Asking

In April 1998, Joan and Sanford Weill announced a gift of $100 million to name Cornell University's Medical Center. Mr. Weill, asked how he and his wife had decided to make this gift, pointed to Cornell's president and medical dean and said, "They asked" (Arenson, 1998). The circumstances surrounding this gift are private, of course, but it can be surmised that the decision was not quite so simple. And yet Mr. Weill's brief, spontaneous answer is poignant. It teaches, once again, the age-old lesson of fundraising at any level: the single biggest mistake in major gift fundraising is failing to ask for the gift; therefore, asking for the gift is the most important thing to do.

This seems obvious, but asking cannot be taken for granted. How many lead gifts have never materialized for your organization because the request was not made, even though all the other factors were in place? How many lead gifts went to "another organization" because that certain nonprofit group made a request and yours did not? How many gifts never reached their maximum potential because the basis of your strategy was insufficient thought and too little homework?

Our intention in this chapter is not to list the elements of a successful solicitation call or to provide stock answers to the typical objections encountered in such meetings. Rather it is to underscore the significance of actively, directly, and aggressively seeking philanthropic investments of the highest possible magnitude. If the proper steps are taken to develop an environment and culture conducive to lead giving, the achievement of significant gift commitments will naturally follow.

Exploring donors' values, fostering mature relationships, engaging volunteers in meaningful ways, personally involving the organization's top leader—all these activities play a part in getting a donor ready to say yes to a direct proposal or to respond to a vision by asking, "How much will it take?" None of this can happen, of course, without your organization's firm commitment to sustained, focused contact with volunteers and donors.

All lead gift solicitations are unique. Each prospect represents a minicampaign requiring specialized attention, creative approaches, and a solicitation grounded in the right strategy. But decisions about how to get these elements right are not made in a vacuum. They evolve from high-quality interactions with volunteers, past and current donors, and prospective donors. Establishing lead gift solicitation strategies requires a significant investment of time on behalf of the organization. The process is labor-intensive and very personalized, and the devotion of ample budgetary resources is essential. Budgetary investments leading to direct contact with prospects will create the most favorable conditions for lead giving.

In the act of asking, one more element deserves emphatic mention: challenge the donor, in terms of both the amount and the purpose of the gift. Stay within the bounds of reason and good professional judgment, of course, but do challenge the donor's competitive spirit by asking the donor to stretch, not just financially but also intellectually and emotionally. The most emotionally and intellectually committed lead gift prospects will expect nonprofit organizations to present them with concepts that respond to their own strong impulses to transform organizations through philanthropy.

The Act of Listening

It is the responsibility of the advancement officer—the staff member in charge of development and community relations—to put these cultivation "mechanics" in place. Doing so requires an often underemployed skill: listening.

Advancement listening, a term not normally found in books on listening skills, requires fundraising professionals and institutional leaders to develop a very keen sense of what a donor is and is not saying. For example, consider one extremely committed donor. The institution's relationships with this donor had followed the classic development track—initial identification of the donor, a visit from the development officer, a strong relationship with the chief executive officer. The donor was not a member of the institution's board. Throughout the evolution of this relationship, the donor's giving had increased. When the chief executive officer began to talk about an investment at the lead gift level, the need to grow the institution's endowment was stressed. Every time the subject was raised, however, the donor listened intently but kept turning the conversation to a specific building project that was also on the drawing board. The building was important—it would be needed within five years—but it was not the institution's highest priority. After repeated conversations, however, the advancement officer and the chief executive officer decided that they should listen to the donor. This act of advancement listening netted a $2 million building gift—the donor's single largest gift ever, by a factor of ten, with tremendous potential for more. Thus the organization chose, in this case, to subordinate a higher priority to an opportunity for matching a donor's interest with another worthy but less immediate project. This decision will probably net the institution millions of additional gift dollars in the years ahead, and the next lead gift from this donor is likely to be for endowment purposes.

Not every act of active listening ends so positively, however. Sometimes an institution must retreat from a gift discussion because the donor's wishes are incompatible with the institution's needs. Such cases are examples of the unique relationship between donors and institutions: donors make tremendous investments in organizations, but they do not run them. The chief executive officer and the institution's governing body determine which gifts can be accepted, and for what purposes; they set the priorities. It is vital for any institution, regardless of its financial condition, to maintain its integrity with respect to the gifts that it does and does not accept. Fortunate is the institution that is not financially dependent on its next lead gift!

Stewardship

Turning away gift support is a rarity at most institutions; a much larger challenge is proper stewardship of the gifts that are accepted.

There are several concepts about stewardship. The original concept predates the Bible, but it is codified in biblical language—that all possessions belong to God and that humanity is responsible for managing those resources while on earth. In feudal Europe, a steward was the person who ran the manor house, particularly the financial aspects of the estate. The green movement of the past few decades also uses the concept, emphasizing the need to be stewards of the earth's natural resources. An underlying element in each context is high moral quality and responsible management. A proper steward is one who is morally responsible and trustworthy.

Stewarding donors may not be thought of as a moral obligation, but it is an important concept. Donors have chosen to invest in your institution. They give time, energy, resources, and talent. As the steward of the manor, the organization has a responsibility to use those gifts wisely and to account for those uses properly. Donors place high trust in institutions, and so institutions should be systematic about telling donors how their money is used. Responses to inquiries about how gifts and other assets are managed should be immediate. Good stewardship also requires communication with donors when institutional needs change and when those changes affect donors' gifts.

There are some extremely practical reasons for being a good steward. No reasonable person would continue sending money to a financial institution that failed to report regularly on the investment. If you want your most committed stakeholders to remain committed, be forthright and regular in reporting on the dividends that their gifts are paying at your institution.

Good stewardship leads quite naturally to stronger existing relationships and to the development of new ones with the organization. Donors are investors, and they are interested in seeing a return on their investments. The stewardship requirement for lead gift prospects and donors goes far beyond sending an annual report on endowment performance or having the organization's chief executive officer pay an annual visit. Good stewardship is a personal process that is carefully managed. It aims not simply to maintain a donor's satisfaction but to increase that satisfaction to the point where the donor asks, "What more can I do?" Good stewardship is not just the end of the solicitation cycle; it is the beginning of a new and higher level of a donor's involvement.

Positioning Lead Gifts in a Campaign Context

In the 1980s, when capital campaign goals first exceeded the billion-dollar mark, some observers speculated that campaigns could not sustain themselves at such rarefied heights. Today, after the record-breaking bull market of the 1990s and the explosion of worldwide wealth, we have to wonder whether there is any ceiling at all to campaign goals.

Campaigns will remain part of the fundraising landscape for one simple reason: they work—they raise money. And lead gifts have never been more important to campaigns. Transformational gifts represent huge percentages of campaign totals. Capital campaigns' goals continue growing at a feverish pace because lead gifts are escalating exponentially.

Do donors really care about goals? Do campaigns provide an excuse to ask for unprecedented gifts? Twenty years ago, donors may not have cared as much about the details of capital campaigns. Today, however, they often care deeply about whether their gifts are made in the context of a campaign. Why is this so?

The decision to make a campaign gift does not always reflect a donor's desire to be included in a mass appeal for funds. Rather, it reflects the evolutionary role of campaigns and the programs that those campaigns seek to fund. It also reflects donors' increased sophistication. A successful capital campaign today is a direct outgrowth of the institution's strategic planning process. Institutional needs are not simply brought to the chief executive officer's desk and converted into a campaign brochure. The needs, goals, ambitions, and mission of the institution should be debated, discussed, and defined. The campaign is an outgrowth of the institution's strategic thinking. Lead gift donors increasingly want to know that their gifts will be used for specific, strategic purposes. For example, in February 1998 the University of Pennsylvania's law school announced the largest outright gift ever to a law school for construction and endowment purposes, and in May 1998 the Wharton School at the University of Pennsylvania announced the largest single gift ever to a business school in the United States (it was an unrestricted gift). In both cases, the donors were key volunteers who had taken a hand in shaping institutional directions and ambitions.

Involving key volunteers and donors in strategic planning is also vital to a campaign's success. Committed outsiders bring a real-world perspective to the planning process. Such donors become much more committed to the process, and they have a greater investment in its successful outcome when they have been consulted. Donors actually cultivate themselves through this process by becoming much more familiar with the strengths and needs of the institution. This is not to suggest that the planning process should be turned over to donors and volunteers, however; institutional representatives must ultimately develop and implement a strategic plan, but the involvement of key constituents will make finding resources much easier when it is time to fund the strategic initiatives. Donors do care about campaigns when the case for support has been clearly developed and can be backed by strategic analysis.

Capital campaigns provide a framework that makes securing lead gifts much easier. Campaigns set deadlines, benchmarks, and goals. Deadlines make decision making more efficient, and donors will be more efficient with their gift decisions when deadlines are set. The deadline concept is further refined in campaigns, too. Most campaigns do not go public until a certain percentage of the goal has been committed—usually between 40 and 60 percent—and lead gifts represent the bulk of the money raised during this quiet phase. Asking lead donors to make their gift commitments early, before the campaign goes public, creates another deadline that can encourage gift decisions. Skillful campaign leaders often set several intermediate deadlines as a way to benchmark progress and help close gifts.

Campaigns also provide a bandwagon effect, and campaign-conditioned donors often expect to play a part. Some donors will not make a gift decision unless they know it will be part of a larger institutional fundraising effort—as one donor said a few years ago, "I don't want to be a lone wolf." Donors at the lead gift level want their gifts to be counted among other large contributions. Campaigns provide a way for that to happen, and this "rising tide" encourages others to join. Donors also want to associate themselves with successful organizations, and successful campaigns provide that association.

Campaigns also offer a formal structure for recognizing philanthropy. Campaigns provide opportunities for regular stewardship and public relations–related events (donor recognition dinners, news releases, periodic campaign updates), and the campaign format increases the visibility of a donor's gift while also providing a larger audience for it. Gift announcements let institutions reinforce the campaign's overarching goals and highlight how the donor's investment supports the institutional mission. Donor recognition undergirds the stewardship process because it provides another way to thank the donor for the gift. It also encourages others to get on the bandwagon.

Not every donor prefers this kind of recognition, however. That was the situation recently when an institution received a very large gift—a record breaker—but both the gift and the donor's identity had to remain unknown; the donor did not want to make headlines with his act of philanthropy. This attitude is uncommon—even refreshing, given our age of hype and self-aggrandizement—but the opportunity to take full advantage of peer-to-peer, leveraged, sight-raising philanthropy is lost in such a situation.

Some major donors also give for reasons other than simple altruism. Ego gratification is often a very important consideration. A major donor may want regional and national publicity for a commitment. The donor may want peers and other volunteer leaders in the organization to know of his generosity and may also want his family and social set to be aware of the gift. Often major donors, highly successful in their professional lives, have developed a strong competitive spirit, and the same drive often motivates them to make major gifts and feel challenged to make even larger commitments. Lead gifts may become a vehicle through which these highly competitive, successful individuals, whose egos are often equally well developed, can make a statement to the business and philanthropic worlds.

Donors like these can and should be exacting about the publicity they receive for their gifts. Organizations cannot guarantee media coverage of gift announcements, of course. Some donors expect it, however, and capital campaigns often help in this area. Campaigns provide a context for a gift announcement and a message complementary to it: the campaign messages give the media something else to report in addition to the donor's gift and how it will be used. Campaign publications can be used, too. They are no substitute for prominent news coverage, but they do ensure that the message is delivered to the audience that you choose and at the time that you set.

An important consideration in announcing lead gifts is the staging, sequencing, and pacing of these announcements around campaign events and meetings. This strategy can have a strong motivational impact on both internal and external audiences. For example, asking a donor couple to announce their gift personally to peers has a tremendous emotional effect on those who have not yet given. These personal testimonies and the life stories behind them can be exemplary in raising the standard for the next cycle of campaign gifts.

A final word about press releases on gifts: keep the donor well informed. It is vital to stay in touch with the donor throughout the gift decision process, but it is equally important to keep the donor informed about announcement strategies. It is better to err on the side of giving the donor too many opportunities to change a news release or the circumstances surrounding an announcement. Putting up with some inconvenience is far preferable to angering a donor who feels insufficiently consulted about the publicity surrounding a lead gift that is, after all, an extremely personal matter.

Other Considerations

In addition to working with a donor or a donor couple, organizations often work with a donor's associates. This group may include spouses, significant others, children, other heirs, administrative staff members, and financial and legal advisers. These individuals can play a crucial role in the gift decision process and in the subsequent stewardship activity; they may be either advocates or adversaries in the giving process. The best rule is to involve them as early as possible: the organization benefits if its representatives know when to involve people associated with the donor.

Family and heirs present special issues in the negotiation of major gifts. They often have a personal stake in the donor's commitment and believe that they have a vested interest in the process. It is up to the institution—and sometimes the donor—to demonstrate that the gift decision is in the donor's best interest. Often, by using creative vehicles for planned giving, an institution can design a strategy that benefits the donor, his or her heirs, and the institution itself.

Negotiating such gift arrangements may involve the donor's financial and legal counsel, and institutional representatives often validate the donor's intended gift for these advisers. This is especially true when an adviser is looking for reasons to stop the donor from making the gift. Institutional representatives should have a working knowledge of the financial and tax implications of charitable gifts or should have ready access to people who do. Most donors make lead gifts for reasons other than the tax and estate benefits, but the tax laws do provide real opportunities for people with an interest in making charitable contributions. Never has this been so true as in today's financial markets, where millions of new fortunes—and potential new major donors—have been created with the dramatic increase in the value of equity markets.

Today, gifts of appreciated securities are becoming the currency of choice for major donors, and institutional staff must be well versed in the nuances of stock gifts. Sometimes a donor will make a gift decision when a stock reaches a specific value, or the donor may time a gift in conjunction with a capital event (such as the takeover of a company or an initial public offering). Gifts of stock in a donor's publicly traded corporation can also create special challenges and opportunities. For example, high-profile executives or board members who use corporate stock as their gift vehicle often worry about a possible adverse market reaction to their liquidation of stock for gift purposes. Some corporate insiders will not make significant stock gifts because they fear that the market will misinterpret their intent to give away securities. In work with donors and their advisers, each circumstance requires flexibility and creativity.

Most people are living longer than their parents did and will be much more active later in life. Therefore, another consideration for most donors is the maintenance of a certain standard of living. Longer life expectancy also holds the possibility of costs associated with long-term care for the donor and the donor's spouse, and this possibility can create tremendous pressure on donors to hold on to resources that might otherwise be given. Despite the old fundraising saw that "no one protects the donor's wallet like the donor," concerns about longer life expectancy are real and must be treated with respect and honesty. The ethics of our profession require us to maintain a fiduciary relationship with donors, especially older ones, and we must work with all major donors to craft gift arrangements that benefit both them and our organizations.

Philanthropic work achieves the greatest joy and the most good when it moves beyond the "mechanics of fundraising" and "sealing the deal." Greater success will be achieved if fundraisers adopt a long-term view of their work and recognize that leadership investments are about building lasting relationships that offer meaning and value to the donor first and benefits to the organization second. Placing the donor's interests and vision above the organization's needs unleashes the potential to move organizations forward through philanthropy.

CHAPTER FIFTEEN

APPROACHING CORPORATIONS AND FOUNDATIONS

This chapter discusses the similarities and differences between corporate and foundation philanthropy, the ever-changing patterns that influence their giving, and the preparation of proposals, the most commonly used method of solicitation with foundations and corporations.

Corporations, corporate foundations, and foundations today provide about 10 to 15 percent of all philanthropic giving. Koch (1998) reports that over the past thirty years, the absolute value of corporate gifts has increased relatively steadily. More than 90 percent of America's largest companies made charitable contributions in 1998, a total of $8.97 billion. This was 5.1 percent of all charitable contributions made in 1998. Corporate contributions have generally represented between 4.0 and 6.5 percent of all charitable giving.

Despite this apparent increase, corporate contributions have not grown faster than the economy as a whole. Over the past forty years, corporate contributions have held steady at about 0.1 percent of gross domestic product (GDP). Total charitable giving, by contrast—including gifts from foundations, individuals, and corporations—is typically around 2 percent of GDP. Corporate giving as a percentage of pretax income has actually declined in recent years. Substantial increases in corporate profits have allowed for increases in the absolute dollar value of contributions, while the percentage of pretax income has nonetheless decreased.

Wasow (1998) concludes that the notion of corporate citizenship is an increasingly ambiguous one. Corporate charitable contributions account for only a small fraction of total charitable giving in the United States, and there is little indication that this is likely to change. Nevertheless, evidence suggests that businesses have become increasingly involved in the nonprofit sector in other ways. Corporate volunteerism, cause-related marketing, and long-term partnerships focused on the exchange of information and expertise all seem to be on the rise, and none is fully captured in IRS data on corporate philanthropy. The Conference Board estimates that 19 percent of U.S. corporate contributions are non-tax-deductible assistance expenditures that are not captured in IRS figures (Tillman, 1998). Although such nonprofit-business relationships are not motivated by philanthropic impulses, they do provide important resources for the nonprofit community.

Critics fear in this climate that nonprofits may sell out, sacrificing their integrity for financial security. This is a legitimate worry. The American Medical Association (AMA) was recently embroiled in a lawsuit with Sunbeam Corporation, a maker of home healthcare products. AMA members forced the organization to back out of what they saw as an inappropriate cause-related marketing deal. Nevertheless, organizations that want to take full advantage of corporate support for the nonprofit sector will likely find that they must broaden their view of philanthropy and develop relationships that will benefit companies as well as recipient organizations. Magazine editor John F. Kennedy Jr. (1999) said shortly before his untimely death, "Looking out for profits and people at the same time just makes good business sense." As the balance point of the corporate-nonprofit pendulum swings, this perspective likely marks the place at which it will settle.

The picture is clearer for foundations. Blum and Dundjerski (1999) report that foundation giving is surging. Most foundations base the amount they give on the value of their endowments the previous year. Federal law requires that foundations disburse at least 5 percent of the value of their assets, on average, each year. Therefore, foundation giving is inextricably tied to two fundamentals: the health of the economy and the amount of new money infused into foundations through additions to existing assets and the creation of new foundations. Because the economy remains strong, numerous big new foundations are being created and several small ones are receiving big infusions of assets. Perhaps the most significant growth has come in the two foundations created by Microsoft's Bill Gates and his wife, Melinda. In the course of one recent year, the assets of the William H. Gates Foundation in Seattle and the Gates Learning Foundation, in Redmond, Washington, tripled. In 1999 the Gateses merged the two to form the Bill and Melinda Gates Foundation with assets of $17.1 billion, making it the wealthiest philanthropy in America (Schneider, 1999).

Blum and Dundjerski (1999) also report four other themes that will affect the direction of foundation giving in the early part of the twenty-first century:

- *Changes in foundation leadership.* Changes in leadership often bring new views and changes in direction
- *Movement to new grantmaking programs.* Even without changes in leadership, foundations on occasion change direction, and the dramatic growth fueled by the economy of the later 1990s swelled the giving ability of a number of foundations.
- *A focus on more strategic grantmaking.* Just like the trend in business away from diversification and toward focus on core business operations, foundations too are moving back to a narrower focus on core areas of interest.
- *A willingness to give to general operating expenses.* The drift has been in the other direction for the past quarter century.

There is one other significant factor. Says William L. Taylor Jr., vice president for development at the University of Texas Houston Health Science Center, "The key decision maker can direct resources irrespective of general guidelines" (personal communication, July 1999). Abzug and Webb (1997) and Galaskiewicz and Sinclair (1997) agree by pointing out that in the vast majority of publicly held companies, gifts are distributed by managers rather than the shareholders who own the company. In theory, managers have a more limited stake in the financial success of the company than shareholders do. They might use contributions to enhance their own prestige within the community or to support organizations whose services they use because they are not directly affected by any small detrimental effects that these gifts may have on corporate profits. Banard (1997) envisions competition between corporate giving programs or even institutionalized giving clubs in which managers and chief executive officers leverage their companies' gifts to advance their personal positions or to support their personal beliefs in these hierarchies.

Taylor sums it up neatly: foundations and corporations give "to established reputations and quality; to well-designed and convincing cases that present vision, not problems, solutions not needs; to ideas that advance the community; and to solicitors who are peers and whom they cannot turn down" (personal communication, July 1999).

For nonprofits that fit Taylor's model, corporations and foundations remain a significant resource, and the potential for growth and expansion in the first quarter of the twenty-first century will keep both in the mainstream of philanthropy.

Researching Corporations and Corporate Foundations

According to Kathy Wilson, director of development services at the Indiana University Foundation (personal communication, Sept. 1998), research on corporate prospects needs to address four vital questions:

1. How financially healthy is the business?
2. What are its current products, and what are its interests in your institution?
3. What existing relationships could be used for moving this prospect to the next step of cultivation or solicitation?
4. How has the corporation supported your institution in the past, and why would it want to give support again? It is more important to the corporation to fulfill its own need than to fund your institution's project.

The following basic information should be gathered on each corporate prospect:

- Full name and correct address
- Corporate assets
- Type of business
- Names of corporate officers and directors
- Names of officers of any existing corporate foundation
- Sales volume
- Previous giving record
- Decision-making process
- Gifts to other institutions (more difficult to determine if there is no corporate foundation)
- Connections with the institution (if yours is an educational institution, names of alumni employed by the corporation; if a hospital, names of patients the corporation employs; and so forth)
- History of dealings with your institution
- Local subsidiaries and the names of their officers
- Information about the corporate gift committee (names, connections, and kindred interests)

Corporate financial analyses are available on the World Wide Web, particularly via the EDGAR database. Fee-based services on the Internet that provide financial information on corporations include Dialog, Lexis/Nexis, and Dun & Bradstreet. CD-ROM- and print-based sources include *The Directory of Corporate Affiliations* (the CD-ROM version is *Corporate Affiliations Plus*), the *Million Dollar Directory, Standard & Poor's*, and the Moody series of industrial manuals. Many of these CD-ROM and book resources are available at local libraries. The Dun & Bradstreet on-line database is one of several that provide information on public and private companies. One of the best places to gather information on public companies (and on some private companies) is the EDGAR Database of Corporate Information at http://www.sec.gov/edgarhp.htm (EDGAR stands for "electronic data gathering analysis and retrieval"), which offers free access to Securities and

Exchange Commission documents that have been filed electronically by public corporations.

From the standpoint of corporate and foundation relations, it is equally important to learn something about company products, research and development, and future marketing plans. An annual report can supply some of this information. Other possible sources are the institution's office of sponsored research (if it has one), which may be aware of research and development interests within the corporation. Philanthropic publications such as *Taft Corporate Giving Web* and *Philanthropic Digest* list corporate contributions, which can be reviewed for trends in grants for research and development. In addition, several databases list awards of government contracts. Finally, newspapers and journals can provide a glimpse of the future. Articles in such magazines as *Fortune* and *Forbes* may provide a vision of the direction in which the corporate prospect is moving. Local newspapers are an equally valuable resource.

Working with the appropriate in-house staff, the institution needs to expand on the basic questions about relationships with corporate prospects. If yours is an educational institution, for instance, how many alumni are employed by the corporation? Do any members of your institution's staff serve on the corporation's advisory board or science advisory panel? Does the corporation in any way rely on your institution for services? What about funding history? Has funding come from the corporation or from the corporate foundation? Enlightened corporate self-interest is the basis of these relationships, and so it is important to understand these components in planning a fundraising approach. Except for a few national corporations and corporate foundations, and the local business community, this category of prospects has become more specialized in recent years. Most do not give outside the areas where they have plants, programs, or people. Very often, quid pro quo considerations—stockholder concerns, for example—determine the granting policies of national corporations.

Besides major corporations, other sources for support of a campaign include local independent businesses, vendors, and businesses that are owned by or employ people who are affiliated with the institution, whatever their geographical location. In dealing with any prospect, but especially a corporate or foundation prospect, a campaign should never extend its boundaries beyond the circle represented by its volunteer leaders. This is a cardinal rule that is often broken in campaigns.

As Richard K. Dupree, executive director of development at Indiana University's Kelley School of Business, and Tracy A. Connelly, director of corporate and foundation relations at the school, point out (personal communication, July 1999), corporations and corporate foundations give to what they know. They know their local communities, local and state educational institutions, and local nonprofit organizations. They also know their business—pharmaceuticals, accounting, or technology, both in their local community and throughout the world.

Most corporations and corporate foundations still prefer to give to organizations located where they operate. There are several possible reasons for this:

- They know the organization and its leadership (they read about it in the newspaper; they attend events sponsored by the organization; corporate executives serve on the organization's board).
- They feel a sense of obligation to the community in which they are located and do business.
- They want to reinvest in the community to help meet short- and long-term business or community objectives (workforce development, neighborhood improvement, diversity).
- They can more easily monitor the impact of their giving by visiting the organization and meeting with local organizational leaders.
- They can effect change on a smaller scale rather than spreading philanthropic dollars across wide areas.
- The goodwill and public relations impact of their philanthropy is vastly increased among employees, customers, suppliers, and community members who know the corporation.

Corporations and corporate foundations that give outside their geographical area do so because they know the organization they are supporting. They can justify that either there is no local organization that can carry out their objective in the same way or that the organization has expertise beyond the ones present locally. Corporation and foundation giving officers are often extremely knowledgeable about their program areas within their geographical areas and beyond. For example, a California-based technology corporation may make a gift to a midwestern college or university because the school is a leader in education and research. That same corporation might also decline a proposal from a college or university in its own community if the school is not a leader in the field or does not meet a specific business objective of the corporation. Conversely, the same corporation would be more likely to support a human services organization in its own California community than a similar organization in the Midwest.

Ways Corporations and Corporate Foundations Give

Corporations give in a variety of ways and for a variety of reasons. Increasingly, corporations and corporate foundations have an objective to carry out with their nonprofit organization partners. If a corporation wants to combat illiteracy, it might donate cash to organize and deliver workshops for children at risk. The company might also encourage volunteerism by its employees to serve as role models and mentors to the children and so might provide, for example, a corporate van to transport children to and from the workshop. Cash, in-kind equipment and services, and volunteerism are just a few of the ways corporations and foundations accomplish philanthropy.

Matching Gifts

Matching gifts, originally designed to encourage and reward employees' personal giving and to allow employees to participate in directing corporate giving, have proved very popular. Indeed, because of the tremendous demands on funds available to provide matches, companies are now reining in these programs in various ways:

- They are leveling out the incentives: 3:1 and 2:1 matches were more prevalent in the past; 1:1 is the norm today.
- They are putting ceilings, or lowering existing ceilings, on the amounts they will match per individual donor.
- They are becoming more selective in the kinds of gifts they will match. Historically, companies would simply follow the employee's gift designation. Now more companies are limiting the scope of what will be matched so as to reflect corporate priorities more closely. A good number prohibit matching certain types of gifts (for example, gifts to college athletic programs), and virtually all choose not to give to religious organizations or organizations they deem "controversial."

Volunteerism

Corporations are becoming more supportive of volunteerism programs. Though growth is hard to quantify and varies by industry, some studies suggest volunteering has more than doubled in the past five years. This is an excellent way for nonprofits without a ready-made way of identifying new prospects to bring additional people into their orbit.

In-Kind Gifts

In-kind gifts represent about 25 percent of all corporate contributions, according to the Conference Board (Tillman, 1998). Pharmaceutical companies, office equipment manufacturers, and manufacturers of scientific and photographic equipment and computers are among the industry leaders in using this form of giving.

Pro Bono Services

The giving of time is a practice often used by professionals and professional groups, such as lawyers, doctors, and accountants. Companies also do this in the form of loaned executives.

Facilities

A growing number of companies are opening up meeting rooms or other facilities at no cost for use by nonprofits.

Cause-Related Marketing

Wasow (1998) notes that other trends in corporate support of nonprofits straddle the line between philanthropy and advertising. Cause-related marketing is potentially a profitable revenue source for nonprofit organizations, and it is becoming increasingly common. Loosely defined, cause-related marketing is the public association of a for-profit company with a nonprofit organization, intended to promote the company's product or service and to raise money for the nonprofit.

Most cause-related marketing is not considered a charitable contribution by the IRS, but it is an important avenue for corporate support of nonprofits. Cause-related marketing agreements can include everything from affinity credit cards to the use of nonprofit logos on products.

Sponsorships

Wasow (1998) further notes that sponsorship of events, like other forms of cause-related marketing, can be classified as either a tax-deductible donation or advertising. The distinction lies in the way the sponsorship is promoted. If a nonprofit bases the size of a funding request on the number of people attending an event, the size of an ad, or the number of pieces to be distributed, or if the nonprofit compares a sponsor's product or service to a competitor's or endorses the product or service, it will be considered advertising and is not tax-deductible.

This legal ambiguity is characteristic of cause-related marketing techniques. While there is little question that nonprofits do benefit from these marketing tactics, they can also be extremely profitable for businesses, which has made this form of corporate "philanthropy" controversial. Critics argue that cause-related marketing, with its focus on the corporation's bottom line, is not a charitable gesture and should not be described as such.

Partnerships

Dupree and Connelly (personal communication, Oct. 1999) indicate that many corporations have formed partnerships with colleges and universities (partnerships need not be limited to educational institutions), whom they see as a supplier for their future human resource needs. The company does some forward buying by creating scholarships, fellowships, or attaching its name to a classroom or lecture hall. If the company strives for visibility among college or university faculty, it might invest in a professorship or endow a chair. Although some observers argue that the quid pro quo associated with corporate contributions is not in the spirit of true philanthropy, it remains true that corporations are not in business to give money away. Corporations exist to make a profit, and so their philanthropy must ultimately further a bottom-line objective. By creating partnerships, nonprofit organizations and corporations and corporate foundations can help each other accomplish their separate goals.

Types of Foundations

Foundations give truth to the adage that charity begins at home. The vast majority of foundations give in their own communities or geographical areas. Some give regionally, a few give nationally, and a handful give internationally. The largest concentration of foundations, in terms of both size and number, is on the island of Manhattan in New York City. The majority of their support is given to organizations within a 250-mile radius of the city. Another cluster of large foundations calls Texas home. The vast majority of them do not make grants outside the state of Texas. It's a strong reminder to keep the home fires burning.

Tromble (1999) identifies five types of foundations:

- *Independent foundations* include America's largest: the Lilly Endowment, Ford, Kellogg, Kresge, Rockefeller. Most were established by individuals or families of wealth.
- *Corporate foundations* like the Exxon Education Foundation and the General Electric Foundation are extensions, some more distanced than others, of their companies and their giving policies usually further the company's interests.
- *Community foundations,* ranging from the New York Community Trust to the Henry County (Indiana) Community Foundation, are local, community-based, and regionally sponsored. They are funded by a number of separate donors, each with their own funding guidelines, as opposed to a single donor. They often serve as distributors and managers of family foundations and fortunes.

- *Operating foundations* like the J. Paul Getty Trust or the Longwood Foundation sponsor their own programs and make few or no grants to outside organizations.
- *Institutional foundations* like the Indiana University Foundation or the British Columbia's Children's Hospital Foundation have a single mission: to support the host institution. They make no grants outside the institution.

Researching Foundations

Billian (1985) says that foundations are the easiest of the three types of prospects to research because they usually have specific funding interests that are known or that can easily be determined by potential applicants. For the most part, these interests are dictated by policy and by the foundation's granting history. The information sought about a foundation is basically the same type of information as that sought about a corporation, and it will include the following elements:

- Full, correct name
- Street address and phone number
- Names of the officers or directors and their professional connections
- Brief historical sketch of the foundation (when it was created, by whom, and for what purposes)
- Current assets
- Amount of recent grants, by year and by individual recipient
- Decision-making process
- Pattern of giving (to what kinds of institutions and for what programs, with specific examples)
- Your institution's best contact with the foundation (the person to visit or send a proposal to)
- The foundation's connections with your institution
- History of your institution's contacts with the foundation
- Copy of a recent PF 990 tax form for the foundation, with a listing of income and grants made (copies of this form are available through the Associates Program of the Foundation Center) and statements of interest published by the foundation
- Most recent annual report (also available through the Associates Program of the Foundation Center)

There are several excellent sources of such information in addition to the Associates Program of the Foundation Center. Three of the most widely used are *Prospector's Choice, FC Search,* and the *Foundation Directory.* All four sources provide information about foundations' financial assets, interests, giving focus, grants to other institutions, and requirements for submitting proposals. One valuable component of these references is their indexing of information according to foundations' giving interests. Many of these materials are also available through Dialog. More information may also be available on a foundation's Web site on the Internet. Always check to see if a foundation you are interested in has a Web site.

William Taylor (personal communication, July 1999) advises that it's often best to submit a proposal at the beginning of a foundation's fiscal year, before the money is given away. And sometimes, in economic boom years, unexpended money that must be given away may remain at the end of a fiscal year. In any event, always obtain submission deadlines directly from the foundation—they change from year to year—and get your submission in on time.

There are several sources of information about where a corporate or foundation prospect has contributed in the past. A few of the most popular are the *Directory of Corporate and Foundation Givers* (Taft), *Corporate Foundation Profiles* (Foundation Center), *Corporate 500* (Public Management Institute), *National Directory of Corporate Giving* (Foundation Center), *Directory of International Corporate Giving* (Taft), *Corporate and Foundation Grants* (Taft), *Chronicle of Philanthropy, Corporate Philanthropy Report,* and *Corporate Giving Watch.*

Preparing Proposals

A proposal is a request for support formally presented or submitted to a prospective donor. In other words, it is a solicitation, an ask. It is most often written, although it may be a verbal request; verbal requests are usually accompanied by or supported by a written document, however. Proposals may be as simple as a one-page letter or may be a comprehensive, elaborate presentation (see Resource 22, "Letter Proposal," and Resource 23, "Full Proposal").

A proposal is designed to do two things:

- To make a potential donor aware that your organization has a program or a project that will accomplish something that the donor wants done
- To invite the potential donor to invest in this program or project, thus filling the potential donor's need to get that something done

Don't think about how a foundation or corporation can help you achieve your goals; rather consider how your organization can help the foundation or corporation achieve its goals, and present your proposal accordingly.

Follow the guidelines provided by the potential funding source. Deviations from these requirements will usually trigger a penalty and may cause the proposal to be dropped from consideration. Foundations and corporations receive far more qualified proposals than they can fund—some report ten to fifteen for every grant made—and one method of pruning the list is to eliminate proposals that do not follow the guidelines. The format to be used will depend on the nature of your organization's relationship with the potential funding source and its requirements for submission. You may find that corporate or foundation giving officers are willing to answer questions as the proposal is developed. This can be crucial. The same principles described in Chapter Sixteen with regard to good writing, effective presentations, and speaking in your institution's distinctive voice apply equally to publications and proposals.

A full proposal should contain all of the following information.

1. Cover letter (very important; use it to emphasize key ideas in the proposal)
2. Proposal cover or title page
3. Table of contents
4. Executive summary (no longer than one page for a long proposal, one paragraph for a short proposal)

    Amount requested

    Specific purpose of the grant

    Anticipated results

5. Introduction (in short proposals, the executive summary may serve as the introduction)

    The issue

    Your plan

    Amount requested

6. Discussion of the issue

    What's wrong

    Why it's important to address the issue

    How you propose to address the issue (what you will do, what others have done, why your way is better)

7. Solution

    What you will accomplish

    How you will accomplish it

    What it will take to address the issue (people, money, other resources)

8. Your organization's qualifications

    What you've done in the past

    What you're doing now

    What you're contributing (talent, time, space, money)

    What you'll do next

9. Methods (ways in which you intend to accomplish the goal)

10. Evaluation plan (how you'll know the goal has been accomplished)

11. Future funding plans (how the project will survive when the grant is gone)

12. Budget (as complete and detailed as possible, with narrative)

13. Conclusion

14. Summary

15. Thanks

16. Appendixes (as brief and informative as possible)

    Evidence of tax-exempt status

    Supporting documents

    Letters of commitment, commendations, support, and the like

    Other specific information

    Other general information

The Fund Raising School (1995) cites twelve primary reasons why proposals do not get funded:

- Project has not been documented properly.
- Project does not strike reviewer as significant; statement of the project does not stimulate interest.
- Prospective client groups have not been involved in planning and determining project goals.
- Proposal is poorly written or hard to understand.
- Proposal objectives do not match objectives of funding source.
- Proposal budget is not within range of funding available.
- Proposed project has not been coordinated with other individuals and organizations working in the same area.
- Funding source has not been convinced that the individuals submitting the proposal are capable of carrying it out.
- Project objectives are too ambitious.

- Proposal does not follow guidelines provided by funding agency.
- Insufficient evidence is provided that the project can sustain itself beyond the life of the grant.
- Evaluation procedures are inadequate.

Proposals, at least those that get funded, seldom arrive unannounced and uninvited. The same principles that apply to the cultivation of individuals apply to the cultivation of corporations and foundations. Letters of inquiry, telephone calls, e-mail exchanges, and personal visits are the precursors to the submission of a proposal that gets funded. It has been said, although it is not proven, that more than 75 percent of grants made by foundations go to organizations and institutions with whom or more members of the board have personal involvement or close associations. The two most significant reasons why people give money to causes are belief in the cause and involvement with the organization. Foundation and corporate giving guidelines direct decisions, but board members and chief executive officers make the decisions.

William Taylor (personal communication, July 1999) concludes:

> Corporation and foundation work is essentially major individual gift work. There are key players who make decisions, and they are swayed by the same considerations any individual of means is—reputation of the institution, fiscal probity, a convincing case, and preeminently, who solicits. As competition increases, the peer volunteer, committed and well versed, becomes ever more the trump card in the deck. We all have good causes, and good institutions; but who believes in us and is willing to turn to us makes all the difference. This is old news, but every day proves it out more and more.

CHAPTER SIXTEEN

PROMOTING THE CAMPAIGN

Publications alone do not raise money, but funds cannot be raised without them. They are especially helpful with people who are not institutional insiders; they also give confidence and provide support and security to volunteers and staff alike. Therefore, fundraising promotional materials and activities must be planned in light of their specific purposes and in the belief that they will make a difference.

Types of Fundraising Communications

The case statement and its derivatives are clearly the most important pieces of fundraising literature (see Chapter Three). Nevertheless, the nonprofit will also need several other written pieces:

- A pledge card or contribution form
- A brochure on taxes and estate planning for people making major gifts
- Instructions to workers
- A fact booklet on the organization
- An impact-of-organization brochure or financial impact study
- A campaign or program newsletter
- Campaign reports
- Transcript materials (major gift presentations, foundation and corporate proposals)

For examples of such materials, see Resource 9, "Annual Campaign Volunteer's Kit"; Resource 10, "Capital Campaign Volunteer's Kit"; Resource 24, "Monthly Financial Report"; Resource 25, "Newsletters"; Resource 26, "Pledge Forms"; and Resource 27, "Letterhead and Envelopes."

A brochure on taxes and estate planning and a companion piece on memorial or named gift opportunities are important pieces of campaign literature. Both are intended to raise sights and encourage larger gifts by pointing out tax advantages and offering an opportunity for personalizing gifts in a permanent and appealing way. These brochures will take a variety of forms, in keeping with the circumstances of an individual campaign (see Resource 10, "Capital Campaign Volunteer's Kit").

Another vital piece of campaign literature is an instruction booklet for workers (see Resource 10, "Capital Campaign Volunteer's Kit"). This volunteer guide should provide a step-by-step program designed to educate volunteer solicitors and make them feel at ease. It should also describe the suggested procedure for cultivating prospects and securing major gifts. Some campaign directors also prepare information for volunteers that focuses on how to close the gift and that details the skills needed to close (opening, questioning, listening, presenting, overcoming objections, and asking for the gift; see Chapter Eleven).

A fact sheet about the institution need not be elaborate. Nevertheless, it should be comprehensive and should provide a variety of important general information that will educate volunteers and provide answers to many of the routine questions that prospects may ask, especially if they are not intimately familiar with the institution.

The campaign newsletter is another piece of literature that takes infinite shapes and forms (see Resource 25, "Newsletters"). It is important that the campaign newsletter be published regularly. It should make liberal use of pictures of volunteers, donors, and others involved in the campaign and, within reason, should include the greatest possible number of people's names. The best campaign newsletter will also have a well-thought-out purpose. It serves not only to provide recognition and reward for volunteers and donors but also to set the tone for the campaign and to move the fundraising effort forward in an organized, efficient, effective manner.

Another important component of the campaign literature is pledge documentation (see Resource 26, "Pledge Forms"). The most basic form of this documentation is the campaign pledge card. The typical pledge card provides space for the name and address of the prospect, a statement indicating that the donor's pledge is made "in consideration of the gifts of others and toward the campaign goal," a place to record the amount of the pledge, a statement of how it will be paid (if in some way other than cash), a statement of the payment period, and a description of the frequency with which payments are to be made, including the starting date. It also provides a place for the donor's signature and a space for indicating both the amount paid, if any, at the time the pledge is made and the balance remaining. It is important that a statement appear on the face of the pledge card that contributions "are deductible for federal and state income tax purposes as provided by law." It should be clearly indicated to whom checks should be made payable.

Also to be included, usually on the back of the card, is a statement indicating whether the soliciting institution intends to treat the pledge as a legally binding obligation. (The majority of campaigns do not treat pledges as legal obligations.) There should be ample space for the donor to indicate a gift designation (if the gift is to be restricted) and any commemorative gift wording that the donor may wish to have used, as well as a place for other information. The pledge card should also include a place for the volunteer's name and the date of the solicitation.

In addition to the basic pledge card, some pledge instruments have two perforated, detachable pieces referred to as ears. The first ear is used for a confidential statement indicating the gift rating of the prospect, to guide the solicitor in making the call. The information included here is highly confidential, and the volunteer should detach it before seeing the prospect; it should never be shown to a prospect. The other ear is a temporary acknowledgment form. If its use is required, this ear should be separated from the pledge card at the time the commitment is made. These forms usually include places for writing the name of the donor, the total amount of the gift, and the amount, if any, at the time of the pledge. There is also a place for the volunteer to sign and date the temporary acknowledgment. The temporary acknowledgment usually indicates that an official gift receipt will be mailed in the near future.

The second instrument used to record pledges is a letter of intent (see Resource 10, "Capital Campaign Volunteer's Kit"). The third form of pledge commitment is a letter written by the donor on personal or corporate stationery and giving the same information that would be recorded on a pledge card or included in a letter of intent.

The number and quality of support materials developed in support of any campaign is going to be influenced by the overall fundraising goal. It is easy to understand that while the same aids are needed to support all campaigns, more funds are available to budget on such expenditures when the goal is $600,000 than when the goal is $150,000. Efforts and expenditures made in all campaigns must be to scale. However, just because the fundraising goal may permit larger expenditures, expenditures should always be dictated by common sense, good taste, and prudent judgment. Never skimp on quality, however. In addition to the various printed documents, appropriate audiovisual materials should routinely be prepared.

These may include a synchronized-sound slide show, motion pictures, audiocassettes, videocassettes, flipcharts, graphs, posters, and mockups or models.

It is also important to design the presentation of the case statement so that it is easy to interpret differently for various market segments. The same information about the organization may be viewed differently from the perspective of a corporate executive, a wealthy philanthropist, a vendor, or a neighborhood group. In designing literature and institutional approaches for various constituencies, it is important to remain flexible so that the approach can be tailored to produce optimal results. With the explosion of technology and the ever-widening possibilities for delivering messages, all materials should be adaptable to distribution via the World Wide Web and through telecommunications media and all the other emerging technologies as well as through more conventional methods.

No function of the campaign literature and audiovisual material can be more important than supporting and sustaining a mood of importance, relevance, and urgency and an atmosphere of optimism and institutional community. This function becomes more and more important as campaign goals go higher and higher and as schedules have to cover more and more time: as solicitation moves from the inside out, from one group of potential givers to another, and as the few traveling teams of official advocates go from group to group—and, in wide-area campaigns, from city to city—the risk of having the campaign die on the vine becomes real indeed.

The key to avoiding this problem is for the campaign chair, the chief executive officer, and others to keep delivering the message of the campaign, actively and continuously engaging in the case-stating process, and never letting up until the job is done. They should never make speeches or write reports without referring to the unfinished task, doing so with all the gravity due its importance and with the confidence of certain and complete success.

What they and the campaign publications say, and keep saying, is important in itself; almost equally important is that everything and everyone say it again and again and carry the same message, even if it is stated with different emphases for different constituencies. Continuity is the business of all institutional communications, whether they are disseminated via magazines, newsletters, or Web sites. Indeed, this is the principal business of campaign bulletins or newsletters, which nevertheless sometimes make the mistake of dealing almost solely with progressive statistics. These bulletins deserve careful planning so that every issue deliberately plays up the attainment of higher standards, the involvement of respected people, praise from outside the institution, significant growth in the campaign, quotations worthy of repetition, and every good thing to be thought of that can boost confidence.

Preparing Campaign Publications

Jana Wilson, director of development publications at the Indiana University Foundation, says that fundraising publications should be to the point—brief, simple, and clear (personal communication, Nov. 1999). In an environment of twenty-second electronic media sound bites and *USA Today*–style print reporting, your audience, unless keenly interested—and most often it is not, at least initially—is not going to respond to lengthy pieces that are poorly designed, written, or presented. Hence the first thing you must know is what the point of a particular publication is. Wilson achieves this by doing a creative strategy for every publication. "No matter what the project is, you need to know what you have to say, who you're saying it to, and how you want to say it," she explains. The basic elements to be considered in formulating a creative strategy are the following:

- *Objective:* What do you want this piece to do?
- *Strategy:* How are you going to use it?
- *Target audience:* Who is the publication for?
- *Primary message (call to action):* What do you want the reader to do? (If you can't state this in a single sentence, you may be trying to do too much with one publication.)
- *Secondary message:* What else needs to be said?
- *Tone:* Is it light and festive? Warm and nostalgic? Edgy and high-tech? Everyone needs to be on the same wavelength.
- *Deadlines:* When must the project be finished? Work backward from that date to determine when the various parts of the project need to be done.
- *Budget:* How much do you have to spend? Do not go over your budget. But be aware that the budget will determine how your publication looks. Usually, you get what you pay for.

If an institution does not have a top-quality publications department, it should seriously consider hiring outside help to produce its campaign publications, especially the major ones. If outside help is used, do not relinquish control over the finished product. Monitor progress, and require periodic checks with the campaign leaders. Do not scrimp on campaign publications. Prestige pieces are a necessity, and they will pay for themselves. In creating the communications package for a campaign, review the proposed strategy, audience message, and goal for each piece. If necessary, restate the message as it should appear in each communication, remembering that different communications are written to address and reach different audiences.

Always develop logic to support the request or message in each communication. Analyze what the audience has indicated it would like to hear; use the feedback process to secure important information. Write, dictate, or design the first draft of a communication, and then edit to eliminate triteness, fuzziness, and pet phrasing. Then test the communication with a segment of its target audience and listen for a response. It may be necessary to revise this communication after audience feedback and review.

A word about style is also in order here: the principles of clear, concise, idiomatic writing that apply to other nonfiction can be the guide for brochures as well. To the point of clear, concise, precise writing, Paula La Rocque (1992) offers these guidelines:

- Keep to one idea per sentence.
- Keep sentences short. Vary lengths, but any sentence that contains more than twenty-three words is long. If you must use a long sentence, place a short one before and after it.
- Don't have more than three numerical expressions of any kind in one sentence.
- Don't use more than three prepositional phrases in any sentence. If the phrases run consecutively or have the same preposition, even three are too many.
- When unraveling an unclear sentence, find the subject-verb-object relationship. Don't resort unnecessarily to the passive voice.
- Reduce long or difficult words to shorter or simpler terms. Recast jargon and journalese, pretentious or repetitive phrasing, in everyday words.
- Don't back into a sentence with unnecessary clauses or clauses that delay the subject. Move those clauses later in the sentence (or omit them entirely).
- Prune all deadwood and redundancy from the sentence (write "now" instead of "at the present time," "soon" instead of "in the immediate future," and so on).
- Don't pack the lead. Specificity is wonderful, but if you can't be specific without weighing down your opening paragraph, choose a general, clear statement and support it with details later.
- Maintain a graceful, conversational manner of expression. Read the work aloud to check rhythm and readability.
- Choose concrete over abstract terms.
- Use strong, direct verbs instead of weak ones or verb phrases ("they decided" instead of "they made a decision," "we can" instead of "we are in a position to," "they intend" instead of "it is their intention").

Campaign promotions too often contain a lot of specialized or insider language—jargon that is familiar to educators, medical staff, or seminary scholars but baffling to almost everyone else. Try to avoid it. Keep in mind that most donors—and all major ones—will be laypeople who respond best to plain language, short sentences, and familiar usages. One rule of good writing that particularly applies to fundraising brochures is to avoid generalities and look for specifics. Every institution has its own history, achievements, and vital statistics. Know them, and include them in the writing.

David W. Barton Jr., retired president of Barton Gillet, is fond of reminding people that the characters in Mark Twain's *Huckleberry Finn* speak in five distinct dialects. He specifically mentions that Twain pointed to this phenomenon in the book's introduction because he had taken pains to get the dialects right: the characters speak authentically, and Twain wanted the reader to appreciate what he had accomplished; what he wrote is a masterpiece in part because he respected his characters enough to get their language right. In the same way, every institution speaks in a different voice, with a different tone and a different stylistic emphasis. If an institution can capture its own flavor and essence in its campaign literature, its constituents will respond to it. The difference between the right word and the nearly right word is the difference between lightning and a lightning bug; in the same way, the right word and the right image aimed at the right person at the right time and in the right way can produce lightning.

The institution must also be concerned about the layout and design of its publications and on-line presentations. Graphics should be done by a professional designer, but it is the writer's responsibility to gather the necessary material and guide the designer on tone and style. It is helpful to give the designer a few samples of the institution's recent literature as a guide to its taste, unless the pieces are unimpressive or the institution wants a new look. Try to give the designer more illustration material than can actually be used so as to provide a range of choices. Avoid extremes, being neither too conservative nor too modern; the institution wants to raise money from fairly traditional individuals, not win graphics or arts awards or impress the avant-garde. Clean, readable, attractive campaign communications are the goal.

Photographs, because of their immediacy, are generally favored over artwork. They should be informal, candid, and unposed. Use pictures that add warmth to the story and bring the institution to the donors. In today's publications, larger pictures are generally favored over smaller ones, and an uncluttered look generally makes the best impression. Some institutions maintain orderly, up-to-date picture files and can simply provide a selection for the designer. If that is not the case, hire a professional photographer to take some fresh pictures for the campaign.

Architectural drawings are essential when an objective of the campaign is a new building. Nobody would contract for a building without some idea of what it might look like, and the same applies to those who put up the funds. Further, an attractive rendering dramatizes the building, and floor plans help clarify the named and memorial gift opportunities. Sometimes there is a problem getting renderings for the brochure because of delays in making decisions about the components. The architects thoroughly understand this problem and are usually willing to cooperate.

In preparing information for campaign workers, package the materials conveniently and compactly. Summarize key information, and do not overload volunteers with unnecessary facts. Provide sample questions and answers as well as simple charts and graphs to aid them in their understanding and acceptance of the campaign.

Developing a Realistic Plan for Marketing and Public Relations

Effective campaign communications are not enough; for a campaign to succeed, a comprehensive plan for public relations and marketing is also required. The objective of any public relations plan in support of a campaign should be to increase awareness, understanding, and appreciation on the part of targeted audiences in selected geographical areas, with the aim of motivating support for the campaign. Target audiences will vary according to the size and kind of institution conducting the campaign. In a capital campaign, with respect to these targeted audiences, the ultimate public relations challenge for an institution seeking to maintain and enhance its reputation is to bring sharp focus to past achievements that have contributed to its current high stature, its current achievements in its area of interest, and its future hopes and aspirations.

Donors at all levels and from all sources are more inclined to contribute to institutions that can make this part of their case. Effective public relations programs produce a climate for fundraising but should not be expected to attract gifts or volunteers directly. As is true in every other phase of the capital campaign, it is paramount that the individuals involved in developing and implementing a public relations plan learn the organization and its cause very well.

Once the institution has done its homework—defined its mission and priorities—and once a fundraising strategy has been established, it becomes a task of the public relations program to identify the audiences to be informed and cultivated, state the campaign's message (understanding what response is being sought from each target audience), and identify potential methods for communicating this message to the selected audiences. Among the instruments available for communicating the message are personal visits; open houses; speeches; audiovisual presentations; letters (personal letters or mass mailings); brochures; leaflets; graphs, charts, and other visual displays; special press conferences to announce significant gifts; films;

radio and television public service announcements or purchased time; ground-breaking or dedication events; regional campaign announcement events (in wide-area campaigns); news and feature stories in newspapers or magazines; newsletter, magazine, or newspaper advertisements; and creative uses of technology.

The ability to attract media attention is going to be affected by a number of variables, including these:

- The size of the institution's media market
- The size of the fundraising goal
- The level of community interest in the campaign (newsworthiness)
- Contacts the institution has with the media
- Participation in the campaign as leaders or volunteers by key media executives and important nonmedia community members

A $5,000 gift in a small farming community in Iowa might make the local weekly newspaper; a gift of $1 million in New York City might fail to attract any media attention. The United Way drive in any community is more likely to receive local coverage than a campaign to build a new chapel being conducted by one of the community's many churches.

It is not enough simply to block out the period of time when the campaign will be conducted and say that during this time the institution is going to have a good public relations program. Good public relations should precede the fundraising activity, accompany it, and go on after the active fundraising period has passed—and good public relations should exist inside the institution as well as outside.

Naming the Campaign

Whatever the campaign is called, its name should have dramatic impact and meaning for the institution as well as its constituents. Symbols, logos, titles, themes, and other identifiable marks should be developed and used throughout the campaign. In this area, a communications advisory committee can often be extremely helpful (Perkins, 1985).

After the campaign has been thoroughly planned—and a significant portion (30 to 50 percent) of the campaign goal achieved—it should be formally announced through a major media event, such as a formal dinner or a major press conference (see Resource 28, "Public Announcement Event Invitation and Program"). Both the annual campaign and the capital campaign deserve and need a public send-off event. As a practical matter, however, fewer and fewer annual campaigns have a kickoff event, and the traditional black-tie dinner to launch the capital campaign is giving way to public announcement events that truly are events, including live testimonials, audiovisual displays, tours, entertainment, and other trappings that make events distinctive and memorable. To do anything less is to fail to meet the challenge of getting the right people, the key ones you really want, to your event given the seemingly endless procession of invitations major donors and corporate and foundation heads receive. To get these people at your event, you have to attract their attention, especially if they are not already on your governing board, a current interested major donor, or a curious or motivated prospect.

Use the media to keep the campaign's progress before the public. In addition to cultivating newspaper and broadcast media coverage, use institutional publications to provide continuing publicity. Printed materials, such as the annual report, and other, external magazines, bulletins, and announcements for institutional events should all be used to keep the campaign in the public eye. Upon campaign completion, a victory dinner should be held, and a final report issued to everyone involved in the campaign.

It is important that community leaders be involved in making decisions about the public relations program. To this end, according to Perkins (1985), a communications advisory committee should be established. This committee is of great importance in any well-planned and professionally administered campaign. Committee members should be experts—public relations executives, marketing experts, media professionals, Webmasters, and senior members of advertising firms. This group should review and recommend program materials, media coverage, and special events. Not only can the members of this committee give professional advice, but they can also offer active assistance in working with the media. They can publicize the institution's efforts in areas where it is not known, accompany representatives of the institution on visits to media outlets and representatives, and make phone calls to say that a story or an idea for one is on the way.

In establishing such a committee, the institution should select members for specific purposes—for areas to be reached or for the kinds of stories the institution is apt to produce more abundantly. Bring these committee members to the institution, if at all possible, to orient them to the institution as it is now, not as it was when they last visited. Be professional, and do not ask members of the committee to help sell what is not legitimate news. Keep the committee informed about successes, and give credit to those who helped. Make sure that committee members know they are appreciated—send letters from the chief executive officer welcoming them to the committee and, at the end of the first year, thanking them for their time and effort and noting their successes. Give them recognition for their efforts in institutional publications, and invite them to institutional events.

The basic steps, generally stated, in a public relations program for a fundraising campaign are as follows:

- To gain support for the campaign from all the organization's constituencies, beginning with members of the institutional family
- To keep all constituencies adequately informed about the campaign's progress
- To secure broad agreement on the plan from all the major parties involved in the campaign
- To work closely with all elements of the development or advancement structure within the organization so as to secure their support and cooperation

If all the advancement efforts are not already combined, it is highly recommended that the organization seriously consider combining them, at least temporarily, in preparation for a capital campaign. If combining these efforts is impossible, at least a pledge of complete cooperation in working toward the campaign goal should be secured from all the members of the institutional advancement program. There should be enough incentive to overcome any future territorial conflicts about who is going to call the shots.

Public relations in a capital campaign cannot operate in a vacuum. The person responsible for the campaign's public relations must be considered an important and integral part of the campaign team. The campaign's public relations director should attend all meetings and special events connected with the campaign—especially meetings held at the highest levels. The public relations director should be allocated time, as appropriate, to discuss the campaign's public relations plans and to report on progress. This person must be thoroughly familiar with the master fundraising plan and should know when, where, and how funds are to be raised. It is also important for the public relations director to know what strata of the population are expected to make contributions, in order to determine what media those people read, watch, and listen to and to develop strategies for reaching them effectively.

Above all, every public relations effort connected with a campaign must be planned and carried out with the dignity and sophistication that the institution merits. A campaign's public relations effort, well done, will pay dividends far into the future.

CHAPTER SEVENTEEN

TESTING FUNDRAISING POTENTIAL AND ASSESSING PROGRAMS

Before a capital campaign is undertaken, it is essential to determine an organization's capacity to succeed. This is achieved through a market survey, an external assessment of fundraising potential. Most astute nonprofits will also conduct a program assessment, an internal review of performance and preparedness. Program assessments may also be conducted periodically as a routine checkup regardless of whether a capital campaign is imminent. This chapter discusses both types of assessment and proposes a new method for assessing preparedness, the Dove Preparedness Index, that can be used as an intermediate step by organizations as they move toward a campaign. Insisting on these undertakings is the responsibility of the board, but they may be initiated by either the board or the staff.

Conducting a Development Program Assessment

For a fundraising program to be successful, it must be well organized and well managed, both internally and externally. Too often institutions devote most of their time and attention to external preparedness while doing little or nothing to address internal conditions, both within the institution as a whole and within the development office itself, that can enhance or handicap efforts. It is unfortunate, in these situations, that so much is done attempting to raise significant sums of money when the institution is not internally prepared to handle the effort or success. As a result, it may forfeit many of the effort's lasting benefits.

One of the first requirements for internal preparedness is to make all the organization's internal constituents aware of the fundraising effort and help them feel that they have an active part to play in it. Key administrators should be consulted or informed about all proposals for fundraising activities that are related to their specific areas. At the same time, key institutional personnel should be actively involved in providing the kind of information that will lead to the eliciting of gifts.

What exactly is an institutional development program assessment? It is a formal, comprehensive evaluation of an institution's development program and of the institution's relationship to the people in the areas it touches. The assessment is conducted by a facilitator (an experienced, qualified fundraising professional or consultant) who gathers both objective and subjective data by observing and interviewing as well as by reviewing institutional literature and written reports. This information is then analyzed to produce an assessment of the institution's fundraising program (see Resource 29, "Program Assessment").

An assessment conducted in advance of a capital campaign, immediately before or upon the arrival of a new chief executive officer or a turnover in board leadership, or as a regularly planned event at periodic intervals can do the following things:

- Establish the facts (as opposed to feelings or perceptions) about the institution's development program
- Suggest, at these critical points, new and better ways of doing things
- Justify the role of the development program and its budget, to both the institutional leaders and the development staff
- Involve managers and volunteer leaders in the development program and encourage their help and support

In addition, an assessment conducted in a timely fashion can help the people at the top of the institution—senior managers and board members—gain a clearer understanding of what the development officers and the program do, how they do it, why they do it, and the results that can be expected. This comprehensive overview can encourage the kind of synergy between top managers, key volunteers, and development professionals that is essential to making a fundraising program or capital campaign a success.

How is this comprehensive overview developed? It is best accomplished on the basis of asking and answering at least twenty fundamental questions:

1. Do you have a reason for being (that is, a mission statement)?
2. Do you have a strategic plan spelling out your purpose and direction for the next five to ten years?

3. In your plan, have you determined the placement and importance of development?

4. Do you have a formal procedure for devising institutional priorities?

5. Have you made an analysis of the programs and projects with the greatest potential for attracting private funding?

6. Have you made a commitment to a comprehensive development program designed to attract annual, special, major capital, planned, and deferred gifts?

7. Do you take a coordinated approach to communications, volunteer services, public relations, publications, and development?

8. Do you provide adequate funding (including salaries and benefits) for employees to conduct a coordinated, comprehensive, productive development program?

9. Do you insist on having an up-to-date organization chart and job descriptions for each discrete fundraising activity, as well as regular performance evaluations for all professional employees?

10. Do you regularly monitor the progress and results of development activity, provide feedback to the staff, and document achievements to the development program's constituents?

11. Do you insist on adequate financial controls, to ensure donors' confidence and the institution's credibility?

12. Do you maintain adequate, up-to-date donor and gift records?

13. Are special attention and consideration for your major donors and prospective donors made mandatory by your fundraising program's system of rating, cultivating, and soliciting prospects?

14. Are your chief executive officer and your development staff actively involved in the cultivation and solicitation process?

15. Do you properly and promptly acknowledge the receipt of all gifts, incorporating meaningful personal touches?

16. Do you encourage key volunteers to participate actively in the fundraising process by providing them with information (through news reports, educational materials, a public relations program) and helping them make efficient use of their time and effective use of their talents?

17. Do you use a comprehensive array of techniques to keep your various constituencies informed and involved?

18. Do you have a plan for interpreting the fundraising process to the institution's family, whose cooperation and understanding are essential?

19. Do you periodically use consultants for the experience and objectivity they can provide?

20. In terms of the scope and effectiveness of your fundraising efforts, do you periodically compare yourself with peer institutions (while realizing the inherent limitations of such comparisons)?

For these questions to be answered, it will be necessary to review at least the following materials and data:

- Any marketing or promotional material about the institution
- The institution's statement of mission and purpose
- Résumés (including salaries) of all professional personnel working in the area of advancement (that is, in development and community relations)
- Organization charts for the institution as a whole and specifically for the advancement area
- Job descriptions of professional personnel in the advancement area
- The organization's budget (by division) and advancement budget (line item)
- The organization's planning document and the year's plan of activity for the advancement effort (if a written plan exists), giving details about goals, objectives, and the annual advancement calendar
- Any management indicators for monitoring the progress of the institution's current efforts
- Any mechanisms, if they exist, for monitoring programs in the development area
- Current standards, if any exist, for measurement and evaluation of the development area
- The personnel evaluation system, if any, as it is currently implemented in the development area
- Any instruments for market research, as well as any data (formal or informal) produced by these instruments that the organization may have used in the past thirty-six months
- A five-year history of giving to the organization, itemized by source and by purpose, as well as an indication, in terms of a ratio of expenditures, of the gifts received in each of the five years
- Comparisons of annual achievement to projections, for each program or project and with respect to overall organizational goals
- Samples of proposals prepared for individuals, corporations, foundations, and organizations
- Samples of the written development publications and fundraising pieces used in the past year
- Any accreditation reports or other, similar reports received in the last three to five years, with a primary focus on any sections or comments directed at the advancement effort
- Histories of all board members and, as applicable, their corporate giving histories

Many people representing the institution's various constituencies should also be involved in providing the answers to the questions that are posed. The facilitator of the development program assessment should interview board members, the chief executive officer, senior managers, the chief development officer, the professional development staff, representatives of the secretarial and clerical staff, other key individuals within the institution, important volunteers and lay leaders, and perhaps influential and affluent community members. The facilitator should make every effort to conduct these interviews objectively and should assure each person interviewed that the conversation will be confidential. This interview process should go on until the facilitator is certain that enough information is available to provide a complete report to the institution. Finally, the facilitator should supplement these interviews with personal observations about such factors as space allocation and the visual impact of publications. The report of the development program assessment, which should be presented in writing, will often be supplemented by an oral report to the board and the chief executive officer.

For the purposes of preparing for a capital campaign, it is best that this assessment be conducted by an external facilitator of some kind, whether that means an individual, a team of individuals, or a professional consultant with expertise in this area. The advantages of using an independent facilitator are that he or she brings special expertise and experience not generally found among institutional personnel and that he or she is free of the biases often found in organizations. It is important to conduct this assessment of the development program at the right point before the capital campaign begins. The stakes are so high that the institution cannot run the risk of having the job done any less professionally, less objectively, or less competently than it can be done.

Conducting a Market Survey

Before a capital campaign is undertaken, the board and the chief executive officer often commission a market survey. This is a recommended step, a requisite in fulfilling the responsibility of the board to prepare as thoroughly as possible.

Setting Goals and Priorities

To determine the goals for a successful capital campaign, an inventory of needs and a determination of priorities are imperative. The needs list is usually generated in-house. It evolves from the planning process, determining all the important needs that might be met with private funding. Be aware that there is a great deal of difference between institutional wants and institutional needs. It is absolutely essential that the initial list of goals be carefully pared down until it contains only substantiated, documented needs. Then the needs must be ranked in order of priority.

One important consideration is that goals must appeal to constituents. This is not to say that legitimate institutional needs should be altered or abandoned if they lack appeal (although a special educational program for constituents may be necessary before a campaign can move forward). It does mean, however, that items of little or no interest to constituents should not be featured as major components of a campaign goal. How much constituent appeal a particular campaign component has can best be determined through selective surveying of the key constituents. In other words, a market survey is a test of an institution's fundraising potential (see Resource 7, "Market Survey Materials").

It is generally recommended that the institution, before conducting a market survey, undertake an assessment of its development program to measure the institutional level of internal preparedness. The institution must also have the following essential elements in place:

- An institutional plan that anticipates funding needs
- A financial plan for approved projects and programs
- Support from board members, in the form of advocacy and gifts
- A sales and production staff
- A comprehensive program for financial development
- Prospects capable of providing the expected support
- A strong case for substantial support

These essentials of fundraising are the threads that run through the fabric of all campaigns.

The market survey itself has a number of objectives:

- To provide an accurate assessment of the factors that may affect the campaign
- To investigate and evaluate external opportunities for the institution to mount and successfully accomplish a large-scale major gifts campaign
- To determine, on the basis of reactions to the case statement (see Chapter Three), attitudes toward the institutional priorities and the campaign goal and, as warranted, to suggest changes in the priorities, the campaign goal, or both
- To educate potential major donors and campaign leaders
- To identify and evaluate the people best suited to providing leadership for workers or for major donors to the campaign
- To afford the institution an analysis of all the information that has been gathered

Preparing the Interviews

No two sets of market survey questions should look exactly alike. Any survey will ask a certain set of standard, basic questions, but each will also ask specific questions focused on the distinctive needs of the institution for which it is being conducted. As important as asking the correct questions correctly is listening to the answers, accurately recording them, and asking appropriate follow-up questions, which should include questions that may not belong to the questionnaire proper.

The questions should be written in such a manner as to be objective and neutral. The best and most valid questionnaires are even taken to market research or opinion survey groups, or to individuals with this type of expertise, to be validated before use. The matrix of questions must also be designed to check and cross-check certain key points, issues, and attitudes that the institution is particularly interested in investigating. It takes trained professionals to ensure this kind of cross-checking.

Market surveys must be conducted by individuals whom the respondents consider "honest brokers." If respondents perceive that an interviewer is carrying institutional baggage or has an institutional agenda, their answers may be less than complete and may severely limit or even invalidate the survey's conclusions and recommendations. An institution that proceeds on the basis of limited or invalid survey findings is at serious risk. To be certain that your market survey is conducted properly, use a valid survey instrument and have your survey conducted by objective, qualified professionals.

A market survey generally takes from thirty to ninety days to complete. The size of the survey population, as well as the geographical area to be covered in the face-to-face interview process, will determine the time needed. For example, it takes longer to conduct fifty interviews for the Canadian Diabetes Association or the Canadian National Institute for the Blind, whose service areas range from Nova Scotia to British Columbia, than it does to conduct fifty interviews for the YWCA of Calgary, all of which can be conducted within the Calgary city limits.

Regardless of the organization's size, the fact is that a correctly and carefully drawn sample of thirty to thirty-five respondents is adequate to provide the data sought through the market survey. Smaller organizations, if they are adept or properly guided, may obtain a valid survey using twenty to twenty-five interviews, but many opt to conduct more so as to include more people. Regardless of whether these interviews improve the accuracy of the survey, they help build important bonds with constituents. Larger organizations often do more interviews simply as a result of their need to be inclusive of the various leadership groups that they do not want to offend by exclusion.

Let's say a large organization decides to conduct a market survey consisting of fifty to seventy face-to-face interviews. At the outset, it should allow up to five days of consultation for the following tasks:

- Developing the design of the survey
- Assembling and evaluating the list of prospects to be interviewed
- Drafting and reviewing the interview contact letter and needs statement

- Developing interview strategies
- Drafting the interview questionnaire
- Assembling and mailing any ancillary marketing materials that may be required

All market surveys must be based on face-to-face interviews with a carefully selected respondent pool; there is no substitute. The interviews used in a market survey should be conducted with a cross-section of board members, community leaders, service users, alumni and friends of the institution, and other key constituents. The people to be interviewed are selected on the basis of their close relationships to the institution, their familiarity with the persons and situations pertinent to fundraising, their potential as donors, and their ability to influence others to work and to give. People experienced in conducting market surveys should be involved in the selection process.

Sophisticated organizations are increasingly supplementing face-to-face interviews with input gathered through phone interviews and direct-mail surveys. These two supplementary approaches permit the institution to gain further validation of the survey's statistical results and, more important, to expand the universe of individuals who are brought into the "inner circle" early in the process of planning and preparing the campaign. The Internet is sure to become another avenue for collecting data. Ultimately, the size of the sample and the nature of the data-collection techniques that are used will be determined by the size and complexity of the institution's constituency, the design and goal of the campaign, and the institution's resources.

Conducting the Survey

Once a properly constructed questionnaire has been achieved, the market survey can begin. For a sample of fifty to seventy people interviewed over a wide area, the interview portion of the study generally requires three to five weeks. The initial list of major constituents should be supplemented by basic profile information on each interview candidate. In order for the appropriate number of interviews to be conducted, the list of names should be about twice as large as the sample that is actually needed.

Every prospective respondent receives an initial contact letter and a brief case statement describing the funding needs of the organization. These letters are followed by telephone calls to each individual, and survey interviews are scheduled. Interviews that must be kept confidential are conducted by professional counsel or by institutional staff under the direction of counsel. A significant but smaller number of interviews can be conducted with selected administrators and staff, although this group is not included in all cases.

Every effort must be made to conduct the interviews objectively. It is important that each person interviewed be assured that the conversation will be held in strict confidence, if that is the respondent's wish. The privileged information thus obtained becomes valuable in the process of evaluating the potential for a successful capital campaign.

In general, the value of face-to-face interviews does not rest solely in the apparent information obtained. Remember that in some instances, things that appear to be facts are merely subjective observations. As the interview process continues, however, the interviewers are in a unique position to check and cross-check the reliability of various opinions and to assess the perceptions of each person interviewed. It usually becomes clear which responses should be given greater weight, and those responses are emphasized in the market survey report.

Normally, each face-to-face interview takes from thirty to sixty minutes to complete. Focus groups, telephone interviews, direct-mail questionnaires, and e-mail surveys are increasingly being used to supplement and further validate the traditional face-to-face interview, but each of these methods has its own limitations, and none should supplant the traditional interview as the principal technique.

Analyzing the Results

It is extremely important for the organization to understand that a market survey used to determine the feasibility of a campaign should not deal at length with the presentation of a campaign plan or timetable. These items should be covered in detail after the market survey has been accepted formally by the organization's board.

After the interviews have been conducted, an additional six to ten days are usually required for evaluation and analysis of the results. This process involves three tasks that absolutely must be performed by experienced, skilled professionals:

- Accurately weighting the responses (reflecting the fact that some respondents and responses are more important than others)
- Correctly analyzing and interpreting the data
- Translating the data into a report that achieves acceptance, inspires confidence, and creates a plan for action or points the institution toward such a plan

These three tasks cannot be left to amateurs, but very few institutions have individuals on staff who can perform them accurately without assistance. Even if an institution does have such people, it may still be advisable to involve outsiders, thereby eliminating potential concerns about objectivity.

Supplementing the Survey

In an organization that is not conducting a development program assessment or making use of ongoing consultation, the market survey should check into the following internal systems:

- Individual, foundation, and corporate records
- Quality and range of information maintained
- Ongoing efforts to expand and update prospect files and other donor records
- The gift processing system and financial record-keeping procedures
- Other data-processing support services (for example, daily and monthly tracking of prospects, donors, and corporate and foundation proposals)
- Quarterly and annual gift progress and management reports
- Word-processing support services that facilitate the development program (for example, correspondence, proposal preparation, other text and manuscript services)
- Basic techniques of donor research and prospect rating by internal staff

Finally, one to two days should be reserved for presentation of the survey to the administration and the board.

Using the Results

The market survey should provide an accurate, perceptive assessment of the constituents' views of the institution, as well as information about how aware and supportive they are of the needs that the institution is putting forward. The survey should also supply information about the correct timing of a capital campaign, about whether the right leadership is available for it, and—undoubtedly most important from a financial standpoint—about whether sufficient money can be raised to undertake the campaign.

Beyond these, a market survey provides other significant benefits:

- Public relations value
- The opportunity for important constituents to review the institution
- The opportunity to develop or strengthen relationships with business and civic leaders by including them in the survey sample
- Valuable information about development gleaned from the interviews
- Other information from the interviews that is helpful not only in formulating the campaign plan but also in doing comprehensive institutional planning

Properly done, a market survey can minimize the cost and maximize the success of the campaign. Moreover, it is very often the first public step taken to cultivate key support for the campaign, especially among constituents who are close to but not directly included in the institution's immediate family.

Using Surveys in Other Ways

Institutions today are increasingly deciding in advance that they will conduct a campaign and then use the market survey both to inform potential volunteer leaders and major donors that a campaign is being planned and to gain the benefit of outside expertise in establishing a strategy for the fundraising effort. The purpose of the market survey is different in these instances; accordingly, its presentation will have a different focus. The organization must understand whether it seeks a true study of financial feasibility or is already committed to a campaign (unless counsel can dissuade it on the basis of the findings of the market survey) and is using the market survey fundamentally as an educational technique to advance its efforts. It must communicate its situation to counsel before the market survey is undertaken so that counsel can appropriately structure its efforts and reports to the organization.

Institutionalizing Market Surveys

One organizational feature that is emerging today is the creation of a market survey committee. The purposes of such a committee are to develop among its members a sense of direct involvement and active leadership during the early, key planning stages of the campaign and to provide knowledge and background information about significant campaign issues. Members of the market survey committee are typically asked to perform the following tasks:

- Review a draft list of those to be interviewed and make recommendations
- Facilitate access for the consultant to the individuals whose views are being surveyed
- Meet with the consultant to review and comment on the detailed design of the survey instrument
- Review and comment on both the draft and final versions of the market survey report

The members of the market survey committee will include its chair, high-level representatives of the major constituency groups that the campaign will target, representatives of the board, and perhaps the individual who will be asked to serve as general chair of the campaign. The committee functions best when there are no more than ten members; in most cases, five to seven members will be the optimum number.

Dedicated volunteer leaders are also essential to a campaign's success. Because their connection with the campaign eventually leads them to make investments of time, energy, and resources, a few wise institutions today are also involving key prospects as volunteers at this very early stage; many more institutions will adopt this approach as it becomes more widely known.

Market surveys are like produce: they do not remain fresh for long. Therefore, the timing of a survey is important. It is conducted only after other prerequisites (planning, setting priorities among needs, completing an assessment of the development program that supports the campaign's moving forward) have been satisfied. The results of a survey, once received, are generally valid for six to nine months, perhaps even as long as one year. If the institution, for whatever reason, does not launch its campaign within a year, the survey probably should be at least partially updated or perhaps even redone.

The Dove Preparedness Index

A useful tool that has been developed and introduced in the past decade is the Dove Preparedness Index (DPI). A DPI review is not obligatory, but institutions are now beginning to use this tool during campaign preparation as a way of evaluating the current state of preparedness at critical decision-making points. It can be administered internally or facilitated by an independent third party. Having a facilitator work with the organization is recommended if the institution has little or no background in conducting campaigns or in evaluating the results.

The DPI individually considers the ten prerequisites discussed in Chapter One. Each is scored on a scale of 1 to 10, with 1 representing the lowest score and 10 the highest score. Three of these ten prerequisites are considered (the "key three," italicized on the following list). If the overall score on all ten prerequisites is 75 or higher, and if the score on the key three is 25–30, the institution is very well positioned to go forward with its campaign. If the overall score is 60–75, or if the key three score is 20–25, the institution is in a gray area—close, but probably not quite ready. If the overall score is lower than 60, or if the key three score is below 20, there is still work to do.

Here is the DPI for a hypothetical organization, with scores indicated in parentheses:

1. Commitments of time and support from all key participants (9)
2. A clear organizational self-image and a strategic plan for organizational growth and improvement (8)

3. Fundraising objectives based on important and legitimate institutional plans, goals, budgets, and needs (8)
4. *A written document that makes a compelling case for supporting the campaign* (3)
5. An assessment of the institutional development program and a market survey addressing internal and external preparedness (8)
6. *Enlistment and education of leaders* (1)
7. *Ability and readiness of major donors to give substantial lead gifts* (5)
8. Competent staff and, perhaps, external professional counsel (5)
9. Adequate, even liberal, funds for expenses (6)
10. Other factors (age of the organization, caliber of the constituency, range of the institution's giving program, size and geographical distribution of the constituency, previous fundraising success, quality of the program and impact of its services, location of the organization, human factors, state of the economy, competing and conflicting campaigns, trends in the nonprofit sector, unfavorable publicity, local issues) (5)

In this hypothetical case, the DPI is 58 and the key three score is 9. This organization is not yet ready to proceed.

What needs attention? Certainly, the case statement needs development; the matter of leadership needs to be addressed, and the major donor pool has to be expanded. Raising these key three scores alone to the level of 8 or 9 each would position the institution to go forward. Moreover, the cultivation process must be expedited, and it appears that the proposed budget is inadequate. There are some issues around staffing, and other factors were noted that either are causing concern or require some attention.

CHAPTER EIGHTEEN

USING PAID SOLICITORS AND CONSULTANTS

Many organizations that have funding needs and wish to launch fundraising programs have very small staffs. One-person offices are common—sometimes fundraising is only one aspect of a staff member's responsibilities—and many grassroots organizations have no professional development staff members at all. A membership survey conducted by the Association of Fundraising Professionals (AFP) in 1999 found that 52.5 percent of its members work by themselves or with three or fewer colleagues. Less than 15 percent work in situations with ten or more staff and support persons. It is possible to conduct a successful fundraising program under these conditions, but the organization usually needs to improvise. In many cases a dedicated volunteer or team of volunteers has conducted a successful program for an organization with no paid development staff. In other instances a member of the administrative staff has carried out the task. Others turn to paid solicitors or consultants.

Fundraising counselors do not solicit or retain custody of contributions. The American Association of Fund-Raising Counsel (AAFRC) guidelines prohibit consulting firms from handling funds. By contrast, paid solicitors—firms as well as individuals—are employed to solicit contributions. In some cases they also take possession of the contributions they receive. Common sense tells us that that situation should be avoided whenever possible, however. Handling money can offer temptation; the best way to resist temptation is to avoid it. There are also the matters of institutional accountability to donors and fiscal integrity—nonprofits themselves ought to receive and handle contributions made to them. It is far better to have the organization pay the solicitor than to have the solicitor retain received funds and forward the organization's portion. If the nonprofit is not capable of receiving and handling its own funds, a third party, such as a bank, an attorney, or an accountant, should receive and handle contributions. (A board member may be of service to the organization by performing this function.) At a minimum, there is a need to establish some kind of reliable verification system if the paid solicitor is to handle the funds.

Contracting for Outside Services

Depending on their particular area of expertise, fundraising consultants or firms may handle any of these services, on-site or off-site:

- Annual campaigns
- Board development
- Capital campaigns
- Development office functions or start-up
- Endowment development
- Executive search
- Foundation and corporate giving services
- Grantwriting
- Interim staffing
- Leadership, staff, volunteer, or board training
- Mail services
- Major gift development
- Market surveys and feasibility studies
- Planned giving services
- Precampaign positioning
- Prospect research
- Publications
- Special events
- Strategic planning
- Telemarketing and communications
- Volunteer recruitment

In the 1999 profile of AFP members, respondents were asked if their organization retained professional fundraising counsel or service firms for any of the following services in the last two years. Approximately three-quarters reported using one or more services. Approximately one-fifth reported using outside services for strategic or long-range planning and budgeting, a campaign market survey, or capital campaign direction. Next most frequently mentioned were direct mail, communications and public relations, and special event services.

Strategic or long-range planning/budgeting	19.8 percent
Campaign market survey	19.6 percent
Capital campaign direction	19.2 percent
Direct mail	14.1 percent
Communications/public relations	13.7 percent
Special event assistance	12.0 percent
Fundraising management	11.0 percent
Grant research/proposal writing	10.3 percent
Executive search	10.3 percent
Planned/deferred giving assistance	9.7 percent
Telemarketing	8.4 percent
Development office audit	7.6 percent
Prospect research	6.7 percent
Market research survey	6.5 percent
Annual fund assistance	6.3 percent
Other	3.2 percent
None	24.9 percent

Selecting Outside Counsel

The selection of outside counsel should follow this process according to the *AAFRC Book on Fund-Raising Consulting* (1998):

Step 1: Identifying Prospective Consultants

Once the board and staff leaders have affirmed the desire to investigate fundraising consultants or consulting firms, they can identify a pool of candidates via three main avenues:

- *Referrals:* Ask board members or colleagues.
- *Directories and Web sites:* Consult the AAFRC, AFP, CASE, and other directories and Web sites for information.
- *Advertisements:* Respond to advertisements in trade periodicals or the Yellow Pages.

Step 2: Preliminary Screening

- *Basic information:* Request basic information from each firm or individual. Find out generally what kinds of services they provide.
- *Detailed information:* Narrow the field to three or four candidates and arrange a face-to-face briefing with each.

Step 3: Request for Proposals

- *Proposal content:* After the briefing, request proposals from each of the firms or individuals with whom you meet. Proposals should clearly state the costs, fees, services, staffing, and a preliminary schedule.

Step 4: Reference Check

- *Calling references:* Always ask for references; always check them carefully. Ask the clients if they would hire the firm or individual again.
- *Successful and unsuccessful campaigns:* Ask for three references from satisfied clients and one reference from a client whose goals were not achieved or from an assignment where the consultant or the organization resigned from the contract. Consultants should treat the request for a reference from a less-than-satisfied client as standard operating procedure.

Step 5: Chemistry

There are many ways of understanding a subject and of applying that knowledge when making a decision.

- *Impressions:* Your personal impression of key staff people will influence your decision.
- *Objectivity:* The search for a consultant should be as objective as possible, focusing on skills and expertise and de-emphasizing such factors as attire and demeanor.
- *Realism:* Nevertheless, personal preferences are part of every professional relationship and every hiring decision. If you really do not relate well to someone who is making every effort to impress you, chances are the relationship will not improve.
- *Professional judgment:* Instincts sometimes arise from wisdom. You should trust them but not allow them to overshadow the facts.

Step 6: Notifying Candidates

- *Notify all candidates* of your decision. It is considered a courtesy to give a brief explanation of your choice to the consultants you did not select.

Step 7: Contracts

The contract is very important and should be specific and detailed. This is the best time to uncover and iron out expectations or potential misunderstandings. Legal counsel should be consulted regarding appropriate terms and their use in the document. The following matters, as well as others recommended by the organization's board or legal adviser, should be outlined or explained in detail in a contract or a letter serving as a contract.

- *Services:* What services will be provided? When and how often will you receive reports, and what will they contain?
- *Schedule:* If the timing is expressed in days, how many hours are in a day? If it is a planning or market study, when will it start, and when will it be finished?
- *Fees:* What specific professional fees will be billed? What is the billing schedule? What additional expenses will be reimbursed by the client, and up to what amount? Fees should always be based on services rendered. Never allow fees to be based on the goal of the campaign. Contingency fundraising is prohibited by premier firms and eschewed by ethical consultants.
- *Custody of funds:* All funds raised should go directly to your organization. Do not permit counsel to maintain custody of funds; however, this does not prevent counsel from helping you track funds.
- *Confidentiality:* A clause should be included to protect the organization's proprietary and confidential information
- *Termination:* Under what conditions may the agreement be terminated by either party?
- *Personnel:* Which people from the firm will provide direct services, and what other professionals may be called on to support them?
- *Financial responsibility:* Who in the organization is responsible for contractual decisions, and who is responsible for rendering payment?
- *Location:* Where will the services be rendered, on-site or off-site?

Step 8: State Regulations

- *Compliance:* Most states require both charities and fundraising professionals to register and follow certain procedures before commencing a campaign. Make sure both the organization and the fundraiser are in compliance.*

---

*A summary of state laws, including the addresses and telephone numbers of state regulatory entities, is available from the AAFRC Trust for Philanthropy, 25 West Forty-Third Street, New York, NY 10036; (212) 354-5799; http://www.aafrc.org

Avoiding Pitfalls

The AAFRC warns to guard against the following situations.

Switching Consultants. Although changing consultants is a completely legal option and one appropriately exercised if you are truly dissatisfied, the consultant that does your feasibility study or begins your campaign develops a knowledge of your organization and constituency that goes beyond the parameters of even the most thorough and detailed report. A great deal of accumulated wisdom is lost when bringing in a new consultant midway through a process.

The Lowest Bid. Each campaign should be designed specifically for your organization and should not be the result of a cookie-cutter approach. Even responsible bids vary, and you have to use professional judgment and fact checking to know what you really want. Sometimes the lowest bid is the best one, but not necessarily.

Communication with Donors. The relationship between a nonprofit organization and its donors is precious and should continue long after counsel has left. Anything that comes between an organization and its constituency is detrimental to long-term viability and the organization's potential to fulfill its mission. Staff, board members, or volunteers, not counsel, should ask for donations. Written communications as well as verbal ones should be developed with scrupulous oversight from the organization.

Interviewing Too Many Firms. After a point, the process of interviewing consultants becomes repetitive, frustrating, and too time-consuming for staff and volunteers. Three firms are plenty; more than four begins to be counterproductive.

Outside Professional Counsel and the Capital Campaign

A successful capital campaign will generally adhere to the principles stated in this book. Nevertheless, the simple memorization of these principles will not guarantee a successful campaign. Success is more likely when the mechanics are supplemented by human experience, insight, strategies, sensitivity, and judgments of the kind that transcend the prescriptions of any written document. These added ingredients are often provided by outside professional counsel.

An institution with a sizable and experienced fundraising staff may decide to proceed without aid from outside counsel, but the majority of institutions find such aid both advisable and necessary. Outside counsel is most often employed when the organization feels that it must supplement its staff's ability to handle a campaign or feels that it needs expert advice or when the development office feels that it needs objective advice.

Gibson (1983), outlining the advantages and disadvantages of using outside counsel, cites the following advantages:

- Consultants can provide an objective viewpoint to the institution, and they often have more credibility with the chief executive officer and board members. Consequently, consultants can be tougher in circumstances where toughness is called for, and they can take the heat when they have to.
- Consultants bring credibility because they can call on a broad range of experience and can share this experience with the institution.
- Consultants are paid fees high enough to motivate the chief executive officer and the board to work with them effectively and efficiently.
- Consultants can apply the brakes to ensure that enough time is being spent on cultivation and solicitation of the critical top 10 percent of prospects while keeping an eye on the entire campaign—anticipating needs, prodding to get things done, giving support to the staff, and suggesting the systems and strategies to be used.
- Consultants offer a sounding board to experienced development directors who have no other knowledgeable people close at hand.

Gibson identifies the following disadvantages, among others:

- In the goal-setting process, outside consultants may be too cautious out of a desire to ensure feasible goals for their clients.
- The best person in the consulting firm—the one who is a match with the institution's needs and chemistry—may not be available at the right time. The consultant actually assigned to the institution may prove incompatible and difficult to work with, and the firm may find it difficult to provide an appropriate substitute to serve the institution's needs in the time available. When a consulting firm is used, there is also the possibility of excessive disparity between the firm's top representative and the day-to-day contact person provided by the firm.
- Because the consultant's function is to show the institution how to raise money, but not necessarily to raise money for the institution, the consultant may be able to provide good strategic counsel but limited operational help—and many campaigns need operational assistance as much as they need strategic guidance.
- If consultants are used on a full-time, in-house basis, much information may not be captured in the files at the end of the campaign and may leave when the consultant leaves.
- Bringing in consultants may eliminate the opportunity to train institutional staff.
- The use of consultants can be costly, even though it may be cost-effective.

In considering the use of outside counsel, it is important to understand that the role of professional counsel is not to raise money but rather to help the institution raise it. The use of professional counsel does not relieve the institution's board and administration of their responsibilities for the success of the campaign. In most cases professional counsel is used to supplement in-house capabilities. Professional counsel enables people to draw on a breadth and depth of experience not generally possessed by a single institution. Counsel is usually retained for one or more of the following purposes:

- To conduct a program assessment in advance of the campaign
- To conduct a market survey
- To prepare the campaign case statement and related materials
- To provide full-time (resident) campaign management
- To provide part-time (periodic) counseling

In the latter two categories, a significant shift occurred in the 1990s. Fifteen years ago, consultants predominantly provided campaign management to their clients through resident counsel. Today, given the growth in the number of institutions with previous campaign experience, as well as the dramatically larger population of professional staff with previous campaign experience and stronger day-to-day management abilities, consultants are increasingly being used to provide strategic direction, advice, and vision through periodic visits and off-site consultation.

Because consultants now generally serve more a strategic than an operational function, it may be time for institutions to consider the minimum standards on which they must insist before engaging outside professional counsel. Inexperienced consultants should not be engaged to manage or offer counsel to campaigns at an institution that finds itself in need of outside counsel: the institution is itself inexperienced and uncertain in this arena, and consultants who have no more, and sometimes less, experience and knowledge than their clients will be of limited use, at best. There are currently no licensing requirements or credentialing programs for consultants, nor are they advocated. At the minimum, however, institutions may want to ask whether a potential consultant meets the requirements of the professional certification program for fundraising executives administered by the NSFRE.

Another change occurring in the consulting field is the emergence of firms, partnerships, and sole proprietorships that primarily serve geographically defined territories. This development is in contrast to the existence of the well-established, recognized national firms that work across wide areas. Given the growth in the number of consultants who work in relatively confined areas, there is a corresponding growth in the potential for conflicts of interest when it comes to the confidentiality of proprietary information belonging to a single organization. It may be tempting to hire a consultant who already knows your service area well thanks to previous assignments in the same market—and to be sure, there is much local knowledge that can be shared legitimately between and among consultants and multiple clients. But there is also a large body of knowledge and a great amount of information that should not be shared or exchanged under any circumstances without the prior written consent of the client organization. Beware the potential consultant who offers to share confidential and proprietary information obtained in service to another organization. The temptation to acquire this information may seem irresistible, but do resist: How would you feel if it were your information being passed along without your knowledge or consent?

During a recent discussion, the chief development officer of a hospital illustrated the problem. The hospital concluded a capital campaign a few years ago. It used a consulting firm, the campaign was a success, and the relationship was a good one. Following the campaign, word came back to the hospital that its consultant was using its proprietary and confidential information in service to other clients in the same market area. This was cause for concern, but what happened next was much more bothersome. The hospital, which had remained in contact with the firm, advised the firm that it was considering a new campaign and that a diagnostic and treatment center including cancer would be the primary focus. At the same time, a cancer agency in the same market area was contemplating a major campaign. The hospital told the firm that if it chose to work with the cancer agency, the hospital could not rehire the firm because of the conflict of interest the situation would present. The firm signed a contract with the cancer agency and then reapproached the hospital seeking its business and made light of the hospital's concerns about conflict of interest. The hospital refused to do business under the circumstances and probably will never work with the firm again.

Incredible as it may seem, during this same time period, another organization in the hospital's market area engaged another firm to do a market survey for it. That firm included the hospital's chief development officer on the potential interview list. Curious, the hospital's chief development officer agreed to do the interview. During the interview, the firm's representative asked the chief development officer direct questions about gifts made to the hospital's campaign and about potential volunteer leaders in the community known to the hospital. The questions should never have been asked given the circumstances, and the hospital officer declined to provide answers to those questions.

The AAFRC has promulgated strict standards for membership and professional conduct, and most of the leading professional firms subscribe to them. Nevertheless, there are consulting firms that are not members of the AAFRC. Other professional organizations such as CASE, the AFP, the Association of Healthcare Philanthropy (AHP), and the Association of Governing Boards of Universities and Colleges, can provide leads on firms and individual consultants who are not AAFRC members but who do have records of reputable service. Also available are individual freelance consultants, senior advancement officers from all third-sector areas, retired chief executive officers, vice presidents and other institutional administrators, and other specialists in specific fields and disciplines that may be applicable to an institution's needs.

Ethics in Fundraising

Ethical conduct and adherence to ethical standards are paramount in fundraising, and governing boards, administrators, and donors should adopt a zero-tolerance attitude toward violations.

There are two model codes, one pointed to fundraisers, the other to donors, that instruct the conduct and operation of nonprofit organizations—the "AFP Code of Ethical Principles and Standards of Professional Conduct" (see Exhibit 18.1) and "A Donor Bill of Rights" (see Exhibit 18.2).

These documents are widely embraced and endorsed throughout the third sector. They should be the basis on which every nonprofit conducts itself, but as in any other field, there are occasional lapses. Like commercial airline crashes, scandals in fundraising are the exception, not the rule. But when they occur, they are big news and receive extensive media coverage and community attention. Too many such instances involve ethical breaches that can reach the level of criminal prosecution. Whenever such an occurrence happens, it's both sad and bad. In instances where dishonesty, deceit, or another form of corruption crops up in the philanthropic sector, the offenders must be identified and appropriately reprimanded or disciplined. Currently, the national organizations have no ability beyond establishing laudatory standards to legislate or to adjudicate. That is now left to the general public, which is increasingly taking action.

Pat Lewis, past president and chief executive officer of the Association of Fundraising Professionals, comments ("Pat Lewis," 1994, pp. 8–9):

> The nonprofit sector must continue to be proactive regarding the federal and state governments' heightened interests in the activities of charitable organizations. Charges of misuse of funds at several highly visible organizations and the search for new sources of revenue have led regulators to look critically at charitable tax exemptions and activities.

EXHIBIT 18.1. AFP CODE OF ETHICAL PRINCIPLES AND STANDARDS OF PROFESSIONAL PRACTICE.

STATEMENT OF ETHICAL PRINCIPLES
Adopted November 1991

The Association of Fundraising Professionals (AFP) exists to foster the development and growth of fund-raising professionals and the profession, to promote high ethical standards in the fund-raising profession and to preserve and enhance philanthropy and volunteerism. Members of AFP are motivated by an inner drive to improve the quality of life through the causes they serve. They serve the ideal of philanthropy; are committed to the preservation and enhancement of volunteerism; and hold stewardship of these concepts as the overriding principle of their professional life. They recognize their responsibility to ensure that needed resources are vigorously and ethically sought and that the intent of the donor is honestly fulfilled. To these ends, AFP members embrace certain values that they strive to uphold in performing their responsibilities for generating philanthropic support.

AFP members aspire to:

- practice their profession with integrity, honesty, truthfulness and adherence to the absolute obligation to safeguard the public trust;

- act according to the highest standards and visions of their organization, profession and conscience;

- put philanthropic mission above personal gain;

- inspire others through their own sense of dedication and high purpose;

- improve their professional knowledge and skills in order that their performance will better serve others;

- demonstrate concern for the interests and well being of individuals affected by their actions;

- value the privacy, freedom of choice and interests of all those affected by their actions;

- foster cultural diversity and pluralistic values, and treat all people with dignity and respect;

- affirm, through personal giving, a commitment to philanthropy and its role in society;

- adhere to the spirit as well as the letter of all applicable laws and regulations;

- advocate within their organizations, adherence to all applicable laws and regulations;

- avoid even the appearance of any criminal offense or professional misconduct;

- bring credit to the fund-raising profession by their public demeanor;

- encourage colleagues to embrace and practice these ethical principles and standards of professional practice; and

- be aware of the codes of ethics promulgated by other professional organizations that serve philanthropy.

STANDARDS OF PROFESSIONAL PRACTICE
Adopted and incorporated into the AFP Code of Ethical Principles November 1992

Furthermore, while striving to act according to the above values, AFP members agree to abide by the AFP Standards of Professional Practice, which are adopted and incorporated into the AFP Code of Ethical Principles. Violation of the Standards may subject the member to disciplinary sanctions, including expulsion, as provided in the AFP Ethics Enforcement Procedures.

Professional Obligations

1. Members shall not engage in activities that harm the member's organization, clients, or profession.

EXHIBIT 18.1. AFP CODE OF ETHICAL PRINCIPLES AND STANDARDS OF PROFESSIONAL PRACTICE, Cont'd.

2. Members shall not engage in activities that conflict with their fiduciary, ethical, and legal obligations to their organizations and their clients.

3. Members shall effectively disclose all potential and actual conflicts of interest; such disclosure does not preclude or imply ethical impropriety.

4. Members shall not exploit any relationship with a donor, prospect, volunteer or employee to the benefit of the member or the member's organization.

5. Members shall comply with all applicable local, state, provincial, federal, civil and criminal laws.

6. Members recognize their individual boundaries of competence and are forthcoming and truthful about their professional experience and qualifications.

Solicitation and Use of Charitable Funds

7. Members shall take care to ensure that all solicitation materials are accurate and correctly reflect the organization's mission and use of solicited funds.

8. Members shall take care to ensure that donors receive informed, accurate and ethical advice about the value and tax implications of potential gifts.

9. Members shall take care to ensure that contributions are used in accordance with donors' intentions.

10. Members shall take care to ensure proper stewardship of charitable contributions, including timely reports on the use and management of funds.

11. Members shall obtain explicit consent by the donor before altering the conditions of a gift.

Presentation of Information

12. Members shall not disclose privileged or confidential information to unauthorized parties.

13. Members shall adhere to the principle that all donor and prospect information created by, or on behalf of, an organization is the property of that organization and shall not be transferred or utilized except on behalf of that organization.

14. Members shall give donors the opportunity to have their names removed from lists that are sold to, rented to, or exchanged with other organizations.

15. Members shall, when stating fundraising results, use accurate and consistent accounting methods that conform to the appropriate guidelines adopted by the American Institute of Certified Public Accountants (AICPA)* for the type of organization involved. (*In countries outside of the United States, comparable authority should be utilized.)

Compensation

16. Members shall not accept compensation that is based on a percentage of charitable contributions; nor shall they accept finder's fees.

17. Members may accept performance-based compensation, such as bonuses, provided such bonuses are in accord with prevailing practices within the members' own organizations, and are not based on a percentage of charitable contributions.

18. Members shall not pay finder's fees, commissions or percentage compensation based on charitable contributions and shall take care to discourage their organizations from making such payments.

Amended October 1999

Source: Courtesy of the Association of Fundraising Professionals.

EXHIBIT 18.2. DONOR BILL OF RIGHTS.

Philanthropy is based on voluntary action for the common good. It is a tradition of giving and sharing that is primary to the quality of life. To assure that philanthropy merits the respect and trust of the general public, and that donors and prospective donors can have full confidence in the not-for-profit organizations and causes they are asked to support, we declare that all donors have these rights:

I.

To be informed of the organization's mission, of the way the organization intends to use donated resources, and of its capacity to use donations effectively for their intended purposes.

II.

To be informed of the identity of those serving on the organization's board, and to expect the board to exercise prudent judgment in its stewardship responsibilities.

III.

To have access to the organization's most recent financial statements.

IV.

To be assured their gifts will be used for the purposes for which they were given.

V.

To receive appropriate acknowledgment and recognition.

VI.

To be assured that information about their donations is handled with respect and with confidentiality to the extent provided by law.

VII.

To expect that all relationships with individuals representing organizations of interest to the donor will be professional in nature.

VIII.

To be informed whether those seeking donations are volunteers, employees of the organization or hired solicitors.

IX.

To have the opportunity for their names to be deleted from mailing lists that an organization may intend to share.

X.

To feel free to ask questions when making a donation and to receive prompt, truthful and forthright answers.

DEVELOPED BY
American Association of Fund Raising Counsel (AAFRC)
Association for Healthcare Philanthropy (AHP)
Association of Fundraising Professionals (AFP)
Council for Advancement and Support of Education (CASE)

ENDORSED BY
(Information)
INDEPENDENT SECTOR
National Catholic Development Conference (NCDC)
National Committee on Planned Giving (NCPG)
National Council for Resource Development (NCRD)
United Way of America

Source: Courtesy of the American Association of Fund Raising Counsel, Inc. Reprinted with permission.

Some states are examining cause-related marketing and questioning both the corporate expense claim and the tax exemption. They are exploring whether corporate contributions and sponsorships are unrelated business income and therefore subject to taxes.

Hartsook (1997, p. 48) has this to say on the subject:

Government oversight, which currently has emerged with regard to tele-marketing sales, will be enforced prominently with regard to philanthropic solicitations—especially solicitations relating to high-cost telephone solicitations made by fringe philanthropic groups. Unfortunately, telemarketing for non-profit organizations has received a bad name because of fringe philanthropic organizations that solicit and collect large sums of money—while dedicating most of those funds to the costs of fund raising and salaries.

State regulators are responding to calls from the public, which is expressing concern about charities. Registration requirements for fund raisers and consul-tants, which sometimes require large bonds, are being enacted. Questions about charitable annuities and charitable life insurance gifts are being raised.

Currently, only three states—Idaho, Montana, and Wyoming—have no laws regulating nonprofits. The AAFRC Trust for Philanthropy (1998a) lists the fol-lowing seven general categories of regulation (the number of states where such regulation exists is shown in parentheses):

- Registration or licensing requirements for charitable organizations (41)
- Reporting dates and requirements for charitable organizations (42)
- State acceptance of uniform registration form (31)
- Solicitation disclosure requirements for charitable organizations (23)
- Requirements for organizations using paid solicitors to note additional disclo-sure requirements if paid solicitors are used (30)
- Requirement for organizations using fundraising counsel to note registration, licensing, or bonding requirements for counsel (28)
- Need for organizations using paid solicitors to note that the state imposes addi-tional requirements for solicitors (42)

Funds spent on legal services and on administration to satisfy the growing number of rules and regulations cannot be used to fulfill the primary missions of third-sector organizations. The creation of and adherence to acceptable standards and practices should be determined by the nonprofits themselves. It should remain the vigilant business of the AAFRC, AFP, CASE, AHP, and other such bodies to impose self-discipline in this field, lest legislators and the general public impose their views on the third sector to an even greater extent.

Compensating Fundraisers

Beyond the issue of compensation paid to solicitors and consultants, discussions about staff compensation are increasing also. Typically, a nonprofit's employees are provided fixed and previously agreed-to compensation for their services. Debate has long raged in the nonprofit sector over pay for performance. Some people feel strongly that such agreements are unethical as well as impractical to administer; Asp (1999) concludes that performance incentives are both ethical and effective. Many institutions use incentive plans.

In general, an incentive is a financial reward based on objective criteria on which the employee and supervisor agree in advance. An incentive should not be confused with a bonus or a commission. A bonus is a financial reward given after the fact according to the subjective judgment of a supervisor to recognize a job well done. An organization could offer both bonuses and incentives; they are not mutually exclusive.

A commission, by contrast, is a payment to a fundraiser based on a percentage of funds he or she has raised. Most professional organizations absolutely discourage the use of commissions in the fundraising community. The implementation of commission-based fundraising can lead to very serious problems in the way staff members perform their jobs, and commission programs can severely hurt a development department. Commissions are to be avoided.

Institutions should reward fundraisers on the basis of merit. An institution should reward fundraisers who perform exceptionally in raising money more than it rewards those whose work is less successful. Fundraisers should know the criteria on which their supervisors will evaluate them. A successful incentive program will require that supervisors and employees be very clear about what criteria and specific numerical measures will be used to evaluate performance. Such explicitness gives the employees definite goals to shoot for. The fundraisers should be accountable to the rest of the institution. With an incentive program, the development office will easily be able to demonstrate the performance of each fundraiser as well as the department as a whole.

Asp (1999) recommends that the development program draw up a statement of values defining the type of development program the institution wishes to promote. This values statement guides the fundraisers' action and reinforces the institution's intent to reward a long-term focus.

The incentive program should use multiple evaluation measures when determining incentives. Using a single measure to evaluate performance can have unintended negative consequences. A well-structured plan should avoid emphasizing the dollar goal to such an extent that fundraisers will try to reach it by any means (this is one problem with commission programs). It should also avoid emphasizing process to such an extent that the fundraisers spend more time filing paperwork than meeting with prospects. An institution should use a wide variety of techniques to spur good performance in all aspects of a fundraiser's job.

The incentive plan must be written clearly. Often the simplest of words can be construed in many different ways when it comes time for the year-end evaluations. An institution should try to define the terms of its plan as specifically as possible. Also, to avoid confusion, institutional managers should meet with their fundraisers quite often so as to make sure everyone clearly understands the terms of the plan.

A well-structured plan should reward teamwork as well as individual accomplishments. The easiest way is to reward all development staffers when an institutional goal is met. However, there are other ways to reward people on an individual basis for keeping the best interests of the entire organization in mind. One option is to give an incentive to development staff members who are instrumental in helping a fundraiser secure a donation. These and other methods can help reward those who keep the best interest of the entire institution in mind.

When it comes time for evaluations and the payment of incentives, managers should remember to use common sense. For example, if a fundraiser falls just short of a personal goal but you had the person working on a long-term project for the institution as well, it would be advisable to give the incentive to reward this team player for being willing to sacrifice time and effort that could have been devoted toward the personal incentive. Such a reward will also instill a sense of teamwork in the staff. But on the flip side, a manager must also stick to his or her guns. An incentive plan and evaluation system will not work if it is not followed strictly most of the time. Generally, people who attain their goals should be rewarded, and those who did not do the work necessary to attain their goals should not be.

Another key component to any incentive plan is the rewards themselves. For most people, money is the strongest of all incentives. However, certain people might be better motivated by days off, public acknowledgment, private recognition, or a better job title. An institution should research which rewards will best serve to motivate its staff. Institutions should also not be afraid to tailor the rewards to each particular individual.

It may also be necessary to educate the rest of the institution about the incentive plan. There could be criticism from other employees. It might be said that the development office is detached from the values of the institution. However, this potential criticism is one of the reasons the statement of values must be developed and the policy must be communicated. When this criticism arises, show the other departments the statement of values, and they should realize that the development officer is still, first and foremost, committed to the overall mission of the institution.

A lot of work goes into developing and maintaining compensation packages and an incentive plan. The institution must be willing to invest the time and money that is required by such a plan. However, if done properly, an incentive plan can be a very big factor in the improvement of a development office's overall work product and productivity.

CHAPTER NINETEEN

APPLYING TECHNOLOGY TO FUNDRAISING

Kent E. Dove
William V. West

This chapter is about the single most important support factor in fundraising: technology. Like fundraising promotions, technology will not in and of itself raise money. Without technology, however, it is difficult if not impossible today to raise money effectively, efficiently, and economically.

Selecting an Information System

One of the most important aspects of an effective fundraising organization is an effective information system to support it. Information systems are electronic data management systems (hardware and software) that allow the transfer of information to take place for such purposes as data warehousing, research, analysis, communication, or e-commerce. Information systems can be as slight as a pocket organizer or grandiose in scale, restricted only by the resources and creativity of the user. In an ideal world, the information system should be as transparent to the fundraising process as the telephone. It has to be available and easy to use, and it has to contain needed information.

For small nonprofits, often information system needs can be met by emerging on-line systems or by purchasing software off the shelf that runs on a personal computer (PC). Access, the database component of Microsoft Windows 2000, is one reliable product for this purpose. In programs with four or more users and

2,500 or more names in the data base, Raiser's Edge, JSI Paradigm, and Millennium are popular products. In settings with twenty or more users and corresponding larger databases, organizations often explore the possibility of developing more individually distinctive information systems and purchasing software applications from established vendors. In this size range, three well-known names are Datatel's Benefactor and Colleague systems and the Iowa and BASF systems. Speaking with organizations of similar size and scope can help you identify producers and vendors that may satisfy your organization's information system needs.

There are two fundamental aspects to establishing a system that is efficient and effective: selecting the right system for your environment and selecting the right people to install and support that system. The 80/20 rule is an important consideration in selecting the right computer system. This rule states that 80 percent of users just want access to data (and want it now); they need to be able to see the data and produce, quickly and easily, reports that support their business. Only 20 percent will actually use the detailed functionality of any system. Remembering the 80/20 rule is fundamental in choosing the right system. Failure to do so will have two consequences. First, the system will contain only features that support its most sophisticated users (the 20 percent). Second, your organization's information system staff will then have the expensive task of building in the features that will support the remaining 80 percent of the users.

The selection of a development information system starts with the composition of the team that will make the selection. This team should strike a balance between the 20 percent of users who enter data and the 80 percent who use the data. Its members should include representatives of the following groups:

- Front-line development officers
- Development administrators
- Research analysts
- Data and gift processors
- Technical support staff
- High-level directors
- Lower-level staff (those who actually use the information system in the course of doing their work)

No one who lacks a thorough understanding of the detailed processes in his or her functional area should be on the selection team.

In the information system selection process, leadership is critical. The keys to selecting the right leader are *accountability* and *involvement*. Therefore, the leader of the information system selection team is accountable not only for the success of the system but also for the success of the organization. The leader must also be heavily involved at every step of the selection process; a leader who simply shows up for project meetings and does not understand the system's details cannot be effective. The leader should not be from the organization's technology department, however. It is best if the leader is from the development office or the executive office. The organization's development function should take ownership of the selection process—but with the technology function serving as a strong partner because the selection of a system that really impresses the development office but is impossible to support or enhance will lead to failure just as quickly as the selection of a system that uses "fresh" technology but does not satisfy development's needs.

Definition of the system's functional requirements—what the system is expected to do—is an important step. The requirements must include a definition of the organization's core processes. These are the essential functions that the organization requires to conduct its business. The only thing more important than carefully defining the system's requirements is making sure that the system has flexibility, in terms of both its software and your own environment. It is often easier to change a process or a report than it is to change a system. Rarely will you find a new system that can still produce, in the same format, every report that you now use. The focus should be on the marriage between functional needs and the system's capabilities. If that focus is achieved, then the system should be flexible enough to enhance its functionality as changes occur in the organizational environment.

We are in the midst of an explosion of new technologies, with new products coming to market literally every week. In their eagerness and excitement, some vendors make exaggerated claims, impossible promises, and empty guarantees. Guard against vendors like these, and make intelligent decisions that address your current and future needs. But how do you do this in a quicksand marketplace? Three techniques work very well:

1. Attend meetings of a user group. (If your vendor does not sponsor a user group, you are talking to the wrong vendor.) Attend the sessions that deal with the technical and functional aspects of the information system being considered. Talk to individuals from institutions that are equivalent to yours in size. This step is vital: some of the systems now on the market work beautifully in small institutions but fail in larger ones, and vice versa. Assess the types of staff people making presentations at user meetings. Ask yourself what type of staff you have and what type you can afford. Talk with users from development, information system, accounting, and other departments. Take the opportunity to get the total picture and identify potential weaknesses.

2. Meet with current users of the information system being considered. Go to these customers' sites—and make sure that you have adequate travel funds in the selection project's budget (a few $300 plane tickets now could save hundreds or thousands of dollars later). A site visit provides a chance to see the information system in action, talk to its users and support staff, learn about the customer's conversion or installation process (never visit a site that has not yet gone live), and assess the customer's satisfaction. It is best to make such a visit without the vendor: most customers are willing to be open, but not when the vendor is there. Do not allow the vendor to select the customers to be visited, and make sure that those visited are selected from a full list of the vendor's current customers. Be sure to bring along representatives from each of the major functional areas that will be using the system.

3. Test the system by installing it at your site. A true pilot installation (meaning that you are not committed to buying the system) will tell you very quickly how easy or hard the system will be to support and use. Pilot tests are not cheap. They take system resources and time. But if you think you are ready to make a selection, a pilot test will either confirm your decision or warn you of impending danger. (It will also quickly identify any phantom functionality that may have appeared in the vendor's demo.) Buy a small server, install the system, configure it for your environment, import some real data, install the system on the desks of your major functional departments, and then try to use it—*really* use it. This will not be an easy phase, and it will make demands on the participants. If this approach seems expensive, remember that nothing costs more than regret.

The information system you select should be easy to support, especially if yours is a small organization with limited resources. The tools used to develop the system should be standard and widely available. Selecting a system built with the vendor's proprietary tools puts an organization in the position of being dependent on this vendor alone for support, and such an arrangement can make the system's future growth and enhancement difficult. Moreover, recruitment and training of staff will be much easier if your system's architecture is a common or popular one. If the vendor is the only source of contract support, that is a sign of a closed system architecture—something you want to avoid. A system developed with a common programming language known as Report Programming Generator (RPG) or with PowerBuilder (Powersoft's tool for access to databases) can be integrated with a wide variety of other systems and platforms, whereas a system developed with a custom-made computer-aided software engineering tool or programming language cannot be easily integrated with other systems without substantial vendor assistance.

The system's database and its operating system should also have an open architecture. A system developed on any of the top databases (Oracle, Sybase, DB2, DB/400, Microsoft SQL server) is much more likely to grow with your needs than a system developed on a proprietary database that you've never heard of. The operating system you select will also have a significant impact on long-term costs. A system that runs on Unix or OS/400 may offer more flexibility but will also require more expensive hardware than a system running on NT.

Also consider the direction of the vendor's software company. The information system you purchase has to grow with your organization and also keep pace with changes in the technology sector. This is the only way to be sure that your organization will have access to the staff it needs for supporting the information system and to people who can easily learn how to use it. For example, if a system is currently running on technology built in the 1980s, its vendor may be unwilling to invest in software that will meet future needs. A vendor who claims to be enhancing a system with new technology should be put on hold until the enhancement has actually been completed, lest an organization make an unwitting investment in "vaporware." For example, information system vendors who are aligned with emerging trends should have developed browser technology by 2000. Much of a development officer's job is conducted out of the office, and access to the World Wide Web makes up-to-date information quickly available. Browser technology also significantly reduces the load that software puts on a PC and may therefore reduce the cost of the computer's support.

Installing the Information System

The information system installation process is never over. For one thing, the needs of the development staff are constantly changing as the organization moves from one campaign to the next, and the installation process has to account for the ongoing enhancements that will be requested. For another, because the installation of a new system is a major distraction from building anything else, be aware that there is certain to be a backlog of priority projects waiting after the information system has been installed. Therefore, you should not imagine that you will be able to hire temporary staffers just for the installation and then let them go.

Let us examine the keys to successful information system installation, in the order of their importance.

Leadership

From the most senior executive in development to the heads of each functional area, you must have solid leadership if the project is to be successful.

Time

Your best friend is time—the time to do things right. Deadlines are important in maintaining a sense of urgency about the project, but unrealistic timelines will damage the project. It is better to say that the project will take three years and then finish it a year early than to say it will take one year and then finish it a year late. Do the math: in both instances, the project takes two years.

Funding

Installing a new information system is expensive, no matter how good your staff is. The budget manager must be accountable at each stage of the project and must continue to demonstrate progress—real progress, not status reports and timelines. It is vital to know that you are getting the most for each dollar.

Involvement

Nobody gets to sit on the sidelines and throw rocks at the project. For the capabilities of the information system to be integrated with the processes in each functional area, the staff and managers of each area have to be involved. They should be involved in the definition of the processes, the data, and the interactions with other departments. This is the area where you are most likely to encounter resistance to change, but strong leadership and executive sponsorship can stifle it. Keep others involved, responsible, and accountable. Make it their project, too.

Communicating and Managing Expectations

Constant, consistent, positive, honest communication has to be the rule. The installation of the information system should not occur in the dark. Expectations need to be communicated clearly in the beginning. *Do not* let staff, employees, or executives believe that the system is going to be a panacea. *Do* tell them all the reasons why they should be excited, but also prepare them for the work associated with the changes they will encounter.

Expertise of the Technical Team

Select an information system you can support. If that is impossible, then get your technical staff into training. Make sure that the most productive people on staff know how to make the system work. Beware of simply hiring someone who has experience in the technical environment of the new information system: doing that may get a system up and running faster, but it could hurt in the long run because it takes time to learn and understand a development environment. Therefore, be sure to harness the institutional knowledge in your existing staff. Contract with outside experts to coach, mentor, and guide you through the installation process, but do not hire contractors to do the installation itself. Contractors will not understand your environment, and ultimately, turning your installation over to contractors will not help your staff support the information system. It is better to contract for education than to contract for labor. Bring in experts from other sites to check your project's quality and double-check your decisions. Your consulting support should ensure that you are asking the right questions, making the right decisions, and learning along the way.

Pilot Testing

Nothing provides better feedback than a good pilot test. Make it a real one. Be sure that there is ample time to conduct the test and to evaluate the results before full installation of the system begins. Use real data, process parallel transactions, and then compare the results of these transactions. Most of all, build some reports that simulate your current ones.

Education and Training

Invest time and money in training. If people lack skill and knowledge, they will either ignore the system or use it incorrectly. It is essential that key users as well as technical staff understand the functionality of the information system. Conduct basic training courses after the system goes live, and conduct refresher training frequently and repeatedly until the users stop attending.

Reports

No functionality is more important than the system's ability to build and produce reports. The information system should offer report capabilities to users at all levels of experience as well as to the system's programmers; any system that requires experienced programmers for the production of simple reports should send you running for the hills. As soon as the system goes live—not after—have several standard reports ready (for example, weekly giving activity, a month-by-month comparison of the current year to the previous year, donor profiles, completed pledges, campaign tracking, account balances). These reports will satisfy most users while additional reports are being developed.

Standards and Procedures

Nothing in a system is harder to fix than bad data. Therefore, standards and procedures must be defined before the system is installed because they are essential to converting and importing historical data, and they will be vital if your data-entry operations are decentralized.

Coding Structure

The coding structure used throughout your information system should be defined by people who understand both the business of the institution and its data. At this stage, it is also crucial to have someone on hand who is an expert in the particular information system that has been installed. Therefore, the team defining the coding structure must include a representative from the vendor's company who knows the system inside and out—that is, who understands how information is processed on the screens and how data are processed by the programs. Failure to define the codes correctly may prevent entire modules of the system from functioning in response to your needs. This expert must also have experience using the system's software in an environment comparable to yours because the coding scheme used by a small institution may be significantly different from the scheme used by a large institution.

Support of Core Processes

With every new decision, ask yourself, "Does this feature support a core process?" Many bells and whistles can be included in a development information system, and many among the sophisticated 20 percent of users believe they've got to have it all. This vocal 20 percent will have a knack for quibbling and distracting the project from its purpose. That is why strong, knowledgeable leadership is so important. An essential part of the leader's role is to ensure that the functions installed are those that support the institution's core processes. A new system also very often requires a fundamental change in mind-set, especially if you are making the change from an existing system: "We've always done it this way" could cripple your project. Your focus should always be the marriage of your functional needs with the capabilities of the system.

Managing an Information System Group

Many factors—skillful leaders, executive support, ample funding, a talented technical staff—promote the successful management of an information system group, but one factor stands out from the rest: the separation of day-to-day operational duties from project-related duties. In general, attempts to blend the staff responsible for day-to-day information system support and the staff responsible for developing and upgrading information system tools and services will prevent both functions from reaching their maximum potential (if they do not fail altogether). Operational duties include user support, service on the help desk, and report development and distribution. Project-related duties include software development, database development, systems integration, business process automation, and of course the installation of a new information system. To the extent possible, the operational staff, at least the help desk, should be physically separated from the other information system staff. This area usually draws high traffic and open conversation and can be a major distraction to programmers.

The processing of ad hoc report requests and the production of reports should also be separated from the functions of the information system programming and project staff. According to the kind of system you have, reports may be produced by support staff, programmers, or high-end users. Regardless of who produces the reports, however, the demands of report production are very different from information system project-related demands and should be kept separate from them. User support is a chaotic environment, where the priorities and the focus change daily, and project-related staff members will fail in this environment. They need a quiet area where focus, concentration, and teamwork are possible. The large majority of organizations (those with fewer than twenty-five fundraising professionals) may be required to use programmers to produce ad hoc reports, but these organizations should still use dedicated programmers for this task, keeping it separate from the work of the project-related programmers.

Setting Clear Priorities for the Information System

One of the key success factors in an efficient and effective information system operation is the setting of clear priorities. These priorities must be set through a balance of the needs of the system's users and the needs of the infrastructure. The information system staff is responsible for defining and clearly communicating the needs of the infrastructure; in order for the needs of users to be defined, however, organizational leaders must be involved. Organizational environments can be hotly political at times, and there is always a slate of high-priority projects under way. It should not be the responsibility of the information system department to determine which projects will receive its attention; saying no is not a successful position to be in. Assigning an information system director the job of saying no can quickly alienate the director and produce animosity between the departments that get top priority and those that do not. Equal access and representation ensures that every priority is set with the best interests of the organization in mind and that all departments will understand why. Moreover, there are never enough information system resources to implement every project, solve every emergency, or design every good idea introduced by users. Therefore, an empowered team of organizational leaders must be responsible for setting priorities.

The forum and process for establishing priorities can be very simple. It starts with a request form—a simple form that states the nature of the project, records who has requested it, says how it will benefit the organization, and provides a place where a programmer can make an assessment and estimate the time needed for the project. All requests should be logged in a database or spreadsheet so that a report of new requests can be produced. The team of organizational leaders should gather periodically to go over the new requests, review the status of current projects, and set priorities for the new requests.

This process has two clear benefits for both the information system staff and the development staff. First, the programmers are given clear priorities: they know what to work on first and can complete projects in order. Second, this process ensures that limited programming resources are focused on the areas of most benefit to the organization as a whole. The needs of the infrastructure may or may not be discussed by way of this forum. These include upgrades to network and server equipment that will be imperceptible to the users. These needs must be factored into the discussion if a shared pool of staff members is required for both project types and will have to be coordinated with upcoming projects, of course. But often the priorities for the infrastructure projects are defined or required by changes in the technology industry; solid leadership in the information system function can ensure that the needs of the infrastructure are well orchestrated with other priorities.

Updating and Maintaining Your Technical Environment

Updating and maintaining your information system is a strategic imperative of your development program. It costs less to maintain a position ahead of the advancement curve than it does to regain a position once it has been lost. As newer technologies have emerged and faster computers have been developed, the cost of maintaining a positive position in technology has actually been coming down. In the early 1990s, PCs had to be upgraded or replaced every three years in order to run current software. This meant that more than 30 percent of an organization's computers had to be replaced every year. In 1998, a PC with the best-valued processor and a fifteen-inch monitor cost between $2,000 and $2,500. A year later, a PC with twice the power and a seventeen-inch screen cost between

$1,200 and $1,800. The newer PCs are able to last four to five years and even after five years will retain enough power to satisfy low-end, occasional users. This means that now only 20 to 25 percent of your equipment needs to be upgraded every year. The price for very powerful PCs will continue to drop.

The updating and upgrading of your primary applications and your operating systems will need to be justified and handled with due diligence. Software vendors commonly try to force an organization to upgrade, but the value added to the system does not always justify the cost of the upgrade. Moreover, a software upgrade can shorten the life of hardware. To protect your investment, control staffing and support costs, and ensure that priorities are focused on the projects that offer the most value to the organization, do not upgrade software unless there is a real need to do so. Any plans for a software upgrade should justify the expense and guarantee that the upgrade will not make current hardware obsolete (this is not an issue, however, if current computer hardware has already outlived its usefulness).

Business managers should be involved in the planning process for a software upgrade, to ensure their understanding of the added benefits and the changes to existing systems. Technical professionals should not be expected to make an upgrade decision alone. The key success factors for an upgrade are similar to those for selecting a new system. The involvement of everyone is essential to making sure the decision that gets made is the right one for the organization.

The budget required to maintain an information system must be in the baseline of the capital budget; it should not be an add-on. Technology is a strategic tool. Those who use it well will gain an advantage over those who do not. Effective use of technology provides the ability to reduce business costs, improve the efficiency of all processes, and increase fundraising. It is difficult to prove that adding technology increases success, but it is often very easy to spot cases in which poor technology or failed technology projects seriously hampered the success of a development program. Therefore, the baseline budget should include the funds required to maintain your position.

The budget for a new technology project should be independent of the operational budget. The funds for new technology should be justified and requested separately as a part of the capital budget on the basis of the value that the technology can add to the organization. The technology-related expenditures and returns should also be tracked separately in the operating budget so that the progress and the success or failure of the project can be monitored. This procedure ensures that the project's performance will not have an impact, positive or negative, on the operational budget (this precaution is most important, of course, when a new technology project runs over budget).

Technologies That Serve Development

Some technologies serve development better than others. A few of these are emerging technologies; others are time-related.

Internet Technology

Information can be a strong asset for a development officer, if it is available when and where it is needed. The emergence of the Internet as an international communications pathway has opened the door for all institutions, large and small, to enhance information sharing, both internally and with peers. Most of the technologies relevant to the development function are now more useful because of the Internet. The truly helpful elements that all development organizations should consider—in addition, of course, to an in-office local-area network (LAN) and an information system—are access to the Internet, e-mail, laptop computers, remote access to databases, and palmtop devices. (If you do not have a LAN or an information system, then you should not yet be looking at these other elements.)

Fortunately, most universities, and many other larger organizations, are wired, one way or another, for Internet access. Therefore, the first step is to get your office connected to your organization's Internet server via your LAN. Once that connection has been made, everything else is possible, and everyone in the development office will have access to a wide array of research services.

A staff constantly on the move, on the road, and in meetings can find e-mail extremely useful. It is an excellent tool for receiving and responding to messages. The disadvantage of e-mail, relative to the phone, is that you cannot have a real conversation; and because a text message contains no audible emotional cues, messages can be misinterpreted. The advantage of e-mail over the phone is that you can read and respond at your own convenience (you are not interrupted), you do not have to take written notes, and you can easily keep a log of correspondence. An e-mail program usually also offers a suite of other tools—an officewide calendar, an officewide address book, a tool for contact management—that make life in the office easier.

If yours is a small development office, you can piggyback your e-mail on someone else's system (your organization's, for example). Supporting an e-mail system is expensive; do not install your own unless your office is large enough to afford the support staff or unless you absolutely have no other choice. The advantage of using an organizationwide system is that you can share an address book and calendar with colleagues and associates. If tying your e-mail to your organization's service is not an option, however, then often you can find an Internet service provider (ISP) in your area that provides e-mail service. One requirement for an e-mail system is that it be accessible via the Internet. Internet access to an e-mail account opens up a larger array of solutions for staff on the road. ISPs can now also offer on-line giving capabilities. These need to be examined carefully, particularly with regard to confidentiality and other security issues.

Portable Computing

Laptop computers have continued to drop in price while increasing in quality and power. A full-powered laptop with a nice monitor now costs the same as a desktop computer did three years ago and provides more power. A laptop with a docking station, which allows it to be connected to your network; a full-size keyboard; and a full-size screen provides all the services of a desktop computer but offers the advantage of portability. After work, or as you head off on a trip, you can detach your laptop from your docking station and take it along. This means that you can take your tools and information—essentially, your whole office—with you.

A laptop becomes a mobile office once you have remote access to your servers and to the Internet. Remote access can be provided in three ways: through an organizational dial-up (another reason to connect your office with your organization's network), through an Internet service provider (the primary reason to ensure that your e-mail is accessible via the Internet), or through your own modem pool (a bank of dedicated phone lines for use in dialing in to the office). These options are listed in increasing order of cost. Supporting your own remote-access server (RAS) is much more expensive than piggybacking on your organization's. The larger an organization, however, the easier it is to support your own RAS. Having your own RAS also provides dedicated lines and the ability to connect toll-free. A toll-free number can save your organization significant money in charges for calling over long distances while it simplifies the dial-in process for the staff.

Palmtop devices are providing increasing power and functionality in a small package. Some staff members on the move may prefer a palmtop to a laptop. A palmtop device will not serve as a fully mobile office, but it will provide many of the essentials (e-mail, an appointment calendar, a contact list, expense reporting, and other features helpful to the traveling development officer). The price of a palmtop is also substantially less than that of a laptop. For an office on a small budget, palmtops and a link to the Internet could provide a very cost-effective functional package.

Another helpful software product is the emerging system for geographical mapping and location finding. Such a system allows you to import a name and an address from your development database. It then plots the location of the address on an interactive map, showing you how to drive to the location. The more advanced systems can work in your car and be integrated with a global positioning system (GPS) that actually tracks current location and plots current position with respect to destination.

Web Technology

Since the introduction of the Web browser in 1993, the World Wide Web has grown from anonymity to becoming the most popular medium in use. Businesses, both for-profit and nonprofit, view the Web with awe and uncertainty. However, there is one thing that is guaranteed: the Web will be the dominant medium going forward. It will be a strategic imperative for every business to have a solid Web presence. Nonprofit organizations that successfully integrate the Web into their plans will have a strategic advantage over those that do not.

The Web offers several unique opportunities that will affect the very heart of any organization. Internally, the Web offers a means to increase the capacity of an organization without increasing its expenses. Business processes that require extensive documentation and paperwork can be replaced with on-line Web transactions between any organization and its constituencies, including the savviest donors. Externally, the Web offers the ability to customize marketing strategies to meet the needs of each donor. Print media and mass mailings cannot offer the degree of customization that a Web-based marketing program can offer. It's equivalent to producing a brochure whose contents dynamically change to meet the interest of each reader.

So nonprofits need a Web presence. But where to start?

Establishing a Presence on the World Wide Web

There are many approaches to developing a Web site. Some organizations hire a developer and train their own staff to develop the entire site in-house. Others contract a company to develop their site. And some do a little of both. There are advantages to each approach.

One guideline is to take baby steps. Do a little at a time, but do each step very well. Recognize your organization's strengths, and then build on those as you branch into the Web's world. Mastering the basics of the Web is quite easy. Most new college graduates enter the workforce with basic Web development skills. However, the world of the Web gets complicated quickly. A conservative and deliberate approach to the Web will ensure that each stage achieves at least one objective, and does it well, while proactively preparing to achieve the next, usually more complicated, objective.

Senior management, with competent facilitation and education, should provide solid direction and input into the overall strategy and design of the Web site. Begin by preparing your staff to support a Web site. Address the five primary components involved in that support: content management, content design and development, programming and integration, systems administration, and training and education. A team approach is best for each of the five components.

Content management needs to be led by someone who fully understands the mission and operations of the organization. The focus of content management is marketing and service. A word of caution: as the Web site grows, the time required for content management will grow. This function needs to work off a well-defined set of priorities to ensure that the strategic goals of the Web are met. The success of content management will be predicated on the implementation of an effective process that enables current content to be maintained without hampering the development of new content.

Content design and development are functions that are traditionally handled by a publication's staff, writers, and graphic artists. Depending on the level of sophistication of the Web site, many individuals in an organization can be trained to be content developers. Basic design and development of Web pages is quickly becoming a common skill, like word processing and desktop publishing. From the standpoint of the publication's staff, the Web is simply a new medium. Development of Web publications is similar to development of print-based publications. The constituencies and desired outcomes are the same.

Programming and integration of Web pages is not trivial. The Web is first and foremost a technology. Simple, static, and noninteractive Web pages are easy to build but boring. Building a Web site that is truly interactive—one that enables constituents to make a gift, update their profile, view their account, register for events, and provide the myriad of services that can truly make a Web site successful, all within a secure environment—requires a trained programming staff that can work as part of the team with the content developers. Most of the programming and integration of a Web site happens behind the scenes. Programmers don't typically make good Web designers. However, a solid, supportive Web programmer gives content developers more flexibility to be creative and really reach the limits of a Web site's potential.

The systems administration functions that are required for fundraising information systems and networks are also required for the Web site. Installation and support of the Web servers is similar in many ways to that of supporting other enterprise (internal) servers, however, there are some nuances that must be learned by each institution's support staff. A solid systems administration function should provide content developers with the tools and environment they need to be creative. A well-designed systems infrastructure will provide a secure and reliable environment that is easy to support and promotes sharing and reuse of Web content.

Training and education are required for the long-term development of the Web site. Content developers need to be trained to use Web-based tools, just as they use word processors, to develop the information that will be placed on the Web. As their skills improve, continuous training will enable them to reach new heights. Senior management and the business managers need to be educated on the possibilities of the Web. Increasing their awareness and understanding of the Web will enable them to create new ideas, strategies, and programs that are incorporated into the Web strategy. The Web offers new and exciting ways to interact with prospects and donors. Understanding the potential that the Web offers and preparing a skilled staff to implement your ideas will enable you to take advantage of this forum to maximize the success of your programs.

The Role of the Web Developer

The typical approach to Web development is to hire a Webmaster, or developer. This person's mission is to provide leadership and ensure that the Web development team works together. Webmasters have proliferated over the past few years as more and more programmers, graphic artists, instructional designers, and other professionals have developed Web skills. However, a new Web developer cannot survive all alone. Hiring an expert Web developer brings new and valuable skills into an organization. A competent Web developer can create solid Web pages while coaching and educating staff about Web development. However, the knowledge and leadership required to develop a Web site must come from within the organization. A new Web developer will need time to learn about the organization and its fundraising process. With the right organizational structure and attitude, this person can become very successful quickly.

The ideal Web developer possesses a combination of skills. These skills are often not found in a single individual, and they present a fundamental challenge when hiring a Web developer. If found in one person, chances are you can't afford the person. This is why a team approach to Web development is often essential. A good Web developer must be

- Technically astute to work within the Web site, which is after all still a technical environment.
- Skilled at marketing, since your Web site will become a major medium used to reveal your organization's image.

- Aesthetically inclined in order to develop Web pages that are clean and well organized. This may be the most important characteristic. There are a lot of really ugly Web pages on the Internet.
- As creative as a graphic designer in the ability to clip and paste images and icons together. The developer need not be a trained artist but must be able to construct and edit graphics in order to assemble pages that are attractive and usable.
- Well organized so that the Web site's appearance, supporting file structure, and the process used to prioritize additions to the site are clear and systematic.
- Able to absorb ideas, knowledge, and facts from the organization and incorporate them into the Web pages.
- Adept at communication and at project management. A skilled developer can facilitate groups of staff from different areas of an organization and lead them to the construction of a solution that meets the needs of the donors while satisfying the demands of the internal business processes.
- Able to accept good ideas, understand the needs of the creator of those ideas, and then produce a result that not only reflects those ideas but takes them to the next level. This may be the most important function of all. Nothing compares to the thrill of working with a Web developer who can take ideas and make them come to life, producing even more than imagined. That's when you know you've hired the right person.

Don't expect the Web developer to support the technical environment used by the Web—the programming, integration, and systems administration tasks. Web developers need constantly to take the time to develop and enhance their Web skills and learn the intricacies of the related systems environment. Both the Web and the systems environments are quickly maturing and changing. Becoming a competent Web developer in an ever-changing technical environment is not a small endeavor for three primary reasons. First, the ability to understand the supporting systems environment often exceeds the abilities of Web developers who emerge from nontechnical backgrounds. Second, programming complex interactions such as on-line forms and reports requires extensive time, which can significantly delay other content-only projects. And third, as the Web site gains popularity, the onslaught of new projects and maintenance work often prevents the Web developer from developing new skills that require time, training, and practice. Surviving this dilemma requires that a solid technical support team is in place to provide the programming and systems administration support so that the Web developer can focus on developing and enhancing the content, without losing time supporting the infrastructure.

In addition to the internal Web developer, begin training other key staff members on basic Web development skills so that they can contribute to the contents of the Web. The publications staff should begin training to develop on-line publications. From this standpoint, publication's constituencies will not change, but the media they use now include the Web. The administrative staff should be trained in the basic Web content development skills, too. As technology progresses, Web content will become as easy to develop as documents on a word processor. Training internal staff members to develop Web content results in two strategic advantages for any organization. It increases the capacity to develop a Web presence by having more staff members with the skills to do so. And it produces a transformation in workers by giving them the ability to be creative, develop new ideas, and interact directly with the target market via the Web site.

Maintaining the Web Site

Once the team is in place, what's next? Many of the important considerations are the same as in any other medium.

Internet, Intranet, Extranet. By simple definition, the *Internet* Web sites are used by prospects and donors, the *intranet* is used by employees, and the *extranet* is used by business partners (external development units, alumni relations, business offices, banking and investment partners). The Internet Web site is your primary window to the world and will enable you to increase gifts; this is the Web site that presents your image and enables you to interact with prospects and donors. The implementation of an intranet and an extranet will enhance productivity, facilitate communications, and reduce costs over the long term. The need for all three is based on the size of the organization, the complexity of the services offered, and the short-term and long-term strategic plans. Every organization needs an Internet site. An intranet or extranet may not be needed by small organizations. However, both might be essential to a large organization with development and administrative personnel spread across a multiple sites.

The Basics. Donors have certain fundamental expectations when they arrive at a Web site. They want the whos, whats, and wheres. Start with a staff directory, a picture of your institution and building, basic statistics that demonstrate your success, and a feedback mechanism that enables two-way communication. At a minimum, your site should contain these easy-to-provide items. From there you can begin introducing your constituents to the programs that support your strategic plans. Here are some key rules of thumb:

- Keep it simple and make it interesting.
- Make the basic information easy to find.
- Make the strategic information interesting and interactive. (Pages of text describing all the forms of giving are good for reference, but are not likely to entertain site visitors.)
- Introduce your goals and success to the visitor in an interactive way that keeps them clicking.

Sell, Sell, Sell. Don't assume that visitors want to be at your site. Give them a reason to stay. Explain to them what you are and what you stand for. Explain why your organization is important, and then back it up with results.

Interactive Service. Find out what your constituents want and need most, and then provide it. This is where an educated senior management team supported by a skilled development team can really begin to create new ideas and methods to interact with and reach out to constituents. Some fundamental services include the ability for a donor to make a gift or pledge, to see his or her own past giving record, or update address and profile information. Many university-related organizations have found success by providing their alumni and donors with a lifetime e-mail address that looks like "YourName@alumni.institution.edu." On-line searchable directories of alumni, friends, business contacts, and others are also a valuable service that can be provided via the Web. Emerging ideas include assistance with tax and estate planning, with education cost projections and savings plans, and with finding and applying for scholarships. These are all areas that allow the development programs to offer service to constituents while reinforcing fundraising efforts. These services pull constituents into the organization by providing services they want while exposing them to important programs like planned giving, endowment funding, and other campaigns.

Implementation of these services requires a strong programming and support staff. Development of Web sites that interact with your information system in a secure and easy-to-use environment is identical to the implementation of a new application system such as telemarketing automation or an investment management system. It shares the same level of complexity.

Note that these services may require a solid partnership with departments within the institution that have traditionally provided services related to these. The Web has required, like nothing else before it, a greater need for cooperation among the departments across the institution.

Sustaining Growth. Start with the information and services that are needed most by your prospects and donors. Then assemble a deliberate plan for adding content and services over time. Do each step very well; then move on, leaving behind a support and maintenance plan that will ensure that the content of existing pages is maintained without distracting from the implementation of new content and services. Set expectations within your organization. You cannot successfully put all programs and departments on your Web site at the same time with equal quality. Senior management must set the priorities. A well-established team can then complete each priority in turn.

PCs and office networks have dramatically changed the way every employee works. The World Wide Web will change the way organizations interact with their prospects, donors, and the world. It will become a primary method used to conduct business at the start of the twenty-first century. Institutions and their supporting development programs will be able to use the Web to launch new services that will attract and cultivate new donors. The Web will give the ability to develop new marketing strategies that are more personal at a much lower cost by allowing organizations to customize strategies to each individual. The only other forum that provides this flexibility is a one-on-one relationship. The Web provides a starting point to build a one-on-one relationship with each and every visitor.

Maintaining Data

Maintenance of the data in a development system can be a complex, time-consuming task. Many factors affect how complex this task will be. Let's examine a few of those factors.

• *The number of prospects and donors in the database.* Complexity increases as the number of records increases. A staff of two or three may be able to maintain a database of 25,000 constituents but cannot maintain a database of 250,000 with the same degree of efficiency. Likewise, a large organization may have 250,000 constituents but may not be able to afford to hire twenty people for its records department. Therefore, you must determine the database priorities, the technologies and techniques to be used, and the acceptance costs to maintain data.

• *The number of gift and accounting transactions completed each year.* The more transactions in a system, and the more added each year, the more efficient data-maintenance processes need to be, especially if there are many years of historical data in the system. Maintaining accuracy in the files that contain the giving history, and in all the subtotal files, requires strict standards for processes. The need for accuracy and for the ability to subdivide these data will increase as the number of transactions increases.

- *The number of fields important to the organization.* Maintaining only donors' home addresses makes for a simple data-maintenance process, regardless of the number of records. If the primary focus is on home mailings, then staff can focus on strategies that enable this level of data maintenance. But if phone numbers and information about prospects' employment, activities, and affiliations are also required, the complexity of the data-maintenance process increases. In sophisticated organizations—those with programs for annual giving, special giving, major gifts, planned and deferred giving, capital campaigns, donor relations, and prospect management—it is not uncommon to maintain more than a hundred data elements for each record.

- *Accuracy requirements.* Accuracy in constituents' records is often measured by addressability, and addressability is a moving target: more than 20 percent of the population may move in any given year. The costs and efficiency of record maintenance will be closely tied to the need for accuracy. Each nonprofit must determine how high a degree of accuracy is required and what price it is willing to pay to achieve it.

Organizing the Records Department

There are many options for organizing the records department. Put the records staff in the department where it will receive the most support, regardless of that department's primary function. This may mean putting the records department in the research area, in the alumni association (if yours is an educational institution), in accounting, in another development office, or somewhere else. The important thing is that it receive the tools, guidance, and direction needed and that it is not expected to carry out duties in addition to maintaining records. Record maintenance is hard, tedious work, and if staff members must choose among competing priorities, record maintenance will inevitably suffer.

Several techniques and technologies can improve the process of maintaining records; what works at a given organization may very well depend on a number of external factors. In a large, complex environment, take advantage of its large core of development officers in order to gather new data from a wide variety of sources (events, meetings, telemarketing, Web pages, and so on).

It is best not to decentralize data entry itself; centralized control of data-entry standards is very important for the long-term integrity of the data. One key to ensuring its integrity is to have a single individual responsible and accountable for that task. This individual is in charge of all code definitions and oversees the data-entry process. It is vital that this individual understand the objectives of the organization and become an integral contributor to its business functions.

With strong and well-defined data standards, you can enable all users to contribute to the accuracy of information. If you do not already have this ability, consider adding a function to your system that allows every user to send updates to the records department directly through the system. Updates are made by the records department, but every user contributes to the update process. Decentralization of access to record maintenance is one of the key success factors in many large, complex organizations.

E-mail and the World Wide Web are excellent mechanisms for further decentralizing the collection of data from constituents. An organization-sponsored e-mail address gives constituents an organizational tie and provides a means of making contact electronically free of charge. The Web also offers the ability to post an on-line form that enables constituents to update their own information as often as necessary. This electronic form should send the updated data to the members of the records staff, who will then enter it in system. A form like this one is easy to create and very cost-effective. Both of these services should be advertised on every publication and mailing sent out.

Postage is an expensive part of record maintenance and development. Coordinating mailing efforts can save expenses and increase the ability to update constituents' information. For example, when mailing a gift receipt to a donor, check to see if the phone number and employment data are complete. If not, include a minisurvey form in the receipt envelope. In addition, pay for the return postage on at least one major mailing a year. When you mail a receipt, solicitation, magazine, or invitation, make sure that you get address correction information from the U.S. Postal Service. If employment data and phone numbers are important, send out a survey form for every address update made: "We've noticed that your address has changed—has anything else?"

New Roles for Technology

Information services and products constitute the world's largest and fastest-growing economic sector. Computers, computer systems, networks, and digital information increasingly dominate every facet of life. This growing dependence on digital information and information technologies is dramatically altering fundraising and will continue to do so. Mal Warwick (1994, pp. 39–41) has the following comments on this development:

> It's impossible to foretell the shape or direction of the future—especially where technology is concerned. But this much I'll predict: the direct response fundraising systems we'll depend on twenty years from now will share the following six characteristics.

1. *Individualized.* Our appeals will be "individualized." By and large, we won't be dealing with donor file "segments" anymore but with individuals—responding to their unique, personal interests and capabilities. We'll know a lot more about our donors, because we'll ask them for more information through frequent surveys and questionnaires and because our information management systems will be capable of storing much more data than most charities now find practical to retain.

2. *Multi-sensory.* Our appeals will be "multi-sensory," using forms of what today are called "multimedia" technologies. We won't be limited to paper, or to voice communications, or to pre-recorded sounds or video images. A single fundraising appeal might consist of sights, sounds and data, and be delivered, separately or simultaneously, through several communications channels: a wallscreen, perhaps, with full-motion sound and video, or a pocket communicator bearing a simplified, two-dimensional version, or a hardcopy printout a little like what today we call a "fax." Donors will choose which method they prefer, and open it up when and where they wish—suiting the mood or constraints of the moment, or following long-established preferences for one form or another.

3. *Information-rich.* Twenty years from now, our appeals will be "information-rich." On-line databases and super-high-speed data transmission will permit us to make veritable mountains of information available to every prospect or donor—and the demands of competition will force us to do so. Meanwhile, flexible database management software will permit every prospect and every donor to select precisely those bits of information they want—and not one word or one image more.

4. *Real-time.* Within two decades, "real-time" transactions will be common in direct response fundraising. "Real-time" is computer jargon for "right now." For example, by authorizing a gift in the course of an on-line videoconference with her favorite charity, a donor may instantaneously transmit funds from her bank account to the charity—before the conference is even over. The response curves we measure today in weeks and months may be viewed in terms of hours or even minutes twenty years from now.

5. *Interactive.* Fundraising thirty years from today will be highly "interactive." Donors will actively participate, not just in selecting the amount and the format of the information they receive, but [in] the role they'll play in the life and work of the charities they support. Today's dedicated donor "hotlines" will become multimedia gateways that offer donors a multitude of new options: to participate in the latter-day equivalent of focus group research, for example, or to share their specialized expertise with program staff, or to integrate what

they're learning from us into ongoing educational programs. Both two-way and small-group communications will be an integral part of the process— freeing fundraisers from the constraints of time and geography, and permitting us to develop rich and rewarding relationships with donors we may never actually meet.

6. *Communal.* The nonprofits that flourish in the fast-moving environment of the twenty-first century will be those that provide their supporters with the experience of community. Today's fast-multiplying computer networks, bulletin board systems, local access cable TV, video teleconferencing and e-mail facilities foreshadow the integrated technologies of the twenty-first century. Within twenty years, charities will be able to engage thousands of their donors in a profoundly personal and meaningful way—simultaneously, and over great physical distances. Meanwhile, as individuals, many donors will find the nearly instantaneous, broadband communications of the New Age will permit them to turn a shared commitment to a charity's work into personal relationships with many of their fellow donors. Just as users of today's converging technologies are forming "virtual communities," often spanning continents and oceans, donors by the thousands may eventually be able to join with a charity's other constituents—staff, board, clients, alumni—in shared access to the daily experience of the charity's work. How? Through a latter-day equivalent to "personals" ads in the newsletters or public forums on the Network of the future. That experience and the personal relationships that result may enrich daily life in the twenty-first century for tens of millions of people.

CHAPTER TWENTY

PROVIDING ACCOUNTABILITY AND EXPRESSING APPRECIATION

M ost fundraisers do not like to consider the handling and internal process-ing of a gift or pledge once it has been received. The fundraiser's tendency is to move along to the next new donor and gift. However, it is essential that gifts and pledges be processed and handled properly. Handling funds properly once received is as important as raising them successfully. Days, months, and even years of careful cultivation can be harmed by an organization's failure in these invisible but very important processes. This chapter touches on the areas of bud-get construction, gift administration and account administration, and investment policy—the financial and administrative processes that secure the fundraising process. It concludes with a discussion of the visible activities associated with good stewardship—saying thank you and showing appreciation.

Annual Budget

The question of budget is a difficult one to address because there are so many variables that affect and influence the discussion, including the factors discussed in Chapter One. Generally speaking, mature nonprofits that hold the cost of fund-raising to 15 to 20 cents per dollar raised (500 to 750 percent return on invest-ment, ROI) are considered productive; those that keep costs around 10 to 15 cents per dollar raised (750 to 1,000 percent ROI) are viewed as highly productive; and those that keep costs at or below 10 cents per dollar raised (1,000+ percent ROI) are deemed extremely productive. For growing nonprofits, costs of 20 to 50 cents per dollar raised (100 to 500 percent ROI) are considered marginally productive and generally represent acceptable returns.

In certain instances, fundraising costs may exceed 50 percent of the total dollars raised. Such a situation can occur in a start-up program or where the fundraising is primarily a broad-based, smaller-gift participation program. It may also occur in a program with such a small staff that the organization must outsource most or all of its program to paid solicitors or one that is attempting to attract new donors in large numbers. All of these are labor-intensive, and the costs can be substantial over the short term.

It is ultimately the responsibility of the governing board, on the basis of recommendations from management and its own careful discernment, to approve the fundraising budget and to determine acceptable ROI guidelines. If the board feels it can comfortably endorse and defend its budget to its donors, friends, and critics, it has a budget that is probably reasonable whether it fits within these guidelines or not.

Campaign Budget

What does it cost to run a professionally managed capital campaign? Again, there is no single answer. Several factors influence the cost of campaign fundraising:

- Proportion of institutional resources already committed to the ongoing development program
- Size of the goal (certain fixed costs that are common to all campaigns—preparation of a case statement, use of professional counsel, major public announcement event, victory celebration—are more easily amortized in large campaign budgets than in small ones)
- Campaign model
- Solicitation method
- Geographical scope of the campaign

Campaign budgets can vary significantly. Costs in large campaigns can sometimes be kept as low as 2 to 3 percent of the campaign goal. For the purposes of planning, however, most institutions should assume that it will cost between 10 and 12 percent of the campaign goal to conduct the campaign, especially if the goal is under $10 million or if the institution lacks appropriate fundraising infrastructure in the beginning. For a large segment of the institutions contemplating capital campaigns, a guideline of 4 percent is applicable. Into this group falls the institution that has a well-developed fundraising program (a program with annual giving, special gifts, major gifts, planned giving efforts, and a research function) and an adequately funded operating budget, with a campaign goal in the range of $25 million to $250 million. This incremental amount of 4 percent of the goal is in addition to the established operating budget.

Several variables must be considered before a final figure is arrived at, but two fundamental points are of primary importance.

First, it takes ample funding to ensure the success of a campaign, and too much attention is focused on fundraising costs. With so much at stake, it is foolhardy to be too restrictive of campaign expenses; to fixate on costs is to adopt the perspective that the glass is half empty. It does matter how much is spent, but isn't the real issue how much is realized? No matter how cost-effective an effort is, it is always possible to argue that even more costs could be squeezed out of the budget if only the campaign managers looked harder. But it is time to change the dialogue, establish a new paradigm, focus on returns—and an investment in a campaign, wisely made, will yield very high returns. *It costs money to raise money.* Is a 1,000 percent return on investment acceptable? How about 2,500 percent? What board member, volunteer, institutional employee, or donor would not be pleased with a 2,500 percent return? That's a 4 percent cost factor.

Second, all the campaign's needs should be considered and included at the outset. Most campaign budgets have lines for the items shown in Exhibit 20.1.

A final important consideration regarding budget is to establish an internal procedure that provides for constant monitoring and scrutiny of budget expenditures. Forms that can be used in conjunction with tracking progress are presented in Exhibit 20.2 for a multiyear campaign and Exhibit 20.3 for an annual campaign.

In addition to the costs of campaigning, there is the little-discussed loss called shrinkage—losses resulting from unpaid pledges. Shrinkage can be as low as 1 to 3 percent of the amount raised in a capital campaign, but 5 to 10 percent is more usual, and even higher rates may be encountered in an annual campaign. The job of the professional staff member is to ensure that shrinkage stays as low as possible.

Some losses are uncontrollable, as in the case of a donor's death or the failure of the donor's business. Some, however, are caused by inadequate pledge reminder and billing systems. The amount of income that short-term investments can earn these days makes it imperative for an organization to collect its pledges on schedule—earlier, if possible. An organization that does not have a responsive system enabling it to bill accurately and on schedule may be headed for collection difficulty. The institution must check this system and, before the campaign is begun, make any necessary corrections. A status report on the campaign and information about what is being done with the funds can be included with the billing statement. This practice can help payments flow and is sound cultivation for later gifts.

EXHIBIT 20.1. BUDGET LEAD SHEET.

	BUDGET LEAD SHEET			
DEPARTMENT:				
LOCATION:				
BUDGET MANAGER:				
Object Code	Description	1998 Budget	3/31/98 Actual	1999 Requested
80005	Admin. Salaries (Net Reimb.)			
80005	Clerical Salaries			
80010	Contract Salaries			
80015	Overtime Wages			
80020	Wages Paid to Hourly Emp.			
80025	Temporary Services			
88000	Salary—Allow for Attrition Alloc.			
	Total Salaries			
80165	Fringe Benefits			
	Total Personnel			
80200	Job Training			
80202	Employee Recruitment			
80205	Employee Recog. & Goodwill			
80210	Organizational Funct.			
80215	Sundries			
81000	Travel			
81005	Representation			
81006	Represent. Activities & Events			
81010	Business Meetings			
81020	Advertising & Promo			

EXHIBIT 20.1. BUDGET LEAD SHEET, Cont'd.

	BUDGET LEAD SHEET			
DEPARTMENT:				
LOCATION:				
BUDGET MANAGER:				
Object Code	Description	1998 Budget	3/31/98 Actual	1999 Requested
81025	Membership Dues			
81030	Art Exhibition Expenses			
81035	Artists' Expenses			
82000	General Office Supplies			
82005	Kitchen Supplies			
82007	Food Service Expense			
82010	Printed Brochures			
82015	Newspapers & Magazines			
82025	Professional Publications			
82030	Art Production			
82035	Framing Supplies			
82050	Photocopying & Microfilming			
82100	Business Reply Postage			
82103	Bulk Mail Postage			
82104	Bulk Mail Postage (Contract)			
82105	Metered Postage			
82110	Postage Stamps			
82115	Shipping & Express Charges			
82120	Shipping Supplies			
83000	Bldg. Maintenance Contract			
83005	Bldg. Rental Expense			
83010	Bldg. Repair & Maint.			
83015	Bldg. Operating Supplies			
83020	Utilities			
83025	Real Estate Taxes			
83030	Property Insurance			

EXHIBIT 20.1. BUDGET LEAD SHEET, Cont'd.

	BUDGET LEAD SHEET			
DEPARTMENT:				
LOCATION:				
BUDGET MANAGER:				
Object Code	Description	1998 Budget	3/31/98 Actual	1999 Requested
83120	Non-Depr. Furnishings			
83200	Computer Repair & Maint.			
83205	Computer Access Expense			
83210	Computer Insurance			
83212	Printer Supplies			
83215	Non-Depr. Computer Equip.			
83300	Computer Software Maint. Fee			
83310	Non-Depr. Computer Software			
83400	Telephone Expense			
83410	Fax Charges			
83500	Copier Lease			
83505	Copier Repairs & Maint.			
83600	Vehicle Gas and Oil			
83605	Vehicle Repairs & Maint.			
83610	Vehicle Insurance			
83615	Vehicle License & Tax			
83620	Non-Depr. Vehicle Parts			
83625	Other Vehicle Expense			
83800	Other Equip. Repair & Maint.			
83805	Other Equip. Rental Expense			
83810	Other Equip. Insurance			
83815	Non-Depreciable Equipment			
84000	Legal Fees			
84001	Non-Budgeted Legal			
84005	Audit, Tax, & Accting. Fees			
84010	Consulting Fees			

EXHIBIT 20.1. BUDGET LEAD SHEET, Cont'd.

	BUDGET LEAD SHEET			
DEPARTMENT:				
LOCATION:				
BUDGET MANAGER:				
Object Code	Description	1998 Budget	3/31/98 Actual	1999 Requested
84011	Reimb. of Consulting Fees (Contract)			
84015	Professional Fees			
84020	Miscellaneous Services			
84050	Bank Service Fees			
84055	Merchant Credit Card Fees			
84060	Filing Fees			
84070	Service Bureau Fees			
84080	Service Bureau Conversion			
85000	D & O Liability Insurance			
85005	Blanket Bond Insurance			
86005	Loss from Damage/Theft			
89000	Miscellaneous Expense			
89020	Allowance for Doubtful Accounts			
	Total Program			
90010	Cap. Exp.—Building Improvements			
90020	Cap. Exp.—Furniture & Fixtures			
90030	Cap. Exp.—Computer Hardware			
90040	Cap. Exp.—Computer Software			
90050	Cap. Exp.—Vehicles			
90080	Cap. Exp.—Other Equipment			
90090	Cap. Exp.—Artwork			
	Total Capital			
	Total Budget			

EXHIBIT 20.2. MULTIYEAR CAMPAIGN BUDGET REPORT FORM.

Expenses to date as of 8/31/98

Line No.	Description	FY '96 Actual	FY '97 Actual	FY '98 Actual	To-Date Actual 8/31/98	'99 Budget	'00 Budget	'01 Budget	To-Date Budget	Total Budget	Amount Remaining	Percent Variance
1	Salaries (net of allowance)											
2	Overtime Wages											
3	Fringe Benefits											
4	Total Personnel											
5	Training & Recruiting											
6	Travel											
7	Representation											
8	Supplies											
9	Printing											
10	Postage & Shipping											
11	Telephone											
12	Copier Maintenance & Supplies											
13	Building Repair & Maintenance											
14	Vehicle Repair & Maintenance											
15	Computer Repair & Maintenance											
16	Other Equipment & Furnishings											
17	Legal Fees											
18	Professional and Other Fees											
19	Insurance											
20	Miscellaneous											
21	Total Program											
22	Capital Expenditures											
23	Total Expenditures											

EXHIBIT 20.3. ANNUAL CAMPAIGN BUDGET REPORT FORM.

For the month of _____

Current Month Actual	Current Month Budget	Percent Variance	Prior Year Actual	Percent Variance	Line No.	Description	Year-to-Date Actual	Year-to-Date Budget	Percent Variance	Annual Budget	Amount Remaining	Prior Year Actual	Percent Variance
					1	Salaries							
					2	Overtime wages							
					3	Fringe benefits							
					4	Less: Allowance for attrition							
					5	Total personnel							
					6	Training and recruiting							
					7	Travel							
					8	Representation							
					9	Supplies							
					10	Printing							
					11	Postage and shipping							
					12	Telephone							
					13	Copier maintenance and supplies							
					14	Building repair and maintenance							
					15	Vehicle repair and maintenance							
					16	Computer repair and maintenance							
					17	Other equipment and furnishings							
					18	Legal fees							
					19	Professional and other fees							
					20	Insurance							
					21	Miscellaneous							
0	0	0.00%	0	0.00%	22	Total program	0	0	0.00%	0	0	0	0.00%
0	0	0.00%	0	0.00%	23	Capital expenditures	0	0	0.00%	0	0	0	0.00%
0					24	Total expenditures							

Creating and Using Report Forms

Before the campaign begins, the institution should create the various printed forms and computer programs needed to record, retain, retrieve, and reproduce the information associated with the wide variety of campaign tasks. There are two types of basic reports for which the professional staff is responsible: financial reports and reports on people, volunteers, and prospects. The number and sophistication of the financial reports will vary according to the size and complexity of the campaign (see Resource 24, "Monthly Financial Report"). In an established development office, of course, a great number of operating procedures will probably already be in place, particularly those pertaining to fiduciary matters but also those pertaining to the wider scope of the office's activities. Two examples of the kinds of forms routinely generated in support of a capital campaign are included here. Exhibit 20.4 shows a sample weekly campaign progress report. A typical prospect status summary is shown in Exhibit 20.5. For both types of forms, information can be maintained and conveyed via hard copy or computerized procedures.

The institution interested in studying a complete library of the variety of materials and tables used in a typical campaign can consult *The Campaign Manuals*

EXHIBIT 20.4. CAMPAIGN PROGRESS REPORT FORM.

Week ending _____

   I. Campaign goal $
  II. New gifts and pledges
 III. Total previous gifts and pledges

              Grand total gifts and pledges

 IV. Amount needed to reach goal
  V. Recent campaign activities

 VI. Appointments scheduled

Donor Category	Campaign Goal	Received to Date	Balance Needed
Board	$	$	$
Individuals			
Corporations			
Foundations			
Other			
TOTALS			

EXHIBIT 20.5. PROSPECT STATUS SUMMARY REPORT FORM.

Major Prospects	Researched	Prospect	Assigned to Staff	Possible Volunteer(s)	Assigned to Volunteer	Meeting Held	Letter and/or Proposal Submitted	Gift/Pledge Made; Seek More	Refused; Try Again	Adequate Gift/Pledge Made	Firm Refusal	Comments

(Builta, 1984), a two-volume scrapbook of a particular campaign. The first volume, *The Campaign,* contains the most important communications between campaign headquarters and volunteers, presented in chronological order. The second volume, *Steps and Procedures,* deals directly with record-keeping systems and contains an index to help the reader find particular forms or sets of instructions.

The organization must be responsible for records and services in all of the following areas:

- Fund and account structure
- Documentation of donor intent—agreements with donors
- Documentation of change or revision of donor intent
- Donor reporting
- Gift substantiation and receipting
- Pledge accounting and write-offs
- Gifts-in-kind policy
- Matching gift processing
- Pledge reminders system

Gift Receipts

Gift receipts must meet five Internal Revenue Service requirements (see Resource 30, "Gift Receipt Templates"):

1. They must state the amount of cash contributed.
2. They must describe—but not value—any property contributed.
3. If the donor received no goods or services in return for the donation, the acknowledgment must so state.
4. If the donor received goods or services in return for the donation—other than an "intangible religious benefit" or token items of "insubstantial value"—the acknowledgment must describe them and provide a "good faith estimate" of their value.
5. If the only benefit the donor has received is an "intangible religious benefit," the acknowledgment must so state.

The IRS does not require a gift receipt for donations of less than $250, but it is both good business practice and good donor relations for nonprofits to formally acknowledge and issue a receipt for all gifts. Gifts of $250 or more must be acknowledged in writing by the nonprofit to enable the donor to claim a tax deduction.

Where membership dues are involved, the donor may deduct only the amount that is more than the value of the benefits received. Membership benefits may be disregarded if the amount is $75 or less. The nonprofit must give a written statement or a gift receipt if the value is $75 or more. It must indicate that the donor can deduct only the amount paid that exceeds the benefits received and must give a good faith estimate of the value of those goods and services (benefits).

Valuing Noncash Gifts

On the gift receipt, noncash gifts are to be described but not valued. However, for the donors' purposes, values need to be established. In order to do this, Taylor (1998) offers the following advice.

Gifts of Stock and Bonds. A gift of securities is not a gift until it is under the control of the donee organization or its legal agent. This means that an organization cannot recognize the gift or record it until the stock or bond is registered in the institution's name and under its control. Stocks are valued at the mean between the high and low trading range on the date of legal transfer. Bonds are different. An institution has a little more leeway with bonds since they are not traded on a central exchange. The usual procedure is to gather data from two or three brokerage firms who make markets in the particular bond being given and use this as a basis for determining the amount of the gift.

Gifts-in-Kind: Artwork, Property, and the Like. In the absence of an established fair market value or already tested IRS guidelines according to which acceptable values can be set, an appraisal is necessary. Have the donor provide a copy of an appraisal that was done within ninety days of the gift date. (The donor will need that appraisal to claim a tax deduction anyway.) Use the figure given by the appraiser as the value for gift-reporting purposes.

If the donor will not have an appraisal by the time the organization needs it, the organization can use the opinion of a local expert, like a curator, although the organization might want to confirm that estimate with a qualified outside source. On the IRS receipt, just describe the gift—don't mention a value.

For an in-kind gift to be tax-deductible, it must further the mission of the donee institution. It can be either something truly needed or something that can be sold to provide funds to further the organization's mission. A complete review of the rules regarding income tax charitable deductions can be found in Resource 20, "Rules Regarding Income Tax Charitable Deductions."

Documenting Pledges

When a donor commits to future charitable contributions, a pledge for the commitment can be entered on the donor record. Any of the following documents will suffice to establish the commitment:

- Signed donor gift or pledge intent memorandum
- Pledge data form
- Solicitation card

- Pledge card
- Contract to make a will
- Signed correspondence from the donor
- Payroll deduction form
- Automated clearinghouse (ACH) form
- Correspondence or memo outlining conversation and commitment of the donor and signed by the development officer

A gift agreement, by itself, is acceptable to record a pledge as long as *all* of the following information appears in the documentation received from the donor or development officer:

- Donor signature (preferred)
- Pledge amount
- Indication of whether the pledge is conditional or unconditional
- Installment structure (annually, semiannually, quarterly, monthly, by a certain date)
- Installment amount
- Donor bank account name and number
- Indication of whether or not the donor should receive a reminder

Verbal commitments should not be recorded on the donor record without the accompaniment of additional signed donor correspondence or a signed memo from the development officer outlining the conversation and commitment.

Conditional Pledge. A pledge is conditional when a donor makes a promised gift contingent on the occurrence of a specified *uncertain* future event or condition. In this case the pledge should be recorded in the gift system but should not be recorded in the audited financial statements until such time as the contingency has been met or waived by the donor. This is because the donor is not bound by the promise until the event or condition occurs.

Unconditional Pledge. A pledge is unconditional when a donor makes a promised gift contingent only on the passage of time (payable on predefined installment due dates, at death, or the like). In this case the pledge should be recorded in the gift system and in the audited financial statements.

Creating Gift Agreements

McLelland (1997) advises that even after the organization and the donor have agreed on an endowment's purpose, you should exercise caution when writing the endowment agreement. Such agreements are legally binding and assumed to last forever, so be sure to word the spending purposes or restrictions very carefully.

The purpose of the fund should be stated broadly, to allow some flexibility. And every endowment agreement should include an "escape clause"—for example, "If, in the opinion of the board of trustees, all or part of the gift cannot appropriately be used in the manner herein described, the board may use the gift for other purposes as nearly aligned to the donor's original intent as the board deems appropriate under the circumstances."

And what if the donor has no specific dream in mind? Try asking for unrestricted support. Endowments with no restrictions can be applied to things the organization would pay for out of its budget even if the special funding wasn't there. This frees up budget dollars to be used elsewhere.

Exhibit 20.6 traces the steps in the gift agreement process. Forms used by one organization are included in Resource 19, "Gift Agreement Templates."

Nonacceptance of a Gift

It does not happen often, but occasionally a donor's intent differs from the current wishes of the nonprofit. What should the nonprofit do? Lyon (1998) says when the basic terms proposed by the donor are unacceptable to the nonprofit—for example, if they are too rigid or compromise the integrity of the nonprofit—the gift should be declined.

Investment and Spending Policies

Investment and spending policies are set by the governing board. As fiduciaries holding a public trust, board members usually adopt investment policies that are designed to maintain purchasing power over time and, in good times, to permit growth. A typical investment mix today is 70 percent in equities (stocks) and 30 percent in fixed-income assets (bonds). Most organizations in today's economic climate pay out 5 percent of income annually on endowed accounts. Also, whether the assets are managed by the organization or by outside managers at the behest of the institution, reasonable and customary administrative and investment fees are paid. The overage, if there is any, is reinvested in the principal as a hedge against inflation and, in good times, to provide growth beyond inflation.

Recognizing, Acknowledging, and Reporting Gifts

Once a donor has made a significant gift, cultivation can move to a new and higher level. A sincere expression of gratitude can show the human quality of an institution. It goes without saying that every gift should be acknowledged when it is received; the donor is expecting acknowledgment. If in fact the gift has played a part in strengthening the institution, the real opportunity to give thanks will come

EXHIBIT 20.6. THE GIFT AGREEMENT PROCESS.

Step 1

- Development officer works with donor to determine donor intent and drafts gift agreement from organization's template.
- Development officer gets approval from appropriate administration.
- Standard template may be shown to donor as appropriate. Deviations from the standard template should be approved in Steps 2–4 before being shown to donor.
- Supporting documents (solicitation card and the like) should be forwarded with gift agreement where no donor signature is required (as when there are multiple donors).
- Development officer should make sure new account request is completed and forwarded to Account Administration along with gift agreement.

Step 2

- Development officer works with Account Administration to review gift agreement and discuss all administrative aspects of the gift.

Step 3

- Account Administration staff forwards agreement for legal review as necessary.
- Gift agreement is prepared in final form with an original copy for each signer.

Step 4

- Development officer has final gift agreement signed by donor and appropriate administrator and returns it to Account Administration.

Step 5

- Account Administration sends gift agreement to chief executive officer for signature.
- Organization's original is filed in Account Administration.
- Remaining originals are sent to development officer for distribution as appropriate internally and to donor.

in six months or a year, when the effect of the gift is more fully known. In the interim period, keep in close contact with the donor, and never fail to follow up and provide the information that will convey the full positive effect of the gift to the donor.

People love recognition, whether they admit it or not. Because recognition is often a major motivation for giving, every development program must have an effective way of acknowledging major donors. Opportunities should be established at the beginning of the campaign, with policy guidelines for naming facilities, providing endowments, and engaging in the many other activities that people will want to support in a comprehensive campaign. Institutions are encouraged to hold events to dedicate buildings, open offices or wings, announce the establishment of endowments, and recognize program support and to engage in other ceremonial activities, as appropriate. The placing of plaques in buildings is always acceptable, as is the giving of distinguished service awards. Recognition should of course be appropriate; this means that individuals who give $100,000 in the annual fund will be treated differently from those who give $5,000, but they all must be recognized. A luncheon or reception, acknowledgment in institutional publications, and thanks expressed personally by key institutional representatives are always appropriate and appreciated.

It is important that the right people thank those who have given. A determination of who should do the acknowledging should be made for every case individually. Continuing recognition is warranted for major donors. If they are treated properly in the recognition process, they are likely to make even greater investments in the future.

From the beginning of the campaign, all gifts should be promptly acknowledged, and each donor should be properly thanked. Saying thank you is essential, and there's no such thing as thanking donors too much:

- Thank them accurately.
- Thank them promptly.
- Thank them gratefully.
- Thank them publicly.
- Thank them privately.
- Thank them frequently.
- Thank them appropriately.
- Thank them innovatively.

Each donor should receive a personal letter of appreciation from the institution, as well as an official gift receipt. Think about the thank-you letter, too: try to make it more than a thank-you. Make it personal, informative, and meaty. Tell the donor about what is happening, about the amount raised, about progress on the building project, about the amount of endowment money, and so forth. This is one of the details that need to be thought about in advance. Who will sign the letters? At what minimum level will institutional administrators and campaign leaders sign? $100? $500? $1,000? More? Does the plan call for the institution to ask each volunteer to thank each donor and send the institution a copy of the thank-you letter? It should. For larger gifts, the chief executive officer should certainly provide a personal acknowledgment. The key volunteer working on the solicitation may also choose to communicate with the donor; so may the chair of the board and the chair of the campaign. Gifts are made individually, and their acknowledgment should be considered individually. If more than one acknowledgment is to be sent, the staff should make certain that the acknowledgments are not redundant but complement and reinforce each other. Long delays in acknowledging and thanking donors for gifts are unprofessional and make a bad impression. Be certain that everyone—donors and volunteers—is thanked as quickly as possible.

The Children's Museum of Indianapolis thanks all of its donors, from the smallest to the largest, in a timely fashion using the following format:

$1–$99

- Thank-you letter from the chief executive officer (within one week of gift)
- Invitation to donor open house
- Invitation to donor shopping day

$100–$249

- All of the above
- Recognition in the publication *Tributes* for new donors
- Copy of *Tributes*
- Copy of the *Newseum* newsletter
- Recognition in the annual report
- Copy of the annual report
- Telephoned thank-you from the donor relations officer (within one week of gift)

$250–$999: Polar Bear Level, Rex Level

- All of the above
- Corresponding benefits sent with a letter from the donor relations officer (within two weeks of gift)

$1,000–$2,499: President's Club Level

- As for $250–$999 donors except thank-you letter is from the chair of the board

$2,500–$4,999: Water Clock Society Level, Reuben Wells Society Level

- As for $250–$999 donors except telephoned thank-you is from the major gifts officer

$5,000+: Carousel Society Level

- As for preceding level
- Additional thank-you letter from the chair of the Carousel Society
- Corresponding benefits sent with a letter from the major gifts officer

Another major consideration is reporting gifts, both internally and to volunteers and the public. As part of campaign planning, the institution must build internal recording and reporting systems that will enable it to handle gifts correctly and with dispatch. These systems must be able to compile the gift data to formulate reports showing the number, sources, and amounts of the gifts received and, more important, the purposes for which the gifts were received. This is essential, not only for practical reasons, such as reporting periodically to campaign leaders and workers, but also for internal audit controls. The staff must be able to report where the campaign stands and will almost certainly be asked for such information daily.

The staff should also consider preparing a weekly or monthly campaign report to be mailed to all volunteers and to others important to the success of the campaign. As noted earlier, the formats of such reports vary widely and can be determined by individual institutions. In some campaigns, a monthly report is all that is required. It helps in keeping the focus on the campaign and can be used to build fires under volunteers who are not performing up to expectations. Each volunteer leader should review the division or team's effort at each report session. The bandwagon effect is important in a campaign.

According to the campaign's organizational structure, the staff may want to be able to report in a number of ways—by division, by team, by area, by class, by source, by amount, by fund, or by all these criteria (see Resource 24, "Monthly Financial Report"). Certainly, a breakdown of this type will be desirable in the institution's final report of the campaign, so why not plan it in advance and have this capacity during the campaign? Most institutions now use technology to make this a simple task if it is programmed carefully. If an institution still uses a manual system, multipart copies can do the trick.

Stewardship

An essential component of any follow-through program is the thoughtful, systematic organization of a stewardship effort. Stewardship effectively begins even before the first gift is received—when the board establishes policies regarding the acceptance, handling, management, and investment of gifts. Once a gift is received, stewardship encompasses a variety of activities, including recognition, appreciation, and reporting. It also, obviously, includes the wise and prudent financial management of the investment.

Stewardship is the ongoing process of saying thank you, giving attention, and expressing appreciation. It is designed not only to recognize past support but also to be a part of the cultivation program that leads to the donor's next gift. Its frames of reference are both the past (for what has already been done) and the future (for what might still be done), but its setting is the present (for what can be done now to achieve the bookend goals of thanking for the past and cultivating for the future simultaneously).

Every organization should prepare a written stewardship plan for its best donors; then follow it, don't file it (see Resource 31, "Stewardship Program at the University of Florida").

The following recommendations can assist in establishing an effective stewardship program:

- Survey donors to discover their preferences, and adhere to their wishes.
- Remember birthdays and anniversaries.
- Respect religious holidays, observances, customs, and dietary restrictions.
- Stop by when you're "in the neighborhood" and say hello; make sure you are occasionally in the neighborhood.
- List names in the annual honor roll of donors.
- If your organization has an electronic reception desk, add a menu choice for donor recognition—list donors' names at this site.
- List donors' names on your Web site.
- Call occasionally just to say hello and keep in touch.
- Clip articles of interest to donors and send them.
- Send an annual donor statement to donors with named and endowed accounts; accompany it with a thank-you letter.
- Provide advance notice of upcoming events and activities; offer to assist with tickets or to provide transportation, as appropriate.
- Offer appropriate courtesies and amenities—for example, a parking pass for use while on campus or in your building is always appreciated.
- Send flowers occasionally or candy (except to diabetics).
- Ask donors how they are doing; ask, too, how they think you are doing.
- Always try to find ways to say thank you, to show appreciation, to remember people, and to let them know they are valued (see Table 20.1).

Treat special donors in a special way. Borrow best practices from the for-profit sector, such as high-end merchandisers Nordstrom or Neiman-Marcus,

TABLE 20.1. DONOR RECOGNITION AT VARIOUS GIVING LEVELS.

	$100	$500	$1,000	$2,500	$5,000	$10,000	$25,000	$50,000	$75,000	$100,000
Acknowledgment letter	X	X	X	X	X	X	X	X	X	X
Information (newsletters, e-mails)	X	X	X	X	X	X	X	X	X	X
Mementos	X	X	X	X	X	X	X	X	X	X
Holiday card		X	X	X	X	X	X	X	X	X
Special events (cultural, academic, athletic, black tie)			X	X	X	X	X	X	X	X
Holiday gift				X	X	X	X	X	X	X
Birthday card				X	X	X	X	X	X	X
Personal letter or phone call from key volunteers or staff					X	X	X	X	X	X
Personalized site visit					X	X	X	X	X	X
Personal letter/or phone call from the chief executive officer						X	X	X	X	X
Reception with chief executive officer and key volunteers						X	X	X	X	X
Letter from recipient of endowment						X	X	X	X	X
Personal report on endowment						X	X	X	X	X
Personal report on annual giving amounts and cumulative lifetime giving								X	X	X
Publicity								X	X	X
Personalized donor recognition event								X	X	X
Personal visit from chief executive officer										X

who specialize in personal attention and attention to detail, or the airline industry, which caters to its frequent flyers by knowing their preferences and satisfying them. For example, send donors with named or endowed accounts an annual statement to show the balance in their fund at the beginning and end of the report period and to show what expenditures have been made, accompanied by a thank-you letter (see Exhibit 20.7).

To sum up, you cannot say thank you enough, but you must say thank you in appropriate ways that please donors. Make sure your program is flexible enough to fit your donors' needs, individually and collectively.

EXHIBIT 20.7. ANNUAL STATEMENT TO DONOR.

NAME OF ORGANIZATION
JULY 1, 1999, TO JUNE 30, 2000
<ACCOUNT TITLE LINE 1>
<ACCOUNT TITLE LINE 2>

FOR THE BENEFIT OF
<AREA OR DEPARTMENT>

Description	Income/Disbursement Amounts	Balances
July 1, 1999: Beginning Market Value		$#,###,###.##
Asset additions (gift value)	###,###.##	
Investment income	##,###.##	
Other income	##,###.##	
Total Contributions/Other Income		###,###.##
Student support	(##,###.##)	
Faculty and staff support	(##,###.##)	
Program support	(#,###.##)	
Total Disbursements		(##,###.##)
Change in Market Value		###,###.##
June 30, 2000: Ending Market Value		$#,###,###.##
Total Estimated Income for Fiscal Year 2000	$##,###.##	

(Based on interest and dividend rates for assets held as of the end of the period)

CHAPTER TWENTY-ONE

CONCLUDING THE CAMPAIGN AND BUILDING ON THE MOMENTUM

Perhaps the greatest enemy in any campaign is volunteers' procrastination. Maintaining volunteers' efforts can be frustrating, especially during the campaign's dog days—that period after the public announcement, when the initial excitement and enthusiasm of the campaign have passed, the arduous and detailed work of concluding the campaign is at hand, and everything seems to have come to a halt. This is almost certainly a point that all capital campaigns reach, but it is also a real factor for annual campaigns that use face-to-face solicitation. Procedures for maintaining momentum should be planned well in advance. The following suggestions from Picton (1982) should prove helpful:

- Use the campaign organizational structure. Require that all chairs keep in touch with the volunteer leaders in their part of the organization and that those leaders keep in touch with their workers, by visit or by phone, on a regular basis. Push for the successful completion of each prospective gift. Each chair, co-chair, and worker is responsible for regularly reviewing the assignments of every volunteer he or she recruits. Do *not* push volunteers for gifts per se. Keep volunteers aware that the suggested level of giving or rating of each prospect must be asked for and received if the campaign is to be successful.
- Try to keep everyone aware of deadlines. When working toward a regular, scheduled report meeting or the final report meeting, push constantly so that each

person will complete assignments on schedule. Most people need deadlines. Arrange to have workers called and reminded of report meetings a day or so in advance and ask if the report will be ready. If not, when?

• Pay particular attention to uncompleted assignments that are of significant importance to the campaign's success—the top 10 to 20 percent of the prospects who collectively contribute most of the campaign objective. Although it is rare for all major gift assignments to be completed by the deadline, every effort should be made to try for that conclusion. Major gifts sometimes take a long time to cultivate. However, careful, thoughtful follow-up is essential. No matter how often they are reminded of the importance of the top few prospects to the success of the campaign, staff members and volunteers are still inclined to spend an undue amount of time and effort on the smaller donors. Do not neglect them, but concentrate efforts where the returns can be greatest.

• A major gifts committee composed of the chief executive officer, chief development officer, campaign chair, and selected key volunteers already committed should be included as a part of the campaign cabinet to concentrate on these key problems and other significant obstacles that will arise. This committee is also a good vehicle to have available when attempting to enlist a powerful individual who may not want or be able to accept major campaign responsibilities.

• Regular reports indicating the status of the program will of course be given at report meetings. Be certain the official report is mailed to all volunteers immediately as a follow-up. Showing comparative results by division or by team can be a helpful tool to help combat procrastination. Keep deadlines before volunteers. Most people work best under pressure. Also send reports to major donors and prospects. It keeps them attuned to the campaign. And remember that many a major donor has increased an original gift, so continued cultivation of donors as well as prospects is essential during the campaign.

• It is useful to have media attend key report meetings, especially if there is something eventful to report. If the media will not attend, see that a report is filed with them. Widespread word of success adds momentum. Any announcement of a significant gift should be carefully planned so that it is given proper media coverage.

Even the best leaders and volunteers, no matter how well trained and committed to the cause, will sometimes find fundraising challenging and difficult. It is the job of the staff to help everyone fight through these periods, to maintain momentum to encourage and lift those who are flagging, and to express the right mixture of confidence and enthusiasm, tempered by sober reality, to carry the campaign through to victory.

Victory on Schedule

Picton (1982) shares the following thoughts on celebrating a victory. Ideally, success on schedule will be the campaign's good fortune, and it is important to plan the victory celebration carefully in the event that this good fortune does come about. Continue to feature the campaign's leaders. All the credit and limelight should be theirs, not the staff's. Be certain that each person who has had a major campaign responsibility or who did an outstanding job is appropriately recognized. Encourage the attendance of major donors who really made success possible. Be certain that all volunteers are invited and recognized, too. The celebration should be a well-organized, happy occasion.

Recognize major donors who agree to be recognized. How they are recognized depends on the institution and on the individual donor (see Chapter Twenty). Being recognized from the dais is enough for some; others like certificates, plaques, or some other imaginative, tangible symbol of their generosity. The institution may want to honor some donors at smaller events—private affairs. A campaign also provides chances to give recognition while the campaign is in progress. This kind of recognition may mean naming a facility after a donor, placing plaques and offering citations, presenting distinguished service awards (or, in the case of a college or a university, awarding honorary degrees), and electing advisory groups or governing boards. Each situation should be examined separately. But by all means, do give recognition, no matter how you choose to do so. Maintain friendly contact with donors, and use direct mail, the telephone, and face-to-face opportunities to report on what their gifts have accomplished. Doing so reinforces donors' appreciation and gives the institution an opportunity to keep donors aware of continuing needs. Additional gifts are often a by-product of the pleasure derived from being recognized and receiving information.

It is equally important to honor campaign workers. In all campaign announcements, reports, and news releases, praise the volunteers for their efforts, and invite them to special events along with donors and prospects. Maintain contact with and seek advice from important workers as well as from major donors.

Prepare media handouts concerning what the campaign gifts have accomplished and will accomplish, and recap the highlights of the campaign. Once again, feature leaders and major donors if they will permit you to do so. If media representatives attend the victory event, a larger audience will be informed of the campaign's triumph, and that will help develop public relations for the institution. Whatever the celebration program, it should be carried out in a thorough but light and entertaining way, leaving everyone feeling good about what has been accomplished. Go first class! Everyone wants to be recognized for accomplishments, and everyone wants to be on a winning team. When these factors are recognized in plans for the victory celebration, volunteers will be more likely to say yes when the organization asks for their assistance in future fundraising activities.

Donors should not be forgotten after the victory is celebrated. They should be invited to special occasions at the institution—lectures, research symposia, special luncheons or dinners, plays or musical productions, gallery openings—anything that brings them on site is sound cultivation. If a capital campaign was conducted for a specific construction or renovation project, be certain to invite all donors to the dedication or opening. If a donor gives a scholarship, it is nice to have the donor meet the student recipient. This is just common sense, but sometimes institutions get so involved in daily activities that they overlook these possibilities for continued cultivation.

If you ask volunteers to do something today, do not forget them tomorrow. Workers and donors have the right to expect to be remembered forever for what they have done. Responsibility for remembering them belongs to the public relations and development departments. All past good deeds should be regarded as promises for the future. The best way to remember donors is to give them further opportunities to serve the institution. Never write anyone off as a future prospect.

Saving the Victory

If victory on schedule should elude an institution, it is important to do two things according to Picton (1982). First, be candid. Announce the results to date, and indicate that all gifts have not been received. Continue in a quiet, determined way to push for a successful conclusion as soon as possible. Second, ask all leaders to call or visit every key prospect in their divisions or on their teams to ask that the prospects keep the campaign in mind until the work is finished, and offer assistance to particular leaders or staff members. For example, if certain volunteers have not been effective, perhaps some reassignment of prospects is called for. It does not take long for a campaign to wither, so push harder than ever. This is where the campaign leaders must be aggressive. Here again, review the status of the major prospects, and look for new approaches if they are needed. Have the campaign cabinet consider going back to key prospects for a second gift; rarely does the initial gift tap out a donor.

Final Reports

At the conclusion of the campaign, be it annual or capital, two types of final reports should be prepared. The first is an internal report (see Resource 32, "Post-Campaign Assessment—Annual Campaign," and Resource 33, "Post-Campaign

Assessment—Capital Campaign"). The second is a public document (see Resource 34, "Final Report—Annual Campaign," and Resource 35, "Final Report—Capital Campaign").

Internal Report

At the end of the campaign, the institution should internally analyze its effort. According to John Grenzebach and Associates (1986), this analysis should be geared to answer the following questions:

- Was the campaign on the whole well received?
- Which expenditures proved the most beneficial and which the least effective?
- Which promotional materials and events were the most effective?
- What was the best method of solicitation?
- Which procedures should be repeated, and which ones should be abandoned?
- What key leaders emerged during the campaign?
- What key prospects emerged?
- Has the institution recorded all the data that turned up during the solicitations?
- Should the organization publish a final report on the effort?
- How well did the campaign, volunteers, staff, and consultants perform?
- Did any individuals identify themselves as prospective board members during the campaign?
- Did others surface who might serve on important institutional committees?
- Did some of the objectives of the campaign fail to be fully funded, even if the goal was met?
- Did the efforts of the campaign bring about a need for increased staff and greater budget to undergird the development effort in the future?

The internal report should include a cover letter from the campaign director to the general chair of the campaign, with a copy to the chair of the board, summarizing the major accomplishments achieved by the campaign and the problems that were encountered. This report should also include any recommendations or suggestions that the campaign director would like to make. It should provide a plan for stewardship, describing activities that can be developed both to recognize donors and to keep them informed about the benefits being derived from their contributions. It may also include other suggestions designed to prepare the institution for a more fruitful long-range development program. The report should contain a list of prospects who have not yet committed themselves to the campaign, a brief plan for approaching those prospects who can still be seen and solicited, and a report on the volunteers, indicating the assignments they have taken, the assignments they have completed, and the assignments yet to be completed. It should also include a suggested collections procedure for any outstanding pledges to the campaign, along with a cash-flow projection, indicating the amount already received and income projections for each of the following years during which pledge payments are scheduled. It may also provide a list of the named and memorial gift pledges that were recorded during the campaign.

Another part of this report should be a statistical review of the campaign, listing the campaign goal, the total subscribed by particular donor groups (corporations, foundations, individuals), the total number of donors, the total commitments received to date, and the number of volunteers involved with the project. In larger and more complex campaigns, there may also be an analysis of the prospects by campaign division. The report should also contain an expense summary, showing expense accounts, budget allocations, and expenditures made against budget allocations.

One of the most important parts of the internal final report is a scrapbook that will serve as a visual record of campaign activity. It should be organized chronologically and should show how the campaign and all its aspects were built. Early in laying the groundwork for the campaign, the institution should prepare a file folder so that materials can be automatically collected and filed as they are generated. Responsibility for preparing the scrapbook is usually assigned to a member of the office staff. It is important to understand that this scrapbook should be compiled as the campaign goes along; the materials should not be reconstructed and assembled at the end of the campaign.

Public Document

The second kind of final report is circulated widely to donors, workers, key constituents, and, according to the circumstances, prospective donors and workers as well. If this type of report is used, it can be designed as part of the transition from the current campaign to the next one, if the organization is using an annual campaign model, or from the capital campaign to the ongoing fundraising effort if that is the case. This report, which can take infinite shapes and formats, should include a list of all donors unless the campaign has been comprehensive or the list of donors is very long, in which case the organization may opt to list only donors of a certain amount—say, $1,000 or more. It is equally important to consider segregating listings of donors, especially if the campaign has encompassed several separate objectives under a total goal or has been run in several separate divisions, and to provide recognition according to the size of the donation: obviously, more attention will be given to donors of $100,000 than to donors of $1,000. Give recognition to key volunteers and workers as well as to donors. A campaign cannot succeed without both groups. The report should also provide an adequate amount of financial detail—amounts pledged, amounts collected to date, and plans for expenditures—to satisfy donors and volunteers alike that their efforts are indeed providing the benefits that the campaign aimed to provide.

Most organizations routinely publish annual reports. However, there is sometimes a temptation to eliminate this report after the capital campaign with the rationale that the campaign is already over, the next capital campaign is years away, and the report represents an additional expense that can be avoided. Do not be rationalized out of preparing this report! Whatever the institutional investment required, it will assuredly be returned in full and plentiful measure in the future as the individuals recognized express their appreciation through future gifts.

Only the Beginning

The institution may think that the conclusion of its campaign marks the conclusion of its intensive work. Actually, its work is just beginning. The end of a campaign is the time for the institution to capitalize on its success and move its development efforts to a new and higher level for the future. It is the time to establish and begin to sustain an ongoing major gifts program. Conducting an assessment to find answers to the important questions just listed is a vital step in this process. Even more vital is taking action once the answers have been obtained.

In almost every campaign in which more than one objective has been included in the overall fundraising goal, not every objective is fully funded during the campaign. This shortfall provides an opportunity, at the end of the announced campaign period, to carry over the funding of an important facility or other unmet needs into an ongoing development program or to develop a short-term campaign separate from the original one. It also presents an excellent opportunity to reconstitute a new, smaller working group of volunteers specifically dedicated to completing the task at hand. In this way the institution has an opportunity to begin integrating into the working group of key volunteers those people who emerged during the campaign as major donors or able workers. This transition period is the time to clean up old business and establish the basis for new, future relationships.

Even as an institution concludes its current campaign, it is planning the next. The ongoing program for major gifts development never truly ends. The methods and contacts developed must sustain the institution and prepare it for its next campaign or special effort. Workers who develop in one campaign are the leaders of the next. They need to be continually developed through active, meaningful, appropriate, increasingly responsible involvement from the time one effort ends until the next one begins. Ask volunteers to continue serving by becoming involved in the ongoing program for annual giving. Many will now be ready and able to solicit top gifts, either on a face-to-face basis or through telephone solicitation programs during the annual campaign. Ask them to continue working as volunteers in single-purpose capital campaigns that may be undertaken after the comprehensive or historical effort is completed. And ask them to continue working in the program for planned and deferred gifts. Find a niche for each and every one, and use them—or risk losing them, possibly to the organization down the street! The cultivation of prospects needs to continue, and weaknesses in the campaign need to be identified and corrected as part of the continuing development effort. It is also important to maintain the abilities of the staff beyond the current campaign period as the institution looks to the future.

In many cases, as much as 90 percent of the dollar objective will come from 10 percent of the constituency. This fact makes it vitally important that the institution treat its potential and actual donors with extreme care. When a campaign has been successful and celebration is at hand, it is time to begin a new period of cultivating current donors and to continue cultivating the prospective major donors to future campaigns. Chances are that the institution will have found new top prospects for continued support because of their gifts to the campaign. A number of major donors may also have disappointed the institution and will need special attention. What will emerge, however, is a new listing of the top 10 to 20 percent of the institution's constituency, and those prospects are the key to future fundraising success, as well as a major source of future institutional leadership.

How this new list is treated is important. First, it must be acted on, not just drawn up. Second, room must be made in the organization to accommodate these people. It is often hard to effect the succession of leaders or make room for new faces, but it is important that this be done and that it be done in creative, enthusiastic, energetic ways so as to let everyone, old and new, feel wanted and welcome.

The key is involvement; that begets investment. The secret to involving volunteers and donors, old and new alike, is simple, well known, and timeless: give them something meaningful to do, and earnestly seek their counsel, advice, and support. What is most important is that the institution proactively and systematically go about involving its key donors and volunteers. *Do not leave involvement to chance.* There should always be a place in the organization for someone who is willing to work and who agrees to give. Further, outstanding volunteers will have come to light during the campaign because of their excellent performance. Do not overlook or forget them. Be certain that they are brought into the institution's planning and that they have a voice in its future activities, and make this a certainty as soon as possible. Name them to committees; nominate them for positions on the board. By tying up all the loose ends, by following through, the institution will have prepared a neat package for its future activities.

Never forget that fundraising is more about people than about process. As Payton (1999) reminds us, fundraising has forever been—and will forever be—of, by, for, and about people.

PART TWO

THE FUNDRAISING RESOURCE GUIDE

RESOURCE GUIDE CONTENTS

MISSION STATEMENTS

EITELJORG MUSEUM

The Eiteljorg Museum of American Indians and Western Art is dedicated to the appreciation and understanding of American Indians and Western American art and the many cultures of North America. The museum will

- Collect, present, and preserve art, artifacts, and related items of the highest quality
- Develop exhibitions and programs of both an educational and entertaining nature
- Endeavor to advance research and knowledge in its chosen fields

While remaining an integral part of the Indianapolis community, the museum will strive to become an institution of national stature.

◆

GREEN CHIMNEYS CHILDREN'S SERVICES

GREEN CHIMNEYS SCHOOL

It is Green Chimneys' mission to provide innovative and caring services for children, families, and animals. The agency serves as a leader in the development of specialized programs that foster individual competencies and self-reliance.

STRATEGIC PLAN

STRATEGIC PLAN

◆

INDIANA UNIVERSITY FOUNDATION

BUILDING SUSTAINED GROWTH
IN PRIVATE FUNDING
FOR THE YEAR 2000 AND BEYOND

June 12, 1998

Table of Contents

◆

I. Situation Analysis: The Need for Sustained Growth in Private Funding

The Indiana University Foundation has maintained a position of strength over many years, with particular success during recent years in the areas of major gifts, consolidation of the annual giving program, investments, administrative processes, and technology. Going forward, the number of private funding opportunities appears significant with alumni, friends, corporations, and foundations.

Current Situation and Challenges

- The Indiana University Foundation (IUF) continues to build from a position of strength. In partnership with the campuses and schools, it has achieved significant growth in private support for IU and is a leader among university and college foundations. Achievements include:
- A consistent ranking in the top 3 percent among all universities and colleges in the U.S. in total voluntary support.
- A consistent top 10 ranking among public universities in market value of endowment.
- The Endowment Campaign for IU Bloomington has doubled giving to that campus. In the eighteen months between July 1, 1994, and December 31, 1995, $53.4 million was committed in gifts, pledges, and expectancies; in calendar 1996, nearly $89 million; and in calendar 1997, more than $105 million.
- Consistent growth in giving for IU, from $40.4 million 1989–90 to more than $70 million in 1997–98, an increase of approximately 73 percent.
- Consistent growth in number of donors to the University, from 62,400 in 1989–90 to 92,000 in 1997–98, an increase of 47 percent.

However, continued growth in private sector funding through the Foundation is essential. Competition for limited funds from the private sector has intensified, with a general decline in corporate and governmental support. Moreover, public funding of the University from the State is under pressure, and the University must look for increased private funding. Therefore, the Foundation must continue to build on its current strengths to achieve considerable growth in private sector support for IU, in order to help enable IU to realize its overall mission and each campus to realize its strategic initiatives. Fortunately, the Foundation's ability to meet the challenge of increased private funding is made easier by our strengths, including:

- Development efforts that have built a superior major gifts and campaign capability and integrated the annual fund;
- Administrative initiatives and policy changes that have resulted in state-of-the-art information databases, compliance with donor intent, and overall efficiencies and work flow improvements;
- An investment program that has generated attractive returns within reasonable risk parameters, helping to stabilize our financial resources;
- An experienced and expert staff dedicated toward achieving even better performance in the future.

II. Our Strategic Vision: Why We Exist

To be a catalyst for maximizing private sector for Indiana University so that IU can contribute to the betterment of individuals and of the human condition.

Our Strategic Purpose: What We Do

Our strategic purpose is, therefore, to develop and implement an institution-wide strategy for maximizing private-sector support of Indiana University.

Our Mission: How We Do It

Designated by the Trustees of Indiana University as the sole fund-raising entity for the University and directed by its priorities:

The Indiana University Foundation seeks to maximize the University's private-sector resources by:

- Developing comprehensive strategies and programs for building lifetime donor relationships;
- Preserving the purchasing power of gifts and providing a major source of consistent, ongoing support to the University;
- Administering these resources for the benefit of the University, in a way that inspires continuing trust and commitment from donors and enhances our partnership with IU.

Institutional Values

The Indiana University Foundation endorses a set of institutional values that govern our conduct and our relationship with donors and with IU.

We will always represent the priorities of the University to the donors. Indiana University rightly sets its own academic and program agenda and, in light of the feasibility of raising private-sector funds for various projects at each of the campuses, presents its fundraising requests to the Board of Directors of the Foundation for review. It is the Foundation's responsibility to present these priorities fully and fairly to donors, with an awareness of and respect for donors' interests, abilities, and welfare.

We ensure compliance with donor intent. We listen to, represent, and recommit ourselves to donors across all segments. This focus on donor stewardship drives all of our development, investment and administrative activities. We will continually seek to reach out to donors, communicate their needs, concerns, and desires, and translate them into effective development, service, and investment programs. In this process, we will celebrate the diversity of donors and treat each donor as an individual, not simply as source of funds.

We respect the privacy of donors. We value the consistent collection and capture of information regarding donors and their relationships with the University and with each campus, and develop and adhere to ethical guidelines regarding the kind of information collected and its use. To serve donors cost effectively, we need to gather information regarding giving patterns and aspects of their University relationships. In the process of using this information, we always respect a donor's request for control, security, and privacy. Ultimate approval for the use of information rests with donors.

We continue to enhance our partnership with the University. To maximize private resources and to extend the best practices across the University, we must continue to build an integrated planning process with campuses, schools, and departments. Although we will initiate the process and develop recommendations proactively, we recognize that the Foundation's goals can be met only through the spirit of active listening and participation in planning and execution of programs and events. Therefore, the Foundation is simultaneously a leader and a partner in this process.

Organizational Values

These beliefs shape the essential character of the Foundation, creating our unique organizational culture and becoming the criteria for shaping policy, making decisions, and for directing our day-to-day behaviors and attitudes.

All our interactions are based on mutual respect and a recognition of the value of each individual. Within the Foundation and in interactions and communications with our Foundation colleagues, our partners at IU on all the campuses, donors, and all others, we are appreciative of each person's contributions and achievements, eager to work with others to accomplish goals and solve problems, open in expressing

Resource 2

and hearing differences of opinion, and committed to making our best effort once a course of action has been chosen. We reach out to our colleagues, partners, and friends, delighting in their successes and encouraging them in times of difficulty.

We accept our individual accountabilities and acknowledge our responsibilities to organizational success. Growth and the increasing complexity of our business require greater specialization and expertise. Individually, we must specialize. Collectively, we must work in teams to meet our goals. By means of effective program and functional teams and of training, we gather the collective expertise needed for success in execution. As much as collaboration, success requires individual accountability within these teams.

We commit to achieving individual and organizational potential. Without staff commitment and a sense of ownership, we cannot build donor commitment and loyalty or offer our best service to the University and to each campus. Without commitment to professional growth and service to the Foundation, we cannot find better ways to achieve our goals. We therefore strive to create an environment that strengthens individuals, relationships, and the organization, and that promotes effectiveness and efficiency. We aim high, realizing that courage and perseverance will be needed to realize our aspirations.

We believe in integrity and ethical behavior. We are committed to the consistent expression of the core values of the Foundation and manifest those values daily. Whether complying with regulations or navigating a difficult and complex ethical dilemma, we remain steadfast in adhering to our core values and encourage others in their efforts to do so, even at the risk of the displeasure of others.

Our Responsibilities

The Foundation has responsibilities to a wide range of individuals and constituencies: to Indiana University and its leadership, faculty, staff, development officers, and students on all campuses; to donors and prospects; to our Board of Directors and other volunteers; and to our own staff.

The Foundation's responsibilities to these constituencies have a number of common threads. We must communicate the importance of private funding to the success of Indiana University; maximize private resources for IU, providing increased gift income and maintaining the purchasing power of gifts; respect the interests, privacy, and individuality of donors; represent the University's interests and priorities; provide for the financial stability of the Foundation without unduly calling on University resources; adhere to the highest standards of service; and meet or exceed the obligations and expectations of a not-for-profit corporation partnering with a great public university.

To Indiana University: We must increase private resources by means of a comprehensive development program based on continuing lifetime relationships, with donors; plan and coordinate an institution-wide strategy for building private support; be guided by the academic mission of the University, as articulated to us by University administration; be sensitive to the needs and concerns of the faculty, staff, and students; represent accurately the University's interests and priorities to donors, prospects, and others; advise the University on the feasibility of proposed projects; manage assets, making every effort to maximize return on gifts; administer funds efficiently and with excellent service; and educate IU staff about our programs, policies, and strategies.

To donors and prospects (alumni, individuals, corporations, foundations, and other organizations): We must communicate to donors and prospects the importance of private resources, fundraising priorities, and avenues for giving; elicit their interests and their perceptions of the University and relay these comments to the appropriate person or group; preserve donors' and prospects' confidentiality by collecting and distributing only appropriate information; in cooperation with the University, have administrative controls in place to ensure that donors' gifts are directed by the Foundation and by the University to the purposes specified; ensure a reasonable return on donors' contributions; report regularly and fully to donors about the use and status of their gifts; and encourage their continuing involvement in the life of the University.

To our Board of Directors: We must keep the Board informed regarding the operation and management of the Foundation; seek its guidance; follow its policies; and reconcile requests from the University with those policies. We continue to encourage the representative mix of members that has provided the Board with a diversity of perspectives and experiences to draw upon.

To our other volunteers: We must inform and educate them about the University and its fundraising priorities; train them as needed; provide logistical support, feedback, and reports on results; recognize volunteers' contributions of time and talents on behalf of the University in an appropriate manner; and make them aware of opportunities for continuing involvement.

To the Foundation staff: We must treat each other fairly and with respect; train and educate; set realistic and appropriate performance expectations with reasonable regard to each individual's personal situation; match talents with tasks to be done and adjust the match if necessary in light of the Foundation's expectations and the person's potential; provide recognition of achievements; communicate openly and freely with one another; and provide a working environment that promotes work-related growth and development and that fosters employee health and well-being.

III. Goals and Priorities: Fiscal Years 1998 through 2002

Goal 1: Fundraising

Maximize private sector support for Indiana University, guided by the priorities of Indiana University and complying with donor intent.

1.1   Total Gift Income

From the base year, 1995–96, increase the three-year moving average of gift income 50 percent by 2002.

1.2   Major Donors

Increase the number of major donors to 300 in FY 1998, 325 in FY 1999, and 350 in FY 2000.

1.3   Planned Giving

Complete 25 planned giving instruments per year, per planned giving officer, for a total of 150 gifts in 1997–98, 175 gifts in 1998–99, and 200 gifts in 1999–2000. Also, realize 120 bequests in 1997–98, 130 in 1998–99, and 140 in 1999–2000, for the total University development effort.

1.4   Annual Giving

Increase the three-year moving average of all annual gifts via best practices by 2,800 donors in 1998, 2,950 in 1999, and 3,100 in 2000, a 5 percent increase each year.

1.5   Alumni Giving

1.5.1   Loyalty Migration: Increase the five-year moving average of loyal alumni by 8.8 percent in 1999 and 8.2 percent in 2000. (Loyal alumni are defined as those who gave in either four or five of the last five years.)

1.5.2   Retention of alumni through continuous lifetime giving: Retain 65 percent of alumni who give in each of the next three years, generating $3.5 million 1998, $3.8 million in 1999 and $4.0 million in 2000.

1.6   Corporations and Foundations

Realize funding of 40 percent of proposals submitted.

1.7   IU Faculty

Continue to work with IU faculty in appropriate ways, respecting the academic culture and its sensitivities to the proper handling of the development process so as to instill confidence in the IUF and to maximize private support from the faculty in support of IU.

1.8   IU Students

Challenge each professor and dean at every school and program to increase participation in specific events.

1.9   Friends

From the base year 1995–96, in which contributions from friends totaled $18.9 million, increase the three-year moving average of friends' donations by $2.0 million in 1998, $2.5 million in 1999 and $3.0 million in 2000.

1.9.1   Develop targeted programs aimed at specific friend segments, both to acquire new donors and cultivate ongoing relationships with the University.

1.10   Best Practices Partnership

Capture and institutionalize best practices that can be used broadly with all campus and degree programs.

1.10.1   Implement the Comprehensive Integrated Development Program (CIDP) begun in 1996.

1.11   Volunteers

Work with the campuses and schools to engage 900 more individuals who are actively involved in fundraising on their behalf. Further educate, engage in service, and staff a volunteer support group for the Foundation of 100 individuals actively involved in fundraising, and maintain this level of volunteerism going forward.

1.12   Contact Management

Develop appropriate and effective contacts to maintain a continuous lifetime giving program.

Goal 2: Investment Management

Preserve and enhance the real purchasing power of contributions, and provide the University with a stable and growing source of income.

2.1   Achieve, within acceptable risk levels, an average total return that meets or exceeds the sums of the Foundation's spending (distribution) rate, plus the inflation rate, plus the investment management and related fees over a long period of time.

Goal 3: Financial Stability

Develop operating fund resources sufficient to achieve the goals and objectives of the strategic plan; minimize the vagaries of changing conditions by identifying multiple, stable sources of income; provide an acceptable return on investment in fundraising; provide funding for future expenditures for technology, campaigns, facilities and related infrastructure, and other contingencies; and build trust and strengthen relationships with constituents by developing a funding structure that is fair and is perceived as fair, and that is consistent with good business practices.

Goal 4: Service and Compliance

Offer exemplary service to our constituents while complying with all regulatory and other external requirements.

4.1   Comply with or exceed mutually agreed upon expectations and requirements of outside agencies and of our constituents; Indiana University and its administrators, faculty, students, and staff; donors and prospects; our Board of Directors; other volunteers; and Foundation staff.

    4.1.1   In coordination with IU, establish procedures to obtain documentation of compliance with donor intent for all transfers to IU.

4.2   Adhere to professional standards, monitor compliance with federal and other regulations, perform all business operations in a timely and accurate manner.

Goal 5: Efficient and Effective Management of Resources

Create and enhance internal programs and processes to add value to the Foundation's services and operations, increase efficiency and effectiveness, and further the mission and goals of the Foundation.

5.1   Technology

The Foundation must provide superior technology services that support the achievement of the missions of the organization. New technology will be cost justified and proven. Information will be timely, accurate, easy to use, and easy to support. Services will be outsourced as appropriate.

    5.1.1   Score the database annually with proven variables that can be leveraged to build targeted marketing programs.

    5.1.2   Provide tools and training that enable quick and accurate analysis for prospective programs.

5.1.3 Continue to eliminate redundant systems and streamline processing throughout the Foundation and University.

5.2 Facilities

The Foundation will provide professional and functional work facilities that will support the staff in achieving the Foundation's goals. Buildings and grounds will be maintained in ways that support professionalism, quality, and security.

5.2.1 For both Bloomington and Indianapolis, renovate, expand, and/or build new facilities with adequate space to accommodate the Foundation's needs for the next 20 years.

5.2.2 Establish regular maintenance programs for buildings, grounds, and equipment.

5.2.3 Ensure correct ergonomics for all offices and workstations.

5.2.4 Develop a Facilities disaster plan.

5.2.5 Reorganize maintenance staff to prove more flexibility, cost efficiency, and security.

5.2.6 Implement a new purchasing and inventory policy.

5.2.7 Research and implement bar coding on outgoing mail where cost effective.

5.2.8 Fully implement records retention schedule.

5.3 Work Flow

The Foundation will periodically assess key processes to ensure that they meet all standards yet flow as efficiently as possible and accommodate current needs.

5.3.1 Conduct a review of all key processes and develop a timeline to evaluate and make appropriate adjustments to every key process over the next three years.

5.3.2 Implement a system-wide Acknowledgment/Receipt Process, which receipts/acknowledges gifts within 72 hours of deposit. Consider sending an annual contribution statement to donors.

5.3.3 Complete review of Gift Agreement or Account Agreement for 3,200 accounts.

5.3.4 Issue annual statement to donors for all endowment accounts on a timely basis, including a report from the unit on how the funds benefited IU, by fall 1998.

5.3.5 Automate gift processing for certain units at IU. Improve efficiency and accuracy of data-entry procedures.

5.3.6 Add capability of filing prospect tracking and contact reports electronically.

5.3.7 Continuously upgrade and refine systems available to users on Benefactor and Affinity.

Goal 6: Organizational Development

Continually evaluate the organization's environment and capabilities to assure its ability to meet its strategic goals and objectives. Align individual and organizational capabilities with the strategic mission and direction.

6.1 Employment practices: Assess, diagnose, and develop practices that attract and retain superior employees.

6.2 Learning: Provide appropriate programs/systems for new and existing employees that focus on business and organizational knowledge, interpersonal proficiency, and the ability to analyze and solve problems.

6.3 Develop an organizational environment which will attract, develop, and retain managers and development professionals whose vision and values are aligned with the organization.

6.4 Communication: Assure that employees have continuous access to accurate and up-to-date information on matters related to their Foundation employment.

Goal 7: Excellence

Be recognized at the local, regional, and national levels for excellence and as a leader among peer organizations. Create strategic alliances to improve our ability to achieve our mission and goals.

7.1 Rank in the top 3 percent of universities and colleges nationwide in total voluntary support.

7.2 Rank among the top 10 public universities in market value of endowment.

7.3 Plan professional volunteer service and other commitments in accordance with our information needs and plans for achieving our goals.

7.4 Benchmark against outstanding organizations in the public and private sector.

7.5 Create communications and activities that facilitate the achievement and recognition of the Foundation's goals and objectives.

In the appendices section of a strategic plan, you would elaborate on some but not all of the goals. Below is an example of more in-depth information provided for two of the goals in this plan.

IV. Appendices

Appendices of the Foundation's strategic plan amplify discussions of the plan's goals and objectives. The number of each item in the Appendix corresponds to its objective number in the plan. [Some objectives were omitted here for the sake of brevity.]

Objective 3: Financial Stability

- The Foundation's resources are all directed to maximizing private support for IU and providing the highest level of service to our constituents. These goals determine our requirements for resources, including expert staff, adequate facilities, and state-of-the-art technology.
- Guidelines and assumptions:

    Assets under management will grow to $1.1 billion by the end of our five-year planning period.

    The fee on the Long Term Pooled Fund is 1.32 percent as of July 1, 1997.

    The Development Services Fee from the University is not expected to grow by more than 2.5 percent per year.

    The Foundation will develop efficient key processes that will allow the organization to reduce expenditures in certain areas or accommodate 10 percent growth while maintaining growth in expenditures at the rate of inflation, which is assumed to be 4 percent over the planning period.

    Contributions will grow by 50 percent in five years.

    Effectiveness should be measured as a relationship between resources expended and returns achieved. Compare our effectiveness to both education-related and non-education-related institutions.

Objective 6: Human Resources

Human Resources has a responsibility to assure value-added services to IUF's customers and employees utilizing fiscal common-sense. HR practices are to be incorporated into business strategy.

The employee dimension is defined in terms of employee attitude and organizational processes that affect employee attitudes (leadership, teamwork, communication, empowerment, shared values, treating with dignity).

6.1   Employment Practices

6.1.1.   Assess, diagnose, and develop practices that attract and retain superior employees.

- Analyze effectiveness of current search techniques by comparing recent hires and the search methods used to find the candidate.

- Investigate alternative search approaches that have the potential for increasing the quality of the candidate pool and the diversity of that pool.

- Work with hiring managers to design interview strategies that effectively identify candidates that can accomplish the strategic goals of the organization and work effectively in the IUF culture.

Resource 2

- Work with IUF managers to assist them with their future staffing needs in order to project and plan staffing costs and strategies.

- Review the total compensation program. Determine which components of the program are most important to our employees. Utilizing the employee benefit committee, identify key improvements to the program. Promote the total compensation program among employees as a retention tool.

6.1.2.   Assure that job descriptions are clearly written and accurately summarize the duties and responsibilities of the job and are properly aligned with business strategy.

- Increase flexibility and usage efficiency of the job descriptions by combining jobs wherever practical.

6.2   Learning

Provide appropriate program/systems for new and existing employees that focus on business and organizational knowledge, interpersonal proficiency, and the ability to analyze and solve problems.

- Continue the supervisor training programs with a more pronounced focus on the strategic plan and management's role in the success of the plan.

- Provide individual coaching and guidance to managers as needed. This practice must be a priority of the HR Director to maintain consistency with IUF HR practices.

- Devise ways for managers to share ideas and problems in a nonthreatening environment and learn from each other.

- Continue to facilitate meetings with secretaries and other employee groups that assist them with job enhancement strategies, problem-solving, and conflict resolution.

- Develop a skills/knowledge inventory of our employee base. Knowing which individuals possess the talent to work on specific problems can help minimize the need to hire outside talent.

6.3   Organizational Environment

6.3.1.   Develop an organizational environment which will attract, develop, and retain managers and development professionals whose vision and values are aligned with the organization.

- Identify key performers and hard to fill positions.

- Design strategies for individuals and positions identified above that increase retention potential and the potential for filling key positions when needed.

- Design a succession plan that incorporates key performers into a long-range strategy of planning for replacement of key management positions and targeted projects (A/FIS in particular must be prepared with the correct talent for rapidly changing technical needs).
- Develop a horizontal progression plan for job rotation and transfer that assures the continuous development of technical and managerial skills for key employees.
- Maintain an interest inventory of our employee base to identify the projects they would like to work on and the skills they would like to develop.

6.3.2. Assist managers with the development of learning strategies for their employees that helps increase knowledge sharing and the application of that knowledge.

6.3.3. Assure that managers identify their key positions and then identify and develop the individuals targeted to fill those positions should they become vacant.

6.3.4. Investigate ways to enhance our reward systems to assure employees feel recognized for their efforts and years of dedication to IUF.

- Improve the service award program
- Continually look for ways to enhance the EOM program
- Investigate ways to recognize and reward community volunteer efforts
- Increase usage of the employee relations committee to identify efforts that the employees feel would be meaningful ways to recognize employee efforts

6.4 Communication

Assure that employees have continuous access to accurate and up-to-date information related to issues related to their IUF employment.

STRATEGIC PLAN PROGRESS REPORT

STRATEGIC PLAN: PROGRESS TOWARD GOALS AND OBJECTIVES IN FISCAL 1999–2000

INDIANA UNIVERSITY FOUNDATION
as of October 1, 1999

◆

*Action plans developed by the staff
of the Indiana University Foundation in support
of the goals and objectives established
through the strategic planning process
and approved by the Foundation's
Board of Directors on June 12, 1998*

GOAL 1: FUNDRAISING.

Maximize private sector support for Indiana University, guided by the priorities of IU and complying with donor intent.
Total gift income: From the base year, 1995–96, increase the three-year moving average of gift income by 50 percent by 2002.

Goal	Obj.	Dept. or Program	Staff	Action Plans	Time Frame	Budget	Progress/Evaluation
1	1	President	Simic	Work with a select group of major gift donors and prospective donors	7/1/99–6/30/20		Strategies and relationships evolving.
1	1	VP Development	Dove	Increase private support by 50% over a five-year period	7/1/97–6/30/00		Private gift support: 1996–97 $59,950,218 (baseline) 1997–98 $71,889,107 1998–99 $75,364,630 25% increase after two years Total gift support: 1996–97 $116,422,088 (baseline) 1997–98 $139,210,524 1998–99 $157,226,958 33% increase after two years
1	1	Endowment Campaign	Dove	Complete campaign successfully by 6/30/00	6/30/00		$373,607,733 toward $350,000,000 goal (106.7%) as of 8/99 (86.1% of the timeline)
1	1	VP Development	Hardwick	Campaign for IUPUI campus			
1	1	Special Gifts and Annual Giving Programs	Madvig	1. Bring together staff to form new office of Special Gifts and Annual Giving Programs.	7/1/98	$0	Complete

Note: Due to space considerations, portions of this report have been omitted.

			Date	Cost	Status
		2. Provide staff opportunities to brainstorm and implement new initiatives that will encourage continuous lifetime giving, and form the nucleus necessary to identify and cultivate the next generation of major gift prospects by creating an environment where creativity is valued and rewarded.	12/31/98	$0	Phase One complete. Ideas continuing to be encouraged.
		3. Provide support and advice to each program within the department, ensuring present and future success.	7/1/98	$0	Ongoing
1	Special Gifts and Annual Giving Programs: Office Management — Daugherty	1. Continue to ensure that support staff is capable and well-trained particularly in areas related to dealing with donors.	6/30/00	$0	Ongoing
		2. Encourage new ideas that will improve team spirit, efficiency, and productivity.			
1	Well House Society — Muehling	3. Strengthen ties to existing associates and cultivate new members, thus increasing overall members by 10%, by: a. Contacting each current member quarterly through a personal visit, a phone call, or personal correspondence. b. Conducting 1 or 2 cultivation/stewardship receptions in the homes of Well House Advisory Board Members.	6/30/00	$3,000	Ongoing
		c. Making an average of 18 to 20 personal visits per month to new prospects.	4/3/00	$0	Ongoing

GOAL 1: FUNDRAISING, Cont'd.

Goal	Obj.	Dept. or Program	Staff	Action Plans	Time Frame	Budget	Progress/Evaluation
				1. Increase membership and maximize current relationships by developing a legacy program. By Spring 2000: a. Identify descendants of current, former, and deceased Well House associates. b. Evaluate prospects for best possible strategy to apply (Under 40, Arts Initiative, Athletics, and so on). c. Complete cultivation and solicitation, realizing at least a 33% conversion rate.			
1	1	Well House Society	Muehling, Bomba	1. Realize 30% additional growth in new Under 40 level, by: a. Creating and following up on 2 new events for this audience in the Indianapolis and Chicago areas. b. Continuing cooperation with Varsity Club, IUSF, and other entities through Young Alumni Committee. c. Continuing to grow the new prospect list, increasing the list of "suspect" names by 54% to reach an ongoing list of 100 qualified prospects.	12/31/99 Ongoing	$5,000 $0	
1	1	Well House Society	Muehling, St. John	1. Recruit additional WHS members through partnerships with IU arts entities, such as IU Auditorium and IU Art Museum. At end of fiscal year, confirm at least a 50% prospect conversion rate. 2. Specifically, sponsor IU Auditorium show during 1999 season.	6/30/00 11/30/99	$3,000 $5,000	Ongoing

		Program	Responsible	Goal/Action	Date	Amount	Status
1	1	Class Campaigns Program	Stuckey, Ellis	1. Use Fiscal Year '98 successes as challenge/benchmark for upcoming classes.	6/30/99	$0	Complete. Each class in question met more than 100% of goal.
1	1	Class Campaigns Program	Stuckey, Ellis	1. Meet or exceed goal for each of reunion classes, including: a. $150,000 for Class of '74 b. $400,000 for Class of '50	10/31/99 6/30/00		Ongoing
1	1	Parent/ Student Programs	Rogers, Ingersoll	Raise funds for Armstrong Stadium renovation and Armstrong Student Foundation. Create endowment in Bill Armstrong's memory.	6/30/00	$5,000	Ongoing. Gifts received to date = $2.3 million.
1	1	Parent/ Student Programs	Ingersoll	Increase awareness of fundraising and development with current students through Senior Gift program, by: 1. Having IUSF serve as ambassadors to educate other students on need for private support. 2. Encouraging the habit of "giving back" before students leave campus. 3. Attaining $2,000 and 100 gifts from personal asks by student development committee and $5,000 and 300 gifts via Telefund program.	6/30/00		
1	1	Regional Campus Services	Lindauer	Increase regional campus development officers' knowledge of and use of IUF resources (Major and Planned Giving Office, Department of Research, Corporate and Foundation Relations Office, Prospect Management Program, and so on).	6/30/00	$0	Ongoing
1	1	Regional Campus Services	Dove	Conduct campaign for Danielson Center in New Castle for IU-East.	6/1/98–12/31/98	$0	$1M+ raised against a $500K goal in four months.

GOAL 1: FUNDRAISING, Cont'd.

Goal	Obj.	Dept. or Program	Staff	Action Plans	Time Frame	Budget	Progress/Evaluation
1	1	Regional Campus Services	Dove	Conduct market survey for IU-Southeast.	11/1/98–3/31/99	$0	Completed Spring 1999. Approved $7M campaign goal.
1	1	Regional Campus Services	Dove	Conduct market survey for IUSB.	3/31/99	$0	Scheduled for Fall 1999.
1	1	Regional Campus Services	Lindauer	Increase regional campus development officers' knowledge of and use of IUF resources (Major and Planned Giving Office, Department of Research, Corporate and Foundation Relations Office, Prospect Management Program, and so on).	6/30/99	$0	Ongoing
1	1	Regional Campus Services	Dove	Conduct campaign for Danielson Center in New Castle for IU-East.	6/1/98–12/31/98	$0	Goal met
1	1	Regional Campus Services	Dove	Conduct market survey for IU-Southeast.	11/1/98–3/31/99	$0	
1	1	Student Foundation	Rogers	Identify plan for renovation of the Armstrong Stadium. 1. Work with proper university officials to identify all needs. 2. Develop time schedule to meet 50th running celebration.	6/30/99		Goal met Construction to begin 10/1/99
1	1	Analytical Services	Thiede	1. Form new Analytical Services Department. 2. Develop strategies and services that will contribute to the success of existing and future fundraising programs.			Ongoing Ongoing

		Major Donors: Increase the number of major donors to 300 in FY 1998, 325 in 1999, and 350 in FY 2000.			
1	2				
1	2	Student Foundation	Develop strategy for the Armstrong Endowment.	Rogers	6/1/00	In process
			1. Identify key members for steering committee.			
			2. Identify major donors for plan.			
			3. Develop plan for participation of past steering committees.			
			4. Develop plan for participation of past riders.			
			5. Work with athletics for proper recognition of soccer program.			
1	2		Communicate to donors how their gifts have helped.	Beggs	12/31/2000	In process
1	2		Review Presidents Circle and revise appropriately.	La Barr	12/31/2000	In process
1	2	Development Services	Establish and formalize policies and procedures for regular reporting to donors of endowed funds account balances, use of funds, identity of recipients, and other such information as may be requested by Development Services and donors.			
			1. Develop a donor statement acceptable to senior management.	Wilson, K.		Completed
			2. Create a cover letter for statements.	Beggs	10/31/99	In process
			3. Work with unit development officers for suggestions for best academic administrator to sign cover letter.	La Barr	3/31/2000	In process
			4. Create biographies of appropriate donors and recipients.	Martin, V.	3/31/2000	Not yet started
			5. Create proposal for senior management—for example, how many will be mailed, what will the package look like, what units do not want to mail.	Wilson, K.	12/31/2000	Not yet started

GOAL 1: FUNDRAISING, Cont'd.

Goal	Obj.	Dept. or Program	Staff	Action Plans	Time Frame	Budget	Progress/Evaluation
1	2	Development Services		Actively encourage and assist in identification and carrying out of stewardship activities within units, with particular emphasis on donors of endowed scholarships, lectureships, professorships and chairs.			
1	2	Development Services	Beggs	1. When data are elected, develop action plan.	6/30/2001		Not yet started
			Beggs	2. Draft stewardship suggestions for review with selected development officers.	3/31/2000		In process
			Wilson, K.	3. Discuss plan with senior management.	12/31/2000		Not yet started
			Wilson, K.	4. Determine next steps for implementing.	6/30/2001		Not yet started
1	2		Martin	Develop an aggressive strategy for identifying prospects for the IUPUI Comprehensive Campaign working closely with the IUF Indy staff.	3/31/2000		In process
1	2		Martin	Initiate plan to form stronger partnership between front-line development officers and the Research Department via geographical assignment of research staff in line with geographical assignment of development staff.	3/31/2000		In process
1	2		Martin	Increase number and quality of proactive names identified and presented to development officers and refine plan for follow-up activity with those identified.	3/31/2000		Not yet started

1	2	Development Services	Establish and implement policies and procedures for a "moves management" program working closely with the goal-setting committee.			
			1. Work with AFIS team for roll out and implementation of new policies and procedures relating to release of AFFINITY 2.0.	Wilson, K.	12/31/99	In process
			2. Consulting with appropriate staff, determine PMP "moves management" needs based on current goals.	Wilson, K.	3/31/2000	In process
			3. Document desired enhancements of current PMP reports to meet policy and provide to programmers.	Wilson, K.	6/30/2000	Not yet started
			4. Test reports with key development officer.	Wilson, K.	8/31/2000	Not yet started
			5. Roll out policies, procedures, implementation plan to senior management and then to development officers.	Wilson, K.	12/31/2000	Not yet started
1	2	IUPUI Campaign	IUPUI Campaign	• Conduct follow-up survey interviews to supplement the Grenzebach Glier market survey and to provide additional, more detailed market information to the schools/units.	6/99–10/99	
				• Establish campaign management council.	10/99	
				• Develop campaign communications plan.	11/99	
				• Enlist campaign leaders; establish campaign executive committee.	10/99–2/00	
				• Establish campaign corporate and foundation committee, planned giving committee, communications committee, and special events committee.	1/00–6/00	

GOAL 1: FUNDRAISING, Cont'd.

Goal	Obj.	Dept. or Program	Staff	Action Plans	Time Frame	Budget	Progress/Evaluation
1	2	IUPUI Campaign	Sloan, Hardwick	1. Finalize formal campaign plan. 2. Working with campus administration, campus development staff, and IUF staff, continue the silent phase of the IUPUI comprehensive campaign. 3. Develop campaign theme/logo. 4. Finalize campus case statement; begin development of campaign marketing materials.	9/99–10/99 7/99–6/00 10/99 10/99		
1	2	School of Law-Indianapolis	Jones	1. Assist the School of Law with the completion of its capital campaign.	Ongoing		
1	2	Herron School of Art	Sloan	1. Assist the Herron School of Art with the silent phase of its capital campaign.	Ongoing		
1	2	Analytical Services	Thiede, Hernandez-Martin	Develop a model that allows development officers to assess the major gift potential in various geographical markets.	12/99		In progress
1	3			Planned Giving: Complete 25 planned giving instruments per year, per planned gift officer, for a total of 175 gifts in 1998–99 and 200 in 1999–2000. Also, realize 130 bequests in 1998–99 and 140 in 1999–2000, for the total university development effort.			
1	3	Development Services		Establish and formalize policies and procedures for regular reporting to donors of endowed funds account balances, use of funds, identity of recipients, and other such information as may be requested by Development Services and donors.			

		Unit	Responsible	Action Steps	Date	Status
1	3	Development Services	Wilson, K.	1. Develop a donor statement acceptable to senior management.		Completed
			Beggs	2. Create cover letter for statements.	10/31/99	In process
			La Barr	3. Work with unit development officers for suggestions for best academic administrator to sign cover letter.	3/31/2000	In process
			Martin, V.	4. Create biographies of appropriate donors and recipients.	3/31/2000	Not yet started
			Wilson, K.	5. Create proposal for senior management—how many will be mailed, what will the package look like, what units do not want to mail, and so on.	12/31/2000	Not yet started
1	3	Development Services		Actively encourage and assist in identification and carrying out of stewardship activities within units, with particular emphasis on donors of endowed scholarships, lectureships, professorships, and chairs.		
				1. When data are collected, develop action plan.		
			Beggs	2. Draft stewardship suggestions for review with selected development officers.	6/30/2001	Not yet started
			Beggs	3. Discuss plan with senior management.	3/31/2000	In process
			Wilson, K.	4. Determine next steps for implementing.	12/31/2000	Not yet started
			Wilson, K.		6/30/2001	Not yet started
1	3	Major Gifts	Spears	1. Analysis of geographical giving patterns produced realignment of territory assignments in order to gain more intense focus on "best areas." 2. Additional staff hired (start Fall '99) to fulfill plans. 3. Regular interaction with planned giving staff provides essential knowledge base for major gift officers.	None	Completed

GOAL 1: FUNDRAISING, Cont'd.

Goal	Obj.	Dept. or Program	Staff	Action Plans	Time Frame	Budget	Progress/Evaluation
				4. Participation in planning and delivery of planned gift matching programs.			
				5. Inclusion of CID's officers in planned/major gift staff meetings leverages major gift strategy plan.			
1	3	Planned Gifts	Spears	Identify new and solicit existing planned giving prospects.			
				1. Provide ongoing assistance to development staff with individual planned giving prospects.	Ongoing		
				2. Identify and meet with existing donors to show them new planned giving calculations and solicit additional gifts.	Ongoing		
				3. Begin annual effort to upgrade selected bequest donors by cultivating them for a life income gift.	6/30/99		
				4. In cooperation with class campaigns, approach appropriate members of classes celebrating their reunions to identify prospects for planned gifts.	6/30/99		Completed
				5. In cooperation with prospect research, identify a minimum of 200 new planned giving prospects each year.	Ongoing		
1	3	Planned Gifts	Spears	Establish a strong marketing effort to promote planned giving.			
				1. Draft planned giving advertisements and articles for existing development newsletters, publications, and alumni magazines.	12/31/99		

2. Develop a book that includes testimonials from current planned giving
donors. — 6/30/99

3. Develop our own planned giving
newsletter, which will be sent at
least three times a year to a targeted
group of prospects and donors. — 12/31/98 — Completed—
"Next Steps"

4. Revise "Guide to Giving" and "Gifts
of Retirement Plan" brochures for
general use. — 6/30/99

5. Mailings:

a. Segment the database to identify
a targeted population of donors
who have made annual gifts of
$100 or more for three consecu-
tive years to receive planned giving mailings. — 6/30/99

b. Segment the database to send
our planned giving newsletter to
prospects and donors age 65 and
above. — 6/30/98 — Completed

c. Begin an annual mailing to select
donors or prospects age 75 or
older to provide information on
charitable gift annuities. — 4/30/99

d. Identify all donors who have cumulatively given $5,000 or more
to the Foundation to receive
planned giving information. — 4/30/99

e. At year-end, send a letter soliciting stock gifts from existing
donors who have made a gift of
stock in the past five years or
have cumulative gifts of at least
$2,000. — 12/31/99

GOAL 1: FUNDRAISING, Cont'd.

Goal	Obj.	Dept. or Program	Staff	Action Plans	Time Frame	Budget	Progress/Evaluation
				6. Events: a. Annually, host seminars for IU faculty. Focus will be on pre-retirement planning, retirement planning, and financial planning, to inform the faculty and motivate potential donors who are capable of making a planned gift.	2/28/99		
				b. In conjunction with our out-of-town board meeting, conduct a seminar on planned giving opportunities for prospects, donors, friends, and alumni living in that area.	3/31/99		
				c. Host annual Arbutus Society recognition event.	6/30/99		
1	3	Planned Gifts	Spears	Raise the visibility of the planned giving program internally and externally. 1. For internal constituents: a. Educate development officers about trends in planned giving so that they are comfortable in presenting planned giving options to donors and prospects.	Ongoing		
				b. Educate and train researchers, Telefund callers, annual fund staff, and class campaign staff to identify planned giving prospects.	6/30/99		
				c. Assign Planned Giving Services staff members to serve as the liaison to specific units.	6/30/99		

1	3	Planned Gifts	Spears	d. Develop planned giving strategies for each academic unit and regional campus.	12/31/98
				2. For external constituents:	
				a. Continue mailings of newsletter to representatives of the banking, financial, and legal communities. Institute personal follow-up with those who request additional information from response cards.	12/31/99
				b. Create professional advisory committees in Bloomington and Indianapolis and on each regional campus to assist in marketing planned gifts.	6/30/99
				3. Conduct an annual charitable gift planning, estate planning, and financial planning seminar for donors and prospects.	Ongoing
				4. Conduct annual continuing education seminars focusing on charitable giving for professionals—one in Indianapolis and one in Bloomington.	4/30/99
				5. Host two receptions per year for outside professionals to educate them about the organization and foster social interaction.	12/31/98
1	3	Analytical Services	Thiede	Conduct market research as needed to facilitate targeted marketing strategies.	Ongoing

GOAL 1: FUNDRAISING, Cont'd.

Goal	Obj.	Dept. or Program	Staff	Action Plans	Time Frame	Budget	Progress/Evaluation
1	4			Annual Giving: Increase the three-year moving average of all annual gifts via best practices by 2,950 donors in 1999 and 3,100 in 2000, a 5% increase each year.			
1	4	Parents Fund Program	Rogers, Ingersoll	1. Change solicitation cycle to fall. 2. Work with IU to find alternative ways to get parent phone numbers.	8/1/98 6/30/00	$0 $0	Complete Phase One complete
				3. Through larger and more involved Parents Fund Steering Committee and new Parents Fund Society, increase the number and size of gifts to the program, including: a. At least two $2,500 gifts b. At least fifteen $1,000 gifts c. At least sixty-seven $500 gifts	6/30/00	$0	Ongoing
1	4	Annual Giving: Telefund	Madvig, Lindauer	1. Identify and select new annual giving chair for 2000–2002 term.	8/31/99	$0	Complete. Isiah Thomas has signed on in this capacity.
				2. Produce 170,000 completed calls resulting in pledges totaling $3.5 million.	6/30/00		Ongoing
				3. Maintain overall pledge rates of 12% on donor acquisition, 33% on lapsed donor retrieval, and 70% on donor renewal.	6/30/00		Ongoing
				4. Maintain 70% pledge fulfillment rate.	6/30/00		Ongoing
				5. Upgrade to newest version of Centenium (automated phone program) in order to ensure Y2K compliance, as well as to provide improved scripting and monitoring capabilities.	8/31/99		Complete

		Program	Person	Action	Target Date	Cost	Status
				6. Design and implement clean-up phase to nondonors on behalf of Bloomington campus academic endowment campaign.	6/30/00		Complete
				7. Enter affiliation/activity codes for all IU graduates of 1980 and after. Use statistician's input to assist in determining additional target pools.	12/31/98	$5,000	Complete
				8. Test three target pools: Residence Hall Association, Singing Hoosiers and IU Student Foundation Steering Committee.	6/30/99	$0	Complete. Segments two and three met with success, but RHA mailing was not particularly productive.
				9. Plan and implement quarterly phone look-ups.	9/1/98	$28,000	Complete
1	4	Annual Giving: Direct Mail	Madvig, Higgins	1. Segment currently planned mailings additionally.	8/1/98	$0	Complete. Direct-mail program achieved one of best years on record, with two mailings garnering best results ever. Ongoing
				2. Use Kearney report and statistician to target new donor acquisition pools, particularly class campaign follow-up and donor acquisition of young alumni.	6/30/00	$0	
				3. Design and implement clean-up phase to current and lapsed donors on behalf of the Bloomington campus academic endowment campaign.	6/30/00	$0	
1	4	Regional Campus Services	Lindauer	Integrate regional campuses into the centralized annual giving program, leaving development officers free to focus on major gifts and other activities.	3/31/99	$0	Ongoing

GOAL 1: FUNDRAISING, Cont'd.

Goal	Obj.	Dept. or Program	Staff	Action Plans	Time Frame	Budget	Progress/Evaluation
1	4	Chancellor's Circle	Bosch	• Hold two cultivation events prior to September '00.	Sept. 2000	$10,000	
				• Assist new membership chair, to be recruited by Chancellor Bepko.	Fall 1999		
				• Increase membership to 85 (+20).	June 2000		
				• Increase revenues to $100,000.	June 2000		
1	4	Campus Campaign	Bosch	• Expand volunteer base to a ratio of 1:10 FTE.	Spring 2000	$12,000	
				• Redesign CC00 materials to reflect/complement comprehensive campaign materials.	Fall 1999		
				• Delegate responsibility for distributing and retrieving pledge packets to deans and development officers.	Spring 2000		
				• Assist three-member Campus Campaign Coordinating Committee.	Fall 1999–Spring 2000		
				• Assist Planned and Major Gifts Subcommittee.	Fall 1999–Spring 2000		
				• Increase participation to 36%.	Spring 2000		
				• Raise $22 million from internal gifts.	Spring 2004		
1	4	Direct Mail	Bosch	• Execute direct-mail calendar in coordination with Telefund	Ongoing	$17,000	
1	4	Women's Fund	Thiede	Establish a women's fund for Indiana University as a means of: 1. Acquiring new donors 2. Upgrading gift levels of current donors	Fall 2000		In progress

GOAL 2: INVESTMENT MANAGEMENT.

Goal	Obj.	Dept. or Program	Staff	Action Plans	Time Frame	Budget	Progress/Evaluation
2	1			Preserve and enhance the real purchasing power of contributions, and provide the University with a stable and growing source of income. Achieve, within acceptable risk levels, an average total return that meets or exceeds the sum of the Foundation's spending (distribution) rate, plus the investment management and related fees over a long period of time.			
2	1	Investments	Koon, Stratten	Review alternative investment classes for possible inclusion in the endowment portfolio	6/30/99		
2	1	Investments	Koon, Stratten	Review and recommend necessary changes to streamline and increase returns in the management of daily cash balances	6/30/99		
2	1	Real Estate	Koon, Wilhite	The new Director will review IUF R/E policies and procedures with an eye toward being able to be of better support to the staff. Also, make an extra effort to be of support for development staff that has not been involved with R/E as a gift.	6/30/00		

GOAL 3: FINANCIAL STABILITY.

Goal	Obj.	Dept. or Program	Staff	Action Plans	Time Frame	Budget	Progress/Evaluation
3		Financial Stability					
3		President	Simic	Ensure the long-term financial stability of the Foundation, including an operating endowment	7/1/99–6/30/00		Operating endowment established by Board in June 1999. Working with Foundation VP for Finance on financial strategies.
3		Finance	Reel	1. Continue benchmarking with Big Ten/Big Twelve/Pac Ten Universities to develop best practices.	Ongoing		Meet regularly with peer group (University Financial Officers UFO).
				2. Work with CASE to develop set of three standard surveys.	3/1/00		UFO group has developed surveys on a one-year test basis. IUF's share of cost will be approximately $500, paid to CASE. Reel has been assigned to a committee of UFO to review the Surveys so that they are more consistent and representative of participating institutions.
3		Finance	Perin/Reel	3. Develop 5 year budget models that provide for contingency plans should revenue sources fall short of projections.	Ongoing		
3		Finance	Perin/Reel	1. Work with IDFA and Bond Counsel to issue second series of tax exempt bonds for the construction of an IUPUI facility.	2000		

Note: Due to space considerations, some goals have been left out.

GOAL 7: RECOGNITION FOR EXCELLENCE.

Goal	Obj.	Dept. or Program	Staff	Action Plans	Time Frame	Budget	Progress/Evaluation
7	1			Excellence: Be recognized at the local, regional, and national levels for excellence and as a leader among peer organizations. Create strategic alliances to improve our ability to achieve our mission and goals. Rank in the top 3% of universities and colleges nationwide in total voluntary support.			
7	1	President	Simic	Raise funds at a level that will keep IU in the top tier of colleges and universities nationwide.	7/1/99–6/30/00		1997–98 rankings reported in 1999 placed IU/IUF 1st in the nation among all universities reporting, placing IU/IUF in the top 2%.
7	2			Rank among the top 10 public universities in market value of endowment.			
7	2	President	Simic	Manage endowment in a way that ensures IU's position in the top tier of public universities.	7/1/99–6/30/99		1999 rankings of market value of endowment in the 1997–98 fiscal year place IU 6th in the Big Ten and 12th among public universities in the nation.
7	3			Plan professional volunteer service and other commitments in accordance with our information needs and plans for achieving our goals.			
7	3	President	Simic	Make presentations under the sponsorship of national organizations	7/1/99–6/30/00		Big Ten Fund Raising Institute, Big Ten Development Officers Conference; worked with individual institutions on visits their campuses and in meetings at IUF
7	3	President	Simic	Serve as the Dean of the Big Ten Fund Raisers Institute	7/1/99–6/30/00		Served first year as dean in 1999. Ongoing commitment.

Resource 3

GOAL 7: RECOGNITION FOR EXCELLENCE, Cont'd.

Goal	Obj.	Dept. or Program	Staff	Action Plans	Time Frame	Budget	Progress/Evaluation
7	4	Benchmark against outstanding organizations in the public and private sector.					
7	4	President	Simic	Represent the IU Foundation at the national level as a leadership organization in its field	7/1/99–6/30/00		Received Ashmore Award for contributions to the Council for the Advancement and Support of Education and to the advancement profession. CASE awards for publications. CASE fund raising award for leadership.
7	4	Student Foundation	Rogers	Update and address Long Range Plan for IUSF 1. Review past plan for updates 2. Identify major areas of focus for after the 50th running			Ongoing
7	4	Planning	Coffman	Record implementation of initiatives and progress toward goals and objectives of the strategic plan.	10/1/99		Completed
7	5	Create communications and activities that facilitate the achievement and recognition of the Foundation's goals and objectives.					
7	5	President's Office	Bishop	Maintain a continuously up-to-date speech file for President, containing the latest IU-IUF information, quotes, anecdotes, statistics, et al. 1. Personally, and with the cooperation of Research, cull existing newspapers and publications for usable speech material. 2. Create separate files cataloquing by topic, source, etc. 3. Maintain links with Alumni Office, and Athletics, et al. to acquire usable information.	7/1/99–6/30/00	NA	Speech materials gathered from various off and on-campus sources. Speeches are written on an as-needed basis, tailored to specific audiences.

7	5	4. Create one or two additional "stock" talks on typical development issues, such as volunteers, Foundation-university relationships, et al.				
		Write and produce two additional 30-second spots for airing on the Cameron and Knight Shows, 1999–2000. Evaluate the appropriateness of campaigns that could be featured. 1. Arrange for taping, B roll. 2. In cooperation with Communications and Marketing and Radio-TV Services, produce final edition of spot.	President's Office	Bishop/ Coffman	7/1/99– 6/30/00	NA	Produced and aired spot on student scholarships. Two other spots will focus on programs in Bloomington and Indianapolis.
7	5	Develop plan to properly recognize the 50th running of the race 1. Work with volunteer committee to represent alumni ideas 2. Create strategy that works with the town of Bloomington 3. Create strategy that works with the university 4. Identify past support and increase alumni involvement	Student Foundation	Rogers	Spring 2000		In process
7	5	1. Identify and review outstanding corporate and nonprofit communications functions. 2. Conduct audit of Foundation communications 3. Develop strategies for addressing communications issues.	Communications	Coffman	7/1/99– 6/30/00	$TBD	Priority focus for Planning and Communications in FY00
7	5	Provide publicity and a set of publicity priorities that reinforce the Foundation's strategic goals and objectives.	Communications	Coffman	7/1/99– 6/30/00		Ongoing

CASE STATEMENTS

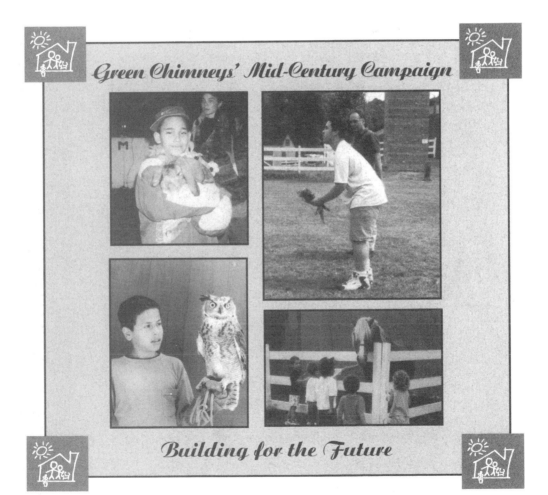

Green Chimneys' Mid-Century Campaign

Building for the Future

Serving New York & Connecticut

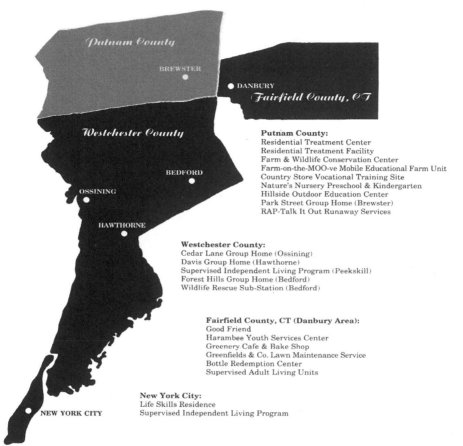

Putnam County:
Residential Treatment Center
Residential Treatment Facility
Farm & Wildlife Conservation Center
Farm-on-the-MOO-ve Mobile Educational Farm Unit
Country Store Vocational Training Site
Nature's Nursery Preschool & Kindergarten
Hillside Outdoor Education Center
Park Street Group Home (Brewster)
RAP-Talk It Out Runaway Services

Westchester County:
Cedar Lane Group Home (Ossining)
Davis Group Home (Hawthorne)
Supervised Independent Living Program (Peekskill)
Forest Hills Group Home (Bedford)
Wildlife Rescue Sub-Station (Bedford)

Fairfield County, CT (Danbury Area):
Good Friend
Harambee Youth Services Center
Greenery Cafe & Bake Shop
Greenfields & Co. Lawn Maintenance Service
Bottle Redemption Center
Supervised Adult Living Units

New York City:
Life Skills Residence
Supervised Independent Living Program

"We have made treatment a normalizing experience within a community atmosphere. Please visit our campus and see the Farm and Wildlife Conservation Center to experience it firsthand."

—*Joseph A. Whalen, Executive Director*

"The child who is loved learns to give love. The child who gives love will receive love. Our children learn nurturing by taking care of animals. Working with the animals prepares them to work with others."

—*Samuel B. Ross, Jr., Founder*

From the Chair

Green Chimneys is a unique agency serving not only those within its own community, but those without as well. It is not an isolated facility, but a multifaceted system of programs serving many needs.

Smiling faces on the children, staff, and even the animals greet you as you walk on campus. Children and animals are being nurtured in a warm, friendly environment. While those in the residential community receive healing and support, others can enjoy the many and varied experiences the agency has to offer.

Green Chimneys has grown and prospered for many years under the direction of its founder, Sam Ross. During this time, no major fundraising campaign has occurred. The celebration of its 50th year is a perfect time to honor this organization by seeking to build its endowment, enhance its capital needs, and renew its annual appeal. We want to assure the future of this exceptional agency so it can continue to serve those in need. Please join us with your support.

Sheila Perrin
Campaign Chair

PAUL NEWMAN

July 10, 1996

Dr. Samuel B. Ross, Jr.
Green Chimneys Children's
Services, Inc.
Putnam Lake Road
Brewster, NY 10509

Dear Sam:

Hotch and I have checked on our annual commitments and I am very pleased to tell you that we will be sending you an annual contribution of $150,000 over the next five years. A check in this amount will be sent to you in our usual funding period in November.

It really is a pleasure to make these contributions in recognition of the marvelous contribution you've made to young people over the years through the Green Chimneys operation.

We need more people like you, Sam.

Best personal wishes,

PN/do

"The love and the tenderness of the mother for her young ones is not produced by reasoning but by imagination; animals feel grief, love, and attachment to their young. If the law provides that grief should not be caused to cattle and birds, how much more careful we must be that we should not cause grief to our fellow man."
—*Maimonides*

Care and Concern for All Living Things

About Green Chimneys

Green Chimneys was founded in 1947 by the Ross Family, who purchased a farm in Patterson, New York, to house a private school where children could interact with farm animals. In 1974 Green Chimneys became a social service agency, serving children and adults with handicapping conditions. It also serves the general population through numerous public programs.

The agency is considered the strongest and most diverse of its kind involving farm, animal, plant, and wildlife-assisted activities. We see our mission as providing care and concern for all living things and target our services at restoring and strengthening the emotional health and well-being of children and families and fostering optimal functioning and independence.

Green Chimneys is a voluntary, nonsectarian, multiservice agency. Its programs facilitate growth in emotional well-being, physical health, basic education, daily living and survival skills, recreation, and vocational pursuit. For those others served, the emphasis is on extracurricular activities which promote skill development, use of leisure time, socialization, and self-actualization.

Understanding Today's Needs

A Case for Support

As we approach our 50th anniversary, we see more and more children and animals in need of help. We are beginning our Mid-Century Campaign to ensure that we will be able to meet their needs.

We see increased violence, neglect, and abuse to children and animals. We see decreased funding from government sources. We are concerned with promoting attachment, nurturance, and caring between humans and animals. We see common problems which affect people in cities, suburbs, and rural areas, and we see similar problems worldwide. We are concerned with reducing violence, neglect, and abuse to children and animals. We see increased demand for the services and training we offer.

We work to improve the quality of life. We work for a better tomorrow. We work to transform service recipients into service providers. We work to bring hope and encouragement to those who have felt helpless and disenfranchised.

Timeline

1948—Green Chimneys opens as boarding school and camp where young children interact with animals.

1971—Farm Center is launched to offer programs for the public.

1974—Green Chimneys Children's Services, a social service agency, is founded.

1981—Group homes begin operating.

1982—Intern program is started.

1983—Gramercy Residence opens in New York City for older adolescents preparing for independent living.

1988—Condominiums for mentally handicapped adults open.

1989—Residential Treatment Facility opens on the campus.

1991—Greenfields work crew for mentally handicapped adults offers lawn care services. RAP runaway services begins.

1992—Good Friend adult/child mentoring program is started.

1994—Greenery Café and Bottleworks, staffed by mentally handicapped adults, opens in Danbury.

1995—Special education day students begin attending classes.

Living and Learning Improvements

A Case for Facility Enrichment   The passing of time, the ability of our residents to accelerate depreciation, and the space restrictions of our present Brewster campus make it absolutely essential to develop a comprehensive building program.

Off-campus projects include the opportunity to purchase and renovate the Gramercy Residence, enabling us to have a permanent home for our adolescent life skills residence in New York City.

The on-campus projects result from a truly epic opportunity—the largest building project ever undertaken by Green Chimneys. We are in the final planning phase of arranging the construction of a new $11 million educational facility which will include school administrative offices. This project is being funded by the Dormitory Authority of the State of New York. This building project will result in the replacement of all the present classrooms, a new library, and a computer center. Additional construction and renovation must be accomplished through the acquisition of private money from individuals, corporations, and foundations.

Green Chimneys Serves . . .

- 102 residents on main campus, Brewster, NY
- 35 day students
- 38 group home residents
- 4 Westchester Co. Supervised Independent Living Residents
- 27 Life Skills Residents in New York City
- 10 New York City Supervised Independent Living Residents
- 5 mentally challenged adult condominium residents in Danbury, CT

$3,000,000: Improved Facilities with Your Help

The Facility Challenge

Renovation of School Buildings
After completion of the new school building, the existing school buildings will be renovated for use as living units, additional offices, more space for children's programs, and expansion of public programs. **Cost: $895,000**

Maintenance/Support Services Building
Construction will relocate maintenance/support services, which will eliminate vehicular traffic on campus roadways that are used as walkways. **Cost: $450,000**

Vocational Arts Training Center
Renovation of the present maintenance/support services building for use as vocational training center will provide a program site for our residents, as well as for developmentally delayed adolescents and adults from local communities. **Cost: $75,000**

Expansion of Crystal House, Old Barn Family Center, and Patio Building
These will be renovated and connected, creating the administrative nerve center of the agency. Renovation will include expansion of visitor waiting areas, establishment of a training center, and consolidation of mail, copying, graphics, and publishing facilities, bringing greater efficiency and savings. **Cost: $250,000**

Off-Campus Building
The opportunity to purchase and renovate the Gramercy Residence will provide a permanent home for the Life Skills program and will increase its capacity to 27 beds. **Cost: $750,000**

Intern House
The home directly across from the Brewster campus will provide much-needed intern housing. The increased internship demand has outstripped current available housing. **Cost: $320,000**

Swimming Pool
An outdoor pool for increased camp enrollment and expanded residential use will bring additional revenue. Current demand is beyond the capacity of the indoor pool. **Cost: $350,000**

Plus $11,000,000 from the State of New York

$1,250,000: Guarantee Permanent Funding

A Case for Endowment Green Chimneys has built its international reputation on its creative, visionary outlook. We believe that involvement with the community and the community's acceptance of our children is one of our strengths.

We see government reducing the amount that it will provide for the services we offer. We are going to need private funding to continue to do the things we do. We need to have reserves available for the times when government funding is late in arriving.

Our Mid-Century Campaign is dedicated to providing permanent funding for Green Chimneys. It seeks to guarantee permanency for the services we provide and expand our services for those in need.

An endowment of $1,250,000 will enable us to continue training programs for our staff and community. It will provide funding for an adult-child mentoring program, parenting classes, and behavior management and crisis intervention training. It ensures the development of training programs in the areas of animal-assisted therapy and animal-assisted activities.

Accredited with Commendation

Green Chimneys has been Accredited with Commendation by the Joint Commission of Accreditation of Healthcare Organizations. This is the highest level of accreditation awarded by JCAHO.

"Receiving Accreditation with Commendation is a significant achievement, one that recognizes exemplary performance by Green Chimneys," said Dennis S. O'Leary, M.D., president, JCAHO. "Green Chimneys should be commended for its commitment to providing quality care."

Resource 4

$1,750,000: Everyday Support Is Necessary

A Case for Annual Giving The mood of the country is changing. People are questioning the way all nonprofits do business. They are rethinking the role that government will play in our lives. They are assessing their position in terms of giving and volunteering. While government and the public decide on how they will react toward the nonprofit sector, Green Chimneys must strengthen its role as a provider and discover new funding streams to provide revenues for its services.

Reduced funding by government continues to alert us to the need to seek private funding. We believe we will survive and thrive, but we need to know that we can depend on the consistent financial support of the Friends of Green Chimneys to help us meet the needs of those who depend on our services. We have the task of coming up with ways to develop an alliance with others so that we can offer services to meet the needs of our customers. We need to raise $700,000 every year to cover the gap in funding. This means we must raise $1,750,000 during the two and one-half years of the Mid-Century Campaign.

Green Chimneys Serves . . .

- 9,000 people annually through guided farm tours
- 6,000 people annually through self-guided farm tours
- 250,000 people annually through the Farm on the Moo-ve
- 5,000 people annually through Hillside Outdoor Education Center
- 400 children annually through Good Friend adult-child mentoring
- 350 animals and 41 permanently disabled wildlife

Resource 4

Summary of Campaign Goals: $6,000,000

We need to raise $6 million over the two and a half years of our Mid-Century Campaign. This includes:

- $3,000,000 for faculty enrichment
- $1,250,000 for endowment
- $1,750,000 through annual giving

The Benefactors Circle: Providing Care and Concern *Forever*

We invite you to join the Benefactors Circle, established to recognize those who, through their future bequests, will provide for the children and animals entrusted to Green Chimneys. We will publish the names of people who have notified us that they will remember us in their wills and ask, if they choose, that they provide a letter stating their intention. For more information about the Benefactors Circle, please contact Samuel B. Ross, Jr., Ph.D., at (914) 279-2995, ext. 200, or (718) 892-6810, ext. 200.

Scale of Gifts for the Campaign

As you consider your ability to make a gift to Green Chimneys, please take a moment to study the table below. Based on the fundraising experience of many organizations around the country, the table projects the approximate number and size of gifts that will be required to reach our goal. No campaign like ours succeeds without substantial gifts from those with the resources to provide campaign leadership, and every successful campaign is driven by the enthusiasm and commitment of many contributors at all levels.

Number of Gifts	Gifts in Range of	Totaling	Cumulative Total
1	$750,000	750,000	750,000
1	$500,000	500,000	1,250,000
4	$250,000	1,000,000	1,750,000
6	$100,000	600,000	2,850,000
10	$50,000	500,000	3,350,000
20	$25,000	500,000	3,850,000
30	$15,000	450,000	4,300,000
50	$10,000	500,000	4,800,000
80	$5,000	400,000	5,200,000
100	$3,000	300,000	5,500,000
250	$1,000	250,000	5,750,000
Many less than $1,000		250,000	6,000,000

As Green Chimneys prepares to celebrate 50 years of care and concern for all living things, we reflect on those we have served in the past and look forward to all that we can do in the future. With your help today, we can continue to work for a better tomorrow for the children who pass through this facility. Green Chimneys is committed to high standards of professional service and to constructive and purposeful use of all the resources available to us.

—*Warren R. Colbert, Chairman, Green Chimneys*

"These are the tears of things, and the stuff of our mortality cuts us to the heart," said the poet Virgil, and so it is with our children. The evidence of their abuse and neglect when they first come to us "cuts us to the heart." But as they are healed, the tears we shed are tears of joy and wonder.

The children are our future. Please join us as we continue to help them. Without your financial generosity we cannot survive.

—*Jules Schwimmer, President, Green Chimneys*

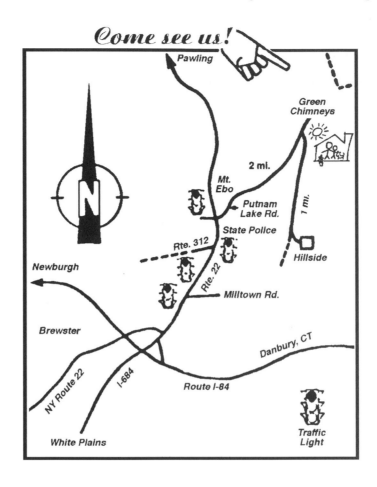

*"A hundred years from now, it will not matter
what my bank account was, the sort of house I lived in,
or the kind of car I drove, but the world may be different
because I was important in the life of a child."*
—Unknown

Green Chimneys' Mid-Century Campaign
Putnam Lake Road • Caller Box 719 • Brewster, NY 10509
(914) 279-2995 • (718) 892-6810 • Fax (914) 279-2714

Green Chimneys' Mid-Century Campaign

Building for the Future

Ways of Giving

You can make your tax-deductible contribution to the campaign in various ways, including:

- *Check, cash, or securities:* Most persons decide to make charitable gifts in the form of cash. The next most frequent way of making a gift is through marketable securities such as stocks and bonds. For gifts of cash, you are entitled to an income tax deduction up to 500 percent of your adjusted gross income with a five-year carryover for any excess. For gifts of long-term appreciated securities, the ceiling is 30 percent of adjusted gross income, and you avoid the capital gains tax that would have applied had you sold the securities.
- *A pledge payable over a multiyear period:* Usually a person is able to make a larger gift by extending the payment schedule over a period of several years. The full value of your pledge will be credited in the year of your commitment. However, you are entitled to a deduction for tax purposes only in the year you make the payment.
- *Real estate:* We would be happy to explore with you a gift of a home, vacation property, condominium, undeveloped land, or other real estate.
- *Life insurance:* You can make a significant commitment through a life insurance gift. This is particularly appropriate for paid-up policies that are no longer needed in your estate planning.
- *Bequests:* In your will, you can include charitable gifts to Green Chimneys in the form of specific property (cash, securities, works of art, etc.), a percentage of your estate, or the residue of your estate. Your attorney can help you plan the most appropriate type of bequest when you make or update your will.
- *Gift annuities:* In exchange for a gift of cash or securities (sometimes real estate can be accepted), Green Chimneys will pay you a fixed annual annuity. The rate of the annuity is based on the age of the annuitant. You will incur no immediate capital gains tax on the transfer; part of the annuity payment will be tax-free, and you will receive an income tax deduction for part of the gift.
- *Charitable remainder trust:* This type of trust, which may be executed by your attorney, provides a lifetime income for you and your beneficiary. At the end of the trust's term, the trust principal is distributed to Green Chimneys. You incur no capital gains tax on the transfer of appreciated long-term securities or real estate to the trust, and you receive an income tax deduction for part of the gift.
- *Charitable lead trust:* The lead trust is the mirror image of the charitable remainder trust. In this arrangement, the trust pays an annuity to Green Chimneys for a specific number of years. On termination of the trust, trust assets revert to the donor or to the heirs at significant transfer tax savings.
- *Pooled Income Fund:* The Pooled Income Fund accepts charitable gifts from many people and invests them in a common fund, like a mutual fund. The donor and designated beneficiary or beneficiaries receive a lifetime interest income from this irrevocable gift. As with mutual funds, the income to the donor varies. The gift may be made in the form of cash or securities. On a gift of appreciated stock, the donor pays no capital gains tax and also receives an income tax charitable deduction. The initial minimum gift is $5,000, and there is no maximum limit. Also, additional gifts of $1,000 or more may be added to the Pooled Income Fund at any time.

Named Gift Opportunities

As a lasting tribute, some donors choose to honor a loved one, mentor, or friend with a named charitable contribution to Green Chimneys. Many named gift opportunities are available.

Facilities (New School Buildings)

North Wing	$500,000
South Wing	$500,000
Swimming Pool	$350,000
Administration Center	$250,000
Student Computer Center	$125,000
Library/Multimedia Center	$105,000

Program

Farm Science and Animal Awareness	$50,000
Wildlife Conservation Program	$20,000
Sports and Recreation	$20,000

Endowment

Founder's Discretionary Fund	$100,000
Library/Multimedia	$50,000
Staff Growth and Development	$50,000
Preveterinary Training	$25,000
Camper Scholarships	$20,000
Preschool Scholarship	$15,000
Staff Training Fund	$15,000
Intern Support	$10,000

Other Programs

Runaway Shelter	$250,000
Training Institute	$100,000
Mentoring Services	$50,000
Public Information	$20,000
Gardening Education/Horticulture	$20,000
Cultural Arts	$20,000

Other Opportunities

One week of family outreach services	$1,000
Camper scholarship for one three-week session	$600
Group home resident's high school graduation	$500
Class field trip	$250
A resident's animal activities for one year	$100
Equipment for a group horticulture activity	$75
A resident's learn-and-earn experience for one year	$50
A resident's family visit	$25
Paperback books for a resident's personal use	$15

$1,000 joins the Committee of the Concerned.
All gifts of $1,500 or more will be recognized on a plaque at the end of the campaign.

Green Chimneys' Mid-Century Campaign
Putnam Lake Road, Caller Box 719, Brewster, NY 10509-0719
(914) 279-2995 • (718) 892-6810

Pledge Card

Green Chimneys'
Mid-Century Campaign

Building for the Future

I/We hereby pledge support for Green Chimneys' Mid-Century Campaign.

Name _____

Address _____

_____

Telephone _____

Pledge: $ _____ beginning _____

☐ In full now
☐ Over a   ☐ three-year period
  ☐ five-year period
☐ Annually
☐ Semiannually
☐ Quarterly
☐ Other _____

Please send reminders
☐ Quarterly   ☐ Semiannually
  ☐ Annually

☐ My/Our gift is unrestricted.
☐ I/We prefer to restrict our gift to

_____

This gift is given in (honor) (memory) of

_____

Signature_____

Date_____

My/Our gift will be matched by

_____
(Company Name)

Named gift opportunities are available. Please contact the Development Office for details on a wide range of options.

It is my/our intention to fulfill my/our pledge to Green Chimneys' Mid-Century Campaign. If unforeseen circumstances occur, the unpaid portion of my/our pledge ☐ shall ☐ shall not be legally binding against my/our estate.

☐ I/We intend to make a bequest and wish to become a member of the Benefactors Circle, providing care and concern forever.

Gifts are tax-deductible to the extent allowed by law. Donors may be acknowledged in the annual progress report to the community. If you would prefer your donation to be anonymous, please check here. ☐

**Green Chimneys'
Mid-Century Campaign**
Putnam Lake Road, Caller Box 719
Brewster, NY 10509–0719

(914) 279-2995 • (718) 892-6810

For more information, please contact Samuel B. Ross, Jr., Ph.D., ext. 200, or Lillian Roode, ext. 203.

Thank You

MAKING A WORLD OF DIFFERENCE

◆

THE ST. LOUIS YMCA

The mission of the St. Louis YMCA is to provide quality programs in fitness, family activities and positive personal values for youth—all at a price to encourage participation across the broadest possible spectrum of economic levels of our society.

The YMCA of Greater St. Louis is serving people—all kinds of people—children of all ages, teens, adults, seniors, and handicapped, every race and religion, every income level, male and female alike. As we seek to improve and expand our considerable array of programs for youth and adults, our basic goal remains ever-constant". . . to assist each individual to grow in body, mind and spirit."

This is the YMCA of Greater St. Louis.

Milestones Along the Way

1853   October 20, 1853. Referring to the founding of the St. Louis YMCA, the *Missouri Republican* says, "It is our privilege to record the beginnings of an enterprise, which contains in it the germs of more good to St. Louis than any undertaking which has ever been entered upon here."

1877   Supported by community business firms, the YMCA organizes to find jobs for the unemployed.

1905   The YMCA initiates the first resident summer camp for St. Louis area youth.

1926   The St. Louis YMCA begins the national movement of Y Indian Guides, a program directed to cement father/son relationships.

1964   Amid the turmoil of the civil rights movement, the St. Louis Y pioneers a detached street worker program for inner-city youth.

1967   To meet the exercise needs of a growing office-bound workforce, the YMCA emphasizes cardio-vascular fitness as a way to prolong active, productive lives.

1977   The St. Louis YMCA successfully completes a major capital campaign for needed expansion.

1983   Resulting from the dramatic rise in both single-parent families and homes with two working parents, the St. Louis YMCA becomes the leader in before-and-after-school child care based in elementary school facilities.

The Path of Progress

In 1953, the St. Louis YMCA consisted of a couple dozen men in a city of 74,000 people. Today, the metropolitan area contains over two million people and the Y serves nearly 150,000 women, men, girls and boys.

In 1977, the City of St. Louis launched a vigorous program of growth and development. That same year, catapulted by a ten million dollar capital campaign adding three new Program centers, the YMCA of Greater St. Louis entered a period of unparalleled growth.

- Total attendance has nearly doubled. The St. Louis Y ranks third in attendance in a comparison of St. Louis leisure time organizations.

ARCH	6,369,640
CARDINALS (baseball)	2,559,709
YMCA	1,986,143
ZOO	1,903,000
BLUES	596,000
BOTANICAL GARDEN	550,000
GRANT'S FARM	515,298
ART MUSEUM	500,000
THE MUNY	387,826
SYMPHONY ORCHESTRA	336,330
STEAMERS	335,805
CARDINALS (football)	309,612

- Y participants represent one-sixth of the people served by United Way agencies.
- 48.7 percent of YMCA memberships are women and girls.
- There are more youth involved in YMCA programs than are enrolled in the St. Louis City Schools.
- A 160 percent increase in participant-generated income has created greater self-reliance and financial stability.

Resource 4

The YMCA of Greater St. Louis . . . Today

Visible	Twelve neighborhood program centers, a branch serving Washington University students and a youth and family camp.
"Of" the community	475 civic and business leaders serve on YMCA Corporate and Branch Boards of Directors.
Well-attended	149,118 individuals actively participate in Y programs and services annually.

Current Programs

Fitness

The YMCA provides much more than quality fitness facilities. Fitness testing, nutritional counseling and many other services support the Y's entire approach to physical conditioning and good health. Over 65 St. Louis corporations recognize the important relationship between physical health and employee productivity. These employers look to the Y to deliver fitness programming to their people. Reduced health costs, lowered absenteeism and employee satisfaction are the valuable by-products of corporate fitness.

Aquatics

The YMCA teaches more people to swim than any other organization in our community. Aquatic enrollments total 39,968.

Youth Sports

Nearly 21,000 girls and boys learn the fundamentals of basketball, gymnastics, T-ball, soccer, hockey and other sports in the YMCA Y-Winners program. Although winning is fun, Y-Winners emphasizes learning the game and giving every kid the chance to participate. Parents are developed as coaches. Kids have fun. Everyone becomes a winner.

Camp Lakewood: Resident Summer Camp

Values development, new experiences and recreation . . . this is a summer camp for over a thousand girls and boys at Camp Lakewood. Building self-reliance and responsibility in children requires a variety of learning experiences. Swimming, canoeing, nature exploration, horseback riding, crafts, campouts and many other activities allow kids to lead, to work independently and to test their abilities. Scholarships are available for children unable to pay full fee.

Trout Lodge

Occupying the same grounds as Camp Lakewood, Trout Lodge offers nearly 14,000 people a beautiful setting for family retreats and outdoor educational experiences. Religious, educational and business groups are booked throughout the year. Trout Lodge is a nationally approved site for Elderhostel and offers seniors a variety of non-traditional educational programs.

Child Care and Development

Over 9,000 children and their parents realize the benefits of YMCA preschools, day care centers, latchkey programs, day camps and summer fun clubs. Far from a baby-sitting service, Y programs instruct, nurture and enhance child development through positive learning experiences.

Leadership Development

782 teenagers develop leadership skills and enjoy responsible involvement in Youth In Government, Camp Lakewood's Counselor-In-Training program and in a variety of Branch volunteer activities.

Adult Sports

19,801 adults enroll in league team sports.

Handicapped Classes

553 handicapped individuals utilize Y facilities for physical therapy, group exercise classes and swim classes.

Youth Employment

In partnership with the business community, the YMCA employs over 2,000 young people, ages 16 to 21.

A Plan for the Future

The YMCA has always followed the philosophy that as long as its core programs meet high standards and attract sufficient volume, they remain. However, new approaches and new programs are being continuously developed in response to constantly emerging needs in an ever-changing society. That is why, after six years of rapid growth, the Y instituted an intensive planning process:

1. The Department of Urban Affairs at St. Louis University provided information on the changing demographic nature of Branch service areas.

2. Y officials interviewed six or more "community knowledgeables" in each of the 12 geographic areas in which YMCA program units are situated asking each person to comment on how changes are impacting lives and how the "Y" might best respond. Y workers were particularly interested in the ramifications of factors affecting family life, the value-developing needs of youth, and the degree to which Y fitness programs meet modern needs.

3. Based on this data plus questionnaire results from members, YMCA staff and board members:

    a. Examined current programs for relevance and projected program design changes appropriate to the findings.

    b. Projected participation levels of redesigned programs in five-year and ten-year intervals.

    c. Determined the personnel, facility and operating revenue changes required in order to achieve projected program levels.

4. A planning committee commissioned by the Metropolitan Board conducted extensive review meetings to determine the validity of the conclusions each contained.

5. In November 1984, the YMCA's Metropolitan Board adopted the master plan, established general priorities for facility development and engaged the national Y's Buildings and Furnishings Service to provide construction cost estimates.

Points in Planning

Some major demographic and lifestyle changes that influenced program and facility decisions were:

- Married couples' share of all households plunged sharply in the '70s, indicating that families will face increasing disruptions and breakdowns.
- The rapid rise of women in the workforce (approaching 50 percent) signals a continuing rate of growth of female participation in the YMCA (now at 48.7 percent). Other "Y" programs that will be in increased demand as a result are after-school youth programs, day care, and teen-age and grade school-age programs with a strong values component.
- The "baby boom" generation has reached child-bearing age increasing the need for activities for young families, fitness and recreation facilities designed for family use, and the expansion of facilities and programs for pre-schoolers.
- Those constituting the "empty nest" family cycle and senior citizens make up an increasing proportion of the population. For most St. Louisans, one-third of life will occur after the eldest child leaves home. Greater need for active and vigorous lifestyles means added pressure on the YMCA to respond with programs and facilities tailored to that age. Adult fitness, camping and social activities are but a few Y programs already experiencing this demand.
- The increase in disadvantaged persons—the physically and culturally handicapped and the economically deprived—calls for creative approaches to the needs of these special populations.

The YMCA Responds

The dramatic expansion of YMCA programs brought about by the highly successful "Path of Progress" capital development program of 1977 is poignant testimony to the impact the YMCA can have on the quality of life in St. Louis given the needed tools. Recent experience indicates that an equally dramatic growth rate will be achieved in the decade ahead with the commitment of all top community leaders. The payoff in enriched lives will be as significant as in any project in recent memory.

YMCA Objectives

Fitness for Living

Expand enrollment in fitness activities from 92,701 youth and adults to 154,000— a 66 percent increase in participation in sports and cardio-vascular programs! New levels will be accomplished through the development of a new fitness center in West County, a leased fitness facility for working youth adults in Downtown St. Louis, and expansion of fitness facilities in several existing centers.

Resource 4

Family Programs

Mount a concerted effort to increase enrollments in family-related activities from 19,848 to 36,000. In order to provide values education and family enrichment experiences to greater numbers of people, a comprehensive new building designed to serve all ages will be built. Extensive family camping facilities are planned at the YMCA of the Ozarks.

Aquatic and Water Safety

A new pool and expanded locker room that will increase the number who can use existing pools will result in a broadening of aquatic and water safety services from 31,850 to 41,000 further strengthening the Y's title as "swim teacher for St. Louis."

Combined Impact

What is planned is a quantum leap in the positive impact of YMCA programs on the lives of St. Louisans. By combining the upgrading and expansion of existing facilities with new construction, limited only in areas in which no YMCA buildings now exist, significant growth will be accomplished at a considerable saving over other alternatives. Participation in YMCA activities will increase an impressive 66 percent.

New and Improved Facilities

To achieve planned objectives, YMCA and community leaders must act now to establish new Y facilities and renovate others.

WEST COUNTY CENTER $4,000,000

Construct a new family program and fitness center accessible to the youth and families of the Parkway and Rockwood school districts.

YMCA OF THE OZARKS   5,000,000

Build a new lodge and family program center, remodel youth camp cabins and build new program areas for resident camping at Sunnen Lake.

NORTH COUNTY CENTER   1,050,000

Completion of the Emerson Fitness Center will expand fitness programs for all ages. The addition will include a gymnasium, indoor track and expanded locker rooms.

DOWNTOWN FITNESS CENTERS   2,600,000

This includes two projects: major renovation of the existing Downtown Y which was constructed in 1962 and the leasing and remodelling of space for a 2nd cardio-vascular fitness center for men and women located closer to the River.

MID-COUNTY FITNESS AND FAMILY CENTER   2,000,000

Renovate and upgrade locker rooms, the gymnasium, the pool, exercise areas, and public use areas to expand capacity and increase service to Brentwood and to those employed in the Clayton Area.

KIRKWOOD/WEBSTER GROVES   1,050,000

Replace older portions of the Kirkwood building to house a gymnasium, indoor track, expanded locker rooms and exercise areas.

SOUTHSIDE & CARONDELET CENTERS   654,000

Renovate these two old but busy buildings in order to extend their useful lives by ten years or longer. Both facilities serve areas whose stability and gradual revitalization are crucial to the further renaissance of the City. Replacement now would cost many times the planned expenditures.

MONSANTO   250,000

This program center was built in 1980 and has far exceeded planned participation levels. It is so successful that it has become a national model of what can be done by non-profit organizations to address the family recreation needs of the inner city. Additional space is needed for more fitness areas and for day care facilities.

JEFFERSON COUNTY AND WEST ST. CHARLES COUNTY   700,000

Property acquisition and outreach facilities are needed in these two remaining major population growth areas. Modest facilities are planned to serve day care needs and provide a command post for community-based Y programs.

WESTPORT FITNESS CENTER   500,000

Plans involve leasing and renovating existing space for a cardio-vascular fitness center for the apartment dwellers and the young adults working in the Westport Area.

WASHINGTON UNIVERSITY—CAMPUS Y   90,000

This Branch addresses the needs of college students to develop socially and to relate meaningfully to the larger community through service projects. An expanded endowment will supplement a budget that is modest in comparison to the impact on values and the broad community service this Center provides.

TOTAL IMMEDIATE PROJECTS: $17,894,000

A Call for Action

The need is now at hand to build upon an earlier investment and a rich legacy, to build for today's needs and for tomorrow's. The goal is challenging but not unreasonably so. Eight years ago, the task of achieving a smaller goal must have seemed much more formidable. Yet, the goal was reached.

While much has been achieved, much remains to be done. Large concentrations of St. Louis families who need and would respond to YMCA programs live too far from existing facilities to participate regularly. Several YMCA buildings reflect heavy use over long periods of time. The quality-seeking people of modern society are not attracted to institutions with buildings that have seen better days and call into question the leadership's ability to either understand the present or anticipate the future. Other YMCA buildings are incomplete due to phased construction and now are ready for completion as earlier planned.

This important bridge on the YMCA's and St. Louis' continuing path of progress needs the generous support of all those who see in the programs of the YMCA of Greater St. Louis an enduring asset in the ongoing life of this community and its people.

Resource 4

CASE STATEMENT WITH COMPANION PIECES

Note: Due to space considerations, only the covers are shown above for the Aliber Hall College of Business Administration booklet and the Drake Law School and Frederick D. Lewis Jr. brochures. Their text has been omitted in this resource.

Second Century Fund

DRAKE UNIVERSITY•DES MOINES, IOWA

BUILDING
for the
FUTURE

This document has one purpose.

That purpose is to answer the question: "Why is it necessary to seek at least $25 million in gifts and grants for Drake University's Second Century Fund?"

Do not be misled by the apparent simplicity of our purpose. The question is a complex one. It focuses attention on the growth and the aspirations of Drake University as it completes 100 years of service to a constituency which includes not only the City of Des Moines and the State of Iowa, but the Midwest and the nation as well.

Since its founding in 1881, Drake University has been successful because it has been more than an educational institution. From the beginning the University established itself as a community. First, Chancellor George Carpenter and the faculty recognized that education involved not only classroom activity and study but also work, play, worship, and community life. They believed that a liberal education must develop a student's ability to integrate all of life's experiences.

Even the name of the University's first building, The Students' Home, is emblematic of the kind of education which Drake University espoused in 1881 and continues to offer today. The Students' Home was a place where students and faculty lived and worked together, where education was value oriented, and where learning occurred as much through social process and close interpersonal relationships as through diligent study.

The truly liberal education which Drake has since offered demands a special type of faculty. They are committed to teaching, but more than that they are scholars—people who believe that education is a lifelong process. They are community-minded individuals who participate in campus life and involve themselves with Drake students as counselors and advisors. They are active in the Des Moines community as well because they know that an educated person has the duty to contribute conscientiously to community life.

"If the traditions and values are to be preserved, the University must build for the future."

In the century since The Students' Home was hastily constructed in the brief span of one summer to encompass a dormitory, classrooms, dining room, chapel, and offices, the school in the countryside has become a distinguished urban institution. The campus facilities have grown to include 128 acres and 40 buildings. Within the past ten years alone, a computer sciences center, law school building, health center, fine arts center, biological science building, student and university center, and health and recreation center have been constructed. The undergraduate student body numbers 4,500 in six colleges, with another 2,000 students enrolled in the Law School, graduate programs and the College for Continuing Education. The current student body comes from nearly every state and several foreign countries. Drake enjoys a national reputation based upon the performance of its graduates.

Drake University must not abandon the principles it has spent 100 years developing, but if the traditions and values are to be preserved, the University must build for the future. Scholarship funds must be increased so that the University can continue to help the kinds of students who will benefit from a Drake education. The endowment must be increased so that the University can reward and retain outstanding faculty. A badly-needed building to house the College of Business Administration must be constructed, the campus modernized, equipment brought up to date, and the library endowed so that Drake students of the future can be educated with the same care as their predecessors.

What Drake has been, is now, and will be in the future all come together in this Second Century Fund campaign. Drake's distinctive 100-year contribution to educational excellence, achieved through the growth and quality of students, faculty, and physical surroundings, must be preserved and passed on to future generations. It is the responsibility of all of us who have concern for this University to see that this takes place.

Wilbur C. Miller
President

Endowment	**$13,000,000**
Faculty Development Endowment	5,000,000
General Purpose Endowment	3,500,000
Library Development Endowment	1,000,000
Scholarship-Fellowship Endowment	3,500,000
One-Time Projects	**$12,000,000**
Aliber Hall—College of Business Administration	5,000,000
Campus Modernization	4,250,000
Equipment Modernization	750,000
Operational Expenses	2,000,000
Total	**$25,000,000**

For one of the few times in its 100-year history, Drake University is undertaking a national campaign to raise a very substantial sum of money—$25 million—from private donors for the comprehensive benefit of the University.

The campaign has evolved over a period of four years. An intensive institutional self-study pinpointed high priority programs and projects for which customary funding is not available and, more importantly, demonstrated that the campaign is needed and justified.

An independent study to examine the financial feasibility of such a campaign followed and was completed during the Summer of 1980. Results of this study revealed an unusually strong interest in Drake University among corporate, professional, foundation, and civic leaders in Iowa and elsewhere. The study indicated that Drake has a legion of supporters whose commitment to the University is sufficiently strong that they will meet its needs if so requested.

Guided by these findings, the Drake University Board of Trustees unanimously approved on October 31, 1980, a $25 million Second Century Fund campaign. This campaign is intended to continue Drake's 100-year tradition of educational excellence, and to build for the University's future.

As Chairman of the Development Committee of the Board of Trustees, I have accepted the privileged position of chairing the Second Century Fund campaign. In this capacity, I will be working with the campaign steering committee, other members of the Board, and volunteer leaders around the country who are as dedicated as I am to the success of Drake University.

Briefly, we are undertaking a three-year campaign to raise $25 million for Drake. The $25 million goal takes into account annual fund support normally to be anticipated during the period of Second Century Fund activities.

Today, in spite of sound financial management, Drake University stands at a crossroads. New channels through which will flow added sources of strength to nurture and revitalize the superiority of our University must be developed. There is no doubt that Drake's alumni and friends have the capacity to see that these needs are met. Our campaign is one that can and will be successful.

While strong volunteer leadership is essential in such a campaign, its success will be reflected in the attitudes of prospective donors who recognize that the strength and betterment of the University are worthy of their philanthropic investments. Here is an opportunity for every friend of Drake to establish a lasting legacy for the advancement of human welfare. Join in this exciting adventure— Drake University's Second Century Fund.

R. N. Houser

R. N. Houser
National Chairman

Building an Endowment for the Future

The major portion of the Second Century Fund will go into Drake University's endowment—those funds which are invested to provide the University with a permanent source of guaranteed income. An endowment is not extra money, something to fall back upon when times demand it. To the contrary, a quality university of national standing can be expected to maintain its position only if its endowment assets are of dimensions similar to those of comparable institutions. Nationally, institutions like Drake consider the endowment base adequate if it is approximately twice the annual operating budget. Currently, Drake's endowment is only about one-third the size of its operating budget. Only by increasing endowment can Drake continue to meet the challenge of providing a superior education to talented and deserving students. The Second Century Fund goal represents a vital and important first step toward the fulfillment of Drake's endowment needs, and clearly signals the path to be pursued in the future.

Faculty Development Endowment: $5,000,000

The heart of any university is its faculty. Drake has traditionally attracted dedicated faculty with the skills to inspire students to achieve their full academic potential while instilling in them a respect for moral and ethical values. It is a faculty well-equipped to provide education for leadership.

Quality faculty come to Drake University because of the extraordinary opportunities to develop a career in an educational climate that fosters innovation and a total commitment to educational excellence. A faculty development endowment will allow the University to continue to attract and retain faculty of high caliber.

Endowed Professorial Chair: $750,000 Endowment for Each Chair. Annual income resulting from an endowed professorship will provide salary, personnel, and program incentives to place an educator of superior qualifications in a college of the University where that person can have a profound effect on the curriculum and on the college's efforts to recruit both excellent faculty and superior students. Colleges for which an endowed chair would be of immediate benefit include the College of Business Administration, the College of Education, the College of Fine Arts, the School of Journalism and Mass Communication, the Law School, the College of Liberal Arts, and the College of Pharmacy.

Professional-Curricular Enhancement. Universities, businesses, industries, and professions face the common challenge of keeping pace with progress by providing the opportunities for those in responsible positions to develop further their skills and knowledge. At Drake, there has been an awareness of this challenge from the time the University was founded. However, funding for faculty development has been implemented only to the extent that the operating budget permits. In recent years, these funds have averaged only $25,000 annually.

Endowment support for professional—curricular enhancement is intended to increase these funds at least seven-fold and make possible the following:

1. Named professorships: Merit awards for outstanding faculty work in enriching curricula, strengthening student achievement, augmenting professional knowledge, and providing public service.
2. Continuing professional educational opportunities:
   a. Supplementary study for faculty to update professional expertise or to convert their knowledge and skills to related disciplines.
   b. Leave time for special study or professional activities.
   c. Participation in key professional meetings and events.
3. Special project funding for:
   a. Assembling specialized materials and equipment.
   b. Additional programs designed to encourage faculty to develop programs of special interest for the community.

General Purpose Endowment: $3,500,000

Endowment for general purposes must be sufficient to assure the continuity of Drake's present level and quality of education and service. The University must be in a position to furnish the support to ensure that each academic discipline and department can adapt to changing needs and rise to its own level of excellence to continue providing students with the quality education they have a right to expect. As the continuity of its programs is assured, Drake's certain of retaining its position of educational leadership is ensured.

Library Development Endowment: $1,000,000

Unprecedented increases in the cost of books, periodicals and materials, have made library development a serious concern of universities today from coast to coast. Drake University is no exception. An escalating inflation rate has made it increasingly difficult for Cowles Library to carry on an aggressive program of acquisitions. In 1973, the library purchased 16,175 books for $180,000. In 1979, over $200,000 was spent to purchase 10,310 books. While its purchase of serials has remained constant at 2,000 per year, the library's budget for that purpose has increased by 76 percent since 1973 and now stands at $180,000. An endowment that would provide an annual base which the University could use to purchase books will lessen the effects of this inflation on the operating budget.

Scholarship-Fellowship Endowment: $3,500,000

Recognizing the importance of helping deserving students finance a college education, Drake University spent $3,951,573 on student financial aid in 1979–80. This represented 27.5 percent of the $14,354,599 which Drake students received from federal, state, and private scholarship aid to attend the University. The need to budget even more money for financial aid is essential for three reasons:

1. Drake University is dedicated to the ideal that students who have the potential deserve an education. Economic class must not prevent a student from receiving an education at Drake.
2. Federal programs are being tightened so that less federal aid will be available to students.
3. The financial needs of students are becoming more difficult for their families to meet because of the effects of inflation on personal incomes.

While there is a great urgency for scholarships based on need, Drake University also is intent upon attracting the brightest and most gifted students with merit scholarships which recognize academic and leadership qualities. Responses to the Drake National Alumni Scholarship program each year prove how heavily financial incentives are weighed by good students. Hundreds of high school graduates in the upper 10 percent of their classes—many valedictorians and salutatorians—compete for these awards, which cover four years' tuition, lodging, board, and fees.

It is the purpose of the substantial scholarship-fellowship endowment to supplement by at least $250,000 annually the funding now provided for need, merit, and combined need-merit scholarships and fellowships at Drake University.

Building and Modernizing for the Future

Aliber Hall, College of Business Administration: $5,000,000

A growing College of Business Administration now enrolling over 1,200 students must be provided with the environment and space necessary for it to function in a manner which befits its stature. This goal will be realized with the construction of a new business administration building which will be named Aliber Hall in recognition of gifts from the Aliber Foundation, the late Robert Aliber, and other members of the Aliber family.

Aliber Hall will be a concrete and masonry structure designed to harmonize with existing campus architecture. The building will be strategically situated near Olmsted Center and Meredith Hall. This will facilitate the College's development of conferences, institutes, and short courses.

"The University must . . . continue providing students with
the quality education they have a right to expect."

Some of the major features planned for the new building include an insurance center, a business development and research center, and a large computer facility which will be connected with the University's Dial Center for Computer Sciences.

Aliber Hall also will provide the College of Business Administration with versatile classroom space. In addition to a seminar room, a 50-seat classroom, and a 160-seat lecture hall, the new building will have two case study rooms with the capacity to serve as a behavioral studies laboratory. There will also be three accounting laboratories, two of which will be partitioned so they can be merged into a large, tabled classroom accommodating 40 students.

One of its important attributes will be office space not only for faculty and administration, but also for student organizations as well. The building will contain offices which will house faculty members from the College of Business Administration and from the Economics Department of the College of Liberal Arts. In addition to departmental offices and seven clerical offices, the new building will contain all of the administrative offices for the College, a conference room, reception area, staff lounge, and secretarial work area. Space for students will include a student reading room and student organizations' headquarters.

The $5 million estimate includes cost of construction, site preparation, fixed and movable equipment furnishings, heating, cooling, and utilities installation.

Campus Modernization: $4,250,000

Drake's 128-acre campus and 40 buildings are located within Iowa's largest community and capital city. The University is a harmonious blend of historically significant buildings sheltered by oak and maple trees older than the University itself and a more modern campus designed by America's leading architects and constructed since the end of World War II. Although much is done each year to keep the campus in a state of repair and emergencies are dealt with expeditiously, the budget has not permitted a comprehensive refurbishment and renovation of those buildings and areas of campus which are beginning to show a century of wear. Economically, renovation is far more cost efficient than beginning anew. Moreover, in every case the older buildings are structurally sound, although they are not use or energy efficient by today's standards. Of even more importance is the traditional and historical value of these buildings, especially the venerable old buildings of the inner campus. In order to meet its educational objectives, Drake University must have a campus which matches in quality the academic programs it offers and which retains the traditional appearance alumni and friends remember and cherish.

The Second Century Fund will ensure that an integrated program of campus modernization will take place.

The general effects of this program will be:

1. The redesigning and rebuilding of areas which need improved access for the handicapped and elderly.
2. Structural and equipment changes which are needed to conserve energy and conform to accepted safety standards.
3. General refurbishment of buildings throughout the campus.
4. Modernization and enlargement of the physical plant administrative center.
5. A number of projects designed to increase the beauty of the campus and its functional capabilities. Among these projects are replacing outdated lighting equipment for greater campus safety and security, establishing new parking areas, acquiring properties surrounding the campus, and landscaping certain campus areas to highlight and enhance the architecture.

In addition to the updated physical plant administrative facilities and the grounds improvements, specific projects in the campus modernization program include:

1. *Cole Hall:* Dedicated in 1904 as the original Law School building, Cole Hall must be remodeled to fit the needs of the departments which will occupy it when the College of Business Administration moves to the new Aliber Hall.
2. *Cowles Library:* In addition to renovating the research and general circulation centers, the University must provide a periodical center and a microfilm reading and storage area for the library.
3. *Harvey Ingham Hall of Science:* Laboratories, installed when the building was erected 31 years ago, must be replaced on all three floors.
4. *Howard Hall:* Completed in 1903 as a Conservatory of Music, the second oldest building on campus needs extensive interior and exterior remodeling in addition to an air-conditioning system.
5. *Memorial Hall:* Constructed in 1905 as the Bible College, the building now houses the College of Education and needs considerable renovation of administrative and classroom areas plus a new air-conditioning unit.
6. *Old Main:* The symbol of Drake University since its dedication on September 18, 1883, Old Main is now the administrative headquarters of the University. As such, its office complexes on each floor must be redesigned to accommodate up-to-date administrative functions.
7. *Old Main Auditorium:* Completed in 1900 as an addition to Old Main, this elegant and venerable structure must be completely restored before it can once again be returned to use. Plans call for the replacement of old seating, the outdated public address system, and the obsolete plumbing. In addition, the stage, green room, auditorium ceiling, walls, and entrance ways must be completely rebuilt. A fire protection system and access ramps for the handicapped and elderly also must be installed.

Equipment Modernization: $750,000

In virtually every field of industry, business, and government, as well as in education, obsolescence of equipment sets in earlier today than ever before. The continued rapid development of technology makes early obsolescence an ever-present fact of modern living.

Equipment modernization needs include: increased computer capabilities, up-to-date laboratory and classroom equipment, new printed and audio-visual aids, added audio-visual equipment, electronic and print media equipment, new musical instruments, new visual arts and performing arts equipment, and up-to-date office equipment.

Support to Help Meet Operational Expenses: $2,000,000

Day-to-day operational expenses also must be taken into consideration. In University financing, no matter how astute the planner or careful the planning, the *present* too often intrudes upon and eventually overshadows the *future.* The Second Century Fund will provide additional revenue to help the University meet these expenses. It also is designed to provide a cushion against inflation so that Drake University can better plan and build for the future without fear of being constantly overwhelmed by the present.

Commemorative Gift Opportunities

Commemorative gift opportunities offer alumni, parents, friends, foundations, and corporations numerous ways to establish named gifts as memorials and testimonials to family, friends, organizations, or other individuals. These gifts embody the donor's ideals and provide essential support to ensure a strong future for Drake.

A University representative will be glad to work with anyone desiring to make a commemorative gift, and explore a number of options through which such a gift may be developed. A few of the more traditional categories are listed below.

Professorships

A named endowed professorship may be established for an existing professorship or a new professorship in a school or a field of study. Such an endowment fund may be established with a gift or gifts to total $750,000.

Lectureships

A named endowment fund to provide a lecture program (that is, one which may be used for the honorarium and expenses of a special guest lecturer) may be established with a fund of not less than $10,000.

Resource 5

Scholarships

A named endowment scholarship may be established with a fund of not less than $25,000 or a guarantee of annual support for one or more recipients totaling at least $1,200.

Fellowships

A named endowed fellowship may be established with a fund of not less than $100,000 or a guarantee of annual support for one or more recipients totaling at least $5,000 but with no award being made which is less than $1,000 to a recipient.

Prize Funds

A named financial award for outstanding accomplishment may be provided through the establishment of a prize fund with an endowment of not less than $5,000 to furnish awards of approximately $200 or more to one or more students each year.

Book Funds

The earnings from an endowed book fund may be used for the purchase of books or other materials in a particular field or library and also may be used as specified by the donor for other expenses of the library. Such a fund may be established with not less than $5,000.

Funds for Student Activities

Gifts and funds will be accepted for the support of recognized student activities if such activities have the approval of the Vice President for Student Life.

For further information regarding these or other named and memorial gift opportunities contact:

Office of Institutional Development
Drake University
319 Old Main
Des Moines, IA 50311
Telephone (515) 271-3154

Methods of Giving

Certainly, the tax rewards alone should not motivate one to give—they are not the starting point. The desire to help Drake University comes first, and those who make gifts to Drake are generously rewarded by tax laws.

Some methods of giving include: outright gift of cash, gift of securities, gift of real property, gift of life insurance, deferred gifts which can take many forms, and gifts through a will.

One or a combination of these methods may have a particular appeal in planning one's gift. Drake University provides estate planning and tax advice to donors; however, it is suggested that professional tax or legal advice be obtained in order to realize the maximum tax benefits from such gifts.

SECOND CENTURY FUND SUMMARY.

Endowment		
Faculty Development Endowment	$5,000,000	
Named Endowed Chairs		
Professional-Curricular Enhancement		
General Purpose Endowment	3,500,000	
Library Development Endowment	1,000,000	
Scholarship-Fellowship Endowment	3,500,000	
Second Century Fund Minimum Endowment Goal		$13,000,000
One-Time Projects		
Aliber Hall, College of Business Administration	$5,000,000	
Campus Modernization	4,250,000	
Projects in Cole Hall, Cowles Library, Harvey Ingham Hall of Science, Howard Hall, Memorial Hall, Old Main, Old Main Auditorium		
Grounds modernization, beautification and expansion		
Expansion of Physical Plant Administrative Facilities		
Equipment Modernization	750,000	
Support to help meet Operational Requirements	2,000,000	
Second Century Fund Minimum One-Time Projects and Operational Support Goal		$12,000,000
Second Century Fund Goal		$25,000,000

On the preceding pages you have read about an exciting program designed to build for the future of Drake University. On the following pages are the names of those who endorse and support the Second Century Fund and who have accepted the challenge of its leadership.

This is more than a campaign designed simply to raise $25 million, or a campaign to build and renovate buildings, to increase endowment, or to generate operating revenues alone. These are mere symbols which represent in concrete terms our real mission—namely, to ensure through thoughtful building the educational quality of Drake University and to keep the promise of our future. This campaign will assure that teaching and learning will continue at Drake in an environment conducive to producing the best possible graduates, to conducting the best possible research, and to providing the best possible service.

Our campaign goal is an ambitious one which cannot be achieved through the contributions of a few prominent individuals or a select group of businesses, corporations and foundations alone. In order to meet the challenge of our program, everyone will need to give generously. As you are asked to join our effort, I am confident you will respond in a manner which befits the magnitude of the undertaking and with the knowledge that the future of Drake University promises to be as distinguished as its past. All of us united in this common cause embodied in the Second Century Fund can make that promise a reality.

Robb B. Kelley
Chairman,
Drake Board of Trustees

Second Century Fund

DRAKE UNIVERSITY•DES MOINES, IOWA

The Case for Aliber Hall

Aliber Hall Fulfills a Need

At Drake University, education for business is not an ancillary program—it is a core educational component. However, the physical environment in which the University fulfilled this accepted responsibility had become outmoded and could no longer provide the educational and administrative quarters to support the programs offered.

The College of Business Administration, now enrolling over 1,500 students, required the educational environment and space necessary for it to function efficiently. Physical improvements were needed to provide specialized instruction, to centralize faculty and administration of the College and to improve student services.

Today, the College of Business Administration's student population of more than 1,500 exceeds one-fifth of Drake's total enrollment and is the second largest college of the University. With the new technologies of the 1980s, expanded use of computer information systems in business and government, and with more women and minorities seeking managerial careers, growth prospects for the College look excellent.

For these reasons, Drake's Board of Trustees realistically recognized the need for a more suitable business education environment and authorized the construction of a $5 million building, housing the College of Business Administration. The project is a major part of Drake's Second Century Fund, a national voluntary fundraising effort designed to raise $25 million for increased endowment and several one-time projects.

Educational Center for Business

Completed this fall, Aliber Hall adds a new dimension to the College of Business Administration. It not only provides resources to improve traditional education areas, it also houses specialized instructional centers and makes possible centralization of the College's faculty and administration.

The new building, located just south of Drake's Olmsted Center, harmonizes in appearance with existing University structures. It contains 47,300 square feet of space on three stories above grade and a lower level. Each level of the facility has been designed to produce a functionally efficient and aesthetically stimulating learning environment.

The main administrative area is situated on the second floor and is equipped with a reception area, conference rooms and a staff lounge. Faculty offices exclusively occupy the third floor. Classrooms, seminar and conference rooms; a computer room and laboratory; a case study room; accounting laboratories; and specialized instructional centers in business development and research, insurance and executive development are located on the lower level as well as the first and second floors.

Structural features include a north arcade, entry ways from both the north and south to accommodate campus traffic and public access from University Avenue and a 148–seat lecture hall with access from the first floor. A focal point of the building is the spiral staircase to the upper levels of the structure. A primary siting consideration was the preservation of the "north-south" green mall-type area through the center of campus.

Commemorative Gift Opportunities

Aliber Hall is providing a suitable environment to ensure the continued growth and distinguished reputation of Drake's College of Business Administration. However, the completion of financing for Aliber Hall remains a challenge. The generosity of The Aliber Foundation and the Robert Aliber family provides impetus for encouraging the commitment of substantive support from alumni and friends of Drake University.

Aliber Hall is a showcase for Drake University. For this reason, we are offering numerous gift opportunities for individual office and room facilities within the Hall. Each area provides a naming or memorial opportunity according to the donor's wishes, and appropriate recognition will be placed in each area so named.

You are invited to share in these naming opportunities and to help complete financing of Drake's new College of Business Administration, Aliber Hall.

The Second Century Fund offers alumni, parents, friends, foundations and corporations numerous ways to provide memorials and testimonials to family, friends, organizations or other individuals. Your commemorative gift can embody the donor's ideals and provide essential support to ensure a strong future for Drake University.

To participate or get further information, call or write Drake University, Second Century Fund, Des Moines, IA 50311. Our telephone number is (515) 271-3154. Your inquiry will receive prompt and courteous attention.

ALIBER HALL: GIFT OPPORTUNITIES.

Building	(Reserved)
Floor (4)	$1,000,000
Lecture Hall	500,000
Dean's Suite	250,000
Conference Room	75,000
Dean's Office	(Reserved)
Computer Suite	250,000
Computer Classroom	100,000
Computer Laboratory	50,000
Insurance Center Suite	200,000
Director's Office	(Reserved)
Business Development/Research Center Suite	150,000
Executive Development Room	150,000
Student Administration Suite	100,000
Case Room	100,000
Accounting Laboratory (First Floor)	100,000
Research Library	75,000
Accounting Laboratory (3) (Lower Level)	75,000
Student Reading Room (Lower Level)	75,000
Staff Lounge (Second Floor)	75,000
Seminar Room (First Floor)	(Reserved)
Student Organization Room	40,000
Conference Room (2) (First Floor)	40,000
Conference Room (2) (Second Floor)	25,000
Faculty Offices (53) (Third Floor)	10,000

**Second
Century
Fund**

The Drake University Second Century Fund is a national voluntary fund raising effort designed to raise $25 million. In order to maintain and improve its position in higher education, Drake University must address itself to a number of urgent needs for which customary funding is not available. There are two major categories of needs: increased endowment, including faculty development, general purpose, library development and scholarship-fellowship totaling $13,000,000; and one-time projects, including Aliber Hall (College of Business Administration), campus and equipment modernization and support to help meet operational requirements totaling $12,000,000.

Drake University admits students without regard to sex, race, color, national or ethnic origin or handicap.

Second Century Fund

DRAKE UNIVERSITY•DES MOINES, IOWA

The Plough Pharmacy Scholarship Fund

Drake University has been honored as the first private educational institution in the country to be awarded a $500,000 gift from the Plough Foundation for the purpose of establishing a scholarship program for Drake's College of Pharmacy.

The Plough Story

Abe Plough, founder of Plough, Inc., a pharmaceutical company, and the Plough Foundation, based in Memphis, Tennessee, established the Plough Pharmacy Scholarship Fund as an expression of gratitude for the support of retail pharmacists who over the years enabled Plough, Inc. to grow and prosper. It is their commitment to today's youth who will be tomorrow's pharmacy professionals.

The Scholarship Fund

Drake University is only one of nine schools nationally that now participate in the Plough Pharmacy Scholarship Fund. This scholarship will provide financial assistance of up to $1,000 per year to selected Drake full-time undergraduate pharmacy students. Dollar awards to Plough Scholars may be increased in subsequent years.

The Challenge

An important element of this generous gift is that Drake University, over the next eleven years, must match the gift with a $500,000 advance to the Plough Scholarship Fund. Beginning in 1998, the Fund will begin to return the $500,000 to Drake until finally in the year 2008, the University will have received all of the money invested plus more than $2,000,000 in endowment.

Help Meet the Challenge

You are invited to help Drake meet the challenge presented by the Plough Foundation. Your generous support of this scholarship fund will ensure that many eligible students will receive their pharmacy education through Drake's College of Pharmacy. Together, we can make a long-term commitment that will help Drake University continue its program of training qualified pharmacy professionals.

To participate or get further information, call or write Drake University, Plough Pharmacy Scholarship Fund, Des Moines, IA 50311. Our telephone number is (515) 271-3154. Your inquiry will receive prompt and courteous attention.

PLOUGH PHARMACY SCHOLARSHIP FUND.

Year	Drake Contribution	Plough Contribution	1/2 of Interest Add to Principal	Total Accumulated Principal	Total Interest at 12 percent[a]	1/2 of Interest Available for Scholarships
1	50,000	50,000	100,000	12,000	6,000	
2	45,000	45,000	6,000	196,000	23,520	11,760
3	45,000	45,000	11,760	297,760	35,731	17,865
4	45,000	45,000	17,865	405,625	48,675	24,337
5	45,000	45,000	24,337	519,962	62,395	31,198
6	45,000	45,000	31,198	641,160	76,939	38,470
7	45,000	45,000	38,470	769,630	92,356	46,178
8	45,000	45,000	46,178	905,808	108,697	54,348
9	45,000	45,000	54,348	1,050,156	126,018	63,009
10	45,000	45,000	63,009	1,203,165	144,380	72,190
11	45,000	45,000	72,190	1,365,355	163,842	81,921
12	—	—	81,921	1,447,276	173,673	86,837
13	—	—	86,837	1,534,113	184,093	92,047
14	—	—	92,047	1,626,160	195,139	97,570
15	—	—	97,570	1,723,730	206,848	103,424
16	(50,000)		103,424	1,777,154	213,258	106,629
17	(45,000)		106,629	1,838,783	220,653	110,327
18	(45,000)		110,327	1,904,110	228,492	114,246
19	(45,000)		114,246	1,973,356	236,802	118,401
20	(45,000)		118,401	2,067,570	245,610	122,805
21	(45,000)		122,803	2,124,562	254,948	127,474
22	(45,000)		127,474	2,207,036	264,844	132,422
23	(45,000)		132,422	2,294,458	275,335	137,667
24	(45,000)		137,667	2,387,125	286,455	143,228
25	(45,000)		143,228	2,485,353	298,242	149,121
26	(45,000)		149,121	2,589,474	310,736	
	$0	$500,000	$2,089,474			$2,089,474

[a]Total annual interest based on estimated 12 percent equals Net

Second Century Fund

The Drake University Second Century Fund is a national voluntary fund raising effort designed to raise $25 million. In order to maintain and improve its position in higher education, Drake University must address itself to a number of urgent needs for which customary funding is not available. There are two major categories of needs: increased endowment, including faculty development, general purpose, library development and scholarship-fellowship totaling $13,000,000; and one-time projects, including Aliber Hall (College of Business Administration), campus and equipment modernization and support to help meet operational requirements totaling $12,000,000.

Drake University admits students without regard to sex, race, color, national or ethnic origin or handicap.

RESOURCE 6

SHORT-FORM CASE STATEMENTS

The Mission

To raise $4,000,000 for capital funding for major expansions of St. Jude Children's Hospital and University of Tennessee Medical Units for expanded pediatric and adult cancer research and clinical treatment. In MEMPHIS, NOW!

This Is the Goal

The attainments of St. Jude Children's Research Hospital in the field of clinical research into catastrophic children's diseases are recognized worldwide.

From a 17% cure rate in 1962, they have progressed to a 51% survival rate in the area of acute lymphocytic leukemia today.

The University of Tennessee Medical Units is currently expanding its own Cancer Research Center, with its thrust in the field of adult cancer. Construction plans envisage a multi-unit center, a headquarters complex, and a major expansion of its present West Tennessee Cancer Clinic.

Thus the goal: To provide $4,000,000 of capital funding to help make possible the seven-story addition currently under construction for St. Jude Children's Research Hospital, plus major expansion facilities to the U.T. Cancer Research Center. The result could be to establish Memphis as one of the preeminent adult and children's cancer centers in the world.

Cancer Must Be Stopped

Cancer remains one of the leading causes of death around the world. In the United States, it ranks second only to heart diseases as the nation's number one killer. With the progress in arresting heart, circulatory, and other major causes, cancer can assume an even greater percentage of deaths if not arrested. Some form of cancer will strike approximately 655,000 Americans in 1974. *Only one out of three* will be cured. And even closer to home, Tennessee reported 6,300 adult and childhood cancers last year. This figure includes 1,101 deaths in Memphis.

Success Can Influence Federal Funding

We are not being asked to raise *all* the money for this vast and continuing Memphis program. But community support will be vital in assuring federal funding in a number of areas. . . . The National Cancer Institute has received from U.T. an application for $4,600,000 as an initial grant. A site team recently visited officials of the Medical Units and a favorable impression was made. Other grants will be sought for both St. Jude and the Medical Units. The success of our Mission for Memphis can be highly influential in securing major grants in coming years.

The Important Economic Benefits to Our Mid-South Economy

The benefits in terms of human progress are apparent. But such a combination of effort can result in contributions to the Memphis and Mid-South economy that are truly impressive. We have been accustomed to rely on cotton, lumber, and heavy industry as our major bulwarks in the past for growth. The medical field has now surpassed these industries in our economic progress. The combined budgets of St. Jude and U.T. for 1974 is $38,400,000. By 1980 this figure is projected to be $75,000,000—with $40,000,000 of that figure devoted to cancer alone!

The Mission That Must Succeed

This is the Mission for Memphis: to show community support of one of the most important challenges ever presented to the business and civic leaders of our city. With the dedication and enthusiasm of those who have risen to the occasion in the past, this Mission for Memphis *cannot* and *must not* fail: Mission accomplished will mean for Memphis what Sloan Kettering means to New York, what the Mayo Clinic means to Rochester, and the M. D. Anderson Clinic means to Houston in the world of cancer research.

The Committee

SAM COOPER, Campaign Chairman
TOM HUTTON, Vice-Chairman
W. W. MITCHELL, Special Gifts Chairman
DON DRINKARD, Initial Gifts Chairman
JOHN F. CANALE, Vice-Chairman—Administrative
FRANK NORFLEET, Finance Committee
MILTON SIMON, PR Chairman

TEAM CHAIRMEN

E. F. BARRY	R. M. HUNT
JOHN F. CANALE	S. L. KOPALD, JR.
S. W. FRY	ALLEN MORGAN
M. M. GORDON	WILLIAM QUINLEN
WILLIAM H. GATCHELL	ALVIN WUNDERLICH, JR.

Headquarters: White Station Towers
5050 Poplar Suite 1402, Memphis, TN 38117
685-7860

Resource 6

Summary

1. THE MISSION

To raise $4,000,000 for capital funding of expanded major additions to St. Jude Children's Research Hospital for pediatric cancer and the University of Tennessee Medical Units Cancer Center for adult cancer.

2. THE NEED

To continue to fight against cancer with expanded research facilities and thereby improve chances for survival for both children and adults in Memphis and the Mid-South.

3. THE CHALLENGE FOR FEDERAL SUPPORT

Community response to this campaign can influence federal authorities, who are selecting fifteen or more cancer centers throughout the United States as part of a $750,000,000 program. Memphis *can* and *must* be selected as one of these cities.

4. THE PLUS FOR THE MID-SOUTH ECONOMY

By 1980 it is estimated that outside income for both of these institutions will approximate $75,000,000, of which $40,000,000 is to be spent on cancer research and treatment.

5. THE ULTIMATE GOAL

To help Memphis become one of the world's leading cancer research centers!

"Only Research Can Conquer Cancer"

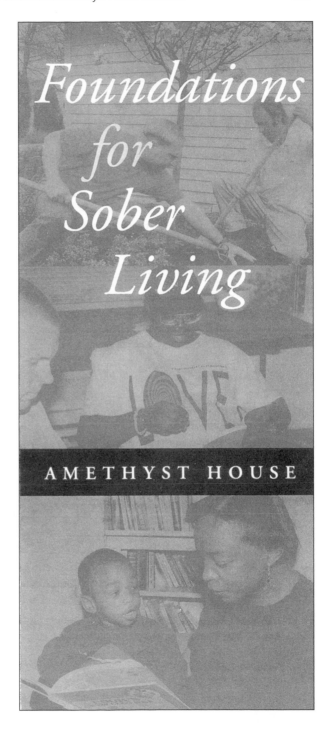

Foundations for Sober Living

AMETHYST HOUSE

Resource 6

Providing Dignity and Hope

Amethyst House: A Local Solution

Amethyst House is a nonprofit agency. We aim to empower men and women in ways that give them dignity, hope, and a healthier sense of themselves and their community as they recover from their addictions.

   We are currently involved in developing an extensive database that links criminal justice and treatment data on individuals involved in drug and alcohol abuse. This database will give treatment providers and criminal justice officials information on the kinds of treatments provided and their outcomes in order to make more effective and efficient treatment plans.

Services at Amethyst House

We run a transitional residential program in separate houses for men and women with their dependent children. Experienced case managers and support staff ensure an alcohol- and drug-free environment and provide a structured setting.

The Program Works!

In the past year:

- We provided residents 4,756 days in a safe and supportive environment.
- More than half of Amethyst House residents leave our houses earning a living wage and having support in the community.

We Need Your Financial Support

- In the new managed care environment, Indiana has reduced payments to all providers of addictions services.
- The rent we charge does not cover the cost of services we provide.
- Help us tap into additional federal funds. *HUD gives us $4 for every dollar donated.*

For more information about Amethyst House, please call (812) 226-2570.

Hope

is the thing with feathers—
That perches in the soul—
And sings the tune without words—
And never stops—at all—

Emily Dickinson

Please help us provide Amethyst House residents the opportunity to build new lives full of promise and optimism for the future.

Name _____

Address _____

_____

Phone _____

E-mail_____

Please accept my tax-deductible donation of:

☐ $25   ☐ $50   ☐ $75   ☐ $100

☐ $250   ☐ $500   ☐ Other amount _____

☐ I would like to donate the following goods or services to Amethyst House:

_____

☐ I can volunteer my time:

_____

Amethyst House

P.O. Box 11
Bloomington, IN 47402

Alcohol and Drug Addiction

A National Problem

- Burdens society with $150 billion in social, health, and criminal costs each year.

- Plays a role in one out of three failed marriages.

- Costs employers up to $100 billion in lost time, accidents, health care and workers comp costs and plays a role in 65% of all workplace accidents.

- Plays a role in 50% of all traffic fatalities, 86% of murders, and 72% of assaults and robberies.

Here in Monroe County

- More than 80% of jail inmates are behind bars for substance-related offenses.

- 65% of the homeless people served by Shelter, Inc., have chronic drug or alcohol addiction problems.

Helping People Rebuild Their Lives

Amethyst House offers:

Experience from playing a vital role in the Bloomington area community for over 17 years.

Strength from our partnership with the Center for Behavioral Health and United Way.

Hope of recovery from drug and alcohol addiction through our supportive living environment and program.

Community and Education Joining Forces to Ensure a Bright Tomorrow

What Is the Goal?

A community effort to raise $650,000 for the establishment of an Indiana University East Center in New Castle to serve the immediate needs of Henry County.

What Is Proposed?

The establishment of an Indiana University East Center in Henry County. The construction of a one-story, 4,100-square-foot education center to include classrooms, a computer laboratory, and space for a variety of services. The building will be an up-to-date instructional facility and can be expanded should future growth warrant.

Where Will the Center Be Located?

On Trojan Lane, adjacent to the Indiana High School Basketball Hall of Fame, on a site donated to the Henry County Community Foundation, Inc., by Ameriana Bank as its contribution to the IU East/Henry County Project.

Why Is It Needed?

Henry County, like many other rural Indiana counties, loses too many of its promising youth who go away to college and never return home. A center in Henry County will permit us to serve the postsecondary educational needs of our citizens without having to go elsewhere.

The new center will permit IU East to offer an expanded and enriched curriculum including Purdue University programs, both day and evening. Classes will not only be taught at the new center but also continue at New Castle High School.

IU East administrators project a doubling of enrollment at the Henry County Center within three to five years.

Not only will this help us keep our students at home, but it will have a significant impact on the county's economy.

An enhanced educational environment will aid in economic development. The quality of our schools, the availability of health care, the size and quality of our workforce, and the range of public services available are all key factors that potential new employers consider when they are looking to locate or to expand in Henry County.

The Henry County Center of IU East will be a source of pride for all our citizens.

What Is the Cost?

The construction cost is estimated to be $650,000. The site has already been donated.

How Will the Funds Be Raised?

By private gifts from the community. Individuals, businesses, and corporations will be asked to participate. Already the campaign is off to a great start. Two donors have stepped forward and pledged $250,000 as a matching gift. A third donor has given $150,000 and will match up to another $100,000! That means for every dollar we give, these donors will match it two for one. Example: If you give $1,000, the matching gifts will be $2,000, for a total of $3,000!

How Can I Help?

Gifts and pledges are welcome. Three-year pledges are encouraged so that everyone can do as much as they'd like to join our friends and neighbors in successfully funding this project.

How Will Donors Be Recognized for Supporting This Project?

Several naming opportunities are present. Classrooms may be reserved with a gift of $50,000. Twenty-four computers are needed to equip the computer laboratory, and each may be reserved with a $3,000 gift. Bricks forming the IU logo will also be incorporated into the landscape design. Large bricks are $300 and small bricks are $150. Gifts and pledges above $3,000 have special recognition within the building.

When Will Construction Begin?

Groundbreaking is scheduled for this summer. Given the excitement this project is generating, it is hoped that the gifts and pledges will be received quickly enough to have the building ready for occupancy in January 1999.

**Named Giving
Opportunities**

All donations above $3,000 to the IU East/Henry County Project will be permanently recognized with special significance within the building.

*Additional opportunities include,
but are not limited to:*

$50,000	To name a classroom
3,000	To purchase a computer for the computer lab
300	To purchase a large landscaping brick
150	To purchase a small landscaping brick

Despite its worldwide reputation, Indiana University has never lost sight of its core constituency. As a public university, IU's roots go deep into Indiana soil. We are here, first and foremost, to serve Hoosiers, and we take seriously our mission to provide quality education to all Indiana's citizens.

The way the community and university are working together to carry out that mission in Henry County is an expression of the Hoosier values we all hold so dear—open-handed generosity, commitment to community, hard work, and optimism about the future. The many volunteers who are leading the effort to build this new learning center exemplify these values.

I am enormously excited about this new initiative.

Myles Brand
President, Indiana University

For the past three years Indiana University East has provided educational opportunities on a limited scale to the residents of Henry County. It is an honor to be invited by the community to expand that role and at the same time advance the mission of Indiana University.

The construction of this new center is an indication of Henry County's strategic commitment to its residents and quality of life. IU East is proud to be a part of that commitment. Together we will provide the educational opportunities that will help secure a healthy and productive future for Henry County and the surrounding region.

David Fulton
Chancellor, IU East

The Committee

This campaign is endorsed by the Henry County Community Foundation, Inc., and the IU East/Henry County Advisory Board. Members of the Campaign Committee are:

Steering Committee

Carol Goodwin
Harry Bailey
Linda Wroblewski

Team Members

Noel Blevins
Dan Conway
Greg Crider
D. C. Danielson
Blake Dye
Libby Edwards
Maurie Goodwin
Nadine Kirkpatrick
Judy Melton
John Pidgeon
Mary Beth Van Arsdal
Larry Williams
Mary Alice Wilson
Doug Zimmerman

Headquarters

The Henry County Community Foundation, Inc.
112 South Main Street, 2nd Floor
New Castle, IN 47362
Phone (765) 529-2235

MARKET SURVEY MATERIALS

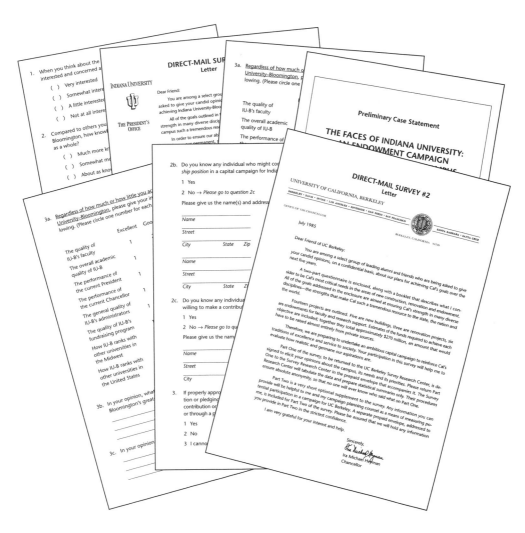

INDIANA UNIVERSITY BLOOMINGTON
ENDOWMENT CAMPAIGN

FACE-TO-FACE
MARKET SURVEY QUESTIONNAIRE

Before we address the questions in this survey, what association, if any, have you had with Indiana University Bloomington?

Over what period of time?

Has your association been satisfactory (pleasing)?

Who is your closest contact at Indiana University Bloomington?

When do you have occasion to see this person?

When did you last have a conversation with him or her?

1. When you think about the future of Indiana University Bloomington, how interested and concerned are you about its welfare?

   ( )   Very interested

   ( )   Somewhat interested

   ( )   A little interested

   ( )   Not at all interested

2. Compared to others you know who are associated with Indiana University Bloomington, how knowledgeable do you think you are about the University as a whole?

   ( )   Much more knowledgeable

   ( )   Somewhat more knowledgeable

   ( )   About as knowledgeable as most people I know

   ( )   Somewhat less knowledgeable

   ( )   Much less knowledgeable

3a. Regardless of how much or how little you actually know about Indiana University Bloomington, please give me your impression of each of the following.

	Excellent	Good	Fair	Poor	No Impression
A. The quality of IUB's faculty					
B. The overall academic quality of IUB					
C. The performance of the current president					
D. The general quality of IUB's administrators					
E. The quality of IUB's fundraising program					
F. How does IUB rank with other universities in the Midwest?					
G. How does IUB rank with other universities in the United States?					

3b. What area(s) stand out among its greatest strengths?

3c. What area(s) need improvement?

4. I would like to suggest some different ideas others have expressed. For each one, please indicate how much you agree or disagree.

	Agree Strongly	Agree Somewhat	Disagree Somewhat	Disagree Strongly
A. Unless IUB receives endowment funds, it will not be possible to maintain its standard of excellence				
B. Private funding is critical to meeting IUB's endowment goals				
C. Above all else, IUB's excellence depends upon the quality of its faculty				
D. It's up to the State of Indiana to provide most of the funding for building improvements at IUB				
E. Matching funds are important in encouraging private support				
F. Today, even private universities are very dependent upon government funding				

5. The University has set forth seven major areas of proposed improvements. Please tell me how important you consider each of the following proposed campaign projects at Indiana University Bloomington.

	Essential	Important but not Essential	Somewhat Important	Not Important
Faculty Support				
Student Support				
Library				
Technology				
Special Programs				
Executive Education Center				
Discretionary Funds				

6. Now, please indicate which you think deserves top priority, second priority, and third priority in the allocation of funds.

Faculty Support
Student Support
Library
Technology
Special Programs
Executive Education Center
Discrete Funds

1. _____

2. _____

3. _____

7. Are there any other campus needs and goals (not included in question 5) that you consider important?

   (   ) Yes   (   ) No

   If yes, what? _____

   _____

   _____

   _____

   _____

8a. In order to accomplish the goal outlined, private funds totaling approximately $224 million will be needed over the next three to five years. Please refer to the Table of Gifts which allows the number and size of gifts that are needed to meet these goals.

TABLE OF GIFTS NEEDED TO RAISE $224 MILLION.

Size of Gift	Number Needed	Total
$25,000,000	1	$25,000,000
15,000,000	1	15,000,000
10,000,000	3	30,000,000
5,000,000	7	35,000,000
2,500,000	10	25,000,000
1,000,000	25	25,000,000
500,000	50	25,000,000
100,000	100	10,000,000
50,000	250	12,500,000
Under 50,000,000	Many	21,500,000

8b. Do you consider this configuration of gifts to be feasible?

   (   ) Yes (Skip to 9a)   (   ) No (Skip to 8c)   (   ) Don't know (Skip to 9a)

8c. What is the *main* reason you feel that way? (Please check only one)

    1. _____ Because the dollar amount of the top gift levels is too high.

    2. _____ Because the dollar amount of most of the gift levels is too high.

    3. _____ Because the number of gifts required at the top gift levels is too high.

    4. _____ Because the number of gifts required at each level is too high.

    5. _____ Some other reason (Please explain): _____

    _____

    _____

    _____

    _____

    _____

    _____

8d. If no, then what dollar goal would you consider to be realistic?

9a. Do you think there are any reasons why Indiana University Bloomington *should not* undertake a major capital fundraising campaign at this time?

    ( ) Yes   ( ) No

9b. Please tell me the reason:

10. Are there other major fundraising campaigns that are currently vying for your support? If yes, what are they?

    ( ) Yes   ( ) No

    ( )   A fundraising campaign for another college or university

          (If so, which one(s)?) _____

          _____

          _____

          _____

          _____

          _____

    ( )   A fundraising campaign for a medical center or hospital

          (If so, which one(s)?) _____

          _____

          _____

          _____

          _____

          _____

    ( )   A campaign for an arts organization (If so, which one(s)?)

          _____

          _____

          _____

          _____

          _____

          _____

    ( )   Some other type of campaign? Please describe: _____

          _____

          _____

          _____

          _____

          _____

11. People have many different reasons for wanting to work for or make a significant financial contribution to a capital campaign. Which of the reasons listed below would provide the *strongest motivation(s)* for you personally to participate in such a campaign for Indiana University Bloomington?

   ( )   Loyalty to Indiana University Bloomington

   ( )   Well-documented needs and rationale

   ( )   Recognition for myself or another person I wish to honor

   ( )   Being part of a prestigious leadership group

   ( )   Being able to make an anonymous gift

   ( )   Having input in the setting of goals

   ( )   Having a major responsibility in the campaign

   ( )   Having a limited responsibility in the campaign

   ( )   Indiana University Bloomington's reputation as an educational institution

   ( )   Income tax considerations

   ( )   Some other reason, please describe:

   ( )   I probably would not be motivated to participate in a campaign for Indiana University Bloomington.

12. Were Indiana University Bloomington to launch a campaign, who would make a good volunteer chair for this effort? _____
_____

13. If asked, would you personally consider taking a leadership position in the campaign?

   ( ) Yes   ( ) No

14. Have you ever participated in any way in a major capital fundraising campaign for a non-profit organization?

   ( ) Yes   ( ) No

15. Do you know any individuals or organizations who you believe might be willing to make a contribution of $50,000 or more?

( ) Yes ( ) No

NAME   NAME

_____   _____

_____   _____

_____   _____

16a. While I am not here to present a solicitation proposal today, some sense of our own participation in this project is important to our study. If properly approached, would you personally consider making a significant contribution to Indiana University Bloomington?

( ) Yes (Ask 16b)   ( ) No   ( ) Don't know

16b. If you would, could you tell me where on the gift range chart you might fall?

17. Do you personally have ties to any corporations or foundations that might be willing to support a campaign for Indiana University Bloomington?

( ) Yes ( ) No (Please skip to question 18)

Corporation/Foundation   My relation to it is:

_____   _____

_____   _____

_____   _____

18. Do you have any specific suggestions to offer regarding any aspect of Indiana University Bloomington that we have not already discussed which you feel would assist us in preparing our report for IUB?

Resource 7

DIRECT-MAIL SURVEY #1
Letter

INDIANA UNIVERSITY   March 10, 1995

THE PRESIDENT'S
OFFICE

Dear Friend:

You are among a select group of leading alumni and friends who are being asked to give your candid opinion, on a confidential basis, about our plans for achieving Indiana University-Bloomington's goals over the next five years.

All of the goals outlined in the enclosed brochure are aimed at ensuring IUB's strength in many diverse disciplines—the strengths that make the Bloomington campus such a tremendous resource to the state, the nation, and the world.

In order to ensure our ability to meet the needs of our constituents, we need to enhance our permanent, stable base of support—the endowment. Increased endowment in the areas of faculty support and student aid, for both graduates and undergraduates, is required in addition to endowment support for our libraries. Support for special programs, technology enhancement, the Art Museum, and the creation of an Executive Education Center is also being considered.

Estimates of the funds required to achieve these objectives are included; together they total approximately $224 million, an amount that must be raised entirely from private sources. We are preparing to undertake an ambitious capital campaign to reinforce IU-Bloomington's traditions of excellence and service to society.

I would appreciate it if you took the time to answer the questions in the enclosed booklet regarding Indiana University-Bloomington. The information you provide will be helpful to me as a means of measuring potential participation in a campaign for the Bloomington campus.

Part One of the survey, to be returned to the IUB Survey Research Center, is designed to elicit your opinions about the campus, its needs and its priorities. Please return Part One to the Survey Research Center in the prepaid envelope that accompanies it. The Survey Research Center will tabulate the data and prepare statistical summaries only. Their procedures ensure absolute anonymity, so that no one will ever know who said what on Part One.

Part Two is a brief supplement to the survey. Any information you can provide will be helpful to me and my campaign planning counsel as a means of measuring potential participation in a campaign for Indiana University-Bloomington. A separate prepaid envelope, addressed to me, is included for Part Two of the survey. Please be assured that we will hold any information you provide in Part Two in the strictest confidence.

Bryan Hall 200
Bloomington, Indiana
47405-1201

(812) 855-4613
Fax (812) 855-9586

I am very grateful for your interest and help.

Sincerely yours,

Myles Brand
President

Preliminary Case Statement

THE FACES OF INDIANA UNIVERSITY: AN ENDOWMENT CAMPAIGN FOR THE BLOOMINGTON CAMPUS

INDIANA UNIVERSITY, BLOOMINGTON
January 1995

Introduction

In his book, *Being Lucky,* Herman B Wells wrote: *"A university can be distinguished only as its faculty is distinguished. . . ."*

Dr. Wells' vision contains a great truth: *It is the people of Indiana University that create this distinguished institution, whether they are first-rate faculty, bright graduate students, or sought-after undergraduates.* Indiana University has been such an institution for a very long time.

Indiana has always done more with less. It is quite remarkable—given limited funding—to see what Indiana University has achieved. For example, in recent years the *Gourman Report* (an objective, comprehensive rating of American universities) ranked 26 departments of the College of Arts and Sciences in the top 20 nationally. The School of Music has been ranked number one consistently in four independent surveys over a 20-year period, and *Business Week* places the School of Business seventh in the country. One of the ten best university art museums in the U.S. is right here, as is the thirteenth best university research library in all of the U.S. and Canada. The Schools of Journalism; Education; Library and Information Science; Public and Environmental Affairs; Law; Optometry; and Health, Physical Education and Recreation—all have programs that are among the best in the country in their respective disciplines. Their quality, and what they can do for their students, is increasingly threatened as resources become more scarce.

Indeed, while some surveys place IU in favorable company, others do not. The latest reports also show that faculty salaries, graduate student stipends, and student/faculty ratios at IU have all drifted to the bottom of the Big Ten. Dr. Wells also stated: *"So keen is the competition everywhere for outstanding faculty that they are difficult to secure, even for institutions with adequate resources; but for institutions such as ours, with limited revenues, the problem is unusually acute."*

The same is true for outstanding graduate students and undergraduates. In this competition with some of the best universities in the nation, we are losing as often as we are winning.

The State of Indiana has been generous within its means. In the 1950s it provided IU Bloomington with more than 50 percent of its total budget. Today, *only 26 percent* comes from the state. This change reflects the growing pressure our legislators and state leaders are under to meet other state needs in health care, social services, the schools, and the criminal justice system.

IU is no longer a state-supported university. Now, at best, it is a state-assisted university. It is clear: as we look to the future, we cannot build our strategy for shaping an even greater Indiana University by relying primarily on state support.

Indiana University must supplement fluctuating and uncertain funding with a steadier source of income. As Dr. Wells observed, *"Peaks of excellence are provided typically by private money."*

The program that now bears his name stands out as an example of how *private endowments* can affect the academic quality of the University. The Wells Scholars Program, created and endowed through a successful fundraising campaign, brings 20 of the nation's best and brightest undergraduates each year to the Bloomington campus. These students have turned down full scholarships to universities such as Harvard, Yale, and Michigan. The high caliber of these young scholars, and the other talented students they attract, has had a positive influence on the entire student body.

Endowments are among the best assets a university can use to build and maintain long-term quality. Endowments mean money invested for future growth, with only a portion of the return being used today. Investment returns that exceed the amount needed for distribution are reinvested to add to the growth of the fund. Endowments therefore provide stable, dependable sources of financial support, protected from the uncertainties of state funding, the economy, tuition, or other factors. Endowment funds give the University the ability to retain and recruit great professors; to provide competitive stipends for the next generation of teacher/scholars—graduate students; to attract more undergraduates like the Wells Scholars; and to build strong library collections and furnish modern technology for these talented people to use.

By building Indiana University's endowment now, we seek to strengthen our ability to serve future generations of Hoosiers, as well as people across the country and around the world. IU's traditions, its history, its core values, all lead us to embrace and renew the University's strong commitment to the ideals of a *public* university: one that daily touches all our lives and helps all members of our community reach their potential.

To realize fully all these possibilities, we seek your financial assistance. We propose to embark upon a $224 million endowment campaign—a campaign that is about people and the tools they need to succeed. What follows are brief descriptions of the priority areas where funding is critical to the future well-being of our University.

Faculty Support

Faculty are the heart of any great university. As teachers and mentors, in classrooms and through one-on-one projects, they guide students through the best that has been thought, said, written, and discovered. As scholars and artists, they help assure that knowledge and ideas live, grow, adapt.

State funds, which help pay faculty salaries and benefits, constitute a diminishing share of IU's support. To compensate, we turn to fundraising—and endowments.

Chairs and professorships are among the most important resources any university can have in assembling and maintaining a distinguished faculty. Such positions provide honor and recognition for the faculty members who hold them, of course. But they provide something more important: stable, dependable sources of income for special teaching and research materials, library acquisitions, salary supplements, and travel assistance, protected from the vicissitudes of state funding, the economy, fee income, or other factors. They are an insurance policy for our excellence.

Indiana University is lagging far behind its peers in establishing these valuable assets. IU has 19 faculty endowments with market values of $1 million or more. Among Big Ten schools alone, Michigan has nearly 100 such endowments; Minnesota has 223.

In appointing faculty to endowed positions, we seek to retain and recruit scholars, scientists, and artists who help set the standards in their disciplines. And we expect each to set another standard: distinction in research, distinction in teaching, and commitment to the University community.

Goal: $84 million

Graduate Student Support

As a top public university in a higher education system that is the envy of the world, IU provides an incomparable range of resources to the state and country. This success is directly tied to our graduate programs (IU has more than any other institution in the state), and particularly to the interactions between students and faculty. Graduate students are the life force of academia and innovations for the future. They come here to assist faculty in research and teaching, bringing new and creative ideas. They help open doors of learning to thousands of undergraduate students; they participate in the discovery and dissemination of new knowledge.

Unfortunately for us, the competition for new graduate students, especially at the PhD level, is intense. Our stipends for fellowships, and teaching and research assistantships, just are not adequate to meet basic living expenses. The most promising graduate students will go to the universities that can offer them sufficient compensation to allow them to devote themselves entirely to study, research, and teaching. We cannot allow Indiana University to fall behind in its ability to attract the best and brightest graduate students, and thereby jeopardize our overall strengths. The links are clear: outstanding faculty attract outstanding graduate students; both participate in the education of undergraduates.

Goal: $29.5 million

Undergraduate Student Support

As the costs of higher education rise, more and more good students are forced to delay or abandon their degree goals, or take on very heavy debts. Over the past decade, as state funds have diminished, tuition increases have taken their place. At the same time, federal assistance for undergraduates has dramatically declined. Students increasingly must borrow to pay the costs of their schooling. Within the last six years, the loan portion of the typical student aid package has jumped from 49 percent to 70 percent. If these trends continue, we risk pricing students out of the education they deserve. When only prosperous families can afford higher education, we will have helped to create a permanent underclass that cannot add value to the economy of the future.

Endowed funds can provide scholarships to help undergraduates stay on a more productive track. These funds will be used especially for students who work part-time to finance their educations. Keeping these students enrolled at IU and making progress toward their degrees is important to the future of Indiana. The large majority of undergraduates, especially those already working, remain to pursue their careers in the states where they earn their degrees. Endowments can help IU students make better academic and career progress and help prevent a "brain drain" of the best young minds.

Goal: $22.3 million

Libraries

When your purpose is acquiring, transmitting, and preserving knowledge, you can only be as good as your information source: your libraries. The success of our teaching, research, and service programs depends on outstanding library collections, high quality information services, and talented personnel. In a world exploding with information, the Libraries enrich learning and scholarship by bringing faculty and students in touch with the resources they need to answer questions, to solve problems. These capabilities are shared by thousands of individuals and businesses across Indiana and the nation, for whom the Libraries serve as a vital resource.

As one of the top teaching and research collections in the world, the Bloomington Libraries are recognized for distinguished holdings in many fields, innovative services, important participation in national cooperative programs, leadership in the use of technology, and valuable contributions to professional research. But this excellence is challenged by the escalating cost and diversity of information; the need to invest in new technology; the demand for librarians and staff with a wide variety of subject, language, and computer skills; and a requirement for modern facilities.

Endowments for the collections will enable the expanded purchase and preservation of books, journals, and the rich electronic resources so central to the work of students and faculty. Endowments for specialized librarian positions will make the Libraries more competitive in the recruitment and retention of experienced professionals and provide the resources to enhance their work. And support for technology equipment and electronic services will enhance dramatically the ability of our students and faculty to take advantage of extraordinary information opportunities.

Goal: $8.5 million

Special Programs and General Endowments

Each school and department has unique needs that do not fit under a simple heading of faculty endowments, scholarships, or technology needs. Many schools have responded to their faculty or students by creating programs that meet a special need. For example, a program in the College of Arts and Sciences is attempting to prepare its students for the workplace by offering classes taught jointly by liberal arts and School of Business faculty.

Or the School of Education, which has created programs to foster new thinking in teacher education. Or the School of Health, Physical Education and Recreation, which is investigating new measures and improvement of human performance. Or the School of Library & Information Science, which hopes to build an observational laboratory to study how people interact with new technology. This is the type of creative programming that has marked Indiana University as a great university in the past. Endowments will ensure it continues.

Goal: $25.65 million

Technology

Two things are certain about IU and technology. First, needs will increase as the role of technology increases and diversifies throughout society. Second, opportunities for students, faculty, and the public will also expand. Communication networks will bring enormous amounts of information to the student's or the professor's fingertips while carrying IU's vast resources to the public.

We must prepare our students for a world increasingly dominated by sophisticated information technologies. Information-seeking and information-management skills must become integral parts of our students' educations. Further, to maintain our prominence in teaching and research, the University must provide access to global networks that will enhance students' and faculty's learning.

For example, in the School of Journalism, students no longer can rely on a sharp pencil and a clean notebook. New communication equipment has reshaped the journalism major. Technology also has reshaped the future of the business student, for whom international communication may be a way of life. Interactive TV and distance learning equipment will be necessary to prepare these students, but it will not come cheaply—nor will the vital scientific equipment needed by students in the College of Arts and Sciences to perform relevant research.

But perhaps nowhere do we become more aware of technology's effect on academia than in the University library system. Electronically connecting IU students and faculty to the vast network of international databases is an exciting vision. And the IU Library System also serves all of the citizens of Indiana, and indeed the nation.

Efforts to create a technology environment are expensive. An interactive university requires major investments for classrooms, learning centers, and libraries.

Goal: $26.5 million

IU Art Museum

Among the best university art museums in the country, this facility brings important international exhibitions, publications, and treasures of the global art community to the people of Indiana. A successful endowment campaign will help keep this jewel in the University's crown polished by supporting new acquisitions, conserving current holdings, planning educational programs, and mounting exhibits.

The excellence of the Museum staff, the quality and depth of the collections, and the leadership roles the staff have taken within the larger Museum community all attest to the Museum's level of excellence.

One of our faculty members recently wrote to the chair of the Museum's advisory board expressing sadness that we live in a time where so many people focus on the differences among human beings. He wrote that the Museum's collection "bears witness to the common desires that all people in all times have had to touch the eternal, to seek the beautiful, and to express their experience of this mystery we call life." This endowment would help us meet those aspirations, those desires.

Goal: $10.8 million

Executive Education Center

As the IU School of Business extends its mission to include life-long partnership with business, it must dedicate more resources to serving the needs of practicing professionals. The Executive Education program was created to meet this need. Upper management professionals from national and international business come to the IU Bloomington campus 38 weeks a year. They participate in stimulating programs designed to refresh their educational background, learn how to work in teams, resolve conflict, increase productivity, discuss international business, and many other topics.

As the program has grown, so have housing, space, and technology needs. Currently, meeting and hotel space are relegated to wherever space allows in Bloomington or Indianapolis. Often, only outdated equipment is available in these hotel meeting rooms. To meet the growing demands of the program, the School proposes to renovate an existing building on the Bloomington campus. The new Executive Education Center would have 50 hotel rooms, office space for the staff, adequate meeting rooms, and state-of-the-art audio-visual equipment.

Goal: $10 million

Chancellor's Initiatives

Organizations require discretionary funds to pursue new opportunities. Flexible resources free leaders to expand organizational reach or fund special one-time projects. IU faces these very demands. Circumstances arise after budgets are set. Urgent needs and great opportunities require immediate action.

As a public institution, IU operates with a fixed, two-year budget. Yet the campus chancellor must be able to move quickly and decisively when there is an opportunity to provide seed money for a promising program, to develop the interdisciplinary work which opens new fields of learning, to assist a new faculty member at the start of her career, to help a student through an emergency. The chancellor's fund will provide this vital flexibility.

Goal: $7.5 million

As the campaign proceeds, the University may discover other targets of opportunity as well. When possible, gifts will also be sought where specific donor interests coincide with special campus programs, such as the Indiana University Press and WFIU public radio.

SUMMARY OF PRELIMINARY OBJECTIVES FOR A BLOOMINGTON CAMPUS CAMPAIGN BY UNIT AND PURPOSE (IN MILLIONS OF DOLLARS).

	Faculty Support	Student Support	Library	Special Programs	Tech	Art Museum	Facilities	Unrestricted Funds	Total by Unit
Art Museum						10.8			10.8
Business	24.3	6.0		4.0	7.0		10.0		51.3
Chancellor's Fund								7.5	7.5
College of Arts & Sciences	25.0	11.0		12.0	7.5				55.5
Continuing Studies		0.3		0.1					0.4
Education	3.0	3.0		6.0					12.0
Health, Physical Education, & Recreation	1.2			1.3					2.5
Journalism	1.0	1.5			1.0				3.5
Law	5.0	8.0	2.0						15.0
Library	6.0	6.0	6.0	2.0	11.0				25.0
Music	10.0	20.0							30.0
Library & Information Science	1.0			.25					1.25
Public & Environmental Affairs	7.5	2.0	0.5						10.0
Total by Purpose	84.0	51.8	8.5	25.65	26.5	10.8	10.0	7.5	224.75

TABLE OF GIFTS NEEDED TO RAISE $224 MILLION.

Size of Gift	Number Needed	Total
$25,000,000	1	$25,000,000
15,000,000	1	15,000,000
10,000,000	3	30,000,000
5,000,000	7	35,000,000
2,500,000	10	25,000,000
1,000,000	25	25,000,000
500,000	50	25,000,000
100,000	100	10,000,000
50,000	250	12,500,000
Under 50,000,000	Many	21,500,000

Resource 7

QUESTIONNAIRE, Part 1

SURVEY OF LEADING ALUMNI AND FRIENDS

INDIANA UNIVERSITY–BLOOMINGTON

Center for Survey Research
1022 East Third Street
Indiana University
Bloomington, IN 47405

Before you complete this questionnaire, please read the packet titled *"The Faces of Indiana University: An Endowment Campaign for the Bloomington Campus."* Some of the questions in this survey will refer to information in the packet.

Feel free to add notes if you think an answer might be unclear or require more explanation.

As soon as you finish filling out the questionnaire, please mail it back to the Center for Survey Research in the enclosed prepaid envelope.

1. When you think about the future of Indiana University–Bloomington, how concerned are you about its welfare? (Please circle one number.)

   1 Very concerned

   2 Somewhat concerned

   3 A little concerned

   4 Not at all concerned

2. Compared to other people you know who are associated with Indiana University–Bloomington, how knowledgeable do you think you are about the campus as a whole? (Please circle one number.)

   1 Much more knowledgeable

   2 Somewhat more knowledgeable

   3 About as knowledgeable

   4 Somewhat less knowledgeable

   5 Much less knowledgeable

3a. <u>Regardless of how much or how little you actually know about Indiana University–Bloomington</u>, please give your impression of each of the following. (Please circle one number for each item.)

	Excellent	Good	Fair	Poor	No Impression
The quality of IU-B's faculty	1	2	3	4	5
The overall academic quality of IU-B	1	2	3	4	5
The performance of the current President	1	2	3	4	5
The performance of the current Chancellor	1	2	3	4	5
The general quality of IU-B's administrators	1	2	3	4	5
The quality of IU-B's fundraising program	1	2	3	4	5
How IU-B ranks with other universities in the Midwest	1	2	3	4	5
How IU-B ranks with other universities in the United States	1	2	3	4	5

3b. In your opinion, what areas stand out among Indiana University–Bloomington's greatest strengths?

_____

_____

_____

3c. In your opinion, what areas need improvement?

_____

_____

_____

> The next set of questions refers to information in the packet *"The Faces of Indiana University: An Endowment Campaign for the Bloomington Campus."* If you have not already done so, please read the packet <u>before</u> answering the next few questions.

4. Below is a list of ideas others have expressed. For each one, please indicate how much you agree or disagree. (Please circle one number for each item.)

	Strongly Agree	Somewhat Agree	Somewhat Disagree	Strongly Disagree
Unless IU-B receives endowment funds, it will not be possible to maintain its standards of excellence	1	2	3	4
Private funding is critical to meeting IU-B's endowment goals	1	2	3	4
Above all else, IU-B's excellence depends upon the quality of the faculty	1	2	3	4
Today, even private universities are very dependent on government funding	1	2	3	4
It's up to the State of Indiana to provide most of the funding for building improvements at IU-B	1	2	3	4
It's up to the State of Indiana to provide most of the funding for technology improvements at IU-B	1	2	3	4
Matching funds are important in encouraging private support	1	2	3	4

5a. The University has set forth several major areas of proposed improvements in the packet materials. Please indicate how important you consider each of the following proposed campaign projects at Indiana University–Bloomington. (Please circle one number for each item.)

	Essential	Important but not Essential	Somewhat Important	Not Important
Art Museum	1	2	3	4
Executive Education Center	1	2	3	4
Faculty support	1	2	3	4
Graduate student support	1	2	3	4
Library	1	2	3	4
Technology	1	2	3	4
Special programs	1	2	3	4
Undergraduate student support	1	2	3	4
Unrestricted funds	1	2	3	4

5b. Please indicate which area from question 5a you think deserves top priority, second priority, and third priority in the allocation of private gift funds.

1 _____

2 _____

3 _____

6. Are there any other campus needs and goals (not included in question 5a) that you consider important?

1 Yes → If yes, what are they? _____

_____

_____

2 No

Resource 7

In order to accomplish the goals outlined in the enclosed preliminary case statement, private gift funds totaling approximately $224 million will be needed over the next three to five years. Please refer to the Table of Gifts below which suggests the number and size of gifts that are needed to meet these goals.

TABLE OF GIFTS NEEDED TO RAISE $224 MILLION.

Size of Gift	Number Needed	Total
$25,000,000	1	$25,000,000
15,000,000	1	15,000,000
10,000,000	3	30,000,000
5,000,000	7	35,000,000
2,500,000	10	25,000,000
1,000,000	25	25,000,000
500,000	50	25,000,000
100,000	100	10,000,000
50,000	250	12,500,000
Under 50,000,000	Many	21,500,000
	Total	$224,000,000

7a. Do you consider this configuration of gifts to be realistic? (Please circle one number.)

   1 Yes → *Please go to question 8*

   2 No → *Please go to question 7b*

   3 Don't know → *Please go to question 8*

7b. What is the *main* reason you feel this way? (Please circle one number.)

   1 Because the dollar amount of the *top* gift levels is too high

   2 Because the dollar amount of *most* of the gift levels is too high

   3 Because the number of gifts required at the *top* levels is too high

   4 Because the number of gifts required at *each* level is too high

   5 Some other reason (Please describe): _____

   _____

   _____

7c. What dollar goal would you consider to be realistic?

8. Do you think there are any reasons why Indiana University–Bloomington should not undertake a major capital fundraising campaign at this time?

    1 Yes → *If yes, please describe:* _____

    _____

    _____

    2 No

9a. Are there other major fundraising campaigns that are currently vying for your support?

    1 Yes

    2 No → *Please go to the instructions in Box 1*

9b. If yes, what are they? (Please check all that apply.)

    ___ 1 A fundraising campaign for another college or university.

        If so, which one(s): _____

        _____

        _____

    ___ 2 A fundraising campaign for a medical center or hospital.

        If so, which one(s): _____

        _____

        _____

    ___ 3 A campaign for an arts organization. If so, which one(s):

        _____

        _____

        _____

    ___ 4 Some other type of campaign. (Please describe.)

        _____

        _____

        _____

Resource 7

> *Box 1*
> *In order to compare the opinions of different groups of people, we would like some information about you. Please answer as many of the following questions as you can, knowing that all the data you provide will be treated in strict confidence.*

10a. Did you ever attend Indiana University–Bloomington?

    1 Yes

    2 No → *Please go to question 11a*

10b. How long were you enrolled at Indiana University–Bloomington? (Please circle one number.)

    1 Less than one year

    2 At least one year, but less than two

    3 At least two years, but less than three

    4 At least three years, but less than four

    5 At least four years, but less than five

    6 At least five years, but less than six

    7 Six years or more

11a. Did you ever attend any other college or university?

    1 Yes

    2 No → *Please go to the instructions in Box 2*

11b. Which other colleges or universities did you attend?

_____

_____

_____

> *Box 2*
> *If you never attended a college or university, please go to question 15.*
> *If you have attended a college or university, continue with question 12.*

12. When you were in college, at Indiana University–Bloomington or elsewhere, in which school or college did you complete the majority of your degree work? (Please circle one number.)

    1 I did not have a major

    2 Allied Health

    3 Business

    4 College of Arts & Sciences

    5 Continuing Studies

    6 Education

    7 Health, Physical Education & Recreation

    8 Journalism

    9 Law

    10 Library & Information Sciences

    11 Music

    12 Nursing

    13 Optometry

    14 Public & Environmental Affairs

    15 Social Work

    16 Other (Please describe): _____

13a. Did you pursue graduate studies either at Indiana University–Bloomington or elsewhere? (Please circle one number.)

    1 Yes, at Indiana University

    2 Yes, at another college or university

    3 No → *Please go to question 14a*

13b. What was your field of specialization? (Please circle *all* numbers that apply.)

1 Biology	14 Languages
2 Business	15 Law
3 Chemistry	16 Mathematics
4 Communications	17 Medicine
5 Computer Science	18 Music
6 Dentistry	19 Optometry
7 Education	20 Political Science
8 English	21 Psychology
9 Environmental Programs	22 Public Affairs
10 Health, Physical Education & Recreation	23 Religious Studies
	24 Sociology
11 History	25 Theater & Drama
12 Jewish Studies	26 Other (Please describe):
13 Journalism	_____

14a. Have any members of your family, other than yourself, ever attended Indiana University–Bloomington?

1 Yes

2 No → *Please go to question 15*

14b. What members of your family? (Please circle one number for each item.)

	Yes	No
1 Parent	1	2
2 Child	1	2
3 Spouse	1	2
4 Brother or sister	1	2
5 Grandchild	1	2
6 Some other relative	1	2

Resource 7

15. Where is your principal place of residence? (Please circle one number.)

    1 Northern Indiana   7 Southwest U.S.

    2 Southern Indiana   8 Great Plains

    3 Indianapolis area   9 Midwest

    4 East Coast   10 Southeast U.S.

    5 West Coast   11 Northeast U.S.

    6 Northwest U.S.   12 Other (Please describe):

        _____

16. How old were you on your last birthday? (Please circle one number.)

    1 Under 35

    2 35–44

    3 45–54

    4 55–64

    5 65–74

    6 75 or older

17. What is your gender?

    1 Male

    2 Female

18. What was your approximate household income (before taxes) in 1994?
    Please include income from all sources. (Please circle one number.)

    1 Under $30,000

    2 $30,000–$49,999

    3 $50,000–$99,999

    4 $100,000–$199,999

    5 $200,000–$499,999

    6 $500,000 or higher

19. Have you ever participated in any way in a major capital fundraising campaign for any college, university or other organization?

    1 Yes

    2 No

20. Would you consider participating in a future fundraising campaign (by working in the campaign and/or making a gift) for Indiana University–Bloomington?

    1 Yes

    2 No

21. Please use the space below to tell us anything else you think we should know about your feelings regarding the proposed campaign.

    _____

    _____

    _____

    _____

    _____

    _____

    _____

    _____

    _____

    _____

    _____

Thank you for your help. Please return this questionnaire to The Center for Survey Research in the prepaid envelope provided.

We would appreciate it if you would take a few minutes to complete Part Two of this survey. The information you can provide will be very helpful.

QUESTIONNAIRE, Part 2

SURVEY OF LEADING ALUMNI AND FRIENDS

INDIANA UNIVERSITY–BLOOMINGTON

President Myles Brand
Indiana University
P.O. Box 500
Bloomington, IN 47402

Volunteer leadership and private gift support are essential to the success of a campaign to meet Indiana University–Bloomington's needs. In order to give us a preliminary indication of the level of interest in supporting a campaign, please take a few minutes to complete this survey.

Most of these questions ask about personal interest in providing leadership or financial support to a fundraising effort. In addition, if you know other individuals, foundations or corporations that you believe might consider participating in a campaign, we would appreciate knowing about them as well. Any information you give us will be extremely helpful.

PLEASE return this form in the enclosed prepaid envelope addressed to President Myles Brand. DO NOT return it to the Center for Survey Research with your larger questionnaire.

You need not put your name on this form, but you are welcome to do so. The information you provide here will be held in strictest confidence by the President and his development counsel. It cannot be linked to the information you provided in Part One.

Again, thank you very much for your help.

1. People have many different reasons for wanting to work for or make a significant financial contribution to a capital campaign. Which of the reasons listed below would provide the *strongest motivation(s)* for you personally to participate in such a campaign for Indiana University–Bloomington? (Please circle one number for each item.)

	Yes	No
Loyalty to Indiana University–Bloomington	1	2
Well-documented needs and rationale	1	2
Recognition for myself or another person I wish to honor	1	2
Being part of a prestigious leadership group	1	2
Being able to make an anonymous gift	1	2
Having input in goal setting	1	2
Having a responsibility in the campaign	1	2
Indiana University–Bloomington's reputation as an educational institution	1	2

Resource 7

	Yes	No
Income tax considerations	1	2
Believe it is important to emphasize the tradition of giving within the community	1	2
Believe non-profit organizations are the most efficient way to solve society's problems	1	2
Enjoy giving to organizations that are supported by my social network	1	2
Give out of a sense of obligation and gratitude	1	2
Believe it is my moral obligation to give back to non-profit organizations	1	2
Enjoy giving as a way to achieve personal development and self-fulfillment	1	2
Feel it is important to emphasize the tradition of giving within my family unit	1	2

Some other reason (Please describe): _____

_____

I probably would not be motivated to participate in a campaign for Indiana University–Bloomington.	1	2

Sometimes Indiana University–Bloomington alumni and others who support the University have helped us by providing names of corporations, foundations or individuals who might be interested in participating in a fundraising campaign.

2a. Do you personally have ties to any corporations or foundations that might be willing to support a campaign for Indiana University–Bloomington?

1 Yes

2 No → *Please go to question 2b*

Please give us the name(s) and address(es) in the space below.

Corporation/Foundation   Your Relationship or Connection

_____   _____

_____   _____

_____   _____

2b. Do you know any individual who might consider taking a volunteer *leader-ship position* in a capital campaign for Indiana University–Bloomington?

1 Yes

2 No → *Please go to question 2c*

Please give us the name(s) and address(es) in the space below.

Name	*Name*
Street	*Street*
City *State* *Zip*	*City* *State* *Zip*
Name	*Name*
Street	*Street*
City *State* *Zip*	*City* *State* *Zip*

2c. Do you know any individuals or organizations who you believe might be willing to make a contribution of $50,000 or more?

1 Yes

2 No → *Please go to question 3*

Please give us the name(s) and address(es) in the space below.

Name	*Name*
Street	*Street*
City *State* *Zip*	*City* *State* *Zip*

3. If properly approached, would you personally consider making a contribu-tion or pledging $50,000 or more to Indiana University–Bloomington? The contribution or pledge could be paid outright over the next three to five years or through a planned gift (e.g., trust, bequest). (Please circle one number.)

1 Yes

2 No

3 I cannot make a commitment at this time

4a. If asked, would you personally consider taking a volunteer leadership position in the campaign?

1 Yes

2 No → *Please go to question 5*

4b. On which of the following committees would you most like to work in a leadership capacity? (Please circle one number.)

1 National committee

2 State committee

3 Local committee

4 Other (Please describe): _____

5. Please use the space below to give us any comments about the proposed campaign or any other aspects of this effort.

_____

_____

_____

_____

You need not put your name on this form, but you are welcome to do so. The information you provide here will be held in strictest confidence by the President and his development counsel. It cannot be linked to the information you provided in Part One.

_____
Your Name

_____
Street

_____
City   *State*   *Zip*

_____
Telephone (Please include area code)

Thank you again for your help. Please return this part of the survey to President Brand in the prepaid envelope provided.

DIRECT-MAIL SURVEY #2
Letter

UNIVERSITY OF CALIFORNIA, BERKELEY

BERKELEY · DAVIS · IRVINE · LOS ANGELES · RIVERSIDE · SAN DIEGO · SAN FRANCISCO   SANTA BARBARA · SANTA CRUZ

OFFICE OF THE CHANCELLOR   BERKELEY, CALIFORNIA   94720

July 1985

Dear Friend of UC Berkeley:

You are among a select group of leading alumni and friends who are being asked to give your candid opinions, on a confidential basis, about our plans for achieving Cal's goals over the next five years.

A two-part questionnaire is enclosed, along with a booklet that describes what I consider to be Cal's most critical needs in the areas of new construction, renovation and endowment. All of the goals addressed in the enclosure are aimed at ensuring Cal's strength in many diverse disciplines—the strengths that make Cal such a tremendous resource to the state, the nation and the world.

Fourteen projects are outlined. Five are new buildings, three are renovation projects, six are endowments for faculty and research support. Estimates of the funds required to achieve each objective are included; together they total approximately $270 million, an amount that would have to be raised almost entirely from private sources.

Therefore, we are preparing to undertake an ambitious capital campaign to reinforce Cal's traditions of excellence and service to society. Your participation in this survey will help me to evaluate how realistic and germane our aspirations are.

Part One of the survey, to be returned to the UC Berkeley Survey Research Center, is designed to elicit your opinions about the campus, its needs and its priorities. Please return Part One to the Survey Research Center in the prepaid envelope that accompanies it. The Survey Research Center will tabulate the data and prepare statistical summaries only. Their procedures ensure absolute anonymity, so that no one will ever know who said what on Part One.

Part Two is a very short optional supplement to the survey. Any information you can provide will be helpful to me and my campaign planning counsel as a means of measuring potential participation in a campaign for UC Berkeley. A separate prepaid envelope, addressed to me, is included for Part Two of the survey. Please be assured that we will hold any information you provide in Part Two in the strictest confidence.

I am very grateful for your interest and help.

Sincerely,

Ira Michael Heyman
Chancellor

QUESTIONNAIRE, Part 1

SURVEY OF LEADING ALUMNI AND FRIENDS

UNIVERSITY OF CALIFORNIA, BERKELEY

Survey Research Center
University of California
Berkeley, CA 94720
I.D. # _____

CONFIDENTIAL   CONFIDENTIAL

> - Before you complete this questionnaire, please read the booklet titled "Preliminary Statement of Goals for a Proposed Capital Campaign." Some of the questions in this questionnaire refer to information contained in the booklet.
> - Please *do not* write your name anywhere on this questionnaire. The number will help tell the Survey Research Center who has returned their questionnaire and who needs reminder letters. But no one will ever know who said what.
> - Feel free to add notes if you feel an answer might be misleading or require more explanation.
> - As soon as you finish filling out the questionnaire, please mail it back to the Survey Research Center in the enclosed prepaid envelope.

1. When you think about the future of the University of California, Berkeley, as a whole, how interested and concerned are you about its welfare?

   1 ☐ Very interested

   2 ☐ Somewhat interested

   3 ☐ A little interested

   4 ☐ Not at all interested

2. Compared to most people you know, how knowledgeable do you think you are about UC Berkeley as a whole?

   1 ☐ Much more knowledgeable

   2 ☐ Somewhat more knowledgeable

   3 ☐ Somewhat less knowledgeable

   4 ☐ Much less knowledgeable

   5 ☐ About as knowledgeable as most people I know

3. Regardless of how much or how little you actually know about UC Berkeley, please give us your impression of each of the following. *(PLEASE CHECK ONE BOX FOR EACH.)*

	Excellent 1	Good 2	Fair 3	Poor 4	No Impression 5
A. The quality of UC Berkeley's faculty	☐	☐	☐	☐	☐
B. The overall academic quality of UC Berkeley	☐	☐	☐	☐	☐

C. The performance
   of the current
   Chancellor ☐ ☐ ☐ ☐ ☐

D. The general quality
   of UC Berkeley's
   administrators ☐ ☐ ☐ ☐ ☐

E. The quality of UC
   Berkeley's fundraising
   program ☐ ☐ ☐ ☐ ☐

THE NEXT QUESTIONS REFER TO INFORMATION IN THE BOOKLET "PRELIMINARY STATEMENT OF GOALS FOR A PROPOSED CAPITAL CAMPAIGN." IF YOU HAVE NOT ALREADY DONE SO, PLEASE READ THE BOOKLET BEFORE YOU ANSWER THE NEXT QUESTIONS.

---

4. Below is a list of different ideas some people have expressed. For each one, please indicate how much you agree or disagree.

	Agree Strongly 1	Agree Somewhat 2	Disagree Somewhat 3	Disagree Strong 4
A. Unless UC Berkeley receives capital improvement and endowment funds, it will not be possible to maintain its standards of excellence	☐	☐	☐	☐
B. *Private* funding is critical to meeting UC Berkeley's building and endowment goals	☐	☐	☐	☐
C. Above all else, UC Berkeley's excellence depends upon the quality of its faculty	☐	☐	☐	☐
D. Today, even private universities are very dependent on government funding	☐	☐	☐	☐
E. It's up to the State of California to provide most of the funding for building improvements at the University of California's various campuses	☐	☐	☐	☐

5. Below is a list of the three major areas of proposed improvements at UC Berkeley. In each column, please check *one and only one* box, indicating which of these areas you think deserves top priority, second priority, or lowest priority in the allocation of funds. Please do not check two in the same column, even if you think two areas are almost equally important.

	Top Priority	Second Priority	Lowest Priority
	1	2	3
A. New buildings and facilities	☐	☐	☐
B. Renovation of existing buildings and facilities	☐	☐	☐
C. Academic enrichment	☐	☐	☐

6. Now please tell us how important you consider each of the following proposed campaign projects at UC Berkeley. (These projects are briefly described in the companion booklet.)

	Essential	Important but not essential	Somewhat important	Not important
	1	2	3	4
BUILDINGS				
A. Biological Sciences Complex	☐	☐	☐	☐
B. Business School	☐	☐	☐	☐
C. Chemistry Building	☐	☐	☐	☐
D. Computer Science Building	☐	☐	☐	☐
E. Faculty Housing	☐	☐	☐	☐
F. Law School Renovation	☐	☐	☐	☐
G. Music Additions	☐	☐	☐	☐
H. Student Services Building	☐	☐	☐	☐
I. Other (*PLEASE DESCRIBE:* _____ _____ _____)	☐	☐	☐	☐

Resource 7

ENDOWMENTS

J. Faculty Chairs ☐ ☐ ☐ ☐

K. Humanities Institute ☐ ☐ ☐ ☐

L. Latin American Studies ☐ ☐ ☐ ☐

M. Moorea Biological
Station ☐ ☐ ☐ ☐

N. Soviet Studies ☐ ☐ ☐ ☐

O. Cal Futures Fund ☐ ☐ ☐ ☐

P. Other (*PLEASE
DESCRIBE:* _____

_____

_____) ☐ ☐ ☐ ☐

In order to accomplish the goals outlined in Question 6, private funds totalling approximately $270 million will be needed over the next three to five years. Please refer to the Table of Gifts below which shows the number and size of gifts that are needed to meet these goals.

TABLE OF GIFTS NEEDED TO RAISE $270 MILLION.

Gift Amount	Number of Gifts Needed	Total
$20,000,000	2	$40,000,000
15,000,000	2	30,000,000
10,000,000	3	30,000,000
5,000,000	6	30,000,000
2,500,000	10	25,000,000
1,000,000	20	20,000,000
750,000	30	22,500,000
500,000	40	20,000,000
250,000	75	18,750,000
100,000	100	10,000,000
Under 100,000	Many	23,750,000
	Total	$270,000,000

CAMPAIGN VOLUNTEER LEADERSHIP: A DISCUSSION OF ROLES, RESPONSIBILITIES, AND POSSIBILITIES

◆

PREPARED BY:

JIM SMITH

VICE PRESIDENT, RESOURCE DEVELOPMENT

UNITED WAY OF CENTRAL INDIANA

Solutions For People®
UNITED WAY OF CENTRAL INDIANA

May 1999

Introduction

Throughout its 80-year history, United Way of Central Indiana (UWCI) has accomplished its mission thanks in large measure to countless volunteers from all walks of life. Committed to improving the quality of life for all local residents, each volunteer's contribution is valued. But the most visible role of all UWCI volunteers during the annual campaign is that of the Annual Campaign Chair.

Those invited to chair the campaign are chosen because they are well known, have a high degree of respect and credibility throughout central Indiana, are proven leaders, and have the capability to bring or leverage greater contributions of volunteers and dollars.

This is a discussion of general concepts and specific tasks involved in chairing a successful United Way annual campaign. The first section reviews the role of the Leadership Giving Chair, which is typically the role a prospective Annual Campaign Chair assumes in preparation for becoming overall chair.

Leadership Giving Chair

Successful leadership giving (contributions of $1,000 and up) is the primary reason UWCI campaign totals are increasing, though the total number of United Way donors has been declining. During the 1990s, the number of leadership givers nearly doubled, from 2,656 in 1990 to about 5,000 in the 1998 campaign. Therefore, the Leadership Giving Chair is a crucial member of United Way's Campaign Cabinet.

Our leadership giving strategy is twofold: (1) to increase the numbers of leadership givers and (2) to advance current leadership givers to higher levels.

To accomplish these objectives, we must increase the number of personal solicitations—especially of qualified prospects outside the workplace—and ask for three-year pledges of increasing amounts.

The Leadership Giving Chair is instrumental in implementing these strategies through various means.

Personal Leadership

The Chair should set an example for volunteers and donors by making a personal leadership giving commitment and by calling on prospects and donors just as other committee members will.

Volunteer Recruitment

The Chair identifies and recruits volunteers to serve on the Leadership Giving Council (LGC). Current leadership givers or those capable of giving at leadership levels are sought. Each member is asked to personally solicit individual leadership gifts from five to seven others.

Overseeing the Process

The Chair convenes and leads meetings of the LGC to ensure that prospects are properly identified, assigned, and solicited on a timely basis. Two subcommittees report to the Chair. Each has two meetings: a prospect rating and assigning meeting at the beginning of the campaign and a final report meeting.

LGC I is aimed at prospects and donors at the $5,000 level and up. It begins in May and ends in July.

LGC II moves donors at the $2,500 to $4,999 level to higher levels. It begins in August and ends in October.

Meetings and Events

Participation by the Leadership Giving Chair at meetings and events is an effective way to get an overall perspective of the campaign. Out of respect for your schedule, we have identified times at which the Chair's presence is most critical and preferred.

Event or Meeting	Date	Chair's Presence
Campaign Cabinet Meetings	Monthly (1999 dates attached)	Highly preferred
Leadership Giving Council (I & II)		
Rating and Screening	May, August	Critical
Report Meeting	July, October	Critical
Alexis de Tocqueville Reception	Varies	Critical
Wine, Art, and Roses	June 20	Preferred
Pacesetter Kickoff	July 29	Preferred
Pacesetter Report Meeting	August	Preferred
Day of Caring	September	Preferred
Platinum Plus Party	October	Critical
Press Conference— Final Campaign Figure	December	Highly preferred

Relationship with Staff

UWCI's director of major and planned giving is your staff contact. On some occasions, UWCI's President or Vice President for Resource Development will be in contact with you.

As lead staff, the director of major and planned giving

- Proposes overall strategy for the campaign
- Provides materials for Leadership Giving Council Meetings
- Accompanies the Chair or LGC members on prospect visits
- Maintains records on results of calls
- Drafts correspondence for the Chair
- Schedules the Chair for meetings and other events
- Performs other duties at the Chair's request

Annual Campaign Chair

Few other volunteer roles equal the level of personal involvement and investment that is required of UWCI's Annual Campaign Chair. But individuals who have served in the position say that while the pressures and responsibilities are great, the rewards are even greater.

Volunteer Recruitment

The Chair's first and most important task is to recruit Campaign Cabinet members by mid-February. The Campaign Cabinet is composed of approximately 15 to 20 individuals who each have responsibility for a specific segment of the campaign. These are the individual contributors whose combined efforts ensure the campaign's success. They should be in a position of community influence, able and willing to open doors and attract attention to United Way's cause.

CEO Calls

In the spring, the Campaign Chair is asked to personally visit as many of the top 60 companies who support United Way campaigns as possible. To expedite the process, UWCI's President and top Campaign Cabinet members will make some of the calls. Typically, discussion at the visits includes the corporate gift and a goal for the company's employee campaign. An individual CEO gift might also be discussed. Existing relationships and the desired objective for each company will influence who makes the call. Companies with the greatest potential for growth in either corporate or employee support and large companies not currently participating in the UWCI campaign get priority.

Overseeing the Process

We rely on the Chair to implement a process to ensure that the complex structure of volunteers, staff, and companies stays on track throughout the campaign. Campaign Cabinet meetings are the traditional means of evaluating our progress, but the Chair should be prepared to offer extra encouragement to keep volunteers motivated and on track, as needed.

Meetings and Events

In addition to monthly Campaign Cabinet meetings, the Chair should make every effort to be available for other important campaign events. United Way staff will work with the Campaign Chair to establish protocol for scheduling the Chair for events, particularly with strategic companies requesting an appearance by the Campaign Chair. Out of respect for your schedule, we have identified times at which the Chair's presence is most critical and preferred.

Event or Meeting	Month	Chair's Presence
Campaign Cabinet Meetings	Monthly	Critical
Executive Roundtable for United Way Campaign Chairs	February	Critical
UWCI Board Meetings	February, May, July, October, December	Highly preferred
Alexis de Tocqueville Reception	Varies	Critical
Wine, Art, and Roses	June	Highly preferred
Pacesetter Kickoff	July	Critical
Day of Caring (Campaign Kickoff)	September	Critical
Platinum Plus Party	November	Critical
Press Conference— Final Campaign Figure	December	Critical

Opening Doors

We must broaden our base of support to ensure long-term growth of United Way resources. The Campaign Chair can be instrumental in either personally visiting or facilitating visits by others with decision makers in companies that have at least

50 employees and do not currently participate in the Annual Campaign. Volunteers and staff in the New Business Development segment of the campaign are trained to identify such businesses, but they may need help in getting access to the right person for an opportunity to present United Way's story. Past Campaign Chairs have been instrumental in gaining access to larger employers and have joined in some visits.

Relationship with Staff

The Director of the Annual Campaign is the staff liaison with the Campaign Chair, though there is often significant contact with other staff, most notably the United Way President and Vice President for Resource Development.

Enhanced Resources

Each Campaign Chair brings to the position unique and potential resources that can greatly enhance our success. United Way is often asked by individuals who are preparing to chair the campaign for suggestions of ways in which they might promote increased giving and involvement. Given your position as the Chairman Emeritus of the most important and influential company in our area, you bring some unique opportunities and the capacity to enable UWCI to accomplish a number of objectives. For example, UWCI has lagged behind other similarly sized cities in attracting megagifts ($100,000 and up) to the annual campaign. Although your own megagift commitment is to the UWCI endowment, you are now uniquely positioned to effectively pursue such commitments as you have personally made such a commitment yourself. Among other opportunities to which new resources could be committed are aggressive advertising to heighten the profile of UWCI throughout the six-county area and initiatives in specific market segments with high potential and low involvement. These are just several examples, and others will be developed as the 1999 campaign runs its course and opportunities for growth in 2000 are identified.

We respectfully request that you consider providing $_____ that would be used to fund these critical initiatives. As you know, our objective is to implement strategies that will result in reaching a $40 million campaign by 2001. While it would certainly be ambitious, reaching that level in the 2000 campaign presents an exciting opportunity that would not only be historic but also set UWCI on a course of success for the next century.

Resource 8

RESOURCE 9

ANNUAL CAMPAIGN VOLUNTEER'S KIT

How to Run a Peak Performance Campaign That Impacts Our Community

Congratulations on being appointed Employee Campaign Coordinator for your organization's United Way of Central Indiana campaign! Your job is critical to our community's success because the funds you raise help improve the lives of thousands of central Indiana people every day. Your efforts positively impact our community by helping meet community needs, making central Indiana a better place to live, work and prosper.

This guide is designed to show you how to achieve outstanding results in your campaign. Use it as a tool to plan and execute your campaign.

Good luck, and remember we're all counting on you to run a successful campaign.

The Keys to Success

Here's what United Way givers tell us about peak performance campaigns. There are specific factors which help the workplace/United Way partnership perform up to its potential—helping both the employer and the employee meet the challenges facing our community.

Information, please! During a United Way campaign, there is no such thing as information overload! The more employees know about the solutions made possible by their gift, the more generous they are!

Motive matters. When employees are asked to participate in the United Way campaign with too little information about "why," it harms the company's relationship with its employees. And it also harms the community. People who have no opportunity to focus on the compelling human services reasons to give are less likely to give generously.

Create a winning team. We suggest you recruit other people to help you make your campaign a success. We realize the composition of your committee will have a lot to do with the size and capabilities of your company, but these job descriptions will help you figure out your lineup. And remember, the more active committee members you have, the more opportunities there are to spread the work around so no one person has to do it all.

Receive respect. Employers who support workplace campaigns and model leadership in positive ways can earn respect and appreciation from their employees.

Best results. Research demonstrates that peak performance campaigns are those that ensure that employees see and hear the campaign materials available, coupled with a positive and supportive campaign atmosphere provided by company leadership.

1 Here's an Example of a Winning Team

CEO, President or General Manager
- Endorse the campaign.
- Ask top management for contributions.

Campaign Coordinator
- Develop goal and campaign plan including determining what Benchmark Campaign Techniques will be used (Benchmark Campaign Techniques are listed on the back of this booklet).
- Assist CEO in top management solicitation.
- Attend and speak at employee briefings.
- Act as liaison with United Way staff.

Assistant Campaign Coordinator
- Coordinate execution of campaign plan.
- Organize the Employee Campaign Committee.
- Arrange employee briefings.
- Monitor results and help collect pledges.

Employee Campaign Committee
Involve people from all levels and divisions of your organization.
Suggested committee members include:

Marketing/Public Relations Representative
- Develop campaign promotion and publicity.
- Plan and coordiate year-round United Way communications.
- Put together entry and application for United Way's Communicator Awards contest.

Finance/Payroll Representative
- Develop payroll deduction procedures.
- Prepare personalized pledge cards.
- Collect completed pledge cards from ambassadors.
- Provide ongoing tabulations to track results *(United Way has software that can do this for you. See Step 7 for details.)*

Personnel Representative
- Recruit ambassadors.
- Plan and organize ambassadors' training.
- Schedule and plan employee briefings and agency tours.
- Work with United Way to develop volunteer projects throughout the year.

Labor Union Representative (if applicable)
- Endorse and support the campaign.
- Attend and speak at employee briefings.

Senior Management Representative
- Coordinate leadership giving campaign among top managers.

Ambassadors (one for every ten employees)
- Attend training sessions(s).
- Organize and/or attend employee briefings.
- Meet one-on-one with assigned co-workers to respond to questions and ask for pledges.
- Collect pledges and report results.

2 Get Top-Level Support

When you run an employee campaign, look to the top for support. Encourage the CEO/senior manager of your organization to personally endorse your United Way employee campaign. This sends a powerful message of support and concern for the community.

Ask your CEO/senior manager to:

- Endorse and promote campaign objectives and goals.
- Continue supporting or join the Key Club for leadership contributors of $1,000 or more.
- Approve time for training, employee briefings, agency tours and special events.
- Schedule a meeting with management staff to secure their support and involvement.
- Attend employee briefings to make a personal endorsement.
- Endorse the campaign in a letter to all employees. Sample letters targeted to specific employee groups that your CEO can use to endorse the campaign are in the back of this kit. The letters may be used as written, or you can tailor them to your company's circumstances.

3 Analyze Past Campaign Plans

Talk to last year's campaign volunteers and Campaign Manager about the previous campaign. Look for strengths, weaknesses and opportunities. Find out . . .

- The composition and structure of last year's committee
- The type of communications, special events and promotions used
- The campaign timetable

Review the previous year's giving and analyze . . .

- Total amount pledged
- Number of employees
- Number of payroll deduction givers
- Number of Key Club ($1,000 and above) givers
- Number of givers by department or level (i.e., finance department, or hourly, labor, management and salary)

This important market research will help you learn how you might improve. Call your United Way Campaign Manager for a copy of your company's giving history.

4 Set a Challenging Campaign Goal

Setting a realistic and challenging goal is an important step. Your United Way Campaign Manager or Loaned Associate may already have a personalized plan and recommendations for a successful campaign to present to you.

There are many different ways to set a goal. You and your committee, along with your United Way representative, can work together to select one that is right for your organization.

Strive to Earn the Coveted "A Company That Cares" Award

Something you might want to strive for in your campaign is the coveted "a company that Cares" award. Last year, over 250 companies earned this prestigious award, which symbolizes community leadership. They were honored at United Way events, in newspaper ads, and in other printed materials.

Leadership Giving

One way to make sure your company reaches its goal is to establish strong leadership giving up-front. Leadership givers donate $1,000 or more and receive special recognition from United Way as Key Club members.

Before the general campaign, have the CEO or upper management conduct executive/management solicitation early to set the pace for the rest of the company. Potential Key Club members can come from anywhere in your organization; however, we recommend that you encourage anyone with a salary of $50,000 or more to become a member of United Way's Key Club.

Key Club members receive special benefits, including a lapel pin and a listing in United Way's Key Club Directory to show they are concerned community leaders. In addition, they are recognized at special United Way receptions.

Key Club Giving Levels

Silver Key . . . . $1,000 to $2,499
Gold Key . . . . $2,500 to $4,999
Platinum Key . . . . $5,000 to $9,999
Alexis de Tocqueville . . . . . $10,000 and more

Please be sure to ask your United Way representative for some of the special materials that we have for leadership giving solicitation.

Here's What Your Company Needs to Do
to Become "A Company That Cares"

Your organization must reach a goal agreed upon by a company representative and a United Way campaign manager. This can be a monetary or participation goal.

The organization must complete eight of thirteen United Way Benchmarks you will obtain from your UWCI Campaign Manager. A company with fewer than 50 employees need only complete six. A first-time employee campaign must complete five.

Stick with the Peak Performance Campaign Techniques listed on the back cover of this booklet and your company can become "a company that Cares." Ask your United Way Campaign Manager or Loaned Associate for an application.

5 Choose Strategies and Messages That Will Work at Your Company

There are many different ways to ask your fellow employees to support United Way. You need to make sure that your employees are well informed about United Way and know that the dollars they donate will be used wisely to help people here in central Indiana. You can educate them in a variety of ways:

- *Show them.* Take small groups of employees or key individuals on a tour of two or three agencies. Put together a group of employees and have a Day of Caring, where they volunteer at an agency and see firsthand how their contributions can touch lives and touch our community.
- *Inform them.* Ask a fellow employee who has benefited from a United Way agency to share his or her story with other employees. You can use the survey with the camera-ready art pages of the Campaign Kit to help locate these people.

You also can schedule an agency speaker to talk to employee groups about the needs that are being met and the people that are being helped because of contributions to United Way.

And in our electronic age, you certainly should consider using the communications capabilities available in many companies today. In the back of this kit is a selection of e-mail messages. Also, many of the campaign materials can be found on our web page.

Two other effective ways to inform employees are employee briefings and the personal ask. Briefings are a quick, efficient way to educate and solicit employees in small groups, while the personal ask is a one-on-one approach. Consult your United Way Campaign Manager or Loaned Associate about which method may be appropriate for your organization.

Employee Briefings

Conducting employee briefings allows everyone to hear the same message about United Way. These meetings should only take 20 to 30 minutes. Be sure you emphasize the key messages about United Way in your meetings. Remember, well-informed contributors are more likely to offer and increase gifts.

How to Get Started

1. Meet with your United Way Campaign Manager or Loaned Associate.
2. Arrange for data, place, entertainment, publicity, etc.
3. Schedule a United Way video, agency speaker, and anything else you might need at the meetings.
4. Schedule time for attendance at meetings by departments, branches, etc.
5. Get the word out! Publicize the meetings so everyone knows about them and wants to come.

The Meeting

1. Top management (and union leaders when applicable) endorse the campaign and acknowledge the organization's commitment to United Way. (5 min.)
2. Show United Way video. (5 min.)
3. Have a short personal talk by a Torchbearer, an employee who has benefited from a United Way agency, or an agency speaker. (5 min.)
4. Employee Campaign Coordinator announces the company's campaign goal, explains incentive programs and how to fill out the pledge card (and donor choice card if applicable). (5 min.)
5. United Way Campaign Manager or Loaned Associate is available to answer questions. (3 min.)
6. Employees turn in pledge cards at the end of the meeting.

Group meetings are flexible and can be adapted to the needs of the organization. To arrange for an agency speaker or additional information, call your Campaign Manager or the United Way Logistics Department, (317) 921-1379.

Personal Ask

The personal ask allows for contributions to be solicited one-on-one by a peer. This allows for everyone's concerns and objections to be addressed on an individual basis.

1. Choose ambassadors who are enthusiastic about United Way to approach employees one-on-one and explain how United Way touches lives and touches our community. Remember, the best givers make the best askers.
2. Work with your United Way Campaign Manager or Loaned Associate to educate ambassadors about United Way of Central Indiana. Ambassadors should be well versed in United Way's key messages.
3. Schedule agency tours for all ambassadors.
4. Personalize pledge cards.
5. Send an endorsement letter to all employees from top management (and labor representative when appropriate).
6. Confirm personal contact with all employees by ambassadors. Make it fun by having a contest for ambassadors who are the first to turn in pledge cards for their assigned employees.
7. Direct follow-up on employees who are absent, retirees, part-time employees and telecommuters.

Key Messages

The following key messages should be communicated to potential contributors. These messages will help them understand why they would want to build the community through United Way.

- United Way provides Solutions For People by supporting proven programs that deliver positive changes.
- United Way is your expert partner . . . constantly researching community needs to improve people's lives.
- You can accomplish more through United Way than you can on your own.
- United Way allows you to have the greatest impact on the community . . . combining your gift with over 100,000 others.
- United Way makes your caring count by focusing on the greatest needs and providing real solutions.
- United Way is extremely efficient. 90%* of your contribution will directly provide Solutions For People . . . only 10% will be used for operating costs.
- United Way demonstrates what's being accomplished.
- United Way's goals for central Indiana are . . .
    Children and Youth will succeed.
    Families and Neighborhoods will be healthy and safe.
    People will have a second chance.
    Seniors will not be alone.

*The recognized industry average is 75%.

6 Train Ambassadors

Depending on the method of asking you choose, the ambassadors can assist during group meetings, follow up with employees who are absent during the meetings or personally solicit them.

Ambassadors are very important to the campaign team. They should be natural leaders, well liked and respected by fellow employees. Recruit key representatives from each department and employee group, making sure to involve labor groups when appropriate. Choose one ambassador for every 10 employees. Make sure they are educated about United Way and its member agencies and know the key messages that will convince people to support United Way. They need to be ready to answer questions, and they need to be enthusiastically committed to serving.

Use United Way training tools and staff members to help prepare volunteers. Remember, videos, materials and agency tours are available.

Here are some basics you'll want to include in your ambassador training program:

- Endorsement of United Way by the CEO/senior manager and labor leadership where appropriate.
- Explanation and review of campaign literature, including information on key messages and tips on how to make a successful solicitation.
- Education about United Way and its member agencies using:
    Campaign video
    Agency tour
    Agency speaker or Torchbearer
    Other United Way programs
- Department captains sharing successes.

7 Promote and Educate

Take advantage of every opportunity to promote the campaign and create enthusiasm. This section lists themes, special event ideas and other resources to make your campaign educational and fun.

Giving Clubs

One of the best ways to make people feel good about giving to United Way is to create giving clubs that recognize employees for their support. Name your club as it relates to your workplace, such as "The Quality Club," and start recognition levels at $500. Publish the names of everyone who joins in the company newsletter. This is a great way to raise morale.

Great Campaign Ideas

Here are some examples of how companies throughout central Indiana have made their campaign fun and successful with events and contests. Use these as inspiration and, who knows, maybe your company will be listed here next year!

Bank One/NBD. Employees at these banks who gave at or above a certain level were rewarded with eight hours that they could use volunteering in the community any way they wished. Between the two banks, over 9,000 community service hours were contributed.

Thomson Consumer Electronics. Try a reverse tour. Children from Mt. Zion and Crossroads Rehabilitation Center visited Thomson to trick-or-treat for Halloween. Employees provided candy and prizes for the children. The children provided smiles.

Special Events

Have fun with your campaign by using special events to promote giving. It's also a great way to raise additional funds for your campaign over and above the annual gifts. Here are some examples:

- Exhibition game with Boys and Girls Clubs
- Friendship jamboree
- Goofy Olympics
- Jingle contest about United Way
- Silent auction
- Talent show
- Crazy tie contest
- Bake sale
- Garage sale
- Flower sale
- Lip-sync contest
- Employee breakfast served by management
- Inter-departmental contests
- Costume party
- Dunk tank
- Children's poster contest
- Car wash
- Golf outing
- Box lunch auction
- Funniest home video contest
- Competitive golf tournament with other companies

Ask your United Way Campaign Manager to provide you with even more ideas, or come to one of the ECC training dates listed on the back if you can. There, you can take a workshop specifically for campaign special events.

Resource 9

Roche Diagnostics. One of the busiest days at Roche Diagnostics (formerly Boer-hinger Mannheim) was the day the Goodwill truck came. One day during the campaign Goodwill brought out a truck so Roche employees could make donations on site. They filled four trucks!

Roche also held an intranet auction the enabled all employees to bid on items through the company's intranet.

Eli Lilly and Company. Used United Way's Day of Caring to encourage new hires to participate in their campaign. In return for making a pledge, each new hire was allowed to participate in Day of Caring and spend a day volunteering at a United Way agency. This showed them the importance of community involvement and the partnership between Eli Lilly and Company and United Way.

Rolls-Royce Allison. Held a summer activity fair. They invited agencies who had summer programs and asked them to bring enrollment forms. The parents were able to see the available programs and enroll their children on the spot. The same idea can be used for a targeted need. For example: child care, elder care, and exercise programs.

Meridian Insurance. Designated one day a week during their campaign month as United Way Casual Day. In addition, their campaign included a craft sale where employees sold their own creations. Each participant was charged a table fee in order to display their homemade items, and many crafters contributed a percentage of their total sales to United Way.

American United Life. Held a "United Way Beach Blast '98" agency fair. It was held in one of their auditoriums which was decorated with flamingos and miniature beach balls. The campaign committee members wore safari hats as they distributed pledge cards to employees and gave out ice cream and popsicles.

IUPUI. Held a Chili for Charity event where employees, students and community members voted on the best chili. The winners had their name engraved on the coveted "Chili for Charity" pot. In addition, there was a haunted conference room complete with all the spooky decorations, tarot card readers, raffles and music.

Campaign Resources

Free resources are available to help you run a better campaign. Your United Way Campaign Manager or Loaned Associate can help you determine which ones are appropriate for your company.

Resource 9

Since thousands of companies are planning their campaigns at the same time, please try to request campaign materials and speakers at least *two weeks in advance.* For tours, fairs and workshops, *three weeks' notice* is appreciated.

United Way Videos. A variety of United Way videos are available.

Speakers. United Way speakers, called Torchbearers, are available to speak at your company. Make arrangements two to three weeks before your meeting.

Day of Caring Volunteer Projects. One way to encourage people to contribute is to have them spend a day volunteering at a United Way agency. United Way has a Day of Caring at the beginning of the campaign where thousands of volunteers from hundreds of companies spend a day volunteering. UWCI can also arrange for a separate Day of Caring for your company if you choose. Call (317) 921-1212 for more information.

Your Fellow Employees. One of your best campaign resources may be there at your company—your fellow employees. If you can find someone at your company who has been helped by a United Way agency and is willing to tell his or her story, either in employee briefings or in your company newsletter, you have an excellent way to demonstrate the benefits of a United Way contribution to fellow employees.

Tours. Agency tours give potential contributors an opportunity to see United Way contributions at work firsthand. Tours take less than two hours and can be arranged to accommodate employees' schedules. Please call (317) 921-1379, three weeks in advance, to make arrangements.

Brochure. The campaign brochure is designed to give employees a quick look at how United Way touches lives and touches our community.

Targeted Brochures. Special brochures are available for new employees, labor, retirees and residents of Boone, Hamilton, Hancock, Hendricks and Morgan counties.

Communication Materials. Other materials have been prepared to help you tell the United Way story better. There are articles, statistics and other items you can distribute to employees to better educate and inform them. Camera-ready art pages of this Campaign Kit are ready to be used creatively in your printed materials or on bulletin boards. Also, check United Way's web page (www.uwci.org) for many of these materials.

Software. United Way has software you can use to make tracking your campaign a breeze. It will allow you to track contributions and print personalized pledge cards and other data you'll need to complete reports. If you're interested in finding out more about this software, call your Campaign Manager.

More Ideas

- Keep the contents of the United Way employee briefing a secret to generate curiosity and excitement. Then, don't disappoint—fill the room with goodies, balloons and fun!

- A great way to kick off your campaign or say thank you at the end is with an ice-cream social. If you can't have employees come to a central area, you can take the show on the road! Load a cart with ice cream and take it to the different departments.

- Take pictures of representatives from different departments looking their most stressed. Hang these pictures in a central location with containers by each picture. People can vote for their favorite stressee at a quarter a vote. The person with the most votes gets a small gift from the company. The quarter votes go to UWCI.

- "That can't be my boss!" Why not let members of your senior management showcase their talents? Have a talent show, lip-sync contest or comedy night featuring upper management. Employees can vote for best, worst and most original performance in return for a $1 donation to United Way.

- Take your campaign high-tech. If your company has e-mail, try an e-mail trivia contest. Ask questions about United Way every day, and have people e-mail their answers to the ECC. The department with the most correct answers wins a pizza party.

- Conduct a "Plus Two" campaign by asking everyone to increase their pledge by $2 per pay period. Give special recognition to those who increase their pledge.

- Design a web page for your employees who want to know more about UWCI and its member agencies.

---

8 Implement Your Campaign Plan

Now is the time to pull the plan off the drawing board and put it to work! All successful campaigns contain these elements:

Strategic Timing. Schedule the campaign when it is most convenient for your company. Remember, the quicker your campaign finishes, the better the results will be and the better people will feel about the process.

Call your UWCI Campaign Manager if you'd like to conduct your campaign at a different time of year.

Pledge Cards. Personalize all pledge cards with employees' names and the previous amount pledged.

Retirees. Include retirees in your campaign.

Payroll Deduction. Promote use of payroll deduction on employee pledge cards.

Employee Briefings and Solicitation. Conduct employee briefings or personal solicitation to build momentum and interest. The campaign should be short and intensive. Strive for completion in two weeks or less.

Follow-Up. Make sure every employee has been asked to contribute.

9 Wrap Up the Campaign and Report Results

We encourage you to complete your campaign by the end of October. Please follow these steps after the campaign is over.

1. Return and account for all pledge cards.
2. Fill out the Key Club Giving Report.
3. Fill out the front of the campaign report envelope. Make a copy for your files. Include the Key Club Giving Report, the United Way copy of the pledge card, direct bill and cash pledge cards, cash and checks, and donor choice cards. All cash, checks and donor choice cards must be attached to the appropriate pledge card.
4. Fill out the Benchmark Survey and return it inside your envelope.
5. Keep the payroll copy of the payroll deduction pledge cards. Turn them in to the company's payroll office. Be sure to check whether the submitted report is partial or final. Record only the amount being turned in when presenting a partial report. United Way will keep the cumulative total for your company's campaign.
6. Attach all donor choice cards to the corresponding pledge cards.
7. Please submit all pledge cards, donor choice cards, Key Club listings, etc., in the appropriate envelope. This allows United Way to thank donors in a timely fashion. Partial envelopes can be submitted as often as you like. United Way will keep the cumulative total for your company. Call your UWCI Campaign Manager or Loaned Associate to pick up your envelopes.

8. Submit your company's "a company that Cares" award application. If you qualify, your company will receive a beautiful sculpture piece for the lobby and special recognition in the media and at special events. Ask your United Way Campaign Manager or Loaned Associate for an application.
9. Submit your company's Communicator Awards application and be recognized for the activity you used to achieve success.

10 Thank You

Develop a program to thank and recognize everyone who volunteered and contributed to United Way. Some ideas include

- Cookies and punch reception
- Pizza party
- Thank you note, card or e-mail from CEO
- Hand-shaking tour
- Special bulletin boards
- A day at a park or zoo

Peak Performance Campaign Techniques Checklist

Follow these tried and true campaign techniques, and you're sure to have campaign success.

Organize for success   Date

Recruit a campaign committee with organizationwide representation.   _____

Recruit and train key employees to follow up on the solicitation process.   _____

Work with a UWCI representative to set meaningful campaign goals.   _____

Promote leadership giving

Conduct a Key Club campaign.

Host an event to thank Key Club members throughout the organization.   _____

Conduct an educational campaign

Invite a UWCI representative to conduct a briefing meeting for
all employees.   _____

Show the United Way video.   _____

Distribute the UWCI brochure to educate and refer people
to useful services.   _____

Use personalized pledge cards.   _____

Allow your employees to see UWCI agencies, firsthand, via tours, fairs
and seminars.   _____

Create excitement and say "thank you"

Conduct an internal kickoff event.   _____

Encourage employee participation in United Way Day's of Caring.   _____

Offer incentives to employees related to your campaign goals.   _____

Conduct an event to thank contributors.   _____

Solutions For Peopl℮ ®
UNITED WAY OF CENTRAL INDIANA

UNITED WAY OF CENTRAL INDIANA

Campaign Solutions

Inspirational ideas that will supercharge your company campaign

Table of Contents

◆

Note: Due to space considerations, portions of this booklet were left out.

Preface

Campaign Solutions is a guide to conducting a creative, effective, entertaining and exciting United Way campaign. This book is a collection of the best ideas that have been used by experienced Employee Campaign Coordinators (ECC) from companies located in the central Indiana area. You will find campaign tips that suit your organizational atmosphere, company size and budget.

Your ideas don't have to end with *Campaign Solutions.* What do you think will work best for your company? Get your co-workers involved and ask for their ideas. You might be surprised at the many possibilities!

Of course, no United Way campaign is complete without a direct ask for personal gifts, preferably through payroll deduction. However, special events can make your campaign easier and help generate teamwork and enthusiastic employees. This can also be a fun way to educate your employees about how their gifts impact the health and human service needs of our community.

United Way of Central Indiana appreciates your efforts in organizing your company's campaign and thanks you for helping to make our community a better place to live!

Employee Meetings

"HOW TO GET 'EM THERE AND GET 'EM IN THE SPIRIT"

Meetings are the perfect venue for presenting information about United Way of Central Indiana to the largest number of people at one time. Here are a few tips for successful meetings.

- Hold United Way meetings on company time and combine the United Way meeting with a regularly scheduled staff or safety meeting. Take the meeting to the employees. Instead of having it in a conference room, why not bring it out into the work area?
- Invite the department head or CEO to say a few words in support of the campaign.
- Have a prize drawing at the end of the meeting by exchanging tickets for completed pledge cards. Make sure this is publicized in advance.
- Arrange to have employees share their experiences of United Way services they've received or of agency tours they've been on with other employees. Take pictures to share at your meeting.

- Smaller meetings involving departments usually work better than a mass meeting for hundreds of people. You can establish more personal contact in a smaller group.
- Large flip charts (or slides) will help to communicate some of the details, like pay periods and giving clubs, more effectively.
- Providing a United Way pin for each employee will help spread the word to others.
- Torchbearers and Agency Speakers are an excellent way to spice up a company meeting. Speakers are available for both educational and inspirational topics. The length of each speech varies from five to twenty minutes. Be sure to publicize the speakers ahead of time.
- Utilize videotapes in meetings. Several different VHS-format videos are available for use in small or large company meetings. Copies of the campaign video and "Celebrate Living" are available.

Themes

"CREATING A CAMPAIGN PERSONALITY"

Campaigns with themes can be very successful. They increase enthusiasm and give the campaign a "personality." Following are some ideas that may be applicable to your company's campaign.

The Big Shot

Great for hospitals or health care professionals. Many campaigns use large thermometers to monitor campaign progress. Instead of the standard thermometer, use a picture of a hypodermic needle.

Pieces of a Large Dollar Bill

Create a large size dollar bill. Cut it into the same number of pieces as there are employees. Distribute the pieces to each employee to be returned for a completed pledge card and/or contribution. At the end of the campaign, all the pieces of the dollar bill puzzle will come together.

United Way Cookie Caper

Use the slogan "United Way Cookie Caper: Help Us Bring in the Dough." Each pledge card is passed out with a cookie and the slogan.

Resource 9

1950s, '60s or '70s Theme

This works well as a campaign kickoff event. Employees dress up in clothes from one of the above eras. Depending on the decade, a theme kickoff (sock hop, disco, etc.) can be planned. Have a penny vote for best dressed.

Wild West Theme

This also works well as a kickoff event. Employees dress in western clothes and tacos are served. Use a cactus as your thermometer.

Halloween Campaign

Throw an at-work Halloween party as a campaign kickoff. Employees come in costume and play bobbing for apples, etc. Have a pumpkin carving or painting contest between departments. Vote for the best with spare change. Use Count Dracula's cape as a thermometer. Have children come in to trick-or-treat for candy and pledge cards!

Need More Theme Ideas? Try Some of These Slogans.
- Paint a Bright Tomorrow
- Caring Is Sharing
- It's Your Chance to Make a Difference
- United We Stand
- Caring Works Wonders
- Build a Caring Community*
- Make a Change for the Better
- You and United Way—A Partnership That Works
- Solutions For People
- Learning to Care
- Touch A Life
- The Power of You*
- Lighting the Way
- Capture the Spirit
- Lift Someone's Spirits
- Caring Hearts Build Hope*

---

*Related incentive products are available in the United Way of America 1999 Campaign Catalog.

Creative Ways to Communicate

"HEY, YOU! IT'S UNITED WAY TIME"

Communication is key. People like to know how they're doing. Giving initial information and regular progress reports during the campaign is very important. It gives your employees a goal. Good communication lets them know how close they are to that goal. Here are some ways to creatively convey the information:

- Use bulletin boards to post weekly progress reports with results (in terms of percent of employees participating) broken down by department or office group. This lends an element of competition.
- A large graphic indicating progress toward the overall goal is effective to let employees know how their company or organization is doing. This is where the thermometer signs shine.
- Send brief reports to every employee's desk or workstation as a memo from the "boss" or from the ECC to encourage employees to finish the job and meet the goal.
- If you have a public address system in your facility, use it to give daily (or regular) reports. Possibly create "commercials" from various staff members asking their colleagues to pitch in and support United Way.

Publicizing Your Campaign

- "Teasers," which can work up to the kickoff announcement, grab employees' attention and create anticipation. *For example: candy treats with catchy phrases.*
- Send regular e-mail messages to remind employees about contributing, participating and campaign updates.
- Publish a calendar of company campaign events.
- Hang United Way posters, banners or thermometers in heavy traffic areas. Place door hangers on office doorknobs. Decorate the elevators, stairwells and the inside of restroom stall doors.
- Ask your United Way representative to help with local media coverage if your company is doing something really original.
- Create a heart-rending booklet to distribute with employee pledge cards. Feature stories and quotes from employees who give to and believe in the United Way. Include a photograph of the employee along with a quote from that employee about giving through United Way. Try to represent all levels of the company. This booklet can dispel myths or support facts about United Way of Central Indiana.

Your Way . . . to Know Who to Help

United Way of Central Indiana is your expert partner . . . continually researching and prioritizing community needs. In fact, we wrote the book on it! Our Community Assessment tells us what human challenges exist, what's already being done to meet them, and what can be done to make a difference.

    Our goals for central Indiana are . . .

- Children and Youth will succeed.
- Families and Neighborhoods will be healthy and safe.
- People will have a second chance.
- Seniors will not be alone.

Your Way . . . to Have the Greatest Impact

- United Way focuses on the community's greatest needs and provides real solutions.
- Your gift is combined with the power of over 100,000 other gifts.
- United Way of Central Indiana supports over 200 proven programs that make positive changes in the lives of thousands of people very day.
- United Way is extremely efficient. 90% of your gift will directly provide Solutions For People. The recognized industry average is 75%.

Now that's impact!

Your Way . . . to Get Results

United Way builds our community by supporting proven programs that deliver positive changes . . . and we tell the community what's being accomplished. This gives us all peace of mind.

Your Way . . . to Touch a Life!

Your Way is a life where the only boundaries are your courage and your ambition . . . a life where setbacks catapult you five steps forward . . . a life where you give of yourself knowing the returns will be endless.

What in the World Does United Way of Central Indiana Do?

We provide Solutions For People . . . including you!

Specifically speaking . . .

We are the critical link in our community . . . bring together experts, residents, human service providers and recipients, government, and funding sources . . . to make positive changes in people's lives.

Proven Programs, Positive Changes

United Way of Central Indiana supports over 200 proven programs that make positive changes in the lives of thousands of local people very day. It's *Your Way* to provide Solutions For People!

Nurturing Children and Youth

United Way–funded programs help youth improve their success in school and avoid involvement in the juvenile justice system.

United Way–funded programs are helping teenagers who are pregnant have full-birth-weight babies and avoid infant mortality.

United Way–funded programs are helping teenagers in central Indiana avoid pregnancy.

Strengthening Families and Individuals

United Way–funded programs are improving family functioning in central Indiana and keeping families intact.

United Way–funded programs are helping central Indiana women who are involved in abusive relationships escape violence and develop independence.

United Way–funded programs are helping infants and toddlers accomplish early developmental milestones that prepare them for a successful start in school.

Building Self-Sufficiency

United Way–funded programs are helping central Indiana adults become employed and economically independent.

United Way–funded programs are helping elderly adults and adults with disabilities avoid placement in institutions and remain in their own homes.

United Way–funded programs are keeping central Indiana individuals and families in their own homes and preventing them from becoming homeless.

Fostering Health and Well-Being

United Way–funded programs are helping people survive serious illnesses, such as cancer, heart disease, and sickle cell anemia.

United Way–funded programs are helping central Indiana youth remain drug-free.

United Way–funded programs are helping reduce tobacco and drug/alcohol dependency in central Indiana.

Supporting a Strong, Safe Community

United Way–funded programs are helping reduce violence in central Indiana families.

United Way–funded programs are improving relations across ethnic boundaries in neighborhoods.

United Way–funded programs are helping neighborhood residents work together to solve problems.

Solutions For ® People
UNITED WAY OF CENTRAL INDIANA

Member Agencies

Nurturing Children and Youth

American Red Cross of Greater Indianapolis

Auntie Mame's Child Development Center, Inc.

Big Brothers of Greater Indianapolis, Inc.

Big Sisters of Central Indiana, Inc.

Boy Scouts of America, Inc.—Crossroads of America Council

Boy Scouts of America, Inc.—Hoosier Trails Council

Boys and Girls Clubs of Hancock County

Lebanon Area Boys and Girls Club

Boys and Girls Clubs of Indianapolis

Boys and Girls Club of Noblesville

Boys and Girls Club of Zionsville

Catholic Social Services of Central Indiana

Catholic Youth Organization

Children's Bureau of Indianapolis, Inc.

Community Addiction Services of Indiana, Inc.

Community Centers of Indianapolis, Inc.

Crossroads Rehabilitation Center, Inc.

Day Nursery Association of Indianapolis, Inc.

Girl Scouts of Hoosier Capital Council

Girls Incorporated of Indianapolis

Happy Hollow Children's Camp, Inc.

Jameson, Inc.

Jewish Community Center of Indianapolis

Kaleidoscope Church and Community Partnership

Marion County Commission on Youth, Inc. (MCCOY)

Mt. Zion Day Care Center, Inc.

St. Elizabeth's Home

St. Mary's Child Center

Social Health Association of Central Indiana, Inc.

Tulip Trace Council of Girl Scouts, Inc.

Volunteers of America of Indiana, Inc.

YMCA of Greater Indianapolis

Barbara B. Jordan YMCA

YWCA of Indianapolis, Inc.

Strengthening Families and Individuals

American Red Cross of Greater Indianapolis

Big Brothers of Greater Indianapolis, Inc.

Big Sisters of Central Indiana, Inc.

Catholic Social Services of Central Indiana

Child Advocates, Inc.

Children's Bureau of Indianapolis, Inc.

Church Federation of Greater Indianapolis

Community Centers of Indianapolis, Inc.

Crossroads Rehabilitation Center, Inc.

The Damien Center, Inc.

Family Service Association of Central Indiana, Inc.

Girls Incorporated of Indianapolis

Indianapolis Legal Aid Society, Inc.

Indianapolis Urban League, Inc.

The Julian Center, Inc.

Legal Services Organization of Indiana, Inc.

Lutheran Child and Family Services of Indiana and Kentucky, Inc.

Mental Health Association in Boone County

Mental Health Association in Hamilton County

Mental Health Association in Hancock County

Mental Health Association in Hendricks County

Mental Health Association in Marion County

Mental Health Association in Morgan County

PACE, Inc.—Public Action in Correctional Effort

Pleasant Run, Inc.

Reach for Youth, Inc.

Visiting Nurse Service, Inc.

YWCA of Indianapolis, Inc.

Building Self-Sufficiency

Alpha Home Association of Greater Indianapolis, Inc.

American Red Cross of Greater Indianapolis

Arc Rehabilitation Services

Boone County Senior Services, Inc.

Bosma Industries for the Blind, Inc.

Catholic Social Services of Central Indiana

Community Centers of Indianapolis, Inc.

Community Service Center of Morgan County, Inc.

Coordinated Aging Services for Morgan County, Inc.

Crossroads Rehabilitation Center, Inc.

Family Service Association of Central Indiana, Inc.

Goodwill Industries of Central Indiana, Inc.

Hamilton County Senior Services, Inc.

Hancock County Senior Services, Inc.

Hendricks County Senior Services, Inc.

Heritage Place of Indianapolis, Inc.

Horizon House, Inc.

Independent Residential Living of Central Indiana, Inc.

Indianapolis Senior Citizens' Center, Inc.

Indianapolis Speech and Hearing Center, Inc.

Jewish Community Center of Indianapolis

Lutheran Child and Family Services of Indiana and Kentucky, Inc.

Meals on Wheels, Inc.

Mental Health Association in Boone County

Mental Health Association in Hamilton County

Mental Health Association in Hancock County

Mental Health Association in Hendricks County

Mental Health Association in Marion County

Mental Health Association in Morgan County

Muscular Dystrophy Family Foundation

Noble of Indiana

Perry Senior Citizens Services, Inc.

St. Mary's Child Center

The Salvation Army

Training, Inc.

United Cerebral Palsy Association of Greater Indiana, Inc.

Volunteers of America of Indiana, Inc.

Youth Works, Inc.

Supporting a Strong, Safe Community

Community Centers of Indianapolis, Inc.

Church Federation of Greater Indianapolis

Indianapolis Urban League, Inc.

Resource 9

Information and Referral Network, Inc.

Marion County Commission on Youth, Inc. (MCCOY)

Mental Health Association in Marion County

Mental Health Association in Morgan County

USO Council of Indianapolis, Inc.

Fostering Health and Well-Being

American Cancer Society—Central Indiana Area

American Heart Association

American Red Cross of Greater Indianapolis

Boone County Cancer Society, Inc.

Community Addiction Services of Indiana, Inc.

Community Centers of Indianapolis, Inc.

Family Service Association of Central Indiana, Inc.

First Step, Inc.

Girls Incorporated of Indianapolis

Indianapolis Speech and Hearing Center, Inc.

Indianapolis Urban League, Inc.

Little Red Door Cancer Agency

Martin Center, Inc.

The Salvation Army

Visiting Nurse Service, Inc.

United Way Services

Bridges to Success

Hamilton County Service Center

Nonprofit Training Center

United Christmas Service

United Way/Community Service Council

United Way Center for Human Services

Volunteer Action Center

Youth as Resources

Your Way . . . to Volunteer

You can watch your pledge work firsthand by volunteering for United Way or one of its member agencies. Call (317) 921-1212 to organize a Day of Caring, where you and your friends spend a day at a United Way agency.

United Way of Central Indiana
3901 N. Meridian Street
P.O. Box 88409
Indianapolis, IN 46208
(317) 923-1466

Hamilton County Service Center
942 N. Tenth Street
Noblesville, IN 46060
(317) 773-1308

United Way Center for Human Services
500 S. Polk Street
Greenwood, IN 46143
(317) 865-3458

Serving Boone, Hamilton, Hancock, Hendricks, Marion and Morgan counties.
e-mail: community@uwci.org
website: www.uwci.org

INFORMATION:
THE KEY TO A SUCCESSFUL
UNITED WAY CAMPAIGN

◆

This section contains . . . feature stories, photos, ads, fact sheets and other items to help you tell the United Way of Central Indiana story. These, coupled with other campaign materials available from your United Way Campaign Manager or Loaned Associate, can make your campaign more effective and allow your company to do more to help people here in central Indiana. The camera-ready reproductions can be used in any way you want.

Communicating how United Way of Central Indiana and its member agencies improve the lives of families in central Indiana is important to the success of your employee campaign. Contributors should understand how their contribution will be used to build a caring community. These materials will help your contributors make an informed choice.

Please pass this on to whoever is doing publicity for your United Way campaign.

Solutions For People
UNITED WAY OF CENTRAL INDIANA

Fact Sheet

Mission

The mission of United Way of Central Indiana is to mobilize people in our community to care for one another.

Background

United Way of Central Indiana (UWCI) has been meeting local needs for over 80 years. UWCI was founded in 1918 as the War Chest and has been known as the Community Chest, Community Fund, United Fund and United Way of Greater Indianapolis during its history.

In 1998, UWCI donors pledged $34 million to UWCI. Contributed dollars support 85 agencies and more than 200 programs in Boone, Hamilton, Hancock, Hendricks, Marion and Morgan counties.

A Volunteer-Run Organization

More than 5,000 volunteers from all walks of life and from all over central Indiana serve on UWCI boards and committees that assess community needs, set priorities, raise money, allocate funds, certify agencies, evaluate programs and oversee financial records.

Member Agencies

UWCI's member agencies total 85 and are located throughout the six-county service area. The agencies include local chapters of national agencies, established local agencies and new agencies that address emerging needs. UWCI's agencies provide a wide range of services, are governed by volunteer boards and meet high standards of accountability.

Community Needs

United Way–supported programs reflect the needs and priorities of our central Indiana community based on periodic research. Currently, United Way's goals for central Indiana are . . .

- Children and youth will succeed.
- Families and neighborhoods will be healthy and safe.
- People will have a second chance.
- Seniors will not be alone.

Other UWCI Services

- **The Volunteer Action Center** provides information about volunteer opportunities, promotes corporate volunteerism and manages three leadership training programs.
- **The Nonprofit Training Center** trains nonprofit managers, boards and staff.
- **United Christmas Service** raises and distributes money and matches groups to needy families during the holiday season.
- **Hamilton County Service Center** provides a centralized location and support for nonprofit agencies to better serve Hamilton County residents.
- **Community Service Council** manages the funding process and community services and provides human service planning, research, coalition building and legislative advocacy in an eight-county area.
- **Youth as Resources** funds community programs designed and run by youth and promotes youth volunteerism.
- **United Way Center for Human Services**, a joint effort of the United Ways of Central Indiana and Johnson County, houses 11 agencies to better serve people in northern Johnson and southern Marion counties.
- **Bridges to Success** is a joint effort of UWCI and Indianapolis Public Schools providing health services, recreation, educational support and social services to students.
- **Leadership Programs** enhance the leadership potential of participants—on the job and in the community—through workshops, experiential education, professional and social networking. (The Ardath Burkhart Series, Executive Women's Leadership Program, Youth Leadership Initiative, Leadership Training and Development Series for Diversity)
- **Loaned Associate Program** trains individuals in customer service, sales presentations and problem solving for use in supervised fundraising campaigns. Better understanding of community need and networking in central Indiana are other benefits. Participants are loaned by their employer or sponsored through grants.
- **Volunteer Involvement Program (VIP)** customizes volunteer experiences at a United Way agency for your organization, to build teamwork and morale and to help make a difference in our community.
- **SAVI (Social Assets and Vulnerabilities Indicators)** database maps programs and resources close to your office or where your employees live.
- **HELPLINE** (317-926-4357) provides information to and makes referrals for persons in need of human services and programs in central Indiana.
- **Youth Mentoring Directory** lists programs to match interested adults with mentoring opportunities. Brown Bag information sessions can also be scheduled for your organization.

- **The Community Assessment** publication provides information about human service assets and needs in central Indiana to help your organization make philanthropic decisions beyond United Way.

Ask Your Fellow Employees to Tell Their United Way Story

One of the most effective ways to demonstrate how United Way touches lives is to have your fellow employees tell how they've been touched by a United Way agency. This form will help you get all the information you need.

Will You Share Your Story?

Have you ever participated in CYO, scouting, YMCA, YWCA, or a boys' or girls' club? Have you or a family member received Red Cross safety training or swimming instructions? Have you, a relative or friend ever had cancer or needed family counseling, senior services, subsidized child care, welfare to work training, mental health services, services for a disability, at-home nursing care or assistance with an adoption? If so, you probably got help from a United Way agency.

Right now, our company is conducting a United Way campaign. We want our employees to know that United Way helps people like you; so we'd like to include some personal stories in our newsletter or group meetings.

If you share your story, you do not have to be identified. However, if you'd like to speak about your experience or be interviewed for a newsletter, that would be great. Please help our United Way campaign by sharing your story.

Yes, I'll Share My Story

Check one:

☐ You may use my name.   ☐ I prefer to remain anonymous.

Name: _____

Department: _____

Telephone number: _____

The following agency or agencies helped me, a friend or a relative: _____

_____

Briefly describe help the agency or agencies provided and how it was helpful:

_____

_____

_____

Continue on the reverse side if you need more space. Thanks!

True Stories

What Money Couldn't Buy

When she was just 20 months old, Monte Chamberlin's daughter, Caitie, was diagnosed with "global delays." But no one knew why. "It was a helpless feeling, not knowing the beast that we faced," recalled Monte, a manager at Thomson Consumer Electronics.

The Chamberlins' first contact with a United Way–funded agency, Crossroads Rehabilitation Center, began shortly after that. Caitie attended the Early Start program to receive therapies for lagging speech and motor skills.

At Crossroads, a doctor noticed subtle handwringing by Caitie and referred the family to a specialist who confirmed that Caitie had Rett Syndrome. Rett is a progressive neurological disorder with no known cause or cure. Most people with the disorder lose purposeful use of their hands, they lose their ability to walk, and their speech never develops. There are fewer than 2,000 Rett cases in the country and less than 25 in Indiana.

For years, Caitie continued to receive physical and communication therapies at Crossroads, and the family was linked to support groups that helped them move through the "why me?" phase to the "what next?" phase, Chamberlin said.

Now 12, Caitie has integrated into the public school environment. She spends shared time with students in art, music and homeroom, goes on field trips, goes bowling, and celebrates birthday parties with classmates.

"I used to think United Way was for the less fortunate families in our community," Chamberlin said. "By economic measures, we are very fortunate. But Crossroads gave us something that money could not buy. They helped us know 'the beast' early on so we could help Caitie with school, friends and peer relationships."

Solutions For People®
UNITED WAY OF CENTRAL INDIANA

United Way Gifts Spin Web of After-School Programs

Seeing 12-year-old Ashley Monroe practice tae kwan do kicks after school at Citizens Multi-Service Center, it's hard to image her mask of quiet focus being used destructively. The class is part of a web of programs designed to help kids develop self-esteem and reduce disruptive behavior so they can focus in school on learning.

Ashley's problems began in the fourth grade and earned her the label of "emotionally handicapped" (EH). The school was on the verge of expelling her when Ashley's mom learned of the community center's programs, which are funded in part through United Way's Targeted Initiatives Fund.

After two grading periods in the program, Ashley made lots of friends and learned how to handle disputes through a mediation process taught at Citizens, a member of Community Center of Indianapolis, a United Way agency.

Ashley was tutored in math and also gardened, played basketball and performed African dance at the Center. Computers to do homework on, a library and quiet place to study were also available.

In its first year, the after-school program, called STAR (Striving to Achieve Respect), exceeded its goals for students to reduce disruptive behavior, increase grade point averages, improve or maintain attendance and reduce conflicts with others. But Ashley's mom doesn't need statistics to judge STAR. "This program is every mother's dream," she concluded.

Solutions For People®
UNITED WAY OF CENTRAL INDIANA

Where the Money Goes

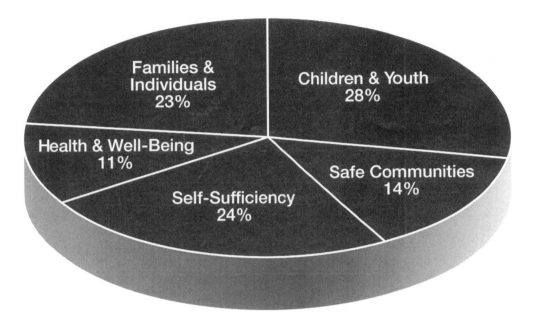

At United Way of Central Indiana, we know you want your contribution to go to people who really need help and to make our community a better place.

The work of 5,000 volunteers helps keep our fundraising and operating costs low, so 90% of funds raised will help strengthen families, nurture children, serve the elderly and disabled, enable people to become self-sufficient, and promote health and well-being. This is more efficient than government-run programs and most individual charities.

United Way of Central Indiana
3901 N. Meridian Street
P.O. Box 88409
Indianapolis, IN 46208
(317) 923-1466

Hamilton County Service Center
942 N. Tenth Street
Noblesville, IN 46060
(317) 773-1308

United Way Center for Human Services
500 S. Polk Street
Greenwood, IN 46143
(317) 865-3458

Serving Boone, Hamilton, Hancock, Hendricks, Marion and Morgan counties.
e-mail: community@uwci.org
website: www.uwci.org

Solutions For People®
UNITED WAY OF CENTRAL INDIANA

Ads, Fillers, Bulletin Board Items . . .

Touch A Life!^{SM}

When you give to the community through United Way of Central Indiana, you're making positive changes in people's lives the most effective way possible . . . dramatically transforming them by changing pain into relief, anger into love, and despair into opportunity.

Payroll stuffer (precampaign)

Your gift will improve our community

THANK YOU for helping United Way provide Solutions For People. You can be sure that your gift will have impact on our community's most critical needs and make positive changes in people's lives.

Payroll stuffer (postcampaign)

How United Way Makes Sure Your Gift Has Impact

1 Research

Before we ask you for a contribution, United Way does extensive research to determine the community's current and emerging needs, along with the resources already in place to meet those needs. United Way is the only organization in central Indiana that does research of this kind.

6 Accountability

Organizations that receive funds from United Way meet high accountability standards and can demonstrate the results they achieve. Funding decisions are based on the performance and impact these organizations have on community needs.

2 Priorities

Once the needs and gaps in resources are known, United Way community volunteers determine what needs are most urgent, and what services will have the most impact on those areas.

3 Strategy

Expert volunteers and staff identify strategies and target dollars to meet the community's most urgent needs.

5 Investment

United Way volunteers and staff invest your contributions in our community by supporting organizations and programs that have proven they can get the results you want for our community.

4 Fund raising

United Way invites you to invest in meeting community needs. Building our community through United Way is efficient and effective. As a trusted partner, United Way has the expertise to focus on tangible problems with real solutions, making your caring count.

Resource 9

_____

Sample Letters

Key Club

(date)
Mark Johnson
Vice President, Marketing

Dear Mark:

United Way of Central Indiana and its member agencies are vital to our community, and giving to United Way is the best way to impact critical community needs. On the occasion of our annual United Way employee campaign, I invite you to demonstrate your support and leadership by joining me as a member of United Way's Key Club. The Key Club consists of people who have demonstrated their community leadership by contributing $1,000 or more to the community through United Way.

When you give through United Way, you are making positive changes in people's lives. Because United Way supports proven programs, you can be sure your caring counts. As a trusted partner, United Way has the expertise to focus your gift on tangible problems with real solutions. Your money stays in our community to help those who really need a second chance.

United Way is efficient; funds raised go directly to over 200 proven services and programs in our community that address critical community needs. United Way–funded programs improve the lives of thousands of our neighbors every day, 365 days a year. Most likely you, a family member or a friend have been helped or served by United Way.

Please join us in building our community. Our goals are that children and youth will succeed, families and neighborhoods will be healthy and safe, people will have a second chance and seniors will not be alone. When you give through United Way, you are making positive changes in people's lives, changing pain into relief, anger into love, and despair into opportunity.

United Way appreciates your gift, will use it to build our community and will let you know what is being accomplished.

Please take time to learn about United Way and its member agencies during the campaign. You can become part of an important group of community leaders when you join the Key Club. Thank you for considering such a significant commitment.

Steve Smith
President

Employee

(date)
Stuart Kennedy
Associate, Manufacturing Division

Dear Stuart:

During the coming weeks, (company) will be conducting our annual United Way of Central Indiana community building campaign. This is your opportunity to touch thousands of lives here in central Indiana by pledging your support to United Way of Central Indiana. I believe United Way is the most efficient and effective way to solve community problems, and I whole-heartedly endorse the campaign.

When you give through United Way, you are making positive changes in people's lives. Because United Way supports proven programs, you can be sure your caring counts. As a trusted partner, United Way has the expertise to focus your gift on tangible problems with real solutions. Your money stays in our community to help those who really need a second chance.

United Way is efficient; funds raised go directly to over 200 proven services and programs in our community that address critical community needs. United Way–funded programs improve the lives of thousands of our neighbors every day, 365 days a year. Most likely you, a family member or a friend have been helped or served by United Way.

Please join us in building our community. Our goals are that children and youth will succeed, families and neighborhoods will be healthy and safe, people will have a second chance and seniors will not be alone. When you give through United Way, you are making positive changes in people's lives, changing pain into relief, anger into love, and despair into opportunity.

United Way appreciates your gift, will use it to build our community and will let you know what is being accomplished.

Thank you.
Steve Smith
President

Information: E-Mail Messages About United Way

Use the latest technology to educate and motivate people at your company. Here are e-mail messages you can send to inform and encourage others. If you wish, you may personalize the messages and add information about your company's involvement with United Way.

- What does United Way do? It provides Solutions For People.
- Before you're asked for a contribution, United Way does extensive research to determine the community's needs. That way, you're assured your gift goes where it's needed most.
- United Way's level of efficiency is unmatched in central Indiana. Ninety percent of funds raised will support programs and services that have impact on the community.
- When you invest in the community through United Way, your dollars stay in your community—Boone, Hancock, Hamilton, Hendricks, Marion and Morgan counties—making it a better place to live, work and do business.
- Expert community volunteers, people just like you, make sure your gift supports programs that have real impact on the community's most important problems.
- United Way is the most powerful way to give to your community. Giving through United Way multiplies your impact by combining your gift with over 100,000 others.
- United Way focuses on tangible problems with real solutions.
- United Way is your best partner because of its expertise and professionalism in addressing human service issues.
- You can feel safe giving through United Way, knowing your money is going to fund programs that really deserve it and will get results.
- Think about what would happen or not happen in our community if United Way wasn't there.
- Wouldn't knowing that you positively changed just one person's life really make you feel good? Through United Way, you'll improve the lives of thousands of people every day, 365 days a year.
- Giving through United Way makes sense because it combines the power of many voices.
- At United Way, we believe. . .
    - . . . that children are our future, and they deserve every opportunity we can give them to learn and grow in an environment free of fear, ignorance and violence.

... that fostering strong families and individuals is the first step in creating a strong and successful community.

... that self-sufficiency is the key to living a fulfilling, productive life and that everyone should have the opportunity to live as independently as possible.

... that individual health, wellness and personal well-being are critical to the well-being of our community as a whole.

... that residents should be able to live in a strong, safe community with affordable and easy access to the services and resources needed to live a healthy, safe and productive life.

... that no frail or elderly person should be alone.

- United Way is the only organization that regularly researches central Indiana's human needs—identifying human problems, working to solve them and suggesting strategies for improving results.

- For human service expertise, community leaders turn to United Way because of its knowledge and understanding of our community.

- United Way must grow to continue the programs already in place that demonstrate measurable and positive outcomes for people in central Indiana.

RESOURCE 10

CAPITAL CAMPAIGN VOLUNTEER'S KIT

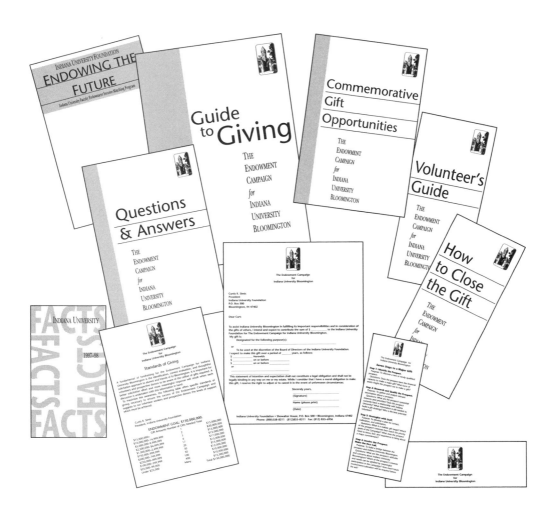

INDIANA UNIVERSITY FOUNDATION

ENDOWING THE

FUTURE

Indiana University Faculty Endowment Income Matching Program

ONE OUTSTANDING TEACHER CAN ENRICH THE LIVES OF THOUSANDS OF STUDENTS.

PERHAPS YOU WERE FORTUNATE ENOUGH TO HAVE ONE OF THESE PROFESSORS WHILE YOU WERE IN COLLEGE.

The kind of teacher who challenged you to set your sights higher, who settled for nothing but your best effort, who helped you to see things in a new light. These educators have always been hard to find, and harder to keep. Today, it's even more difficult.

Consider the following:

Big Ten Public Universities

Number of Endowed Faculty Positions (reported by main campuses in 1995)

1.	Minnesota	239
2.	Wisconsin	226
3.	Michigan	186
4.	Penn State	118
5.	Iowa	115
6.	Ohio State	67
7.	Illinois	62
8.	**Indiana**	**31**
9.	Michigan State	27
10.	Purdue	14

AS YOU KNOW, WELL-DESIGNED FACULTY ENDOWMENTS DO MUCH MORE THAN FUND SALARIES.

They strengthen libraries, laboratories, and computing resources; they attract talented undergraduate and graduate students. We're seeking faculty endowments that will help us address all of these needs and more.

The entire Indiana University family is grateful for the loyalty and generosity of so many donors. And now we can show our appreciation in a different way as we prepare for the future: by matching the income your new endowment generates.

We invite you to establish a legacy at IU by becoming a member of this select group of supporters. And we pledge our commitment to you by matching your gift's income. By helping IU attract and keep more distinguished faculty members, you provide more of today's and tomorrow's students with an opportunity to enrich their lives.

Resource 10

The Indiana University Faculty Endowment Income Matching Program

1. Endowment funds received after December 1, 1995, for the purpose of direct faculty support, especially for Chairs and Professorships, are eligible for this match.

2. The full match, that is 1:1, will consist of a payout equal to 5 percent of the principal on an annual basis and will be available for gifts of at least $1,000,000. If the gift falls between $500,000 and $1,000,000, the match will be based on a ratio of 1:2. Payouts will be in perpetuity. A contractual commitment will be provided to the donor.

3. The match opportunity will be in effect until December 31, 1999. A maximum of $4,000,000 will be allocated during this time. Allocations will be made on a first-come, first-served basis, open to all campuses. Unspent available match funds will not be carried forward.

4. The source of funds for the match will be one-half from University administration and one-half from campus administration. At their option, Chancellors may choose to charge the successful unit for all or part of the campus's portion of the match, or they may distribute all or part of the charges to the entire campus.

5. To take an example, Mary Jones donates $500,000 for endowment for a faculty position in the School of Public and Environmental Affairs at IU Bloomington. Assume that the payment from the endowment is $25,000 per year (that is, 5 percent of $500,00, the current spending policy of the IU Foundation Board of Directors).* The match is 1:2 on this principal amount ($500,000) in perpetuity. Thus, in addition to the $25,000, SPEA receives an additional $12,500 per year for support of this position. Of the $12,500, University administration will provide $6,250. The remaining $6,250 is the responsibility of, in this case, the Bloomington campus.

6. Gifts may be paid over a maximum of five years. The match will be available only if there is a firm, written commitment. However, matching funds will be provided only to the extent that payment has been received (with one exception noted below). So, if there is a gift of $1,000,000 to be paid over four years and $250,000 is received the first year, then the matching funds for the first year are $12,500. Here the match rate is 1:1, and the payout is 5 percent of $250,000.

7. In the case of irrevocable trusts established during the match period with no payout until termination of the trust, one-half of the institutional payout will

---

*The actual payment from an endowment fund is determined by the current spending policy and the investment policy set by the IU Foundation Board of Directors.

Resource 10

begin when the trust is established. The remaining matching funds will become available when the trust terminates, as will, of course, the trust income. Thus, if there is an irrevocable trust of $1,000,000 established during the match time-frame, then the payout from institutional funds (that is, University administration plus the campus) will be $25,000 per year until the trust matures. After that, institutional funds will equal $50,000 per year (at the 1:1 payout ratio) plus the income generated from the trust itself based on its value at maturity.

8. The University President, in consultation with the IU Foundation President, reserves the authority to limit eligibility. In particular, it should not be possible for a single mega-gift to deplete all matching monies. In order to determine the upper limit of a specific gift, a brief written proposal should be submitted to the IU President. The IU Foundation Executive Director, Capital Campaigns will be the initial qualifier of matches under this program.

9. A qualified gift for a 1:1 match may be distributed between more than one endowed faculty program, where each would qualify on its own for a lesser match of 1:2, or no match at all. For example, a $1,000,000 gift will qualify for the 1:1 match regardless of how the gift is distributed among qualified programs. It is the size of the gift that matters, not how it is distributed among qualified programs at IU.

10. Any gift that is eligible for the match must be administered by the IU Foundation or IU and not by an outside trustee.

11. Responsibility for authorizing exceptions to this policy rests with the University President.

Gift Vehicles Eligible for the Matching Program

A DONOR MAY USE ANY OF THE FOLLOWING GIFT VEHICLES, IN ANY COMBINATION, IN ORDER TO REACH THE $500,000 MINIMUM REQUIREMENT FOR THE INCOME MATCHING PROGRAM.

Outright Gifts (Cash and Securities)

Outright gifts of cash or securities that meet the minimum amount of $500,000 or above are eligible for the matching program. These commitments may be received (between 12/1/95 and 12/31/99) all at once or as a pledge paid over five years. Gifts of securities will be recorded at their fair market value on the date of transfer. Personal property will not qualify for the match.* Other types of funds will be handled on a case-by-case basis.

*Please note: Gifts of personal property will not qualify for the match because personal property held by the Foundation will generate no income, and selling the property may have adverse tax consequences for the donor.

Charitable Remainder Trusts

Charitable remainder trusts qualify for the match. However, the payout on the match will be based on the face value of the donor's gift to the IU Foundation, even if the remainder value exceeds the face value at the time the trust terminates. For example, if a donor funds a charitable remainder trust during the match period with $1,000,000, and assuming the annual income will be $50,000, the match of a gift at this level by the University will be 50 percent of the annual income, or $25,000. The ultimate payout of the trust to the IU Foundation depends upon the payment rate to the beneficiary(ies) and investment performance. The age of life income beneficiaries will be considered when deciding whether or not to match gifts of trust.

Charitable Gift Annuities and Pooled Income Funds

The charitable remainder trust criteria (as described above) also apply to charitable gift annuities and the pooled income funds. Because of the irrevocable nature, these gifts qualify for a match from the University based upon the face value of the gift at the time it is initially received by the IU Foundation.

Charitable Lead Trusts

Since charitable lead trusts pay the income they generate directly to the IU Foundation, they qualify if the income generated by the trust to the IU Foundation meets the minimum amount required to qualify for the match. For example, a charitable lead trust funded with assets that will produce at least $500,000 over a five-year period will qualify for the match. If this payout is received or pledged to IU during the match period, it qualifies in the same way as an outright gift.

Bequests

Newly established bequest expectancies will qualify as long as they meet the minimum levels, are first documented during the matching period, and represent a legally binding obligation upon the donor's estate at the time of the donor's death. Age guidelines will be considered when deciding whether or not to match individual bequests. One of the following types of documentation on file at the IU Foundation is sufficient: a copy of the will or excerpt from the will, Arbutus Society enrollment, a signed gift agreement, a letter of intent from the donor, or a letter from the donor's attorney or financial adviser.

Life Insurance

Life insurance qualifies only if the policy is fully paid-up when given to the IU Foundation or will be paid-up within a five-year period after the date of the gift. The donor must make the IU Foundation the irrevocable owner and beneficiary of the policy for the matching fund program to apply. The match will be based on the death benefit of the policy, and it will apply at the time the policy is received by the Foundation. For example, if a donor makes a gift of a life insurance policy with a $500,000 death benefit, when the policy matures, that account will qualify for the match. Age guidelines may be considered when deciding whether or not to match life insurance gifts.

Remainder Interest in Real Estate

Gifts of real estate will be considered on a case-by-case basis. Each gift of real estate must have a documented value to determine qualifications for, and the amount of, the match.

For further information, contact Curtis R. Simic, President, IU Foundation at (812) 855-6679.

Questions & Answers

The
Endowment
Campaign
for
Indiana
University
Bloomington

"In all of the areas in which IUB has major academic programs, it should be second to none. Indiana University Bloomington has the spirit and the will to succeed. This campaign will provide us with the resources."

—Myles Brand

Myles Brand
President,
Indiana University

THE ENDOWMENT CAMPAIGN FOR INDIANA UNIVERSITY BLOOMINGTON is the largest fundraising campaign for one campus in the University's history. It includes all components of the Bloomington campus, with the primary purpose of increasing the number of endowed chairs, professorships, fellowships, and scholarships available to the campus. The Campaign goal is $350 million—$150 million for new endowment and $200 million in ongoing support.

The following pages contain Indiana University President Myles Brand's answers to some of the most frequently asked questions about the Endowment Campaign.

Why is Indiana University Bloomington launching a campaign at this time?

It has become clear that Indiana University's margin of excellence increasingly depends upon the support of friends and alumni. In the past, IU could count on state and federal governments to provide funding for operations and some quality improvement efforts, but that's no longer true. At the state level, other priorities, such as K–12, entitlement programs, and corrections, are absorbing greater portions of public resources. Higher education cannot expect to receive support for anything beyond the basic necessities. At the same time, the federal government, in its attempt to balance the budget, is allocating fewer dollars for research opportunities. There is absolutely no doubt that the continuation of IU Bloomington's tradition of excellence and quality will require the direct support that comes through a campaign.

What is your vision for the University upon successful completion of this campaign?

My vision is simple and straightforward: In all of the areas in which IUB has major academic programs, it should be second to none. Indiana University Bloomington has the spirit and the will to succeed. This campaign will provide us with the resources.

The single most important characteristic of an excellent university is the quality of its faculty, students, and staff. To attract and retain the world's leading faculty members, we must be able to provide endowed chairs and professorships.

Resource 10

IUB is already one of the great university campuses in the country, indeed the world. Unfortunately, however, we lag behind many Big Ten institutions and other major research universities in the number of endowed chairs and professorships. This is more than a matter of numbers, but speaks to the defining essence of IU.

How does this campaign differ from the University's usual fundraising efforts?

IU Bloomington, like other major college campuses across the country, seeks funds on an annual basis to support its faculty, students, and physical facilities. A campaign, by contrast, focuses on specific, high-priority goals, and the campus organizes itself, school by school, to reach those goals. The IU Foundation, the deans, the chancellor, and the president also dedicate their energy to achieving campaign goals.

How was the goal of $350 million established?

We discussed campus needs with the faculty, and the chancellor prioritized them. The Indiana University Foundation then undertook a comprehensive market survey to determine the financial feasibility of a campaign. The goal is the result of determining the financial feasibility and matching it with Bloomington campus priorities.

What do endowments accomplish that other types of gifts do not?

All gifts are important. What makes endowment gifts especially important is their permanence—they continue giving in perpetuity. Properly managed, they not only continue to provide an annual operating income but also grow to meet the eroding effects of inflation. Endowments are a permanent, stable source of income.

IU already has an outstanding faculty. Why are more endowments to support faculty a focus for this campaign?

Indiana University does have an outstanding faculty. In fact, other major universities would very much like to have some of these faculty members on their campuses. But to retain them, we must provide resources and honors, such as endowed professorships and chairs. By the same token, when Indiana University competes with other outstanding universities for the world's most accomplished teachers, scholars, and creative artists, it needs endowed chairs and professorships to provide the necessary incentives and competitive edge.

Remember, excellent faculty members can go to any major university they choose. Such faculty members raise the level of the intellectual enterprise and they provide the stimulant for creative and innovative work in all disciplines. It is these faculty members who make the difference between a good and a great university. The intellectual environment that they create affects everything we do, from classroom teaching to laboratory research to recital hall performances. Creating this superior intellectual environment is the desired end of a great university. IU Bloomington needs to retain these highly accomplished individuals and to bring others to the campus.

What is the University doing to encourage endowments that support faculty?

We have created an endowment matching program for faculty chairs and professorships. Our goal, which is ambitious but eminently achievable, is to generate 100 new chairs and professorships by the end of the Campaign, thereby quadrupling the number of chairs and professorships in existence before the Campaign began. It will be a startling accomplishment, to say the least.

The payout of the endowment for these positions is being matched through dedicated funding,* enabling a donor to significantly enhance the effect of a major gift. Indiana University took this step in order to emphasize the importance of faculty chairs and professorships in the development of the Bloomington campus.

I understand some donors want to support graduate fellowships. Why is graduate student support so important?

Graduate education is part of the core of IU's mission. Training the next generation of faculty members and providing the best-educated leaders for business and the creative arts is, at a deep level, what we are about.

Additionally, good faculty members prefer to work with good graduate students, and good graduate students seek out opportunities to work with a superior faculty in a supportive environment. To attract these superior graduate students to Indiana University Bloomington, we must find means to support their endeavors. Doing so perpetuates our high-quality intellectual environment.

The Campaign for Indiana in the 1980s was system wide. Why is this campaign specific to the Bloomington campus?

A large, multi-campus university, such as IU, has two choices when it comes to fundraising. One is the university-wide campaign that includes all campuses and all schools at the same time, such as our successful Campaign for Indiana. The other, especially apropos for a mature university, is to conduct sequential

---

*The Indiana University Faculty Endowment Income Matching Program is designed to encourage gifts with the goal of raising endowment for faculty positions. President Brand and the Board of Trustees have set aside $2 million in available matching funds for those gifts qualifying for the match before December 31, 1999. Gifts of $500,000 and above, from a single source, designated for chairs and professorships, and received within five years qualify for the match. All income on gifts is to be matched in perpetuity. (Full details are available upon request.)

campaigns for major areas of the institution, such as the recently completed and very successful three-year fundraising campaign at the IU School of Medicine in Indianapolis. It is now time to focus all our energies on the Bloomington campus. One advantage of this approach is that it enables all University resources, especially those of the IU Foundation, to be singularly directed towards a major goal. A sequential approach enables us to utilize existing staff in key areas and is a more efficient and effective way to proceed. This approach works only when a university has achieved a certain level of expertise and experience in fundraising, as IU has done.

How are the Bloomington faculty and administration involved in the Campaign effort?

They are involved in many ways. Some are working directly with major gift prospects. Others are out taking the Campaign to our many publics. And our faculty is financially supporting this campaign. An effort is now underway to solicit each member of the faculty for the Campaign. The faculty co-chairs are Norm Overly (Education), Susan Gubar (English), and Gary Hieftje (Chemistry).

My daughter will be entering IU as a freshman in a couple of years. How will the success of this campaign benefit her?

She can expect to have a richer undergraduate experience, both in terms of the quality of the faculty members she will encounter while here and the quality of her classmates (many of whom are highly competitive students who will choose IU not only because of our academic quality but also because of our ability to successfully compete for them through enhanced scholarship offerings).

My son graduated from IU last year. Why does a successful campaign make any difference to him?

All IU degrees are well regarded today. This campaign is designed to ensure future quality, as well. As IU stays strong and competitive, so will the value of our degrees and their holders.

I always make an annual gift to IU. Why is it important for me to contribute to this campaign over and above that?

Annual support is essential, and we deeply appreciate it. But this is a special time when our alumni and friends can ensure their support in perpetuity. This is an effort to ratchet up the margin of excellence for IUB through a special gift to the Endowment Campaign for Indiana University Bloomington.

I've been supporting a particular program at IU for years. Can I still do that with my campaign contribution?

Absolutely. Because the entire campus and every discipline is involved in the Campaign, we encourage those who choose to support a particular school or program to follow their own interests.

I might not be able to make a significant contribution this year. How long will I have an opportunity to give to the Campaign?

The Campaign will run through June 2000.

This is your first campaign as president of IU. How do you feel about the way it's going so far?

I am extraordinarily pleased by the rapid progress we have made on the IU Bloomington campaign. As I speak to many of our friends and alumni, I am pleased by their positive feelings about our University. Many individuals have already risen to the occasion in supporting the IU Bloomington campaign. They understand, as I do, the importance of private support. We are a Hoosier family. I look forward to a very successful campaign as we move into the future together.

I would like to discuss the Campaign goals and issues further. What is the best way for me to communicate with the University?

I encourage such communication and invite your comments. Should you have an interest in a particular area, be it Journalism, Business, Athletics, etc., I suggest you contact the development officer for that unit. Should you wish to contact me, my mailing address is Bryan Hall 200, Bloomington, IN 47405-1201, and my email address is pres@indiana.edu. We look forward to hearing from you.

Volunteer's

Guide

The
Endowment
Campaign
for
Indiana
University
Bloomington

"To furnish the means of acquiring knowledge is the greatest benefit that can be conferred upon mankind. It prolongs life itself and enlarges the sphere of human existence."
—John Quincy Adams

THE ENDOWMENT CAMPAIGN FOR INDIANA UNIVERSITY BLOOMINGTON IS a significant undertaking. The success of our combined efforts to raise $350 million ($150 million for new endowments and $200 million for ongoing support) hinges primarily upon the success of you—our volunteer solicitors. Your knowledge of the prospect and your experience in approaching the individual make you uniquely qualified to handle your assignments. Only you can best judge the amount of preparation and period of cultivation needed prior to actual solicitation. The following suggestions have been found to be helpful by successful volunteers in major university campaigns. They are offered for your consideration.

1. Get to know your prospect.

As a volunteer for the Endowment Campaign for IU Bloomington, knowledge of your prospect and an assessment of the size of gift you want to secure are logical starting points. Both your Campaign chair and the Capital Campaign staff can provide an evaluated level of giving for each prospect. Campaign pledge cards are included with your volunteer's kit. If more information is needed, either the Capital Campaign Office at the IU Foundation or the individual academic units will provide supplementary information.

2. Cultivate an interest in Indiana University Bloomington.

With prospect-qualifying information in hand, an initial meeting with your prospect to discuss Indiana University Bloomington, its position in higher education, and the urgent needs of the Endowment Campaign, will help open the door. This meeting should be one of cultivation and exploration, not specifically solicitation, and should permit uninterrupted discussion about IU Bloomington. A private luncheon or dinner meeting, or a meeting in a home often proves successful for this purpose. Throughout this initial meeting, try to pinpoint your prospect's particular field of interest. You may be offered a gift; then again, you may not. A gift suggested at this time usually represents a level of giving below that which the prospective donor will make when more fully appreciative of the University's needs. If offered a gift during your first meeting, suggest that you want your prospect to think over the need, the worthiness of an investment in IU Bloomington, and the extent of participation. Also suggest a meeting at a later date to further discuss an endowment commitment.

3. Plan for follow-up.

At the end of your first meeting, you should have learned the prospect's particular interest for participation in the Campaign. If your prospect lacks a discernible specific priority, you may decide to suggest a gift opportunity for your prospect. Preparing your prospect's personalized proposal now becomes a critical consideration, and the Capital Campaign staff will help you develop the proposal for whatever gift rationale you suggest. A written proposal can be prepared and appropriate Endowment Campaign support materials assembled to assist you in matching your prospect's interest with institutional priorities. Your carefully prepared proposal should be delivered with the understanding that you want your prospect to review it. Assure the prospect that you will allow time for consideration of the proposal, and soon will arrange a meeting to discuss a commitment.

4. Ask for the gift.

After allowing your prospect time to review the proposal and to learn more about the priorities of the Endowment Campaign, it is time to close the gift. Only you will be able to decide the propitious moment for this final meeting, during which you will ask them to make a specific giving decision. You should come away from this meeting with a letter of intent, a pledge card, or some other firm commitment to the Endowment Campaign. This is your last chance, so help the prospect decide the level of gift, discuss with candor and diplomacy the amount the prospect should consider, and conclude your solicitation. Ask for the gift!

5. Review incentives for giving.

Remember, working with every prospect should be treated as a "campaign" in and of itself, and every prospect should be motivated to the point of maximum participation. A number of incentives designed to maximize participation in the Endowment Campaign for Indiana University Bloomington can help you achieve success: spreading the pledge payment over three to five years; the possibility of making a capital gift; tax advantages of various methods of giving; the opportunity to establish a permanent named or memorial fund to honor the donor, a close friend, relative, or loved one; the positive effect a gift will have on raising the sights of others; and the specific advantages of planned giving.

6. Use the pledge card wisely.

The pledge card can make the difference between asking your prospect to be a token giver or to be a full participant in the Endowment Campaign for Indiana

University Bloomington. Ask your prospect to study the pledge card with you. Note that the pledge card details the purpose of the Endowment Campaign, offers different commitment options, and requires the prospect to personally write in the total gift amount(s) and designate a specific purpose for the gift(s). The prospect should be reminded that a specific payment plan can be selected to accommodate individual preferences. Be sure your prospect writes in the date of the pledge, for this becomes the date on which the pledge collection system will be based. Clearly point out to your prospect that the pledge is a moral commitment, not a legal contract, so that if circumstances make cancellation a necessity, the donor's wishes will be honored. An official receipt will be mailed to the donor by the University, of course.

7. Above all, be flexible.

Flexibility is the key in approaching a prospect. Special situations might call, for example, for a lunch or dinner with IU's president, a dean, or the head of an academic department. Perhaps a tour of the campus could be scheduled. The Capital Campaign Office and the IU Foundation, as well as the individual academic units, will assist in these special situations. Many times the question of an unrestricted gift arises. You should keep in mind that such gifts, to be used at the discretion of the Campaign, are most desirable and appropriate, if your prospect is not committed to a particular area of interest.

8. Let us know how you're doing.

A close association among you, your Endowment Campaign chair, and the University's professional development staff is mutually beneficial. Strategic as well as moral support is readily available and can make your voluntary job of solicitation easier. Periodic reports on gift negotiations are helpful and provide invaluable progress information on solicitation assignments.

9. Keep your sights high.

Not many people find it easy to ask for large gifts. Remember most prospects are fortified by strong convictions about Indiana University and possess a firm resolve to perpetuate its mission. The prospect (like you) is being asked to represent IUB and to ask others to join them in supporting its goals, so never underestimate your prospect's ability to give. Use your enthusiasm to cultivate enthusiasm in your prospect. Stress the personal satisfaction he or she will enjoy from providing essential and vital support to Indiana University Bloomington.

10. Be proud of your role.

You are bringing to your prospect the opportunity to provide support to an institution of the highest quality. You are seeking private investments in one of our most valued human endeavors—education. Your volunteer efforts are the key to the success of the Endowment Campaign for Indiana University Bloomington. What you are doing is important. Be proud of your role. We certainly are!

The Indiana University Foundation is designated by the trustees of Indiana University as the official fundraising agency for the University. A not-for-profit corporation chartered in 1936 under the laws of the State of Indiana, the Foundation raises and receives gifts from the private sector, administers funds, and manages assets to enhance the quality of education at Indiana University.

How
to Close
the Gift

The
Endowment
Campaign
for
Indiana
University
Bloomington

THE ENDOWMENT CAMPAIGN FOR INDIANA UNIVERSITY BLOOMINGTON is a national and international fundraising effort being conducted into the year 2000. This campaign seeks to add at least $150 million to the campus's endowment and to augment annual giving by at least $200 million. The Endowment Campaign is the largest fundraising campaign for a single campus in the University's history. Since it includes all components of the Bloomington campus, gifts to the Endowment Campaign will enrich every aspect of teaching and learning at IU Bloomington.

Objectives

Each Endowment Campaign volunteer needs to meet three important objectives before beginning solicitation of major gifts:

1. Know the Six Basic Closing Stages.
2. Know How to Handle Objections.
3. Know the Major Errors to Avoid in Solicitation.

Six Basic Closing Stages

Here are the six stages necessary for soliciting and closing a major gift:

1. Opening
2. Questioning
3. Listening
4. Presenting
5. Overcoming Objections
6. Asking for the Gift

1. Opening

In any person-to-person encounter, the opening, to a large extent, will determine the outcome. It does not matter whether you are asking for a luncheon date, talking with a colleague, requesting something from an assistant, or soliciting a major gift, your opening will have a definite effect on the outcome of the conversation.

One of the primary goals you are trying to accomplish in the opening is to light a fire under your prospect. It is critical that you involve the prospect in what you are saying. One of the most effective ways to do this is to talk about the prospect's favorite subject—himself or herself.

Try to get the prospect to talk about himself or herself as soon as possible. Be warm and friendly, carry a smile, and give compliments as honestly as possible, whenever possible. Remember to be as specific and sincere as you can be. Keep in mind that you never talk *to* a prospect, but rather you talk *with* him or her. Ask for responses, listen closely, and reinforce positive statements. By drawing a prospect out, you have a better chance of bringing him or her into a meaningful relationship with IU Bloomington.

The key here, as always, is involvement. Always speak from the prospect's point of view; always ask for reactions; above all, talk about his or her accomplishments. This is true whether you are dealing with an individual major donor, a foundation, or a corporation. Foundations and corporations are people. People make decisions. People carry your proposal to other people.

Make your opening as dynamic and intriguing as you possibly can.

2. Questioning

If you have done a good job of getting the prospect's attention in the opening, your task now is to keep that attention and deepen his or her involvement. That can be easily accomplished through questioning.

Questions are wonderful things. They allow you to talk *with* the prospect rather than *to* the prospect. Questions automatically force the prospect into involvement. Good questions fall into a number of categories—questions that call for a feeling response, fact-finding questions that verify your research, or challenging and new questions that help uncover your prospect's motivations and needs.

Be careful not to ask questions that require a yes or no answer. This type of question will give you little information. Ask open-ended questions. Do not ask questions like, "Do you think we need more research in the area of human attitudes and values?" but rather, "How do you think we could improve research in human attitudes and values?"

Oftentimes, you can draw a prospect out by making a statement you have heard from a respected third party, then following that by a question like, "How do you feel about this?" Try to emphasize needs and problems as much as possible.

The biggest mistake you can make at this point is to begin talking about the Campaign. During the questioning stage, it is very important that you make sure the prospect is aware of the needs of Indiana University Bloomington before you show him or her how those needs may be met.

3. Listening

Listening is probably the most difficult skill to master; however, if you are going to take advantage of all the questions you ask, you will have to do more listening and less talking. That is not easy. The only way a prospect will invest in your solution is if the prospect thinks you have understood his or her position.

A good listener is a participant who understands communication is both an active and selective process. Most people speak at the rate of 100 to 150 words per minute. You are capable of perceiving approximately 400 words per minute.

This gives you a lead time of between 250 and 300 words. You can use this lead time to evaluate what your prospect is saying—anticipating the points he or she will make, judging what has already been said, and judging the importance of each word and each statement.

The technique of listening ahead gives you an opportunity to be discerning in your listening process. Listen with a purpose. Do not interpret. Ask questions and give feedback to your prospect so that he or she knows you are hearing what is being said. You will notice that as you give feedback, your prospects will have a tendency to reinforce the topics that are most important to him or her.

Be empathic in your listening. Put yourself in your prospect's position. By doing this, you will build respect and therefore have a better chance to achieve your desired results.

Listen with your whole body, not just your ears. Lean forward into the conversation. Listen with your eyes as well; you can pick up a lot of information by watching the body language of your prospect. Your own body language and responses will show your prospect that you are alert and interested in what he or she has to say. Use phrases such as, "Let me be sure I have understood what you said" and "Let me see, do I understand this correctly?" These kinds of questions give evidence that you are listening; they encourage the prospect to listen more actively to what you are saying; they help build a common ground between you and your prospect.

Good listening, then, involves your active and meaningful participation. Your feedback to the prospect's responses helps you to qualify and understand his or her position. Probably the most important benefit of active listening is that it makes the prospect feel good about himself or herself. It makes the prospect feel that he or she has something important to say, and that you are listening intently to what is being said.

Developing good listening skills can help you become a more effective solicitor.

4. Presenting

This particular skill may seem like the easiest part of your solicitation effort; however, you must be careful not to fall into the common trap of over-simplification. The natural tendency is to emphasize Indiana University Bloomington and its needs, rather than the benefits IU Bloomington can bring to the prospect's needs. Basically, prospects want four questions answered about the University or a specific program:

1. Is it the best?
2. Will it perform the way you say it will?
3. Will it become or remain the best in the future?
4. How will I be paid back for my investment?

Knowing that your prospect wants these questions answered, you can construct your presentation to answer these questions before they are asked. One of the best ways to do this is to talk about benefits and advantages rather than about the Campaign and its needs.

When discussing the Campaign, always try to use dialogue with the prospect:

- Use people stories.
- Make your language vivid and descriptive.
- Make the benefits for donors seem real enough to touch.

Remember Bell Telephone's marvelous slogan, "Reach out and touch someone." It sells the company's benefits rather than the features of the service. Emphasizing the Campaign's benefits rather than focusing on specific features is what you are trying to do with your prospect. Your objective is to show real people solving real problems through IU Bloomington.

5. Overcoming Objections

Most of us become uncomfortable when objections are raised. Remembering that an objection is not an attack, but rather a question, will help you overcome this discomfort.

When answering an objection, always show understanding of your prospect's position. Try to gain your prospect's respect by making statements such as, "I see your point of view" or "I can understand why you would have that concern." Take the objection and turn it into a positive statement such as "Myles Brand, IU's president, feels the same way you do about this particular problem. He has talked to the administration about it and the administration has come up with a number of ideas to overcome this problem."

The main point is to let the prospect know his or her objection is acceptable, that others feel the same way, and that this type of question has helped us find constructive solutions to other problems. You can even turn the objection into the very reason the prospect should support the Campaign.

Never let the objection lead into an argument. Do not make the objection bigger than it is. Respond to it with facts and never make excuses. If the objection is weak, however, pass over it. Ignore it and move on with your proposal. It is perfectly legitimate to compromise on minor objections if, in fact, they will not be a hindrance to reaching your primary goal.

Remember that all objections are really questions, and that the prospect's investment in the Campaign will help overcome the cause of the objection. This will help you to convert the objections into reasons for giving.

Resource 10

6. Asking for the Gift

This skill is commonly called "the closing." After you have dealt with all the prospect's questions and concerns, it is time to ask for the gift. Most failure in a face-to-face solicitation is a result of not asking for the gift.

It is important that you know how and when to ask. If you have mastered the five previous skills, you will be able to observe when your prospect is ready for you to ask.

Always give the prospect alternatives. Never ask for a yes or no answer. Keep in mind that many prospects will say no two or three times before they say yes.

It is common practice to ask for a larger gift than is expected. This gives you a stronger negotiating position, and in most cases it helps get the gift needed. The prospect knows that this is no ordinary meeting, but that you are there to discuss serious concerns that interest both him or her and the University.

Mastering these six skills will give you a much better chance of closing major gifts for the Endowment Campaign for IU Bloomington.

Handling Objections & Closing Techniques for Major Gifts

1. Assume you already have the gift.

Do not ask for the gift; act as if you already have it.

2. Tell a story.

Use a story you have heard about another prospect who had a similar objection. The prospect in the story should overcome his or her objection and make a major gift to IU Bloomington, a specific program, or an academic unit. Always use the prospect's name in your story. Remember to make the story entertaining.

3. Reverse the question.

Have the prospect ask you a yes or no question, and then reverse it into a question that you ask. For example:

Prospect: "Will the building be named after me?"
 Solicitor: "Would you like your name on the donor plaque?"
Prospect: "If I can afford the gift to get it there. . . ."

4. Close on the major objection.

Use this technique when a prospect offers objection after objection.

 a. Hear out each objection completely.
 b. Restate and put greater emphasis on the major objection.
 c. Ask the prospect if he or she would donate, were it not for the objection.
 d. If no, deal with other minor objections in turn.
 e. If yes, work through the last objection and close.

5. Last resort.

If all else fails, you may want to try the last resort.

Solicitor: "Mr. Stockwealth, I believe Indiana University has a number of great programs, strong leadership, and real vision. All it needs to continue being one of the country's great universities is more support for its faculty and student endowments. Is there anything I did wrong that kept you from making a gift?"

Prospect: (Will bring up an objection.)

Solicitor: "Of course, I should have thought of that! Thank you for being so honest with me and clarifying your feelings. I do not know how I forgot to clear that up for you."

Then deal with the objection and close.

6. Reconsider.

As you start to leave, ask the prospect, "Won't you reconsider?"

Overcoming Obstacles

You may run into a number of problems in your solicitation presentation that will keep you from closing. Here are a few suggestions to help you overcome these obstacles:

Problem #1

Prospect says, "I have to talk to my spouse."

Strategy

a. Ask, "May we both meet with him/her?"
b. Hypothesize, "Just suppose he/she agreed."
c. Ask, "Are there any other questions to which you think he/she will want the answer?"
d. Do your research—be sure to speak with both spouses on the first visit.
e. Get the spouse involved in the Campaign before you visit.

Problem #2

Prospect imposes a time limit on the meeting.

Strategy

a. Condense your presentation.
b. Ask, "Is this the only time we will be able to spend together?"
c. Ask, "How long do you think this will take?"
d. Continue with the presentation.
e. Set new agenda and proceed.
f. Reschedule the meeting for a more convenient time.

Problem #3

Prospect offers a gift that is too small.

Strategy

a. Say, "Our expectations are greater."
b. Suggest the offered gift as first payment on a larger one.
c. Check the prospect's financial position.
d. Apologize for misleading him or her about the amount you need.
e. Take the smaller gift and upgrade later.
f. Say, "If you could make four or five gifts this size, look what we could do!"
g. Say, "Before I can accept this gift, I have to check with my Campaign chair."

Problem #4

Prospect is a non-talker or silent.

Strategy

a. Ask questions.
b. Use gestures to put the prospect at ease.
c. Look and act interested when prospect does talk, and then ask more questions.

   d. Do not let the silence rest on you.

   e. Get another volunteer to play devil's advocate to stimulate the conversation.

   f. Go golfing, fishing, etc. with the prospect, a situation in which it is not necessary to have a lengthy conversation.

   g. Ask a good friend of the prospect to volunteer information about the prospect. Ask questions the friend knows the prospect is thinking about.

   h. Go into your presentation.

Problem #5

Prospect is aggressive or talkative.

Strategy

   a. Let him or her talk until he or she runs down.

   b. Hang tough.

   c. Use a high status volunteer to counter lower status person references.

   d. Do not press. Set up another meeting.

   e. Ask questions to change the focus of the conversation.

   f. Ask why he or she came to the meeting.

   g. Look for a bridge to your presentation.

   h. Ask to meet with prospect's spouse.

   i. Playback.

Problem #6

Lack of coordination among team members.

Strategy

   a. Clarify roles in advance.

   b. Set an agenda of questions.

   c. Match complementary personalities and styles.

   d. Role-play and practice in advance.

   e. Be flexible.

   f. Work out signals.

Major Errors to Avoid in Solicitation

In your presentation, be sure to avoid the 14 critical errors that commonly occur when soliciting major gifts.

   1. Not asking for the gift.

   2. Not asking for a large enough gift.

   3. Not listening/Talking too much.

4. Not asking questions.
5. Not talking about benefits to the prospect.
6. Not being flexible/Not presenting alternatives.
7. Not knowing enough about the prospect before the solicitation.
8. Forgetting to summarize before moving to solicitation.
9. Not practicing with team members before solicitation.
10. Asking for the gift too soon.
11. Speaking, rather than remaining silent, after asking for the gift.
12. Settling on too small a gift.
13. Not cultivating the prospect before soliciting.
14. Not sending out trained solicitors.

Campaign Contacts

[*Note:* Names and addresses of the contacts here were omitted to protect privacy.]

The Indiana University Foundation is designated by the trustees of Indiana University as the official fundraising agency for the University. A not-for-profit corporation chartered in 1936 under the laws of the State of Indiana, the Foundation raises and receives gifts from the private sector, administers funds, and manages assets to enhance the quality of education at Indiana University.

The Endowment Campaign for
Indiana University Bloomington

Seven Steps to a Major Gift

Step 1: Identify the Prospect.

Purpose: To discover a new or newly qualified prospect.

Questions: Does the prospect have the financial capacity to make a major gift? What form of assets might the prospect use to make a gift?

Step 2: Research and Qualify the Prospect.

Purpose: To gather and analyze relevant information about a prospect.

Questions: What are the prospect's potential interests and priorities? Does the prospect currently have a relationship with Indiana University? What information is still needed to build a gift strategy? Who is the best potential volunteer?

Step 3: Strategize with Staff.

Purpose: To develop a plan for contact, cultivation, and solicitation.

Questions: What is a realistic gift target? Which of the prospect's interests best match the priority goals of the Campaign? What does the prospect need to know, feel, and experience to bring about a major commitment?

Step 4: Involve the Prospect: Make the First Call.

Purpose: To build a bridge between the prospect and Indiana University Bloomington.

Questions: What are the prospect's attitudes and concerns about Indiana University Bloomington? Which of the prospect's interests and needs can be satisfied by meaningful participation in the Campaign? How much future involvement/cultivation will be required before the ask?

Step 5: Make the Ask.

Purpose: To invite the prospect to consider an investment in the Endowment Campaign.

Questions: What is the prospect's reaction to the ask? What are the crucial objections or concerns? What needs to be done to facilitate an actual gift or pledge commitment?

Step 6: Make the Close.

Purpose: To lead the prospect to a commitment.

Questions: What further attitudes and concerns must be addressed? What alterations may be necessary to the original request? What professional help is needed (legal counsel, investment advice, etc.)?

Step 7: Follow Up.

Purpose: To express appreciation and thanks.

Questions: What kinds of personal attention can be shown to the donor? Where should ties to Indiana University Bloomington be strengthened? What further interests and needs of the donor may be served by another gift?

Five Prospect Attitudes and Reactions

1. Agreement—Proceed to the next step.
2. Misunderstanding—Clarify the misunderstanding; gently correct with facts.
3. Indifference—Use "closed-ended" questions to discover needs and interests.
4. Skepticism—Overcome with an "expert witness."
5. "Real objections"—Use the four-step process:
   a. Clarify the objection to make sure you understand it.
   b. Meet the objection but never beat it. Restate the objection as a question; use further questions to narrow the objection to one specific, manageable issue.
   c. Minimize the impact of the objection; try to emphasize the greater good or bigger picture.
   d. Try to gain a neutral position. Ask if the objection will keep the prospect from joining in the Endowment Campaign. Summarize graciously and move on.

Resource 10

Guide
to Giving

The
Endowment
Campaign
for
Indiana
University
Bloomington

THE ENDOWMENT CAMPAIGN FOR INDIANA UNIVERSITY BLOOMINGTON is a national and international fundraising effort being conducted into the year 2000. It is the largest campaign in the University's history and includes all components of the Bloomington campus. The Campaign goal is $350 million—$150 million for new endowment and $200 million in ongoing support. Endowment is one of the most cost-effective and manageable ways to achieve the University's goals and prepare for the future. The primary purpose of this campaign is to increase the number of endowed chairs and professorships, fellowships, and scholarships available to the campus. Gifts to the Endowment Campaign will enrich every aspect of teaching and learning at IUB.

Contents

A Message from Curt Simic

Every year, Indiana University benefits from the generosity of thousands of people. Their reasons for giving vary as widely as their interests and their financial circumstances. What they all have in common is the desire to help make a great university even greater, to enable it to better serve the state and the nation.

You share that desire, and IU is pleased to count you among its supporters. Yet your situation, like everyone else's, is unique; your motivations, your goals, and your available resources combine to make your situation unlike that of any other donor. What may seem to be the most obvious way to make your gift may not be the best way for you.

Fortunately, there are many options for setting up a gift to IU. I am sure one of them will suit your purposes. This booklet is designed to help you become familiar with these choices and, I hope, help you identify the ones that are right for you.

While philanthropic impulses may have prompted your decision to support the University—indeed, few gifts are as personally rewarding as a gift to education—you should also consider the potential tax advantages provided by certain types of gifts. Some arrangements offer you other financial benefits—life income, for instance, or professional management of your assets.

The fundraising professionals at the IU Foundation are here to answer any questions or concerns you or your financial advisers may have. We want you to be confident, right from the start, that you have all the information and informed advice you need. In short, we want you to know that you are choosing the best path.

Curtis R. Simic

Curtis R. Simic
President, Indiana University Foundation

The Basics

You will find a wide variety of giving options in this booklet. Some are simple, others more complex. The general information in this section may be useful to you whichever ones you choose.

Designating Your Gift

What you choose to support is entirely up to you. You may designate your gift for any purpose that contributes to Indiana University's three-fold mission of teaching, research, and service, and that is acceptable to the trustees of the University or the board of directors of the IU Foundation. Among the most useful gifts, however, are those designated for "wherever the need is greatest." These unrestricted gifts offer much-needed flexibility to an otherwise rigid state-appropriated budget. They allow the University to take advantage of unexpected opportunities and meet challenges that arise after state budgets are set. Donors who make unrestricted gifts can be confident that their gifts will be put to the best possible use.

Endowed Funds: The Gifts That Keep On Giving

An endowment is an investment in the future. When you use your charitable gift to establish an endowment, the gift is invested with two goals in mind: to make the principal grow faster than inflation, and to provide spendable income for whatever specific purpose you have designated. The principal is never invaded, and any earnings over a certain amount—usually five percent—are channeled back into the fund to keep it healthy and growing. Well-managed endowments can generate income indefinitely. That fact makes them uniquely valuable to the University, and therefore especially attractive to donors who wish to leave a legacy at IU.

Gift Agreements

Whenever a gift fund is set up, it is wise to create a gift agreement. The agreement sets out your specific criteria for how the University will utilize your gift. It ensures that the gift will always be used exactly as you intend. It also may set out provisions for alternative uses, should it become impossible or impractical for the University to carry out your original intention (as when, for instance, advances in knowledge render a given field of study obsolete). For these reasons, the IU Foundation now requires that all new funds have a written gift agreement on file. The Foundation staff will work with you to draw up the agreement.

Donor Recognition

Indiana University appreciates its supporters. Regardless of what form your gift to the Indiana University Foundation takes, it may qualify you for one of IU's donor recognition groups. The best reward for your contribution, of course, is the knowledge and satisfaction that you have made a difference in the lives of the individuals your gift touches. Nevertheless, the University wants to publicly thank its major donors and recognize them for their philanthropy. Below are the University-wide recognition groups. In addition, the different schools may have their own donor societies.

The Presidents Circle. The Presidents Circle honors the University's most generous benefactors, those who make irrevocable gifts at leadership levels. Lifetime giving of $100,000 or more qualifies a donor for inclusion in the Presidents Circle. One may also become a member if others donate $100,000 or more in his or her honor.

The Arbutus Society. The Arbutus Society recognizes those individuals who inform the IU Foundation of their intention to invest in the future of Indiana University through planned or deferred gift arrangements.

The Well House Society. The Well House Society is unique among college and university donor recognition groups. Donors make annual gifts that are unrestricted, that is, they may be used for whatever purpose Indiana University's president and the IU Foundation's board of directors deem best. Alternatively, Well House Society donors may choose to combine their unrestricted gift with one directed to a school, department, or program of their choice. Because a very small percentage of gifts for the University are unrestricted, the Well House Society gives IU a vital source of flexible funds.

Outright Gifts

Most gifts to the IU Foundation for the benefit of Indiana University are simple, outright transfers of property. They range from $30 checks for the Annual Fund to multimillion-dollar real estate transactions. Regardless of their size or method, however, all have tax advantages for the donor, with the added appeal that the University can put an outright gift to work immediately.

Gifts of Cash

The most common type of gift is the gift of cash—and with good reason. It is simple, straightforward, and as easy as writing a check. And, because charitable gifts qualify for federal tax deductions, the real out-of-pocket cost of a cash donation is usually much less than its face value: you save whatever tax you would have owed on the amount of the gift. Likewise, some state tax laws offer additional deductions or credits for gifts to education.

For record purposes, a gift of cash is considered made on the date it is mailed or hand delivered. Please make checks or money orders payable to the Indiana University Foundation, the designated fundraising agency for Indiana University.

Resource 10

Features & Benefits

- Simple and quick
- Charitable income tax deduction
- IU can make immediate use of your gift
- Estate tax and probate savings

Gifts of Appreciated Property

Charitable gifts of appreciated property—whether real estate or capital gain securities—can provide even greater tax benefits than a cash gift of equal value. You may take a charitable deduction for the full fair market value of the property, while avoiding capital gains taxes. The IRS currently allows you to deduct the full fair market value of the property up to 30 percent of your adjusted gross income for the year. Any amount over that ceiling can be carried forward for future deduction, for up to five years, subject to the same percentage limitations.

A gift of appreciated property is considered made on the day the transfer is completed. Please contact the IU Foundation for specific instructions.

Features & Benefits

- Opportunity to make a substantial gift to IU
- Charitable income tax deduction
- IU can make immediate use of your gift
- Avoid capital gains tax
- Estate tax and probate savings

Gifts of Tangible Personal Property

A gift of tangible personal property—such as furniture, art works, jewelry, antiques, books, coin or stamp collections, and so on—is deductible for its full fair market value (up to 30 percent of your adjusted gross income) if it meets two conditions: 1) it must be documented by a legitimate appraisal, and 2) it must satisfy the "related use" standard.

"Related use" means that the University must be able to use the gift in a way that is related to or furthers its educational mission. For example, books donated to the library will meet the standard, as will classroom or office furniture, or computers, or business machines. A painting will meet the standard if it is displayed for viewing, but will not if the University sells it. Property that does not satisfy the "related use" standard may still be deducted, but only for your cost

Resource 10

basis in the property, subject to a limit of 50 percent of your adjusted gross income. The five-year carryover rule for the deduction applies in both cases. Please note, however, that in order to protect its tax-exempt status, the University must severely limit the non-related-use gifts that it accepts.

A gift of tangible personal property is considered to be made on the date when ownership or legal title is transferred. To make the formal transfer, you may write up a simple "letter of intent to donate" that identifies the property and includes a signed statement of your intent to transfer it to the Indiana University Foundation.

Features & Benefits

- Opportunity to make a unique and substantial gift to IU which may be of significant value to teaching, learning, or research
- Charitable income tax deduction
- IU can make immediate use of your gift
- Avoid capital gains tax
- Estate tax and probate savings

Bargain Sales

You may have property that has appreciated in value, but you only want to give part of that value to the IU Foundation. You may make a "bargain sale" of the property to the Foundation for less than its fair market value, usually your cost basis. You thereby get cash in hand to recoup your original investment, while getting a charitable deduction for the donated difference. You should note, however, that some of the cash recovered will be treated as a capital gain.

For record purposes, the date of the sale is considered to be the date of the gift. Bargain sales require careful planning. Please consult your tax adviser, legal counsel, or other financial planner, and contact the IU Foundation's Office of Planned Giving Services for further information.

Features & Benefits

- Possible recovery of original investment
- Opportunity to make a substantial gift to IU
- Charitable income tax deduction
- Reduction in capital gains tax
- Increased cash flow
- Estate tax and probate savings

Gifts of Closely Held Stock

If you are a business owner and you contribute closely held stock, you may take a charitable deduction for the stock's appraised fair market value. Besides increasing your cash flow, you also avoid the potential capital gains tax on the appreciated value of the stock. The corporation may buy back the stock, but so long as the IU Foundation is not legally obligated to sell back the stock, you may enjoy significant tax savings.

For record purposes, the date of a gift of closely held stock is considered to be the date the stock is transferred.

Features & Benefits

- Opportunity to make a substantial gift to IU
- Charitable income tax deduction
- Avoid capital gains taxes
- Positive impact on cash flow
- Estate tax and probate savings
- Excellent estate planning opportunity for yourself and your heirs

Life Income Plans

You can make a substantial gift to Indiana University while still earning income from the donated assets. These life income plans are some of the most flexible and fruitful options available to donors. They allow you to provide income for yourself, your heirs, or both; avoid significant capital gains and estate taxes; and satisfy your wish to make a substantial gift to IU.

This is how it works: You fund the trust with a significant, irrevocable gift to the IU Foundation to benefit Indiana University. (The gift must be irrevocable to qualify for the federal charitable deduction.) The Foundation invests the gift, and you or your designee receive income for as long as you choose: for a definite term of not more than 20 years, or for the rest of your life. At the end of that time, the remaining principal benefits the University in whatever way you specify.

You may establish a trust using assets such as real estate, stock, or cash. Funding it with appreciated long-term property enables you to protect your profit or reinvest for a higher yield, while avoiding capital gains taxes. You thereby maximize the value and the benefit of the property, both as income and as a gift.

There are two basic types of life income trusts: annuity trusts and unitrusts. The annuity trust pays a fixed *dollar amount,* while the unitrust pays a fixed *percentage.*

With the annuity trust, your income will be the same each year, regardless of the value of the trust. With the unitrust, your income will go up or down as the value of the trust itself fluctuates.

Annuity Trusts

A charitable remainder annuity trust pays a fixed amount (at least five percent of the fair market value of the trust assets when the trust is established) to you or your beneficiaries at least once a year. The payout is determined when you set up the trust, based on such factors as your age, the number of beneficiaries, your desired income, and the length of the trust term. If the trust earns more income than the agreed amount, the additional earnings are reinvested. If the earnings are less, withdrawals from the trust's principal make up the difference. Once the annuity trust is created, you may not make additional contributions to it.

You will receive an income tax deduction for the value of the charitable remainder interest in the trust at the time you set it up (calculated from tables based on your age), and you avoid capital gains taxes on the transfer of appreciated long-term assets such as real estate or securities. Because the assets are effectively removed from your estate, you also avoid estate taxes.

Features & Benefits

- Opportunity to make a substantial gift to IU while receiving life income
- Fixed payout offers the security of guaranteed income
- Can unlock appreciated assets for diversification or increased yield
- Professional asset management
- Can receive an attractive equivalent rate of return
- Immediate tax deduction
- Avoid capital gains taxes
- Estate tax and probate savings

Unitrusts

A charitable remainder unitrust differs from an annuity trust by paying a fixed percentage—at least five percent—of the fair market value of the trust's assets each year, rather than a fixed sum. That means the income will fluctuate from year to year as the trust's value fluctuates, but because the long-term market pattern is usually one of growth, you can generally expect payments to increase over time. In this way a unitrust can be an effective hedge against inflation.

Choosing a lower percentage may actually increase your income over time because it allows the principal to grow more quickly. As the principal increases, so will the amount of your payment. The difference can be significant. And the more the principal grows, of course, the larger the ultimate gift to Indiana University will be, and the more completely it fulfills your philanthropic goals. You may also make additional contributions to a unitrust.

Your charitable deduction depends on the fair market value of the initial assets you transfer, the payout percentage you choose, the number and ages of beneficiaries, and other such factors. As with an annuity trust, you effectively remove the funding assets from your estate, and you likewise avoid capital gains taxes.

Features & Benefits

- Opportunity to make a substantial gift to IU while receiving life income
- Variable percentage payout may protect against inflation as your trust's assets grow
- Larger gift to IU than might otherwise be possible
- Professional asset management
- Receive an attractive "real" rate of return on your assets
- Can unlock appreciated assets for diversification or increased yield
- Immediate tax deduction
- Avoid capital gains taxes
- Estate tax and probate savings

Pooled Income Funds

Another kind of trust is called a pooled income fund. It allows separate donors to pool their gifts for investment purposes. Two or more donors must irrevocably transfer property into the trust, contributing the remainder interest in the property to the IU Foundation. The Foundation then acts as trustee, investing the combined fund and distributing the annual proceeds to the donors in direct proportion to the assets each one contributed. The actual dollar amount is not specified: it depends on the amount earned by the fund. You may designate yourself as beneficiary, or anyone else living at the time the fund is created.

Your charitable deduction would be the present value of the remainder interest in the property, as determined by IRS tables, on the day you transfer it. You may add to the fund at any time.

Features & Benefits

- Opportunity to make a substantial future gift to IU
- Competitive rate of return

- Professional asset management
- Income for yourself or other beneficiary
- Can unlock appreciated assets for diversification or increased yield
- Immediate tax deduction
- Avoid capital gains taxes
- Estate tax and probate savings

Charitable Gift Annuities

One of the most common and popular ways to make a planned gift is with a charitable gift annuity. It is a simple contract between you and the IU Foundation. In exchange for an irrevocable gift, the Foundation agrees to pay one or two annuitants a fixed dollar amount each year for life. The amount is based on life expectancy: the older you are at the time of the gift, the greater the amount can be. The payments are guaranteed by the general resources of the Foundation.

Charitable gift annuities can be funded with cash, real estate, or appreciated securities. You receive a tax deduction based on your age, the payout rate, and the federal discount rate. If you use an appreciated asset, a portion of each payout will be capital gain, which is therefore spread out over your lifetime. Likewise, a part of each payment would be a tax-free return of principal, increasing the after-tax value of each payment. And because you have effectively removed the assets from your estate, you avoid estate taxes.

A similar type of annuity is the deferred charitable gift annuity. The arrangement is essentially the same; the difference is that the IU Foundation waits to begin your fixed payout until some specified point in the future (at least one year). In either case, at your death the proceeds of the gift annuity become available for Indiana University to use in whatever way you wished.

A deferred charitable gift annuity can be an excellent way to supplement your retirement income. The Foundation receives the gift today and invests it for years; you receive a current tax deduction, but you don't receive the payments until you retire, when you may be in a lower income tax bracket.

Features & Benefits

- Fixed payout offers the security of guaranteed income
- Attractive rate of return
- Can unlock appreciated assets for diversification or increased yield
- Professional asset management
- Opportunity to make a substantial gift to IU
- Favorable income tax position now and at retirement
- Immediate charitable tax deduction
- Estate tax and probate savings

Other Planned Gift Arrangements

Life income plans are not the only kind of planned gift. Many others exist that offer particular advantages for specific circumstances. The following pages present a sampling of the most popular. If you believe your own situation requires something not described here, a specialist from the Office of Planned Giving Services at the IU Foundation will be happy to discuss other options with you.

Charitable Lead Trusts

A charitable lead trust is like a charitable remainder trust in reverse. You select the assets used to fund the trust and decide how long it will last, and the IU Foundation receives income from the trust while it exists. There is no minimum payout. When the trust terminates, its assets return to you or your designated beneficiary.

This type of trust can be useful if you want to reduce your current income but wish to retain the assets for your family. A charitable lead trust can be a means to transfer substantial amounts of wealth from generation to generation, free (or largely free) of estate, inheritance, and gift taxes.

A charitable lead trust is a complex giving vehicle with many income, estate, and gift tax consequences. You should discuss your goals with your legal and financial advisers to determine whether a charitable lead trust would suit your plans. You are also encouraged to contact the planned giving professionals at the IU Foundation for more detailed information.

Features & Benefits

- Reduces current income while retaining assets
- Can be a low-cost means of transferring property to heirs
- Opportunity to make a substantial current gift to IU
- Potential estate, inheritance, and gift tax savings

Gifts of Real Property Subject to Life Estate

Your personal residence or farm may be the single most valuable asset you own. If it has appreciated significantly in value, you could owe tremendous capital gains taxes if you or your heirs sold the property. An alternative is to give the property to the IU Foundation subject to life estate, which simply means that you or your designees retain the use of the property for life.

You gain an immediate tax deduction for the remainder interest in the property, and you escape the potential capital gains taxes. Best of all, you get to make a substantial gift for Indiana University without disrupting your lifestyle.

Gifts of this kind require detailed language tailored to your specific situation and needs, and the advantages and benefits vary accordingly. The Foundation's planned giving staff will be happy to work with you and your advisers to help you arrange the best plan for you.

Features & Benefits

- Opportunity to make a substantial gift to IU while retaining lifetime use
- Immediate tax deduction
- Avoid capital gains taxes
- Estate tax and probate savings
- Can provide a favorable income tax position

Wealth Replacement with Life Insurance

When you make a gift to the Indiana University Foundation for the benefit of Indiana University, you may use a life insurance trust to replace the value of the donated assets. In this way, you can protect the interests of your heirs while still fulfilling your philanthropic goals. The life insurance provides the dollar amount, and the trust, provided it is irrevocable, removes the proceeds from your estate for tax purposes.

In this arrangement, you create a trust to buy insurance on your life, with your children as beneficiaries. You can use the tax savings from your charitable gift, or the payout from a life income arrangement, to cover the premiums. After your death, the proceeds from the policy pass to the trust free of estate taxes, thereby replacing the value of the original charitable gift.

Wealth replacement life insurance trusts can be set up in several different ways, and all have strict technical requirements. You should discuss them with your financial and legal advisers before deciding to pursue this option. The Foundation's planned giving staff will be happy to answer your questions.

Features & Benefits

- Restores asset value to your estate at relatively low cost
- Opportunity to make a substantial gift to IU without consequence to your heirs
- Estate tax and probate savings

Wills and Estate Plans

A carefully prepared will or estate plan is the best way to ensure that your loved ones are provided for after your death, and that your preferred charities are supported as you intend. They allow you to retain full use of your assets during your lifetime and still make a significant gift for Indiana University. They are technical documents that should therefore be drafted by an attorney, but they may be revised and updated whenever you like, as your wishes and circumstances change.

Types of Gifts

By far the most common means of making a charitable gift is through a personal trust or will. It's no wonder: such gifts allow you to contribute to Indiana University at a level you might never have managed during your lifetime.

Your bequest can take a variety of forms. Here are a few samples for you to consider.

Specific Bequest. The most popular type of charitable bequest, a specific bequest provides that the IU Foundation receive a specific dollar amount, percentage of your estate, or piece of property.

Residuary Bequest. A residuary bequest provides that the IU Foundation receive all or a stated portion of your estate after all other bequests, debts, taxes, and expenses have been distributed.

Contingent Bequest. A contingent bequest can ensure that if circumstances make it impossible to carry out your primary provisions (as when your spouse or other heirs do not survive you), your assets will then pass to the IU Foundation for Indiana University rather than to unintended beneficiaries.

Trust Under Will. You can bequeath a portion of your estate to be held in trust for a specified purpose, as stated in your will.

Bequest Language

Because the Indiana University Foundation has been designated by the trustees of Indiana University as the official entity for receiving and administering gifts for IU, please incorporate the following language into your will:

> *"I give, devise, and bequeath the (sum of/percentage of/residue of my estate) to Indiana University Foundation, a not-for-profit corporation with principal offices located in Bloomington, Indiana, to be utilized for the benefit of Indiana University as specified in a gift agreement on file at said Foundation."*

Appreciation and Recognition

If you decide to include a gift to Indiana University Foundation for the benefit of IU in your will, we invite and encourage you to let the Foundation know about your decision ahead of time, for several reasons. First, so you can complete a gift agreement and ensure that there will be no question as to how your gift will be used. Second, so that IU and the Foundation can make note of the gift as they plan for the future. And finally, so that we may recognize your generosity and show our appreciation, if you so desire, by including you in the roster of major donors to Indiana University.

The Indiana University Foundation is designated by the trustees of Indiana University as the official fundraising agency for the University. A not-for-profit corporation chartered in 1936 under the laws of the State of Indiana, the Foundation raises and receives gifts from the private sector, administers funds, and manages assets to enhance the quality of education at Indiana University.

Commemorative

Gift

Opportunities

The
Endowment
Campaign
for
Indiana
University
Bloomington

THE ENDOWMENT CAMPAIGN FOR INDIANA UNIVERSITY BLOOMINGTON is a national and international fundraising effort being conducted into the year 2000. This campaign seeks to add at least $150 million to the campus's endowment and to augment annual giving by at least $200 million. The Endowment Campaign is the largest fundraising campaign for a single campus in the University's history. Since it includes all components of the Bloomington campus, gifts to the Endowment Campaign will enrich every aspect of teaching and learning at IU Bloomington.

Commemorative Gift Opportunities

Commemorative gift opportunities available through the Endowment Campaign for Indiana University Bloomington offer alumni, parents, friends, foundations, and corporations numerous ways to provide memorials and testimonials to family, friends, organizations, or other individuals. These gifts can embody their donor's ideals and provide essential support to ensure a strong future for IU Bloomington.

Each commemorative gift provides a naming opportunity for the donor according to his or her wishes, and appropriate recognition will be given. Methods of making commemorative gifts include outright gifts of cash, gifts of securities, gifts of real property, gifts of life insurance, planned gifts which can take many forms, and gifts through a will.

An IU Foundation representative will be happy to work with anyone desiring to make a commemorative gift and explore the options through which that gift may be given. For details on these and other named and memorial gift opportunities, see the *Guide to Giving* or contact the Indiana University Foundation Office of Planned Giving Services at (800) 558-8311 or (812) 855-8311.

Guidelines for Naming Opportunities and Endowed Funds

The monetary amounts listed are University thresholds. Each unit may establish higher minimums for certain endowments based on unique requirements of the individual unit, the discipline involved, and the scope of the program relative to budget and other factors.

Support for Faculty*

Deanship. To endow the deanship of a school requires a gift of $3 million or more.

Directorship or Departmental Chair. To establish a directorship or departmental chair requires a gift of $2 million or more.

*The position, not the person, is endowed.

Faculty Chair. To establish a faculty chair requires a minimum gift of $1 million.

Professorship. To establish an endowed professorship requires a minimum gift of $500,000.

Faculty Research Fund. To establish a faculty research fund requires a minimum gift of $250,000.

Visiting Professorship. To establish an endowed visiting professorship requires a minimum gift of $250,000. The annual proceeds will be used to invite a distinguished scholar to campus for a finite period of time.

Lectureship. To establish an endowed lectureship requires a minimum gift commitment of $100,000. The annual proceeds from this endowment will be used to pay for honoraria, publicity, and the expenses of a member of the faculty or a visiting lecturer from another institution or organization on the campus.

The Indiana University Faculty Endowment Income Matching Program has been designed to encourage gifts with the goal of raising endowment for faculty positions. President Brand and the Board of Trustees have set aside $2 million in available matching funds for those gifts qualifying for the match before December 31, 1999. Gifts of $500,000 and above, from a single source, designated for chairs and professorships, and received within five years, qualify for the match. All income on gifts is to be matched in perpetuity. (Full details are available upon request.)

Support for Students

Graduate Student Fellowship. Establishment of an endowed graduate student fellowship requires a minimum gift of $200,000. A fellowship is ordinarily awarded to a student who is working toward an advanced degree in any of the graduate fields. An endowed fellowship should provide support for the majority of the recipient's expenses.

Herman B Wells Scholarship. A scholarship in the Herman B Wells Scholarship Program can be established with a minimum gift of $150,000.

Undergraduate Scholarship. To establish a full-tuition undergraduate endowed scholarship requires a minimum gift of $25,000.

Support for Programs and Facilities

School. Opportunities exist to name several of the schools and the main library on the campus, by providing a gift for the general endowment to benefit the unit. The minimum gift commitment required to do so varies with the respective schools, but the minimum gift to name a school is $10 million.

New or Renovated Building. To name new or renovated buildings generally requires a gift of one-half of the construction cost of the capital project.

Research Center, Institute, or Academic Program. To name a research center, institute, or an academic program requires a gift commitment of $1 million or more; the size of the gift is to be determined by the specific center, institute, or program to be named.

Campus Library. To establish a campus library, a gift commitment of $1 million or more (depending on the size of the library) is required. Endowment income will benefit the collections, service, and technology needs of the particular library.

Laboratory. To establish an endowed laboratory requires a minimum gift commitment of $1 million. The annual earnings from the endowment will be used for equipment, technology, enhancements, and research.

Classroom. To establish an endowed classroom requires a minimum gift commitment of $500,000. The annual earnings will be used for equipment, technology, enhancements, refurbishment, and modernization.

Collection Fund. To establish an endowed collection fund requires a minimum gift of $250,000. The income from an endowed collection fund may be used for the purchase of books or other materials in a specific field and, to the extent not needed for purchases, for the preservation of books. The income may also be used for book repair, cataloguing, or other expenses of the library.

NOTES

Five-year pledges can be made to create these endowments.

The Indiana University Faculty Endowment Income Matching Program has been designed to encourage gifts with the goal of raising endowment for faculty positions. President Brand and the Board of Trustees have set aside $2 million in available matching funds for those gifts qualifying for the match before December 31, 1999. Gifts of $500,000 and above, from a single source, designated for chairs and professorships, and received within five years, qualify for the match. All income on gifts is to be matched in perpetuity. (Full details are available upon request.)

All gifts to the Endowment Campaign for Indiana University Bloomington are tax deductible within the regulations of the Internal Revenue Service. Prospective donors to the Endowment Campaign may wish to consult their attorney or tax advisor to determine which gifts are most appropriate to their financial situation.

The Bloomington campus chancellor, or his designee, has the latitude to approve the establishment of named funds in amounts less than those stated above, provided that it is understood that, within a reasonable period of time from the establishment of the fund, the principal of the fund, excluding interest income, will equal the stated minimum.

It is the general policy of Indiana University that the University President shall approve the establishment and activation of named funds upon receipt of the gifts by the IU Foundation. The president of the University, in consultation with the Bloomington chancellor and deans and the IU Foundation president, sets minimum gift level amounts and establishes guidelines for gift-naming opportunities as approved by the IU Board of Trustees. Approval cannot be granted until the donor's name is known or until the name or names of the person or persons being memorialized are known.

Commemorative Gift Opportunities for Individual Units

Selected gift opportunities have been established for all academic units participating in the Campaign. For details on a unit's specific needs and objectives, please refer to its individual case statement or contact the unit's chief development officer.*

IU Art Museum

Name the Museum	$10 million
Name the Director's Chair	$2 million
Name the Education Chair	$1 million
Name the Curatorship for African Art, Oceania, and the Americas	Reserved
Name the Curatorship for Ancient Art	Reserved
Name the Curatorship for Western Art through the 18th Century	$1 million
Name the Curatorship for 19th and 20th Century Art	$1 million
Name the Curatorship for Works on Paper	$1 million
Name the Curatorship for Asian Art	$1 million
Name the Conservatorship of Objects	$750,000
Name the Conservatorship of Paintings	$500,000
Name the Conservatorship of Works on Paper	$500,000
Endow a Graduate Fellowship	$300,000

College of Arts & Sciences

Name the College of Arts & Sciences . . . . $25 million

Name the College Honors Program . . . . $5 million

Name the Liberal Arts Management Program . . . . $3 million

Name the Women's Studies Program . . . . $3 million

Endow the Dean's Chair . . . . $3 million

Endow a Departmental Chair . . . . $2 million

Endow a Science, Social Science, or Humanities Chair . . . . . $1 million

Endow a Laboratory . . . . $1 million

Endow a Professorship in Science,
Social Science, or Humanities $500,000

Endow a Classroom $500,000

Endow a Graduate Fellowship $400,000

Endow a Visiting Professorship $250,000

Endow a Faculty Research Fund $250,000

Endow a Dean's Scholar $200,000

Endow an Undergraduate Scholarship $25,000–200,000

Endow a Lectureship $100,000

Endow a Summer Fellowship $100,000

Endow a Teaching Award $40,000

Endow a Book Fund $25,000

Athletics

Endow the Academic Counseling Office for IU Athletes . . . . $2 million

Endow the Marching Hundred Band . . . . $2 million

Endow Computer Labs for Athletes . . . . $1 million

Endow the Student Athletic Board . . . . $1 million

Endow the University Softball Complex . . . . $1 million

Endow the University Cheerleading Squad . . . . $1 million

Endow an Undergraduate Scholarship for an IU Athlete* $250,000

Name an Undergraduate Scholarship for an IU Athlete* $100,000

Create a Sustaining Endowment Fund
to Support IU Athletics $25,000

*Donors may designate these gifts to particular varsity sports, including the following: men's and women's basketball, men's and women's cross country, men's and women's golf, men's and women's soccer, men's and women's swimming and diving, men's and women's tennis, men's and women's track and field (indoor and outdoor), football, baseball, wrestling, volleyball, softball, and water polo.

School of Business

Name the School of Business . . . . Reserved

Name the Corporate and Graduate Center . . . . $9 million

Name the Existing School of Business Building . . . . $9 million

Endow the Deanship . . . . $3 million

Establish Named Directorships or Departmental Chairs . . . . $2 million

Name the Business Library . . . . $2 million

Endow a Faculty Chair . . . . $1 million

Endow a Professorship $500,000

Endow a Visiting Lectureship $250,000

Endow a Faculty Research Fund $250,000

Endow a Graduate Fellowship $200,000

Endow an Undergraduate Scholarship $50,000

School of Continuing Studies

Endow a Professorship in Labor Studies $500,000

Endow an Undergraduate Scholarship $25,000

School of Education

Name the School of Education . . . . $25 million

Name the School's Auditorium . . . . $5 million

Endow the Deanship . . . . $3 million

Name the School's Atrium . . . . $3 million

Name the Distance Education Studio . . . . $2 million

Endow a Faculty Chair . . . . $1 million

Name the Education Library . . . . $1 million

Create an Endowment for Technology Support . . . . $1 million

Endow a Professorship $500,000

Endow a Lectureship $250,000

Endow a Graduate Fellowship $200,000

Endow an Undergraduate Scholarship $25,000

School of Health, Physical Education, & Recreation

Name the School of HPER . . . . $20 million

Endow the Deanship . . . . $3 million

Endow a HPER Research Center . . . . $1–3 million

Endow a Departmental Chair . . . . $2 million

Endow a Faculty Chair . . . . $1 million

Name the HPER Library . . . . $1 million

Endow a Laboratory . . . . $1 million

Endow a Professorship $500,000

Endow a Classroom $500,000

Endow a Faculty Research Fund $250,000

Endow a Graduate Fellowship $200,000

Endow a Lectureship $100,000

Endow an Undergraduate Scholarship $25,000

Endow a HPER Book Fund $25,000

School of Journalism

Name the School of Journalism . . . . $10 million

Endow the Deanship . . . . $3 million

Name a Research Center . . . . $1–3 million

Name the Journalism Library . . . . $1 million

Endow a Faculty Chair . . . . $1 million

Endow a Professorship $500,000

Endow a Visiting Lectureship $250,000

Endow a Graduate Fellowship $200,000

Endow a Professional Internship for Faculty $150,000

Endow a Travel and Internship Fund for Students $100,000

Endow an Undergraduate Scholarship $25,000

School of Law

Name the School of Law . . . .$25 million

Name the Law Library . . . .$10 million

Endow the Deanship . . . . $3 million

Endow the Moot Courtroom . . . . $2 million

Endow a Distinguished Chair . . . . $1 million

Endow a Public Interest Law Fellowship . . . . $1 million

Endow a Loan Reduction Program . . . . $1 million

Endow the Community Legal Clinic Program . . . . $1 million

Name the Reading Room of the Library . . . . $1 million

Endow a Program . . . . $1 million

Endow a Professorship $500,000

Name the Library Lounge $500,000

Endow a Full-Tuition Scholarship $250,000

Endow a "Dean's Scholar" $250,000

Endow a Research Fund $250,000

Endow a Journal $250,000

> Indiana Law Journal
>
> Federal Communications Law Journal
>
> Indiana Journal of Global Legal Studies

Name a Classroom

> Seating for 100–150 Students $250,000
>
> Seating for 75 Students $200,000
>
> Seminar Rooms with Seating for 30 Students $150,000

Name the Career Services Resource Center $100,000

Name a Placement Interview Room $50,000

Name a Room within the Library $50,000

University Libraries

Name the Main Library . . . . $20 million

Name the Main Library East Tower . . . . $5 million

Name the Main Library West Tower . . . . $5 million

Name a Campus Library . . . . $1 million

Endow Librarian Positions

    Dean of the University Libraries . . . . $2 million

    Head of the Lilly Library or a Campus Library . . . . $1 million

    Head of Preservation, Reference,
    or Manuscript Curator $750,000

Name the Preservation Laboratory $500,000

Endow Collections . . . .$10,000 and above

[*Note:* For space considerations, some of the schools were omitted from this section.]

Campaign Contacts

For more information on the Endowment Campaign or questions or concerns you may have, please contact any of the following individuals at Indiana University Bloomington or the IU Foundation. To discuss options for giving to the school or program of your choice, contact the chief development officer for the specific school on the Bloomington campus.

[*Note:* Names and addresses of the contacts here were omitted to protect privacy.]

The Indiana University Foundation is designated by the trustees of Indiana University as the official fundraising agency for the University. A not-for-profit corporation chartered in 1936 under the laws of the State of Indiana, the Foundation raises and receives gifts from the private sector, administers funds, and manages assets to enhance the quality of education at Indiana University.

The Endowment Campaign for Indiana University Bloomington

Standards of Giving

A fundamental of fundraising for the Endowment Campaign for Indiana University Bloomington is the identification, correct evaluation, and thoughtful solicitation approach to alumni and friends of IU Bloomington. It is important for volunteers and prospective donors to be aware of the caliber of gifts required. A better solicitation effort and more meaningful response will result when each discussion is undertaken with this information in hand.

To maximize this awareness, the following table offers specific standards of giving necessary to ensure the success of the Endowment Campaign and suggests to our volunteer workers and prospective donors the levels of support which must be achieved.

Curtis R. Simic

Curtis R. Simic
President, Indiana University Foundation

ENDOWMENT GOAL: $150 MILLION

Gift Amounts	Number of Gifts Needed	Total
$15,000,000+	1	$15,000,000
10,000,000–14,999,999	2	20,000,000
5,000,000–9,999,999	3	15,000,000
2,500,000–$4,999,999	6	15,000,000
1,000,000–2,499,999	17	17,000,000
750,000–999,999	20	15,000,000
500,000–749,999	30	15,000,000
250,000–499,999	50	12,500,000
100,000–249,999	100	10,000,000
25,000–99,999	400	10,000,000
Under 25,000	Many	5,500,000
Total		$150,000,000

The Endowment Campaign
for Indiana University Bloomington

Curtis R. Simic
President
Indiana University Foundation
P.O. Box 500
Bloomington, IN 47402

Dear Curt:

To assist Indiana University Bloomington in fulfilling its important responsibilities and in consideration of the gifts of others, I intend and expect to contribute the sum of $ _____ to the Indiana University Foundation for The Endowment Campaign for Indiana University Bloomington.

My gift is:

❑ Designated for the following purpose(s):

_____

or

❑ To be used at the discretion of the Board of Directors of the Indiana University Foundation.

I expect to make this gift over a period of _____ years, as follows:

$ _____ Herewith

$ _____ on or before _____

$ _____ on or before _____

or

_____

_____

This statement of intention and expectation shall not constitute a legal obligation and shall not be legally binding in any way on me or my estate. While I consider that I have a moral obligation to make this gift, I reserve the right to adjust or to cancel it in the event of unforeseen circumstances.

Sincerely yours,

_____
(Signature)

_____
Name (please print)

_____
(Date)

INDIANA UNIVERSITY FOUNDATION • SHOWALTER HOUSE, P.O. BOX 500 • BLOOMINGTON, INDIANA 47402
Phone: (800) 558-8311   (812) 855-8311   Fax: (812) 855-6956

Resource 10

Contents

Officers of Indiana University

Myles Brand, *President of Indiana University*

Herman B Wells, *Chancellor of the University*

Kenneth R. R. Gros Louis, *Vice President for Academic Affairs and Chancellor, Indiana University Bloomington*

Gerald L. Bepko, *Vice President for Long-Range Planning and Chancellor, Indiana University–Purdue University Indianapolis*

J. Terry Clapacs, *Vice President for Administration*

Judith G. Palmer, *Vice President and Chief Financial Officer*

George E. Walker, *Vice President for Research and Dean of the Graduate School*

Christopher Simpson, *Vice President for Public Affairs and Government Relations and Special Counsel to the President*

Michael A. McRobbie, *Vice President for Information Technology*

Steven A. Miller, *Treasurer of the University*

David J. Fulton, *Chancellor of Indiana University East (Richmond)*

Michael A. Wartell, *Chancellor of Indiana University–Purdue University Fort Wayne*

Emita B. Hill, *Chancellor of Indiana University Kokomo and Chancellor Liaison, Office of the President*

Hilda Richards, *Chancellor of Indiana University Northwest (Gary)*

Kenneth L. Perrin, *Chancellor of Indiana University South Bend*

F. C. Richardson, *Chancellor of Indiana University Southeast (New Albany)*

John W. Ryan, *President Emeritus of the University*

Thomas Ehrlich, *President Emeritus of the University*

Presidents of Indiana University

Andrew Wylie, 1829–51

Alfred Ryors, 1852–53

William Mitchel Daily, 1853–59

John Hiram Lathrop, 1859–60

Cyrus Nutt, 1860–75

Lemuel Moss, 1875–84

David Starr Jordan, 1885–91

John Merle Coulter, 1891–93

Joseph Swain, 1893–1902

William Lowe Bryan, 1902–37

Herman B Wells,* 1937–38 (acting); 1938–62; 1968 (interim)

Elvis Jacob Stahr, 1962–68

Joseph Lee Sutton, 1968–71

John William Ryan,** 1971–87

Thomas Ehrlich,*** 1987–94

Myles Brand, 1994–

*Appointed University Chancellor in 1962.
**Appointed President Emeritus in 1987.
***Appointed President Emeritus in 1994.

Trustees of Indiana University

The Trustees of Indiana University are charged with policy- and decision-making authority granted by the Indiana General Assembly to carry out the programs and missions of the university. In 1820 the General Assembly created this governing body when it established the State Seminary, which in 1838 became Indiana University.

Appointed by the Governor	*Term Expires*
John D. Walda, President	1999
Frederick F. Eichhorn Jr., Vice President	1999
P. A. Mack Jr., Vice President	1998
William A. Cook	1998
Rose E. Gallagher*	1999
Robert H. McKinney	1998

*Appointment is made from the Indiana University student body.

Elected by Indiana University Alumni

Cora Smith Breckenridge	2000
Ray Richardson	1998
James T. Morris	1999

ADDITIONAL OFFICERS,
APPOINTED BY THE TRUSTEES

Steven A. Miller, Treasurer

James P. Perin, Assistant Treasurer

J. Susan Parrish, Secretary

Dorothy J. Frapwell, Assistant Secretary

Alumni Association

Indiana University's more than 400,000 alumni live in all 50 states and in 143 international locations and are organized in 100 alumni clubs. During the first year of the "Pride of Indiana" membership campaign, IUAA has grown to more than 73,000 members, making it the sixth largest association in the country.

The goal is to have 100,000 members by the year 2000. The association sponsors a variety of programs. Among them are Mini University each summer on the Bloomington campus; family camping at Elkhart Lake, Wisconsin; a worldwide educational travel program; the Good Friends volunteer program for students in grades K–12; and the Alumni Student Recruiters program. More than 21,000 Hoosiers are driving cars with IU license plates. Alumni Publications puts out a magazine for members six times a year, a mini-magazine for nonmembers twice a year, more than 50 constituent publications, and a dozen club newsletters.

IU's alumni have a new home on the Bloomington campus. The successful completion of the Virgil T. DeVault Alumni Center campaign was celebrated during Cream and Crimson Weekend with a grand opening attended by more than 1,200 persons. More than 7,000 alumni and friends contributed $5.3 million to renovate an existing university building. Six meeting rooms are available for university and association meetings and events. All offices of the IUAA are located in the building. More than 600 personalized bricks have been sold for $1,000 and are laid on the Haugh Plaza just outside the Kelley Dining Room. The sale of bricks will continue to build an endowment for maintenance and future expansion.

Jerry Tardy is the university director of alumni affairs and executive director of the alumni association; John D. Hobson and Janet C. Shirley are associate executive directors.

Resource 10

Alumni directors across the state:

Stefan Davis, *Indianapolis*

Bette Davenport, *Richmond*

Jennifer Bosk, *Fort Wayne*

Suzanne Wallace, *Kokomo (Interim)*

Thomas Higgins, *Gary*

Joann Phillips, *South Bend*

Deborah Baird, *New Albany (Interim)*

University Traditions

School Colors: Cream and crimson were chosen by the class of 1888 as the Indiana University colors.

School Song: "Hail to Old I.U." is the alma mater song of Indiana University. It was composed in 1892 by J. T. Giles, class of 1894. Hoagy Carmichael's "Chimes of Indiana," written and dedicated to the university in 1935, is also part of IU's heritage.

School Flower: The trailing arbutus, found by Professor Herman B. Boisen on a hill east of Bloomington in 1877, is the Indiana University flower. The school yearbook carries its name.

Well House: The T. F. Rose Well House was presented to the university in 1908 by IU trustee Theodore F. Rose. Its stone arches originally were the portals of the "Old College Building" erected on

Seminary Square in 1855. In earlier times, tradition held that a female student attained coed status by being kissed in the Well House during the 12 strokes of midnight on the Student Building clock.

Chimes: The classes of 1899 through 1902 raised the funds to install an 11-bell chime in the tower of the Student Building in 1906. The bells were destroyed by a fire in late 1990 and were replaced by 14 new bells in 1991.

Old Oaken Bucket: This trophy, a symbol of the football rivalry between Indiana and Purdue, was donated in 1925 by the IU and Purdue alumni of Chicago. It resides for a year with the winning team, or in the event of a tie, for six months with each school.

Little 500: Beginning in 1951 as a one-day 50–mile men's bicycle race, the Little 500 now consists of several events including the Mini tricycle race. A women's bicycle race was added in 1988.

Founders Day: Although the university was established on January 20, 1820, its anniversary is celebrated in March on Founders Day (called Foundation Day before 1950). Students are recognized for scholastic achievement and faculty members for outstanding teaching during Founders Day ceremonies.

Note: Certain sections of this booklet were omitted for the sake of brevity.

Resource 10

YOUR GIFT TO THE ENDOWMENT CAMPAIGN FOR INDIANA UNIVERSITY BLOOMINGTON

The Endowment Campaign is the largest in the University's history and includes all the components of the Bloomington campus. The Campaign goal is $350 million–$150 million for new endowment, and $200 million in ongoing support.

Endowment is one of the most cost-effective and manageable ways to achieve the University's goals and prepare for the future. The primary purpose of the Campaign is to increase the number of endowed chairs and professorships, fellowships, and scholarships available to the campus. Gifts to the Endowment Campaign will enrich every aspect of teaching and learning at IU.

The Indiana University Foundation is designated by the trustees of Indiana University as the official fundraising agency for the University. A not-for-profit corporation chartered in 1936 under the laws of the State of Indiana, the Foundation raises and receives gifts from the private sector, administers funds, and manages assets to enhance the quality of education at Indiana University.

800 558-8311 or 812 855-8311
Bloomington, IN 47402
P.O. Box 500
Indiana University Foundation
Capital Campaign Office

INDIANA UNIVERSITY BLOOMINGTON
for
THE ENDOWMENT CAMPAIGN

THE ENDOWMENT CAMPAIGN
for
INDIANA UNIVERSITY BLOOMINGTON

Investing in the future of Indiana University Bloomington

This is my/our commitment to The Endowment Campaign for Indiana University Bloomington

Name _____

Home Address _____

_____

Business Address _____

Please distribute each gift as follows:

Amount: Program

$ _____   _____

$ _____   _____

$ _____   _____

_____

Home Phone _____

Business Phone _____

Preferred mailing address (check one):   ❑ Home   ❑ Business

Is this gift from you and your spouse?   ❑ Yes   ❑ No

If so, spouse's name: _____

_____

_____

I/we pledge and invest $_____ in the future of Indiana University Bloomington.

Please send me courtesy reminders for gifts of $_____
to be contributed:

I/we wish to make my/our gift or initial pledge amount by
(please check one):   ❑ Mastercard   ❑ Visa   ❑ Check enclosed

Credit Card Number _____

Expiration Date _____

Signature _____

❑ I/we prefer this gift remain anonymous.

❑ Please send information about giving through wills and trusts.

Special Notes _____

_____

_____

_____

_____

❑ annually   ❑ semi-annually   ❑ quarterly   ❑ other_____

beginning _____ / _____ and ending _____ / _____
           (mo)   (yr)   (mo)   (yr)

*My/our gift will be matched with $_____

from _____ (Matching Company Name),

making the total commitment $_____.

*Note: Your company requires that each subsequent pledge payment must be
accompanied by a complete matching gift form.*

_____

Donor Signature _____

Date _____ / _____ / _____

Donor Signature _____

Date _____ / _____ / _____

IU Representative _____

Thank you for your valuable investment in the future

ANNUAL CAMPAIGN PLAN

PLAN OF ACTION
1998 UNITED WAY OF CENTRAL INDIANA
ANNUAL CAMPAIGN

◆

Mission

The mission of United Way of Central Indiana is to mobilize people in our community to care for one another.

Vision Statement

Our vision is that Central Indiana will be a community where we are proud of the quality of life for all citizens. In support of this vision, United Way of Central Indiana will strive to improve the present and be known and recognized for the following:

- A voluntary means for every citizen to feel connected to the Central Indiana community
- A resource which is accessible to any citizen

Goal

The annual campaign solicits for the financial and volunteer support needed to fund the critical health and human service programs identified through the Community Needs and Assets Report. The campaign will endeavor to accomplish the following:

1. Solicit all previous corporate, public and private sector donors for their financial support
2. Identify and cultivate leadership giving prospects through the Key Club initiative
3. Identify and cultivate nonparticipating companies and donors to give through the United Way campaign and/or participate in event or volunteer activities

Objective

By raising sufficient contributions, United Way of Central Indiana will be able to fund the members' agencies' programs and targeted initiatives that impact the critical health and human needs in Marion and the surrounding counties.

Plan of Action

The 1998 campaign will concentrate on the following initiatives:

Workplace Campaigns

- Conduct personal calls on top 300 accounts and 100 underperforming accounts
- Train Employee Campaign Coordinators and Key Club Coordinators
- Conduct a Pacesetter Campaign
- Recruit and train Loaned Associates for fall campaign
- Provide volunteer opportunities for employees (Day of Caring)
- Oversee first-time initiatives:
    Hospital and Health Care
    Sports
    United Way of Central Indiana Member Agency
    CEO Briefings with UWCI President

Leadership Giving

- Establish a Leadership Giving Council to identify and arrange for personal calls on prospects and current donors
- Initiate a 3-year leadership giving ask for targeted donors
- Promote Lilly Endowment Inc. Challenge grant

New Business Development

- Identify and personally call on targeted companies with significant potential as well as mid- and small size companies
- Conduct Park 100 Blitz
- Fax "Rolling 20" list to cabinet and board members bimonthly
- Attend CEO Briefings with UWCI President
- Recognize New Business Development companies at a luncheon

Allocation of Resources

Funding Sources

- Corporate and donor solicitation in the workplace
    Marion County (Region A & B portfolio of accounts)
    Hamilton County
    Boone, Hancock, Hendricks & Morgan Counties
    Combined Federal Campaign (CFC)
- Leadership
    Leadership Giving
        Ordre d' Égalité ($50,000–$74,999)
        Ordre de Liberté ($25,000–$49,000)
        Membres de la Société ($10,000–$24,000)
        Platinum ($5,000–$9,999)
        Gold ($2,500–$4,999)
        Silver ($1,000–$2,499)
    Individuals and Retirees solicitation
- New Business Development
    Targeted accounts
    Previous donors

Management

The following job descriptions outline the responsibilities of those involved in the planning and implementation of the campaign. All Campaign Cabinet members are encouraged to attend Campaign Cabinet meetings and kickoff and campaign events as listed in the enclosed calendar.

General Campaign Chair   *(Name here)*

- Recruit and manage campaign volunteer leaders
- Personally call on CEO's of targeted accounts; new business prospects, when appropriate; and selected major donors
- Set the campaign goal, in conjunction with the Community Service Council and the Board of Directors
- Represent UWCI's annual campaign to the community
- Attend United Way's Community Leaders Conference (April 23–25)

General Campaign Co-Chair *(Name here)*

- Serve as chair of Leadership Giving Council
- Contribute at Alexis de Tocqueville level or higher
- Select Leadership Giving Council members
- Recruit new Alexis de Tocqueville/Platinum contributors
- Encourage retention or upgrade of existing contributors to Alexis de Tocqueville level or higher
- Actively pursue first million-dollar contributor

CAMPAIGN CABINET

Combined Federal Campaign *(Name here)*

- Organize the local Combined Federal Campaign (CFC)
- Determine eligibility of local agencies in the CFC
- Select and supervise the Principal Combined Fund Organization
- Ensure that campaign is conducted in compliance with Office of Personnel Management (OPM) rules and regulations. Due to OPM rules and regulations, CFC chair is not permitted to call on nonfederal employees

County Campaign Chairs *(Name for each county)*

- Responsible for all facets of the campaign
- Recruit county campaign volunteers
- Plan and attend county campaign kickoffs and Day of Caring
- Plan county reporting meetings and thank-you events
- Identify and cultivate new county accounts and leadership giving prospects

Hamilton County Chair *(Name here)*

- Recruit and manage five top-level Hamilton County campaign volunteers
- Call on selected key firms in Hamilton County for a corporate gift, CEO Key Club gift and improved or new employee campaign
- Identify and cultivate leadership giving prospects within Hamilton County
- Attend Hamilton County Advisory Board meetings, UWCI campaign cabinet meetings, Day of Caring and other UWCI events
- Serve as member of Hamilton County Service Center Advisory Board as the Hamilton County Campaign Chair

Loaned Associate Chair   *(Name here)*

- Direct the recruitment process of Loaned Associates by recruiting a team of key volunteers that promotes company involvement
- Assist in the quality assurance of the training and management of the Loaned Associates
- Assist in the creation of a Loaned Associate Alumni Group
- Assist in the recognition of Loaned Associates and their sponsors

Marketing Chair   *(Name here)*

- Obtain commitment from the local TV stations for continued support and production of the annual simulcast
- Obtain commitment of radio stations and print publications for "radio-cast" and "print cast"
- Obtain pro bono or at-cost production services
- Request good placement of PSA spots
- Guide market research projects
- Advise on public relations and campaign marketing issues
- Approve campaign marketing plans

Minority Key Club Chair   *(Name here)*

- Contribute to the United Way campaign at the Key Club level
- Recruit Minority Key Club Committee of 10 volunteers to identify and solicit donors
- Promote Lilly match of first-time minority Key Club gifts
- Personally solicit colleagues for leadership gifts
- Host the Victory Celebration, a reception to honor those who contributed to the campaign
- Sponsor or secure a sponsor for the Victory Celebration

New Business Development Chair   *(Name here)*

- Meet monthly with New Business Development staff to develop and implement strategies
- Recruit, assist, train and manage 40 community volunteers
- Host one monthly meeting and thank-you celebration
- Call on a minimum of five new business accounts
- Promote Lilly match for first-time corporate donations and employees campaigns

Hospital/Health Care Initiative Chair (Name here)

- Encourage United Way giving at employee level through personal calls or meeting with president/CEO of targeted organizations
- Encourage personal giving at Key Club level of doctors and appropriate staff in these organizations
- Formulate marketing and/or public relations initiatives that would encourage giving to the United Way and public awareness about the campaign

Sports Initiative Chair (Name here)

- Encourage United Way giving at employee level through personal calls or meeting with president/CEO and/or general manager of targeted organizations
- Encourage personal giving at Key Club level of key leaders and staff in these organizations
- Formulate marketing and/or public relations initiatives that would encourage giving to the United Way and public awareness about the campaign

Region A and Region B Chairs (Names here)

- Recruit and manage four or five community volunteers who will be asked to recruit five additional volunteers each to call on designated companies in Marion County
- Personally call on five companies to secure campaign commitment and ensure that all strategic accounts (1997 contributions of $5,000+) have been contacted
- Call on the new accounts or prospects that are appropriate for your participation
- Assist in problem solving on targeted accounts
- Call on targeted accounts for inclusion in the Pacesetter campaign
- Attend monthly meeting to report account progress

UWCI Agency Co-Chairs (Names here)

- Report campaign strategies and progress to member agencies
- Oversee co-marketing efforts by ensuring that all agencies have the UWCI marketing kit, display yard signs and recognize membership on all literature
- Ensure that 100% of UWCI member agencies conduct employee campaigns and solicit their board members for leadership giving.

Note: The campaign timeline appears in Exhibit 7.3 in Chapter Seven.

CAPITAL CAMPAIGN PLAN

The Academic Endowment Campaign

◆

Indiana University–Bloomington Campaign Plan

September 22, 1995

Table of Contents

◆

Introduction

Premises of the Campaign Plan

Perspective

Plan for the Advance/Major Gifts Phase

Campaign Committees

Role of Chairpersons of Academic Unit Component Committees

The Campaign Timetable: Broad Outlines of Activity

Public Relations and Public Information

Staffing

Staff Organization

Annual Giving During the Endowment Campaign

Budget

Campaign Operations

Endowment Matching Program

<table>
<tr><td>Appendix I</td><td>Nucleus Fund Organization</td></tr>
<tr><td>Appendix II</td><td>Endowment Campaign Leadership Structure</td></tr>
<tr><td>Appendix III</td><td>Activity Report</td></tr>
<tr><td>Appendix IV</td><td>By Project: Indiana University Foundation
Major Gift Proposal Update</td></tr>
<tr><td>Appendix V</td><td>Major Gifts Fundraising Guidelines</td></tr>
<tr><td>Appendix VI</td><td>Annual Giving Program During the Endowment Campaign</td></tr>
<tr><td>Appendix VII</td><td>Memorandum</td></tr>
<tr><td>Appendix VIII</td><td>Prospect Rating Sessions and Techniques</td></tr>
<tr><td>Appendix IX</td><td>General Guidelines for Recognizing and Counting Gifts
to the Endowment Campaign</td></tr>
<tr><td>Appendix X</td><td>Guidelines for Naming Opportunities and Endowed Funds
for the Bloomington Campus Campaign</td></tr>
<tr><td>Appendix XI</td><td>Indiana University and Indiana University Foundation
Prospect Management Program Policies and Procedures</td></tr>
<tr><td>Appendix XII</td><td>Gift Vehicles Eligible for Matching Endowment Program</td></tr>
</table>

Resource 12

Introduction

Indiana University–Bloomington (IU-B) is engaged in a planning process and advanced gift program to prepare for a large and comprehensive capital fundraising campaign focusing on the need for endowment. With the authorization of the Trustees of the University for most of the major components of the campaign, and operating under the aegis of the Board of Directors of the Indiana University Foundation (IUF), the Campaign's intensive planning phase began in 1994; the advance gift phase began July 1, 1994; and the public phase of the Campaign is expected to begin by 1998. Before the public phase of the Campaign begins, the Trustees of the University will be asked to formally approve the full Campaign program and plan, which will be specified in two detailed Campaign documents:

1. The *Case Statement* will specify the objectives for which funds are to be sought.
2. The *Campaign Plan* will map out the course of action by which these funds are to be raised.

THIS DOCUMENT IS THE *CAMPAIGN PLAN*. It has been prepared to accomplish several objectives:

1. To establish the basic fundraising principles on which a campus-wide capital funding program can be developed.
2. To outline the overall or "core" plan for the Campaign including the organizational structure, both volunteer and professional, which will be required.
3. To define and describe the relationships implicit on such an effort:
   a. Academic planning and participation
   b. Prospect identification, management and research
   c. Formation of the Nucleus Fund
   d. Major gifts phase
   e. Annual giving and its relationship to the Capital Campaign
   f. Goal setting
   g. Cultivation and involvement of prospects and leadership
4. To establish a timetable for key activities required for the Campaign.
5. To suggest the main elements of supporting publications, public communications and cultivation programs.

Upon approval of this Campaign plan, the University will have a unifying master blueprint for all operations of the campus' development program for 1995 through 2000.

Premises of the Campaign Plan

The Campaign Plan is based on the following assumptions:

1. The Campaign will be authorized by the Trustees of Indiana University and conducted under the aegis of the Board of Directors of the IUF as an exercise of their chartered responsibility as the official fundraising agency of Indiana University.
2. The period of intensive fundraising will be from July 1, 1994, through December 31, 2000, or that academic year.
3. The goal will be large—in the $150 million range for endowment and $350 million overall.
4. The personal solicitation of prospects will be concentrated on those believed to be able to contribute $25,000 or more.
5. The Campaign will have its own identity, but it will be managed in conjunction with other ongoing fundraising activities. It will be carefully coordinated with the University's various annual fund programs and continuing promotional and event schedules. Every major officer of the campus will have a role.
6. The structure and scope of the Campaign will reflect both the campus' evolving emphases and its internal operating structure. This will be a campus-wide Campaign, but development efforts on behalf of particular schools or other units that have their own constituency may occur as campaign components within the overall program.
7. Ongoing support programs will be treated as an "operating component" of the Campaign and all alumni, whether or not they are capital prospects, will be asked to participate in annual giving and other ongoing development programs. Thus, the specific capital fundraising targets of the campaign will be presented as an enhancement to—rather than in place of—ongoing private support.
8. Gifts will be sought in all forms, including cash and securities, real and personal property, trusts, life income agreements, pledges in the form of bequests and any combination of these. Commitments may be paid over three to five years, or longer in the case of special circumstances.
9. Funds raised for the University through the efforts of this Campaign will supplement, but in no way supplant, the operating and capital support for the campus from the State of Indiana.
10. The projected effects of inflation will be taken into account in calculating the amounts needed to fund Campaign objectives.
11. The condition of the stock market and the nation's economy over the next five years will be a variable factor in the giving capacity of many prospects.

12. Tax laws affecting charitable contributions are subject to change; any deleterious changes during the Campaign will require new strategies or adjustments in the Campaign Plan.

13. Corporate and foundation giving is increasingly oriented toward specific programs with well-defined goals. This implies a need for an imaginative packaging of existing and proposed programs based on detailed descriptions and renderings as applicable for these programs.

14. The readiness of various component units of the Campaign may vary and influence the timetable of the public phase of the Campaign. For example, if one of the major components is not ready to proceed at the target date of the Campaign kickoff, inhibiting the Campaign's ability to conduct the advance gift phase for that program on a timely basis, the public announcement of the overall Campaign may necessarily be delayed.

Perspective

This plan encompasses the basic requirements for organizing and seeking contributions to the "Academic Endowment Campaign." The Campaign is designed to appeal to graduates of the University, other special friends, foundations, corporations, corporate foundations and businesses located and headquartered both within and outside the State of Indiana. The Campaign will seek a total of $350 million during the period from July 1, 1994, through December 31, 2000, or the conclusion of that academic year, to enhance the endowment and supplement on-going programs.

The total Campaign goal is comprised of two major elements: 1) Ongoing support accounts for $200 million of the overall goal; 2) Endowment goals amount to $150 million. During the past four years, private support to Bloomington's various programs including schools with joint programs on the Indianapolis campus, has averaged $33 million, of which about $15 million each year has been designated for endowment purposes. A portion of those funds has been contributed for purposes which will be "featured objectives" in the "Academic Endowment Campaign"—faculty and student support. As the Campaign begins, of course, those gifts must not be counted twice, so they will be included in the appropriate category of Campaign objectives.

However, continuing the support of programs outside those objectives is critical to the well being of the campus. As a result, the total Campaign goal is a combination of ongoing support added to the Campaign's "featured objectives." It is our expectation that increases in ongoing support will increase 30 percent to 50 percent during the campaign time period as a consequence of the publicity, increased cultivation activities and a deepening awareness of IU's need for private support.

The endowment goal of $150 million includes funds for those academic endowments which have been assigned the highest priority by the Bloomington Chancellor. Campaign efforts to raise this $150 million that is above and beyond ongoing support programs will focus on major gifts of $25,000 or more. Pace-setting gifts of $100,000 or more will be sought during the Nucleus Fund phase to stimulate the Campaign toward a quick and successful completion. (See Standards of Giving Table below.)

The primary requisite governing this entire undertaking is that the Academic Endowment Campaign will seek to fulfill documented needs of the campus.

Planning for this capital venture is being undertaken with great care and deliberation. The plan which follows documents steps which must be taken to ensure success in the *initial* phases of the Campaign. Except for brief discussions of public relations and campaign policy, the plan which follows deals almost exclusively with the preparatory phases—Advanced and Major Gifts—of the Campaign. Plans for subsequent phases—Special and General—will be developed at the appropriate times in the campaign schedule.

Plan for the Advance/Major Gifts Phase

A. Advance/Major Gifts: The Critical Factors

The Advance/Major Gifts phase of the Campaign is the all-important phase. For this reason, it is urged that, in the initial stages of the campaign organization, all planning and action be directed primarily toward gifts of $100,000 or more (except in relation to the necessarily smaller gifts of a few members of the IUF Board of Directors and the Advanced/Major Gifts Committee). The following figures are targets and illustrate the pattern in which gifts should be sought to achieve the Campaign goal.

TABLE OF GIFTS NEEDED TO RAISE $150 MILLION.

Gift Amount	Number of Gifts Needed	Total in Range
$15,000,000+	1	$15,000,000
10,000,000–14,999,999	2	20,000,000
5,000,000–9,999,999	3	15,000,000
2,500,000–4,999,999	5	12,500,000
1,000,000–2,499,999	20	20,000,000
750,000–999,999	20	15,000,000
500,000–749,999	40	20,000,000
250,000–499,999	50	12,500,000
100,000–249,999	100	10,000,000
25,000–99,999	400	10,000,000
Totals	641	$150,000,000

Resource 12

A table of standards of giving is a sobering thing, and rightly so. It says, in effect, that without gifts of the order of magnitude indicated, the entire effort has little, if any, chance of succeeding. In a mood of urgency created by this awareness, Endowment Campaign leaders are better prepared to offer specific suggestions to prospective donors.

Large amounts of money are not raised by casually saying, "Anything you can spare will be quite all right." In advance of any asking, the Campaign leadership must know what standards of giving are necessary to succeed. When so informed, they can and must communicate a sense of these standards to the entire constituency of workers and prospective donors.

A fundamental of fundraising—one which we must practice throughout the Campaign—is the identification, correct evaluation and thoughtful approach to alumni and friends of IU. The volunteer is better able to do a good job when he/she: 1) proceeds with an awareness of the caliber of gifts required for success; and 2) makes each major gift approach fortified by a specific evaluation of the prospect's capacity to give.

B. Nucleus Fund

The Advance Gifts phase of the Campaign will develop and gain its momentum from the pace-setting gifts of Directors of the IU Foundation, board members of academic unit advisory committees, and 50 to 100 other donors. The success of the Nucleus Fund depends, to a large degree, on securing 100 percent participation from these groups. Once their commitments are made, these leaders are in position to help secure the additional gifts and pledges needed to fulfill the Nucleus Fund goal. A total of approximately 40 percent of the Campaign endowment goal—that is at least $60 million—should be secured before public announcement of the Campaign in 1998.

We realize that some of the gifts from various Board members may be modest; however, sufficient giving ability exists within the present Boards to help make the Nucleus Fund figure an impressive demonstration of tangible leadership. The Nucleus Fund when completed will offer the following advantages:

1. It will give the Boards an opportunity to set an example which will show the way for all the University's constituencies.
2. It will demonstrate that the University has been realistic in setting the objectives for the capital components of the Campaign at $150 million, over and above the $200 million goal for ongoing support.
3. It will set the tone for the remaining major gifts effort, and thus, for the Campaign.
4. It will inspire every major gift prospect subsequently solicited.

The building of a Nucleus Fund (screening, rating and formation of the Campaign committee structure) will occur under the general direction of the President of the IUF and under the specific direction of the Nucleus Fund/Executive Committee. The organizational chart included in Appendix I illustrates the Nucleus Fund organization, which also forms the framework for the overall Campaign leadership structure that will emerge during the Nucleus Fund/Advance Gift phase of the Campaign.

C. Organizing for the Advance Gifts Phase

The chart included in Appendix II presents the Major Gifts leadership structure for the Endowment Campaign. Listed below is a brief description of each component of the Campaign and the summary of the responsibilities and objectives to be assumed by each committee chairperson.

Campaign Committees

[Some material was omitted from this section for the sake of brevity.]

It is proposed that the Academic Endowment Campaign be operated under the direction of a national chairperson or persons.

The duties of the chairperson(s) are as follows:

1. Serve as the Campaign Chief Executive Officer
2. Enlist chairpersons and other top volunteer leaders for the principal functioning units of the Campaign organization
3. Make a significant gift to the Campaign commensurate with his/her own ability
4. Spearhead and/or accompany President Brand in cultivation and solicitation visits with top-level prospects
5. Assume specific responsibility for the personal and/or corporate commitments for members of the nucleus fund-executive committee and of appropriate principal component chairpersons
6. Preside at executive committee meetings
7. Act as primary spokesman, with President Brand, for Campaign goals, themes, objectives and strategies
8. Serve as keynote speaker at Campaign kickoff and other critical Campaign functions and cultivation affairs
9. Provide inspiration and motivation for volunteer leaders to fulfill Campaign commitments
10. Review and approve all major strategy and marketing plans for the Campaign

The campaign committees are as follows:

1. The Nucleus Fund Committee*
2. Endowment Campaign Executive Committee
3. Academic Unit Campaign Committees
4. Other Campaign Committees

> Faculty-Staff Committee

> Public Relations Committee

Role of Chairpersons of Academic Unit Component Committees

The Academic Unit Committee chairpersons perform the most important roles in the Campaign organization. It will be the chairperson's responsibility to put together the respective committees just described, to persuade committee members to accept appropriate assignments, and to keep them on a steady and productive pursuit of their prospects. The chairperson should, if possible, be a resident of the state and/or very knowledgeable about Indiana University, be capable of making major personal gifts, be active in business with considerable influence and should not be hesitant to ask for large gifts. In brief, the tasks of the Academic Unit Campaign chairpersons are as follows:

1. To put together strong committees willing to seek gifts in the $25,000 and up range from individuals and their personal and family foundations
2. To work closely with the National Campaign Chairperson in all matters affecting the committee's responsibility
3. To make a significant personal gift commensurate with his/her own ability.
4. To ask personally for certain major gifts
5. To hold meetings of the committees regularly in which its members can screen and rate new prospects, take additional assignments and report on progress
6. To follow up periodically with members of the committee and make regular reports to the Executive Committee on the progress of the unit campaign
7. To see that members of the committee are fully informed about the Campaign and then to see that each member of the committee has made a personal commitment in accordance with his or her ability
8. To participate in cultivation events as desirable

*The "Nucleus Fund" designation will cease being used once the $60 million Nucleus Fund is achieved and the public phase begins.

The Campaign Timetable: Broad Outlines of Activity, July 1, 1994–December 31, 2000

I. Planning Phase

    Draft Preliminary Timetable

    Draft Initial Statement of Campaign Goals

    Conduct Market Survey of Leading Alumni and Donors

    Build Major Gift Prospect Lists, Research IU Relationships

    Develop Communications and Marketing Plans

    Begin Case Stating Process

    Develop Staff Organization Plan and Campaign Budget

    Present Preliminary Plans to Trustees and Directors

    Recruit and Hire Campaign Staff As Needed

    Refocus Existing Staff on Major Gifts

    Begin Corporate and Foundation Advance Gifts Efforts

    Begin Soliciting Major Leadership Gifts

II. Advance Gifts and Leadership Recruitment

    Conduct Prospect Screening and Rating Programs

    Enlist Nucleus Fund Chair

    Begin Solicitation of Board of Directors

    Identify, Enlist and Educate Campaign Chair(s)

    Identify, Enlist and Educate Academic Unit Chairs

    Produce Pre-Campaign Literature and Case Statement

    Obtain Approval of Full Campaign by Trustees of IU and Directors of the IUF

    Solicit Campaign Committees and Others for Nucleus Fund

       JUNE 30, 1998: DEADLINE FOR COMPLETION OF NUCLEUS FUND GOAL

III. Public Phase of Campaign

    Public Kickoff Event—Fall 1998

    Continue Activity of Academic Unit Campaigns

Resource 12

Continue Adding Names to Major Gifts Prospect List

Continue Prospective Donor Contact and Cultivation as Required

Continue Major Gifts Solicitations

Continue Distribution of Campaign Information to News Media and Prospects

Continue to Enlist, Organize and Train Volunteer Leadership

Ongoing Recognition of Donors of Major Gifts

Campaign Victory Celebration

DECEMBER 31, 2000: DEADLINE FOR
100 PERCENT OF CAMPAIGN DOLLAR OBJECTIVE

Public Relations and Public Information

The results of the Campaign market survey indicate a need to develop a strong communications program for the Bloomington campus to address identity and image concerns uncovered during the survey. This effort should begin in earnest immediately and parallel and complement campaign communication efforts.

A vigorous effort will be made to interpret the Campaign through various written and audio-visual materials, public events and special events for Campaign leaders and volunteers. Eventually, a Campaign newsletter may be published to keep volunteer leaders and donors informed of the progress of the Campaign. Through the IU News Bureau, the campus will also seek to keep the general public informed of the Campaign and the importance of the program to the future of the University through various forms of printed and electronic media as may be appropriate.

Staffing

The IUF is responsible for providing the following:

1. Liaison with the President, Chancellor and Board of Directors of the IUF Board
2. Under the coordination of the President of the IUF, assistance in the development of the Nucleus Fund
3. Assistance in the formation of the Academic Unit Campaign Committees
4. Coordination of ongoing development activities with the Campaign

5. Liaison for the Campaign with annual fundraising programs
6. Maintenance of the President's, Chancellor's and the Chair of the Campaign's schedule
7. Research on major gift prospects by phases in the Campaign
8. Service to Campaign solicitation activities, that is, corporate, faculty-staff, annual fund, planned giving, and so on
9. Handling of gifts, gift records and acknowledgments
10. Production of campaign status reports in compliance with approved guidelines.
11. Supervision of budget and control of expenses
12. Development and production of a publication supporting the case for all components of the Campaign
13. Assistance in the development of specific component case statements to ensure thematic and design consistency
14. Production of written proposals for major gift solicitations
15. Prospect management and maintenance of the Campaign prospect files

Staff Organization

In large measure, the effectiveness of the Campaign will depend upon staffing. The leadership and chairpersons of all of the operating divisions of the Academic Endowment Campaign will need to have the full-time assistance of the most experienced and able staff available.

Many if not all of the present officers in the University will be involved in the operation of the Campaign in one way or another. Among the officers who will have key responsibilities are the following:

IU President—It has been pointed out before that the role of the President in the Campaign is crucial. Dr. Brand is among the University's most persuasive representatives, and it will be essential for him to be available to undertake certain key negotiations in the early stages of the Campaign and for closing on some prospect solicitations as the Campaign moves through its various phases.

IU Vice President and Chancellor—As one of the campus' most articulate spokespersons, Dr. Gros Louis must play a key role in interpreting the case for support to various constituencies and conveying the positive impact of the campaign to donors. He must also play a key role in working with the Deans of the campus on all campaign related matters.

IUF President—Mr. Simic will advise Campaign leadership and Campaign staff in matters which affect the University. He will play a major role in meetings of the

Executive Committee and will be the University's principal liaison with the Campaign. He will also play a key role in numerous nucleus fund solicitations.

IU Vice Presidents—All must be available for advice and counsel on Campaign matters as they relate to their areas.

Deans—All must be available for advice and counsel on Campaign matters as they relate to their counterparts. Active leadership in each academic unit campaign will be required as well as participation in the solicitation of lead gifts for the unit.

IUF Senior Vice President-Development—Mr. Kirsch is responsible for directing the activity of all Foundation staff involved with the campaign and assisting the campaign management team in strategic and operational aspects of the campaign.

Campaign Director—As director of the Campaign, Mr. Dove will serve as chief campaign strategist. He will have jurisdiction in all important aspects of the Campaign. He will play a key role in ensuring that all elements of the campaign plan are executed in proper sequence and on schedule.

Campaign Development Staff—The Campaign development staff will be organized with regional responsibilities carefully coordinated with component project responsibilities. This will require constant communication and cooperation between Foundation staff and directors of academic unit campaigns.

- *Executive Director of Development*—The Executive Director of Development will participate in directing specified Foundation staff and certain constituent units involved with the Campaign and provide leadership for annual support initiatives within the Foundation and on the Bloomington campus.
- *Associate Director of the Campaign*—An Associate Director may be appointed to work with constituent unit programs and to manage certain operational aspects of the Campaign as designated by the Director. The Associate Director will also provide staff support to the Campaign Executive Committee.
- *Academic Unit Campaign Directors*—The Academic Unit Campaign Directors, namely the chief development officer of each unit, are responsible for staffing the members of their various campaign committees and are responsible for directing the component campaigns assigned them within the parameters set forth in the Campaign Plan. Accordingly, each unit campaign director will be asked to submit to the Campaign Director by November 15, 1995, a campaign plan for their respective unit.

- *Director of Planned Giving*—The Director and staff are responsible for identifying, cultivating and soliciting planned gifts—anticipated to be a major component of the campaign—and for providing service to the academic units in this area.
- *Director of Corporate and Foundations Relations*—The Director is responsible for that portion of the Campaign relying on corporate and foundation support, as well as for other ongoing campus, corporate and foundation relations programs.
- *Senior Development Directors*—These individuals are responsible for the identification, cultivation and solicitation of major prospects in their assigned territories. They are also responsible for the training and staffing of any regional Campaign volunteers.
- *Staff Reporting Expectations*—Beginning December 1, 1995, every IUF and academic unit development officer with Campaign responsibilities will be expected to complete a monthly activity report to be shared with the Dean/Director and with the Campaign Director. The format for such a report is included in Appendix III.

Additionally, on a monthly basis, all individuals with campaign solicitation responsibility will be asked to submit to the campaign director's office a report to include new solicitations, the status of outstanding solicitations and the closure on any solicitations. A form is attached as Appendix IV.

Development officers will be expected to perform under the guidelines established by and for major gift officers in the summer of 1994 subsequent to the development program review conducted by Grenzebach and Associates. These expectations are attached as Appendix V.

Annual Giving During the Endowment Campaign

It is recommended that during the life of the campaign, the IUF assume responsibility for annual giving programs on the campus, thereby enabling development officers to meet the new responsibilities and expectations imposed by the campaign through devoting a maximum amount of time to major gift fundraising. A brief plan for this approach is included as Appendix VI.

Budget

The Campaign is budgeted at 5 percent of the endowment goal. The proposed campaign budget is attached as Appendix VII.

Campaign Operations

There are many keys to success in a fundraising enterprise. The following, however, cannot be overlooked.

A. Board Participation

We have stressed the importance of the Nucleus Fund and Director support. We look to these Boards, as well as to leadership from academic unit campaign committees, to provide vigorous leadership in the enlistment of committee members and in the actual solicitation of funds from prospects for significant gifts.

B. A Voluntary Effort

Major gift solicitation should be undertaken principally by volunteers except in special cases of the involvement by the President and members of the University's administration and faculty. The principle of voluntary participation in Advance and Major Gift solicitation also applies straight down the line in the whole Campaign organization. The effectiveness of workers comes as much from their readiness to commit their own time, energy and money as from their persuasiveness in selling the campus' case for support.

C. Solid Prospecting

Major gift prospecting is a "sights-raising" search for giving potential. Potential is an indication of a person's capacity to give, not to be confused with propensity, which is a factor of interest and our ability to cultivate and to sell the program.

At the moment there are about 400 prospects identified with significant gift potential. Experience would indicate that this number of prospects is inadequate to achieve the gift tables as indicated in a previous section of this plan. Peer screenings and ratings will bear this out. The approximate number of solid prospects needed in each of the major gift categories are indicated as follows:

NUMBER OF PROSPECTS NEEDED TO RAISE $150 MILLION.

Gift Amount	Number of Gifts Needed	Total in Range	Number of Prospects Needed
$15,000,000+	1	$15,000,000	4
10,000,000–14,999,999	2	20,000,000	8
5,000,000–9,999,999	3	15,000,000	12
2,500,000–4,999,999	5	12,500,000	20
1,000,000–2,499,999	20	20,000,000	80
750,000–999,999	20	15,000,000	60
500,000–749,999	40	20,000,000	120
250,000–499,999	50	12,500,000	150
100,000–249,999	100	10,000,000	300
25,000–99,999	400	10,000,000	1,000
Totals	641	$150,000,000	1,754

Resource 12

D. Pledges

Pledges over a period of several years are a necessary factor in making possible on every level the size of gifts essential to success in a capital campaign. The standard provided for payment of pledges to the Campaign should be up to five years. Provision should be made for extending the payments beyond that in special cases.

E. Prospect Identification and Rating

Because the number of prospects needed is not sufficient, prospect identification and rating will be vital to the success of the campaign. In particular, intensive efforts on the part of all campaign development officers need to be undertaken immediately and extend through the pre-public phase. An explanation of the rating process is offered in Appendix VIII. It is recommended that of the various methods proposed for rating, the individual one-on-one method be used predominantly. IUF will offer training sessions and track results.

F. Gift Credits

All pledges and gifts will be counted in accordance with the guidelines published by the Council for Advancement and Support of Education (CASE). A summary of those guidelines is attached as Appendix IX.

G. Naming Opportunities

Named and memorial gift opportunities are available to donors to encourage and recognize support. The University guidelines are outlined in Appendix X.

H. Prospect Management

Management of prospects will be accomplished under the established terms of the University's prospect management system. These are outlined in Appendix XI. Priority in all cases will be given to the Campaign in prospect assignment.

I. Matching Funds

The Indiana University Board of Trustees has approved a program to match the endowment income on certain gifts throughout the University. This program will be available for certain gifts made to the Bloomington campaign. The general guidelines are outlined below.

Endowment Matching Program

1. Endowment funds received after December 1, 1995, for the purpose of direct Faculty support, especially for Chairs and Professorships, are eligible for this match.

2. The full match, that is 1:1, will consist of a payout equal to 5 percent of the principle on annual basis and will be available for gifts of at least $1,000,000. If the gift falls between $500,000 and $1,000,000, the match will be based on a ratio of 1:2. Payouts will be in perpetuity. A contractual commitment will be provided to the donor.

3. The match opportunity will be in effect until December 31, 1997. A maximum of $500,000 will be allocated each year during this time for a total of $1,000,000. Allocations will be made on a first-come, first-served basis, open to all campuses. Unspent available match funds will not be carried forward.

4. The source of funds for the match will be one-half from University administration and one-half from campus administration. At their option, Chancellors may choose to charge the successful unit for all or part of the campus' portion of the match, or they may distribute all or part of the charges to the entire campus.

5. To take an example, Mary Jones donates $500,000 for endowment for a faculty position in SPEA at IUB. Assume that the payment by the IUF is $25,000 per year (that is, 5 percent of $500,000). The match is 1:2 on this amount. Thus, in addition to the $25,000, SPEA receives an additional $12,500 per year for support of this position. Of the $12,500, University administration will provide $6,250. The remaining $6,250 is the responsibility of IUB.

6. Gifts may be paid over a maximum of five years. The match will be available only if there is a firm, written commitment. However, matching funds will be provided only to the extent that payment has been received (with one exception noted below). So, if there is a gift of $1,000,000 to be paid over four years and $250,000 is received the first year, then the matching funds for the first year are $12,500. Here the match rate is 1:1, and the payout is 5 percent of $250,000.

7. In the case of irrevocable trusts established during the match period with no payout until termination of the trust, one-half the institutional payout will begin when the trust is established. The remaining matching funds will become available when the trust terminates, as will, of course, the trust income. Thus, if there is an irrevocable trust of $1,000,000 established during the match timeframe, then the payout from institutional funds (that is, University administration plus the campus) will be $25,000 per year until the trust matures. After that, institutional funds will equal $50,000 per year (at the 1:1 payout ratio) plus $50,000 from the trust itself.

8. The President, in consultation with the IUF President, reserves the authority to limit eligibility. In particular, it should not be possible for a single megagift to deplete all matching monies. In order to determine the upper limit of a specific gift, a brief written proposal should be submitted to the President.

9. Appendix XII details the various gift vehicles eligible for this match and payout qualifications for each vehicle.

Appendix I

NUCLEUS FUND ORGANIZATION.

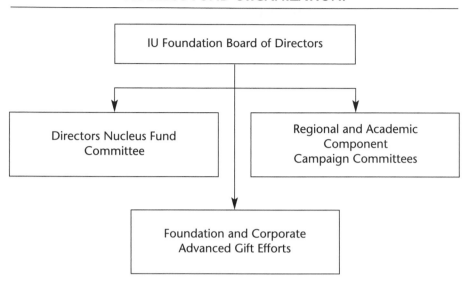

Appendix II

ENDOWMENT CAMPAIGN LEADERSHIP STRUCTURE.

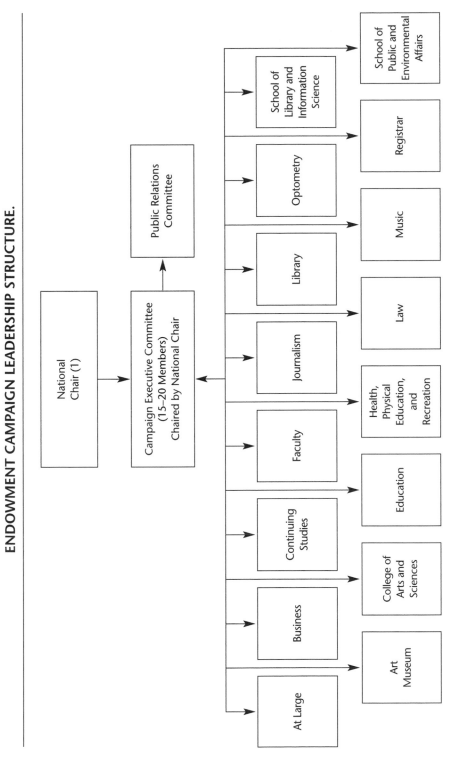

Appendix III

ACTIVITY REPORT.

Development Officer:

Today's Date: Covers (   ) Working Days

1. Prospect/Volunteer Contacts {(*) first time contact; (#) prospect rating/screening session}:

2. Solicitations: A) Proposals Submitted B) Gifts Closed (list name/amount/purpose):
   A) Proposals Submitted

   B) Gifts Closed

3. New Volunteers Recruited:

4. Important Campus Meetings/Contacts:

5. Major Activity/Meetings Scheduled for Next Two Weeks:

Appendix IV

BY PROJECT: INDIANA UNIVERSITY FOUNDATION MAJOR GIFT PROPOSAL UPDATE.

Month

Staff/Vol.	Project	Prospect	Date of Solicitation	Amount of Solicitation	Written Verbal	Last Report Status	Current Status

Appendix V

Major Gifts Fundraising Guidelines

Indiana University implemented a constituency-based development program in 1983, delegating a major part of the responsibility for fundraising to campuses throughout the University system and to constituent schools, colleges, and departments on all campuses. The constituency-based development program:

- allows Foundation staff to work in cooperation with the development officer(s) of each constituent fundraising unit on behalf of University-wide priorities;
- is successful because it is conducted by and for the former academic homes of alumni and allows for a broad range of giving opportunities to the University (more than 95 percent of gifts received from donors are restricted to specific units or programs);
- provides an opportunity for administrators and faculty, system-wide, to be involved in development programs which identify academic needs and priorities through the University administrative structure.

Major gifts are an integral part of the total development program. Each year approximately 50 percent of the total voluntary support to Indiana University through Indiana University Foundation comes from gifts of $50,000 or greater. Individuals who are responsible for major gifts acquisition include faculty members and administrative staff. There are significant differences in the amount of time units and individuals allocate to major gifts, ranging from full time to a small percentage of time due to other responsibilities.

In order to place appropriate emphasis on major gifts, the Committee on Standards, Expectations and Measurement of Major Gifts recommends that the following guidelines be adopted as a set of general expectations for professional development personnel. These expectations are offered as general guidelines for a *full time* major gift officer. They may be altered by a variety of circumstances identified in the guidelines or as agreed upon by the fundraiser and her/his supervisor.

I. The major gifts threshold is currently defined as an outright or deferred gift of a minimum of $25,000 over a five-year period or a single year commitment of $5,000 or greater. This definition may be modified for a given unit upon consultation with the unit head and the Indiana University Foundation. Some units which have a more mature development program or are involved in a capital campaign may adopt a higher base. Gifts at levels below those described above, while possibly significant to a particular program, are typically not characterized as major gifts or produced with the methodology or intensity of efforts desired or described in this document.

II. Guidelines for Annual Expectations of a Full-Time Major Gifts Officer:

A. Manage a pool of approximately 150 individuals. This pool should represent a balance of individuals at various stages in the development continuum. As a guideline the following distribution is recommended: (the mix might change based on the status of a campaign or project)

Cultivation	65	43 percent
Solicitation	35	24 percent
Stewardship	50	33 percent

It is assumed that most or all volunteers will fall into one of these categories. Everyone in the pool should receive *at least* one meaningful contact each year. Individuals in the solicitation stage require several substantive personal contacts yearly, with particular attention paid to the value of the contact in moving the prospect towards closure of a gift.

B. Make or cause to be made an average of 180 meaningful calls per year. Based on past experience, a full time major gifts officer can be expected to make 180 face to face personal calls per year. However, other forms of meaningful contacts may be included, as well as those defined by each unit head, dean or director in consultation with the development officer. Each meaningful contact should be reported through the prospect management system.

C. Make or cause to be made a minimum of 30 major gift solicitations per year. This should produce 15–20 gifts.

D. Identify 15–25 new prospects to be managed through the prospect management system who have the inclination and capability which qualify them as major gift prospects. In general, 50 individual contacts will be made to identify and qualify 15–20 new prospects and these prospects will replace individuals who have been removed from the prospect pool.

E. Make or cause to be made stewardship calls on all donors in the pool. Using the proposed pool distribution, this could require 50 individual contacts. The nature of stewardship contacts may take a variety of forms ranging from individual meetings to invitations to special events. As the major gifts officer expands their donor base it will be essential to rely on a variety of institutional contacts to accomplish the stewardship function. *Summary.* Given the capacity of 180 face to face personal calls for a full time major gifts officer and the need to make calls in all areas—solicitations (30–35), cultivation (65), stewardship (50), and prospect identification (50), it is clear that the number of calls may exceed the capacity of a staff member. Solicitation calls should receive the highest priority, with cultivation calls and new prospect identification secondary. Stewardship calls, although critical, may require the use of other institutional contacts to accomplish the stewardship function in some cases.

III. The comprehensive nature of these guidelines is designed to assist Indiana University in maintaining and coordinating the solicitation of major gifts. These guidelines will be helpful in setting goals and measuring the performance of major gift development officers. Considerations which may affect the prospect pool each staff member is expected to maintain includes the following:

A. Percentage of time spent in major gifts solicitation
B. Geographic proximity to prospects
C. Complexity/size of gifts being sought
D. Campaign/noncampaign mode
E. General experience as a development officer
F. Nature of constituency

IV. The importance of major gift acquisition should be part of the strategic plan of every unit. The President, deans, directors, and unit heads should have a defined role in major gift fund raising. As part of the planning process, it is essential that support be provided within each unit for the acquisition of major gifts. This support includes:

A. Budget
    1. Travel
    2. Special Events
B. Provision for administrative support
    1. Clerical
    2. Writing Services
    3. Research
    4. Equipment—access to the IUF database
C. It is assumed that the IUF will continue to make available support services including, but not limited to, consultation for legal questions, planned giving, and corporation and foundation relations, as well as prospect management, research services, donor records, and proposal writing.

In carrying out the duties of major gift fundraising, it is expected that each representative of Indiana University will observe the highest standards of personal and professional conduct. Accordingly, major gift officers are expected to carry out their duties in a manner which inspires and assures the confidence of fellow major gift and development officers, donors, alumni and friends of the University as directed in the IUF code of ethics.

It is also expected that each major gift fundraiser will meet with his/her supervisor throughout the year to discuss and adjust these goals as appropriate to each individual position.

Appendix VI

Annual Giving Program During the Endowment Campaign

Background

Currently, the Indiana University Foundation's Annual Giving Office produces three major mailings each year and provides Telefund services which are used extensively by the academic units. Additionally, each academic unit, and many departments within some units, make multiple mailings each year. Combined, it is estimated that more than 140 mailings and over 565,000 pieces of mail are sent each year. The actual number is unknown and is likely much higher. At the present time there is no reliable mechanism in place to track this information.

The system has become increasingly cumbersome and too complex to effectively coordinate. This lack of coordination has resulted in duplication, higher printing costs, increased staff, and confusion and sometimes ill-will on the part of alumni who receive overlapping fundraising letters and phone calls.

The Annual Fund is the cornerstone of a comprehensive fundraising program. However, it is expensive based upon cost per dollar raised, and labor intensive. Staff resources dedicated to direct mail and telefund programs are resources lost for the Endowment Campaign. A central annual giving program will result in efficiencies which will allow more time for unit development officers to focus on major gifts for the campaign and other unit priorities.

Advantages

A centralized annual giving program has many advantages:

1. It will reduce work loads within the various units, allowing development officers to make additional major gift contacts for the upcoming endowment campaign.
2. Economies of scale would be an option for the first time. By centralizing the annual giving program, large mailings will help to reduce the overall costs.
3. It will provide a coordinated annual giving calendar, which does not currently exist. This calendar will maximize everyone's efforts, and avoid our current problem of "oversoliciting" our alumni.
4. It will allow for a specific identity to be created for the Annual Fund with a campus-wide theme. Penn State University is just one example of how this approach has reaped significant rewards. *For instance, their alumni participation increased from 16 percent to 20.5 percent after centralization, and net income on mailings alone went up 29 percent.*

Resource 12

Technology

Technologies associated with direct mail have eliminated the problems involved with personalizing individual mailings. Today, even with a campus-wide unified mailing, the mailing can be tailored to represent a specific unit. While costs might dictate that donor acquisition and lapsed retrieval mailings remain somewhat generic, donor renewal mailings would include significant personalization.

Telefund automation, the next logical enhancement of our annual giving program, will allow for an increased number of calls to be made each year and for a corresponding increase in income. While the Telefund has seen steady growth in dollars pledged, from $2,190,566 in 1990–91 to $3,221,309 in 1994–95, automation would increase dollars pledged to as much as $4,266,000 over a twelve-month period. It will also allow additional personalization by providing more data about our donors both before and after phone contact is made. Automation will also allow for more contacts to be made, further enhancing the ability to speak with IU's alumni on a personal basis.

Summary

Overall, the centralization of the annual giving program is the next logical step in the evolution of fundraising on the Bloomington campus, particularly as we prepare for the campaign. A centralized annual giving program should allow unit development officers to concentrate on major gifts, reduce costs, increase gifts, and foster goodwill with our alumni. These outcomes will benefit the university not only during the campaign but for many years thereafter. Centralization could be accomplished after the successful automation of the Telefund.

The differences between the current and proposed systems are summarized below:

CURRENT SYSTEM:	PROPOSED SYSTEM:
Focus on Annual Giving in most constituent programs	Focus on major gifts in all constituent programs
Level or modest growth in donors and gift income	Significant increases in donors and gift income
Multiple, overlapping solicitations leading to confusion and sometimes ill-will toward IU	Reduced mailings and fewer overlapping solicitations
High printing costs due to a number of small mailings	Lower printing costs due to volume discounts
No effective campus coordination of mailings or direct mail tracking system	One comprehensive solicitation calendar managed by the Foundation

Appendix VII

Memorandum

TO: Rod Kirsch
FROM: Kent Dove
RE: Budgeting the Academic Endowment Campaign
DATE: December 19, 1994

For the purpose of initiating discussion, I write to make recommendations as to how the additional funds that will be needed to underwrite the Academic Endowment Campaign might be generated. The underlying premise here is that it costs money to raise money and that the University and the Foundation both should share in assuming these costs.

My view of the needs of the campus and who should pay these costs are:

Major Gifts Officers

Two academic areas, Business and the College of Arts and Sciences, will need to add a full-time major gifts officer. Both currently have already budgeted positions open. Given appropriate job descriptions and corresponding selection, these new hires could meet the campaign's needs. I recommend that these respective academic units be responsible for their costs plus the support help that will be needed. In the first year, I have budgeted each of the major gift officers at $65,000 plus 25 percent benefits for a total of $81,250 per position. Support staff, one for each major gift officer, is projected at $18,000 plus benefits for a total of $22,500 each. I recommend that these persons be housed in the academic units.

Two other academic areas, Education and the School of Public and Environmental Affairs, could share a major gifts officer. The costs are the same as above. I recommend that the University assume these costs and that these people be housed in the IU Foundation.

Next, there is a grouping of units, all of which will require attention, but only on a part-time basis: Music*, School of Health, Physical Education & Recreation, Art Museum, University Libraries, School of Library & Information Science, Optometry, Continuing Studies and Journalism. I recommend two major gifts officers and one support staff to service all these areas to be paid for by the University and to be housed in the Foundation.

*Staffing needs may be met by a new person when hired in early 1995.

One unit, Law, is sufficiently staffed and will require only advisory assistance from the Executive Director of the Campaign.

Planned Gifts Officers

Additionally, I recommend that three planned gifts officers be added to the staff to serve the entire campus during the campaign and that the University provide for these positions which should be housed in the Foundation.

Campaign Administration

The IU Foundation should provide for the campaign administration officer, the Executive Director of Capital Campaigns and his assistant.

Operating Costs

It is further recommended that the other direct costs of the campaign, communications, training (volunteer and staff), office supplies and printing, telephones, representation, etc., be paid out of unrestricted gifts to the campaign and/or that costs be recovered from the units on their gift income from the campaign.

DRAFT IU ENDOWMENT CAMPAIGN BUDGET.

	1994–95	1995–96	1996–97	1997–98	1998–99	1999–2000
Salaries and Benefits						
Professional		$731,250(a)*	$767,812(a)*	$806,203(a)*	$846,513(a)*	$888,839(a)*
		Six major gift officers at $65,000 a year; three planned giving officers, two at $70,000 a year, one at $55,000 a year, plus 25% benefits for all nine.				
Secretarial/Clerical $196,760(a)			$161,875(a)	$169,969(a)	$178,467(a)	$187,390(a)
		Seven support staff at $18,000, plus 25% benefits.				
Administration	$166,250	$174,563(a)	$183,291(a)	$192,456(a)	$202,079(a)	$212,183(a)
		Executive Director, Capital Campaign and Assistant to Executive Director of the Capital Campaign.				
Fees for Consultants	$50,000	$50,000	$50,000	$50,000	$50,000	
		Contingency funds to be used if outside assistance is desirable, i.e., audio visual needs, case statement, planned giving.				
Market Survey	$60,000					
	See attached outline.					
Office Supplies and Printing		$25,000	$25,000	$22,500	$20,000	$15,000
Telephone and Other Communication Networks	$25,000	$25,000	$25,000	$25,000	$25,000	
Publications/Print and AV Materials		$300,000	$30,000	$18,500	$10,000	$10,000
Public Announcement Event	$40,000					
Representation		$12,000	$20,000	$20,000	$20,000	$15,000
Travel		$20,000	$50,000	$60,000	$40,000	$40,000
Special Events/ Leadership Training		$15,000	$25,000	$15,000	$10,000	$10,000
Space and Office Furnishings				To be determined		
Campaign Victory Celebration						$35,000
Undistributed		$20,000	$40,000	$30,000	$20,000	$15,000
Totals	$226,250	$1,574,688	$1,386,072	$1,418,126	$1,430,982	$1,512,782

(a) Includes 5% annual adjustment.

*The Foundation does not necessarily have to assume all personnel costs. They may be shared with the academic units.

FUNDING THE ACADEMIC ENDOWMENT CAMPAIGN.

Position	Personnel Cost*	Travel Budget	Funded by	Housed by
Major Gifts Officer, Business	$81,250	$5,000	Academic Unit	Academic Unit
Support Staff, Business	22,500		Academic Unit	Academic Unit
Major Gifts Officer, COAS	81,250	5,000	Academic Unit	Academic Unit
Support Staff, COAS	22,500		Academic Unit	Academic Unit
Major Gifts Officer, Education and SPEA	81,250	5,000	Indiana University	IU Foundation
Support Staff, Education and SPEA	22,500		Indiana University	IU Foundation
Major Gifts Officers, Group	162,500	7,500	Indiana University	IU Foundation
Support Staff, Group	22,500		Indiana University	IU Foundation
Planned Giving Officers	243,750	12,500	Indiana University	IU Foundation
Support Staff, Planned Giving	45,000		Indiana University	IU Foundation
Campaign Administration	175,000	3,000	IU Foundation	IU Foundation
Support Staff, Administration	22,500		IU Foundation	IU Foundation

Costs Allocated to:	Personnel	Travel		
Academic Units	$207,500	$10,000		
Indiana University	581,250	25,000		
IU Foundation	197,500	3,000		

*First year only. Campaign to be budgeted for five years. Totals include salary plus benefits.

Resource 12

Summary of Professional Staffing Needs

Need Full-Time Position	College of Arts & Sciences (COAS)
	School of Business
Need Split Position	School of Education
	School of Public & Environmental Affairs (SPEA)
Need Share Positions	Health, Physical Education & Recreation (HPER)
	University Libraries
	Journalism
	School of Library & Information Science (SLIS)
	Optometry
	Continuing Studies
	Art Museum
	Music*
Adequately Staffed	Law
	Music*

*Depending on person hired early in 1995.

Appendix VIII

Prospect Rating Sessions and Techniques

The purpose of prospect rating is to determine accurately within a range an individual's ability to give. The evaluator should not be concerned with what the individual might give—or even that he/she will give. Further research subsequent to the evaluation will address these questions. The sole criteria during the evaluation should be to establish what a donor can do given his/her personal circumstances.

The purpose of the rating session *is not* to have the professional staff member offer evaluations. The staff member should not participate in the evaluation other than to explain the purpose of the session, to keep the session moving and to clarify and answer questions as to form and procedure. The professional staff member should make no comments to the evaluator which could influence a rating. Pertinent information on the prospect held by the professional staff member should be noted and conveyed directly to file.

Small Group Discussion: In this procedure the leader calls out the name of the prospect and a roundtable discussion ensues. A rating is agreed to. Pertinent comments are recorded by the professional staff member. This is the best method of evaluation, but its success is dependent on the group leader's ability to initiate discussion and the group's willingness to participate in an open and forthright fashion.

Group Individual Rating: In this procedure each member of the group is given a rating book and works individually without discussion to rate the prospects and offer appropriate written comments. The professional staff member collects the evaluations and tabulates the information after the meeting. The major disadvantage here is that there is no exchange of ideas or information within the group. The advantage is that there is the feeling on the part of the evaluator that he/she has more confidentiality; hence, the possibility of a more realistic evaluation and more pointed and useful comments.

Individual One-on-One: In this procedure the professional staff member meets individually with the evaluator and verbally goes through the list recording on the evaluation form pertinent comments. The advantage of this process is that the evaluator can feel he/she has complete assurance of confidentiality. No one else will hear the comments or know his/her personal feelings about the prospect. The disadvantage is that the validity of the evaluation is limited to the extent of the evaluator's knowledge. There is no second and third opinion. And, the single evaluator may not know a number of the prospects well enough to rate them thus necessitating additional rating sessions involving other evaluators.

Individual Solitary: In this process the evaluator is given or mailed a list of prospects and rating instructions and then is left on his/her own. The evaluation is either picked up or mailed back on or before a mutually agreed upon date. This procedure should be used only in special instances. Its advantage is that it gives the evaluator time to reflect and to substantially consider his/her rating and comments. It leads, generally, to a very thoughtful, thorough evaluation when done properly. The disadvantage is that often the individual will put off doing the evaluation thereby frustrating the process.

The evaluation should be done by knowledgeable individuals. Secondhand and hearsay information is of little or no value. Speculation is just that. Bankers, lawyers, investment counselors, insurance executives, the socially prominent and those actively involved in organized philanthropy in communities with organized efforts make the best evaluators.

Resource 12

Appendix IX

General Guidelines for Recognizing and Counting Gifts to the Endowment Campaign

All gifts and pledges to Indiana University-Bloomington during the campaign period July 1, 1994, through December 31, 2000, or the end of that academic year, will be counted toward the total campaign goal in accordance with the following guidelines. (The guidelines described below in summary form generally conform to the CASE Campaign Standards issued in April of 1994.)

1. All *outright gifts* in the form of cash, marketable securities, closely held stock, real property and gifts of tangible personal property.

2. All *pledges* of five (5) years or less which are initiated between July 1, 1994 and the conclusion of the campaign and documented in writing by the donor(s).

3. All gifts for *ongoing support* received during the campaign period.

4. The face value of all *realized bequests* received during the campaign period.

5. *Future bequest commitments* from donors, if properly documented, will be reported in campaign totals at face value and recorded at discounted present value for internal purposes.

6. *Charitable remainder trusts* held by the Foundation or another trustee and *pooled income funds* will be reported in campaign totals at their face value and will also be recorded at discounted present value for internal purposes.

7. The face value of the income interest received or pledged during the campaign time period from *charitable lead trusts* on trusts held by the Foundation or another trustee.

8. The face value of *charitable gift annuities* will be reported in campaign totals; the present value also will be recorded for internal purposes.

9. *Matching gifts* awarded in support of the campaign.

10. Gifts of *life insurance* will be recognized as provided in the CASE Campaign Standards based on the nature of the policy, i.e, paid-up; existing, but not fully paid-up; new policy.

11. The following types of gifts or intentions will not be recognized in campaign totals: oral pledges, gifts previously counted in the Campaign for Indiana, earnings on gifts, governmental funds, contracted research revenue.

12. *Exceptions* to the foregoing may be made for good cause on a case-by-case basis. Such exceptions shall be approved by the Executive Committee of the Bloomington Endowment Campaign.

Appendix X

Guidelines for Naming Opportunities and Endowed Funds for the Bloomington Campus Campaign

General Policy

It is the general policy of Indiana University that the University President approve the establishment and activation of named funds upon the receipt of gifts by the IU Foundation as described below.

The President of the University in consultation with campus Chancellors, Deans and the IU Foundation President sets minimum gift level amounts and establishes approved guidelines for gift naming opportunities.

The Board of Trustees, in all gift naming opportunities, reserves the final right of approval for the name or names designated for any of the gift naming opportunities which follow. Approval cannot be granted until the donor's name is known or until the name or names of the person or persons being memorialized are known.

The gift levels described below are intended as minimum amounts needed to name the respective opportunity. In most cases, gifts may be made outright over a multi-year pledge period, through a trust or similar irrevocable instrument. The selection of holders of all endowed positions is the responsibility of the cognizant deans in consultation with the affected department and the campus Chancellor.

Specific Gift Naming Opportunities

The monetary requirements cited in the paragraphs below are University minimums. In each category both numbers represent the minimum amounts needed for endowments in various sized programs. The larger number is not a cap; it is a minimum figure for a larger or more comprehensive program. Each school or college may establish higher minimums for certain endowments based on unique requirements of the individual unit, the discipline involved and the scope of the program relative to budget and other factors.

1. The opportunity exists to name several of the schools on the campus by providing a gift for the general endowment to benefit the unit. The minimum gift commitment required to do so varies with each respective unit.
2. To name a *research center, institute* or *academic program* requires a minimum gift commitment of $1 to $3 million for endowment.

3. To name a *branch library,* a minimum gift commitment of $1 million is required. Endowment income will benefit the collections, service and technology needs of the particular library.

4. To establish a *deanship,* $3 million or more is necessary. In such cases, the position—not the person—is endowed.

5. To establish *directorships* or *departmental chairs,* gifts of $2 million or more are necessary. The position, not the person, is endowed.

6. To establish an *endowed faculty chair* requires a minimum endowment of $1 million.

7. To establish an *endowed professorship,* a minimum gift of $500,000 is required.

8. To establish an *endowed visiting professorship* requires a minimum gift of $250,000. The annual proceeds will be used to invite a distinguished scholar to campus for a finite period of time.

9. To establish an *endowed lectureship* requires a minimum gift commitment of $100,000. The annual proceeds from this endowment will be used to pay for honoraria, publicity and the expenses of a member of the faculty or a visiting lecturer from another insitution or organization to present a lecture on the campus.

10. To establish an *endowed laboratory* requires a minimum gift commitment of $1,000,000. The annual earnings from the endowment will be used for equipment, technology enhancements and research.

11. To establish an *endowed classroom* requires a minimum gift commitment of $500,000. The annual earnings will be used for equipment, technology enhancement, refurbishment and modernization.

12. To establish an *endowed faculty research fund* requires a minimum gift of $250,000.

13. To establish an *endowed graduate student fellowship* requires a minimum gift of $200,000. A fellowship is ordinarily awarded to a student who is working toward an advanced degree in any of the graduate fields. An endowed fellowship should provide support for the majority of the recipient's expenses.

14. To establish a scholarship in the *Herman B Wells Scholarship Program* requires a minimum gift of $150,000 for endowment.

15. To establish an *undergraduate endowed scholarship* requires a minimum gift of $25,000.

16. To establish an *endowed book fund* requires a minimum gift of $25,000 for endowment. The income from an endowed book fund may be used for the purchase of books or other materials in a specified field. It may also be used, to the extent not needed for purchases, for preservation of books. It may also be used for repair, cataloging and other expenses of the library.

17. To name new or renovated buildings and facilities generally requires one-half the construction cost of the capital project.

Exceptions for Endowments and Funds

The campus Chancellor, or his/her designee, shall have the latitude to approve the establishment of named funds in amounts less than those stated above, provided that it is understood that, within a reasonable period of time from the establishment of the fund, the principal thereof, including interest income and additional gifts, shall equal the stated minimum. If the stated minimum is not achieved, then the fund may be terminated and the funds expended for the college, school or department originally designated by the donor. The annual income from a fund established hereunder and not terminated as provided shall continue to be accrued to the principal until the minimum endowment level is reached.

Appendix XI

Indiana University and Indiana University Foundation Prospect Management Program: Policies and Procedures

(Draft 4/5/94, Jim Smith) (Revised 8/4/95, Kathy Wilson)

INTRODUCTION

Mission

The prospect management program (PMP) is designed to provide effective management of cultivation, solicitation and stewardship activities with individuals, corporations, foundations and other prospects determined as having the interest and capability of making a major gift to Indiana University.

Means

PMP fulfills its mission by: 1) creating and maintaining a database that includes major gift prospects, the staff and volunteers assigned to those prospects, documentation of significant contacts and "moves" with prospects, and background research information; 2) regularly convening a prospect assignment committee to act on requests for assignment and to address other issues; and 3) periodically conducting prospect review sessions to ensure effective and coordinated management of top-level prospects.

Role of Development Professionals

PMP functions at its optimum level when development staff contribute in the following areas: 1) Communication—staff who are co-assigned to a prospect utilize a team approach and proactively share plans, activity and information with each other; 2) Documentation—documenting significant contacts and "moves" in the Benefactor major prospects module, and share that documentation with all appropriate staff.

Prospect Management Program Authority and Administration

The Prospect Management Program is managed on behalf of Indiana University by the Indiana University Foundation, in accordance with its designation by the Indiana University Board of Trustees as the officially designated fundraising agency for Indiana University. The Senior Vice-president for Development of the IU Foundation, in consultation with the President of the IU Foundation, has ultimate administrative authority for the program, including formulation and revisions of the policies and procedures governing the program.

POLICIES AND PROCEDURES

1. Prospect Assignment

Policy. Prospects submitted for assignment in PMP should, through prior activity or research, have been determined to 1) be capable of fulfilling a commitment of at least $25,000 over 5 years or $5,000 in 1 year; and 2) have a demonstrated interest in supporting the University and the specific program or project for which support is being sought. In particular, evidence of linkage with the prospect should include personal contact leading to qualification between the prospect and the staff or unit requesting assignment.

Procedures

1.1 *Request for Assignment*—Development staff may request assignment to a prospect by completing and submitting a "Request for Prospect Assignment" form to the Director of Research at IUF.

1.2 *Assignment Committee Action*—The prospect assignment committee meets on alternate Mondays. All requests received by the Wednesday prior to the meeting will be considered.

1.3 *Clearance Levels*—The prospect assignment committee will assign a clearance level of cultivation, solicitation or stewardship. The request may be denied, in which case the committee will provide a written explanation of its decision.

1.4 *Deferred Action*—The prospect assignment committee may defer action on a request when: 1) the request form is not complete, i.e., a rating is not provided or there is no evidence of personal contact, in which case the form will be returned to the requester; 2) clarification or further information is needed from other parties, in which case such information may be sought by committee members, or the requester may be instructed to secure the information and forward it to the committee.

1.5 *Primary Manager*—The prospect assignment committee will act upon requests for assignment as primary manager and will make final decisions in instances where more than one individual has requested primary manager status.

1.6 *Appeals of Assignment Committee Decisions*—Decisions made by the prospect assignment committee may be appealed in writing to the IUF Senior Vice-President of Development within 20 working days after the committee decision is received.

1.7 *Length of Assignment and Clearance*—Assignment for cultivation and stewardship clearance levels will be for up to one year, at which time the assignment must be renewed with a written justification. Clearance for solicitation will be for a six-month period, and may be renewed and justified as already described. If there is a lack or absence of documented contact between the assigned staff and moving the prospect to closure, requests for reassignment may be denied.

1.8 *Rating of Prospects*—All prospects in PMP must have a rating assigned to them at the time the request is made.

1.9 *Committee Members*—The prospect assignment committee consists of the following: Sr. Vice-President Development, Vice-President Indianapolis, all IUF Sr. Development Directors, Director of Corporations, Exec. Director of Development, Director of Development Services, and Director of Research who chairs the committee. One representative from each of the Bloomington and Indianapolis Development Councils will be selected to serve a one-year term on the committee for the period September–August.

2. Documentation

Policy. All relevant prospect contacts must be documented on a "Contact Report" and on the prospect's Benefactor record in the Major Prospects module. Further, this information is to be shared with all co-assigned staff and, if applicable, with the unit development officer from the prospect's academic home and with the IUF staff assigned to the geographic area in which the prospect resides. Written documentation should NOT preclude verbal communication among co-assigned staff.

Procedures

2.1 *Documentation of Contacts*—Within twenty (20) working days after the contact, the IUF development officer should arrange for summary information about the contact to be entered into the Benefactor database. The unit development officers should send their contacts to the Director of Research at IUF to arrange for that information to be entered into the Benefactor database. Every development officer should complete a contact report and send it to the Director of Research at IUF, indicating the appropriate IUF staff, co-assigned staff and unit development officers who should receive copies. Also, the development officer should note on the form whether this contact is to be considered as "meaningful."

2.2 *Distribution of Contact Reports*—Each development officer will be responsible for distributing their own contact reports to individuals requiring copies. Individuals requiring copies are: 1) Senior Vice President of Development; 2) Director of Research; 3) all development officers assigned to the prospect; 4) development officer(s) where prospect holds degree(s); and, 5) to those development officers with geographic responsibility where the prospect resides.

2.3 *Documentation Standards and Conventions*—Information entered into the Benefactor Major Prospects Module must be in accordance with the conventions established to ensure consistency of data stored in that module. Special care should be taken in entering information that does not directly impact the cultivation, solicitation or stewardship strategy for an individual, or may be sensitive in nature.

3. Prospect Review

Policy. On an as needed basis, the Director of Research will convene a meeting for the purpose of reviewing current activities with selected major gift prospects and determining how to maximize support from each prospect. Such meetings will be held on a regularly scheduled basis during large capital campaigns.

Procedures

3.1 *Selection of Prospects for Review*—Prospects may be selected for review on the basis of their rating, their status as a prospect for a specific project, or other reasons specified by the Senior Vice-President for Development.

3.2 *Notification of Development Staff*—Notification of all staff assigned to a prospect to be reviewed will be sent at least 15 working days prior to the scheduled review session. Included in this notification will be the names of those prospects to be reviewed.

3.3 *Attendance*—All staff assigned to prospects being reviewed are expected to attend and be prepared to discuss current strategy with each prospect. If attendance is impossible, written comments on each prospect should be sent to the Director of Research at least seven working days prior to the scheduled meeting. A copy of those comments should be sent to the primary manager of each prospect.

3.4 *Meeting Summary*—Research and PMP staff will record highlights of discussion and decisions made regarding each prospect reviewed. PMP staff will enter this information on the prospect's PMP record and will distribute copies of the meeting summary to all attendees, assigned staff and others not in attendance but determined as appropriate to receive all or portions of the information.

4. Management Reports

4.1 *Solicitation Expiration Report (XSER)*—Clearance for solicitation will be for up to a six-month period, at the end of which time the assignment must be renewed and justified. On the report the development officer is asked whether to 1) extend the solicitation for another six (6) months; 2) change the level to cultivation or stewardship; or 3) remove the assignment. If no response is received, the prospect will automatically be moved to cultivation. This report is run monthly for solicitation requests made 6 months prior.

4.2 *Manager's Activity Report (XPMP)*—Bi-monthly reports regarding overall prospect and Development Officer activity will be prepared and distributed to the development officers for their review in order to keep the PMP database clean. If no response is received, the assignment will be removed.

4.3 *Contact Summary Report (MPCS)*—All contacts entered 20 working days after contact will be tracked by IU Foundation and included on the previous month's activity report which will be distributed to development officers and appropriate IUF staff.

Appendix XII

Gift Vehicles Eligible for Matching Endowment Program

1. Outright Gifts

All outright gifts that meet the minimum amount of $500,000 or above qualify for the match. An outright gift is one of $500,000 or above that is received all at once or as a pledge paid over five years. The amount to be matched will be the current value of the outright gift. Outright gifts may consist of cash, securities, or real estate. With regard to real estate, the amount matched will be the proceeds from the expected sale of the property.

2. Charitable Remainder Trusts

Charitable remainder trusts qualify for the match. However, the payout on the match will be based on the face value of the donor's gift to the Foundation, even though the remainder value may exceed the face value at the time the trust during the match period with $500,000, with an annual payout rate of 5 percent, the annual income will be $25,000 and the match of a gift at this level will be 50 percent of the annual income, or $12,500. This will apply to all charitable remainder trusts which meet the basic criteria, irrespective of trustee.

3. Charitable Gift Annuities and Pooled Income Fund

The same criteria apply for charitable gift annuities and the pooled income fund as applied to the charitable remainder trust. That is, because of the irrevocable nature of the gift, they qualify for the match based upon the face value of the gift at the time it is initially received by the Foundation.

4. Life Insurance

Life insurance qualifies only if the policy is fully paid-up when given to the Foundation or will be paid-up within a five year period after the date of the gift. The donor must make the Foundation the irrevocable owner and beneficiary of the policy for the matching fund program to apply. The match will be based on the death benefit of the policy and it will apply at the time the policy is received by the Foundation. For example, if a donor makes a gift of a life insurance policy with a $500,000 death benefit with an annual payout rate of 5 percent when the policy matures, the annual income will be $25,000 and the match of a gift at this level will be 50 percent of the annual income, or $12,500. Age guidelines may be considered when deciding whether or not to match life insurance gifts.

5. Bequest

Newly established bequest expectancies will qualify as long as they meet the minimum levels, are documented during the matching period and represent a legally binding obligation upon the donor's estate. Age guidelines may be considered when deciding whether or not to match individual bequests.

6. Personal Property

Personal property will not qualify for the match primarily due to the fact that personal property held by the Foundation will generate no income, and selling the property may have adverse tax consequences for the donor.

7. Remainder Interest in Real Estate

Remainder interest in real estate will qualify for the match when the Foundation receives its remainder interest and completes the sale of the real estate. The match will be based on the amount realized from the sale of the real estate.

8. Charitable Lead Trusts

Since charitable lead trusts pay the income they generate directly to the Foundation, they qualify if the income generated by the trust meets the minimum amount required to qualify for the match. For example, a charitable lead trust funded with $2 million in assets with a 5 percent annual payout rate will produce $100,000 in annual income. If this payout is received or pledged during the match period, it qualifies in the same way as an outright gift.

DIRECT-MAIL SOLICITATION LETTERS: SEQUENTIAL ANNUAL MAILINGS

LETTER #1

Indianapolis Museum of Art

Date

Name
Address
City, State, ZIP

Dear 1997 Donor:

Visit the IMA throughout the year!

The Indianapolis Museum of Art's 1998 calendar of exhibitions and events is one of the most exciting in memory. *More than 300,000 individuals will visit the museum in 1998—please be among them.* Because you contributed to the museum last year, I encourage you to see and appreciate all that your annual contribution helps to make possible.

For more than 100 years, the IMA has offered so much to so many. For some visitors, the IMA is visual art—maintaining a permanent art collection of national importance. For some, it's a center for the study of world culture, history, art and humanities. For some, the IMA is special exhibitions, member openings, workshops, lectures, the Summer Nights concert and film series and summer festivals like Africafest. With the historic relevance of the Lilly Pavilion and the beauty of the grounds, some visitors never make it inside the museum's galleries. Others come to browse in the Alliance Museum Shop, find a bargain at the Better Than New Shop or simply enjoy lunch at the Garden on the Green. Whether you enjoy the serious pursuit of art appreciation or a more leisurely experience—the IMA has something for everyone.

You may be surprised to learn that your membership dues do not support the museum's daily operations and maintenance. The museum's daily operations depend mostly on the Annual Giving Campaign. The goal for the 1998 Annual Campaign is $3,000,000 from individuals and businesses. It costs about $30,000 a day to operate the museum. As costs continue to increase, so do annual goals to fund daily operations.

Please consider making a gift now to support the museum's daily operations. You may make your gift in tribute or memory of a friend or family member. If you'd prefer, you can make your pledge now and we will send a pledge reminder in the month indicated.

Please visit the museum and experience everything that your support makes possible.

Sincerely,

Don E. Marsh
1998 Annual Campaign Chair

1200 West 38th Street	317.923.1331
Indianapolis, Indiana	317.926.8931 Fax
46208-4196	

LETTER #2

Indianapolis Museum of Art

July 6, 1998

Mr. & Mrs. John Carreron
7812 Ashtree Lane
Indianapolis, IN 46259

Dear Mr. & Mrs. Carreron:

Experience art inside and out at the IMA.

As you head outdoors this summer, I hope you will make the Indianapolis Museum of Art part of your summertime plans. There are a variety of programs and activities for you to enjoy at the IMA—and the grounds of the IMA create a magnificent backdrop for museum events.

Each time I visit the IMA I'm always so impressed with how extraordinary the grounds are maintained. It is a big job to keep the 153 acres of the museum up. Today nine full-time groundskeepers keep the grounds of the museum impeccably maintained. A stark comparison to the 32 groundskeepers the Lilly family employed when they lived on the grounds at the turn of the century. Every time you visit the IMA you can see your annual fund gift at work. As a result of 1997 operating gifts more than 2,952 perennials, 83 trees, 20,222 bulbs, 512 shrubs and 5,279 annuals were planted and enjoyed by museum visitors.

When you visit the IMA, you will notice the renovation of the Lilly Pavilion and the ravine garden. Upon completion, this historic country home, and one of the few remaining ravine gardens in the nation, will be the IMA's single largest piece of art in the museum's collection. I am writing to encourage you to participate in the annual operating campaign. It is a message that can be put very simply: we could really use your help around the house and garden this summer. Please support the 1998 campaign by making your tax-deductible gift. Participation from every museum member is critical to attaining this year's goal.

Grab your picnic basket and a blanket, and take in a concert or classic film under the stars during the IMA's Summer Nights series. The current special exhibition celebrates ten years of art donations from members of our local community. A Decade of Treasures is an important exhibition which, as IMA supporters, I urge you to see. But hurry because the exhibition will end on July 19. Everyone's favorite art fair, Penrod, will take place on September 12. I urge you to support this year's campaign, which makes possible all you see and do at the IMA.

Sincerely,

Don E. Marsh
1998 Annual Campaign Chair

1200 West 38th Street   317.923.1331
Indianapolis, Indiana   317.926.8931 Fax
46208-4196

LETTER #3

Indianapolis Museum of Art

October 12, 1998

Mrs. Irving Joffe
7450 Lions Head Drive
Indianapolis, IN 46260

Dear Mrs. Joffe:

On October 5, 1998, the Alliance of the Indianapolis Museum of Art celebrated its 40th anniversary of service to the community through its support of the museum.

As part of the Alliance 40th anniversary celebration, art objects in the IMA galleries which were purchased with the assistance of Alliance funds will be identified with a small ribbon during the month of October. Congratulations!

Each year, volunteers contribute thousands of hours to the museum by serving on the governing boards, working at the information desk and in the shops, guiding visitors through the galleries, organizing events and raising funds. Your commitment of time, talent and treasures has been vital to the IMA.

This year, one of the goals of the Annual Campaign is to increase participation. Businesses and individuals help to raise one-third of the museum's annual operating budget, approximately $3 million. As costs to operate the museum continue to increase annually—currently about $30,000 a day—it is crucial that we increase the number of donors to the campaign.

The Development Committee, an eleven-member volunteer group made up of business and civic leaders, has generously offered to match gifts—up to $25,000—through December 31. *Your gift will essentially be doubled.* The amount of your gift is not as important as increased participation throughout the Alliance membership base.

For your convenience, I have enclosed an Annual Campaign brochure and a return envelope. The brochure can give you even more reasons to join other Alliance members and friends in providing the support needed for responsibly operating the museum daily. I hope you will give special consideration to supporting the museum's Annual Campaign. If you have already mailed your check, thank you.

Sincerely,

Judy Rush
Alliance Member

Resource 13

1200 West 38th Street   317.923.1331
Indianapolis, Indiana   317.926.8931 Fax
46208-4196

LETTER #4

Indianapolis Museum of Art

December 2, 1998

Ms. Gayle Lewis
1638 North Pennsylvania Street
Indianapolis, IN 46202

Dear Ms. Lewis:

Thank you for contributing to the Indianapolis Museum of Art's 1998 Annual Operating Campaign. Your financial investment allows the museum to present outstanding special exhibitions, educational programs for children and adults, classic films, exciting concerts, horticulture study, in-depth lectures, family festivals and so much more.

We are proud of all that was accomplished in 1998, but we still have $120,000 to raise in order to meet this year's annual operating goal and to ensure programs and special exhibitions already scheduled for 1999. I hope you will consider making an additional gift of support. Only by meeting our financial goals by December 31 can we be sure that necessary repairs, art exhibitions and educational programs continue to meet your expectations. If we begin our new fiscal year with a deficit, this will be a real challenge.

As we continue our year-end fundraising, we are preparing many events for you and your family to enjoy this winter, including our traditional holiday musical concerts and family holiday studio activities, storytelling and children's gift making. Whether you browse the IMA gift shop for a unique holiday gift, enjoy lunch with a friend at The Garden on the Green or introduce a friend or co-worker to the splendor of the Lilly Pavilion bedecked for the season, the IMA is a beautiful place for holiday entertaining.

Your support of the museum's Annual Campaign makes all that you see and do at the IMA possible. Every gift, regardless of the amount, is important as we work toward meeting 1998's goal. Participation from all museum members is crucial. I hope you will spend some time at the IMA this holiday season, and thank you for your support of the Annual Operating Campaign.

Sincerely,
Don E. Marsh
1998 Annual Campaign Chair

P.S. The IMA's Development Committee will match all pledges received by December 31, 1998, dollar for dollar. Your gift at this time may provide you with additional year-end tax benefits.

1200 West 38th Street   317.923.1331
Indianapolis, Indiana   317.926.8931 Fax
46208-4196

RESOURCE 14

DIRECT-MAIL SOLICITATION WITH INSERT

Indianapolis Museum of Art

March 1999

Dear Mr. & Mrs. Dafforn:

Would it surprise you to learn that some important people like Rembrandt, Rodin, Rubens, Seurat, Picasso, Cézanne, Van Gogh, and O'Keeffe rely on your support of the museum's Annual Operating Campaign? Your contribution helps to conserve and protect these artists' great masterworks. And now, the permanent collection continues its reputation of national importance with recently acquired works from the Samuel Josefowitz collection, featuring the works of Paul Gauguin (1848–1904).

Enjoy the inaugural viewing of *Gauguin and The School of Pont-Aven: The Samuel Josefowitz Collection* through August 1. This important exhibition features 101 paintings and prints by Paul Gauguin and the followers who gathered around him nearly a century ago in the French village of Pont-Aven. View this impressive collection, installed in its entirety.

> *". . . Vibrant color, decorative patterns, and vivid images. The paintings of Pont-Aven offer a superb look at a fresh and powerful approach to painting"*
> —IMA Chief Curator, Ellen Lee

The paintings and prints come from the renowned collection of Swiss entrepreneur Samuel Josefowitz, considered one of the world's foremost art collectors. *This group of works establishes the IMA as the leading American museum featuring art of the Pont-Aven School.* Your support of the museum's Annual Operating Campaign helps to attract significant works to the collection and present community-wide special exhibitions.

Your gift to the Annual Operating Campaign helps to offset costs associated with presenting art that educates and inspires all people of central Indiana. When you give $150 or more, you will be invited to attend an exclusive *Gauguin Director's Reception* on Thursday, May 6, from 6 to 8 p.m. IMA Director Bret Waller welcomes you with refreshments followed by a special docent-led tour of the Gauguin collection.

I hope you will support the museum's Annual Operating Campaign. Through your generous gift, you verify the importance of the Indianapolis Museum of Art to the community and to your life.

Sincerely,

Linda Hardwick
Director of Development and Membership

P.S. To attend the IMA's Gauguin Director's Reception, your gift must be received no later than Tuesday, May 4, 1999.

IMA 2000 RAFFLE

The raffle is an idea I got from the Chicago Art Institute.

We have 20 major gifts over $1,000 each in value. You conduct the Raffle by mail at $10 per ticket and so that you can direct your tickets to any prize you wish. We will mail 100,000 packets in March and have the drawing in May.

Everything has been donated, including printing. Olive LLP is coordinating all of the tickets for us.

We hope to net about $50,000 to $100,000 for the unrestricted annual operating fund.

Resource 14

TELEMARKETING SCRIPTS

DONOR ACQUISITION

◆

Greeting: Hello! May I speak with Mr./Mrs. *Firstname Lastname?*

Introduction: Hi, Mr./Mrs. *Lastname,* my name is *Caller's Firstname Lastname,* and I'm calling on behalf of the School of Business here at the University of Anywhere. How are you tonight? *(Respond appropriately.)*

Case: I'm with a group of students tonight, calling alumni and friends of the School of Business to generate support for the 1999 Annual Fund. As you may know, alumni support is *so important* for the School of Business because it provides the much-needed funding for additional student scholarships, classroom equipment, new technologies and more

First Ask: Without alumni support, we'd probably be a good business school, but it's the support of alumni and friends that make the School of Business at the University of Anywhere a *great* business school!

Mr./Mrs. *Lastname,* I'd love to get you involved with this effort tonight, and the first thing I'd like to mention is a gift of $1,000 which could be done in four installments. This would qualify you for the President's Council, one of our most elite donor recognition groups. Is this something you'd like to do for the School of Business this year?

(If answer is yes, proceed to confirmation. If not, proceed to second ask.)

Second Ask: That's understandable, Mr./Mrs. *Lastname;* that's not something everyone is comfortable with—it's just a starting point. The important thing is to find a way for everyone to participate this year. As the costs associated with higher education continue to rise, more and more students need financial aid to attend the School of Business. We just want to make sure these students have an opportunity to receive a fine education here at the University of Anywhere. Many more of our alumni and friends feel comfortable with a pledge of $500, which could also be done in installments. This is called the Chancellor's Council, and I'd love to put you down for that this year!

(If answer is yes, proceed to confirmation. If not, proceed to third ask. Don't forget to deal with any objections and talk about the person's experiences here at the University of Anywhere!)

Third Ask: Mr./Mrs. *Lastname,* I can certainly appreciate your situation. And I must thank you for speaking with me tonight. As I said before, participation is our goal for this program. We know that if we can get everyone on board with this effort, we can meet our goals and continue to offer the best to our students both today and in the future. Let me share one of our more popular gifts. It's just two installments of $125 for a total of $250. It's our Dean's Circle gift, and it would be *terrific* if you could join us with that this year!

(If answer is yes, proceed to confirmation. If not, proceed to fourth ask.)

Fourth Ask: I appreciate your time this evening, let me mention just one more thing. The School of Business really wants us to find something everyone would be comfortable with for the 1999 Annual Fund. I think this might be something you could do—it's just $50 next month and $50 after that for a total pledge of $100. It would be *just great* if you could join our efforts with that, Mr./Mrs. *Lastname!*

(If answer is yes, proceed to confirmation. If not, proceed to closing.)

Closing: Thank you again for your time, Mr./Mrs. *Lastname;* it's been a pleasure speaking with you. While I have you on the phone, let me just check your address *(check home and business address information).* I hope you'll consider supporting the School of Business next year. You have a great night!

Pledge Confirmation: Thank you so much, Mr./Mrs. *Lastname,* for your pledge of *(specify amount)* to the School of Business at the University of Anywhere! Your support will go a long way at the school! Let me make sure I have your address right *(check home address).* I also have your business information as *(read and confirm business information).* Do you or does anyone in your household work for a company that would match that gift? *(If yes, please note.)*

Let me make one final check that I have everything correct: that's a total gift of *(state total amount)* done in *(discuss installment options)* for the School of Business at the University of Anywhere. I'll send you a pledge card in the morning with your pledge of *(specify amount)* noted on it. Will you be able to make that first payment in the next 30 days? Terrific! *(If not, renegotiate.)*

Thank you again, Mr./Mrs. *Lastname!* You have a great night!

DONOR RENEWAL: $50–$500 DONORS

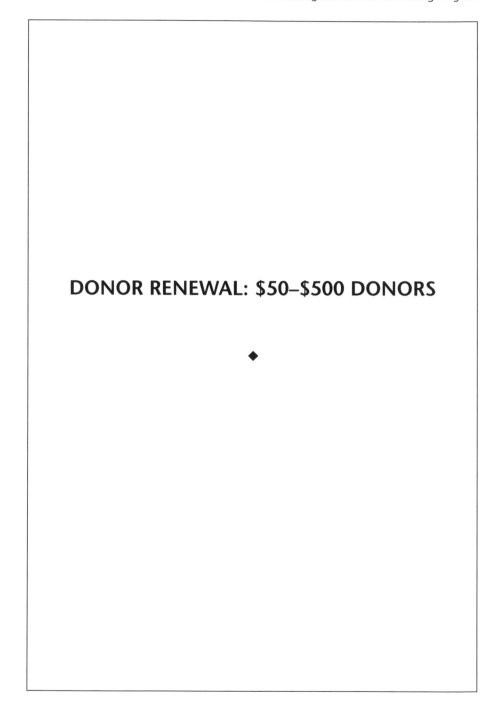

Greeting: Hello! May I speak with Mr./Mrs. *Firstname Lastname?*

Introduction: Hi, Mr./Mrs. *Lastname,* my name is *Caller's Firstname Lastname,* and I'm calling on behalf of the School of Business here at the University of Anywhere. How are you tonight? *(Respond appropriately.)*

Case: I'm with a group of students tonight, and I'm calling to say *thank you* for your continued support of the School of Business! As you already know, your support is *so important* for the School of Business because it provides the much-needed funding for additional student scholarships, classroom equipment, new technologies and more!

First Ask: Without alumni support, we'd probably be a good business school, but it's the support of alumni and friends *like you* that make the School of Business at the University of Anywhere a *great* business school!

Mr./Mrs. *Lastname,* I'd also like to renew your support for 1999, and the first thing I'd like to mention is a gift of $1,000, which could be done in four installments. This would qualify you for the President's Council, one of our most elite donor recognition groups. Would you be able to make a President's Council gift this year?

(If answer is yes, proceed to confirmation. If not, proceed to second ask. Keep last year's gift in mind for the renewal.)

Second Ask: That's understandable, Mr./Mrs. *Lastname;* that's not something everyone is comfortable with—the important thing is to renew your support again this year. As the costs associated with higher education continue to rise, more and more students need financial aid to attend the School of Business. We just want to make sure these students have an opportunity to receive a fine education here at the University of Anywhere. Some of our alumni and friends have been able to increase to a pledge of $500, which could also be done in installments. This is called the Chancellor's Council, and I'd love to renew your support with that this year!

(If answer is yes, proceed to confirmation. If not, proceed to third ask. Don't forget to deal with any objections and talk about the person's experiences here at the University of Anywhere! This is a donor, and we love our donors!)

Third Ask: Mr./Mrs. *Lastname,* I can certainly appreciate your situation. And I must thank you for speaking with me tonight. As I said before, our goal is to renew everyone's support for the 1999 Annual Fund. We know that if we can get everyone on board again with this effort, we can continue to offer the best to our students both today and in the future. Let me share one of our more popular gifts. It's just two installments of $125, for a total of $250. It's our Dean's Circle gift, and it would be *terrific* if you could renew your support again this year with a pledge of $250.

(If answer is yes, proceed to confirmation. If not, proceed to fourth ask.)

Fourth Ask: I appreciate your time this evening; let me mention just one more thing. The School of Business really wants us to find a way for everyone to renew their commitment to the 1999 Annual Fund. I think this might be something you could do—it's just $50 next month and $50 after that, for a total pledge of $100. It would be *just great* if you could join our efforts with that, Mr./Mrs. *Lastname!*

(If answer is yes, proceed to confirmation. If not, proceed to closing. If the donor gave less than $100 last year, ask for a renewal. If the person gave $50 last year, you might consider a $75 ask.)

Closing: Thank you again for your time, Mr./Mrs. *Lastname;* it's been a pleasure speaking with you. While I have you on the phone, let me just check your address *(check home and business address information).* I hope you'll renew your support for the School of Business next year. You have a great night!

Pledge Confirmation: Thank you so much, Mr./Mrs. *Lastname,* for your pledge of *(specify amount* to the School of Business at the University of Anywhere! Your continued support will go a long way at the school! Let me make sure I have your address correct *(check home address).* I also have your business information as *(read and confirm business information).* Do you or does anyone in your household work for a company that would match that gift? *(If yes, please note.)*

Let me make one final check that I have everything correct—that's a total gift of *(state total amount)* done in *(discuss installment options)* for the School of Business at the University of Anywhere. I'll send you a pledge card in the morning with your pledge of *(specify amount)* noted on it. Will you be able to make that first payment in the next 30 days? Terrific! *(If not, renegotiate.)*

Thank you again, Mr./Mrs. *Lastname,* for your continued support! You have a great night!

RESOURCE 16

MEMBERSHIP CLUB, DONOR CLUB, AND GIVING SOCIETY BROCHURES

Membership Brochure: Indianapolis
  Museum of Art Membership 700
Donor Club Brochure:
  Young Friends of Art 706

Giving Society Brochure: Second
  Century Society 712

Note: Due to space considerations, only the covers are shown above for The Corporate Partner Program and Discover Art. Their text has been omitted in this resource.

The Benefits of an IMA Membership

The Privileges

- 10% discount in Alliance Museum Shop
- 10% discount in Madeline F. Elder Greenhouse
- Access to Stout Reference Library and Jane S. Dutton Resource Center
- Members-only domestic and international travel program
- Discount on Civic Theatre main stage productions

The Collections

- Free admission to IMA permanent collection and temporary exhibitions for one year
- Free admission to IMA—Columbus Gallery
- Members-only guided art tours and Behind-the-Scenes tours
- Invitations to members-only exhibition openings and receptions
- Invitations to join specific IMA art interest groups

The Connections

- Discounted admission on classes, lectures, family activities, films and concerts
- Subscription to members magazine, *Previews,* a bi-monthly publication
- Members-only garden tours

Indianapolis Museum of Art Membership Categories

Individual ($35) Membership card and benefits for one adult

Family/Dual ($50) Two membership cards and benefits for two adults and all children 18 and under in same household

Guest Benefit ($20 additional) One guest can join you for any activity. Member must accompany guest. Guest benefit is available with any of the above memberships. Please limit one per membership.

Sustaining ($100) All benefits of Family membership plus:

- 10% discount to *Taste of the IMA*
- Guest Benefit membership enhancement

Reciprocal: $150 All Sustaining membership benefits plus:

- Reciprocal member benefits at 14 major art museums around the country
- Invitations to international and domestic travel programs

Membership Add-on Benefits

These additional benefits are not tax-deductible donations.

Kids Club ($10 additional per child)
Enhance your membership and inspire your child's imagination through art. Benefits include:

- Your child's own membership card
- Free Family Studio Guides
- Postcards or e-mails reminding your family to join us for Family Days at the IMA
- *Annual Summer Social Event*

Educators Club ($10 additional per educator)
Enhance your membership and inspire your student's imagination through art. Benefits include:

- Art alert postcards
- Teacher Newsletters
- *Annual Evening for Educators*

Young Friends of Art ($10 additional)
Young professionals aged 21 through 40 will enjoy a signature series including: *Unwind with Art, The Great Gallery Mix-up, The Inside Scoop: Curator's Tour* and a special event in the summer.

Membership Application

Please print clearly and return with payment to the IMA.

IMA Attn: Membership Services
1200 West 38th Street
Indianapolis, IN 46208-4196

To charge your membership, please call 317.920.2651.

☐ Ms.   ☐ Miss   ☐ Mrs.   ☐ Mr.   ☐ Mr. and Mrs.

☐ other (please indicate)_____

_____
Your Name

_____
Second Name (Family Membership & above)

_____
Street

_____
City   State   Zip

_____
Telephone (home)   (business)

_____
e-mail

Membership Categories

☐ Individual   ($35)
☐ Family/Dual   ($50)
☐ Guest Benefit   ($20)
    per membership
☐ Sustaining   ($100)
☐ Reciprocal   ($150)

Additional Levels of Support

☐ Advocate   ($250)
☐ Patron   ($500)
☐ Benefactor   ($900)

Membership Add-on Benefits
(Not tax deductible)

☐ Young Friends of Art ($10)
    per membership
☐ Educators Club ($10) per educator
☐ Kids Club ($10) per child

    Children's names

    _____

    _____

    _____

Method of Payment:

☐ Check $ _____ ☐ Cash $ _____ ☐ Credit Card $ _____

_____
Credit Card Number   Expiration Date

_____
Name as it appears on card

_____
Signature

Membership card(s) will be mailed following payment. Please allow two weeks
for processing. Memberships are renewable annually.

☐ *Yes! I want to give an IMA gift membership.*

Recipient of the Gift Membership:

_____
Name

_____
Second Name (if Family Membership)

_____
Street

_____
City   State   Zip

Corporate Matching Gifts and Tax Information

Based on IRS guidelines and the fair market value of your benefits, the following amount of your membership is tax deductible and may be matched by your employer: Individual ($35), Family/Dual ($50), Sustaining ($100), Reciprocal ($150), Advocate ($250), Patron ($500), Benefactor ($850), Guest Benefit ($20)

Customize your membership!

Birth Date _____

Please rank your preferred visual art interest (1=high, 5=low):

____ European Art

____ Asian Art

____ African Art

____ Contemporary Art

____ Decorative Art

____ Grounds & Gardens

____ Photographs

Please rank the programs in terms of your interest (1=high, 3=low):

____ Exhibition Openings

____ Adult Studio classes

____ Children's Workshops

____ Lectures

____ Self-Guided Tours

____ Docent-Guided Tours

____ Video Orientation

Membership Services
Indianapolis Museum of Art
1200 West 38th Street
Indianapolis, IN 46208-4196
317.920.2651

Richard Marquis

Membership Reply Enclosed
Membership
Service

BUSINESS REPLY MAIL
FIRST-CLASS MAIL   PERMIT NO. 4101   INDIANAPOLIS IN

POSTAGE WILL BE PAID BY ADDRESSEE

ATTN: MEMBERSHIP SERVICES
INDIANAPOLIS MUSEUM OF ART
1200 West 38th Street
Indianapolis, IN 46208-4196

NO POSTAGE
NECESSARY
IF MAILED
IN THE
UNITED STATES

Discover Art-
Inside&Out

Inside, find treasures from around the globe. Outside, explore 52 acres of magnificently landscaped grounds, dine at our restaurants, explore our shops, and enjoy many exciting special events.

Jean-Baptiste-Claude Odiot

Central Africa

Admission to the museum is free.

There is a charge for special exhibitions.

Free tours of the museum's collections are offered every day. Call 317.920.2649 for information on group tours.

Membership Services
317.920.2651

Museum Hours

Tuesday-Saturday,
10 am-5 pm
Thursday, 10 am-8:30 pm
Sunday, noon-5 pm
Closed Mondays and
major holidays.

Outdoor parking is free.

Indoor parking is also available.

**NATIONAL
ENDOWMENT
FOR THE ARTS**

**ARTS COUNCIL OF
INDIANAPOLIS**

This activity is made possible in part by the Indiana Arts Commission, a state agency, with funds from the Indiana General Assembly and the National Endowment for the Arts

A portion of the museum's general operating funds for this fiscal year has been provided through a grant from the Institute of Museum and Library Services, a Federal agency serving the public by strengthening museums and libraries.

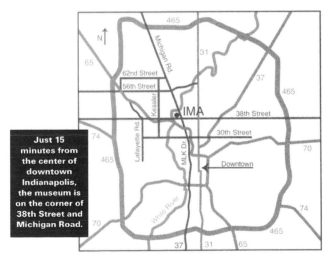

Just 15 minutes from the center of downtown Indianapolis, the museum is on the corner of 38th Street and Michigan Road.

Indianapolis Museum of Art

**1200 West 38th Street
Indianapolis, IN 46208-4196
317.923.1331
24-hour information line: 317.920.2650**

Young Friends of Art

You are invited to join one of the most dynamic civic groups in Indianapolis. Young Friends of Art (YFA) is a group of young professionals, couples and families who are members of the IMA. Our diverse members all have in common an appreciation of art and a desire to share that passion with others.

As a YFA member, you can serve the museum and work closely with the staff, the art and other Indianapolis professionals. You will be a critical link in the museum's volunteer service structure, providing hands-on help for exciting special events. You will also be a critical link to the community, sharing your love of art through engaging outreach programs.

YFA Members Involved at the Museum

Collector's Series. This series is designed for those who have an interest in beginning their own art collections. YFA members tour local fairs, studios, homes and galleries in search of affordable works of art. Experts explain the collecting process and offer suggestions on what to buy and when to buy it.

Exhibition Series. This series allows for in-depth exploration of the special exhibitions through private tours and discussion with IMA curators. A wine-and-cheese reception follows each tour.

Taste of the IMA. YFA members act as hosts for these special evenings. They began with a reception in Clowes Courtyard, followed by a spotlight-tour of three original works of art. Then feast on a savory gourmet meal and lift your spirits by visiting with others interested in art.

First Fridays. Mix and mingle on the first Friday of the month. Enjoy the sounds of traditional and contemporary jazz, view the current special exhibition or the permanent collection and enjoy cocktails and hors d'oeuvres with friends and colleagues. YFA members provide volunteer support for these monthly art mixers.

Young Friends of Art was created in the spirit of service. Please consider participating in a volunteer committee as a YFA member.

YFA Volunteer Committees

Membership Services Committee—recruits new YFA members at events such as First Friday, Taste of the IMA, the Summer Nights series, Penrod and AfricaFest.

Education Committee—coordinates the Collector's Series and the Exhibition Series in an effort to broaden YFA members' knowledge of art and the IMA.

Marketing Committee—assists with the production of YFA promotional materials such as postcards and invitations.

Special Events Committee—helps plan and coordinate YFA social and fundraising events, both at the museum and at other locations.

Volunteer Committee—develops and maintains a volunteer network for all YFA programs and special events.

Public Relations Committee—calls on new members, encouraging their participation in this dynamic group.

To join Young Friends of Art, please call the YFA hotline at (317) 920-2683 or complete this form and mail it with your payment to the Indianapolis Museum of Art.

☐ Yes! I want to become a member of the Indianapolis Museum of Art and participate in Young Friends of Art.

☐ Ms.   ☐ Miss   ☐ Mrs.
☐ Mr.   ☐ Mr. & Mrs.   ☐ Rev.
☐ Dr.   ☐ Drs.   ☐ Other _____

_____
(Name)

_____
(Second Name—Family Membership and above)

_____
(Street)

_____
(City)   (State)   (Zip)

_____
(Telephone) (home)   (work)

Please begin my IMA membership at the following level:

☐ Individual—$35   ☐ Advocate—$250
☐ Family—$50   ☐ Patron—$500
☐ Sustaining—$100   ☐ Benefactor—$900
☐ Reciprocal—$150

☐ *Young Friends of Art*—$5 in addition to membership

Method of Payment:

☐ Check $_____
☐ Cash $_____
☐ Credit Card $_____

_____
(Credit Card Number)

_____
(Expiration Date)

_____
(Name as it appears on card)

_____
(Signature)

Membership card(s) will be mailed following payment. Please allow two weeks for processing. Memberships are renewed annually and are fully tax deductible.

Membership Services
Indianapolis Museum of Art
1200 West 38th Street
Indianapolis, IN 46208
317.920.2651

The Benefits of Membership

The Collections

- Free admission to IMA permanent collection and special exhibitions for one year
- Free admission to IMA-Columbus Gallery
- Members-only guided art tours and behind-the-scenes tours
- Invitations to members-only exhibition openings and receptions
- Invitations to join IMA special art interest groups

The Connections

- Discounted admission to classes, lectures, family activities, films and concerts
- Subscription to members' magazine, *Previews,* a bimonthly publication
- Members-only garden tours

The Privileges

- 10% discount in Alliance Museum Shop
- 10% discount in Madeline F. Elder Greenhouse
- Access to art reference library and Jane S. Dutton Resource Center
- Members-only domestic and international travel opportunities
- Discounts on main-stage Civic Theatre productions

Please check the art topics that interest you most:

☐ African Art	☐ European Art
☐ American Art	☐ Grounds & Gardens
☐ Asian Art	☐ Photographs
☐ Contemporary Art	☐ Prints & Drawings
☐ Decorative Arts	☐ Textiles

Please check the format(s) in which you like to learn about art:

☐ Exhibition opening receptions	☐ Self-guided tours
	☐ Docent-guided tours
☐ Adult studio classes	☐ Video orientation
☐ Children's workshops	of special exhibitions
☐ Lectures	

I would like to participate on the following YFA volunteer committees:

☐ Membership Services	☐ Special Events
☐ Education	☐ Volunteer
☐ Marketing	☐ Public Relations

Indianapolis Museum of Art Membership Categories

Individual: $35
- Membership card and benefits for one adult.

Family/Dual: $50
- Two membership cards and benefits for two adults and all children 18 and under in same household.

Sustaining: $100
- *All benefits of Family membership plus:*
- 10% discount on Taste of the IMA
- Guest Pass Admission to special exhibition

Reciprocal: $150
- *All benefits of Sustaining membership plus:*
- Reciprocal member benefits at 14 major art museums around the country
- Invitations to international and domestic travel programs

Advocate: $250
- *All benefits of Reciprocal membership plus:*
- Complimentary subscription to *Expressions*
- Recognition in the Annual Report

Patron: $500
- *All benefits of Advocate membership plus:*
- Invitations to selected major donor events

Benefactor: $900
- *All benefits of Patron membership plus:*
- Complimentary catalogue of special exhibitions organized by the IMA

Young Friends of Art—$5 additional.
Young professionals in their 20s, 30s and 40s enjoy additional special events including Collector's Series, artful travel, wine and beer tasting, jazz concerts and more.

IMA memberships are fully tax-deductible.

Indianapolis Museum of Art	317.923.1331
1200 West 38th Street	
Indianapolis, Indiana	
46208.4196	
Membership Services	317.920.2651
YFA Hotline	317.920.2683

Second Century Society

Indianapolis Museum of Art

"Membership in the Second Century Society has enriched my life in many ways. Through my involvement in the Society's activities, I have made new friendships with those who share my love of art and of the museum. It has also given me the opportunity to intimately learn about the workings of the museum and more about the world's great art."

Roberta Walton
Second Century Society member

A Special Invitation to Join the Second Century Society

"You are invited to join the Second Century Society and to contribute to the growth and improvement of the Indianapolis Museum of Art.

For almost two decades, Second Century Society members have been at the forefront of planning, financing and implementing changes, making the Indianapolis Museum of Art a leader in the cultural community. Please help continue the Society's rich history of support by joining me and fellow Second Century Society members in advancing the horizons of children and adults."

John L. Krauss
Trustee & Chairman, Development Committee

Serving the Central Indiana Community

For more than one hundred and fifteen years, donors and volunteers have been an essential part of the Indianapolis Museum of Art's ability to flourish into a multi-faceted cultural organization. In addition to collecting, preserving and interpreting world-class art, the IMA offers symposia for scholars and educators, distance learning opportunities, educational resources for Indiana teachers, school tours, performing arts events, special exhibition-associated programs including poetry, music, lectures, gallery talks and much more.

As a Second Century Society member, you can join your peers, fellow cultural leaders, in maintaining the established tradition of philanthropy and involvement that has been at the heart of the IMA's growth over the last sixteen years.

The Second Century Society is an essential resource for financial support of the museum's collections, programs and activities through unrestricted and restricted gifts.

Since the Society's inception, the museum has added the Paul Textile Arts Gallery, DeBoest Lecture Hall, Long Gallery and educational classrooms.

Please become part of this special group by sending back the reply form today.

Privileges of Membership

The Society honors and identifies those individuals who make an unrestricted or restricted gift of $1,250 or more. As key partners in the volunteer and philanthropic leadership of the Indianapolis Museum of Art, Second Century Society members' invaluable support is recognized in many ways, including:

- a diverse schedule of unique programs and special events
- exciting travel opportunities to visit the great art collections of the U.S. with the director of the IMA
- private tours of major exhibitions
- visits to regional private and corporate collections
- behind-the-scenes tours with curators to view conservation work
- the annual Founder's Day Dinner celebration in October.

You can join the Second Century Society at several membership levels or Circles. Please find the level of support and involvement that best suits you and indicate the Circle on the response card.

Membership Levels*

T.C. Steele Circle $1,250–$2,499

Born in Indiana, T.C. Steele (1847–1926) studied in Munich for five years before returning to his home to paint landscapes. One of the five members of the noted Hoosier Group, he is considered the Dean of Indiana artists.

- Complimentary invitations for two to the annual Founder's Day Dinner
- Complimentary invitations for two to major exhibition opening receptions
- Complimentary invitations for two to Second Century Society events and receptions
- Discounts on purchases in the Alliance Museum Shop and the Madeline F. Elder Greenhouse
- Free parking in the IMA garage
- Voting privileges at the museum's annual meeting
- Special recognition in select museum publications

Mary Cassatt Circle $2,500–$4,999

Mary Cassatt (1845–1926) is considered to be the greatest nineteenth-century American woman artist. Associated with the French Impressionists, Cassatt is noted for her studies of mothers and their children.

- All the benefits listed at the T.C. Steele Circle
- Opportunity to arrange a curator-led tour of a special exhibition for up to twenty-five friends or business associates

William Merritt Chase Circle $5,000–$9,999

William Merritt Chase (1849–1916), born and reared in Central Indiana, was one of the greatest American artists of his time.

- All the benefits listed at the Mary Cassatt Circle
- Complimentary invitations for two to a private event with the Director

J.M.W. Turner Circle $10,000–$19,999

J.M.W. Turner (1775–1851) was an English landscape painter who excelled in watercolors. The museum holds one of the largest collections of Turner paintings outside the United Kingdom.

- All the benefits listed at the William Merritt Chase Circle
- Complimentary invitations for two to attend private contributors dinner

Georges Seurat Circle   **$20,000 and above**

The French artist Georges Seurat (1859–1891) is well known for developing the Neo-Impressionist style. The museum's collection boasts many Neo-Impressionist works, including one of Seurat's last landscape paintings.

- All the benefits listed above

* All but $200 of your Second Century Society membership will be tax-deductible.

"Second Century Society members are leaders of the community—women and men of vision and foresight who take pride in supporting the Indianapolis Museum of Art, an institution they know to be one of the great cultural assets of this city and the state of Indiana."

Bret Waller
Director

Please help

- expand the Indianapolis Museum of Art's permanent collection
- develop special exhibitions
- maintain the IMA as a cultural focal point in the community
- support many educational opportunities

  by joining the Second Century society today.

SPECIAL-EVENTS PLANNING CHECKLISTS

Special Events:
Planning for Success

April L. Harris

Published by the Council for Advancement and Support of Education

Budget Planning Checklist

When planning a special-events budget, take costs for the following items into account:

1. Facilities

☐ rental of meeting or reception room(s)
☐ overnight accommodations:
_____ number of rooms at _____ rate

☐ setup charges _____   ☐ cleanup charges _____

Rental of:
☐ chairs   ☐ tables
☐ props   ☐ lectern
☐ tent   ☐ canopy
☐ lighting   ☐ extra help
☐ coat checkroom   ☐ electrical generators
☐ additional telephone lines

2. Food Service

☐ number of people to be served: _____
☐ the cost per person for:
☐ coffee breaks   ☐ soda breaks
☐ luncheon   ☐ dinner
☐ cocktail hour   ☐ liquor
☐ wine   ☐ other beverages
☐ table linen   ☐ gratuities
☐ rented table service   ☐ test meal
   (flatware and dishes)

3. Equipment Rental

☐ tables   ☐ canopy or tent
☐ flooring or carpeting   ☐ risers
☐ ropes or stanchions   ☐ props
☐ registration desks and stools   ☐ outdoor toilets
☐ booths   ☐ lighting
☐ backdrop   ☐ trash containers
☐ fencing

4. Decor

- ☐ flowers
- ☐ extra plants
- ☐ corsages, boutonnieres
- ☐ direction signs
- ☐ table decorations
- ☐ props
- ☐ candles
- ☐ other decorations (ribbon, balloons)

5. Design and Printing

- ☐ fee for design concept and package
- ☐ advance announcements
- ☐ programs
- ☐ posters
- ☐ maps
- ☐ signs
- ☐ name badges and holders
- ☐ invitations
- ☐ promotional fliers
- ☐ tickets
- ☐ placecards
- ☐ registration packets
- ☐ any other printed materials

6. Postage and Shipping

- ☐ postage for invitations and reply cards
- ☐ mailing-house charges
- ☐ overnight shipping charges
- ☐ bulk mailing of promotional materials
- ☐ shipping

7. Recognition Items

- ☐ awards, plaques, trophies
- ☐ calligraphy
- ☐ shipping and handling
- ☐ engraving
- ☐ framing

8. Miscellaneous

- ☐ VIP travel and expenses
- ☐ gifts
- ☐ extra help
- ☐ insurance
- ☐ taping and transcribing proceedings
- ☐ electrical connections
- ☐ cellular phone charges
- ☐ honoraria
- ☐ mementos
- ☐ security
- ☐ first-aid station
- ☐ visitors' center materials and staff
- ☐ water hookups

9. Transportation

- ☐ buses
- ☐ parking
- ☐ vans
- ☐ valets

10. Entertainment

☐ fees   ☐ additional equipment
☐ instrument rental   ☐ rehearsal-time fees
☐ promoter fees   ☐ accommodations
☐ travel

11. Publicity

☐ advertising   ☐ photographer
☐ printed photos   ☐ slides
☐ duplicating   ☐ mailing
☐ signs   ☐ press-room hospitality
☐ press-room equipment   ☐ banners
  (computers, faxes, regular and modem phone lines)

12. Audiovisual Equipment

☐ slide and video projectors   ☐ screens
☐ extension cords   ☐ projector carts
☐ microphones   ☐ mixers
☐ speaker system   ☐ tape recorders
☐ pointers   ☐ flip charts/markers
☐ blackboards   ☐ technician services

13. Office Expenses

☐ staff time   ☐ overtime and compensatory time
☐ data processing   ☐ phones
☐ additional staff   ☐ supplies (pens, pads, decals,
  (students, temporaries)   folders)
☐ duplicating   ☐ postage for general
☐ committee materials   correspondence
☐ complimentary tickets   ☐ hospitality for committee
☐ staff travel and expenses   members
☐ staff accommodations

Room Setup Checklist

Date: _____

Event title: _____

Date/time: _____

Institution sponsor: _____

Event planner: _____

Office phone: _____ Cellular phone: _____

Fax: _____

E-mail: _____

Address: _____

Facility name: _____

Address: _____

Facility manager: _____

Office phone: _____ Cellular phone: _____

Fax: _____

E-mail: _____

Rooms being used: _____

Caterer: _____

Contact person: _____

Office phone: _____ Cellular phone: _____

Florist: _____

Contact person: _____

Office phone: _____ Cellular phone: _____

Fax: _____

E-mail: _____

Specifications

Setups: _____

Stage: _____ Lights: _____

Sound: _____

Bandstand: _____

Podium: _____

Microphones (type needed): _____

Number needed: _____

Location of microphones: _____

Bars and serving areas

Bar needed: _____ Location(s): _____

Coat check room needed: _____ Location: _____

Registration area needed: _____ Location: _____

Floor plans

On a separate sheet, diagram the floor plan for each area to be used. Show setups for all areas; note traffic patterns and all entrances and exists. Attach.

Equipment Checklist

Date: _____

Event title: _____

Date/time: _____

Institution sponsor: _____

Event planner: _____

Office phone: _____ Cellular phone: _____

Fax: _____

E-mail: _____

Address: _____

Facility name: _____

Address: _____

Facility manager: _____

Office phone: _____ Cellular phone: _____

Fax: _____

E-mail: _____

Rooms being used: _____

Times being used: _____

Rental company/on-campus source: _____

Address: _____

Contact person: _____

Office phone: _____

Equipment needed and quantity: _____

_____

_____

_____

Color scheme: _____

Cost: _____

Deposit required: _____

Balance due: _____

Delivery and setup instructions: _____

_____

_____

_____

Pickup instructions: _____

_____

_____

_____

Audiovisual Checklist

Date: _____

Event title: _____

Date/time: _____

Institution sponsor: _____

Event planner: _____

Office phone: _____ Cellular phone: _____

Fax: _____

E-mail: _____

Address: _____

Facility name: _____

Address: _____

Facility manager: _____

Office phone: _____ Cellular phone: _____

Fax: _____

E-mail: _____

Rooms being used: _____

Equipment supplier:

Address: _____

Contact person: _____

Office phone: _____

Check equipment needed:

☐ **Slide projectors:**

   No. needed: _____   For room: _____   Time: _____

☐ **Slide trays:**

   No. needed: _____   For room: _____   Time: _____

☐ **Projector cart needed:**   ☐ yes   ☐ no

   For room: _____   Time: _____

☐ **Extension cords:**   ☐ Length: _____

   No. needed: _____   For room: _____   Time: _____

☐ **Spare bulbs:**   Size: _____

   No. needed: _____   For room: _____   Time: _____

☐ **Screens:**

   No. needed: _____   For room: _____   Time: _____

☐ **LCD projector:**

   No. needed: _____   For room: _____   Time: _____

☐ **Video projector:**

   No. needed: _____   For room: _____   Time: _____

☐ **Computer needed:**   ☐ yes   ☐ no

   Kind: _____

   Software requested: _____

☐ **Overhead projectors:**

   No. needed: _____   For room: _____   Time: _____

☐ **Microphones:**   ☐ Type: _____

   No. needed: _____   For room: _____   Time: _____

☐ **Tables:**   ☐ Size: _____

   No. needed: _____   For room: _____   Time: _____

☐ **Chairs:**

   No. needed: _____   For room: _____   Time: _____

☐ **Podiums:**

No. needed: _____ For room: _____ Time: _____

☐ **Televisions:**

No. needed: _____ For room: _____ Time: _____

☐ **VCRs:**

No. needed: _____ For room: _____ Time: _____

☐ **Flip charts:**

No. needed: _____ For room: _____ Time: _____

Miscellaneous (check all that apply and note special instructions below):

☐ **Laser pointer**   ☐ **Computer hookups**

☐ **Telephone**   ☐ **Hand truck**

☐ **Extra extension cords** (specify length) _____

☐ **Other:** _____

Estimated cost: _____ Amount of deposit: _____ Balance due: _____

Operator instructions: _____

_____

_____

Special instructions: _____

_____

_____

Equipment to be delivered on: Date: _____ Time: _____

Deliver to: _____

Equipment to be picked up on: Date: _____ Time: _____

Pickup instructions: _____

_____

_____

_____

Catering Checklist

Date: _____

Event title: _____

Date/time: _____

Institution Sponsor: _____

Event planner: _____

Office phone: _____ Cellular phone: _____

Fax: _____

E-mail: _____

Address: _____

Caterer: _____

Address: _____

Contact person: _____

Office phone: _____ Cellular phone: _____

Facility name: _____

Address: _____

Facility manager: _____

Office phone: _____ Cellular phone: _____

Rooms being used: _____

Time to serve: _____ Projected number of guests: _____

Date, time for final guarantee: _____

Cost per person: _____ Total projected cost: _____

Deposit required: _____ Paid on date: _____

Balance due: _____

Menu: _____

_____

_____

_____

Wines: _____ Toasting: _____

Linen colors: Napkins: _____ Tablecloths: _____

Uniform for wait staff: _____

Placecards: _____ Menu cards: _____

Programs: _____ Favors: _____

Cocktails: _____

Time to serve: _____ Time to close: _____

Location(s) of bar(s): _____

Equipment to be supplied: _____

_____

_____

_____

_____

Bar Checklist

A well-stocked bar should have these supplies:

Alcoholic beverages

☐ vodka   ☐ gin

☐ whiskey   ☐ scotch

☐ bourbon   ☐ rum

☐ beer, regular and light   ☐ white wine

☐ dry vermouth   ☐ red wine

Non-alcoholic beverages and mixes

☐ water   ☐ soda water

☐ tonic water   ☐ sparkling, flavored water

☐ tomato juice   ☐ orange juice

☐ selection of soft drinks (including diet drinks)

Garnishes

☐ lemon and lime wedges   ☐ cherries

☐ olives   ☐ cocktail onions

☐ Angostura bitters   ☐ sugar

Tools

☐ paring knife   ☐ measuring spoons

☐ pitchers   ☐ strainer

☐ jigger   ☐ towels

☐ shaker   ☐ can/bottle opener

☐ corkscrew   ☐ cocktail napkins

☐ bartender's guide of drink recipes   ☐ ice

☐ toothpicks   ☐ ice tongs

Florist/Decor Checklist

Date: _____

Event title: _____

Date/time: _____

Institution sponsor: _____

Event planner: _____

Office phone: _____ Cellular phone: _____

Fax: _____

E-mail: _____

Address: _____

Facility name: _____

Address: _____

Facility manager: _____

Office phone: _____ Cellular phone: _____

Rooms being used: _____

Florist: _____

Address: _____

Contact person: _____

Office phone: _____ Cellular phone: _____

Color scheme: _____

Type of flowers ordered for: _____

Tables: _____

Dais: _____

Reception area: _____

Foyer: _____

Corsages: _____ Boutonnieres: _____

Ushers/hosts/hostesses: _____

Other: _____

Time for deliveries: _____

Containers to be returned: _____

Rented equipment: _____

Return by: _____

Florist to pick up by: _____

Other decorations: _____

_____

Supplier: _____

Contact person: _____

Office phone: _____ Cellular phone: _____

Special instructions: _____

_____

Program Checklist

Date: _____

Event title: _____

Date/time: _____

Institution sponsor: _____

Event planner: _____

Office phone: _____ Cellular phone: _____

Fax: _____

E-mail: _____

Address: _____

Facility name: _____

Address: _____

Facility manager: _____

Office phone: _____ Cellular phone: _____

Rooms being used: _____

Program content: _____

Honored guests/VIPs: _____

Musicians/Band: _____

Contact person: _____

Office phone: _____

Address: _____

Time to begin: _____   Time to end: _____

Time to set-up: _____

Fee: _____   Deposit paid: _____

Check needed at performance: _____   Yes: _____   No: _____

Amount: _____   Pay to: _____

Master of ceremonies: _____

Office phone: _____   Cellular phone: _____

Address: _____

Speakers: _____

Name: _____   Name: _____

Address: _____   Address: _____

Office phone: _____   Office phone: _____

Audiovisuals to be used: _____

Equipment supplied by: _____

Contact person: _____

Office phone: _____

Address: _____

Program Participant/VIP Checklist

Date: _____

Event title: _____

Date/time: _____

Institution sponsor: _____

Event planner: _____

Office phone: _____ Cellular phone: _____

Fax: _____

E-mail: _____

Address: _____

Facility name: _____

Address: _____

Facility manager: _____

Office phone: _____ Cellular phone: _____

Rooms being used: _____

Participant's name: _____

Title/affiliation: _____

Office address: _____

Home address: _____

Office phone: _____ Home phone: _____

Fax: _____

E-mail: _____

Secretary's name: _____

Contact person: _____

Office (area code/phone): _____

Home (area code/phone): _____

Audiovisual requirements: (List equipment needed. If none, state "none.")

_____

_____

_____

Academic regalia:

☐ Will furnish own   ☐ Need to order:

Gown size: _____   Cap size: _____   Colors: _____

To receive: ☐ Award   ☐ Medal plaque   ☐ Citation   ☐ Honorary degree

☐ Other: _____

Presentation item ordered: _____ From: _____

Travel plans: _____

Arrival date: _____ Time: _____

Driving: _____

Flight (airport/airline/flight number and time): _____

To be met by: _____

Meeting place: _____ Time: _____

Accommodations:

Hotel name: _____

Address: _____

Phone: _____

Dates of reservations: _____

Special requests: _____

Departure:

Date: _____ Time: _____

Flight (airport/airline/number/time): _____

To be escorted by: _____ Phone: _____

Will meet for departure at: _____

Expenses:

☐ To be paid by participant   ☐ To be reimbursed, receipts required

☐ To be paid by: _____

Address: _____

Account number or billing information: _____

Honorarium to be paid: $_____ Budget: _____

Other needs:

Special diet: _____

Non-smoking accommodations: _____

Handicapped parking/seating: _____

Is spouse accompanying? _____ If so, name: _____

NONPROFIT KEY WORD SEARCH

Adolescent health issues
African American affairs
After-school/enrichment programs
Agricultural education
AIDS/HIV
Air/water quality
Alzheimer's disease
Animal protection
Art history
Arthritis
Arts and humanities general
Arts appreciation
Arts association and councils
Arts centers
Arts festivals
Arts funds
Arts institutes
Arts outreach
Arts/humanities education
Asian American affairs
At-risk youth
Ballet
Bible study/translation
Big Brothers/Big Sisters camp
Botanical gardens/parks
Business education
Business/free enterprise
Business-school partnerships
Cancer
Chambers of commerce
Child abuse
Child welfare
Children's health/hospitals
Churches

Civic and public affairs
Civil rights
Clinics/medical centers
Clubs
Colleges and universities
Community arts
Community centers
Community foundation
Community service organizations
Community/junior colleges
Continuing education
Counseling
Crime prevention
Criminal rehabilitation
Dance
Day care
Delinquency
Diabetes
Dioceses
Domestic violence
Economic development
Economic education
Economic policy
Education
Education associations
Education funds
Education reform
Elementary education (private)
Elementary education (public)
Emergency relief
Emergency/ambulance services
Employment/job training
Energy
Engineering education

Environment

Ethnic and folk arts

Ethnic organizations

Eyes/blindness

Faculty development

Family planning

Family services

Film and video

First Amendment issues

Food/clothing distribution

Foreign arts organizations

Foreign education

Forestry

Gay/lesbians affairs

Geriatric health

Gifted and talented programs

Health

Health and physical education

Health care/hospitals (international)

Health funds

Health organizations

Health policy/cost containment

Heart

Hispanic affairs

Historic preservation

History and archaeology

Home care services

Homes

Hospice

Hospitals

Hospitals (university-affiliated)

Housing

Human rights

Inner-city development

International

International affairs

International development

International environmental issues

International exchange

International law

International organizations

International peace and security
  issues

International relations

International relief efforts

International studies

Jewish causes

Journalism/media education

Kidney

Law and justice

Leadership training

Legal aid

Legal education

Libraries

Literacy

Literary arts

Long-term care

Lung

Medical education

Medical rehab

Medical research

Medical training

Mental health

Ministries

Minority education

Missionary activities (domestic)

Missionary/religious activities

Multiple sclerosis

Municipalities/town

Museums/galleries

Music

Native American affairs

Nonprofit management

Nursing services

Nutrition

Observatories/planetariums

Opera

Outpatient health care

Parades/festivals

People with disabilities

Performing arts
Philanthropic organizations
Prenatal health issues
Preschool education
Preventive medicine/wellness
    organizations
Private and public education
    (precollege)
Professional/trade associations
Protection
Public broadcasting
Public health
Public policy
Recreation/athletics
Refugee assistance
Religion
Religious education
Religious organizations
Religious welfare
Research
Research/studies institutes
Resource conservation
Rural affairs
Safety
Sanitary systems
Science
Science exhibits/fairs
Science museums
Science/mathematics education
Scientific centers/institutes
Scientific labs
Scientific organizations

Scientific research
Secondary education (private)
Secondary education (public)
Seminaries
Senior services
Sexual abuse
Shelters/homeless
Single-disease health associations
Social science education
Social services
Social/policy issues
Special education
Speech and hearing
Student aid
Substance abuse
Synagogues/temples
Theater
Trade
Transplant networks/donor banks
Trauma treatment
United Funds/United Way
Urban/community affairs
Veterans
Visual arts
Vocational/technical education
Volunteer services
Watershed
Wildlife protection
Women's affairs
YMCA/YMHA/YWCA/YWHA
Youth organizations
Zoos/aquariums

GIFT AGREEMENT TEMPLATES

**XYZ CHARITY
ENDOWED GIFT AGREEMENT**

◆

The _____ Scholarship

```
For XYZ Charity Use Only

ACCOUNT NUMBER: _____
```

XYZ Charity's Name
Name of Account

DONOR(S): _____ ("Donor(s)")

AUTHORIZATION: XYZ Charity _____ ("Charity")

WHEREAS the XYZ Charity ("Charity") receives, invests, administers, and manages private gifts for the benefit of XYZ Charity; and

WHEREAS the Donor(s) wishes (wish) to honor _____, and has (have) irrevocably given to the Charity the sum of $_____ for the purpose of establishing The _____ Scholarship/Fellowship ("Scholarship/Fellowship");

NOW, THEREFORE, IT IS AGREED:

"scholarship/fellowship"   1. It is the intent of the Donor(s) that income from this gift be used to support scholarships. [criteria for selection of recipient can be spelled out here, i.e., "a student enrolled in the school who has an interest in the study of _____, and who has a record of academic excellence as demonstrated by a GPA of _____ on a 4-point scale, and that in selecting recipients, preference be given to (a woman, a graduate of _____ High School, an African American, etc.)."] The number, amount, and recipient(s) of the scholarship will be determined by the Scholarship Committee of the School.

-or-

"professorship/chair"   1. It is the intent of the Donor that [criteria for selection of recipient can be spelled out here]. The use of income generated from this gift may include, but not be limited to, a salary or salary supplement for the designated holder of the professorship [chair], support for research, manuscript preparation, graduate research assistance, library and equipment acquisitions, and other requirements of an active scholar and teacher.

2. The use of this gift will be authorized by the Charity for the reasonable and customary requirements of authorized expenditures as indicated above in accordance with internal operating policies governing investments and administration as established by the Charity. An annual report on the status of the fund will be provided to the Donor(s).

3. The Charity acknowledges that the Donor(s) intend(s) that the original gift amount exist in perpetuity with the income being used to support the purposes of the gift. The Board of Directors of the Charity has established a spending policy which provides for the distribution of both income and a portion of the capital appreciation resulting from investment activity. This policy is consistent with the Charity's investment philosophy to maintain the purchasing power of the original gift so that the endowments may keep pace with inflation.

4. The officers and directors of the Charity have the power, and final decision, to invest, to change investments, to accept property, to sell, to hold, or to reinvest all or any of the monies or property transferred to the Charity under the terms of this Agreement in such manner as they deem proper, and any additional gifts received in support of this purpose are subject to the terms of this Agreement.

5. In the event that the original purposes stated here can no longer be fulfilled, the Charity, through its Board of Directors, and in consultation with the [Dean, campus Chancellor], shall review the circumstances and shall modify this Agreement to the extent necessary to enable the gift to be used in a manner which coincides with the Donor's (s') original intent as closely as possible, and consistent with governing rules/regulations policies/procedures and the internal operating policies of the Charity.

6. The Agreement shall be governed by and interpreted in accordance with the laws of the State of _____.

Signed and dated this _____ day of _____, 200__.

DONOR

_____

[Name(s)]

XYZ Charity

By:_____
, President

INDIANA UNIVERSITY FOUNDATION
ACCOUNT AGREEMENT

For Foundation Use Only

ACCOUNT NUMBER: _____

XYZ Charity's Name
Name of Account

AUTHORIZATION: School of _____ ("School") [Department of _____ ("Department"); Indiana University _____ ("IU_____")]

SOURCE OF FUNDS: [add source of money coming into the account]

WHEREAS the Indiana University Foundation ("Foundation") receives, invests, administers, and manages private funds for the benefit of Indiana University in an account designated for institutional funds (the "Account"); and

WHEREAS [state any information on how the account was created if known].

NOW, THEREFORE, IT IS AGREED:

1. This Account shall be used for . . . (choose from descriptions below or modify as needed). It is further agreed that funds in this Account will not be co-mingled with donor contributions.

Choose one of the following account descriptions or modify as needed:

faculty and staff development   Expenditures may include but are not limited to continuing education, research, departmental awards, travel expenses of faculty and staff, and faculty development.

-or-

capital and equipment needs   Expenditures may include but are not limited to minor renovations to a building or rooms, improvements to the grounds, and purchase of equipment.

-or-

awards, fellowships, or scholarships   The [award, fellowship, or scholarship] will be given out to [spell out specific criteria here]. The number, amount, and recipient(s) of the Scholarship will be determined by the scholarship Committee of the School.

-or-

representation funds   Expenditures from representation accounts shall meet four criteria: a direct benefit to the University, reasonable in amount, a necessary

Resource 19

expenditure which may or may not be made from University funds, and have the appearance of proper use. Expenditures may include employee goodwill, membership dues, meals and entertainment (when the purpose is conducive to conducting university business), and memorabilia given in recognition of support of the institution.

-or-

research   Expenditures may include but are not limited to faculty and staff travel, lodging and travel of visiting scholars, lecturers and research collaborators, supplies and other items which may best serve the needs of the research program.

-or-

general purposes   Expenditures may include but are not limited to faculty and staff recruiting, faculty development, faculty travel, program promotion, and other expenses which may best serve the [academic program or department].

2. The use of the funds in this account will be authorized by the [School, Department, or Campus] for the reasonable and customary requirements of authorized expenditures as indicated above in accordance with internal operating policies governing investments and administration as established by the Foundation, Indiana University, and the [School, Department, or Campus].

3. The Foundation will annually make available the Account balance for the purpose(s) stated above. The Board of Directors of the Foundation established a spending policy which provides for the distribution of both income and a portion of the capital appreciation resulting from investment activity. This policy is consistent with the Foundation's investment philosophy to maintain the purchasing power of the original funds so that the account may keep pace with inflation. This Agreement is subject to the provisions of the Uniform Management of Institutional Funds Act (Indiana Code 30-2-12) ("UMIFA").

4. The officers and directors of the Foundation have the power, and final decision, to invest, to change investments, to accept property, to sell, to hold, or to reinvest all or any of the monies or property transferred to the Foundation under the terms of this agreement in such manner as they deem proper, and any additional funds received in support of this purpose are subject to the terms of this agreement.

5. In the event that the original purposes stated here can no longer be fulfilled, the [Dean, Chairperson or Chancellor], has the power and responsibility to review the circumstances and, if appropriate, modify the purpose of the Account to enable the funds to be used.

6. This Agreement will be terminated no later than one year after all funds received for this purpose have been expended according to the terms stated here.

7. The Agreement shall be governed by and interpreted in accordance with the laws of the State of Indiana.

Signed and dated this _____ day of _____, 200__.

INDIANA UNIVERSITY SCHOOL OF _____

By: _____
       [Name, Dean/Chairperson/Chancellor]

INDIANA UNIVERSITY FOUNDATION

By:_____
       [Name, Executive Director, Administration]

INDIANA UNIVERSITY FOUNDATION
GIFT AGREEMENT

For Foundation Use Only

ACCOUNT NUMBER: _____

XYZ Charity's Name
Name of Account

DONOR(S):_____ ("Donor(s)")

AUTHORIZATION: School of _____ ("School") [Department of _____
("Department"); Indiana University _____ ("IU_____")]

SOURCE OF FUNDS: [add source of money coming into the account if funded by
transfers]

WHEREAS the Indiana University Foundation ("Foundation") receives, invests,
administers, and manages private gifts for the benefit of Indiana University in an
account designated for gifts (the "Account"); and

WHEREAS [state any donor wishes (i.e. in honor or memory of someone) or information on how the account was created if known].

NOW, THEREFORE, IT IS AGREED:

1. This Account shall be used for . . . [choose from descriptions below or modify as
needed].

Choose one of the following account descriptions or modify as needed:

faculty and staff development   Expenditures may include but are not limited to
continuing education, research, departmental awards, travel expenses of faculty
and staff, and faculty development.

    -or-

capital and equipment needs   Expenditures may include but are not limited to
minor renovations to a building or rooms, improvements to the grounds, and
purchase of equipment.

    -or-

awards, fellowships, or scholarships   The [award, fellowship, or scholarship] will be
given out to [spell out specific criteria here]. The number, amount, and recipient(s) of
the Scholarship(s) will be determined by the Scholarship Committee of the School.

    -or-

representation funds   Expenditures from representation accounts shall meet four criteria: a direct benefit to the University, reasonable in amount, a necessary expenditure which may or may not be made from University funds, and have the appearance of proper use. Expenditures may include employee goodwill, membership dues, meals and entertainment (when the purpose is conducive to conducting university business), and memorabilia given in recognition of support of the institution.

-or-

research   Expenditures may include but are not limited to faculty and staff travel, lodging and travel of visiting scholars, lecturers and research collaborators, supplies and other items which may best serve the needs of the research program.

-or-

general purposes   Expenditures may include but are not limited to faculty and staff recruiting, faculty development, faculty travel, program promotion, and other expenses which may best serve the [academic program or department].

2. The use of this gift will be authorized by the [School, Department, or Campus] for the reasonable and customary requirements of authorized expenditures as indicated above in accordance with internal operating policies governing investments and administration as established by the Foundation, Indiana University, and the [School, Department, or Campus]. An annual report on the status of the fund will be provided to the Donor(s).

3. The Foundation will annually make available the Account balance for the purpose(s) stated above. The Board of Directors of the Foundation established a spending policy which provides for the distribution of both income and a portion of the capital appreciation resulting from investment activity. This policy is consistent with the Foundation's investment philosophy to maintain the purchasing power of the original gift so that the account may keep pace with inflation. This Agreement is subject to the provisions of the Uniform Management of Institutional Funds Act (Indiana Code 30-2-12) ("UMIFA").

4. The officers and directors of the Foundation have the power, and final decision, to invest, to change investments, to accept property, to sell, to hold, or to reinvest all or any of the monies or property transferred to the Foundation under the terms of this agreement in such manner as they deem proper, and any additional gifts received in support of this purpose are subject to the terms of this Agreement.

5. In the event that the original purposes stated here can no longer be fulfilled, the Foundation, through its Board of Directors, and in consultation with the [Dean, campus Chancellor], shall review the circumstances and shall modify this Agreement to the extent necessary to enable the gift to be used in a manner which coincides with the Donor's(s') original intent as closely as possible, and consistent with the provisions of UMIFA and the internal operating policies of the Foundation.

6. This Agreement will be terminated no later than one year after all funds received for this purpose have been expended according to the terms stated here.

7. The Agreement shall be governed by and interpreted in accordance with the laws of the State of Indiana.

Signed and dated this _____ day of _____, 200__.

DONOR

By: _____
      [Name(s)]

INDIANA UNIVERSITY SCHOOL OF _____

By: _____
      [Name, Dean/Chairperson/Chancellor]

INDIANA UNIVERSITY FOUNDATION

By: _____
      Curtis R. Simic, President

INDIANA UNIVERSITY FOUNDATION
ENDOWED GIFT AGREEMENT

◆

The _____ Scholarship

XYZ Charity's Name
Name of Account

DONOR(S): _____ ("Donor(s)")

AUTHORIZATION: School of _____ ("School") [Department of _____ ("Department"); Indiana University _____ ("IU__")]

WHEREAS the Indiana University Foundation ("Foundation") receives, invests, administers, and manages private gifts for the benefit of Indiana University; and

WHEREAS the Donor(s) wishes (wish) to honor _____, and has (have) irrevocably given to the Foundation the sum of $_____ for the purpose of establishing The _____ Scholarship/Fellowship ("Scholarship/Fellowship");

NOW, THEREFORE, IT IS AGREED:

"scholarship/fellowship"   1. It is the intent of the Donor(s) that income from this gift be used to support a scholarship. [criteria for selection of recipient can be spelled out here, i.e., "a student enrolled in the School who has an interest in the study of _____, and who has a record of academic excellence as demonstrated by a GPA of _____ on a 4-point scale, and that in selecting recipients, preference be given to (a woman, a graduate of _____ High School, an African American, etc.)."] The number, amount, and recipient(s) of the Scholarship will be determined by the Scholarship Committee of the School.

   -or-

2. The use of this gift will be authorized by the [School, Department, Campus] for the reasonable and customary requirements of authorized expenditures as indicated above in accordance with internal operating policies governing investments and administration as established by the Foundation, Indiana University, and the [School, Department, Campus]. An annual report on the status of the fund will be provided to the Donor(s).

3. The Foundation acknowledges that the Donor(s) intend(s) that the original gift amount exist in perpetuity with the income being used to support the purposes of the gift. The Board of Directors of the Foundation has established a spending policy which provides for the distribution of both income and a portion of the

capital appreciation resulting from investment activity. This policy is consistent with the Foundation's investment philosophy to maintain the purchasing power of the original gift so that the endowments may keep pace with inflation. This Agreement is subject to the provisions of the Uniform Management of Institutional Funds Act (Indiana Code 30-2-12) ("UMIFA").

4. The officers and directors of the Foundation have the power, and final decision, to invest, to change investments, to accept property, to sell, to hold, or to reinvest all or any of the monies or property transferred to the Foundation under the terms of this Agreement in such manner as they deem proper, and any additional gifts received in support of this purpose are subject to the terms of this Agreement.

5. In the event that the original purposes stated here can no longer be fulfilled, the Foundation, through its Board of Directors, and in consultation with the [Dean, campus Chancellor], shall review the circumstances and shall modify this Agreement to the extent necessary to enable the gift to be used in a manner which coincides with the Donor's (s') original intent as closely as possible, and consistent with the provisions of UMIFA and the internal operating policies of the Foundation.

6. The Agreement shall be governed by and interpreted in accordance with the laws of the State of Indiana.

Signed and dated this _____ day of _____, 200__.

DONOR

By: _____
      [Name(s)]

INDIANA UNIVERSITY SCHOOL OF _____

By: _____
      [Name, Dean/Chairperson/Chancellor]

INDIANA UNIVERSITY FOUNDATION

By: _____
      Curtis R. Simic, President

Resource 19

INDIANA UNIVERSITY FOUNDATION
GIFT AGREEMENT

◆

The _____ Scholarship

For Foundation Use Only

ACCOUNT NUMBER: _____

XYZ Charity's Name
Name of Account

DONOR(S): _____ ("Donor(s)")

AUTHORIZATION: School of _____ ("School") [Department of _____ ("Department"); Indiana University _____ ("IU__")]

WHEREAS the Indiana University Foundation ("Foundation") receives, invests, administers, and manages private gifts for the benefit of Indiana University; and

WHEREAS the Donor(s) wishes (wish) to honor _____, and has (have) irrevocably given to the Foundation the sum of $_____ for the purpose of establishing The _____ Scholarship/Fellowship ("Scholarship/Fellowship");

NOW, THEREFORE, IT IS AGREED:

"scholarship/fellowship"   1. It is the intent of the Donor(s) that this gift be used to support a scholarship. [criteria for selection of recipient can be spelled out here, i.e., "a student enrolled in the School who has an interest in the study of _____, and who has a record of academic excellence as demonstrated by a GPA of _____ on a 4 point scale, and that in selecting the recipients, preference be given to (a woman, a graduate of _____ High School, an African American, etc.)."]. The number, amount, and recipient(s) of the Scholarship will be determined by the Scholarship Committee of the School.

2. The use of this gift will be authorized by the [School, Department, Campus] for the reasonable and customary requirements of authorized expenditures as indicated above in accordance with internal operating policies governing investments and administration as established by the Foundation, Indiana University, and the [School, Department, Campus]. An annual report on the status of the fund will be provided to the Donor(s).

3. The Foundation acknowledges that the Donor(s) intend(s) both income and principal, as required, may be used to support the purpose of the gift. The Board of Directors of the Foundation established a spending policy which provides for the distribution of both income and a portion of the capital appreciation resulting from investment activity. This policy is consistent with the Foundation's investment philosophy to maintain the purchasing power of the original gift so that the

account may keep pace with inflation. This Agreement is subject to the provisions of the Uniform Management of Institutional Funds Act (Indiana Code 30-2-12) ("UMIFA").

4. The officers and directors of the Foundation have the power, and final decision, to invest, to change investments, to accept property, to sell, to hold, or to reinvest all or any of the monies or property transferred to the Foundation under the terms of this Agreement in such manner as they deem proper, and any additional gifts received in support of this purpose are subject to the terms of this Agreement.

5. In the event that the original purposes stated here can no longer be fulfilled, the Foundation, through its Board of Directors, and in consultation with the [Dean, campus Chancellor], shall review the circumstances and shall modify this Agreement to the extent necessary to enable the gift to be used in a manner which coincides with the Donor's (s') original intent as closely as possible, and consistent with the provisions of UMIFA and the internal operating policies of the Foundation.

6. The Agreement shall be governed by and interpreted in accordance with the laws of the State of Indiana.

Signed and dated this _____ day of _____, 200__.

DONOR

By: _____
      [Name(s)]

INDIANA UNIVERSITY SCHOOL OF _____

By: _____
      [Name, Dean/Chairperson/Chancellor]

INDIANA UNIVERSITY FOUNDATION

By: _____
      Curtis R. Simic, President

RULES REGARDING INCOME TAX CHARITABLE DEDUCTIONS

PREPARED BY ALAN M. SPEARS, DIRECTOR,
OFFICE OF PLANNED AND MAJOR GIFTS,
INDIANA UNIVERSITY FOUNDATION,
ON THE BASIS OF
INTERNAL REVENUE SERVICE INFORMATION
(As of November 2000)

Income Tax Charitable Deductions

I. *Total amount of the charitable deduction*
   A. Cash: face amount
   B. Securities and real estate owned over one year: fair market value
   C. Securities and real estate owned one year or less: cost basis or fair market value, whichever is less
   D. Tangible personal property
      1. "Related use," owned over one year: fair market value
      2. "Related use," owned one year or less: cost basis or fair market value, whichever is less
      3. "Unrelated use," owned over one year: cost basis or fair market value, whichever is less
      4. "Unrelated use," owned one year or less: cost basis or fair market value, whichever is less
   E. Inventory (excluding inventory contributed for research and other special cases): cost basis or fair market value, whichever is less

Note: The above amounts apply to public charities, pass-through foundations, and private operating foundations. If the gift is made to a private, nonoperating foundation, the amount of the deduction is the face amount for cash and the fair market value for publicly traded securities, but for all other property the deduction is limited to cost basis (or fair market value if less than cost basis).

II. *The amount of the charitable deduction that can be reported in any one year depends on the type of property contributed and the type of nonprofit organization to which the donor makes their gift*
   A. Type of property contributed
      1. Cash and all ordinary income property: 50 percent of adjusted gross income (AGI)
      2. Appreciated long-term capital gain property: 30 percent of AGI
   B. Type of organization
      1. Public charities: educational institutions, churches, tax-exempt hospitals, governmental units, publicly supported organizations such as the American Red Cross or a symphony orchestra, broadly supported and private operating foundations—50 percent or 30 percent of AGI, depending on type of property.
      2. Private nonoperating foundations
         a. Cash and ordinary income property: 30 percent of AGI
         b. Long-term capital gain property: 20 percent of AGI

III. *Carryovers,* when the total allowable deduction cannot be reported in a single year. Donor has year of gift plus five carryover years in which to use it. (Carryovers apply to private nonoperating foundations as well as to public charities and operating foundations.)

IV. *Pledges.* The deduction is taken in the year the pledge is paid, not when it is made. The IRS takes the position that a written commitment or a promissory note is merely an intention to pay and not a payment. This is true even if the donor makes provision in his or her will to ensure that any outstanding balance on the pledge will be covered by bequest.

   If all or a portion of the pledge is unfulfilled at the time of the donor's death, and the donor's promise is enforceable against his estate, the payment of the pledge qualifies for an estate tax deduction.

V. *When a gift is completed*

   A. *Gift by check.* The effective date of the contribution is the day the check is mailed or hand-delivered, provided there are no restrictions on the cashing of the check. A check dated December 31, 1999, mailed and postmarked the same date, is deductible in 1999. It does not matter that the charity receives the check in the new year and that it is actually charged to the donor's account in January. However, a check dated in December but not mailed or handed to the charity until January cannot be deducted on the prior-year return. Neither can a check that is mailed in December but postdated so that it cannot be cashed until the next month.

   B. *Gift of securities.* If the certificate is registered in the name of the donor and property endorsed or accompanied by a separate stock or bond power assignment, the date of the gift is the date on which the security is hand-delivered or mailed.

   If the certificate is in "street name" and held by the donor's broker, the date of the gift is the day when, on proper instructions from the donor, the broker charges the donor's account and credits the charity's account with the particular shares or bonds donated.

   If the donor has a certificate re-registered in the name of the charity, the date of the gift is the date on the certificate. This procedure is not advisable for year-end gifts, as re-registration by the transfer agent can take several weeks.

   C. *Gift of real estate.* The gift is complete on the day when the signed deed is delivered or mailed to the charitable organization.

VI. *Valuation of securities.* For publicly traded securities, the deduction is the mean between the "high" and the "low" on the date of the gift. For unlisted securities (for example, those sold over the counter), it is the mean between the "bid" and "asked" prices. In short, the deduction is the average value of the securities on the day the donor relinquishes control. Value is not dependent on the net proceeds actually received by the charity when the securities are sold.

The valuation of some securities—such as certain municipal bonds and closely held stock—are not quoted and may not be readily ascertainable. A broker can usually ascertain market values of bonds. Closely held stock presents a different set of problems and must be valued by a qualified appraiser's accounting procedures that takes into consideration a number of factors about the company.

VII. *Volunteers' expenses*

   A. *Gifts of services.* The value of a volunteer's time is not deductible. For example, if an attorney who normally charges clients $150 per hour gives two hours of free legal service to the charity, the attorney may not deduct $300. Neither may volunteers who serve on committees and boards deduct the value of their time. Likewise, newspapers that grant free advertising space and radio and television stations that offer free broadcast time are not allowed a deduction. These are all treated as gifts of services and thus are not deductible.

   B. *Out-of-pocket expenses.* Out-of-pocket expenses incurred by a volunteer while working for the charity are deductible. Examples of deductible items are telephone calls, stationery, postage stamps, and travel between home and the places where the volunteer renders services. A volunteer who uses a personal automobile may deduct the actual costs of gas, tolls, and parking (but not insurance or depreciation) or may calculate a flat 12 cents a mile. If the volunteer attends an out-of-town convention representing the charity in an official capacity, lodging, meals, and transportation are also deductible. These items are not deductible if the volunteer attends the convention merely to enhance knowledge and skills.

VIII. *Substantiation requirements (gift receipts)*

   A. Gift of $250 or more—no goods or services provided to the donor
      1. Donor must obtain a receipt from the nonprofit to support the deduction. A canceled check is insufficient.
      2. Receipt must state that no goods or services were provided to the donor.
      3. The $250 requirement applies to each gift. The gifts to a single charity are not cumulative.

   B. Gift of $75 or more—goods or services provided to the donor.

1. Nonprofit is required to provide a receipt, informing the donor of the amount of the contribution that is deductible.
2. The receipt could contain either of three statements:
   a. If the value of the premium does not exceed $71 (adjusted for inflation each year) or 2 percent of the gift, whichever is less, the receipt could say something like "Under IRS guidelines, the value of the benefits is within the allowable limits; therefore, the full amount of your payment is a deductible contribution."
   b. If the benefits exceed these *de minimis* limits, the receipt must provide a good faith estimate of the value of those benefits and indicate the deductible amount.
3. Intangible benefits such as a name on a building or endowment are not counted.

C. Failure to provide the required information can subject the charity to penalties—$10 per contribution and up to $5,000 per fundraising event.

IX. *Substantiation requirements*

A. Form 8283: Information About Donated Property
   1. *Form 8283 is required* if the total value of all property contributed, other than cash, exceeds $500. Depending on the value and type of property contributed, the donor may need to complete Section A, Section B, or both.
   2. Types of contributions reported in Section A
      a. Publicly traded securities
      b. Real estate and tangible property (paintings, boats, and other items) valued between $500 and $5,000
      c. Closely held securities (not traded publicly) valued between $500 and $10,000
   3. Types of contributions reported in Section B
      a. Real estate and tangible property (paintings, boats, and other items) valued between $500 and $5,000. Section B must be completed if the aggregate claimed value of all similar items exceeds $5,000, even if the value of each single item is less than $5,000.
      b. Closely held securities (not traded publicly) valued in excess of $10,000.
   4. *Qualified appraisal.* To receive a charitable deduction for gifts of property covered by the requirement, the donor must obtain a qualified appraisal and attach an appraisal summary to the tax return on which the deduction is first claimed.

      A qualified appraisal must meet the following criteria.

Resource 20

   a. It is completed not earlier than 60 days prior to the date of contribution.
   b. It is prepared by a qualified appraiser—a person who is professionally qualified to appraise the type of property being valued. The appraiser should be independent of both donor and donee. The appraisal cannot be done by anyone affiliated with the charity.
   c. It does not involve a prohibited type of appraisal fee. The fee should not be based on a percentage of the appraised value of the property. It should rather be a flat fee based on the time and expenses of the appraiser.
5. *Appraisal summary.* The appraisal summary should be made on Section B of Form 8283 and include the following information as required.
   a. Donor's name and taxpayer identification number (social security number in the case of an individual)
   b. Description of the property
   c. Date of acquisition
   d. Donor's cost or other tax basis for the property
   e. Nonprofit's name, address, and tax identification number
   f. Date on which the nonprofit received the property
   g. Name, address, and tax identification number of the appraiser (Section B only)
   h. Fair market value of the property
   i. The appraiser's declaration that he or she is qualified and did not charge a fee under a prohibited method (Section B only)
      After completing the form but before filing it with the tax return, the donor should have it signed by the nonprofit. The nonprofit should retain a copy.
B. Form 8282: Information About Sale of Donated Property
   1. *Form 8282 is required* if the nonprofit sells or otherwise disposes of the property (real estate valued in excess of $5,000, closely held stock valued over $10,000) within two years after receiving it.
   2. The nonprofit must file the form.
   3. Information reported on form
      a. Name and tax identification number of the donor
      b. Name, address, and tax identification number of the charity
      c. Description of the donated property
      d. Date of gift and date of disposition
      e. Appraised value
      f. Selling price or amount received from other type of disposition

4. Donor is entitled to a copy. The nonprofit should send a copy of this information to the donor.

C. Form 1040: Income Tax Return

1. Documents and information to be included for outright gifts
   a. For cash contributions of more than $3,000 to any one charity, state name of charity and amount given.
   b. For noncash gifts over $500, attach Form 8283.

2. Documents and information to be included for irrevocable deferred gifts
   a. Name of charity, type of gift vehicle, and amount contributed
   b. Form 8283 for noncash gifts over $500, same as for outright gifts
   c. Computation form showing value of remainder interest
   d. Copy of the trust agreement, gift annuity agreement, or instrument of transfer

D. Form 709: Gift Tax Return

1. Form 709 is required in the following circumstances:
   a. For gift annuities where gift value exceeds $10,000. Also if the annuitant is neither the donor nor the donor's spouse and the actuarial value exceeds $10,000.
   b. For bargain sales where gift value exceeds $10,000
   c. For charitable remainder trusts, pooled income fund gifts, and retained life estates where charity has a future interest, whatever the amount
   d. For charitable lead trusts in most instances
      Note: The donor should file Form 709 even when no gift tax is due.

2. Documents and information to be included: name of nonprofit, type of gift, amount contributed, and computation form showing value of remainder interest or other charitable interest

X. *Corporate contributions.* Same rules as for individual contributions, but with the following differences.

A. The maximum amount of charitable deductions the corporation can use in one year is 10 percent of taxable income.

B. Corporations may contribute inventory for research purposes or for the care of the ill and needy and deduct up to twice the manufacturing costs (see Section XI for details).

XI. *Corporate gifts of inventory.* Normally, if a corporation donates inventory to a charity, the deduction is limited to the cost basis (the actual manufacturing cost if the company produced the item). There are, however, two exceptions:

A. For a contribution of newly manufactured scientific equipment to colleges and universities for research and experimentation, including

Resource 20

research training, the corporation is allowed a deduction of either cost basis plus 50 percent of the appreciation or twice the corporation's cost basis, whichever is less.

The contribution must be to the physical and biological sciences—engineering, medicine, chemistry, physics, zoology, or the like. The increased deduction does not apply to gifts to the social sciences and humanities. Further, the following requirements must be met:

1. The corporation must have manufactured the equipment.
2. The contribution must be made no later than two years after the property was completed.
3. The original use of the property must be by the donee.
4. The donee cannot sell the property for money, services, or other equipment.
5. The donee must provide the corporation with a written statement that the use of the property will fulfill the requirements.

B. For a contribution of inventory to be applied for the care of the ill, the needy, or infants, corporations may also receive a deduction of either cost basis plus 50 percent of the appreciation or twice the corporation's cost basis, whichever is less.

Gift and Estate Tax Charitable Deductions

1. *Gift tax* is levied on a person's right to transmit property during his or her lifetime. The amount of the tax depends on the size of the gift.
2. *Estate tax* is levied on the right to transmit property at death. The amount of the tax depends on the size of the estate the deceased leaves.
3. *Historical background.* The federal government adopted the estate tax first, followed by the gift tax. The purpose of the estate tax was to raise revenue and redistribute wealth. The purpose of the gift tax was to reinforce the estate tax by discouraging people from giving property during their lifetime in order to avoid the estate tax. Until 1976, the estate and gift taxes were largely independent of each other. If a person made a taxable gift during his or her lifetime, the tax was computed using the gift tax rate schedule. If the gift was made at death, the tax was imposed on the estate of the deceased and was computed using the estate tax rate schedule. It was generally advantageous for a wealthy person to give away as much as practical while living because the total tax would be less.

   The 1976 act eliminated the dual tax system and thereby removed most of the incentive for transferring property during one's lifetime. The two tables were replaced by a single progressive rate schedule that applies to the cumulative total of all transfers during life and at death. Thus if a person made $400,000 of taxable gifts during life and died with a taxable estate of $600,000, the transfer tax could be computed on a total taxable estate of $1,000,000.

   Another revision brought about by the 1976 act was the substitution of a single "unified" credit for the lifetime $30,000 gift tax exemption and the $60,000 estate tax exemption. Today, a person may transfer $675,000 of bequests to noncharitable beneficiaries without incurring tax. This will increase progressively to $1,000,000 by 2006.
4. *Annual gift tax exclusion.* An individual may give another individual up to $10,000 in cash or property each year without having to report the gift or incurring a gift tax. There is no limit to the number of individuals to which such gifts may be made. Husbands and wives may join together and give up to $20,000 (indexed for inflation under 1997 law) to any individual without tax (this is known as *gift-splitting*).

   To qualify for the annual exclusion, the gifts must be present-interest gifts. That is, the donee must have a right to benefit from the property now.
5. *Marital deductions.* Gifts of any size between spouses are not subject to gift tax. Likewise, the first spouse to die can now leave an unlimited amount to

the surviving spouse completely free of federal estate tax. The amount passing to the surviving spouse can qualify for this marital deduction if it is given
outright or under certain approved trust agreements.

6. *Deductibility of lifetime gifts to charity.* A donor is allowed an unlimited charitable gift tax deduction for lifetime gifts to qualified charities. However,
the donor is required to complete a gift tax return (Form 709) if making a
future-interest gift such as a charitable remainder trust or a gift annuity.

7. *Deductibility of bequests to charity.* A donor is allowed an unlimited charitable
estate tax deduction. If the bequest is in the form of a charitable remainder
trust with survivor as income beneficiary, the deduction is for the present
value of the remainder interest. If a surviving spouse is the only income
beneficiary, the combination of the marital deduction and charitable deduction will eliminate estate tax on the property.

TEMPLATES FOR DRAFTING TRUSTS

CHARITABLE REMAINDER
ANNUITY TRUST

◆

Inter Vivos (Between Two Living Persons),
Consecutive and Concurrent Interests

On this _____ day of _____, 200_, I, _____, (hereinafter referred to as "the Donor"), of _____, County of _____, State of _____, desiring to establish a charitable remainder annuity trust, within the meaning of Section 5 Rev. Proc. 90-32 and Section 664(d)(1) of the Internal Revenue Code of 1986, as amended from time to time (hereinafter referred to as "the Code") hereby create the _____ Charitable Remainder Annuity Trust and designate the XYZ Charity (hereinafter referred to as the "Trustee") as the initial Trustee.

1. *Funding of Trust.* The Donor hereby transfers to the Trustee the property described in Schedule A attached hereto, and the Trustee acknowledges the receipt of such property and agrees to hold, manage and distribute such property of the Trust under the terms set forth in this Trust instrument.

2. *Payment of the Annuity Amount.* In each taxable year of the Trust, the Trustee shall pay to _____ and _____ (hereinafter referred to as "the Recipients"), in equal shares during their lifetimes an annuity amount equal to the following percentage: _____ (__) percent of the net fair market value of the Trust assets valued as of the date of transfer to the Trustee of the property indicated on Schedule A. The annuity amount shall be paid from income in equal quarterly installments on or after March 31, June 30, September 30 and December 31, and, to the extent income is not sufficient, from principal. If necessary, a fifth payment will be made on or before the date by which the Trustee is required to file the Federal Income Tax return for the Trust, to bring the total payment to the actual amount to which the Recipient was entitled for that year pursuant to this paragraph. Any income of the Trust for a taxable year in excess of the annuity amount shall be added to principal. If for any year the net fair market value of the Trust assets is incorrectly determined, then within a reasonable period after the value is finally determined for federal tax purposes, the Trustee shall pay to the Recipients (in the case of an undervaluation), or shall collect from the Recipients (in the case of an overvaluation), an amount equal to the difference between the annuity amount which the Trustee should have paid if the correct value had been used and the annuity amount which the Trustee actually paid.

3. *Proration of the Annuity Amount.* In determining the annuity amount to paid under paragraph 2., the Trustee shall prorate the same on a daily basis for a short taxable year in accordance with the Treasury Regulation Section 1.664-2(2)(1)(iv)(a) and, for the taxable year of the death of the survivor Recipient in accordance with Treasury Regulation Section 1.664-3(a)(1)(iv)(b). In the case of a taxable year which is for a period of less than 12 months, the amount required to be distributed under Paragraph 2. Hereunder shall be the fraction of such percentage of which the numerator is the number of days in the short taxable year of the Trust

and of which the denominator is 365 (366 if February 29th is a day included in the numerator).

4. *Distribution to Charity.* Upon the death of the survivor Recipient, the Trustee shall distribute all of the then principal and income of the Trust (other than any amount due either the Recipients or their estates, under the provisions above) to the XYZ Charity, a charitable organization, to be used for _____. If the Charity is not an organization described in each of Sections 170(b)(1)(A), 170(c), 2055(a), and 2522(a) of the Code at the time when any principal or income of the Trust is to be distributed to it, then the Trustee shall distribute such principal or income to such one or more organizations described in each of Sections 170(b)(1)(A), 170(c), 2055(a), and 2522(a) as the Trustee shall select in its sole discretion.

5. *Additional Contributions.* No additional contributions shall be made to this Trust after the initial contribution.

6. *Prohibited Transactions.* If the Trust is continued after the termination of all noncharitable interests, there shall be distributed amounts at least sufficient to avoid liability for the tax imposed by Section 4942(a) of the Code. Except for payment of the annuity amount and notwithstanding any other provisions of this Trust, the Trustee shall not engage in any act of self-dealing, as defined in Section 4941(d) of the Code, and shall not make any taxable expenditures, as defined in Section 4945(d) of the Code. The Trustee shall not make any investments that jeopardize the charitable purpose of the Trust, within the meaning of Section 4944 of the Code and the Treasury Regulations thereunder, or retain any excess business holdings, within the meaning of Section 4943 of the Code.

7. *Taxable Year.* The first taxable year of the Trust begins with the date the Trust is first funded with property and shall end on December 31 of that year. Subsequent taxable years shall be on a calendar year basis.

8. *Governing Law.* This Trust having been delivered in the State of _____, the laws of the State of _____ shall govern the validity and interpretation thereof, notwithstanding the residence in another jurisdiction of the Donor or of any persons who may have an interest in this Trust. For purposes of this Paragraph 8, in any conflict with Section 664 of the Code and the Treasury Regulations thereunder, that Code Section and the corresponding Treasury Regulations shall govern.

9. *Trust Not Liable for Estate or Inheritance Taxes.* No gift, legacy, inheritance, estate, or generation-skipping transfer taxes which may be assessed against the property of this Trust by reason of the Donor's death or transfer of property to this Trust shall be paid out of any property held in trust hereunder. If the payment

of any such taxes are due, the surviving Recipient shall provide for payment of such taxes that may arise as a result of his or her survivorship interest from sources other than property held by this Trust and failure to do so shall cause his or her income interest to terminate as if he or she predeceased the Donor.

10. *Limited Power of Amendment.* The provisions of this Trust shall be irrevocable and not subject to amendment, alteration, or revocation by anyone, except the Trustee shall have the power and duty, acting alone, to amend the Trust in any manner required for the sole purpose of ensuring that the Trust qualifies and continues to qualify as a charitable remainder annuity trust within the meaning of Section 664(d)(1) of the Code and the corresponding Treasury Regulations.

11. *Powers.* In administering this Trust, the Trustee shall have all of the trustee powers and discretions conferred upon it by the laws of the State of _____. These include those powers described in (State) Code Section 30-4-3-3 (as amended from time to time), including but not limited to the power to:

(A) sell, exchange or otherwise dispose of any asset held in this Trust at either public or private sale, for cash or on credit;

(B) invest and reinvest the funds of the Trust in any kind of property, real or personal, including (by way of example and not limitation) stocks of any class, shares of regulated investment companies ("mutual funds"), bonds and debentures, real estate investment trusts, shares or interests in common trust funds, and life insurance policies, all notwithstanding any laws or rules of law that would otherwise require the diversification of trust investments solely to types appearing on a statutory list, or prohibit the holding of underproductive property.

(C) vote shares of stock or other corporate securities, in person or by proxy, on any and all corporate matters, and to exercise conversion privileges, warrants, and options, and to hold shares of stock and any other corporate securities in the name of a nominee, without disclosure of a fiduciary relationship;

(D) prosecute, defend, compromise, abandon, or pay any claim by or against it; to employ agents, attorneys, brokers, or other counsel, or employees to aid it in performance of its duties hereunder, and to pay them reasonable compensation for their services; and the Trustee shall not be liable for any negligence, omission, or mistake of any such agent, attorney, broker, or other counsel or employee selected or retained by it with reasonable care;

(E) borrow money for any Trust purpose (including the payments to be made to the Recipient or other beneficiaries under this Trust) either without security or secured by part or all of the Trust property; and to allocate receipts and disbursements between income and principal in accordance with Chapter _____ of the (State) Trust Code, as amended.

12. *Trustee Compensation and Bond.* The Trustee shall not receive any compensation for services rendered under this agreement, excepting a reasonable investment management fee. Such fees shall be charged to income first, but if income is insufficient, to principal. Any such fees paid shall in no way reduce the annuity amount required to be paid to the Recipient under this Trust. No bond or other security shall be required of the Trustee for the faithful performance of its duties in such capacity.

13. *Investment of Trust Assets.* The Trustee's powers and discretions referenced in Paragraph 11. shall not include any power or discretion that is in conflict with Code Section 664 and the Treasury Regulations thereunder or any specific provision of this Trust. No provision of this Trust shall be construed to restrict the Trustee from investing the property held in Trust hereunder in a manner that would result in the annual realization of a reasonable amount of income or gain from the sale or disposition of such property.

14. *Effective Date.* This agreement shall be effective upon the receipt of the Trustee of the property or title to the property listed in Schedule A.

IN WITNESS WHEREOF, the parties hereby execute this Trust on this _____ day of _____, 200_.

DONOR

_____

XYZ Charity

By:_____
                                , President

ATTEST:

_____

Corporate Secretary

CHARITABLE REMAINDER UNITRUST

On this _____ day of _____, 200_, I, _____, (hereinafter referred to as "the Donor"), of _____, County of _____, State of _____, desiring to establish a charitable remainder unitrust, within the meaning of Rev. Proc. 89-20 and Section 664(d)(2) of the Internal Revenue Code of 1986, as amended from time to time (hereinafter referred to as "the Code") hereby create the _____ Charitable Remainder Unitrust and designate the XYZ Charity (hereinafter referred to as the "Trustee") as the initial Trustee.

1. *Funding of Trust.* The Donor hereby transfers to the Trustee the property described in Schedule A attached hereto, and all property that may be added to the Trust at any time. The Trustee acknowledges the receipt of such property and agrees to hold, manage and distribute such property of the Trust under the terms set forth in this Trust instrument.

2. *Payment of the Unitrust Amount.* In each taxable year of the Trust, the Trustee shall pay to _____ (hereinafter referred to as "the Recipient") wholly for the Recipient's lifetime a unitrust amount equal to the following fixed percentage: _____ ( ) percent of the net fair market value of the Trust assets valued as of the last business day of the first calendar month in each taxable year of the Trust (the "valuation date"). The unitrust amount shall be paid from income in equal quarterly installments on or after March 31, June 30, September 30 and December 31, and to the extent that income is not sufficient, from principal. If necessary, a fifth payment will be made on or before the date by which the Trustee is required to file the Federal Income Tax return for the Trust, to bring the total payment to the actual amount to which the Recipient was entitled for that year pursuant to this paragraph. Any income of the Trust for a taxable year in excess of the unitrust amount shall be added to principal. If for any year the net fair market value of the Trust assets is incorrectly determined, then within a reasonable period after the value is finally determined for federal tax purposes, the Trustee shall pay to the Recipient (in the case of an undervaluation), or shall collect from the Recipient (in the case of an overvaluation), an amount equal to the difference between the unitrust amount which the Trustee should have paid if the correct value had been used and the unitrust amount which the Trustee actually paid.

3. *Proration of the Unitrust Amount.* In determining the unitrust amount to paid under paragraph 2., the Trustee shall prorate the same on a daily basis for a short taxable year in accordance with Treasury Regulation Section 1.664-3(a)(1)(v)(a), and for the taxable year ending with the death of the Recipient in accordance with Treasury Regulation Section 1.664-3(a)(1)(v)(b). In the case of a taxable year which is for a period of less than 12 months, the amount required

to be distributed under Paragraph 2. hereunder shall be the fraction of such percentage of which the numerator is the number of days in the short taxable year of the Trust and of which the denominator is 365 (366 if February 29th is a day included in the numerator).

4. *Distribution to Charity.* Upon the death of the Recipient, the Trustee shall distribute all of the then principal and income of the Trust (other than any amount due the Recipient or the Recipient's estate, under the provisions above) to the XYZ Charity, a charitable organization, to be used for _____. If the XYZ Charity is not an organization described in each of Sections 170(b)(1)(A), 170(c), 2055(a), and 2522(a) of the Code at the time when any principal or income of the Trust is to be distributed to it, then the Trustee shall distribute such principal or income to such one or more organizations described in each of Sections 170(b)(1)(A), 170(c), 2055(a), and 2522(a) as the Trustee shall select in its sole discretion.

5. *Additional Contributions.* The Donor or any other person may at any time make additional contributions to this Trust with the consent of the Trustee. If any additional contributions are made to the trust after the initial contribution in Trust, the unitrust amount for the taxable year in which the assets are added to the Trust shall be _____ percent (__) of the sum of (1) the net fair market value of Trust assets (excluding the assets so added and any income from, or appreciation on, such assets) and (2) that proportion of the value of the assets so added that was excluded under (1) which the number of days in the period that begins with the date of the contribution and ends with the earlier of the last day of the taxable year or the Donor's death bears to the number of days in the period which begins on the first day of such taxable year and ends with the earlier of the last day in such taxable year or the day of the Donor's death. The assets so added shall be valued at the time of contribution. If any property is added to the Trust by the Will of any person, the obligation to pay the unitrust amount with respect to such property shall commence with the date of death of such person, but payment of the unitrust amount with respect to such property may be deferred from the date of such person's death to the end of the taxable year of the trust in which the full amount of such property is finally transferred to the Trust. Within a reasonable time after the occurrence of said event, the Trustee shall pay to the Recipient (in the case of an under valuation), or shall collect from the Recipient (in the case of an over valuation), an amount equal to the difference between the unitrust amount which the Trustee should have paid if the correct value had been used and the unitrust amount which the Trustee actually paid. In the case where there is no valuation date after the time of contribution, the assets so added shall be valued as of the time of contribution.

6. *Prohibited Transactions.* If the Trust is continued after the termination of all noncharitable interests, there shall be distributed amounts at least sufficient to avoid liability for the tax imposed by Section 4942(a) of the Code. Except for payments of the unitrust amount and notwithstanding any other provisions of this Trust, the Trustee shall not engage in any act of self-dealing, as defined in Section 4941(d) of the Code or make any taxable expenditures, as defined in Section 4945(d) of the Code. The Trustee shall not make any investments that jeopardize the charitable purpose of the Trust, within the meaning of Section 4944 of the Code and the Treasury Regulations thereunder, or retain any excess business holdings, within the meaning of Section 4943 of the Code.

7. *Taxable Year.* The first taxable year of the Trust begins with the date the Trust is first funded with property and shall end on December 31 of that year. Subsequent taxable years shall be on a calendar year basis.

8. *Governing Law.* This Trust having been delivered in the State of _____, the laws of the State of _____ shall govern the validity and interpretation thereof, notwithstanding the residence in another jurisdiction of the Donor or of any persons who may have an interest in this Trust. For purposes of this Paragraph 8., in any conflict with Section 664 of the Code and the Treasury Regulations thereunder, that Code Section and the corresponding Treasury Regulations shall govern.

9. *Trust Not Liable for Estate or Inheritance Taxes.* Notwithstanding anything herein to the contrary, the assets of the Trust shall not be subject to claim for any federal, state or other gift, estate, inheritance, succession or generation-skipping transfer taxes or duties which may be assessed against the estate of the Donor, and the Donor agrees to make no inconsistent provision in his or her will.

10. *Limited Power of Amendment.* The provisions of this Trust shall be irrevocable and not subject to amendment, alteration, or revocation by anyone, except the Trustee shall have the power and duty, acting alone, to amend the Trust in any manner required for the sole purpose of ensuring that the Trust qualifies and continues to qualify as a charitable remainder unitrust within the meaning of Section 664(d)(2) of the Code and the corresponding Treasury Regulations.

11. *Powers.* In administering this Trust, the Trustee shall have all of the trustee powers and discretions conferred upon it by the laws of the State of _____. These include those powers described in _____ Code Section _____ (as amended from time to time), including but not limited to the power to:

(A) sell, exchange or otherwise dispose of any asset held in this Trust at either public or private sale, for cash or on credit;

(B) invest and reinvest the funds of the Trust in any kind of property, real or personal, including (by way of example and not limitation) stocks of any class, shares of regulated investment companies ("mutual funds"), bonds and debentures, real estate investment trusts, shares or interests in common trust funds, and life insurance policies, all notwithstanding any laws or rules of law that would otherwise require the diversification of trust investments solely to types appearing on a statutory list, or prohibit the holding of underproductive property.

(C) vote shares of stock or other corporate securities, in person or by proxy, on any and all corporate matters, and to exercise conversion privileges, warrants, and options, and to hold shares of stock and any other corporate securities in the name of a nominee, without disclosure of a fiduciary relationship;

(D) prosecute, defend, compromise, abandon, or pay any claim by or against it; to employ agents, attorneys, brokers, or other counsel, or employees to aid it in performance of its duties hereunder, and to pay them reasonable compensation for their services; and the Trustee shall not be liable for any negligence, omission, or mistake of any such agent, attorney, broker, or other counsel or employee selected or retained by it with reasonable care;

(E) borrow money for any Trust purpose (including the payments to be made to the Recipient or other beneficiaries under this Trust) either without security or secured by part or all of the Trust property; and to allocate receipts and disbursements between income and principal in accordance with Chapter _____ of the (State) Trust Code, as amended.

12. *Trustee Compensation and Bond.* The Trustee shall not receive any compensation for services rendered under this agreement, excepting a reasonable investment management fee. Such fees shall be charged to income first, but if income is insufficient, to principal. Any such fees paid shall in no way reduce the unitrust amount required to be paid to the Recipient under this Trust. No bond or other security shall be required of the Trustee for the faithful performance of its duties in such capacity.

13. *Investment of Trust Assets.* The Trustee's powers and discretion referenced in Paragraph 11. shall not include any power or discretion that is in conflict with Code Section 664 and the Treasury Regulations thereunder or any specific provision of this Trust. No provision of this Trust shall be construed to restrict the Trustee from investing the property held in Trust hereunder in a manner that

would result in the annual realization of a reasonable amount of income or gain from the sale or disposition of such property.

14. *Effective Date.* This agreement shall be effective upon the receipt of the Trustee of the property or title to the property listed in Schedule A.

IN WITNESS WHEREOF, the parties hereby execute this Trust
on this _____ day of _____, 200_.

DONOR

_____

XYZ Charity

By:_____

, President

ATTEST:

_____

By,

CHARITABLE REMAINDER UNITRUST

◆

Income-Only, with Flip Provisions,
and Without "Makeup" Provision
Inter Vivos (Between Two Living Persons),
Consecutive Interests

On this _____ day of _____, 200_, I, _____, (hereinafter referred to as "the Donor"), of _____, County of _____, State of _____, desiring to establish a charitable remainder unitrust, within the meaning of Section 4 of Rev. Proc. 90-31 and Section 664(d)(2) and (3) of the Internal Revenue Code of 1986, as amended from time to time (hereinafter referred to as "the Code"" hereby creates the _____ Charitable Remainder Unitrust and designates the XYZ Charity (hereinafter referred to as the "Trustee") as the initial Trustee.

1. *Funding of Trust.* The Donor hereby transfers to the Trustee the property described in Schedule A attached hereto, and all property that may be added to the Trust at any time. The Trustee acknowledges the receipt of such property and agrees to hold, manage and distribute such property of the Trust under the terms set forth in this Trust instrument.

2(a). *Payment of the Unitrust Amount.* Subject to the conditions contained in paragraphs 2(b) and 2(c) below, in each taxable year of the Trust, the Trustee shall pay to _____ during his or her lifetime, and after his or her death to _____ (hereinafter referred to as "the Recipients") for such time as he or she survives, a unitrust amount equal to the smaller of (i) the Trust income for such taxable year (as defined in Section 643(b) of the Code and the Treasury Regulations thereunder), and (ii) the following fixed percentage amount: _____ ( ) percent of the net fair market value of the Trust assets valued as of the last business day of the first calendar month in each taxable year of the Trust (the "valuation date"). The unitrust amount shall be paid from income in equal quarterly installments on or after March 31, June 30, September 30 and December 31, and to the extent that income is not sufficient, from principal. If necessary, a fifth payment will be made on or before the date by which the Trustee is required to file the Federal Income Tax return for the Trust, to bring the total payment to the actual amount to which the Recipient was entitled for that year pursuant to this paragraph. Any income of the Trust for a taxable year in excess of the unitrust amount shall be added to principal. If for any year the net fair market value of the Trust assets is incorrectly determined, then within a reasonable period after the value is finally determined for federal tax purposes, the Trustee shall pay to the Recipient (in the case of an undervaluation), or shall collect from the Recipient (in the case of an overvaluation), an amount equal to the difference between the unitrust amount which the Trustee should have paid if the correct value had been used and the unitrust amount which the Trustee actually paid.

2(b). The method of computing the unitrust amount payable to the Recipients as set forth in the foregoing provisions of Paragraph 2(a) shall continue until _____. Commencing on _____ {*the beginning of the following taxable year*}, the method of computing the unitrust amount payable to the Recipients shall be converted to the method provided for in the following Paragraph 2(c).

2(c). Commencing on _____, and continuing for each taxable year of the Trust, the Trustee shall pay to _____ during his or her lifetime, and after his or her death to _____ for such time as he or she survives, a unitrust amount equal to ___% of the net fair market value of the assets of the Trust valued as of the Valuation Date of each taxable year of the Trust. The unitrust amount shall be paid in equal quarterly amounts from income and, to the extent that income is not sufficient, from principal. Any income of the Trust for a taxable year in excess of the unitrust amount shall be added to the principal.

3. *Proration of the Unitrust Amount.* In determining the unitrust amount to be paid under paragraph 2., the Trustee shall prorate the same on a daily basis for a short taxable year in accordance with Treasury Regulation Section 1.664-3(a)(1)(v)(a), and for the taxable year ending with the death of the Recipient in accordance with Treasury Regulation Section 1.664-3(a)(1)(v)(b). In the case of a taxable year which is for a period of less than 12 months, the amount required to be distributed under Paragraph 2 hereunder shall be the fraction of such percentage of which the numerator is the number of days in the short taxable year of the Trust and of which the denominator is 365 (366 if February 29th is a day included in the numerator).

4. *Distribution to Charity.* Upon the death of the survivor Recipient, the Trustee shall distribute all of the then principal and income of the Trust (other than any amount due the Recipients or the Recipients' estates, under the provisions above) to the XYZ Charity, a charitable organization, to be used for _____. If the Foundation is not an organization described in each of Sections 170(b)(1)(A), 170(c), 2055(a), and 2522(a) of the Code at the time when any principal or income of the Trust is to be distributed to it, then the Trustee shall distribute such principal or income to such one or more organizations described in each of Sections 170(b)(1)(A), 170(c), 2055(a), and 2522(a) as the Trustee shall select in its sole discretion.

5. *Additional Contributions.* The Donor or any other person may at any time make additional contributions to this Trust by gift or bequest with the consent of the Trustee. In any taxable year in which additional contributions are made to the Trust, the unitrust amount for the year in which the additional contribution is made shall be equal to the lesser of: (a) the Trust income for the taxable year, as defined in section 643(b) of the Code and the regulations thereunder, and (b) _____% of the sum of (1) the net fair market value of Trust assets as of the valuation date (excluding the assets so added and any income from, or appreciation

on, such assets) and (2) that proportion of the fair market value of the assets so added that was excluded under (1) that the number of days in the period that begins with the date of the contribution and ends with the earlier of the last day of the taxable year or the day of the Recipient's death bears to the number of days in the period that begins on the first day of such taxable year and ends with the earlier of the last day in such taxable year or the day of the Recipient's death. In the case where there is no valuation date after the time of contribution, the assets so added shall be valued as of the time of contribution. However, any additional contributions received as described in this paragraph are also subject to the conditions of paragraphs 2(b) and 2(c) hereinabove, which define the circumstances when a change of payout method shall be initiated by the Trustee.

6. *Prohibited Transactions.* If the Trust is continued after the termination of all non-charitable interests, there shall be distributed amounts at least sufficient to avoid liability for the tax imposed by Section 4942(a) of the Code. Except for payments of the unitrust amount and notwithstanding any other provisions of this Trust, the Trustee shall not engage in any act of self-dealing, as defined in Section 4941(d) of the Code or make any taxable expenditures, as defined in Section 4945(d) of the Code. The Trustee shall not make any investments that jeopardize the charitable purpose of the Trust, within the meaning of Section 4944 of the Code and the Treasury Regulations thereunder, or retain any excess business holdings, within the meaning of Section 4943 of the Code.

7. *Taxable Year.* The first taxable year of the Trust begins with the date the Trust is first funded with property and shall end on December 31 of that year. Subsequent taxable years shall be on a calendar year basis.

8. *Governing Law.* This Trust having been delivered in the State of _____, the laws of the State of _____ shall govern the validity and interpretation thereof, notwithstanding the residence in another jurisdiction of the Donor or of any persons who may have an interest in this Trust. For purposes of this paragraph 8, in any conflict with Section 664 of the Code and the Treasury Regulations thereunder, that Code Section and the corresponding Treasury Regulations shall govern.

9. *Trust Not Liable for Estate or Inheritance Taxes.* Notwithstanding anything herein to the contrary, the assets of the Trust shall not be subject to claim for any federal, state or other gift, estate, inheritance, succession or generation-skipping transfer taxes or duties which may be assessed against the estate of the Donor, and the Donor agrees to make no inconsistent provision in his or her will.

10. *Limited Power of Amendment.* The provisions of this Trust shall be irrevocable and not subject to amendment, alteration, or revocation by anyone, except the Trustee shall have the power and duty, acting alone, to amend the Trust in

any manner required for the sole purpose of ensuring that the Trust qualifies and continues to qualify as a charitable remainder unitrust within the meaning of Section 664(d)(2) of the Code and the corresponding Treasury Regulations.

11. *Powers.* In administering this Trust, the Trustee shall have all of the trustee powers and discretions conferred upon it by the laws of the State of Indiana. These include those powers described in (State) Code Section 30-4-3-3 (as amended from time to time), including but not limited to the power to:

(A) sell, exchange or otherwise dispose of any asset held in this Trust at either public or private sale, for cash or on credit;

(B) invest and reinvest the funds of the Trust in any kind of property, real or personal, including (by way of example and not limitation) stocks of any class, shares of regulated investment companies ("mutual funds"), bonds and debentures, real estate investment trusts, shares or interests in common trust funds, and life insurance policies, all notwithstanding any laws or rules of law that would otherwise require the diversification of trust investments solely to types appearing on a statutory list, or prohibit the holding of underproductive property.

(C) vote shares of stock or other corporate securities, in person or by proxy, on any and all corporate matters, and to exercise conversion privileges, warrants, and options, and to hold shares of stock and any other corporate securities in the name of a nominee, without disclosure of a fiduciary relationship;

(D) prosecute, defend, compromise, abandon, or pay any claim by or against it; to employ agents, attorneys, brokers, or other counsel, or employees to aid it in performance of its duties hereunder, and to pay them reasonable compensation for their services; and the Trustee shall not be liable for any negligence, omission, or mistake of any such agent, attorney, broker, or other counsel or employee selected or retained by it with reasonable care;

(E) borrow money for any Trust purpose (including the payments to be made to the Recipient or other beneficiaries under this Trust) either without security or secured by part or all of the Trust property; and to allocate receipts and disbursements between income and principal in accordance with Chapter _____ of the (State) Trust Code, as amended.

12. *Trustee Compensation and Bond.* The Trustee shall not receive any compensation for services rendered under this agreement, excepting a reasonable investment management fee. Such fees shall be charged to income first, but if

income is insufficient, to principal. Any such fees paid shall in no way reduce the unitrust amount required to be paid to the Recipients under this Trust. No bond or other security shall be required of the Trustee for the faithful performance of its duties in such capacity.

13. *Investment of Trust Assets.* The Trustee's powers and discretion referenced in Paragraph 11 shall not include any power or discretion that is in conflict with Code Section 664 and the Treasury Regulations thereunder or any specific provision of this Trust. No provision of this Trust shall be construed to restrict the Trustee from investing the property held in Trust hereunder in a manner that would result in the annual realization of a reasonable amount of income or gain from the sale or disposition of such property.

14. *Effective Date.* This agreement shall be effective upon the receipt of the Trustee of the property or title to the property listed in Schedule A.

IN WITNESS WHEREOF, the parties hereby executive this Trust
on this _____ day of _____, 200_.

DONOR

_____

XYZ Charity

By:_____
, President

ATTEST:

_____

Corporate Secretary

RESOURCE 22

LETTER PROPOSAL

Date

Name
Title
Company
Address
City, State, ZIP Code

Dear _____:

We respectfully invite you to consider a gift to The University of Texas–Houston Health Science Center to support the important work of Dr. K. Lance Gould's P.E.T. (Positron Emission Tomography) Center for Preventing and Reversing Atherosclerosis.

Cardiovascular disease claims more lives than any other illness in America today.

Most victims of heart disease never know that their heart's blood vessels are silently closing, choked by cholesterol accumulating in artery walls. A few experience early warning symptoms that prompt them to seek help, but for many of the million Americans who develop cardiovascular disease each year the first symptom is a catastrophic heart attack. Those fortunate to survive or who have warning symptoms receive limited benefit from traditional therapies, which may relieve symptoms but have little effect on extending life or improving the relentless course of the disease.

Few people with cardiovascular disease have a second chance.

Some have found their way to a new approach for identifying and reversing heart disease at the P.E.T. (Positron Emission Tomography) Center for Preventing and Reversing Atherosclerosis developed by Dr. K. Lance Gould at The University of Texas–Houston Health Science Center.

The initial path to Dr. Gould was circuitous—P.E.T. coexists outside of traditional invasive procedures, and it is not yet reimbursed by many insurance companies. Those who come to see Dr. Gould are worried about their heart or health and intrigued by the knowledge that here was someone who could show them in a picture the condition of their heart and a program to preserve its health.

In short, many people know the anxiety leading to Dr. Gould and the profound relief that his program offers. Now we ask that you help in making this relief and program available to others.

Resource 22

An Enormous Opportunity: The Weatherhead Challenge

The work of Dr. K. Lance Gould so impressed Al and Celia Weatherhead, patients from Cleveland, Ohio, that they have made the P.E.T. Center a very generous gift and a challenge. The Weatherheads have given $3 million and pledged another $1 million, provided we raise $3 million by December 31, 1999. Last month, we met that challenge. The Weatherheads were so excited that they immediately pledged another $1.5 million provided you and others will contribute $1.5 million by December 31, 1999, in order to expand the program into the mainstream of medicine as the only documented way of preventing heart attacks and prolonging quality, productive life. To date, we have only $720,000 remaining to raise to meet the second challenge, which when met will provide Dr. Gould a total of $10 million. A gift from you at this time will bring us closer to meeting our goal.

The aim of this expansion is to make P.E.T. and reversal treatment widely accessible to women and men throughout the nation. However, at the same time the Center must expand its research program, refine the P.E.T. technology, train more doctors and nurses, and use computers to link Dr. Gould with the nation's other P.E.T. centers and their patients, creating a "virtual center" for the collection and sharing of new knowledge.

Far too many Americans know what it's like to be told they have coronary heart disease, and far too many die of sudden heart attack without showing warning symptoms. Through Dr. Gould, many have learned that they can prevent or halt the damage and return to robust health—free from fear of heart attack, stroke, or sudden death.

Dr. Gould has invested twenty-nine years in developing P.E.T. technology for the heart, the reversal program, and the knowledge that has helped many. Now you have an opportunity to help provide others a second chance for life by your generous financial support of the P.E.T. Center—support that will trigger the additional $1.5 million donation. By giving to the P.E.T. Center for Preventing and Reversing Atherosclerosis you will help change the course of cardiovascular medicine. I believe such an opportunity comes but "once in a lifetime."

We are deeply grateful for your thoughtful consideration of this request to help us meet the second Weatherhead Challenge by contributing to UT-Houston's P.E.T. Center. Gifts to support the Weatherhead Challenge may be paid in a lump sum or pledged over a five-year period. Please call me at (713) 500-3000 or Tripp Carter at (713) 500-3220 if we can answer any questions for you. Thank you.

Sincerely,

M. David Low, M.D., Ph.D.

Enclosures

RESOURCE 23

FULL PROPOSAL

Date

Name
Title
Company
Address
City, State, ZIP Code

Dear _____ :

At the request of our good and mutual friend, _____ , I respectfully invite _____ to consider a leadership gift of $_____ to The University of Texas–Houston Health Science Center for a new *Nursing and Biomedical Sciences Building.* This facility will be a permanent home for our School of Nursing and will also house new classrooms, laboratory facilities, and auditoriums and conference areas available to all students in the Health Science Center.

This building has been a priority and a dream of this institution since long before my arrival in 1989. With the endorsement of The University of Texas system and generous funding commitments, we are now initiating a campaign that is fundamental to the future growth and success of UT-Houston and, when completed, will put in place a building that will become the heart of our campus and a central setting for students, faculty, and Houstonians to gather.

As is fitting for a new millennium, we will build a structure that will equip the School of Nursing to stand shoulder-to-shoulder with our nation's most admired institutions—a structure that reflects and reinforces its uses and occupants. Multilevel glass walls overlooking Grant Fay Park, one of the rare green spaces remaining in the Texas Medical Center, give the building warmth and an open and spacious feel. Students will prepare for real-life situations by practicing and perfecting their skills in virtual reality skill labs. Computer terminals located throughout the facility will allow students collaborating on research projects to instantly connect to UT-Houston's computer network. Our students' patient care skills and technical expertise will be enhanced because we are designing these features into the building's core.

As you can see, we are demanding a great deal from this new building, and we have invested an enormous amount of planning into it. If you and other trustees of the Foundation would like to learn more about the building and our School of Nursing, please let me know. I would enjoy meeting with you to go over our plans in greater detail and respond to your questions.

At the end of January, we received news that has given this campaign a tremendous start. Houston Endowment Inc., a generous and long-standing benefactor of UT-Houston, initiated the campaign with a gift of $3.6 million. This wonderful news augurs well for our efforts in the coming months, and those efforts would be immeasurably enhanced were our request to engender the gracious support of the Foundation.

We are deeply grateful for your generosity over the years and for your thoughtful consideration of this request. Please call me at (713) 500-3000 or Dr. William Taylor at (713) 500-3200 if we can answer any questions for you. Thank you.

Sincerely,

M. David Low, M.D., Ph.D.

Enclosures

A PROPOSAL
FOR THE CONSTRUCTION OF
THE NURSING AND
BIOMEDICAL SCIENCES BUILDING
AT THE UNIVERSITY OF TEXAS–HOUSTON
HEALTH SCIENCE CENTER

EXECUTIVE SUMMARY

FROM: The University of Texas–Houston Health Science Center
                P.O. Box 20036
                Houston, TX 77225-0036

CONTACT: M. David Low, M.D., Ph.D., President, (713) 500-3000
                William L. Taylor, Ph.D., Vice President, Development, (713) 500-3200
                Rodney H. Margolis, Chair, Development Board, (713) 625-3570
                Robert Cizik, Chair, Steering Committee, (713) 222-7300

PROJECT: Construction of a Nursing and Biomedical Sciences Building
                220,000 gross square feet

PURPOSE: To provide a home for the UT-Houston School of Nursing and for the
                School of Allied Health Sciences, a center for student activities, and a
                university center for faculty and community gatherings

SITE: Adjoining Grant Fay Park in the Texas Medical Center, on Holcombe
                Boulevard, adjacent to the UT-Houston School of Public Health

TOTAL PROJECT COST: $60 million

TOTAL COMMITTED: $50 million

FUNDRAISING GOAL: $10 million

THE UNIVERSITY OF TEXAS–HOUSTON
HEALTH SCIENCE CENTER
THE NURSING AND
BIOMEDICAL SCIENCES BUILDING

Introduction

Those who have carefully observed The University of Texas–Houston from its founding 25 years ago know that in the last 10 years the University has come into its own. Its teaching and research enjoy national stature; UT-Houston plays a pre-eminent role in the depth of its commitment to the underserved of our community; its professional and graduate students are among the nation's best and go on to important careers of service and accomplishment; and the University is beginning to be justly known for its leadership role in forging new models of health care education and delivery, so needed in the coming decades. Most of all, those observers note a flowering of purpose and self-confidence that marks an institution that has come of age.

As a critical part of the next 25 years, UT-Houston plans to construct a key-stone building to complete its campus, providing a home for its superb nursing school, a base for a pioneering program in allied health, a university center for its students, and a welcoming front door to the Houston community.

We plan to build a Nursing and Biomedical Sciences Building next to Grant Fay Park, one of the last remaining natural spots in the Texas Medical Center. This building will be home to the School of Nursing and the School of Allied Health Sciences and will serve as an important student and faculty campus center. The building, along with the School of Public Health, which also faces the park, will form two sides of a "UT-Houston Quadrangle." Together, both buildings will complete the campus begun a quarter-century ago and celebrate the emergence of UT-Houston, which in its dedication to quality and progressive approaches to health care will continue to be a leader for many quarter-centuries to come.

The cost of the Nursing and Biomedical Sciences Building project is $60 million. A broad coalition of UT-Houston students, the State Legislature, and the University have committed $50 million to the project. It is our profound hope that Houston's philanthropic community will join this coalition by providing the final $10 million needed to complete this project.

A New Home

The UT-Houston School of Nursing

The new building will be the first permanent home for the UT-Houston School of Nursing, a school that has been on a fast trajectory. Far different from the fledgling undergraduate school its first students found 25 years ago, today the School is an important national presence focusing on master's and doctoral level training. With over 600 students and 80 faculty, it is recognized as one of the top nursing schools in the nation and is resolved to reach top ten stature. It is committed to educating the graduate-trained nurses and nurse-educators who define and lead the profession, provide the highly specialized care required today, and train coming generations of nurses to the highest standards.

- Last year *U.S. News and World Report* ranked the UT-Houston School as one of the top 40 nursing schools in the nation (in Texas, only UT-Austin's School of Nursing also ranked).
- From 1995 to 1996 the School advanced from 66th to 32nd position in the total number of dollars awarded by the NIH to schools of nursing, tying with Columbia University, Emory University, the University of Florida, and the University of Virginia. This represents an increase from $85,000 to $494,000. The School's five-year goal is to exceed $4 million in NIH support.
- Admission to the School's student body, 95% from Harris County and Texas, is highly competitive; 30% are minority students and 15% are males (a high percentage for nursing schools). Graduates perform very well on licensing exams, averaging in the 95%–100% range, and in national certification exams.
- With a strong graduate orientation, the School offers the Doctor of Science in Nursing degree, the only clinical doctoral nursing program in Texas. The School offers the only Oncology Nursing Program in Texas and the only Emergency Nurse Practitioner Program in the Country.

Resource 23

- The School has one of the finest nurse practitioner programs in the nation, producing master's degree nurses who work with physicians to diagnose, prescribe, and treat patients in family practice, critical care, emergency, cancer, aging, and many other clinical areas.

For all of these achievements, however, this fine school is at a crossroads: if it is to reach its goal of becoming one of the top ten nursing schools in the nation, it must now move to its next challenge—building a facility to buttress the School's pursuit of excellence. In its 25-year history it has established a national reputation for academic excellence, attracted some of the nation's finest teachers and students, and developed a first-rate graduate nursing program.

Our faculty and students have accomplished this remarkable growth in quality, even as they have learned to adapt and remodel, improvise and borrow in cramped, inadequate space. Since 1974 the School has leased space in a building designed for insurance offices, almost 50 years old, never intended for teaching and learning, and with structural and systems problems costing $80 million or more to fix. Its deteriorating condition has forced its owner, the M. D. Anderson Cancer Center, to plan to mothball or demolish the structure by 2002. The School of Nursing needs a new home.

Making an old office building work for academic purposes for over 20 years is a tribute to our nursing students' and faculty's determination to succeed. But now it is time to move beyond these years of paint, partitions, and patience into a new building expressly designed to meet educational and University needs. This graduate nursing school needs a facility with the technological infrastructure critical to advanced nursing educational programs: state-of-the-art virtual reality and interactive technology, multimedia and distance learning capa-bilities, fiber-optic cabling, and easily accessed, comprehensively networked communications.

The UT-Houston School of Allied Health Sciences

The new building will also be the home of the School of Allied Health Sciences and the site of its state-of-the-art Computer Laboratory for Health Informatics. For many of us, personal medical records are spread across many caregivers—the many physicians, HMOs, hospitals, and consulting specialists we have seen. Health informatics, a specialized form of information science, seeks to devise computer-based systems to ensure that these vital facts are available precisely when and where they are needed. The School of Allied Health Sciences is a pioneer in this emerging field. Its advanced degrees and continuing education programs will enable future generations of health professionals to provide better and more efficient care.

Students from many disciplines at UT-Houston—dentistry, medicine, biomedical science, nursing, and public health—will use the facilities of the flagship Informatics Computer Laboratory to learn and develop new ways of storing, organizing, and reporting medical information. Streamlined data will be recorded and sorted in a giant electronic "filing cabinet." The goal is a system that is simple to use yet incorporates "smart" technology to search, sort, and format information—and can also act as a decision support tool. With capabilities such as this in the physician's office, the emergency room, the ICU, and at the patient's bedside, we will help meet one of the greatest needs in health care today.

The School of Allied Health Sciences will offer advanced degrees in health informatics. As the only institution in Texas to offer these programs, and the only institution in the nation to adopt a completely interdisciplinary approach to the teaching of health informatics, UT-Houston is poised to enter the 21st century in the vanguard of the field.

The new building, with its built-in networking and communications infrastructure, is an ideal base for this pioneering educational program. Intrinsically practical, the courses involve cooperation and collaboration with many of Houston's leading institutions, including Rice University, Baylor College of Medicine, The University of Houston, and branches of Texas A&M, Texas Women's University, and Prairie View A&M. The accessibility and visibility accorded the School of Allied Health Sciences within the new building will help secure its future as a center of excellence in a discipline that promises to greatly benefit patients and practitioners.

A Student and University Center

In addition to providing a home for the School of Nursing and the School of Allied Health Sciences, the new building will fill a long-felt need at UT-Houston for a central gathering place for students, faculty, and community friends. Although it is the largest and most comprehensive academic health science center in Texas, UT-Houston has never had a place where students can have a "home," with student government and other student organization offices; the registrar's, financial aid and student counseling offices; student lounges, and dining areas. Faculty, too, feel the need for a place where they can meet colleagues from all the University's six schools both individually and in committee and other faculty gatherings. The Nursing and Biomedical Sciences Building will also fill a critical role as a meeting place between UT-Houston and the University, providing areas for dining, conferences, receptions, and lectures.

The Nursing and Biomedical Sciences Building

An International Design Concept Competition

We did not decide lightly to undertake a project of this magnitude. For the past three years the University has worked hard to develop comprehensive plans for the building. Hundreds of students and faculty members have been involved in the process, which climaxed in a professionally juried, international architectural competition, led by the Dean of the UT-Austin Architecture School. In early 1997 the design concept by Patkau Architects, of Vancouver, Canada, was selected as the winner from submissions from Canada, Mexico, and the United States.

The winning design concept is flexible and will gracefully serve students and faculty for many years to come. It is innovative and responds to our challenge to the architects to design a facility that will meet today's needs with the built-in flexibility to adapt to future space and technology requirements. One of the building's most striking elements is the openness with which it embraces Grant Fay Park—large multilevel glass-walled atrium spaces, staircases, and promenades overlook the park and open onto it through decks, patios, and bridgeways. The building will be spacious but at the same time will encourage the kind of intimate, professional meetings so critical to a graduate-level environment.

A key aspect of the building will be its reliance on "green architecture," using a variety of means to reduce operating costs through passive structural and engineering features—solar panels, natural ventilation and lighting, natural construction materials, natural water conservation and reuse (both within the building and for park irrigation), and respect for the adjoining parkland in both design and construction processes.

The Building

There are certain core elements of academic buildings, and these will be present— classrooms of varying sizes and configurations, a 300-seat auditorium, deans' and faculty offices, conference and tutorial rooms, and teaching laboratories. Throughout the building there will be a major investment in state-of-the-art technology. From virtually any place in the building students and faculty will use fiber-optic cabling to "plug in" to the computer and telecommunications network—from faculty offices, study areas, graduate student carrels, student lounges, classrooms, even hallways.

Faculty will use technology built into the core of the building to facilitate their own research and their students' learning, with the ability for instant Internet communication with scholars across the globe. Classrooms and conference rooms will have immediate access to all the media technologies that advance teaching and learning. Nursing and medical school students will learn and practice their bedside skills through virtual reality skills labs with specially programmed patient dummies. Students will have individualized learning on-line with their faculty and counselors via e-mail and the Internet, as new technology allows an ever more individualized and immediate learning experience.

The student services aspects of the building will include student government and other organization offices, the registrar's and financial aid offices, student lounges, and dining areas. There will also be a penthouse-level dining, conference, and reception area overlooking the park, filling a critical need at UT-Houston for a commons area for faculty gatherings and University functions.

The Site

This site for the Nursing and Biomedical Sciences Building offers significant advantages. It forms the western side of Grant Fay Park on Holcombe Boulevard, a lovely ravine garden filled with shade trees and green spaces, an ideal setting for students, and a rare spot of green in the congestion of the Texas Medical Center. In addition, because the site includes the School of Public Health, the two buildings will complete two sides of a "UT quadrangle" around the park. This new quadrangle will be home to three UT-Houston schools (Nursing, Public Health, and the School of Allied Health Sciences) and will be the focus of many of the University's student activities and programming. Over 1,400 students in these three schools will have immediate access to the student facilities, along with more than 400 pursuing studies through UT-Houston's Graduate School of Biomedical Sciences, which is relocating to a nearby building. An additional 860 medical and dental students, although more distant, will use the new building for some of their student activities and will take academic course work in its classroom facilities.

Funding

Funding for the Nursing and Biomedical Sciences Building will come from a broad base of public and private sources, including a commitment from our students for one-third of the costs. This partnership demonstrates the unity of resolve and purpose at all levels to construct a building that serves so many important purposes for the City of Houston, the State of Texas, and The University of Texas–Houston.

Recognizing the importance of the Nursing and Biomedical Sciences Building to the academic program, and most especially to creating a better sense of community and campus for future students, UT-Houston's students have agreed

SITE PLAN.

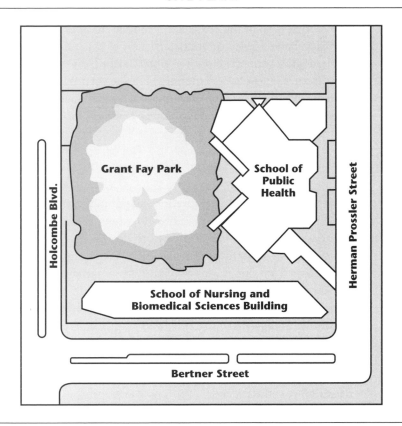

SOURCES OF FUNDING FOR THE NURSING
AND BIOMEDICAL SCIENCES BUILDING.

Source	Amount	Percentage of Total	Status
Students of UT-Houston	$20.0 million	33%	Committed
Texas State Legislature	17.5 million	29%	Committed
UT-Houston	12.5 million	21%	Committed
Private philanthropy	10.0 million	16%	To be raised
Total	$60.0 million	100%[a]	

[a]Percentages do not add to 100 due to rounding.

to a substantial increase in their general use fee that will service bonding for $20 million of the construction costs.

The 75th Session of the Texas State Legislature approved the expenditure of $17.5 million bond servicing for construction of the building. An important element in legislative support of our request was our plan to secure a portion of the total cost from the private community.

UT-Houston has identified, through energy cost savings, attrition, lease revenue, and other resources, funds to service bonding for $12.5 million.

Conclusion

When we call for help in a hospital room late at night, the one who answers is a nurse. Nurses are most often the ones who attend to our needs and are often as important as the physician in restoring us to health and comfort. Less well appreciated are the increasing responsibilities that nurses are assuming in health care today. Fulfilling front-line duties previously reserved for physicians, bringing to bear very specialized knowledge in disease areas, performing important research in patient care and management, moving into very responsible positions in hospital administration—these are new and important roles for nurses, and it is imperative that they be well educated and trained. UT-Houston's School of Nursing is a leader in providing this training, and in its new home it will have the resources to better serve the Houston community.

All students at the University learn best in an environment that supports and encourages them in their lives as students—providing opportunities for talk and reflection, study and play that are so critical in students' lives and to their academic and professional success. This new building will, for the first time, address these needs in a focused way, providing a campus center for students, faculty, and staff alike and a welcoming front door to the Houston community. We believe that the building is fundamental to the future growth and success of The University of Texas–Houston, and we invite and earnestly hope for the generous support of UT-Houston's friends and supporters in making this new center possible.

Resource 23

NURSING AND BIOMEDICAL SCIENCES
BUILDING PROJECT: FACTS.

Sponsor: University of Texas–Houston Health Science Center

Architects: Patkau Architects, Vancouver, British Columbia, Canada

Site: Holcombe Boulevard at Bertner Street, Houston, Texas

Size: 220,000 gross square feet; 12 floors

BUDGET (in millions of dollars)

Necessary Relocation		
Human Genetics Center		
(to the Institute of Molecular Medicine)	3.50	
Graduate School Administration		
(during construction)	0.10	
Subtotal		3.60
Site clearing, asbestos abatement		2.00
New Facility		
Construction (includes contingency)	42.30	
Furnishings, fittings, and equipment	2.90	
Audiovisual equipment	5.30	
Computer equipment	3.00	
Equipment contingency	1.12	
Professional fees	0.09	
Subtotal		54.71
Total Project Budget		$60.31

Resource 23

MONTHLY FINANCIAL REPORT

Confidential

**INDIANA UNIVERSITY
BLOOMINGTON CAMPUS
ENDOWMENT CAMPAIGN**

Reports

For Period Ending September 30, 1999

INDIANA UNIVERSITY CAMPAIGN PROGRESS REPORT, JULY 1, 1994–SEPTEMBER 30, 1999 (DOCUMENTED GIFTS, PLEDGES, AND EXPECTANCIES).

The Bloomington Campus Endowment Campaign

Components	Campaign Goal	Thru September 30, 1999		Thru August 31, 1999		Thru March 31, 1999		Thru September 30, 1998	
		Total Raised	% of Goal	Total Raised	% of Goal	Total Raised	% of Goal	Total Raised	% of Goal
Art Museum	$6,500,000	$5,515,321	84.9%	$5,465,256	84.1%	$3,839,520	59.1%	$3,589,220	55.2%
Athletics	$10,000,000	$17,753,704	177.5%	$17,592,440	175.9%	$14,928,171	149.3%	$13,691,756	136.9%
Business	$37,000,000	$37,426,188	101.2%	$37,367,882	101.0%	$36,399,844	98.4%	$31,696,508	85.7%
College of Arts & Sciences	$30,000,000	$46,845,429	156.2%	$46,553,241	155.2%	$43,333,534	144.4%	$40,225,986	134.1%
Continuing Studies	$500,000	$1,278,414	255.7%	$1,278,414	255.7%	$278,154	55.6%	$277,449	55.5%
Education	$6,000,000	$9,759,716	162.7%	$9,757,291	162.6%	$9,692,364	161.5%	$8,669,385	144.5%
Health, Physical Education & Recreation	$4,000,000	$7,039,597	176.0%	$6,964,898	174.1%	$6,917,121	172.9%	$6,224,905	155.6%
Journalism	$4,000,000	$2,836,560	70.9%	$2,815,210	70.4%	$2,696,668	67.4%	$2,420,039	60.5%
Law	$13,000,000	$15,561,984	119.7%	$15,358,469	118.1%	$14,943,099	114.9%	$14,925,261	114.8%
Library	$4,000,000	$4,884,534	122.1%	$4,883,709	122.1%	$4,761,329	119.0%	$4,624,840	115.6%
Library & Information Science	$1,500,000	$1,527,552	101.8%	$1,527,351	101.8%	$1,227,147	81.8%	$1,021,819	68.1%
Music	$12,000,000	$18,679,561	155.7%	$18,650,475	155.4%	$18,481,798	154.0%	$17,548,348	146.2%
Optometry	$3,000,000	$844,782	28.2%	$796,482	26.5%	$637,337	21.2%	$345,790	11.5%
Public & Environmental Affairs	$6,000,000	$3,395,661	56.6%	$3,395,662	56.6%	$2,842,772	47.4%	$2,583,232	43.1%
Campuswide Support Not Designated to Above Units	$12,500,000	$19,680,758	157.4%	$19,382,048	155.1%	$17,068,662	136.5%	$15,569,571	124.6%
Endowment Total	$150,000,000	$193,029,761	128.7%	$191,788,828	127.9%	$178,047,520	118.7%	$163,414,109	108.9%
Ongoing Private Support	$200,000,000	$183,686,223	91.8%	$181,818,905	90.9%	$153,242,016	76.6%	$138,386,172	69.2%
Campaign Total	$350,000,000	$376,715,984	107.6%	$373,607,733	106.7%	$331,289,536	94.7%	$301,800,281	86.2%

INDIANA UNIVERSITY CAMPAIGN STATUS REPORT, JULY 1, 1994–SEPTEMBER 30, 1999 (DOCUMENTED GIFTS, PLEDGES AND EXPECTANCIES).

The Bloomington Campus Endowment Campaign

Components	Total Campaign Goal	Documented Gifts & Pledges	Documented Expectancies	Total Raised	Percent of Goal Raised
Art Museum	$6,500,000	$3,207,955	$2,307,366	$5,515,321	84.9%
Athletics	$10,000,000	$10,276,358	$7,477,346	$17,753,704	177.5%
Business	$37,000,000	$10,436,180	$26,990,008	$37,426,188	101.2%
College of Arts & Sciences	$30,000,000	$25,295,429	$21,550,000	$46,845,429	156.2%
Continuing Studies	$500,000	$28,414	$1,250,000	$1,278,414	255.7%
Education	$6,000,000	$2,563,672	$7,196,044	$9,759,716	162.7%
Health, Physical Education & Recreation	$4,000,000	$2,374,597	$4,665,000	$7,039,597	176.0%
Journalism	$4,000,000	$1,688,110	$1,148,450	$2,836,560	70.9%
Law	$13,000,000	$5,154,802	$10,407,182	$15,561,984	119.7%
Library	$4,000,000	$4,198,535	$685,999	$4,884,534	122.1%
Library & Information Science	$1,500,000	$25,023	$1,502,529	$1,527,552	101.8%
Music	$12,000,000	$9,398,179	$9,281,382	$18,679,561	155.7%
Optometry	$3,000,000	$144,083	$700,699	$844,782	28.2%
Public & Environmental Affairs	$6,000,000	$1,645,661	$1,750,000	$3,395,661	56.6%
Campuswide Support Not Designated to Above Units	$12,500,000	$11,800,354	$7,880,404	$19,680,758	157.4%
Endowment Total	$150,000,000	$88,237,352	$104,792,409	$193,029,761	128.7%
Annual Gifts, Pledges & Expectancies		$116,387,832	$5,423,872	$121,811,704	60.9%
Non-Governmental Grants		$61,874,519		$61,874,519	30.9%
Ongoing Private Support Total	$200,000,000	$178,262,351	$5,423,872	$183,686,223	91.8%
Campaign Total	$350,000,000	$266,499,703	$110,216,281	$376,715,984	107.6%

Period of Campaign: July 1, 1994–June 30, 2000

Percent Completed: 87.5 percent

INDIANA UNIVERSITY CAMPAIGN
STATUS REPORT, JULY 1, 1994–SEPTEMBER 30, 1999
(DOCUMENTED GIFTS, PLEDGES AND EXPECTANCIES).

ONGOING PRIVATE SUPPORT

Components	Documented Gifts & Pledges	Documented Expectancies	Total Raised
Art Museum	$2,991,787	$181,000	$3,148,787
Athletics	$28,746,962	$220,000	$28,536,374
Business	$18,076,721	$1,843,020	$19,236,521
College of Arts & Sciences	$9,297,356	$220,500	$9,419,553
Continuing Studies	$101,269	$0.00	$99,741
Education	$1,750,264	$5,000	$1,743,847
Health, Physical Education & Recreation	$1,050,161	$50,000	$1,094,129
Journalism	$963,681	$0.00	$959,426
Law	$2,616,777	$40,000	$2,631,486
Library	$3,537,486	$85,000	$3,601,656
Music	$8,195,289	$411,252	$8,561,802
Library & Information Sciences	$180,603	$0.00	$179,628
Optometry	$723,793	$60,000	$800,512
Public & Environmental Affairs	$256,067	$0.00	$272,155
Campuswide Support Not Designated to Above Units	$37,899,616	$2,308,100	$39,658,769
TOTAL ONGOING ANNUAL SUPPORT	$116,387,832	$5,423,872	$121,811,704

Resource 24

INDIANA UNIVERSITY CAMPAIGN
STATUS REPORT, JULY 1, 1994–SEPTEMBER 30, 1999
(DOCUMENTED GIFTS, PLEDGES AND EXPECTANCIES).

Campuswide Endowment Support Not Designated to Primary Components

Components	Documented Gifts & Pledges	Documented Expectancies	Total Raised
Alumni Association	$132,426	$160,615	$268,041
Dean of Students	$193,449	$117,358	$310,687
Class Campaigns*	$2,638,035	$267,299	$2,890,715
Indiana Memorial Union	$127,862	$282,304	$350,499
IU General	$1,810,197	$2,690,619	$4,632,066
International Programs	$81,099	$25,000	$106,959
Office of Student Financial Aid/Wells Scholars Program	$6,071,899	$3,803,259	$9,847,969
Radio & Television	$92,076	0	$92,076
Other	$653,311	$533,950	$883,036
Campuswide Endowment Support Not Designated to Primary Units	$11,800,354	$7,880,404	$19,680,758

*Figures do not include $624,236 raised by the Class Campaigns program for the benefit of the Art Museum.

INDIANA UNIVERSITY BLOOMINGTON CAMPUS ENDOWMENT CAMPAIGN: GIFTS NEEDED AND GIFTS RECEIVED, JULY 1, 1994–SEPTEMBER 30, 1999.

Gift Amount	Number of Gifts Needed	Total in Range	Number of Gifts Received to Date	Total Received to Date	Percent of Total Campaign Goal
$15,000,000+	1	$15,000,000	1	$15,000,000	100.0%
10,000,000–14,999,999	2	20,000,000	0	0	0.0%
5,000,000–9,999,999	3	15,000,000	2	12,850,296	85.7%
2,500,000–4,999,999	6	15,000,000	5	15,646,872	104.3%
1,000,000–2,499,999	17	17,000,000	40	54,265,324	319.2%
750,000–999,999	20	15,000,000	13	10,895,157	72.6%
500,000–749,999	30	15,000,000	36	20,154,104	134.4%
250,000–499,999	50	12,500,000	46	14,748,673	118.0%
100,000–249,999	100	10,000,000	176	23,893,032	238.9%
25,000–99,999	400	10,000,000	274	12,121,671	121.2%
Under 25,000	Many	5,500,000	Many	13,454,632	244.6%
TOTALS		$150,000,000		$193,029,761	128.7%

INDIANA UNIVERSITY BLOOMINGTON CAMPUS ENDOWMENT CAMPAIGN: DOCUMENTED EXPECTANCIES OF $25,000 OR GREATER, JULY 1, 1994–SEPTEMBER 30, 1999.

Donor	Amount	Gift Type	Purpose of Gift

INDIANA UNIVERSITY BLOOMINGTON CAMPUS ENDOWMENT CAMPAIGN:
DOCUMENTED GIFTS AND PLEDGES OF $25,000 OR GREATER, JULY 1, 1994–SEPTEMBER 30, 1999.

Donor	Account Number	Amount	Account Name

NEWSLETTERS

NEWSLETTER

Second Century Fund aided by gifts of all sizes and types

A Gift from the William Friedman Memorial Book Fund

Established by Gifts from his family and friends

In memory of William Friedman L'25, longtime trustee and former secretary of the Board of Trustees who died earlier this year, a book fund in the Law Library has been established by gifts from his family and friends as part of the Second Century Fund. Books purchased through the memorial book fund will be affixed with the book plate shown above.

Every gift and pledge to the Second Century Fund, regardless of amount, brings the University closer to its $25 million fund raising goal and helps ensure a thriving future for Drake during the next 100 years.

Many donors are contributing a variety of gifts to the three-year capital campaign.

Some highlights include:

Marlyn C. "Mike" Augustine — A liberal arts graduate of 1944, Mr. Augustine deeded a five-acre parcel of land in Phoenix, Arizona, to Drake as a contribution to the Second Century Fund. Value of the land is estimated at $80,000.

Jean A. Bandy — Namesake for a new mineral discovered by her late husband Mark Chance Bandy, Mrs. Bandy Ed'21 Ed'56, an Arizona resident, pledged $10,000 to the Second Century Fund for earth sciences study.

Bertram Holst — A liberal arts graduate of 1913, Mr. Holst enjoys a long record of giving to Drake's annual fund. This year, in addition to his annual giving, Mr. Holst made a surprise outright gift of $50,000 to the Second Century Fund in support of the University's capital campaign efforts to assist the College of Liberal Arts.

Yosh Inadomi — A former alumni trustee and a 1945 business administration graduate, Mr. Inadomi pledged $25,000 to establish an endowed scholarship in his father's name. The John K. Inadomi Scholarship Fund will be used to assist students studying business administration.

Jeffry R. and Sharyn Kopriva Jontz — The Jontzes pledged $5,000 to Drake's annual scholarship fund as a Second Century Fund contribution. Now a Florida attorney, Mr. Jontz is a 1966 liberal arts graduate; Mrs. Jontz is a 1968 journalism graduate.

R. Wayne Skidmore — A life member of the Board of Trustees and a 1933 business graduate, Mr. Skidmore, along with his wife Maxine, have established a named gift in Aliber Hall, the new College of Business Administration building. The seminar room in Aliber Hall will bear the Skidmore name because of their generosity.

The Second Century Fund offers donors a number of methods of giving, including outright gifts of cash, gifts of securities, gifts of real property, gifts of life insurance, planned gifts (which can take many forms) and gifts through a will.

One or a combination of these methods may have a particular appeal in planning a gift. Drake University provides donors with help and advice in planning their gifts.

For more information regarding these or other named or memorial gift opportunities, contact:
Office of Institutional Development,
Drake University, 319 Old Main,
Des Moines, Iowa 50311,
telephone 515/271-3154.

Resource 25

Alumni work for Second Century Fund campaign

Alumni attending a Boca Raton, Fl., reception sponsored by the Second Century Fund campaign included Larry Winker FA'62, Dwight Machesney B'34, his wife Helen LA'36, and Sol Glick L'32.

The Boca Raton, Fl., reception also brought together Rob Carney L'75, Larry Witte B'66, his wife Jan Witte Ed'67, Paula (Mrs. Larry) Winker, and Dr. Wilbur C. Miller.

The Second Century Fund campaign is gaining momentum across the country, with fund raising efforts now actively underway in more than a dozen cities nationwide.

Alumni in many cities are forming local committees to assist with fund raising activities, giving generously of their time and talents to help guarantee a successful campaign.

Local committee efforts are being guided by alumni in the following cities:

Des Moines area: L. Donald Easter, chair; Paul Ashby, Virginia Neff Chase; Donald Cook; Robert Frampton; Dorothy Goldberg; William Goodwin, Jr.; David Hawkins; Russell Johnson, Jr.; Kenneth Miller; Dean Mitchell; Rolland Nelson; R. Dale Peddicord; Roscoe Riemenschneider; W. A. Schultz; and William Wimer.

Newton/Jasper County area: Murray Nelson, chair; Virginia Bennett; Donald Byers; John Erickson; Harold Forsyth; Ed Hagen; Myrtilla Levin; Delores Matthews; L. D. Norris; Ed Trost; James Tyler; Robert Underwood; and Eleanor Wheeler.

Cedar Rapids area: Marion Koontz, chair; Mary Heabel; Kent Johnson; Hyla Lehman; Ken Lemke; Robert Newland; John Sackett; John Siebenmann; Ray Stefani; Ray Stefani II; Mrs. Ray Stefani II; Georgene Stapleton; Rod Teachout; and Larry Zirbel.

Mason City area: Diane McNulty, chair; June DeVries; Warren DeVries; Gil Lettow; Kathy Minette; Richard Minette; David Pruess; Don Siefken; and Inez Siefken.

Dallas/Ft. Worth area: Larry Katzen, chair; John Bauer; Jayne Buckroyd;

Shelly Dawson; Jim Feaster; Dwight W. Heaberlin; Ray Hotchkiss; Jerry Nelson; and Jeannette Oehring.

Peoria area: Grant Mathey, chair; Richard Chapman; Marilyn Efinger; Carl Johnson; Peter Johnson; Philip Johnson; Robert Schnarr; and James Yoder.

Denver area: Lois Hobson, chair; John R. Coffey; Phil Doty; Robert Harmon; Robert Poulson; and Leo E. Rostermundt.

Phoenix area: James D. Bruner, chair; David S. Baker; Donald L. Cross; William Don Carlos; and John Harper.

San Diego area: Keith E. McWilliams, chair; Richard T. Cubbage; Robert B. Goode; and Edward Lyon.

Los Angeles area: Ronald T. Olsen, chair; Yosh Inadomi; Gerald Knippenberg; Clifford C. Larson; and Stephen T. Pettise.

Kansas City area: Patrick Kelly, chair; Don Burger; Lawrence Engel; W. Homer Jennings; Leo Mangels; Russell Reynolds; Michael Rissler; and Elwood Thomas.

St. Louis area: James H. Ewoldt, chair; Joann Ewoldt; Norman Handshear; and Robert A. Maddocks.

San Francisco area: Dean Showers, chair; George M. Carr; and Richard Marquart.

Chicago area: Howard S. Haft.

Minneapolis/St. Paul area: Dwight Opperman.

Rockford area: Sherwood Anderson.

Alumni interested in joining or forming a local committee helping with Second Century Fund campaign efforts are invited to contact either the chairperson in their area for more information or the Office of Institutional Development, Drake University, 319 Old Main, Des Moines, Iowa 50311, telephone 515/271-3154.

The Newton/Jasper County area alumni volunteers working on the Second Century Fund campaign include committee chairman Murray Nelson LA'35 L'37, Myrt Levin LA'60, Virginia Bennett FA'65 G'78, Robert Underwood B'39, Edward Hagen B'46 and Edgar Trost B'64.

Gift annuities may provide income for life

Ernest K. Henderson of California receives a check from Drake every month and will continue to do so as long as he lives.

How? Through a charitable gift annuity that pays him a guaranteed income for life.

Mr. Henderson, whose only previous acquaintance with Drake was through his neighbor, Duwayne "Bud" Hartzell B'70, had stock in a national company that paid him stock dividends instead of cash dividends. When he decided he would rather have additional income than stock, through his Drake connection he arranged to enter into a gift annuity with Drake funded by his appreciated stock. As a result, Mr. Henderson was entitled to an immediate charitable contribution deduction on his income tax and has since been receiving a monthly check based on the value of his stock and his age at the time of his gift, a rate of return which is established by the Conference on Gift Annuities and currently ranging from 5 to 14 percent based upon the age of the donor.

This is a good way to give highly appreciated stock, according to Bob Clark, director of planned giving at Drake. Since his stock fortunately was highly appreciated, Mr. Henderson would have been required to pay a large capital gains tax if he had sold the stock. By entering into a gift annuity with Drake, he was able to deduct more than half of the stock's appreciated value and

paid much less in capital gains taxes. Plus, he receives his monthly check of a guaranteed amount for life.

Mr. Henderson's case is not at all unusual. To encourage gifts to institutions like Drake, the Federal government provides tax benefits to those who transfer money or securities in exchange for Drake's agreement to pay the donor (and a survivor beneficiary, if desired) a fixed income for life.

The annual income paid depends on the beneficiary's age at the time of the gift and is a guaranteed annual rate of return, remaining constant for life. A large portion of the annual income is tax-free; the tax-free amount also depends on the beneficiary's age at the time of the gift and is determined by official U.S. Treasury tables. Treasury tables also establish the amount of the immediate charitable contribution deduction to which the donor is entitled, and the charitable contribution deduction often completely eliminates the capital gain. There are several other capital gains implications when gift annuities are funded by appreciated property.

Drake has had a charitable gift annuity program for some time, according to Clark, who feels the program could be advantageous for a number of people who might want to help Drake and still retain a life income from their gifts.

"We have plans tailored to fit any amount and any age," he said.

Law scholarship to honor Lewis

A fund raising effort is being headed by Patrick Kelly L'53 of Kansas City to establish a scholarship fund in honor of Frederick D. Lewis, Jr., professor of law in the Drake Law School from 1949 to 1959 and former executive director of the American Judicature Society.

As part of the Second Century Fund, the Frederick D. Lewis, Jr. Honor Scholarships will help the Drake Law School continue to attract the most gifted students with the potential for outstanding achievement in law and public service and will be awarded on a merit basis.

The Kansas City Area Drake Law Alumni also are involved in fund raising efforts for the Lewis Honor Scholarships.

Fund reaches 60 percent of goal

Every day brings new gifts and pledges to the Second Century Fund, and as of December 1, the total amount in the Fund was $15,062,689, more than 60 percent of the $25 million goal.

Of the total $9,070,357 were gifts from Drake's Board of Trustees (both personal and company), $1,259,675 from corporations, $2,082,729 from foundations, $501,946 from alumni, $99,392 from others (including parents and friends), and $1,369,815 in 1980-81 annual funds. The total also includes $688,775 in 1981-82 annual funds received as of December 1.

Larry Katzen B'67 and his wife Susan Ed'68 met with Drake President Wilbur C. Miller at the Dallas/Ft. Worth meeting of alumni volunteers working on the Second Century Fund campaign.

Mrs. and Dr. Wilbur C. Miller met with Becky and Bob Taylor B'62 at the Naples, Fl., alumni get-together sponsored by the Second Century Fund campaign.

Aliber Hall construction continues on schedule

Construction of Aliber Hall, the new College of Business Administration building and the only major new construction financed through the Second Century Fund, has progressed well in the past few months, with the size and design of the building now clearly evident to passers-by.

Exterior stud walls are being erected, some brick has been put up and the electrical system is about five percent completed, according to construction supervisors. Construction is basically ahead of schedule, according to Richard G. Peebler, dean of the College of

Business Administration, who said he was very pleased with the architect and contractors.

All colors, fabrics and carpets for interior decoration have been approved by the buildings and grounds committee of the Board of Trustees and materials are on order, Dean Peebler said.

Contractors plan the building will be completed by mid-summer.

Major funding for the new structure resulted from gifts of $1 million from the Aliber Foundation of Des Moines and $315,000 from the late Robert Aliber and other members of the Aliber family.

Construction work on Aliber Hall, the new College of Business Administration building financed through the Second Century Fund, is progressing well.

Parents establish scholarship fund

For the next three years, gifts and pledges to Drake from the parents of Drake students will be used to establish the Parents Second Century Scholarship Fund as the Parents Association's contribution to the Second Century Fund campaign.

Vince Nelson, director of the parents program, said that the Parents Second Century Scholarship Fund will be included in the $3.5 million set aside for scholarship and fellowship endowment out of the campaign's total $25 million goal.

The Drake Parents Board, which adopted the scholarship fund program at its semi-annual meeting during the Oct. 2-3, 1981 Parents Weekend, set a $250,000 goal for the scholarship fund. The money will be administered by the Financial Aid Office, with scholarships awarded to students based upon academic excellence and financial need.

Parents Board members Bud and Anne Crowl of Council Bluffs, whose son Matt is a sophomore in liberal arts and an Alumni Scholar, are serving as chairpersons of the scholarship campaign.

Solicitation for the Parents Second Century Scholarship Fund will occur through personal visits by Parents Board members, by direct mail and during the annual telethon.

Second Century Fund

DRAKE UNIVERSITY·DES MOINES, IOWA

Resource 25

VOLUME 2, NUMBER 3

UPDATE

THE ENDOWMENT CAMPAIGN
for INDIANA UNIVERSITY   SEPTEMBER 1998

BLOOMINGTON

Additional $2 Million Investment Could Reap Large Returns·

TRUSTEES EXPAND ENDOWMENT MATCHING PROGRAM

A $6 million investment that could well bring back $150 million?

It's no dream: Indiana University officials can expect such results, because this particular investment is via the University's innovative Faculty Endowment Income Matching Program.

On May 8, the IU Board of Trustees authorized adding another $2 million to the $4 million already allocated to the successful matching program, which encourages private donors to set up faculty endowments by dedicating University funds to match endowment earnings.

The brainchild of IU president Myles Brand, the program began in 1995 when the trustees agreed to set aside $1 million to match the payout (the spendable income generated by the invested principal) of new endowment gifts of $500,000 or more. The program proved so popular with donors that they added $3 million in 1997. With the latest infusion, a total of $6 million has been set aside for the matching of endowment income. Half of the money comes from the president's budget, and the other half comes from the campuses.

Has it been worth it? Brand thinks the numbers speak for themselves. "It's really quite startling," he says. "In its entire 175-year history before the Bloomington Endowment Campaign, the University had received only 31 faculty endowments. I challenged the IU Foundation to increase that number by 100. There was some hard swallowing and a few ashen faces," he chuckles, "but I was optimistic." He convinced the Foundation board of directors and the University trustees that with the matching program as an incentive, donors would give at the high levels needed for endowment support: $500,000 for a professorship, $1 million for a chair. The strategy worked.

As a result of the first $4 million investment, the IU Foundation has already recorded $101 million in gifts. That translates to 105 new faculty endowments. "We've more than tripled our endowed positions in just two years," says Brand.

By that measure, the new $2 million will result in another $40 million in gifts: 50 more endowed positions. "I believe that's a conservative estimate," adds Foundation president Curt Simic. "When this is over, I think we will have leveraged over $150 million."

> "we've more than tripled our endowed positions in just two years."
>
> — PRESIDENT MYLES BRAND

The Foundation is so confident, in fact, that it has raised Brand's original challenge—with scarcely a gulp. The goal is now *150* new endowed faculty positions. "That is definitely feasible," says Simic. "Our donors have been remarkably enthusiastic about the idea. That shouldn't surprise us, really. These folks know a good deal when they see one."

As Brand points out, "It's a win-win situation for everyone. The University gets the financial stability and competitiveness the endowments provide, and the donors get the satisfaction of seeing the results of their gifts right away. Suppose a donor

more on page 2

> "The loyalty and support of Indiana University's donors continues to impress me. They have taken advantage of the matching program at a much faster rate than anyone anticipated. Twice we've had to go back to the trustees to add more funds, just to keep pace with the demand."
>
> — PRESIDENT MYLES BRAND

en•dow•ment (ĕn-dou´mənt) *n.*

1. Money invested for future growth, with only a portion of the return being used today. 2. One of the best vehicles a university can use to keep tuition costs affordable. 3. A good strategy to offset the effects of inflation and reduced state appropriations. 4. An important aid in attracting and retaining today's outstanding faculty, as well as tomorrow's brightest scholars.

Resource 25

VOLUME 2, NUMBER 1

UP DATE

THE ENDOWMENT CAMPAIGN
for INDIANA UNIVERSITY   FEBRUARY 1998
BLOOMINGTON

CONTENTS

Campaign Scores on Kickoff

'LET THE PLAY BEGIN'

On Saturday the 25th of October, amid the renowned splendor of the fall foliage, nearly 500 people gathered on the Bloomington campus. They came from every corner of Indiana, from its cities, suburbs, towns and farms. They came from New York, from California, and many points in between. They were volunteers, benefactors, faculty, alumni, administrators, staff and students. And they had come together to celebrate the launch of one of the most significant events in IU history: the public announcement of the

went public with nearly 68 percent of its total $350 million goal already met: as of October 26, $236 million had been committed, including $100 million in ongoing support; $57.5 million from the IU Foundation Board of Directors; and $13 million from IU Bloomington faculty and staff.

In addition, $136 million had been raised in support of the endowment. That figure represents 335 newly endowed funds, and more than 90 percent of the endowment goal.

The Campaign, in a "quiet" stage since July 1, 1994, went from a whisper to a shout October 25 with a full day of festivities to introduce the public phase.

Kickoff events formally began with a luncheon for Campaign leadership, IU Bloomington deans and administrators, and development staff. In Memorial Union's Alumni Hall, which proudly displayed the colorful blazons of IU Bloomington's schools and units, about 100 participants enjoyed a casual lunch. After introductions by IU Foundation president Curt Simic (BS '63), remarks were made by IU president Myles Brand and Kenneth R.R. Gros Louis, academic vice president and chancellor of the Bloomington campus. Campaign National Co-chair Barbara Jacobs

Master of Ceremonies Ken Beckley

(BS '48) calmly and graciously addressed the audience, while a thousand miles away her Cleveland Indians faced Game 6 of the World Series. Campaign General Co-chair Danny Danielson (BS '42, LLD '94) pledged the support of the Campaign leadership and led an inspirational cheer, while National Co-chair Jack Kimberling (BA '47, JD '50) delivered the best news of the day with a Campaign financial progress report.

The festivities continued in the afternoon when IU Bloomington schools, colleges and units invited the public to open houses, tours, lectures and laboratory demonstrations.

Kickoff events culminated Saturday evening with a black-tie gala at Wright Quadrangle. After a reception in the Quad's nostalgic lounge, guests moved to the historic dining hall to enjoy dinner. Dignified by artist Garo Antreasian's (Honorary DFA '72) enormous murals depicting the University's past, the hall was elegantly decorated, equipped with four stages, and outfitted with an impressive array of electronic wizardry. Video vignettes featuring testimonials of donors and the beneficiaries of their gifts were displayed on 40-inch monitors around the room, and on two overhead video screens.

Lasting relationships was the theme throughout the evening, as Master of Ceremonies Ken Beckley (BS '62) introduced a distinguished list of speakers from the IU family. From the stage or on video, many shared the stories of their unique experiences with the University, and

why supporting it now means so much to them. Among the five testimonials was John Campbell, who spoke movingly of how he and his wife, Johneva, had established an undergraduate scholarship in the name of their late daughter, Mary Diane Campbell; and Mildred Ball (BS '60), who told the story of how the exceptional kindness of an IU dean changed the course of her life more than 40 years ago.

While Wright Quad's one thousand student residents studied or slept in their rooms, elsewhere in their dorm, alumni who were students generations before them pledged to endow their University's future into the next century.

Peg and Myles Brand

Endowment Campaign for Indiana University Bloomington.

The Endowment Campaign, the largest national and international fundraising effort ever undertaken by Indiana University, seeks to add $150 million to the University's endowment and to provide annual gifts of at least $200 million over the next four years. The Campaign

Myles Brand receives a gift of $5 from Sarah Morrison, IU's first woman graduate (portrayed by Jennifer Murphy), in a re-enactment of Morrison's 1883 gift to the University.

Campaign National Co-chair Jack Kimberling (left) and IU Foundation president Curt Simic.

The gala at Wright Quad concludes with the singing of the Alma Mater.

E.W. KELLEY MEANS BUSINESS

HOOSIER PHILANTHROPIST GIVES LARGEST GIFT IN IU HISTORY

(SEE PAGE 2)

YMCA Of Greater St. Louis
CONTRIBUTORS' NEWSLETTER

Corporate Offices • 1528 Locust Street • St. Louis, MO 63103-1897 • 314-436-1177

SAM EDGAR
President

JULY, 1986

DICK STOLL
Vice President
Development

Thank You . . .

Your contributions to the YMCA enable children throughout the Metropolitan area to develop and grow in mind, body and spirit. You are indeed a "Partner With Youth" and this newsletter describes only a handful of benefits your generosity makes possible through Y programs.

"Y" pre-school provides important learning experiences for the future while teaching how to share both verbally and socially in a group situation.

Bright lively bundles of energy are entranced with learning new skills in tumbling and beginning gymnastics.

CAPITAL CAMPAIGN
"Down the Final Mile"

The "Making A World of Difference" capital campaign of the YMCA of Greater St. Louis is moving strongly through its final stage of solicitation. Gathering $14,000,000 in pledges to date, 78% of the $17.9 million goal, determined campaigners continue their efforts to fund buildings and expand programs for 60,000 - 70,000 more people. Projects made possible by this campaign include:

- West County Y - Construct a new family program and fitness center.
- YMCA of the Ozarks - Build a new lodge and family program center, replace and remodel cabins and develop new program areas.
- North County Y - Complete the Emerson Fitness Center adding a gymnasium, indoor track and expanded locker rooms.
- Downtown Fitness Center - Renovate the existing facility and add a second fitness center east of 9th Street.
- Mid-County Y - Remodel and add additional program space.
- Kirkwood/Webster Y - Construct a gymnasium at the Kirkwood Center and air-condition the Webster Groves Center.
- South Side Y - Improve facilities for expanded latch-key and adult fitness programming.
- Carondelet Y - Enhance building access for senior citizens and revitalize existing facilities.
- Monsanto Y - Add fitness and day-care facilities.
- Northwest County/Westport Y - Establish a cardio-vascular center in the Westport business/residential community.
- Washington University Campus Y - Increase the endowment supporting student services.
- Jefferson County Y - Acquire property and construct facilities to provide day-care and other community based programs.
- St. Charles County/Wentzville Y - Acquire property and construct a program building to serve western St. Charles Co.

Source: YMCA of Greater St. Louis, St. Louis, Missouri.

Resource 25

PLEDGE FORMS

Iowa Endowment 2000: A Covenant with Quality
Testamentary Provision Statement of Intention
(Confidential)

As an indication of my support of the Major Gifts Campaign for The University of Iowa "Iowa Endowment 2000: A Covenant With Quality," I/we are pleased to certify that I/we have made an estate provision for The University of Iowa Foundation as follows:

_____ Outright Bequest
_____ Bequest in the Will of the Survivor of Husband and Wife
_____ Testamentary Trust
_____ Life Insurance Agreement

Description of Type/Value of Estate Provision:

General Description: _____
_____
_____

Life-Income Provisions, if any: _____
_____
_____

Definition of Value of Provision (percentage of estate, description of gift property, specific amount, etc.): _____
_____

With the understanding that values are subject to change, at this time I/we expect the value of my/our future provision to be approximately: $ _____

Our Birth Dates Are: _____ _____
                       Husband   Wife

Description of Purpose of Future Gift:

_____ My/our gift is unrestricted to meet Iowa Endowment 2000 Campaign objectives as the President of The University of Iowa and the Board of Directors of The University of Iowa Foundation shall direct.

_____ I/we have specified that the future gift be used for the following Iowa Endowment 2000 Campaign purpose: _____
_____

Other Descriptive Information: _____
_____

A copy of the above-described testamentary provision relative to The University of Iowa Foundation is enclosed.

It is understood that this statement is not binding upon the Donor or his or her estate as to the value or the receipt of the provision herein described.

Signature of Donor(s) _____ Date _____
                       _____ Date _____

Data Documents 03–425520–01 1F2 1

_____
CARD NO.

A TOTAL GIFT OF:

$ . . . .

$ . . . .
Payment Herewith:

$ . . . .
BALANCE
Campaigner:

"MAKING A WORLD OF DIFFERENCE"

Capital Development Program

The Young Men's Christian Association of Greater St. Louis

FOR THE EXTENSION OF YMCA PROGRAMS AND IN CONSIDERATION OF THE GIFTS OF
OTHERS, I/WE PLEDGE THE SUM OF:

$ . . . . To Be Paid as Follows:

PAYABLE OVER A _____ YEAR PERIOD AS FOLLOWS:

☐ ANNUAL   ☐ SEMI-ANNUAL   ☐ QUARTERLY   ☐ MONTHLY

PAYMENT AMOUNTS	1ST PAYMENT DUE:
OTHER PAYMENT ARRANGEMENTS:	

SIGNED: _____ DATE _____

. . . .

Data Documents 03–425520–01 1F2 1

_____
CARD NO.

A TOTAL GIFT OF:

$ . . . .

$ . . . .
Payment Herewith:

$ . . . .
BALANCE
Campaigner:

"MAKING A WORLD OF DIFFERENCE"

Capital Development Program

The Young Men's Christian Association of Greater St. Louis

FOR THE EXTENSION OF YMCA PROGRAMS AND IN CONSIDERATION OF THE GIFTS OF
OTHERS, I/WE PLEDGE THE SUM OF:

$ . . . . To Be Paid as Follows:

PAYABLE OVER A _____ YEAR PERIOD AS FOLLOWS:

☐ ANNUAL   ☐ SEMI-ANNUAL   ☐ QUARTERLY   ☐ MONTHLY

PAYMENT AMOUNTS	1ST PAYMENT DUE:
OTHER PAYMENT ARRANGEMENTS:	

SIGNED: _____ DATE _____

CARD NO.

CARD NO.

CARD NO.

Campaigner

Campaigner No.:

1. Detach this stub.
2. Do not show to Prospect.
3. Contact only those for whom you hold a Prospect Card.
4. See Prospect Personally.

DIV	TM	CPR

YMCA Affiliation:

$

Make Checks Payable to:
St. Louis YMCA—Capital Campaign
1528 Locust St., St. Louis, MO 63103
(314) 436–1177

The YMCA of Greater St. Louis Acknowledges with Thanks the

Contribution of

Name

Amount Subscribed $

Amount Paid $

Received By

Date

Amount suggested
By Appraisal
Committee

Sign, detach and leave this
stub when you select this
Prospect Card.

PART 1

PART 2

PART 3

· ·

CARD NO.

CARD NO.

CARD NO.

Campaigner

Campaigner No.:

1. Detach this stub.
2. Do not show to Prospect.
3. Contact only those for whom you hold a Prospect Card.
4. See Prospect Personally.

DIV	TM	CPR

YMCA Affiliation:

$

Make Checks Payable to:
St. Louis YMCA—Capital Campaign
1528 Locust St., St. Louis, MO 63103
(314) 436–1177

The YMCA of Greater St. Louis Acknowledges with Thanks the

Contribution of

Name

Amount Subscribed $

Amount Paid $

Received By

Date

Amount suggested
By Appraisal
Committee

Sign, detach and leave this
stub when you select this
Prospect Card.

PART 1

PART 2

PART 3

A Pledge to
The University of Iowa Foundation for
Iowa Endowment 2000:
A Covenant with Quality

_____
name(s) (please print clearly)
_____

_____
address
_____
city, state, zip

As an investment in human resources at The University of Iowa and in consideration of the gifts of others, I (we) hereby subscribe and agree to pay The University of Iowa Foundation for the Iowa Endowment 2000 Campaign the sum of:
_____ Dollars ($ _____)
to be paid in either cash, securities or other property of equivalent value.

_____
signature   date

_____
spouse's signature (when joint gift)   date

Total pledge $ _____
Paid herewith $ _____
Balance due $ _____
_____
Balance to Be Paid as Follows:

Month	Year	Amount
_____	19 ___	$ _____
_____	19 ___	$ _____
_____	19 ___	$ _____
_____	19 ___	$ _____
_____	19 ___	$ _____

Payment schedules other than annual may be arranged.

___ I (we) have made provisions for an estate/testamentary gift to support the Iowa Endowment 2000 Campaign. A description of the deferred gift arrangement is attached.

Please make checks payable to:
The University of Iowa Foundation.
Your gift is tax deductible.

RESOURCE 27

LETTERHEAD AND ENVELOPES

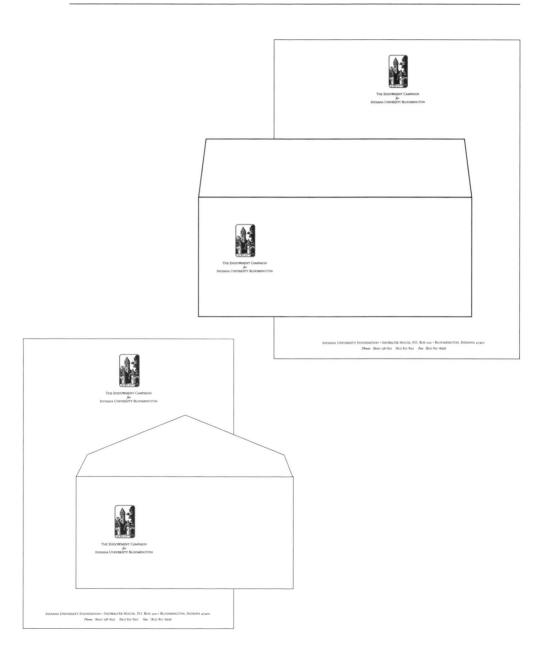

Resource 27

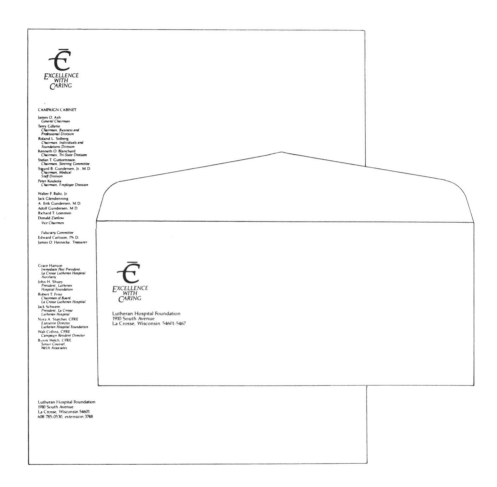

RESOURCE 28

PUBLIC ANNOUNCEMENT
EVENT INVITATION AND PROGRAM

Resource 28

"Dear Invited Guest" Letter

LIBRARY
SQUARE

Dear Invited Guest,

Over five years ago, Vancouver created a dream that demanded strength, courage and dedication. Soon to be realized, this vision stands as a magnificent testament to our enduring civic values. In May of this year, the community will unveil that dream—the new Vancouver Public Library at Library Square.

Ceremony and celebration are traditions important to every society. The opening events for Library Square will be a time for the community to gather, contemplate and applaud an achievement that will forever make us proud. The Main Branch of the Public Library will provide universal access to information and inspire the human spirit to lifelong learning.

"Literazzle: A Family Festival" is a week-long public celebration of the opening of Library Square which will be entirely funded by private donations. To help make this possible, we invite you to purchase tickets to Literazzi, the gala evening, on May 24, 1995. By doing so, you will be among the very first citizens to preview Moshe Safdie's great building. Perhaps even more importantly, your support will make the opening festival a *public* success.

Let us describe for you the evening that awaits your pleasure. . . . An affair of sophisticated literary and gastronomic fantasy, *Literazzi* promises to be a "never before" and "never again" evening. Enter the Promenade, a glass-walled atrium of soaring vertical space. Martinis and champagne await, as a twilight melody draws you closer. A profusion of irises and delphinium glow purple and blue in candle-light; cross a bridge to nooks rich and flowing with the finest vintages and epicurean delights presented by Vancouver's most celebrated chefs. Onward still, to delectable desserts—a sweet finale to a cornucopian feast. Distinguished authors, local luminaries and celebrity guests to engage you, entertainment extraordinaire to surprise you—an evening to enchant you.

We hope that you will celebrate with us our community's newest landmark.

Please order your tickets early to avoid disappointment.

Sincerely,

Philip Owen
Mayor
City of Vancouver

Kyle Mitchell
Chair
Board of Trustees
Vancouver Public Library

Three-by-Five-Inch Card

The Library Capital Campaign Committee would also like you to know about donation and recognition opportunities at Library Square. If you wish more information about naming opportunities that will provide a lasting legacy within the Library, please contact:

Marilyn Wright
Capital Campaign Office
681-8834

In addition to your purchase of Literazzi tickets, a donation to the Capital Campaign would be greatly appreciated.

By supporting the Vancouver Public Library you will be investing in the future of our children, our city and our quality of life.

Brochure

Mayor Philip Owen and members of the Vancouver City Council
and Chairman Kyle Mitchell and members of the
Vancouver Public Library Board

request the pleasure of your company at a Gala Evening to celebrate
the Opening of the new Vancouver Public Library
7:00 – 10:00 p.m., Wednesday, May 24, 1995

LITERAZZI

Library Square
350 West Georgia Street
Black Tie optional

Tickets $175 per person
Valet Parking available

*A gala evening of grand gourmet and fine vintages—join Vancouver's celebrated
chefs, distinguished authors and entertainers extraordinaire in
Vancouver's new jewel, Library Square.*

W E DO NOT LIVE by words alone, despite the fact that sometimes we have to eat them. *Adlai Stevenson* ▪ The things I want to know are in books; my best friend is the man who'll get me a book I ain't read. *Abraham Lincoln* ▪ A book is the only place in which you can examine a fragile thought without breaking it, or explore an explosive idea without fear it will go off in your face. *Edward P. Morgan* ▪ My education was the liberty I had to read indiscriminately and all the time, with my eyes hanging out. *Dylan Thomas* ▪ In two words: im possible. *Samuel Goldwyn* ▪ In literature as in love, we are astonished at what is chosen by others. *Andre Maurois* ▪ I write at high speed because boredom is bad for my health. I also avoid green vegetables. They are grossly overrated. *Noel Coward* ▪ The best time for planning a book is while you're doing the dishes. *Agatha Christie* ▪ Book love is your pass to the greatest, the purest, and the most perfect pleasure that God has prepared for His creatures. *Anthony Trollope* ▪ Hemingway's re-

Colours fade, temples crumble, empires fall, but wise words endure.

Edward Thorndike

I am part
of all that I have
read.

John Kieran

marks are not literature. *Gertrude Stein* ▪ The worst thing about new books is that they keep us from reading the old ones. *Joseph Joubert* ▪ The two most beautiful words in the English language are: "Check enclosed." *Dorothy Parker* ▪ Book— what they make a movie out of for television. *Leonard Louis Levinson* ▪ No passion in the world is equal to the passion to alter someone else's draft. *H.G. Wells* ▪ Reading is to the mind what exercise is to the body. ▪ *Sir Richard Steele* ▪ Never judge a cover by its book. *Fran Lebowitz* ▪ Children don't read to find their identity, to free themselves from guilt, to quench the thirst for rebellion or to get rid of alienation. They have no use for psychology. They detest sociology. They still believe in God, the family, angels, devils, witches, goblins, logic, clarity, punctuation and other such obsolete stuff . . . When a book is boring, they yawn openly. They don't expect their writer to redeem humanity, but leave to adults such childish illusions. *Isaac Bashevis Singer* [*Speech on receiving the Nobel Prize for Literature*].

Menu

LITERAZZI

Prelude....
7:30 pm– 7:35 pm

Introduction: Kyle Mitchell
Chair, Vancouver Public Library Board

Comments: Moshe Safdie
Architect, MSA/DAP

Toast: Phillip Owen
Mayor, City of Vancouver

... to a gastronomical and entertainment gala on seven levels

PROMENADE:

CinCin:
Applewood Smoked Breast of Quail with Spicy Aioli
Roulade of Lamb Tenderloin and Pesto on Peppered Focaccia
Aldergrilled Cured Scallop Ceviche
Tartar of Sesame-Basil Scented Yellowfin Tuna
Middle Eastern Tabouleh with Mint and Persil
Pate of Sun Dried Tomatoes and Goat's Cheese with Onion Crisps

Mescalero:
Southwestern Lambchops
Taquitos with Smoked Chicken Serrano Pesto & Roasted Peppers
Mussels with Sun Dried Tomato Chipotle Cream
Mescalero Marinated Prawns
Chimichangas: Chorizo, Cambazola & Carmelized Red Onions

Lesley Stowe Fine Foods / Terra Breads:
Assorted Antipasto (primarily grilled vegetables)

The Four Seasons:
House Marinated B.C. Salmon on Poppyseed Bagel Chips,
topped with Horseradish and Chive Dip
Roasted Bell Pepper and Peppered Goat Cheese Terrine with
Black Olive Crostini
Hommous and Pita Chips
Shrimp and Potato Fritter with Tomato Salsa

HORS D'OEUVRE SERVICE:

Major the Gourmet
Smoked Tuna
Gravlax on a Rye Croute
Shrimp Mousse on a Blini
Crab Cakes
Orange Grilled Prawns

Culinary Capers:
Crepe Purses filled with Brie and Papaya Salsa
Moo Shu Pancakes filled with Peking Duck and Scallion
Tortilla Roll Ups filled with Black Bean, Grilled Chicken,
and Roasted Pepper
Risotto Cakes filled with Gorgonzola
Phyllo Triangles with Italian Sausage and Monterey Jack Cheese
Lamb Loin and Tamarind Chutney Wellington
Mini Pizzas with Capicolo and Mozarella
Quesadilla with grilled Vegetables, Artichoke Hearts,
and Monterey Jack Cheese served with Guacamole

Bollinger Champagne
sponsored by MacMillan Bloedel

Finlandia Martini Bar

Select Wine Merchants

Featherstone & Company Ltd.
Sebastiani Vendage Chardonnay
Sebastiani Vendage Merlot
Rocca della Macie

Marquis Wine Cellars
Swanson Chardonnay
Swanson Merlot

LEVEL TWO – LIBRARY:

The Sutton Place:
Library Square: A Sculpture in Chocolate
Assorted Chocolate Desserts

Portuguese Trade Commission
Ramos Pinto

Continental Importers
Kopke 1977

LEVEL ONE (Lower) – CHILDREN'S LIBRARY:

The Pan Pacific Hotel / Aromaz Catering:
Strawberry and Lemon Tartlets
Sautéed Pears with Vanilla Ice Cream
Playing Card Sugar Cookies

Murchie's Tea & Coffee

Grady Wine Marketing
CedarCreek 1993 Riesling Ice Wine VQA

Magnum Consultants
Bollinger Champagne

LEVEL ONE (Lower) – MULTI-PURPOSE ROOM:

Regency Caterers
Oyster Bar

Victoria Chinese Restaurant
Steamed Shrimp Dumpling (Har Gow)
Baked Pork Pie 'Hsiang Qiao' Style
Taro Spring Roll (Egg Roll)
Deep Fried Minced Pork Turnover
Vegetarian Goose (Mock Goose)
Moon Cake
Deep Fried Egg White
Steamed Plain Bun (Man Tou)

Theodore Allan
Pyramid Special Bitter
Pyramid Hefeweizen Ale
Pyramid Apricot Ale

International Cellars
Heineken Beer

LEVEL THREE:

The William Tell:
Swiss Cheese Raclette
Beef Steak Tartare

The Raintree:
Cornmeal Crusted Fresh Pacific Salmon served with
Sea Asparagus Tartare
Salad of Fennel and English Cucumber
Cilantro Mint Dressing

Theodore Allan
Quail's Gate Pinot Noir
Tahtani Shiraz
Deer Valley Chardonnay

Termes Agencies
Kendall Jackson Sauvignon Blanc
Kendall Jackson Chardonnay
Covey Run Merlot

LEVEL FOUR:

Quattro on Fourth:
Rotolo Farcito

Granite Cafe:
Jerk Pork with Mango Chutney

Clearly Canadian Beverages

LITERAZZI

~ ENTERTAINMENT ~

Bard on the Beach • Christopher Gaze
The Casual Brothers • Duo
The Colorifics • Jazz Quartet
David Johanns & Co • Jazz Trio
Elizabeth Mabee • Mezzo Soprano
The Euphorics • a Cappella
The Greater Vancouver Historical Performance Society • Dance
Harpist • Zena's Musical Staff
Mark Hasselbach • Horn
Mortal Coil • Medieval Stilts
Pleasantry Valets
Richard Epp • Piano Accompanist
Siegel Entertainment • Mad Hatter
Sandy Winsby • Tenor
String Quartet • Zena's Musical Staff

LIBRARY SQUARE

Grady Wine Marketing
CedarCreek 1994 Ehrenfelser VQA
CedarCreek 1993 Pinot Blanc VQA
Wildflower Gamay
Moeuex Merlot

LEVEL FIVE:

Raku Kushiyaki:
Calamari Salad with Black Bean & Ginger

RainCity Grill:
Lamb Osso Bucco

The Vancouver Sushiman:
Assorted Sushi

U.S. Consulate
Assorted American Wines

Sumac Ridge

LEVEL SIX:

Regency Caterers:
Oyster Bar
Vegetable and Fruit Display

Okanagan Springs Brewery

Bowen Island Brewery

LEVEL SEVEN:

Major the Gourmet:
Mint Cured Salmon
Julienne Smoked Salmon Platter

Joseph E. Seagram & Sons Limited
Scotch Bar

Vincor
Jackson Triggs 1993 Chardonnay
Jackson Triggs 1993 Merlot
Jackson Triggs 1993 Cabernet Sauvignon

PROGRAM ASSESSMENT

GREATER VICTORIA
HOSPITALS FOUNDATION

◆

ASSESSMENT OF THE
GREATER VICTORIA HOSPITALS FOUNDATION
DEVELOPMENT PROGRAM

Table of Contents

Introduction

In December 1999, Melanie McKenzie, executive director of the Greater Victoria Hospitals Foundation (GVHF), retained Kent E. Dove and Associates (KED&A) to perform an assessment of GVHF's development program. Specifically, KED&A agreed to examine institutional planning; development office planning; development office organization; development and community relations office staffing; development office control; records and prospect research; communications; volunteer utilization and organization; prospect rating; cultivation and solicitation; acknowledgment and recognition; clerical and office support; the role of the foundation's board; the role of the hospital's chief executive officer in development; and the role of the executive director.

In completing the review and assessment, KED&A constantly and continually sought to answer twenty fundamental questions:

1. Does GVHF have a reason for being (mission statement)?
2. Does GVHF have a strategic plan spelling out its purpose and direction for the next five to ten years?
3. Has the Capital Health Region (CHR) determined the placement and importance of development within its plan?
4. Does CHR/GVHF have a formal procedure for devising institutional priorities?
5. Has CHR/GVHF made an analysis of the programs and projects that possess the greatest potential for attracting private funding?
6. Has GVHF made a commitment to a comprehensive development program designed to attract annual, special, major, capital, planned, and deferred gifts?
7. Does CHR/GVHF take a coordinated approach toward communications, volunteer services, public relations, publications, and development?
8. Does GVHF provide adequate funding, including salaries and benefits, for employees to conduct a coordinated, comprehensive, productive development program?
9. Does GVHF insist on having an up-to-date organization chart and job descriptions for each discrete fundraising activity and regular performance evaluations for all professional employees?
10. Does GVHF regularly monitor progress and result within the development activity, provide feedback to the staff, and document its achievement to constituents?
11. Does GVHF insist on adequate financial controls to ensure donor confidence and institutional credibility?
12. Does GVHF maintain adequate and up-to-date donor and gift records?
13. Is GVHF's fundraising program based on a system of prospect rating and solicitation that makes mandatory special attention and consideration for its major donors and prospects?

14. Are CHR's chief executive officer and GVHF's board and development staff actively involved in the cultivation and solicitation process?
15. Does GVHF properly and promptly acknowledge all gifts with meaningful personal touches incorporated?
16. Does GVHF encourage active participation of key volunteers in the fundraising process by providing information (news reports, informational materials, and a public relations program) and assistance to make efficient use of their time and effective use of their talents?
17. Does GVHF use a comprehensive array of techniques to keep its various constituencies informed and involved?
18. Does GVHF have a plan for interpreting the fundraising process to the CHR institutional family, whose cooperation and understanding are essential?
19. Does GVHF use consultants periodically to provide experience and objectivity?
20. Does GVHF periodically compare itself with peer institutions (realizing the inherent limitations of any such comparison) in the scope and effectiveness of its fundraising efforts?

The findings and recommendations of this report have been grouped in accordance with these topic areas. Many of the topics discussed are interrelated, and there may be some overlap present in this report. While some of the recommendations involve minor changes that can readily be adapted to current functions, other major actions needed will be more difficult and time-consuming to accomplish.

There are many perspectives to consider in making changes—some fundamental, others less dramatic—to ongoing programs, and the people closest to the situation are best equipped to make judgments regarding the benefits of different approaches. All findings and recommendations in this report are, of course, subject to discussion and adaptation by the foundation's board, its executive director, and CHR's chief executive officer and other involved participants.

The findings in this report reflect analysis of information provided in response to a request by KED&A (see Appendix A). In addition, information gathered from structured and unstructured interviews conducted during March 2000 (see Appendix B), observations made during visits, telephone conversations, and electronic exchanges, which were completed as a part of the preparation, are incorporated. Work was conducted between December 1999 and March 2000. Recommendations are made on the basis of KED&A's experience within related and relevant areas as both a practitioner and a consultant.

Special thanks to Melanie McKenzie, executive director, GVHF, and her staff, most especially Mary Jane Edmonstone, executive assistant, for facilitating this assessment process.

This assessment comes at a most opportune time. Clearly, GVHF is at a point where it is poised to take the next step up in its growth and development, and CHR is at a point where its need for private support has never been greater.

Fundraising Effectiveness

The figures provided for the year ended March 31, 1999, show gift revenue of $3,581,138, and expenses of $839,706. This contrasts with the figures for the previous year of $2,912,456 in gift revenues and $973,434 in expenses. This represents a positive trend. Supporting this is the fact that the number of major gifts and grants jumped from 32 to 56 in this same period. Generally speaking, mature nonprofits that hold the cost of fundraising to 15 to 20 cents on the raised dollar are considered productive; those that keep costs in the range of 10 to 15 cents per dollar raised are viewed as highly productive; and those that keep costs at or below 10 cents on the raised dollar are deemed extremely productive. For growing nonprofits like GVHF, costs in the range of 20 to 50 cents on the dollar raised are considered marginally productive and generally represent acceptable returns on investment. Governing boards ultimately determine the cost-to-return ratio that is acceptable for a given organization.

Based on GVHF's size and complexity and realizing its fundraising potential, it should be expected that the expense-to-income figure can be reduced to the range of 15 to 18 cents on the dollar raised within the next three to five years. Amalgamation could drive the costs even lower, possibly to 12 to 15 cents per dollar raised, presuming the costs of promoting CHR by GVHF can be lowered too.

What will it take to lower GVHF's costs and provide more available funds to CHR? Three things top this list:

- More emphasis (and more time spent) on major gift fundraising and planned giving
- A more coordinated, focused, directed, and consolidated fundraising effort on behalf of CHR to address current apparent inefficiencies (duplication of services) and detriments to effective fundraising (lack of fundraising specialists on staff)
- An organizational structure and overall vision that will permit the implementation of an overall strategic plan (business, fundraising, or combined plan) designed to lift the support of CHR to a higher level

Organizational Structure

As GVHF grows, its organizational structure needs to be under constant evaluation. Today the organization is horizontal. A more vertical approach will probably be needed to move forward. The executive director is very hands-on and is an exceptional person, but her day is only 24 hours long. There is a limit to what she can personally do.

A recent hire, a major gifts officer who wants to spend some focused time on planned giving, offers promise. But more important, more of the executive director's time should be spent on fundraising. She has rare and extraordinary abilities in the areas of board relations, major donor cultivation and solicitation, supporting key volunteers, and putting a public face on GVHF in the community. More time, energy, and effort need to be expended here.

The staff is young and relatively inexperienced in terms of working in a nonprofit organization but, on average, well educated, eager, and motivated. There is little evidence of a mid-level staff presence, and the turnover rate has been higher than usual. In part this can be attributed to the fact that GVHF's size and complexity are now such that changes in the organizational management structure are needed to eliminate bottlenecks and to give staff adequate mentoring, which requires not only experience to share and the ability to teach but also time enough to do it. The addition of a director of operations is recommended.

One staff need not presently addressed is the need for someone to do prospect research. This function will be critical not only to supporting a capital campaign effort but also to sustaining a viable and productive major and planned gifts program.

A high premium is placed on outsourcing (special gifts) and direct mail. A further look should be taken to see if some of this can be brought back in-house. The question is, How can the most money be raised for the least expenditure without sacrificing quality standards? The answer to this question may suggest a change or may support the status quo. Either way, it needs to be asked and answered.

Publications, Publicity, Public Relations, Communications

This is a strong and impressive area. It is comprehensively planned and thoughtfully done. Publications and fundraising literature are tasteful, appealing, and satisfactorily incorporate effective design features and fundraising principles. In fact, much work in this area is exemplary, among the best in fundraising.

The challenges of more and greater visibility and exposure are present and will remain for the reasons outlined in the communications plans reviewed. Suffice it to say that more coverage will always be the desired end, no matter how much is achieved. The CHR public affairs staff spends much time putting out fires. Fire prevention and proactive community relations fall to GVHF, which spends a disproportionate percentage of its budget pursuing a positive public relations image on behalf of CHR. With a change in the CHR chief executive officer impending, the time is right to review this approach. The basic question to be explored is, Should CHR be more proactive in the area of community affairs, and if not, does CHR understand that GVHF is expending resources that might otherwise be directed to CHR fundraising priorities?

Development Services

The "infrastructure" that supports GVHF's fundraising program—development services, information systems, donor recognition and stewardship, gift and account information—is solid. All processes are at or above standard in virtually every aspect. Whether in the continuous day-to-day operations of GVHF's fundraising programs or being prepared to support a capital campaign, this area is basically prepared.

GVHF Board

This is an impressive group. It seems intent on taking the foundation to new and great levels of success. There is a willingness not only to enact policy but also to actively participate in the fundraising process and function. It is a strong, dynamic board and a real asset to both GVHF and CHR.

Patron's Advisory Council

This group, formed before GVHF's first capital campaign, serves in effect as the major gifts volunteer fundraising organization. GVHF's executive director has wisely maintained relations with this key group, which appears to stand ready to serve GVHF again when called on. The council is a most valuable community resource, and its willingness to serve de facto as the major gifts volunteer team for GVHF is an extraordinary asset. Among other things, it permits the GVHF board to concentrate more fully on policy matters pertaining to management and administration, solid in the knowledge that the council stands ready to enhance and promote CHR's capital needs.

Fundraising Plan

It is striking that GVHF does not now have a fundraising plan. (Interestingly, it does have a communications plan.) Whether it's called a strategic plan, a business plan, or a fundraising plan, GVHF needs one. It's hard to achieve one's ends when the ends are not clearly defined. Currently they are not. Indeed, the number of funding requests coming to the foundation is growing. Each new initiative needs to be evaluated as to its priority, and those that are deemed of highest priority should be subjected to a feasibility review or study. Resources, both people and operating budget, need to be added to pursue the initiatives accepted, or else they should not be undertaken.

A couple of variations on the GVHF mission statement were provided. Of significance is the matter of whether the mission should take the long view or reflect the pressures and priorities of the moment. It appears that at present, the latter has superseded the former—but should it?

The big-tent, long-view approach, which should be preferred, suggests that the mission should be a broad one: "To raise money in support of our hospital's efforts to improve patient care." Today's immediate needs, capital acquisition (equipment) and new initiatives, are narrower. The problem is that this does not give proper attention to some vitally important notions.

1. Giving is more emotional than it is rational. Donors (especially of big gifts) give where their interests are and not necessarily where CHR's needs are.
2. Money is fungible as long as the donor's terms and conditions, if any, are met. The GVHF board and CHR have latitude to apportion and spend funds given by donors within guidelines established by donors.
3. No one area of giving—equipment, research, construction, renovation, operations, program or endowment support—appeals to all donors. Giving opportunities across a broad spectrum, creatively packaged for marketing purposes, will yield the greatest return over time.

A narrow focus leaves out too many people who would give if properly approached. Therefore, the marketing strategy (business plan) needs to encompass all ways and forms of giving and encourage appropriate and tasteful donor recognition for all types of gifts at all giving levels.

Why not seek a gift to name the MRI suite in the hospital rather than a gift to buy the MRI? This way the money can be made available to purchase the MRI plus, possibly, additional funds to create an operating endowment or to purchase additional equipment.

There are also now a number of new giving opportunities based on CHR's program management model. These should prove to have interesting potential as fundraising priorities.

There are myriad ways to go, but the critical points to understand are three:

1. *Giving is donor-driven.* Donors decide where their interests are and where their gifts, especially the larger ones, will go.
2. *One size doesn't fit all.* Different donors respond to different stimuli—some like equipment, some like bricks and mortar, still others prefer supporting programs, and the list goes on.
3. *Giving is more emotional than rational.* A logical, rational case for support often loses out to the pure emotional appeal, so the giving opportunity must be wrapped into a presentation that satisfies the potential donor's interests and evokes emotion.

In the end, it may not be so much what you ask for as how you ask for it.

It would also be prudent at this stage of GVHF's growth to begin to encourage gifts of endowment, either designated or undesignated, to permit the gradual building of an operating reserve (if possible), and to encourage less restricted or undesignated gifts, so that the GVHF board and CHR have as much latitude and stability as possible to apportion gift revenues not only to the places where the needs are greatest but also to the places where flexible funds can create the greatest leverage or synergy to "improve patient care." It is time for GVHF to become both broader and bigger in its thinking.

Preparedness to Do a Capital Campaign

Sufficient support systems are in place, and the staffing pattern is reasonable to accomplish a campaign. The executive director will have to free up more time to do major gift fundraising. And as appropriate, some additional staffing will be needed—particularly a researcher and another major gifts officer. Fundraising counsel, more likely a consultant than a resident, should be considered too. As to budgeting for a capital campaign, the GVHF board should plan to budget 4 to 6 percent of the new money campaign goal as an addition to the current operating budget.

No campaign should be undertaken until a market survey is conducted. It is reasonable to assume that such a study can be undertaken and completed before the end of the year 2000.

APPENDIX A
INDIVIDUALS INTERVIEWED
[Names deleted for reasons of confidentiality.]

APPENDIX B
MATERIALS REVIEWED

Marketing Materials

1999–2000 Communications Plan

1996–1997 Communications Plan (Draft)

Statement of Mission and Purpose

Vision and Mission Statement, 1999

Strategic Directions

Healthy People in a Healthy Community

Résumés of Professional Personnel Development and Community Relations

Melanie Louise McKenzie

Dianne Dunnett

J. Garnet Nelson

Organization Charts for Institution and GVHF

Organization of the Capital Health Region

GVHF Organizational Chart, 1999

Salaries for GVHF

Job Description of Professional Personnel (GVHF Only)

Receptionist-Secretary

Secretary to the Executive Director

Donor Relations Assistant

Development Officer

Manager, Research and Major Gift Support

Personnel Evaluation System

Employee Performance Assessment

CHR Budget/GVHF Budget

Sources of Revenues (Reports, Chart)

Budget-to-Actual Variance Analysis

Unaudited Financial Statements

IPS Consulting Financial Report and Budget, March 1999

IPS Consulting Financial Report and Budget, March 1998

Capital Health Region

Organization's Planning Document:
GVHF Annual Goal, Objectives, and Calendar

Health Services Plan

Regional Priorities

GVHF Capital Commitments for 1998–1999

Approved Capital Requests

Regional Priorities (Draft)

CHR Management Indicators

Indicator Charts

GVHF Five-Year Analysis of Programs

Retention of Donors

Current Standards for Measurement and Evaluation of Development

Rankings of Projects

Active Estate Files

Summary of Commitment Form

Over $250 List, January 2000

Campaign Summary List

Fund Summary List, January 2000

Appeal Summary List, January 2000

GVHF Market Research

GVHF Research

Donations: Qualitative Research Evaluation of Attitudes and Behaviors

Donor Prospect Information Form

Five-Year Giving History by Source/Purpose Ratios of Expenditures

Retention of Donors

Samples of Proposals: Individuals, Corporations, Foundations, Organizations

Individual Letter: Golf for the Cure 2000

Organization: Golf for the Cure 2000

Corporation: C-FAX

Individual Letter: Visions 1999 Gala Ball

Foundation Letter: Pediatric Care

Donor Recognition

Donor Recognition Policy, September 1998

Report to Patron's Council, January 2000

Thank-You Letters

Donor Recognition Coding

Samples of Publications and Fundraising Pieces

Direct Mail: "Heart Disease Affects All of Us. You Can Help"

Direct Mail: "With Your Help, We Can Heal"

Visions 1999 Brochure

Report to the Board: "Communications," December 1999–January 2000

"The Advocate," Issue 1, Volume 1, Fall 1997

"The Advocate," Issue 1, Volume 2, Winter 1998

"The Advocate," Issue 1, Volume 3, Spring 1998

"The Advocate," Issue 1, Volume 4, Spring 1999

"Memory of Life" Brochure

Planned Giving: "It Is Not to Live, but . . ."

Report to the Board: "Communications," November 1999

GVHF Informational Folder

Board Members' and Corporate Giving Histories

Members of the 1999–2000 Board of Directors

Board Giving Histories

Patron's Advisory Council

RESOURCE 30

GIFT RECEIPT TEMPLATES

Resource 30

851

FRONT

Indiana University Foundation
P.O. Box 500
Bloomington, IN 47402

January 1, 2000

Indiana University Foundation salutes:
Hubert T. Steerherder
P.O. Box 12345
Fort Somewhere, TX 12345-6789

DONOR - INDIANA UNIVERSITY

999999-9999999
For your commitment and generosity to
Indiana University, the Officers and the
Board of Directors of the Indiana University
Foundation want to thank you for your gift
of $250.00 to IU Alumni Association.

Benefit Received by Donor:
IU Alumni Outing
Value of Benefit Received: $ 99.95
Deductible Amount of Gift: $150.05

Indiana University Foundation
P.O. Box 500
Bloomington, IN 47402

January 1, 2000

Indiana University Foundation salutes:
Hubert T. Steerherder
P.O. Box 12345
Fort Somewhere, TX 12345-6789

DONOR - INDIANA UNIVERSITY

999999-9999999
For your commitment and generosity to
Indiana University, the Officers and the
Board of Directors of the Indiana University
Foundation want to thank you for your gift
of $250.00 to IU Alumni Association.

Benefit Received by Donor:
IU Alumni Outing
Value of Benefit Received: $ 99.95
Deductible Amount of Gift: $150.05

Indiana University Foundation
P.O. Box 500
Bloomington, IN 47402

January 1, 2000

Indiana University Foundation salutes:
Hubert T. Steerherder
P.O. Box 12345
Fort Somewhere, TX 12345-6789

DONOR - INDIANA UNIVERSITY

999999-9999999
For your commitment and generosity to
Indiana University, the Officers and the
Board of Directors of the Indiana University
Foundation want to thank you for your gift
of $250.00 to IU Alumni Association.

Benefit Received by Donor:
IU Alumni Outing
Value of Benefit Received: $ 99.95
Deductible Amount of Gift: $150.05

BACK

INDIANA UNIVERSITY FOUNDATION

Showalter House, Bloomington
(812) 855-8311, fax: (812) 855-6956
50 South Meridian Street, Suite 400, Indianapolis
(317) 673-4438, fax: (317) 274-8818

"People who have been touched by Indiana University have developed a strong loyalty and have expressed that in faithful support and generous gifts. . . . They help to make a difference for the future, building the foundation of one of the great universities for the twenty-first century."

Herman B Wells
University Chancellor

Thank you for your generous gift to Indiana University.

The many dollars in private support contributed each year by people like you add up to a wealth of opportunities for Indiana University to serve the citizens of the state, the nation, and the world. Your gift enables the University to provide greater access to quality educational opportunities, enhance Indiana's tradition of excellence in higher education, contribute to economic development, and conduct research that will change the quality of human life for the better.

Your support is gratefully acknowledged.

Curtis R. Simic

Curtis R. Simic, President
Indiana University Foundation

INDIANA UNIVERSITY FOUNDATION

Showalter House, Bloomington
(812) 855-8311, fax: (812) 855-6956
50 South Meridian Street, Suite 400, Indianapolis
(317) 673-4438, fax: (317) 274-8818

"People who have been touched by Indiana University have developed a strong loyalty and have expressed that in faithful support and generous gifts. . . . They help to make a difference for the future, building the foundation of one of the great universities for the twenty-first century."

Herman B Wells
University Chancellor

Thank you for your generous gift to Indiana University.

The many dollars in private support contributed each year by people like you add up to a wealth of opportunities for Indiana University to serve the citizens of the state, the nation, and the world. Your gift enables the University to provide greater access to quality educational opportunities, enhance Indiana's tradition of excellence in higher education, contribute to economic development, and conduct research that will change the quality of human life for the better.

Your support is gratefully acknowledged.

Curtis R. Simic

Curtis R. Simic, President
Indiana University Foundation

INDIANA UNIVERSITY FOUNDATION

Showalter House, Bloomington
(812) 855-8311, fax: (812) 855-6956
50 South Meridian Street, Suite 400, Indianapolis
(317) 673-4438, fax: (317) 274-8818

"People who have been touched by Indiana University have developed a strong loyalty and have expressed that in faithful support and generous gifts. . . . They help to make a difference for the future, building the foundation of one of the great universities for the twenty-first century."

Herman B Wells
University Chancellor

Thank you for your generous gift to Indiana University.

The many dollars in private support contributed each year by people like you add up to a wealth of opportunities for Indiana University to serve the citizens of the state, the nation, and the world. Your gift enables the University to provide greater access to quality educational opportunities, enhance Indiana's tradition of excellence in higher education, contribute to economic development, and conduct research that will change the quality of human life for the better.

Your support is gratefully acknowledged.

Curtis R. Simic

Curtis R. Simic, President
Indiana University Foundation

Resource 30

GIFT-IN-KIND LETTER
FOR PERSONAL GIFTS UNDER $500

June 30, 1999

Mr. Happy Day
1200 Sunshine Lane
Bloomington, IN 47401

Dear Mr. Day:

On behalf of Indiana University Foundation, the official gift receiving and administering entity for the Indiana University Libraries, we wish to acknowledge your gift on June 1, 1999, of books. Private gifts are a great aid to the University in continuing and maintaining the excellent quality of its programs, and Indiana University Foundation, together with the Indiana University Libraries, thanks you.

Our records reflect that you did not receive any goods or services of value in exchange for this gift.

We appreciate very much your support of the Indiana University Libraries through this gift. If we can ever be of assistance to you, please do not hesitate to contact us.

Sincerely,

Director, Gift Administration

GIFT-IN-KIND LETTER
FOR PERSONAL GIFTS OVER $500

June 30, 1999

Mr. & Mrs. Jenner Ross
1000 Development Drive
Bloomington, IN 47401

Dear Mr. & Mrs. Ross:

On behalf of Indiana University Foundation, the official gift receiving and administering entity for the Indiana University School of Health Physical Education and Recreation, we wish to acknowledge your gift on June 1, 1999, of a sailboat. Private gifts are a great aid to the University in continuing and maintaining the excellent quality of its programs, and Indiana University Foundation, together with the Indiana University School of Health Physical Education and Recreation, thanks you.

Our records reflect that you did not receive any goods or services of value in exchange for this gift.

For gifts valued at over $500, you must file Internal Revenue Service Form 8283 with your federal income tax return when claiming the deduction for the gift. Section A of this form must be completed. I am enclosing this form for your convenience.

We appreciate very much your support of the Indiana University School of Health Physical Education and Recreation through this gift. If we can ever be of any assistance to you, please do not hesitate to contact us.

Sincerely,

Director, Gift Administration

GIFT-IN-KIND LETTER
FOR PERSONAL GIFTS OVER $5,000

June 30, 1999

Mr. I. M. Rich
500 Golden Way
Bloomington, IN 47401

Dear Mr. Rich:

On behalf of Indiana University Foundation, the official gift receiving and administering entity for the Indiana University School of Business, we wish to acknowledge your gift on June 1, 1999, of ten computer systems. Private gifts are a great aid to the University in continuing and maintaining the excellent quality of its programs, and Indiana University Foundation, together with the Indiana University School of Business, thanks you.

Our records reflect that you did not receive any goods or services of value in exchange for this gift.

For gifts valued at over $5,000, you must file Internal Revenue Service Form 8283 with your federal income tax return when claiming the deduction for the gift. We believe Section B of this form must be completed, and you may need to submit a formal appraisal. In the event your tax adviser determines that this is necessary, we would appreciate receiving a copy of the completed form along with a copy of the appraisal for our records. I am enclosing this form for your convenience.

We appreciate very much your support of the Indiana University School of Business through this gift. If we can ever be of any assistance to you, please do not hesitate to contact us.

Sincerely,

General Counsel

Resource 30

GIFT-IN-KIND LETTER
FOR BUSINESS GIFTS UNDER $500

June 30, 1999

Art Solutions Group
Attn: Ms. Painter
700 Creative Drive
Bloomington, IN 47401

Dear Ms. Painter:

On behalf of Indiana University Foundation, the official gift receiving and administering entity for the Indiana University Art Museum, we wish to acknowledge your gift on June 1, 1999, of an African clay pot. Private gifts are a great aid to the University in continuing and maintaining the excellent quality of its programs, and Indiana University Foundation, together with the Indiana University Art Museum, thanks you.

Our records reflect that you did not receive any goods or services of value in exchange for this gift.

We appreciate very much your support of the Indiana University Art Museum through this gift. If we can ever be of any assistance to you, please do not hesitate to contact us.

Sincerely,

Director, Gift Administration

GIFT-IN-KIND LETTER
FOR BUSINESS GIFTS OVER $500

June 30, 1999

XYZ Music Company
Attn: Mr. U. R. Helpful
500 Baldwin Boulevard
Bloomington, IN 47401

Dear Mr. Helpful:

On behalf of Indiana University Foundation, the official gift receiving and administering entity for the Indiana University School of Music, we wish to acknowledge your gift on June 1, 1999, of a grand piano. Private gifts are a great aid to the University in continuing and maintaining the excellent quality of its programs, and Indiana University Foundation, together with the Indiana University School of Music, thanks you.

Our records reflect that you did not receive any goods or services of value in exchange for this gift.

Your gift may qualify for the federal income tax charitable deduction subject to the applicable tax laws. If it is inventory property, the gift value must reflect your out-of-pocket, wholesale cost, rather than its retail value. It is also possible in certain circumstances to claim a deduction for such gifts as a business expense as opposed to a charitable deduction. Your tax adviser will need to make that determination. If you are claiming a charitable deduction for the property, it is necessary to file Internal Revenue Service Form 8283 with your federal income tax return. I am enclosing a copy of this form for your use.

We appreciate very much your support of the Indiana University School of Music through this gift. If we can ever be of any assistance to you, please do not hesitate to contact us.

Sincerely,

Director, Gift Administration

Resource 30

STEWARDSHIP PROGRAM
AT THE UNIVERSITY OF FLORIDA

STEWARDSHIP PROGRAM
AT THE UNIVERSITY OF FLORIDA

PREPARED BY

DEBBIE MEYERS

DIRECTOR OF STEWARDSHIP AND DONOR RELATIONS

UNIVERSITY OF FLORIDA FOUNDATION, INC.

Contents

◆

Resource 31

Overview of Stewardship and Donor Relations

At the University of Florida Foundation, Stewardship and Donor Relations staff includes a Director, a Coordinator and a half-time Program Assistant. The Director reports to the Associate Vice President of Administration, who reports to the Vice President of Development and Alumni Affairs, who reports to the President. The Director works closely with the Director of Operations in many stewardship procedures and events, and SDR staff members work daily with the Records Department (Gifts Processing and Biographical Services) in exchanging gift and biographical information about donors.

The Coordinator reports to the Director and oversees a Senior Clerk and a half-time Clerk Typist. Along with the Director and Coordinator, the two clerks are responsible for generating more than 9,000 personalized gift acknowledgment letters and postcards for gifts of $500 or more. To verify accuracy in salutations, SDR staff coordinates information with the Vice President's Administrative Assistant and the President's Administrative Assistant. (Job descriptions are included in the Appendix.)

The Director position was created and filled in July 1996 in anticipation of the University of Florida's $500 million "It's Performance that Counts" capital campaign. This campaign is built on the belief that this institution is and will continue to be accountable to its constituents for how it performs with their donations. Donors cannot be expected to contribute to an institution that has not properly thanked them for or kept them informed of the progress of their previous contributions.

The Foundation strongly believes in the ethical value of stewardship. Each member of the Foundation staff, at some level, is a steward for each gift that comes into our trust. Furthermore, donors deserve appropriate stewardship, regardless of their capacity for further gifts. Donor relations does not end when the gift agreement is signed or even at the donor's death. For deceased donors, we make every effort to find a surviving family member or friend for whom stewardship should be performed on that donor's behalf.

Following those tenets, these are the major stewardship programs in place at the University of Florida Foundation.

President's Council

Begun in 1971, President's Council is the donor recognition program at the University of Florida. Donors who give $2,000 to $49,999 cumulatively within a year are enrolled at the "Annual" level. The beginning giving threshold for faculty, staff and recent graduates (ten years or less) is $1,000. As "annual" implies, benefits cover one fiscal year only. Donors who pledge $5,000 a year for five years to unrestricted funds are enrolled in the Excellence Society.

Lifetime levels for cumulative giving are Distinguished ($50,000), Society ($100,000), Academy ($500,000) and Cabinet ($1 million or more). Cash and pledges are counted at full value. Deferred gifts are counted at a one-to-five ratio— e.g., a $500,000 bequest is counted the same as $100,000 cash for recognition purposes. (A "benefits" card is included in the Appendix.)

One benefit of President's Council is an on-campus parking decal, which is mailed out each June to correspond with annual membership lapses. Request forms for football parking passes also are mailed to donors during the summer at Distinguished level and above, first-come, first-served. As it is at most major universities, parking at UF is a highly valued privilege, and donors welcome this benefit. (A sample of the parking decal is included in the Appendix.)

Each year, President's Council donors are invited to attend President's Council Weekend, a tribute to their generosity. Because we are a charitable institution, we do ask that they pay a registration fee to attend and cover their own hotel accommodations. This fee defrays only a small portion of the total cost, but it does help and reassures donors that we are not spending their donations on thanking them.

Activities are held at resort areas around the state, including the Renaissance Vinoy at St. Petersburg and the Breakers at Palm Beach. The weekend also encompasses a quarterly meeting of the UF Foundation Board of Directors. A typical agenda for PC members includes a President's Luncheon on Saturday, a tour or recreational activity on Saturday afternoon, a cocktail reception and black-tie banquet on Saturday evening, and a brunch on Sunday morning.

Board committees meet all day on Friday and on Saturday morning. On Friday evening, we host a reception for board members then afterwards, a "Past Presidents' Dinner" for former board presidents and former university presidents. Board presidents devote much time and energy for many months during their tenure, then step down as president. Activity can stop abruptly. This dinner is our way of keeping in touch with them, showing our gratitude and maintaining their tie with the university. During the Saturday morning board meeting, we offer a "First Lady's Coffee," hosted by the President's wife, for spouses of board members.

Donors at Society level and higher are honored at the Saturday night recognition banquet. Their names are printed in the program. They also are called forward by the President, who reads biographical information about them and presents them with a commemorative item (plaque, medallion or other item) on which their names are engraved. (Samples of all printed pieces are included in the Appendix.)

Gift Acknowledgments

All gifts to the University of Florida receive a gift receipt from the Records Department (see Appendix), which is completely separate from Stewardship and Donor Relations. For gifts of $500 to $999, a postcard (see Appendix) goes out under the President's signature. For gifts of $1,000 to $1,999, a personalized letter goes out under the Vice President's signature. Donors with gifts of $2,000 or more receive a personalized letter from the President. The Senior Clerk will indicate which of several form letters is appropriate for these two types of letters.

The Director and Coordinator will draft special letters as requested by the Vice President and President, as well as letters for all gift agreements of $100,000 or more.

For each acknowledgment letter, SDR staff analyze the gift, checking to see if an individual gift will qualify a donor for President's Council or move that donor up to a higher (cumulative) giving level. Staff members also double-check for accuracy of gift and biographical information as processed by Records Department staff, who processed about 97,000 gifts last fiscal year. Our donor database uses ADVANCE software and contains more than 410,000 records for donors, alumni, parents and friends.

Stewardship Checklists

At the beginning of each fiscal year, stewardship checklists are circulated to development officers. This checklist is a menu of stewardship activities, suggestions for the kinds of stewardship activities that development officers can perform for their donors.

In addition to the checklist, development officers receive a list of donors for whom they are responsible for performing stewardship—donors who had gifts of $100,000 or more. The gift could be endowed, unrestricted, capital or for any purpose, but stewardship is monitored for one-time gifts (including pledges), not for cumulative giving.

Original checklists called for the officers to put a planned date and a completed date on the sheet of paper, but that information is now input in our database. Planned activities and dates go in the "Next Activities" tickler system, and completed activities become "Stewardship Contact Reports." Once a next activity is completed, it disappears from the database. Contact reports stay on permanently.

The SDR Director receives quarterly reports on all stewardship next activities and contact reports as a way to monitor what stewardship is being planned and done. If a development officer appears to be lacking in the stewardship area, the Director notifies that person's manager.

Currently, we are experimenting in "layering" donors according to the level of stewardship they would require—high, medium and low maintenance. The level has nothing to do with the amount of giving, for sometimes donors who give the least expect the most, and vice versa. Development officers assign these levels to help them plan their stewardship throughout the year. (A list of suggested activities and frequency for each level is included in the Appendix.)

Annual Endowment Reports

After the close of each fiscal year, as soon as accounting figures are available, a financial statement is issued listing the amount of funds in each endowment account, or "net assets at market value." Using that information, the Director generates Annual Endowment Reports (see sample in Appendix) for each endowed fund to send to the largest donor to each fund. For the first several years, these reports were sent to funds that had $100,000 or more. The threshold last year moved down to $50,000, and this year it will be at $20,000, the amount required to endow a fund.

Whenever possible, the Director asks development officers to generate a personalized letter to accompany the report. The letter can be from a scholarship recipient, a professor, a dean or whoever is directly benefitting from the gift. The report itself functions as a financial statement, showing donors how much interest has been generated from their gifts. A personalized letter, on the other hand, strives to show the direct affect of that donation: the scholarships that were awarded, the professorships that were created or the research that is being performed. Sometimes these letters generate more contributions.

These letters are a most valuable, meaningful stewardship tool. Donors who endow scholarship funds like to hear from students who receive the scholarships to find out where they are from, what they are studying, what they intend to do after graduation. As a charitable institution, it is our duty to be accountable for how we spend these funds.

Proposed Activities

Our biggest renovation project is our acknowledgment letters. Recognition procedures have become too cumbersome to get simple acknowledgment letters out within two months of the gift. We are in the process of simplifying the letters and cutting back on the amount of detail in each letter. Somewhere in our new process lies an ideal balance between personalizing the letter with complete, accurate information and getting the letter done in a timely manner.

For instance, rather than cite the specific fund that the gift went to ("Thank you for your gift of $1,000 to the John Smith Scholarship Fund in the College of Fine Arts"), we would thank the donor for his gift to the college or unit the fund is in. Whenever possible, we would refer to all gifts as gifts, as opposed to pledges, pledge payments, first pledge payments or any other differentiation. All the specific detail of the gift is mentioned in the gift receipt anyway, which donors receive within three days of our booking it.

And finally, rather than choose from among 18 form letters that take into account any number of specific situations, we would cut the list down to two (one from the Vice President, one from the President) and rotate them quarterly with different drafts of the same kind of letter. All details about the President's Council would be mailed separately in a non-personalized form letter. We are redesigning our letterhead and collateral materials as well. (See samples in Appendix.) Our goal is to get the thank you letter turnaround time down to less than one month.

This year, we will begin sending an annual letter to all companies who match gifts. The challenge will be to find out the most appropriate person to send the letters to.

For stewardship checklist activities, Development Officers can perform stewardship for donors of $100 if they chose, but practicality dictates that they be required to do it only for donors of at least $100,000. They have fundraising goals as their top priority, and stewardship often takes a back seat to solicitation and cultivation, particularly for donors who have no more to give. Officers are aware, however, that they are responsible each year for providing stewardship to all their major donors at some level. Eventually, it would be great to track stewardship for donors of $50,000 or more, or for amounts that reflect cumulative giving rather than one-time gifts.

At some point, we would like to begin hosting scholarship luncheons, where donors meet with their scholarship recipients. The SDR Director has been interviewing each Eminent Scholar Chair and is encouraging them to have more contact with their donors, where necessary. The next step is begin meeting with endowed professors.

Another goal is to have a web page that lists all endowed scholarship funds, with a brief biography of the person the fund is named for and a description of the scholarship requirements. This listing would act as a clearinghouse of all university scholarships. Endowed professorships could be included too.

The College of Business Administration has produced a brochure listing all endowed professorships and chairs, and ultimately it would be ideal for all colleges to have such a brochure for all endowed funds. Another goal is to work with fund administrators of all scholarship funds to coordinate efforts in requiring students to write thank-you letters to their donors.

Our office used to coordinate the mailing of holiday cards to our President's Council members, but we have decided this year that this is not an efficient use of time and funds for stewardship purposes. The cards may come across as insincere or impersonal, since many institutions send cards to their clients and customers. Instead, however, we may choose to begin sending a card at the beginning of the academic year ("thanks to your generosity, we're off to another outstanding year") or at the end of the year ("thanks to you, we had a great year").

Summary

Stewardship is a duty that many people share at various levels and in various ways. In a business sense, it is keeping your customer happy. As an ethical duty, it is making sure your donor knows you have honored your agreement, and how. It is not cultivation, for you may be obliged to provide stewardship to donors who will never give another gift. In its simplest form, stewardship is good manners and accountability.

Working with faculty and students to perform stewardship duties is often a challenge. Many do not feel it is their responsibility to thank donors or to keep in touch with them. Others welcome the opportunity to meet with the donors and let them know what is going on with their fund. And who better to tell the donor than the person who is most directly affected? Overall, it is the Stewardship Department's responsibility to make faculty and students aware of the positive impact they can have on the donor's outlook toward the university.

Likewise, working with Development Officers to provide stewardship is not always an easy task. They have many other priorities and administrative duties. They forget things. They lose papers. They are prone to neglect donors who probably will not give any more to the institution. Again, it is the Stewardship Department's role to take care of those donors who are not receiving stewardship by working with the appropriate staff to get them that care and attention.

APPENDIX

ORGANIZATION CHART

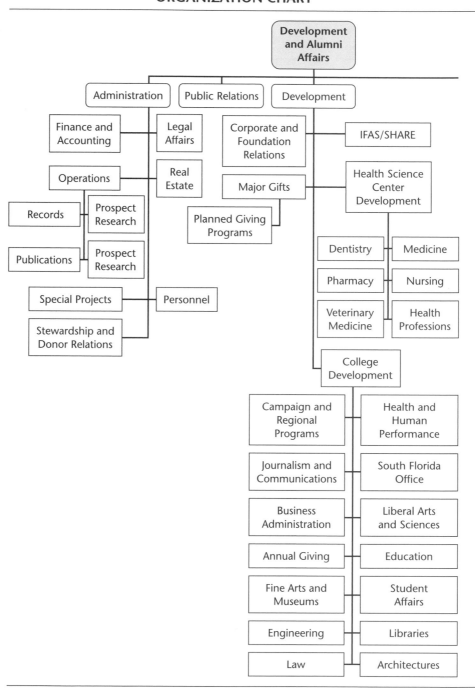

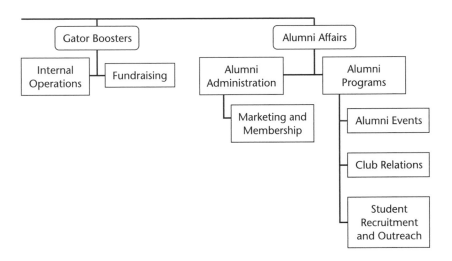

JOB DESCRIPTIONS

Title: **Director of Stewardship and Donor Relations**

Department: **Stewardship and Donor Relations**

Responsible to: **Associate Vice President of Administration**

Major function: **Coordinate all stewardship activities with ODAA donors, including President's Council**

Duties and Responsibilities:

Duties will include but not be limited to:

E 1. Coordinates production and completion by development officers of annual stewardship checklists.

E 2. Coordinates production and distribution to donors of annual endowment reports.

E 3. Coordinates production and distribution of "Thank You" letters for gifts of $50,000 or more.

E 4. Ensures stewardship and/or coordinates events for endowed professorships and scholarships.

E 5. Supervises President's Council programs, activities and staff.

E 6. May supervise special events coordinator.

   7. Other duties as assigned.

"E" indicates essential functions, which are the functions that this position exists to perform. Any incumbent in this position must be able to perform all of these essential fundamental duties, with or without reasonable accommodations. Management retains the right to modify or add duties at any time.

Qualifications

Education

College degree minimum; master's degree preferred.

Experience and Job Knowledge

Must have the ability to communicate clearly and accurately in both written and verbal communication. Excellent writing skills essential.

Experience in development and/or working with volunteers preferred.

Proficiency in WordPerfect and Windows.

MUST be creative, and have excellent interpersonal and customer relations skills.

Additional Considerations

Approved by:

_____ Date: _____
Incumbent

_____ Date: _____
Immediate Supervisor

_____ Date: _____
Personnel

Official title: **Program Assistant**

Department: **Stewardship and Donor Relations**

Responsible to: **Director of Stewardship and Donor Relations**

Major functions: **Assistant to the Director of Stewardship and Donor Relations**

Duties and Responsibilities

1. Assists Director of Stewardship and Donor Relations in preparing annual endowment reports.
2. Assists Director of Stewardship and Donor Relations in preparing stewardship checklist documents.
3. Helps to plan, organize and coordinate the operation of the President's Council Weekend and other stewardship special events, as needed.
4. Handles vendors for stewardship and donor relations special events and recognition programs.
5. Arranges meetings and travel as needed for Director of Stewardship and Donor Relations, attending meetings when necessary.
6. Performs other duties as assigned.

Qualifications

Education

High school education plus two years of business or vocational school training, or associate's degree in secretarial sciences (bachelor's degree preferred), or an equivalent combination of education and experience.

Experience

Minimum of four years of responsible secretarial experience. Public relations experience helpful. Strong verbal and written communications skills essential. Background in research, working with vendors, mailing and printing helpful. Must be able to work independently.

Job Knowledge

Expertise in word processing, data entry and spreadsheet programs necessary. Desktop and presentation software knowledge helpful. Ability to type 50 wpm.

Additional Considerations

Must take initiative and demonstrate the ability to manage various projects simultaneously in a support position. Attention to detail is essential. Strong organizational skills, ability to meet deadlines and problem-solving capabilities are important.

Approved by:

_____   Date: _____
Incumbent

_____   Date: _____
Immediate Supervisor

_____   Date: _____
Personnel

UNIVERSITY OF FLORIDA FOUNDATION, INC.

STEWARDSHIP CHECKLIST

The following list will help you choose stewardship next activities for donors to your college or unit who have made gifts of $100,000 or more during their lifetimes. Choose as many activities that apply, and enter them into your next activities plans.

General Recognition of the Gift

Standard Responses (New Gifts Only)

- Gift acknowledgment (UFF Records Dept.)
- Thank you letter from president (President's Council)
- Thank you letter from vice president for development and alumni affairs (President's Council)
- Thank you letter from dean/director and department chairman (where applicable)
- Thank you letter from development officers
- Press release (UFF Publications Dept.)

Special Recognition of Donor

- Article in campus publication
- Special event, opening, reception*
- Groundbreaking ceremony*
- Commendation
- Permanent recognition (e.g., wall plaque on campus building)*

Stewardship Suggestions for All Gifts

Stewardship Visits

- President
- Vice president ODAA
- Unit vice president
- Dean/director & dept. chair
- Development officer

Invitations

- President's box (football)
- President's area (basketball)

- President's Council weekend
- Other University events
- College/unit events

Other Communications

- Annual Endowment Report
- College/unit (newsletters, magazines)
- Birthday card
- Holiday card
- Other

Stewardship Possibility by Gift Type

Eminent Scholar Chairs/Endowed Professorships

- Personal contact with chair holder/professor
- Letter from chair holder/professor about scholarly work
- Letter from president
- Letter from dean/director and dept. chair (where applicable)
- Letter from development officer

Endowed Scholarships*

- Thank you letter from scholarship recipient(s)
- Letter from president about importance of scholarship
- Letter from dean/director
- Letter from development officer
- Invitation to annual UF scholarship recognition event**
- Invitation to college's annual scholarship recognition event

Buildings (New and Extensive Renovations)*

- Invitation to groundbreaking
- Invitation to dedication
- Commemorative photo album of building (inside and outside)
- Letter from president re use of building
- Letter from dean/director and dept. chair (where applicable)
- Letter from development officer

*Is there a videotaping opportunity?
**Proposed.

PROPOSED STEWARDSHIP ACTIVITY LEVELS

Level A—Most Activity

- Three or more phone calls or two visits by development officer and faculty member, student, dean, Vice President, President or other meaningful individual
- Annual Endowment Report, individualized letter if appropriate
- College/unit mailings
- President's Council mailings (newsletter, invitation to PC Weekend, annual decal, parking pass request)
- Holiday card
- Birthday card, if appropriate

Level B—Middle Activity

- Two phone calls and one visit by development officer *and* faculty member, student, dean, Vice President, President or other meaningful individual
- Annual Endowment Report, individualized letter if appropriate
- President's Council mailings (newsletter, invitation to PC Weekend, annual decal, parking pass request)
- Holiday card
- Birthday card, if appropriate

Level C—Least Activity

- One phone call or visit by development officer or other university representative
- Annual Endowment Report, individualized letter if appropriate
- College/unit mailings
- President's Council mailings (newsletter, invitation to PC Weekend, annual decal, parking pass request)
- Holiday card
- Birthday card, if appropriate

1. Phone calls and visits would have to be logged in as next activities.
2. For annual endowment report, a next activity would be included if a letter will accompany it. Not all funds need accompanying letters. Journalism, for example, sends out its own letters in spring.
3. College/unit mailings will not go to donors who request "no mail" or "restricted mail," unless the restricted mail code has "include" codes for specific publications.
4. PC mailings will not go to donors who request "no mail" or "restricted mail," unless the restricted mail code has "include" codes for specific publications.
5. Not all donors wish to receive birthday cards. This is optional.

GIFT ACKNOWLEDGMENT

UNIVERSITY OF FLORIDA
University of Florida Foundation, Inc.
P.O. Box 14425
Gainesville, FL 32604
A direct support organization of the University of Florida

Thank You!

. . . for your thoughtful gift to the University of Florida.

Private support like yours provides essential resources for our students and faculty, enhances teaching, strengthens research and extends our service programs. Your gift helps the University of Florida sustain the excellence that is the hallmark of a great university.

On behalf of our faculty and students, we thank you for your generous support.

Sincerely yours,

John V. Lombardi
President
University of Florida

Paul A. Robell
Executive Vice President
University of Florida Foundation, Inc.

UNIVERSITY OF FLORIDA FOUNDATION, INC.
ANNUAL ENDOWMENT REPORT

We are pleased to provide you with this annual endowment report. Your investment in the University of Florida is an important part of our endowment, which surpassed $496 million in assets as of June 30, 1998. Spendable income generated by our endowment pool is vital in the support of scholarships, professorships, Eminent Scholar Chairs, program enhancements, and other academic pursuits. Virtually every aspect of the University benefits in some way from endowed gifts such as yours.

Investment of endowment monies is managed by the Investments Committee of the Board of Directors of the Foundation. The investment policy established by this Committee is designed to protect the "purchasing power" of your gift over time and provide steady, predictable amounts of spendable income free from cyclical fluctuations in the market.

We strive to be good stewards of the gifts invested in the University of Florida by local alumni and friends. Thank you again for your investment in the University of Florida.

Paul A. Robell
Executive Vice President

Endowed fund: John Q. Donor Eminent Scholar Chair in Banking
Net assets at market value (6/30/98): $1,262,130

If you have any questions, please contact me (352) 392-5407 or Debbie Meyers, Director of Stewardship and Donor Relations (352) 846-2816.

ENDOWMENT ASSET MANAGEMENT
UNIVERSITY OF FLORIDA FOUNDATION, INC.

The University of Florida Foundation, Inc., is the primary endowment investment organization of the University. The Foundation currently oversees the investment of more than $471 million of endowment securities. (The endowment includes assets other than securities—primarily real property.)

These investments are managed for long-term growth utilizing the expertise of the Foundation's investment advisor Callan Associates, Inc. and eighteen external money managers. Internal oversight and management decisions are the responsibility of the Foundation's Investments Committee.

Asset Allocation Strategy

The Foundation adopted the following asset allocation strategy effective July 2, 1996.

Asset Allocation

Domestic Equities	55%
Domestic Fixed	15%
International Equities	20%
International Fixed	5%
Real Estate	5%
Total	100%

This strategy is designed to provide sufficient annual total return to cover endowment spending, fees, and growth in principal, while attempting to provide for annual increases in purchasing power.

Management of the Endowment

Each manager is evaluated quarterly. Callan rates each manager against its database for similar style and presents this information to the Investments Committee. The Committee expects the managers to provide a return greater than the median performance of their respective databases and benchmarks.

Each quarter, any new monies in the pool are invested to insure compliance with the asset allocation.

POLICY ON THE ESTABLISHMENT OF NAMING OPPORTUNITIES AND ENDOWED FUNDS

General Policy

The Development Committee of UFF's Board of Directors, in conjunction with the President of the University, sets minimum gift level amounts and establishes approved guidelines for gift naming opportunities. UF, in all gift naming opportunities, reserves the right of approval for the name or names designated for any of the gift naming opportunities in the sections which follow. University approval cannot be granted until the donor's name is known or until the name or names of the person or persons being memorialized are known. The gift levels described below are intended as minimum amounts needed to name the respective opportunity. In most cases, gifts may be made over as long as a five-year period. The selection of holders of all endowed positions is coordinated by the Office of the Provost.

Specific Gift Naming Opportunities

Note: The dollar ranges cited in the paragraphs below are minimums. In each category both numbers represent the minimum amounts needed for endowments in various-sized programs. The larger number is not a cap; it is a minimum figure for a larger or more comprehensive program.

Where state matching funds are available, they may be used in conjunction with the donor's gift to reach the minimum level.

College

To name a college at UF, a minimum gift commitment of $10 million to $50 million for endowment is required, depending on the college's size and scope of program.

School

To name a school at UF, a minimum gift commitment of $5 million to $10 million for endowment is required, depending on the school's size and scope of programs.

Department

To name a department, a minimum gift commitment of $3 million to $5 million for endowment is required, depending on the department's size and scope of programs.

Center

To name a university-wide center, a minimum gift commitment of $1 million to $3 million for endowment is required, depending on the disciplines involved and the size and scope of the programs. To name a center that is wholly within a college or department, a minimum gift commitment of $500,000 to $1.5 million for endowment is required, depending on the center's size and scope of program. [Document continues with additional naming opportunities.]

POST-CAMPAIGN ASSESSMENT—ANNUAL CAMPAIGN

DEVELOPMENT AND MEMBERSHIP
YEAR-END REPORT FOR 1998

Indianapolis Museum of Art

◆

February 9, 1999

The Development and Membership staffs focused on bringing in new members and donors and upgrading current members and donors in 1998. To achieve these goals the staff integrated all of the development and membership functions into one unified program that was responsible to the museum event and marketing schedules. All renewal and acquisition projects were centered around the museum's main event for 1998—the King of the World exhibition and its marketing thrust. Additional emphasis was focused around the Ravine Garden and Lilly Pavilion renovations.

The members of the staff also strove to diversify the donor and members giving options by producing multiple appeals throughout the year to yield multiple gifts and offering restricted and unrestricted giving appeals to individuals, corporations, and foundations. This method is exemplified in the broader calendar spread of received gifts and the increase in giving amounts form previous donors caused by moving their gift appeal from unrestricted to restricted.

An ad hoc committee was used to prioritize the major grant initiatives, the curators to determine possible future incoming gifts of art, and a greater use of volunteers to help cultivate prospective donors and to plan cultivation events. Corporate volunteer groups basically took over the phonathons throughout the year with the help of some individual volunteers. The Corporate Advisory Council was instrumental in identifying new corporate contacts and following through with current corporate donors. The Trustee Development and Donor Relations Committees were used to direct donor cultivation and identification. This more directed use of volunteers and staff seemed to be more productive than using volunteers in the more traditional mode of team calling and follow up.

The prospect research efforts were heightened as a staff member was dedicated full time to the endeavor and computer support was provided. As a result, area entrepreneurs and corporate heads were identified for solicitation and restricted giving reports, and resources for current donor research were established.

The foundation base was broadened tremendously through increased research made possible by the on-site access to the Internet. Some 30 new funding sources were approached for funding, and others were asked for multiple gifts for the first time. This area really reaped the rewards of hiring a full-time Foundation Relations Coordinator in mid-1997 (a position that had been eliminated four years earlier).

Corporate funding for unrestricted gifts continued to be a challenge. A decision was made to continue seeking unrestricted support but to move more aggressively to sponsorships of existing and new programs, exhibitions, etc. A policy for sponsorship recognition was put into place with the help of the curatorial and marketing departments.

The staff was given a better computer software system and upgraded hardware to aid them. It took the entire year to make the transition to the point that policies and procedures can be determined in the first quarter of 1999.

Linda Hardwick

**CONTRIBUTIONS AND MEMBERSHIP
ACTIVITY REPORT—DECEMBER 1998**

◆

CONTRIBUTIONS AND MEMBERSHIP
ACTIVITY REPORT—DECEMBER 1998

Annual Unrestricted

	Goal 1998	YTD 1998	YTD 1997
Individual gifts over $1,250	$490,000	$544,536	$524,386
Staff gifts	10,000	11,334	7,777
Individual gifts under $1,250	280,000	230,695	179,775
Corporate	430,000	371,317	427,605
Membership	454,940	343,476	367,701
Subtotal	$1,664,940	$1,491,358	$1,507,244
Satellite gallery	60,000	57,612	64,718
GOS Grants	132,000	278,327	137,725
Federal		56,240	
City/state		221,965	137,725
Private foundation	450,000	450,000	450,000
Total	$2,306,940	$2,277,297	$2,167,412

Annual Restricted

Corporate	$290,000	$422,831	$426,142
Individual	45,000	1,526,624	870,753
Grants	268,000	219,688	55,400
Total	$603,000	$1,949,455	$1,352,295
TOTAL ANNUAL GIVING	$2,909,940	$4,226,752	$3,407,207

Permanently Restricted

Operational endowment		$264,593	$983,901
Restricted endowments		140,602	1,419,014
Art endowments		20,560,682*	1,401,560
Undesignated			41,133,825*
Annuities			40,786
Total		$20,965,877	$43,977,016
TOTAL 1998 REVENUE	$2,909,940	$25,187,018	$45,730,677
Total memberships	9,500	9,036	8,408
Total new members	3,600	3,106	1,777
Value of donated art		$3,225,329	$4,453,890
TOTAL 1998 REVENUE PLUS VALUE OF DONATED ART		$28,412,347	

*The art endowment figure for 1998 and the undesignated bequest for 1997

Development and Membership 1998 (Compared to 1997)

Second Century Society

- 24 new members and 40 upgrades
- 24 members not renewing
- Total membership 294 households
- 3 percent increase in revenue

Staff Giving

- 46 percent increase in revenue

Individual Giving to $1,250

- 25 percent increase in revenue
- 3 percent increase in the number of donors making multiple gifts
- Goal increased 81 percent over 1997's; 80 percent of increased goal received
- 2,969 gifts received (2,466 in 1997)
- 75 percent of gifts from museum members

Corporate Giving

- 49 new corporate donors
- 50 percent increase in number of corporate gifts
- Restricted giving revenue increased by 70 percent
- Unrestricted giving revenue down by 16 percent
- Average unrestricted gift decreased by 46 percent

Membership

- 3,108 new members joined—86 percent of total goal
- 7 percent growth in total membership over 1997
- 77 percent retention rate of current members
- 209 new Young Friends of Art members

Grants

- 100 percent increase in grant revenue (excluding Lilly Endowment's annual grant)
- 40 percent decrease in government restricted project giving
- 11 percent increase in private foundation restricted project support
- 66 percent increase in government unrestricted support

Summary

- 24 percent increase in revenue for all annual giving
- 99 percent of the unrestricted goal raised
- 44 percent increase in revenue for restricted giving (November figures)
- 223 percent of the restricted goal raised

General Observations

- Completion of first full year of new staff team
- Conversion to new computer system
- Completion of corporate sponsorship policy
- Integration of development and membership solicitations and donor/member cultivation with overall museum marketing, event, and exhibition calendars
- Implementation of use of the Internet for individual, corporate, and foundation prospect research

Trends in Fundraising

1. Collaborations, community service, and outreach are the most important cases currently for fundraising.
2. The new fundraising is donor-driven rather than methodology-driven
3. The institution that will survive will make continuous asks throughout the year.
4. There is more professionalism in the field and less use of volunteers.
5. Donor base is moving from an older, civic-minded generation to the baby boomers.
6. There is greater use of technology.
7. Corporate donations are turning almost entirely to restricted programs.

Trends in IMA Fundraising

1. Annual giving is relatively flat in all areas and is keyed directly to the number of new members acquired.
2. Increasing numbers of annual fund donors are inquiring about restricted gifts.
3. Membership retention is relatively flat, but new member growth is increasing.
4. Corporate giving is shifting to restricted projects with funds coming from marketing budgets rather than contributions budgets.
5. Grant income from private foundations is the area of fastest growth.
6. Cost to raise $1 is 36 cents.

How the Development and Membership Staff Is Responding to the Trends

1. Focus on IMA's community outreach and service programs as the cases for giving and the varied "lines of business" to create appeals.
2. Segment prospects and current donors for solicitations and cultivation.
3. Incorporate the museum's marketing plan and special exhibition calendars to drive appeals and events.
4. Begin to use more technological resources in procedures.
5. Survey membership to determine lapsing reasons.
6. Use the related trustee committees to identify and cultivate prospects.
7. Implement the Corporate Advisory Council's recommendation to shift the major focus of corporate giving to sponsorships.
8. Consider merging the financial goals for unrestricted and restricted annual gifts into one annual giving goal.

A RECOMMENDATION
FOR CORPORATE SUPPORT
FROM THE
IMA CORPORATE ADVISORY COMMITTEE
TO THE
IMA BOARD OF GOVERNORS

January 19, 1999

The Corporate Advisory Committee has been reviewing the trends in corporate giving nationally and within the Indianapolis community since its creation in 1994. Many of its members are concurrently on the boards and committees of other nonprofit organizations and have seen similar trends in those organizations. Philanthropic allocations that provide unrestricted support are decreasing, causing corporations to structure their giving around projects that tie directly to their corporate mission, product, employee interests, or location.

To fulfill their role as community supporters and to align themselves with prestigious arts organizations for image building, corporations are looking to their marketing budgets as the resource pool for providing arts support. To justify the allocation of marketing resources on indirect expenditures, corporations are seeking sponsorship opportunities in which they receive at least a two-for-one return on their investment. For instance, if the arts organization requests a $50,000 sponsorship, the corporation is seeking $100,000 in tangible benefits as a direct result of its investment. In addition, many corporations are seeking specific demographic information regarding audience served and the direct impact their sponsorship had on revenue. They are most interested in working with arts organizations that are flexible enough to allow them to be a part of the sponsorship structure process—less client-driven and more customer-driven in approach.

Because of these trends, the Corporate Advisory Council recommends the following:

1. Shift development resources of time, budget, and effort into the development and maintenance of sponsorships.
2. Restructure museum policies to allow more flexibility and visibility regarding sponsor benefits.
3. Develop marketing plans when possible for major projects and exhibitions at least one year prior to the opening of the exhibition.
4. Investigate the possibility of using outside council to provide an in-depth look at the museum's assets and assist with the development of sponsorship proposal policies, procedures, and fee structures.
5. Endorsement from the museum to provide the support and resources necessary to build a sponsorship program.

Resource 32

POST-CAMPAIGN ASSESSMENT—CAPITAL CAMPAIGN

Final Report

VANCOUVER PUBLIC LIBRARY

"FOR THE LOVE OF LEARNING"
LIBRARY SQUARE CAPITAL CAMPAIGN

December 1995

Prepared by

Marilyn Wright Fundraising Counsel Inc.
Vancouver, British Columbia

Table of Contents

Introduction

The active phase of the Library Square Capital Campaign is now virtually complete. The objective is $12 million and at November 27, 1995, we have documented gifts totalling $8,831,261. Several gifts are expected to be realized before the end of December.

The campaign will have been conducted over a 24-month period: January 1994 through December 1995. This report outlines the activity of the capital campaign, which included the recruitment of strong leadership, the formulation of a strong and convincing case, the identification of viable prospects, and the implementation of a successful plan.

This report gives a campaign chronicle and has appended charts, which show the progress of the campaign as it progressed. (See Appendix I and Appendix II.)

Although this phase of the campaign is winding down, additional gifts are anticipated to be received during the next several months.

The Library will continue to monitor major decisions pending, i.e., 1 Service Club, 11 individual major gift calls, and 1 national company major gift. Receipting of donations for the Library Card Christmas campaign will be ongoing into the new year.

This is a report on professional service and outlines the purpose and strategy used in the campaign. It is impossible to detail and account all incidents and events surrounding the campaign. The specific details are documented in the weekly reports to the leadership of the campaign, which are on file in the Campaign Office.

As the campaign draws to a close, it is vitally important that pledge control for long-term commitments be carefully handled. This process must be fully integrated into the ongoing fundraising endeavours of the Library, directed and in a manner satisfactory to the City's Director of Finance.

In submitting this Final Report for the Library Square Capital Campaign, I want to express my sincere appreciation to the Vancouver Public Library Board, who have assisted the Campaign in this extraordinary financial endeavour, with special thanks to Kyle Mitchell, Madge Aalto, and the senior management of the Library, and Ken Dobell, City Manager, for their leadership and determination to support the fundraising campaign. The entire campaign staff has benefited from this experience and feel privileged to have been a part of this project.

An important element of the campaign was the leadership given by the Campaign Co-Chairs, John and Kip Woodward. Their leadership and dedication were the key factors in making this fundraising effort successful.

Sincere appreciation is extended to all of the campaign committee members for the time and commitment given for the past two years. It is impossible to mention each individual who has contributed to the success of this project. A special thank-you must be given to the Library staff, Friends of the Library, and the 100+ community volunteers who help build "a love of learning" at the new Central Branch.

I am grateful for the confidence placed in my procedures, methods, and systems of fundraising. Please accept my gratitude to all of you, who through your involvement, leadership, and kindness have made the work of counsel successful. Respectfully submitted,
Marilyn Wright Fundraising Counsel Inc.

Initial Activity

Having outgrown its 1957 home, the Library Board looked to the people of Vancouver to find out what people wanted in a new building. Community input was the foundation of the library planning process and the community spoke on the design of what was to be the new downtown signature building.

A unique partnership with the federal and provincial governments, the City of Vancouver, and private donors was conceived to create a library to serve people across British Columbia.

The Library was responsible for $12 million for equipment and furnishings and the governments would provide the construction cost. It was determined that new sources of income over and above anticipated income would be required to meet the Library's projected needs for furnishings and equipment. The Board decided to launch a major capital campaign.

A key constituent market survey was undertaken in March 1990. A campaign committee was formed with James Cleave as Chair. Early in the campaign the Chair was transferred out of Vancouver and the new campaign co-chairs, Kip and John Woodward, were enlisted in December 1993.

Marilyn Wright was contacted and retained by the City of Vancouver to direct the capital campaign for a period of 18 months, beginning January 1, 1994, and was extended for six months to end December 31, 1995. Support staff were hired and a Library Square Capital Campaign office was established at 1075 West Georgia. Work began immediately on preparation of the database, research on prospects, foundations, and service clubs. At the same time Counsel worked closely with Kip and John Woodward and Kyle Mitchell, Chair of the Library Board, in recruiting the Campaign Leadership Board.

After careful consideration, the following were invited and agreed to become the Leadership Board who would put their energies to actively solicit funds from the private sector to support the new Vancouver Public Library: Graham Bender, Gordon Campbell, Graham Clarke, W.R.P. (Bill) Dalton, Virginia Greene, Michael Horsey, Terry Hui, Robert Hungerford, Lyall Knott, Peter Ladner, Peter Lamb, David Laundy, Gregory McKinstry, Kyle Mitchell, Nancy Self, Ross Smith, and Marie Taylor.

Each member accepted the responsibility for calling on five to ten key prospects and worked with counsel and staff in developing a campaign strategy for each one. Most members made more than ten calls.

The Campaign Plan

It should be noted that when this campaign began there was no history of organized giving by the private sector to the Vancouver Public Library. A decision was made early in the planning of the campaign to help the public take ownership of their new Library. At the same time a program of educating and involving the internal Library family about the long-term benefits of a capital campaign to the Library system was undertaken. Both external and internal support early in the campaign needed to be backed up by a broad-based public relations program.

The scheduling of campaign activity by phases put a strong focus on target objectives, which helped not only to elevate donor sights but also developed momentum by creating a campaign atmosphere.

Campaign leadership was effective throughout the appeal because of their belief in the following recommended concepts:

- Recruitment and solicitation was conducted on a personal face to face basis.
- Larger gifts were solicited early in the program to develop momentum.
- Long-term commitments were encouraged.
- Recognition opportunities were available for consideration.
- A gift made to the VPL through the British Columbia Library Foundation was available.
- Planned gifts were sought.
- Donors were asked for specific gifts or gift plans.

Gifts

Essential to the campaign plan was a strong emphasis on receiving Major Gifts from corporations, financial institutions, service clubs, individuals, foundations, etc. It was hoped that there would be several gifts in the $2–3 million range. This has not as yet been realized.

The Vancouver Foundation's lead gift of $1,000,000 and the Hong Kong Festival '92 Gala Dinner gift of $200,000 that was matched by the Hongkong Bank were both made during Jim Cleave's time.

The plan was to announce the campaign to the public with a significant amount of the money in hand. At the same time we wanted to build the awareness of the campaign through a media programme. Pacific Press joined with the Library campaign as a media partner and agreed to place recognition display ads in the Vancouver Sun and to support all the events leading up to and including the opening of the Library. The campaign kicked off January 24, 1995, with the announcement of $4,676,000 raised.

To encourage gifts, tours were conducted with prospects almost daily during the construction phase of the building and continued well after the Library was opened. These tours were conducted by the Leadership Board, Campaign Staff, and members of City Council, and I would be remiss if I did not recognize the tremendous effort and support put forth by Shelagh Flaherty of the Library Staff, who always made time to conduct tours.

From January 1995 through to the opening, the Campaign Office Staff became integrally involved with the events around the opening of the Library. Much time and energy was spent in ensuring that the campaign and opening would both be successful and that all activities would be positive for the donors.

Partnerships were formed with Concord Pacific and Fletcher Challenge. This is a new concept for the Vancouver Public Library and with thoughtful and careful planning shows promise as a source of revenue to future endeavours.

"Great Libraries of the World," a contest supported by the Vancouver Sun and Vancouver Bank branches, was held in conjunction with the opening of the new Library. This popular contest introduced the commemorative Library card.

A mailing to 10,000 Business in Vancouver Subscribers was sent in May 1995.

The Ismaili Community chose to support Library Square with the proceeds of their annual Walk. Six months of intensive planning went into this event, which was chaired by Councillor Lynne Kennedy and Alnoor Samji. A committee of 20 comprised of Ismaili members, Friends of the Library, Library staff, and campaign staff worked together to ensure a most successful event on October 1, 1995 (see Appendix III).

Recognition ads have appeared in the Vancouver Sun throughout the campaign thanking donors who have made gifts of $50,000 or more for their contribution to Library Square. The placement of these ads in the newspaper was part of the Pacific Press gift (see the Ronald McDonald Children's Charities ad).

The Chinese Community Support the Library Week was held October 28–November 5, 1995. This very dedicated, hardworking committee chaired by Bill Yuen and Vice Chairs Councillor Maggie Ip and John Cheng were assisted by Honourary Chairs Maria Ko and Stella Wong. They brought together 18 people who planned a week of cultural events at Library Square. To date the total raised from this event is $520,000.

Money Raised

To date, money raised by category:

Individuals—13 gifts totalling $3,435,000, ranging from $25,000 to $1,000,000.

Corporations—43 gifts totalling $2,021,600 ranging from $5,000 to $200,000.

Foundations—8 gifts totalling $1,405,000 ranging from $5,000 to $1,000,000.

Service Clubs—4 gifts totalling $268,500.

Community phase generated gifts totalling $646,161.

- Banks Financial Program (Gift-a-lopes in Banks)
- Commemorative Library Cards
- Downtown Rotary Bike-a-thon
- Ismaili Walk for the Vancouver Public Library
- Chinese Community Support the Library Week
- Wine and Dine British Columbia (not received, not included in total)
- The Vancouver Bank (anticipate proceeds next year)

Gifts-in-kind total $330,000.

Included in the total raised is $1,850,000 in Planned Gifts (Insurance Based)

Total raised to date: $8,831,61.

Of note: The Forest Industry gave over $1,000,000 and the Financial Institutions gave $620,000.

It is encouraging for future fundraising endeavours that the campaign has attracted cash donations and in-kind gifts to the Library that are not included in the campaign total because it is for programs and books.

Recommendations

At the end of any major campaign, there are a number of items that must be dealt with after the departure of counsel. The transition plan is in place and two of the campaign staff will be staying on for two months to help ensure the smooth conversion to a full development program. The Library will be reporting to Council on a continuing development program.

There are outstanding calls that show real potential and there must be continued cultivation and contact with the prospects to realize this possibility.

Communication with the cash donors and pledgors is critical for the next five years. Every effort should be made to keep the donors informed on activities at the Library and any special event that is held should offer these special friends an invitation. In fact opportunities to invite major donors into the Library should be encouraged—keeping those who supported the campaign close will benefit everyone. It is very important to keep current with pledge reminders. As much as possible the practice of a forty-eight-hour maximum receipt turnaround for gifts should be supported.

A complete listing of every donation to the capital campaign is on confidential record in the Development Office. A chronological history of the campaign has been kept by the campaign office and will be presented to the Library Board at the completion of the active phase of the campaign.

Appendix I

DECEMBER 1995 GIFT LEVEL ANALYSIS.

Dollar Amount	Number of Gifts	Dollar Value
1,000,000	2	2,000,000
500,000	2	1,000,000
425,000	1	425,000
300,000	1	300,000
250,000	2	500,000
200,000	4	800,000
150,000	1	150,000
120,000	5	600,000
100,000	9	900,000
60,000	1	60,000
50,000	6	300,000
40,000	1	40,000
30,000	2	60,000
27,500	1	27,500
25,000	5	125,000
20,000	2	40,000
15,000	6	90,000
10,200	1	10,200
10,000	10	100,000
6,900	1	6,900
5,000	5	25,000
4,500	1	4,500
Under 4,500	Many	636,161
In-kind	Many	330,000
		$8,530,261

Appendix II

VANCOUVER PUBLIC LIBRARY CAPITAL CAMPAIGN CUMULATIVE DONATIONS (JANUARY 1994–NOVEMBER 27, 1995).

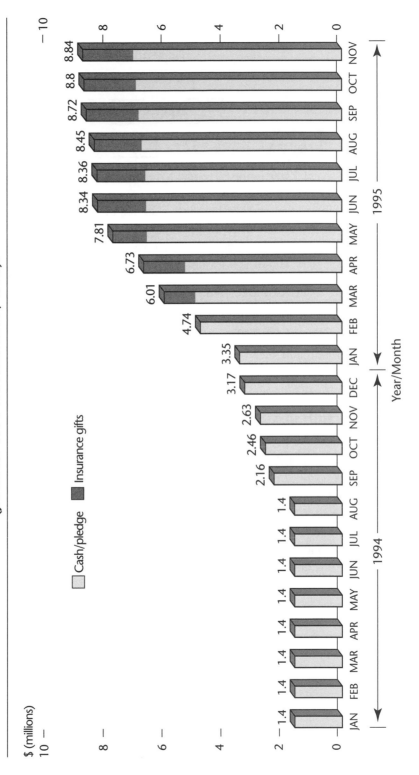

☐ Cash/pledge ■ Insurance gifts

$ (millions)

Appendix III

FOR THE
LOVE OF LEARNING...

Your opportunity to support Library Square

Library Square is an immense resource for us all – students, children
and explorers of all stripes. Vancouverites have proven themselves
to be voracious readers – 5,000 people visit the Central Library each day.
Each hour, 450 business people call for research assistance.

SMALL BUSINESS	LITERAZZI

RECOGNITION
Gifts of $5,000 to $9,999

- Naming of shelving
  (compact and open stacks)
- Listing in *Business in Vancouver*

Gifts of $1,000 to $4,999

- Naming of furnishings
- Listing in *Business in Vancouver*

Additional naming
opportunities are avail-
able for contributions
over $10,000. For more
details on how to support
this remarkable project,
please contact the
Library Square Capital
Campaign Office at
(604) 681-8834.

A gala fund raiser in support of
Library Square and the Open
House Family Weekend, *Literazzi*
welcomes guests to a magical
evening within the seven dramatic
floors of Library Square.

Join prominent British Columbian
and Canadian authors, special
celebrity guests and
award-winning chefs for
a taste of the city's finest
wines, gourmet cuisine
and best entertainment.
Literazzi promises to
be a once-in-a-lifetime
event you won't want
to miss.

Tickets are $175 – call
257-3818 soon to order.

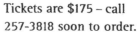

**LIBRARY
SQUARE**

The goal of the capital campaign is to raise $12 million
to furnish and equip Library Square.

Thanks to the Sounding Board for making this advertisement possible.

Appendix III, cont'd.

Resource 33

Appendix III, cont'd.

Ismaili Walk for The Vancouver Public Library

Sunday, October 1

The Walk kicks off at the Plaza of Nations at 10 a.m.

Mark your calendar and join in the fun! Bring the whole family!

Walk, stroll or run the 5 km route which takes you through The Vancouver Public Library.

After the Walk join in the fun, food and festivities of the Family Fair at the Plaza of Nations

All proceeds to the Vancouver Public Library in support of a Children's Exploration Gallery

Pick up a pledge sheet at your nearest Library Branch. For more information call 331-3895.

The Ismaili Walk for The Vancouver Public Library
Co-chairs Lynne Kennedy and Alnoor Samji
Advertising space donated by The Vancouver Board of Trade

Resource 33

Appendix III, cont'd.

LIBRARY
SQUARE

*For the Love
of Learning.*

Ronald McDonald Children's Charities wants each child to know the joy of reading.

On behalf of Vancouver and the Library Square Campaign Leadership Board, John and Kip Woodward, co-chairs, acknowledge the generous contribution Ronald McDonald Children's Charities has made to Library Square.

Ronald McDonald Children's Charities of Canada is dedicated to improving the quality of life for children. Their gift makes it possible to purchase information technology and reading equipment for special needs children at Library Square, ensuring universal access to learning and education.

Thank you Ronald McDonald Children's Charities — you are building a legacy of learning for generations to come.

Library Square thanks the Vancouver Sun for making this advertisement possible.

FINAL REPORT—ANNUAL CAMPAIGN

Mission

The Eiteljorg Museum of American Indians and Western Art is dedicated to the appreciation and understanding of American Indians and Western American art and the many cultures of North America. The museum will:

- Collect, present and preserve art, artifacts and related items of the highest quality.
- Develop exhibitions and programs of both an educational and entertaining nature.
- Endeavor to advance research and knowledge in its chosen fields.

While remaining an integral part of the Indianapolis community, the Museum will strive to become an institution of national stature.

On the Cover

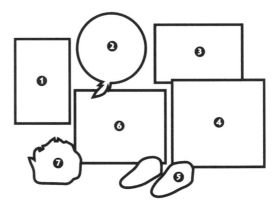

1. Cooks from the "Some Like It Hot!" Chili Cookoff
2. Shield, 19th c.
   Dog Men Warrior
   Tsistsistas (Cheyenne) Artist
   Photo by Mark Sexton from the exhibition *Gifts of the Spirit*
3. White Mountain Apache Crown Dancers from Arizona
   From the Indian Market
4. *The Twins*
   E. Martin Hennings
   Oil on canvas, 1923
   Collection of Eiteljorg Museum
5. Moccasins
   Miami
   Courtesy of the Cranbrook Institute of Science
   Photo by Tim Thayer
   From the exhibition *In the Presence of the Past*
6. *Thunderhead*
   Joe Maktima (Laguna Pueblo/Hopi)
   Acrylic on canvas, 1997
   From *New Art of the West 6*
7. *The Headache Pot*
   Clancey Gray (Osage)
   1995
   Loan of the Bartlesville Community Center, Bartlesville, OK
   Courtesy of Peabody Essex Museum
   Photo by Mark Sexton
   From the exhibition *Gifts of the Spirit*

Eiteljorg Museum Board of Directors *(as of 12/31/98)*

Robert R. Baxter, retired president, Riley Memorial Assoc.

Tom Binford,* Binford Miles Rodgers & Associates

Ronald W. Dollens, president, Guidant Corp.

Michael L. Eagle, vice president, manufacturing, Eli Lilly & Co.

Roger Eiteljorg, senior vice president, Citimark Management Co.

Sonja Eiteljorg, M.D.

Richard J. Freeland, president, Pizza Hut of Ft. Wayne Inc.

Charles Garcia, president, GM Construction

Mrs. Thomas Gellenbeck

Mari H. George, board chairman, Indianapolis Motor Speedway

James D. Holton, HIGLP

Stan Hurt, chairman, Indiana Supply Corp.

Glenn W. Irwin Jr., M.D., Indiana School of Medicine

Kathy Jordan, director of community relations, Pacers Basketball Corp.

Chris Katterjohn, president, Indianapolis Business Journal

James D. Kemper, partner, Ice Miller Donadio & Ryan

Carolyn W. Kincannon, civic volunteer

William K. McGowan Jr., president/CEO, Indiana Convention & Visitors Assn.

Gerald Paul, retired CEO & chairman, Paul Harris

Alexander G. Peacock, vice president of sales, Hindostone Products Inc.

John E. D. Peacock Jr., president, Hindostone Products Inc.

Mel Perelman, Ph.D.

Steve Radcliffe, executive vice president, American United Life Insurance Co.

Bonnie Reilly, civic leader

Frank E. Russell, trustee/chairman of the board, Nina Mason Pulliam Trust

Robert J. Salyers, partner, Salyers & Eiteljorg

A. H. "Hutch" Schumaker II, president, Coca-Cola Bottling Co.

Lora Siders, Miami Nation of Indians

Michael P. Skehan, managing director, R. J. Pile & Co.

Michael Smith, COO, American Health Network

Richard Thompson, president, R. F. Thompson Investments

Jean Whitcraft, educator

Christine Woodward-Duncan, senior vice president/market manager, Emmis Communications

Eiteljorg Museum Board of Advisors *(as of 12/31/98)*

Russell Breeden III, Community First Financial Group
George P. Broadbent, president, The Skinner & Broadbent Co.
Harrison Eiteljorg II
James S. Eiteljorg
Majie Failey
Fred Fehsenfeld, president, Asphalt Materials Inc.
Dan Fitzgibbon, Barnes & Thornburg
Karen Glaser
J. Joseph Hale, president, Cinergy Foundation
James Kittle Jr., chairman & CEO, Kittle's Furniture
Wendy Kortepeter
Skip Lange, Pictorial Inc.
Dave Lucas, president, Sunshine Productions
H. Roll McLaughlin, retired
Hilary Salatich, regional marketing director, Conseco Capital Management
Fay W. Williams, attorney
Tim Wright, managing director, KeyBank

Board Officers

Michael L. Eagle, chairman
Roger Eiteljorg, vice chairman
Glenn W. Irwin Jr., vice chairman
Michael P. Skehan, treasurer
Jean Whitcraft, secretary

Founding Directors

Robert Baxter
Tom Binford*
Harrison Eiteljorg*
J. B. King
Glenn W. Irwin Jr.
William K. McGowan Jr.
Chris Schenkel
June Swango
Donald Tanselle
Jean Whitcraft

*deceased

From the Chairman

The Eiteljorg Museum has begun its push into the next century with the beginning of Phase II of the expansion plan. The construction of the new underground parking facility and entry tower starts the first step in the growth of the museum. This growth will allow the Eiteljorg to continue its commitment to excellence in the arts of Native Americans and the West, and also to offer more programs that will maintain the tradition of distinction the museum has set in the past.

The enabling force behind the expansion has been the *Eye on the Future* capital/endowment campaign. I am happy to report that the campaign has been a great success, generating more than $17 million in two years. This accomplishment will allow the museum to offer larger gallery spaces, artist-in-residence programs and educational activities to supplement exhibitions. I would like to thank all the individuals and organizations that have contributed to the *Eye on the Future* campaign.

Expansion is not contained to our corner of White River State Park, however. The park is alive with the construction of three cultural facilities. Construction will begin this summer on what will become the Eiteljorg's closest neighbor, the new Indiana Museum. Just west of that will be the new home of the NCAA headquarters, featuring the Hall of Champions, a museum dedicated to collegiate athletes. Just across White River will be White River Gardens, the newest addition to an already wonderful Indianapolis Zoo. On the north side of the canal will stand a beautiful monument to Congressional Medal of Honor recipients. And the new Indiana Historical Society is within walking distance of the park and will open this summer. These additions to an already impressive list of cultural sites in Indianapolis will greatly increase the city's reputation as a center for the arts.

The Eiteljorg Museum was excited this past year to be part of an important, nationally traveling exhibition. *Powerful Images: Portrayals of Native America* opened in September of 1998 and was created by Museums West, a consortium of which the Eiteljorg is a part. This exhibition, which featured multimedia displays chronicling the images of Native Americans in "popular" culture and in their own art, became a traveling ambassador for the museum and Museums West.

Sadly, the Eiteljorg lost a long-time friend when Tom Binford died at the age of 74. Tom was one of the 10 founding directors of the museum and sat on the board of directors until his death. Tom involved himself in many community-related causes and served Indianapolis as one of its finest citizens. He will be greatly missed not only by his friends at the Eiteljorg, but by Indianapolis as a whole.

On behalf of the Eiteljorg Museum board of directors, I would like to thank the staff and volunteers of the museum for their dedication and hard work in 1998. I also would like to thank all the guests and especially the members of the museum, whose continuing support has made the Eiteljorg one of the gems of Indianapolis. With expansion underway, a larger endowment, Phase II of *Eye on the Future* progressing, and many exciting programs and exhibitions planned, the Eiteljorg Museum will become a more significant regional and national institution.

Michael L. Eagle

Michael L. Eagle
Chairman, Eiteljorg Museum Board of Directors

From the President

This past year was one of excitement and a glimpse into the future for the museum!

Phase I of our expansion plans began with the ground breaking of our new parking facility and entry tower on July 7. The new parking garage will add 191 spaces to the existing IMAX" underground garage dedicated to the Eiteljorg. We would like to thank all of our guests for enduring our growing pains, and we're excited to bring back to the community the museum's famous landmark, our deer fountain, as construction is completed.

The expansion has been made possible by the continuing success of the *Eye on the Future* capital/endowment campaign, which by 1998 raised more than $17.7 million in funds through the generosity of the entire community in just over two years.

In June 1996, the museum proposed and Lilly Endowment Inc. agreed that if the museum's *Eye on the Future* campaign raised up to $10 million by November 1998, the Endowment would pledge 50 cents on the dollar of all funds donated. Gifts by philanthropist Allen W. Clowes, a joint gift by Eli Lilly Co. and Guidant Corp., and the first gift ever by the Nina Mason Pulliam Charitable Trust pushed the campaign over the $10 million mark, and I'm happy to report that the maximum Endowment donation of $5 million was achieved. The museum also received a generous $1 million donation from Christel De Haan to name the new outdoor sculpture garden and courtyard alongside the canal north of the museum.

This year, the museum saw the creation of its first nationally touring exhibit, *Powerful Images: Portrayals of Native America.* This multimedia exhibition brought together the treasures of 10 of the nation's most important museums of Native Americans and Western art and demonstrated the power of national collaboration. In addition, education programs such as lectures, family classes and workshops, family activity guides and other public programs all were held in conjunction with the exhibition.

The museum's Great Hall received a new occupant this year as "Morning Prayer," a bronze statue by renowned Native American artist Allan Houser, was unveiled in November. This magnificent piece, which portrays an Apache serenely murmuring the daily prayer, was acquired with the help of Mel and Joan Perelman. The bronze sculpture is a significant work by one of the most influential contemporary Native American artists, and we are proud to say that a piece of Allan Houser's legacy is now in our collection.

The museum welcomed more than 100,000 visitors in 1998! The museum's festivals were once again a success, with our annual Indian Market drawing 8,000 visitors in June and our Western Festival drawing more than 4,600. We also welcomed 10,000 visitors through facility rentals, which in 1998 numbered more than 130.

I would like to welcome our new chairman of the board, Mike Eagle, and thank our outgoing chairman, Robert Salyers, for all the leadership, hard work and love he has given to this organization.

This was an exciting year for the museum in all aspects. With the success of the *Eye on the Future* capital/endowment campaign, the beginning of the museum's expansion plan, and the continued dedication of the museum's staff, volunteers and members in 1998, I am sure that 1999 will bring even greater achievements for the Eiteljorg.

John Vanausdall

John Vanausdall
President and CEO

"A very thoughtful combination of artifacts, art, and oral histories."
Visitor quote from *Powerful Images*

Tonto Poster
Wheaties cereal premium
Autry Museum of
Western Heritage
From the exhibit
Powerful Images: Portrayals of Native America

Radio
Richard Swanson
From *New Art of the West 6*

American Indian Gothic
David Bradley (Chippewa/Lakota)
From the exhibit *Powerful Images: Portrayals of Native America*

Shield
19th c.
Dog Men Warrior
Tsistsistas (Cheyenne)
From the exhibit
Gifts of the Spirit

*"I am very impressed.
I don't usually like modern art,
but this is very enjoyable."*
Visitor quote from *New Art of the West 6*

Celebrating Voices of America

The Cinergy Foundation gave the Eiteljorg Museum a generous grant of $50,000 grant to support *1998: Celebrating Voices of America,* the name given to the museum's year-long cultural calendar of exhibitions, events and educational programs addressing various cultures.

Celebrating Voices of America represented the museum's focus on reaching out to the community and delivering educational programs to and about people who have not traditionally been served by museums.

That effort will continue in 1999 and beyond. We're grateful to Cinergy for making this first step possible.

"Gifts of the Spirit" Exhibition Shows Humor

"People take art and Native American culture so seriously. But there's humor there, and one can learn from it," said Jennifer Complo, curator of contemporary art.

Gifts of the Spirit: Works by Nineteenth-Century and Contemporary Native American Artists featured some of the finest ancient artworks in existence, as well as works by today's foremost Native American artists.

Several pieces made viewers smile or even laugh out loud. A "Winking Mask," made by an Inuit artist in the late 19th century, is a fox who appears to be winking. Was he teasing a hunter? And was Richard Glazer-Danay teasing viewers with his "Bingo War Bonnet"—a construction worker's hard hat decorated with stars, leather, a watch face, letters that spell BINGO and plastic, rolling eyes?

The older pieces were gathered early in the 19th century by sea captains and missionaries in Salem, Mass., and included exceptional works and rare masterpieces. The newer pieces were selected for this exhibit based on their artistic quality and their relationship to the historical works in the exhibition.

Continent-wide Collaboration Produces Powerful Exhibition

The Eiteljorg's collaboration with the Museums West group of museums produced great dividends as the exhibition *Powerful Images: Portrayals of Native America* opened in September.

Powerful Images: Portrayals of Native America was a thought-provoking multimedia exhibition about the perceptions and stereotypes surrounding Native American images in cultural history. The exhibit compared the "popular" images of Native Americans in mainstream literature, art, film, and how Native Americans represent themselves through their own art. The pieces in the exhibit were a varied collection from the Museums West group and featured works of popular culture, art, and contemporary pieces by Native Americans.

National sponsors were Ford Motor Co., National Endowment for the Humanities, the Rockefeller Foundation and the National Endowment for the Arts.

Museums West is a consortium of 10 of North America's most important museums of Native America and Western art and includes U.S. and Canadian museums. The exhibition was developed by these institutions, funded by a few lead project donors and by the institutions themselves, and created for circulation to virtually all of the members of the group. The Eiteljorg's contribution to the exhibit included much of the contemporary art and the design of the exhibit itself, done by the Eiteljorg's long-time designer, Larry Samuels, who passed away before he could see the exhibit assembled.

The concept of a collaboration among the Museums West institutions took many years to build into a wonderful traveling exhibition, but with the framework in place, the Eiteljorg's involvement with this respected group will continue to produce exhibitions of the highest cultural and educational quality.

Acquisitions

Collection Is Enriched by Acquisitions

The museum adds to its collections through gifts of artworks by individuals, corporations and groups and through purchases from the biennial exhibition *New Art of the West.*

New Art of the West 6 in 1998 resulted in sales totaling $80,815, a record for the series. The museum earned more than $19,000 in commissions, also a record, and acquired nine pieces—yet another record—for its permanent collection. We thank those who bought works from the exhibition. Twenty artists each displayed three juried works in this eclectic exhibit, which featured oil paintings, oversized straw tops, granite and bronze sculptures and large paintings inspired by and resembling old family photographs.

The museum bought:

- "Plateau Geometric #103," 1997, by Joe Feddersen (Colville Confederated Tribes)
- "Thunderhead," 1997, by Joe Maktima (Laguna Pueblo/Hopi)
- "Radio," 1997, by Richard Swanson
- "Bucephalus," 1997, by Ashley Collins
- "Rain of Words," ca. 1990, by Larry Samuels, a former museum employee who died in 1997.

In addition, these generous friends donated artwork from the exhibition:

- Gail Kirchner donated Feddersen's "Plateau Geometric #122," 1998
- Stan and Sandy Hurt donated "Blue Evening Colorado," 1996, by Ken Holder
- Artist Mary Koga donated two of her black-and-white photos of the Hutterites, "Making Noodles" and "Nursery School," both 1995

Other 1998 Acquisitions

Suzann R. Gates gave the following works by artist Gene Kloss:

Penitente Fires, 1939, Drypoint, aquatint

Taos Pueblo Stream, 1983, Etching, drypoint

Cherry Blossom Time, 1960, Drypoint, soft ground

Clouds at Sunset, 1953, Drypoint and aquatint

Navajo Canyon Cliffs, 1974, Etching, drypoint

Winter Sunrise, 1977, Etching

Return of the Pack Train, 1983, Etching, drypoint, aquatint

Along the Roaring Fork, 1973, Etching, drypoint

The Journey, 1967, Intaglio

Christmas Eve–Taos Pueblo, 1946, Etching

Rifle
ca. 1900
Winchester Repeating Arms Co.
Steel, wood
Gift: Courtesy of Ralph E. Armstrong & John R. Armstrong

Woman's Ensemble
ca. late 1940s/early 1950s
Navajo
Cloth, silver, leather, wool
Gift of Bruce O. Young

Ribbon Dress Dancer
1995, Laurie Houseman-White Hawk (Winnebago/Santee Dakota)
Gouache
Gift of Charlotte Mittler

Flute–"Thanks for the Memories"
1998, Eugene Brown (Miami)
Wood, paint, sinew, pipe stone
Gift: Courtesy of Eugene Brown

Resource 34

Girl Talk

1998, Linda Haukaas (Native American)

Ink and color pencil

Museum purchase, with funds provided by Arnold & Carol Jolles

Deer and the Moon

1942, Woodrow "Woody" Wilson Crumbo (Creek/Potawatomi)

Oil on canvasboard

Gift: Courtesy of Raymond and Billie Lee on the occasion of their 50th wedding anniversary

Beaded Pictorial Basket

ca. 1930, Paiute

Willow, glass beads

Museum purchase

Beaded Pictorial Basket

ca. 1930, Paiute

Willow, glass beads

Museum purchase

Morning Prayer, 1987

Cast 1997, Allan Houser

(Chiricahua Apache)

Cast bronze

Museum purchase, with funds provided by Joan and Mel Perelman

Bison of North America

1991, William Arthur Galloway

Indiana limestone

Gift: Courtesy of NBD, N.A.

Wisdom Keepers

1998, Bruce La Fountain

(Turtle Mountain Chippewa)

Cast bronze

Gift of Mike & Juanita Eagle, Terry & Becky Rader & the artist

Four Worlds

1972, Milland Lomakema (Hopi)

Gouache

Anonymous gift

1997 Acquisitions

Direction of the Center of My Heart

1995, Bernadette Vigil

Oil on canvas

Gift: Courtesy of Mr. & Mrs. C. D. Anderson

Flute

1997, Eugene Brown (Miami)

Poor man's walnut, red cedar, oak, sinew, paint

Presented to the Eiteljorg Museum in recognition of the opening of the exhibition "In the Presence of the Past"

The First Time He Saw Her Face

1997, Thomas F. Haukaas

(Rosebud Sioux)

Colored pencil and ink on ledger paper

Gift: Courtesy of Gail C. Kirchner in memory of her parents, Edwin and Evalyn Carroll

The Parley
1907, after Frederic Remington
Color halftone
Gift: Courtesy of Patricia Brown Snyder

The Great Explorers IV—Raddison
1907, after Frederic Remington
Color halftone
Gift: Courtesy of Patricia Brown Snyder

The Howl of the Weather (The Squall)
1907, after Frederic Remington
Color halftone
Gift: Courtesy of Patricia Brown Snyder

Downing the Nigh Leader (The Attack)
1907, after Frederic Remington
Color halftone
Gift: Courtesy of Patricia Brown Snyder

Self-Portrait
ca. 1960–73, Norval Morriseau
(Ojibwa)
Acrylic on paper
Gift: Courtesy of Dr. & Mrs. Hanus Grosz in memory of Jim Lawton, founder of the Museum of Indian Heritage

Bust of Harrison Eiteljorg
1997, George Carlson
Cast bronze
Gift: Courtesy of the Eiteljorg Museum Board of Directors

Gauntlets
ca. 1890, Yakima
Leather, glass beads
Gift: Courtesy of Albert T. Chapman III (Lafayette, IN) in memory of Albert T. Chapman Sr. (1887–1953)

Night Guard
1851, Robert A. Scott
Casein
Gift of the Robert A. Scott family in his loving memory

Eiteljorg Museum Now Owns Another Houser

An imposing figure now graces the Grand Hall of the Eiteljorg Museum. The larger-than-life Native American figure is "Morning Prayer," a bronze statute by acclaimed Native American artist Allan Houser (Chiricahua Apache). The acquisition of the sculpture, which is 9½ feet tall and weighs 1,200 pounds, of an Apache serenely murmuring the daily prayer was made possible by the Perelman Charitable Fund.

Allan Houser, who died in 1994, is known as the patriarch of contemporary Native American fine art. He has influenced countless artists and has left a legacy of artwork of immeasurable, timeless beauty.

Members of Houser's family attended the unveiling of the sculpture on Nov. 10, 1998. The sculpture is the third of only five castings.

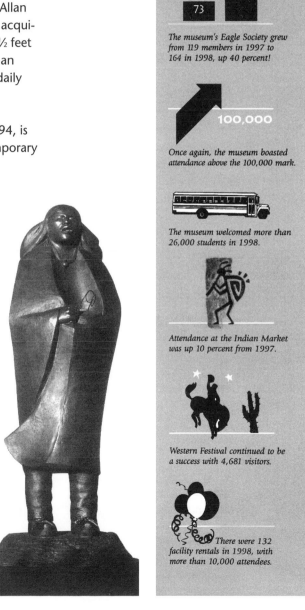

Morning Prayer, 1987
cast 1997, Allan Houser (Chiricahua Apache)
Cast bronze
Museum purchase, with funds provided by Joan and Mel Perelman

CONTINUED GROWTH IN 1998

73   164

The museum's Eagle Society grew from 119 members in 1997 to 164 in 1998, up 40 percent!

100,000

Once again, the museum boasted attendance above the 100,000 mark.

The museum welcomed more than 26,000 students in 1998.

Attendance at the Indian Market was up 10 percent from 1997.

Western Festival continued to be a success with 4,681 visitors.

There were 132 facility rentals in 1998, with more than 10,000 attendees.

Resource 34

Indian Market

A Year of "Firsts" at Indian Market

This was a year of firsts for the sixth annual Indian Market.

For the first time, the museum received 175 applications from artists wanting to take part in the event—a new record!

For the first time, the market featured a menu of Native American food prepared under the direction of a Native American chef, Lucille Calabaza-King (San Ildefonso). All American Catering prepared the Native American and the festival food.

Two Native American dance groups made their first appearances at the Indian Market: The White Mountain Apache Crown Dancers from Arizona and the Western Tennessee Choctaw Dance Group.

For the first time, White River Trader, the museum store, sold games and activities related to the people and events spotlighted at the Indian Market. These affordable items helped children and adults carry the Indian Market experience home with them.

And for the first time, the Indian Market was named to the Top 100 Events in North America by the American Bus Association and was listed in Indian Artist Magazine's Top 10 list of national Indian markets.

Indian Market Division Winners

Clarence Lee (Navajo) won Best of Show at the Eiteljorg Museum's sixth annual Indian Market, June 27 & 28. The winning piece, "Squaw Dance," was a stunning box embellished inside and out with people, animals, buildings and windmills made of silver, copper, turquoise, coral, tiger eye, malica, jet and lapis.

Best of Show	*Pottery (Traditional)*
Clarence Lee	Steve Lucas
Paintings, Drawings, Prints	*Pottery (Nontraditional)*
Dawn Dark Mountain	Pahponee
Fine Art Sculpture	*Basketry*
Cliff Fragua	Squirrel Croslin
Carvings and Dolls	*Weavings*
Tom Haukaas	Mona Laughing
Jewelry (Traditional)	*Textiles and Attire*
Joe and Terry Reano	Emil Woody Richards
Jewelry (Nontraditional)	*Miscellaneous Art*
Clarence Lee	Chandler Good Strike

Marsh Supermarket's Harvest Celebration
Explores Centuries-Old "Thanksgiving"

In November, the museum celebrated harvest time the way Native Americans have done for centuries. The Eiteljorg's second annual Harvest Celebration consisted of four authentic Native American meals and allowed guests to sample and learn about food sources from Native American food expert Carolyn Raine of Seneca heritage. Guests also were treated to Native American music and a six-course meal, which was organized by event manager Gwen Yeaman of Ottawa/Chippewa and Penobscott heritage. Don Secondine (Delaware) treated guests to live flute music and enchanting stories.

The Harvest Celebration was expanded from the first event in 1997 due to its overwhelming popularity. About 240 people took part in the event. The 1998 Harvest Celebration was presented by Marsh Supermarkets.

As the Miami Indians Exhibition Closed, a Miami Leader
and Museum Friend Passed Away

Best Closing Exhibit

Eiteljorg Museum's bold two-year mega-installation about the Miami Nation of Indiana, which closed last week, broke records for attendance. Over 150,000 visitors, including students from 79 of Indiana's 92 counties, experienced five centuries of Miami culture through state-of-the-art exhibits to learn about our region's original settlers.

Visitors came away with more than wonderment about sophisticated tools, clothing, mobile homes, sustenance agriculture and transcontinental trade. They learned, too, of the military leadership of Chief Little Turtle, whose confederation of tribes defeated two American armies in 1790 and 1791; a blow not to be repeated until the attack on Pearl Harbor in 1941.

Not until 1794 could General Anthony Wayne's forces overcome the Indians' defense of their jurisdiction over their traditional homeland.

Non-Indians swarmed over the lands that had supported a people since before Columbus. By 1846 the Miami population in Indiana decreased to a mere fourth of their usual number. Three hundred and twenty-seven, against their will, were removed to a reservation in Kansas. One hundred and forty-eight Miamis remained in Indiana.

Defying extinction, both groups furtively clung to traditional ways. This is perhaps the amazing gift of our state's namesake people: endurance in the face of unspeakable inhumanity. The exhibit is gone but the Miami People are still here, intending to walk with determination into the new century.

—Rita Kohn, *NUVO,* 10/8/98

On Nov. 5, 1998, the museum lost a great friend in Frances Dunnagan. Frances was vice chief of the Miami Nation of Indiana and was instrumental in creating *In the Presence of the Past: The Miami Indians of Indiana.* She helped the museum form a Miami Advisory Group, supported our presentations to the Miami Tribal Council, was a representative of the Miami to the media, and played a leading role in the video "Being Miami" that was shown in the exhibition.

We miss her kindness, her wisdom, her advice and her friendship.

Volunteers Are the Heart of the Eiteljorg

A gift that can't be forgotten is the spirit of volunteerism at the Eiteljorg. It is a gift to the community and to the museum's future.

In 1998, 817 volunteers logged a total of 11,620 hours of work as guides, greeters and volunteers for special events, including Indian Market and Western Festival, along with volunteers in the curatorial, fund-raising and administrative areas of the museum.

The volunteers not only assist our staff, but help create an environment focused on the community and community involvement. They also bring fresh ideas to the museum along with their energy and eagerness to share their knowledge.

The spirit of volunteerism starts at the very top of the organization, with a volunteer board of directors, *Eye on the Future* capital/endowment campaign, and board councils.

The museum welcomed its newest group of volunteers, the Adobe Society, in 1998. This group raised $25,000 for the museum with its first fund-raiser, the Buckaroo Bash.

The passing of knowledge, the help in understanding issues, and the "daily grind" of work volunteers give to the Eiteljorg are priceless gifts. Thank you, volunteers, for your time, effort and enthusiasm.

Volunteers Make Library a Reality

One of the most daunting tasks here at the Eiteljorg Museum has been the cataloguing our library holdings. This collection of more than 4,000 titles represents a valuable source of accurate information on all the subjects that are presented to the public.

In 1998, dedicated volunteers catalogued nearly 1,000 publications. This achievement, which was double the goal of 500, is the foundation for a professional resource open to staff, guides and colleagues. The museum extends a great deal of gratitude to all the dedicated individuals who have helped with this project.

Adobe Society Hits the Ground Running

The museum welcomed its newest volunteer group, the Adobe Society in 1998. The Adobe Society's goal is to assist, promote and support the mission of the Eiteljorg Museum through fund-raising, major events and community involvement.

The first Adobe Society-sponsored event was the opening gala for *New Art of the West 6*. Largely due to the Society's efforts, *New Art of the West 6* resulted in the highest sales ever for a *New Art* show.

The Society's next event was the first Buckaroo Bash. This outdoor event to kick off the museum's Western Festival featured a Western fashion show, a live auction of Western items including works by nationally known artists, and a live performance by the Alligator Brothers band.

Through its events in 1998, the Adobe Society raised $25,000 for the museum. If you're interested in joining this band of shakers and movers, call (317) 636-9378, ext. 111.

Adobe Society Steering Committee *(as of 12/31/1998)*

Karen Glaser *(Chair)*	Wendy Kortepeter	Cristy Sagalowsky
Mindy Eiteljorg	Carla Leppert	Ann Shane
Nancy Elder	Nancy McLane	Lisa Stewart
John Guggenheim	Mary McDowell	Janet Swiss
Linda Gray	Kim McManama	Roberta Walton
Debby Holton	Martha Plager	

1998 Notes of Interest

Huge Technological Strides Help Museum Better Serve Its Audiences

The Eiteljorg began not only its external expansion in 1998, but also its long-overdue technology upgrade. The museum purchased new computers and file servers to replace obsolete equipment that could no longer be serviced or supported, and upgraded from a 10-year-old, outdated DOS system to a Windows NT network. This upgrade provided staff with the tools needed to greatly increase productivity and efficiency, and also improved internal and external communications via a new e-mail/scheduling program.

Other major changes included the conversion to a new accounting system and to a new fund-raising software program. These upgrades also were a big step toward making sure that the museum's technical systems are Y2K compliant by the end of 1999.

The network required a major upgrade of the museum's infrastructure to Ethernet wiring, which was accomplished in part through a donation from the Indianapolis Rotary Club. The old computers were donated to the Boys and Girls Clubs of Indianapolis, which will use them at children's camps to teach the basics of computers. The museum also added a new graphic design workstation and vinyl cutter, which will allow the in-house production of signs and exhibition materials.

Toward the end of 1998, plans were finalized to purchase and install a new telephone/voice mail system. This new system, which replaces the museum's original, 10-year-old telephone system, allows the museum to better serve its constituents.

Two Awards Recognized the Excellence of the Eiteljorg's Programs and Staff

"Year of Miami Campaign" Presented with a VISTA. The Eiteljorg received a VISTA (Visitor Information, Service and Travel Award) at the 5th annual Indiana Travel Industry Awards. This award honors organizations that have had a lasting effect on Indiana tourism. The museum received a first-place award in the category of Advertising and Promotional Material for the "Year of the Miami" campaign that promoted the exhibition *In the Presence of the Past: The Miami Indians of Indiana.* Indiana's governor and lieutenant governor presented the award during the annual Hoosier Hospitality and Tourism Conference and Expo in March.

Tourism and Marketing Projects Manager Honored with Enjoy Indiana Hospitality Award. Lisa Duda, tourism and marketing projects manager at the Eiteljorg Museum, was the recipient of the first Lt. Governor's Enjoy Indiana Hospitality Awards for Central Indiana. The award, which honors those who make "Hoosier Hospitality" a reality, was presented at the Eiteljorg during National Tourism Week in May.

Educational Programs Expanded the Museum's Reach Beyond the Exhibition Audience

The museum was full of skeletons and ghosts as the Eiteljorg took part in the celebration of *El Dia de los Muertos.* "The Day of the Dead" at the end of October is a traditional holiday from Mexico and the Southwestern United States. During this colorful festival, the spirits of the dead are said to return and visit the living.

Museum visitors learned about this festival and created their own traditional sugar skulls and paper skull masks to take home.

A popular holiday event returned to the Eiteljorg this year.

Las Posadas, which is Spanish for "the inns," tells the story of how Joseph and Mary searched Bethlehem for a place to stay just before Jesus was born. *Las Posadas* participants recreated this journey in song. A candlelit procession formed behind two chorale leaders and made its way along a specified route, then stopped at the doors of the museum to ask if there was any room at the "inn." The doors swung open in welcome, and visitors entered the museum for refreshments, games and shopping at White River Trader.

This holiday tradition comes from the Southwest and Mexico, where it has been celebrated for centuries. The program was co-hosted by St. Patrick Church. In lieu of an admission fee, *Las Posadas* participants brought canned food to donate to the St. Patrick food pantry.

EYE ON THE FUTURE

Eye on the Future Campaign Celebrates Success in Raising $17.7 Million

Staff, volunteers and donors gathered in November to celebrate the success of Phase 1 of the *Eye on the Future* capital/endowment campaign. More than $17.7 million was raised during the first two years with gifts and pledges from more than 450 donors. Special thanks were given to:

- Lilly Endowment, Inc.
- Dr. Sonja Eiteljorg
- Nina Mason Pulliam Charitable Trust
- Christel De Haan Family Foundation
- Joan and Mel Perelman
- Eli Lilly & Company/Guidant Corporation and their corporate families
- The Indianapolis Foundation, an Affiliate of the Central Indiana Community Foundation

The Eiteljorg thanks all those who have contributed to the *Eye on the Future* campaign, particularly those who also continued or increased their annual gifts.

Eye on the Future Campaign Cabinet

Ronald W. Dollens, Co-Chair	John E. D. Peacock Jr.
Stan C. Hurt, Co-Chair	Steve Radcliffe
Elizabeth R. Dietz	Bonnie A. Reilly
Michael L. Eagle	Frank E. Russell
Roger S. Eiteljorg	Hilary Stout Salatich
J. Joseph Hale Jr.	Robert J. Salyers
Betsey Harvey	Michael L. Smith
Douglas W. Huemme	E. Andrew Steffen
Carolyn Kincannon	Sam B. Sutphin
Leslie D. Michael	Richard F. Thompson
Gerald Paul	J. Smoke Wallin
Alexander G. Peacock	Christine Woodward-Duncan

Harrison Eiteljorg Society

The Harrison Eiteljorg Society was established in the spring of 1998 to honor those donors who have made bequests to the Eiteljorg, and to encourage others to do so.

Individuals who notify the museum of bequests by Dec. 31, 1999, will be recognized as charter members of the society.

Charter Members

In July, the Eiteljorg Museum broke ground for its 200-space, underground parking garage and new entry tower. The first phase of construction is scheduled for completion in the summer of 1999.

A special thanks to the following contributors for their gifts and pledges to the museum's *Eye on the Future* Campaign as of Dec. 31, 1998:*

Grand Canyon Society   Sonoran Desert Society

Rocky Mountain Society   Sierra Nevada Society

Great Plains Society   Cascades Society

Yellowstone Society   Mesa Society

Rio Grande Society   Black Hills Society

Grand Teton Society

*Names of contributors in each category have been omitted due to space considerations.

A special thanks to the following in-kind contributors for their services to the museum's *Eye on the Future* campaign:

All-American Picnic Co.   Mario Noche

Browning Day Mullins Dierdorf Inc.   National Wine & Spirits

Carey Color   Pearson Crahan Fletcher England

Carmel Trophies Plus   Shepard Poorman
                                        Graphic Arts Center
Jan & French Eason
                                        Telematrix
Hyatt Hotel & Resorts
                                        Susan Thomas
InstyPrints

Operating Income and Expenses

Income: $4,122,954

Grants: $1,492,531

Contributions & In-Kind: $835,199

Interest: $488,250

Admissions: $156,183

Memberships: $119,765

Merchandising & Product Development: $593,974

Special Events: $314,677

Building Rental: $119,405

Miscellaneous: $2,970

Expenses: $3,878,464

Development: $252,154

Public Relations & Marketing: $396,207

Building Services: $701,102

Exhibitions/Education/Events & Programs/In-Kind: $986,764

Administration: $660,350

Merchandising & Product Development: $509,862

Collection/Design: $372,025

A detailed Audited Financial Statement is available upon request.

Donations and Memberships*

President's Society, *$5,000 and up*

Golden Eagle Society, *$2,500–$4,999*

Eagle Society, *$1,000–$2,499*

Patron Society, *$500–$999*

Sustaining Members, *$250–$499*

Contributing Members, *$100–$249*

*Names of contributors in each category have been omitted due to space considerations.

1998 Annual Contributions

Harrison Eiteljorg Society

General Museum In-Kind Donors

Matching Gift Companies

In Memory of . . .

In Honor of . . .

Corporate and Foundation Gifts and Contributions

$5,000 and above

$1,000–$4,999

$500–$999

$250–$499

$50–$249

Grants

Indian Market

Sponsors

In-Kind Donors

Prize Money Sponsors

Western Festival

Sponsors

In-Kind Donors

Jammin' at the 'Jorg

Sponsors

In-Kind Donors

New Art of the West 6

Exhibit Sponsors

In-Kind Donors

Gifts of the Spirit: Works by 19th Century and Contemporary Native American Artists

Exhibit Sponsors

Harvest Celebration

Sponsor

Powerful Images: Portrayals of Native America

Exhibit Sponsors

In-Kind Donors

Splendid Heritage: Masterpieces of Native American Art from the Masco Collection

Exhibit Sponsor

Buckaroo Bash

Sponsors

Corporate Sponsors

Auction Donors

Staff Organization Chart *(as of 12/31/98)*

John Vanausdall, *President/CEO*

    Joyce Helvie, *Executive Assistant*

    Cynthia Schoolcraft, *Festivals Manager*

Arnold Jolles, *Vice President and Chief Curatorial Officer*

    Tricia O'Connor, *Administrative Assistant to the Vice President*

    Jennifer Complo, *Curator of Contemporary Art*

    Ray Gonyea, *Curator of Native American Art and Culture*

    Cathy Burton, *Director of Education*

        open, *Public Programs Manager*

        Carol Schilling, *Education Assistant (p-t)*

        Jan Eason, *Education Assistant (p-t)*

        Andy Mehall, *Education Assistant (p-t)*

    Bob Tucker, *Curator of Collections*

        Richard Harvey, *Preparator*

    Steve Sipe, *Director of Exhibition and Graphic Design*

Doug De Armond, *Facility Director*

    Ken Jackson, *Museum Safety and Security Manager*

    Steve Ham, *Maintenance Technician*

    Dzintars Sture, *Maintenance Assistant*

    Bob Schaaf, *Carpenter*

    Sandra Whitfield, *Event Operations/Housekeeping*

    Benny Grider, *Housekeeping*

    Bo Thomas, *Housekeeping*

    Jeff Young, *Housekeeping*

    Angela Morrow, *Administrative Assistant (p-t)*

Lynn Lambuth, *Director of Development*

    Sharon Hunt, *Capital/Endowment Campaign Manager*

        Kevin Roy, *Capital Campaign Associate*

    Phyllis Olson, *Manager of Volunteer Services*

    Julie Seward, *Corporate Campaign Manager*

Susie Berling, *Administrative Assistant*

Cara Lane, *Membership Manager*

Sally Dickson, *Grants Manager*

Julie Klaper, *Director of Marketing and Public Relations*

Cindy Dashnaw, *Manager of Communications*

Lisa Duda, *Tourism and Marketing Projects Manager*

Sherry Corbin, *Marketing and PR Assistant*

Judy Clayton, *Special Events Manager*

Susan Lewis, CPA, *Director of Finance and Administration*

June Padgett, *Accounting Assistant*

Fabiola Alcalde, *Accountant/Customer Service*

Ann Benthin, *Personnel Coordinator*

Dee McConville, *Manager of Technologies*

Antionette Maio, *Customer Service Manager*

Sherri Lay, *Receptionist/Office Assistant*

Kirsty Claffey, *Admissions Coordinator*

Phil Hundley, *Admissions & Reception Assistant (p-t)*

John Lippke, *Admissions Assistant (p-t)*

Kris Olson, *Administrative Assistant (p-t)*

Brenda Dillon, John Wyre, *Telephone Operators (p-t)*

Dru Doyle, *Director of Merchandising and Product Development*

Dawn Bridgwaters, *Merchandising Operations Manager*

Mary Downey, *Operations Assistant*

Gayle Decker, *Shipper/Receiver (p-t)*

Veronica McGlothlin, *Retail Supervisor*

Nicki Kasting, *Assistant Retail Supervisor*

Janice Young, *Sales Associate (p-t)*

This Annual Report Is Dedicated to the Memory of Tom Binford

The Eiteljorg Museum suffered a great loss this year when Tom Binford died on Jan. 14, 1999, at the age of 74.

Tom was a respected Indianapolis businessman, who also contributed to civic, educational and sporting causes. He served as director or chairman of numerous Indianapolis companies and organizations, was co-founder of the Urban League of Indianapolis, and was chief steward of the Indianapolis 500 from 1973 to 1995.

Tom was also a great supporter of the Eiteljorg Museum. Tom was one of the original 10 Founding Directors of the museum in June of 1988, served on the Eiteljorg Museum board of directors since that time, and was chairman of the Merchandising Council since its inception in 1995.

Tom Binford's dedication, not only to the Eiteljorg Museum but also to all the community groups and organizations he served during his lifetime, will be greatly missed.

Special thanks to John Messner for compiling this report.
Annual report designed by Honeymoon Image & Design Inc.

FINAL REPORT—CAPITAL CAMPAIGN

Table of Contents

Resource 35

Leadership Committee

Campaign Chair
Clark G. Quintin
V.P. & General Manager
Western Canada
IBM Canada Ltd.

Committee Members
Donald A. Calder
Vice President
Business Planning
B.C. Tel

Robert B. Findlay
President and CEO
MacMillan Bloedel Ltd.

Gerald F. Franciscovich (retired)
Former President
Chevron Canada Ltd.

Robert E. Kadlec
President and CEO
B.C. Gas Inc.

Alex E. Klopfer
President and CEO
Epic Data Inc.

William N. Palm
Senior VP, Information Services
Canadian Airlines International

Michael E. Phelps
President and CEO
Westcoast Energy Inc.

G. Wynne Powell
Vice President
Marketing & Retail Services
Technical Group
London Drugs Limited

J. J. Quinn
President
CIBC Mortgage Corporation

John P. Sheehan
Chief Financial Officer
& Senior V.P.
British Columbia
Hydro and Power Authority

Thomas A. Simons
President
H.A. Simons (International) Ltd.

Brian D. Sung
Regional Comptroller
Canadian Broadcasting
Corporation

Marie Taylor
Chairman
The Laurier Institute

John Watson
President
British Columbia
Institute of Technology

**Chair, School of Health
Sciences Campaign**
Dr. Peter Cooperberg
Professor of Radiology
UBC

**Chair, Campus Centre
Campaign**
Dr. Donald Rix, MD
President
Metro-McNair
Clinical Laboratories Ltd.

Chair, Public Affairs Committee
David A. Laundy
VP Public Affairs
Vancouver Stock Exchange

Chair, Family Campaign
Jim Mitchell
Director Campus Life/
Recreation & Athletic Services
BCIT

Campaign Chair's Message

In a world marked by falling trade barriers and new strategic alliances, there remains one constant essential to our global competitiveness and future prosperity—education. Through the High Tech, High Promise: The Drive for BCIT capital campaign, we have added over $13 million in capital to keep BCIT on the leading edge of advanced technology training in Canada. Such investment not only benefits B.C. business and industry but Canadian competitiveness as well. Our "High Tech" investment will undoubtedly yield many dividends through the "High Promise" of BCIT graduates.

While most contributions were directed to the acquisition of equipment and the upgrading of labs, we also established new scholarships and bursaries to help attract talented students to BCIT.

The President's Enterprise Fund was established to help keep BCIT innovative, flexible and technologically advanced through faculty and staff development.

The Campus Centre will create a hub of activity and interaction for the BCIT community and will serve as an enduring legacy of the success of our campaign.

As Chair of the High Tech, High Promise capital campaign, I thank every donor for their contribution. Your confidence in BCIT and support of their efforts are greatly appreciated. I would also like to thank each member of our campaign Leadership Committee, the Public Affairs Committee, the Campus Centre Committee and the BCIT Family Campaign Committee for their time, energy and commitment to raising funds on BCIT's behalf.

Also, my thanks to BCIT faculty and staff who dedicated countless hours in planning for and acquiring needed equipment.

The Drive for BCIT has brought new friends to BCIT and strengthened existing partnerships. As technology continues to advance, so too does the challenge to keep BCIT current. I hope you will all continue to support BCIT generously as "The Drive" continues.

Clark G. Quintin
Vice President and General Manager
Western Canada
IBM Canada Ltd.

[The report lists committee members' names here. They have been omitted for the sake of privacy.]

Public Affairs Committee	Campus Centre Campaign Committee	BCIT Family Campaign Committee	BCIT Development Office

President's Message

Throughout the High Tech, High Promise capital campaign, I have had the opportunity to talk with many of B.C.'s business leaders about their needs for advanced technology and trades training. Their message is clear: they like our job-ready graduates for two key reasons. First, their training is practical and applied, they are comfortable in technology-intensive environments and they quickly become productive employees. Second, our graduates are noted for their ability to work in teams and they have the drive, attitude and ability to succeed. I am committed to ensuring that the excellence in these skills and attributes employers value most will continue to be the hallmark of BCIT graduates.

As a result of the generous investment by our donors through the High Tech, High Promise capital campaign, we have added significantly to the capital resources we urgently require to modernize labs and equipment. Our resources to attract top students and enhance faculty and staff development have also expanded.

Perhaps the most significant accomplishment of the campaign has been the renewal of our partnership with business to meet our province's advanced technology, trades training and applied research needs. Together we can work to enhance the competitive position and future prosperity of British Columbians.

I would especially like to thank the B.C. Government for providing a $5 million fund to match private donations to the campaign. This initiative proved a tremendous asset in attracting private funds to the Institute.

My sincere thanks also to Clark Quintin, for his skillful and dedicated leadership of this campaign and to IBM Canada Ltd. for supporting the philanthropic efforts of their employees and BCIT. Our campaign Leadership Committee and BCIT faculty and staff also deserve our gratitude for their efforts raising funds on BCIT's behalf.

With the completion of this campaign, we will build on our new and existing partnerships to continue fundraising for institute priorities. With your continued support, BCIT will become Canada's leading Institute in advanced technology training, supplying business and industry with the work force and entrepreneurial spirit they need to prosper in our changing society.

John Watson
President
BCIT

Campaign Achievements

The major challenge of the High Tech, High Promise capital campaign was to update equipment and labs for advanced technology and trades training. Much of our equipment had outlived its usefulness and needed to be replaced in order to continue to produce job-ready graduates. Of the $10 million goal, $7.5 million

was earmarked for these purposes. Thanks to the generosity of our donors, with the added incentive of B.C. government matching funds, a total of $11.14 million was raised in gifts-in-kind and cash donations for equipment and labs at BCIT. Throughout the Institute, students and faculty are benefitting from access to current equipment and modern labs.

HIGH TECH, HIGH PROMISE
CAPITAL CAMPAIGN FUNDS RAISED

Gifts of Equipment	$ 4,888,860	
Gifts of Cash		
Allocated to a program area	$ 379,462	
Unrestricted	$ 1,100,759	
New Endowed Funds	$ 229,500	
B.C. Government Matching Funds	$ 5,000,000	
Total Campaign	$11,598,581	**$11,598,581**

ADDITIONAL FUNDS RAISED

Endowed Funds		
(includes B.C. Government Match)	$ 1,200,161	
Non-endowed Funds	$ 513,457	
Total	$ 1,713,618	**$ 1,713,618**
Total funds raised throughout		
the duration of the campaign		**$13,312,199**

School of Engineering Technology

From oscilloscopes to Geographic Information Systems software, gifts to the capital campaign have had a wide impact on the School of Engineering Technology. One highlight, in the Electronics Technology department, was the development of a complete state-of-the-art industrial controls systems lab centered around the donation by GE Fanuc Automation Canada Inc. and Gescan Ltd. of Programmable Logic Controllers, automation software and related computer circuit boards. This donation generated matching dollars sufficient to provide 12 new specialized workstations complete with 486 PC computers. The new facility provides students with the opportunity to analyse and program PLC equipment directly from the computer-based workstation.

In the Instrumentation option, Black and Baird Ltd. and Rosemount Instruments Ltd. both donated "smart" instrumentation in the form of flow, pressure, PH and conductivity sensor/transmitters. This equipment provides state-of-the-art equipment for measurement and control systems found in the pulp and paper, mining, petrochemical and other industries.

In the Power Option of Electronics Technology, a substantial donation of control equipment was received from Telemecanique Ltd. This equipment is similar in function to the PLC's given to the Instrumentation Option and provides an essential alternative in technology so that students receive training in various approaches as taken by different manufacturers.

In Telecommunications, the capital program generated the funds necessary for the purchase of highly sophisticated communications analyzers of the type currently used in the mobile radio and cellular communications industry.

The Erdas Inc. donation of the Erdas Software Lab Kit brought a new level of sophistication to the Geographic Information Systems technology. Not only does the software enable students to experience a powerful image processing system, it also links directly to the ARC/Info system providing access to computerized geographic modelling.

The Lynx Geosystems Inc. donation of Microlynx software brought leading mine planning technology to the Mining department. This comprehensive software package, developed partly in collaboration with BCIT Mining staff and students, enables students to experience mine planning as actually practiced in many mines throughout the world.

School of Business

Updating equipment that no longer met industry standards in the Broadcast Communications program was the major focus of fundraising activity in the School of Business. Thanks to the generosity of Sony of Canada Ltd., we now have five new studio cameras and the back-up support material to replace our existing 20 year old studio cameras. For the first time in years, BCIT has cameras which are fully operational and reliable. Faculty now use current equipment to demonstrate proper procedures to train our students. In addition, the technical quality of student video productions, including a weekly show called "BCIT Magazine," which is broadcast on cable systems throughout the province, has increased dramatically. Now students can direct more energy towards the creative elements of video production. At the recent national Jeffrey Reneau Awards Festival, BCIT won two of seven "Bessies" (out of 68 entries), the only Canadian post-secondary institute to win more than one award.

The matching funds for the Sony of Canada Ltd. donation were further used to update other areas in Broadcast Communications. The Radio program will enter the digital era with new production and on-air facilities and some new practice rooms. Further, Broadcast Journalism will receive a re-vamped newsroom for operation of our campus radio station, CFML.

Other Schools Benefitting

[Some descriptions have been omitted here for the sake of brevity.]

School of Trades Training

School of Health Sciences

Institutewide Gifts

Through their generous donation of equipment and services, IBM Canada Ltd. substantially increased the computing capability at BCIT both at institutional and student levels. Of particular benefit to students will be two new advanced microcomputer labs to be located in SW3 2675 and SW3 2625.

Cash Donations

Unrestricted cash donations are the foundation to a successful fundraising campaign. Through the High Tech, High Promise capital campaign, a total of $2,201,518 (including matching) in cash gifts and pledges was raised for BCIT to direct to areas of greatest need. We would like to extend our sincere thanks to the following donors for their gifts of cash and pledges to the campaign: Unitel Communications, Chevron Canada Ltd., Rogers Cable TV Ltd., Seaspan International Ltd., Royal Bank of Canada, B.C. Gas Inc., CIBC, MacMillan Bloedel Ltd., Canadian Energy Services, Westcoast Energy Inc., Sandwell Inc., Toronto Dominion Bank, Imperial Oil, B.C. Tel, Pacific Foundation of Applied Technology, Weldwood of Canada Ltd., Bank of Montreal, Bank of Nova Scotia, and the Larkspur Foundation.

New Endowments

B.C. Hydro Library Renewal Trust

The B.C. Hydro Library Renewal Trust was established to provide funds for new acquisitions by BCIT's permanent library collection in order to ensure quality and accessibility of the library resource to students and faculty.

President's Enterprise Fund

With a donation from the Hongkong Bank of Canada, the President's Enterprise Fund was established. Designed to foster staff development, the fund will be used to keep BCIT innovative, flexible and advanced, and will enable the BCIT President to pursue creative strategies for promoting advanced technology and entrepreneurship in B.C.

Scholarship and Bursary Endowments

In addition to contributions to existing endowments, many new endowments were established during this campaign.

Constructions Specifications Canada

The Constructions Specifications Canada endowment will provide an annual award to a student in the School of Engineering Technology, Building Technology program.

The George Nelson Muir Memorial Fund

This endowment was established by the Real Estate Board of Greater Vancouver to support students in the Marketing Management program, Real Estate Option.

The D. Letkeman and D. Utz Memorial Endowment Fund

With matching funds from the B.C. Government, Gulf Canada Resources Limited made a contribution towards this endowment, which provides an annual award to a student in the Surveying and Mapping Technology program.

Pacific Foundation of Applied Technology, Otto A. Kloss Entrance Awards

The Pacific Foundation of Applied Technology made a substantial contribution towards this existing endowment with B.C. Government matching funds, through the campaign. The endowment provides entrance scholarships for students entering specific entry-level trades training programs and other preemployment programs in the School of Trades Training.

The BCIT Staff: High Tech, High Promise
Capital Campaign Bursary and Award

This endowment was established through the fundraising efforts of BCIT faculty and staff in support of BCIT students. By October 30, 1992, the BCIT Family Campaign had raised in excess of $14 thousand towards the High Tech, High Promise capital campaign through a variety of activities and events including the Drive for 500 Lottery, Christmas poinsettia sales, Mother's Day hanging basket sales and Country Hoe Down '92, a barn dance. The endowment will provide bursaries for students with financial need and will recognize students who participate voluntarily in support of their school.

Donors

Our sincere thanks to the following corporations, groups, and individuals who gave generously to the Capital Campaign from December 1, 1989, to November 30, 1992 (list of donors follows here).

And the Drive Continues . . .

The High Tech, High Promise Capital Campaign has modernized equipment and labs to meet the training needs of the 1990s. To continue to meet the challenges of rapidly advancing technology, particularly in times of government restraint, BCIT will continue to look to the private sector for leadership and support. Together, we can prepare B.C. for the challenges of a global society.

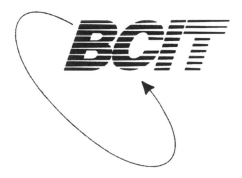

REFERENCES

Abzug, R., and Webb, N. "Rational and Extrarational Motivations for Corporate Giving: Complementing Economic Theory with Organizational Science." *New York Law School Law Review*, Apr. 1, 1997, pp. 1035–1058.

American Association of Fund-Raising Counsel. *AAFRC Book on Fund-Raising Consulting 1998*. New York: American Association of Fund-Raising Counsel, 1998.

American Association of Fund-Raising Counsel Trust for Philanthropy. *Giving USA, 1986*. New York: American Association of Fund-Raising Counsel Trust for Philanthropy, 1986.

American Association of Fund-Raising Counsel Trust for Philanthropy. *Giving USA, 1997*. New York: American Association of Fund-Raising Counsel Trust for Philanthropy, 1997.

American Association of Fund-Raising Counsel Trust for Philanthropy. "Annual Survey of State Laws Regulating Charitable Solicitations as of January 1, 1998." *Giving USA Update*, 1998a, *1*, pp. 1–7.

American Association of Fund-Raising Counsel Trust for Philanthropy. *Giving USA, 1998*. New York: American Association of Fund-Raising Counsel Trust for Philanthropy, 1998b.

American Association of Fund-Raising Counsel Trust for Philanthropy. *Giving USA, 1999*. New York: American Association of Fund-Raising Counsel Trust for Philanthropy, 1999.

Anderson, G. M. "At Home on the Gift Range." *CASE Currents*, May 1986, pp. 42–44.

Arenson, K. W. "$100 Million Donation to Cornell for Medicine." *New York Times*, May 1, 1998, p. A27.

Asp, J. W., II. "Pay for Performance." *CASE Currents*, July-Aug. 1999, pp. 29–33.

Association of Fundraising Professionals. *The Survey Course on Fund Raising Fundamentals*. Alexandria, Va.: NSFRE Institute, 1985.

Association of Fundraising Professionals. *Certified Fund Raising Executive (CFRE) Candidate Handbook*. Alexandria, Va.: CFRE Professional Certification Board, National Society of Fund Raising Executives, 1998.

Association of Fundraising Professionals. *1999 Membership Survey Profile.* Alexandria, Va.: National Society of Fund Raising Executives, 1999.

A. T. Kearney, Inc. *Indiana University Foundation: Building a Long-Term Strategic Plan.* Chicago: A. T. Kearney, Inc., 1997.

Banard, J. "Corporate Philanthropy, Executives' Pet Charities, and the Agency Problem." *New York Law School Law Review,* Apr. 1997, pp. 1147–1178.

Barth, S. "Finding the Needle in the Haystack: Use Computer Screening and Database Analysts to Discover the Hidden Major-Gift Prospects Among Your Alumni." *CASE Currents,* June 1998, pp. 32–36.

Baxter, F. R. "Prospect Management." Unpublished paper, University of California–Berkeley, 1987.

Berry, M. *Native American Philanthropy: Expanding Social Participation and Self-Determination.* Cultures of Caring Council on Foundations, 1999.

Billian, J. M. "Prospect Research, Evaluation, Cultivation, and Solicitation." Presentation made at the annual Council for Advancement and Support of Education conference, Nashville, Tenn., Mar. 1985.

Blum, D. E., and Dundjerski, M. "Foundation's Giving Surges." *Chronicle of Philanthropy,* Feb. 25, 1999, pp. 1–22.

Broce, T. E. *Fund Raising.* Norman: University of Oklahoma Press, 1979.

Bryson, J. M. *Strategic Planning for Public and Nonprofit Organizations: A Guide for Strengthening and Sustaining Organizational Achievement.* (Rev. ed.) San Francisco: Jossey-Bass, 1995.

Builta, J. *The Campaign Manuals* (2 vols.). Cleveland, Ohio: Third Sector Press, 1984.

Campbell, D. A., Jr. "The Capital Campaign: Soliciting the Lead Gift(s)." Presentation made at the annual Council for Advancement and Support of Education District VI conference, St. Louis, Mo., Jan. 1985.

Capek, M.E.S. *Women and Philanthropy: Old Stereotypes, New Challenges.* Princeton, N.J.: Princeton University Press, 1997.

"Charitable Giving by People of Color: African Americans, Asian Americans, Latinos, and Native Americans." *Giving USA Update,* 1999, *2,* 1-2, 11-12.

Chesterman, M. *Charities, Trusts, and Social Welfare.* London: Weidenfeld & Nicholson, 1975.

Chewning, P. B. "The Attitudes of Alumni Nondonors, Donors, and Consecutive Donors Toward Drake University." Unpublished doctoral dissertation, Drake University, 1984.

Conrad, D. L. *How to Solicit Big Gifts.* San Francisco: Public Management Institute, 1978.

Contract with America: The Bold Plan by Rep. Newt Gingrich, Rep. Dick Armey, and the House Republicans to Change the Nation. New York: Times Books, 1994.

Council for Advancement and Support of Education. *CASE Campaign Standards: Management and Reporting Standards for Educational Fund-Raising Campaigns.* Washington, D.C.: Council for Advancement and Support of Education, 1996a.

Council for Advancement and Support of Education. *CASE Management Reporting Standards.* Washington, D.C.: Council for Advancement and Support of Education, 1996b.

Dove, K. E. "Changing Strategies for Meeting Campaign Goals." In A. W. Rowland (ed.), *Handbook of Institutional Advancement.* San Francisco: Jossey-Bass, 1986.

Dove, K. E. *Conducting a Successful Capital Campaign: A Comprehensive Fundraising Guide for Nonprofit Organizations.* (1st ed.) San Francisco, Calif.: Jossey-Bass, 1988.

Dove, K. E. *Conducting a Successful Capital Campaign: The New, Revised, and Expanded Edition of the Leading Guide to Planning and Implementing a Capital Campaign.* (2nd ed.) San Francisco: Jossey-Bass, 2000.

"Drake University Receives $50 Million Gift from Dwight Opperman and Launches $190 Million Campaign." Press release, Drake University, Nov. 1, 1997.

Dunlop, D. R. "Suggestions for Working with Volunteers." Presentation made at the Council for Advancement and Support of Education Summer Institute in Educational Fund Raising, Dartmouth College, July 1981.

Evans, G. A. "Relationship of Capital Campaign to Annual Fund and Deferred Giving Program." Presentation made at the annual Council for Advancement and Support of Education conference, Detroit, Mich., Aug. 1978.

Evans, G. A. "Decisions About the Big Three." *CASE Currents,* Mar. 1979, pp. 34–37.

"Exploring Women and Philanthropy: Interview with Gwinn Scott." *Counsel,* Summer 1998, pp. 1–2.

Fund Raising School. *Fund Raising: Principles, Dynamics, Techniques.* Indianapolis: Fund Raising School, Indiana University Center on Philanthropy, 1988.

Fund Raising School. *Principles and Techniques of Fund Raising.* Indianapolis: Fund Raising School, Indiana University Center on Philanthropy, 1995.

Galaskiewicz, J., and Sinclair, M. "Corporate Nonprofit Partnerships: Varieties and Covariates." *New York Law School Law Review,* Apr. 1997, pp. 1059–1090.

Gallup Organization. *Patterns of Charitable Giving by Individuals II.* Report commissioned by the 501(c)(3) Group, INDEPENDENT SECTOR, and the National Society of Fund Raising Executives. Washington, D.C.: INDEPENDENT SECTOR, 1982.

Gallup Organization. *An Analysis of Charitable Contributions by Upper-Income Households for 1986 and 1987.* Report commissioned by the American Association of Fund-Raising Counsel Trust for Philanthropy. New York: American Association of Fund-Raising Counsel Trust for Philanthropy, 1987.

Gibson, E. B. "The Role of Professional Counsel." Discussion notes from a presentation made at the annual Council for Advancement and Support of Education conference, Philadelphia, Mar. 1983.

Gibson, E. B. "Raising the Bar for Major Gifts: Special Report. *Counsel,* Spring 1999, pp. 1–3.

Hale, E. E. Remarks made at the annual Council for Advancement and Support of Education conference on capital fundraising, Atlanta, Apr. 1980.

Harris, A. L. *Special Events: Planning for Success.* Washington, D.C.: Council for Advancement and Support of Education, 1998.

Hartsook, R. F. "Predictions for 1997." *Fund Raising Management,* Jan. 1997, p. 48.

Havens, J. J., and Schervish, P. G. "Millionaires and the Millennium: New Estimates of the Forthcoming Wealth Transfer and the Prospects for a Golden Age of Philanthropy." An unpublished paper by the Social Welfare Research Institute, Chestnut Hill, Mass. [http://www.bc.edu/bc_org/avp/gsas/swri/m&m.html]. Oct. 19, 1999, p. 1.

INDEPENDENT SECTOR. *Giving and Volunteering in the United States, 1994.* Washington, D.C.: INDEPENDENT SECTOR, 1994.

INDEPENDENT SECTOR. *Giving and Volunteering in the United States, 1996.* Washington, D.C.: INDEPENDENT SECTOR, 1996.

Indiana University Center on Philanthropy. *The Philanthropy Giving Index (PGI).* Indianapolis: Indiana University Center on Philanthropy, 1998.

Indiana University Center on Philanthropy. *The Philanthropy Giving Index (PGI) Executive Summary.* Indianapolis: Indiana University Center on Philanthropy, 1999.

John Grenzebach and Associates. *Campaign Evaluation Questionnaire.* Chicago: John Grenzebach and Associates, Inc., 1986.

Kennedy, J. F., Jr. CNN interview, July 19, 1999.

Koch, K. "The New Corporate Philanthropy." *CQ Reporter*, Feb. 27, 1998.

Kughn, J. C., Jr. "Using Volunteers Effectively." Presentation made at the annual Council for Advancement and Support of Education conference, Nashville, Tenn., Mar. 1982.

La Rocque, P. "More Precise Writing." Handout given with a presentation at the Council for Advancement and Support of Education Writing Institute, Philadelphia, Dec. 1992.

Legon, R. D. *The Board's Role in Fund Raising.* Washington, D.C.: Association of Governing Boards of Universities and Colleges, 1997.

Livingston, H. J., Jr. "The Role of Trustees in a Capital Campaign." *Bulletin on Public Relations and Development for Colleges and Universities*, Mar. 1984, pp. 1–4.

Lord, J. G. *The Raising of Money.* (3rd ed.) Cleveland, Ohio: Third Sector Press, 1996.

Lyon, J. B. "Considerations in Respecting Donor Interests." *Trusts and Events*, Sept. 1998, pp. 108–120.

McLelland, R. J. "Essentials of Endowment Stewardship." *CASE Currents*, Sept. 1997, pp. 1–3.

Miller, A., and Nayyar, S. "The New Hands-On Philanthropy: Women Are Going the Distance to Make Their Money Count." *Working Woman*, July-Aug. 1998, pp. 52–57.

Murphy, M. [http://www.valpo.edu/home/staff/mmurphy/]. May 20, 2000.

Panas, J. *Mega Gifts.* Chicago: Pluribus Press, 1984.

"Pat Lewis on Fund Raising in the 1990s." *Nonprofit Management Strategies*, June 1994, pp. 8–9.

Payton, R. L. "A Tradition in Jeopardy." In C. T. Clotfelter and T. Ehrlich (eds.), *Philanthropy and the Nonprofit Sector in a Changing America.* Bloomington: Indiana University Press, 1999.

Pendel, M. H. *What Is a Case Statement?* Arlington, Va.: Thompson and Pendel Associates, Inc., 1981.

Perkins, D. R. "Public Relations Support for the Capital Campaign." Presentation made at the annual Council for Advancement and Support of Education conference, Nashville, Tenn., Apr. 1985.

Pickett, W. L. "What Determines Fundraising Effectiveness?" *CASE Currents*, Sept. 1984, pp. 45–48.

Picton, R. R. "Effective Follow-Through." Presentation made at the annual Council for Advancement and Support of Education conference, Nashville, Tenn., Mar. 1982.

Price, A. P., and File, K. M. *The Seven Faces of Philanthropy: A New Approach to Cultivating Major Donors.* San Francisco: Jossey-Bass, 1994.

Rose, S. J. *The American Profile Poster: Who Owns What, Who Makes How Much, Who Works Where, and Who Lives with Whom.* New York: Pantheon Books, 1986.

Schervish, P. G., and Havens, J. J. "Wherewithal and Beneficence: Charitable Giving by Income and Wealth." In W. Ilchman and C. Hamilton (eds.), *Cultures of Giving, Part Two: How Heritage, Gender, Wealth, and Values Influence Philanthropy.* New Directions for Philanthropic Fundraising, no. 8. San Francisco: Jossey-Bass, 1995.

Schneider, A. "Gateses Merge Foundations to Create America's Wealthiest Philanthropy." *Chronicle of Higher Education*, Aug. 23, 1999, p. 1.

Seymour, H. J. *Designs for Fund Raising.* New York: McGraw-Hill, 1966.

Shaw, S. C., and Taylor, M. A. *Reinventing Fundraising: Realizing the Potential of Women's Philanthropy.* San Francisco: Jossey-Bass, 1995.

Smith, B., Shue, S., Vest, J. L., and Villarreal, *Ethnic Philanthropy.* San Francisco: Institute for Nonprofit Organization Management, University of San Francisco, 1994.

Smith, D. H. "The Rest of the Nonprofit Sector: Grassroots Associations as the Dark Matter Providing 'Flat Earth' Maps of the Sector." *Nonprofit and Voluntary Sector Quarterly*, June 1997, pp. 117–118.

Smith, J. P. "Rethinking the Traditional Capital Campaign." In F. C. Pray (ed.), *Handbook for Educational Fund Raising: A Guide to Successful Principles and Practices for Colleges, Universities, and Schools.* San Francisco: Jossey-Bass, 1981.

Stuhr, R. L. *Gonser Gerber Tinker Stuhr on Development.* Chicago: Gonser Gerber Tinker Stuhr, 1977.

Taylor, J. H. *Your Noncash Gift Questions Report, 1996.* New York: Conference Board, 1998.

Thiede, J. A. "Establishing a Marketing Department at the Indiana University Foundation." Unpublished report, Indiana University Foundation, 1998.

Thomas Aquinas. "Charity." In *Summa Theologiae,* Vol. 43 (R. J. Batten, trans. and ed.). London: Eyre & Spottiswoode, 1975.

Thompson, D. M., and others. *Typical Outline for the Case Statement.* Arlington, Va.: Frantzreb, Prey, Ferner, and Thompson, 1978.

Tillman, A. *Corporate Contributions Report, 1996.* New York: Conference Board, 1998.

Timmins, N. *The Five Giants: A Biography of the Welfare State.* London: Fontana, 1996.

Tromble, W. W. *Excellence in Advancement.* Gaithersburg, Md.: Aspen, 1999.

United Auto Workers. "Focus On: The Distribution of Wealth." [http://uaw.org/publications/jobs_pay/1097/stat1097_03.html]. Fall 1997.

U.S. Census Bureau. [http://www.census.gov]. Mar. 23, 1999.

U.S. Trust. "Affluent Participation in Charitable Giving." [http://www.ustrust.com/afff-chvsrv.htm]. Nov. 17, 1998.

Veyne, P. *Bread and Circuses: Historical Sociology and Political Pluralism.* London: Allen Lane/Penguin, 1990.

Warwick, M. *Technology and the Future of Fundraising.* Berkeley, Calif.: Strathmore Press, 1994.

Wasow, M. "Corporate Involvement in the Nonprofit Sector." *Giving USA Update,* 1998, *2.*

Wesley, J. "The Use of Money." In *John Wesley's Fifty-Three Sermons* (E. J. Sugden, ed.). Nashville, Tenn.: Abingdon Press, 1983.

White, A. H. *The Charitable Behavior of Americans.* Washington, D.C.: INDEPENDENT SECTOR, 1986.

Whittaker, F. M. "Prospect Research, Evaluation, Cultivation, and Solicitation." Outline of presentation at the annual Council for Advancement and Support of Education conference, Philadelphia, Mar. 1983.

Williams, C. "Tax Checkoffs and Credits as a Policy Mechanism to Encourage Voluntary Contributions for Public Goods." Unpublished dissertation, George Washington University, 1995.

Wolpert, J. *Patterns of Generosity in America: Who's Holding the Safety Net?* New York: Twentieth Century Fund, 1993.

Women's Philanthropy Institute. (Fact sheet.) [http://www.women.philanthropy.org]. July 31, 1999.

INDEX

The Full Proposal in Resource 23 is reprinted with the permission of The Health Sciences Center, University of Texas Houston.

The Monthly Financial Report in Resource 24 is reprinted with the permission of Indiana University Foundation, Bloomington, Indiana.

Update, the Indiana University newsletter in Resource 25, is reprinted with the permission of Indiana University Foundation, Bloomington, Indiana.

Contributors' Newsletter of the YMCA of Greater St. Louis in Resource 25 is reprinted with the permission of the YMCA of Greater St. Louis.

The Pledge Forms in Resource 26 are reprinted with permissions from the University of Iowa Foundation and the YMCA of Greater St. Louis.

The Letterhead and Envelopes in Resource 27 are reprinted with the permission of Indiana University Foundation, Bloomington, Indiana, and Lutheran Hospital Foundation, La Crosse, Wisconsin.

The Public Announcement Event Invitation and Program in Resource 28 are reprinted with the permission of the Fundraising Counsel, Inc., Vancouver, B.C., Canada.

Program Assessment in Resource 29 is reprinted with the permission of Greater Victoria Hospitals Foundation in Victoria, B.C., Canada.

The Gift Receipt Templates that constitute Resource 30 are reprinted with the permission of Indiana University Foundation, Bloomington, Indiana.

The Stewardship Program at the University of Florida in Resource 31 is reprinted with the permission of the University of Florida Foundation, Inc., Gainesville, Florida.

Post-Campaign Assessment—Annual Campaign in Resource 32 is reprinted with the permission of the Indianapolis Museum of Art, Indianapolis, Indiana.

Post-Campaign Assessment—Capital Campaign in Resource 33 is reprinted with the permission of the Fundraising Counsel, Inc., Vancouver, B. C., Canada.

The Final Report—Annual Campaign in Resource 34 is reprinted with the permission of Eiteljorg Museum, Indianapolis, Indiana.

The Final Report—Capital Campaign in Resource 35 is reprinted with the permission of Fundraising Counsel, Inc., Vancouver, B. C., Canada.